ANALECTA BIBLICA

INVESTIGATIONES SCIENTIFICAE IN RES BIBLICAS

158

THOMAS STEGMAN

THE CHARACTER OF JESUS

The Linchpin to Paul's Argument in 2 Corinthians

EDITRICE PONTIFICIO ISTITUTO BIBLICO - ROMA 2005

ISBN 88-7653-158-0

Editrice Pontificio Istituto Biblico
Piazza della Pilotta, 35 - 00187 Roma, Italia

Table of Contents

Acknowledgments

This study is a revised version of the dissertation I completed in the Spring of 2003 at Emory University under the direction of Dr. Luke Timothy Johnson. It is to him that I owe my greatest debt of gratitude, one that I will never be able to repay. Dr. Johnson was the ideal director, knowing when to encourage, when to challenge, when to comfort, and when to push. His love for and passion to understand the Sacred Page are what I find to be his most inspiring qualities as a scholar. Although I am happy to have launched into my own career, I very much miss the time spent with him in his office – toiling with the text, batting around ideas, and growing in our friendship. Dr. Johnson has not only been a great mentor, but has become a close and valued friend.

I also wish to express my sincere appreciation to the other members of my dissertation committee: Dr. Carl R. Holladay, Dr. Vernon K. Robbins, Dr. Don E. Saliers, and Dr. Walter T. Wilson. I consider myself fortunate to have had such an illustrious group of scholars read and critique my work. I am grateful to Rev. Richard J. Clifford, S.J. and Rev. John S. Kselman, S.S. of Weston Jesuit School of Theology, both of whom submitted helpful comments on sections of the manuscript. A word of thanks is also in order to Rev. Daniel J. Harrington, S.J., another Weston Jesuit colleague, who invited me to present some of my work to the New Testament Colloquium of the Boston Theological Institute, where I received critical feedback and encouragement. I am also deeply indebted to Anna Dawn Aberg for her expert editorial assistance, her generous help with the indices, and her personal support.

In addition, I want to acknowledge the personal and financial support of the Wisconsin Province of the Society of Jesus – especially Rev. James E. Grummer, S.J., Provincial – and the St. Peter Canisius Jesuit Community at Marquette University – especially Rev. G. Thomas Krettek, S.J., Rector. I am most grateful to Rev. Eugene F. Merz, S.J., a confidant and friend, for his love and support. The competent and courteous staff at Marquette University Memorial Library was extraordinarily helpful to me in my research needs.

Many family members and friends have loved and encouraged me through my years of study. Most especially, I wish to express my profound gratitude to and love for my parents, Dennis and Kay Stegman, who have always been my strongest supporters and staunchest fans. They have modeled forth Paul's advice in 2 Cor 12:14b-15a: that parents store up treasure for their children, and be willing to give themselves entirely to them. I am eternally grateful for the unconditional love that my parents have bestowed upon me. As a small token of that appreciation, I dedicate this book to them.

Thomas D. Stegman, S.J.
Weston Jesuit School of Theology
Cambridge, Massachusetts, U.S.A.

Abbreviations

AB	Anchor Bible
ABD	*Anchor Bible Dictionary*. Ed. D.N. Freedman. 6 vols. New York: Doubleday, 1992.
ACNT	Augsburg Commentary on the New Testament
AJBI	*Annual of the Japanese Biblical Institute*
ALBO	Analecta Lovaniensia Biblica et Orientalia
AnBib	Analecta Biblica
AUSS	*Andrews University Seminary Studies*
BBB	Bonner biblische Beiträge
BDAG	Bauer, W., F.W. Danker, W.F. Arndt, and F.W. Gingrich. *A Greek-English Lexicon of the New Testament and Other Early Christian Literature*. 3rd ed. Chicago: University of Chicago, 2000.
BDBG	Brown, F., S.R. Driver, C.A. Briggs, and W. Gesenius. *The New Brown – Driver – Briggs – Genenius Hebrew and English Lexicon*. Peabody, Mass.: Hendrickson, 1979.
BDF	Blass, F., A. DeBrunner, and R.W. Funk. *A Greek Grammar of the New Testament and Other Early Christian Literature*. Chicago: University of Chicago, 1961.
BETL	Bibliotheca ephemeridum theologicarum lovaniensium
BHT	Beiträge zur historischen Theologie
Bib	*Biblica*

BJRL	*Bulletin of the John Rylands University Library of Manchester*
BNTC	Black's New Testament Commentary
Bsac	*Bibliotheca sacra*
BT	*The Bible Translator*
BTB	*Biblical Theology Bulletin*
BZ	*Biblische Zeitschrift*
BZNW	Beihefte zur Zeitschrift für die neutestamentliche Wissenschaft
CBET	Contributions to Biblical Exegesis and Theology
CBQ	*Catholic Biblical Quarterly*
Colloq	*Colloquium*
ETR	*Etudes théologiques et religieuses*
EvT	*Evangelische Theologie*
FRLANT	Forschungen zur Religion und Literatur des Alten und Neuen Testaments
Greg	*Gregorianum*
HB	Hebrew Bible
HNTC	Harper's New Testament Commentary
HR	*History of Religions*
HTR	*Harvard Theological Review*

DB	*The Interpreter's Dictionary of the Bible*. Ed. G.A. Buttrick. 4 vols. Nashville: Abingdon, 1962.
IDBSup	*The Interpreter's Dictionary of the Bible: Supplementary Volume*. Ed. K. Crim. Nashville: Abingdon, 1976.
ICC	International Critical Commentary
Int	*Interpretation*
IVPNTCS	InterVarsity Press New Testament Commentary Series
JAAR	*Journal of the American Academy of Religion*
JB	Jerusalem Bible
JBL	*Journal of Biblical Literature*
JRelS	*Journal of Religious Studies*
JSNT	*Journal for the Study of the New Testament*
JSNTSup	Journal for the Study of the New Testament: Supplement Series
JSOT	*Journal for the Study of the Old Testament*
JTC	*Journal for Theology and the Church*
JTS	*Journal of Theological Studies*
KJV	King James Version
KNT	Kommentar zum Neuen Testament
LCL	Loeb Classical Library
LS	*Louvain Studies*

LXX	Septuagint
Mils	*Milltown Studies*
MBPS	Mellon Biblical Press Series
NAB	New American Bible
NAC	New American Commentary
NCB	New Century Bible
Neot	*Neotestamentica*
NIB	*The New Interpreter's Bible*. Ed. L.E. Keck. 12 vols. Nashville: Abingdon, 1994-2002.
NIBC	New International Biblical Commentary
NICNT	New International Commentary on the New Testament
NIV	New International Version
NIVAC	New International Version Application Commentary
NovT	*Novum Testamentum*
NovTSup	Novum Testamentum Supplements
NRSV	New Revised Standard Version
NTC	New Testament in Context
NTL	New Testament Library
NTS	*New Testament Studies*
NTT	New Testament Theology (Cambridge)

PCB	*Peake's Commentary on the Bible*. Ed. M. Black and H.H. Rowley. London: T. Nelson, 1962.
PIBA	Proceedings of the Irish Biblical Association
PTS	Patristische Texte und Studien
RB	*Revue biblique*
ResQ	*Restoration Quarterly*
RHPR	*Revue d'histoire et de philosophie religieuses*
RSV	Revised Standard Version
SANT	Studien zum Alten und Neuen Testaments
SBLDS	Society of Biblical Literature Dissertation Series
SBLSymS	Society of Biblical Literature Symposium Series
SBT	Studies in Biblical Theology
SJT	*Scottish Journal of Theology*
SNTSMS	Society for New Testament Studies Monograph Series
SP	Sacra pagina
ST	*Summa theologiae*
TDNT	*Theological Dictionary of the New Testament*. Ed. G. Kittel and G. Friedrich. Trans. G.W. Bromiley. 10 vols. Grand Rapids, Mich.: Eerdmans, 1964-76.
TLNT	*Theological Lexicon of the New Testament*. C. Spicq. Trans. and ed. J.D. Ernest. 3 vols. Peabody, Mass.: Hendrickson, 1994.

TS	Theology series
TS	*Theological Studies*
TynBul	*Tyndale Bulletin*
WBC	Word Biblical Commentary
WUNT	Wissenschaftliche Untersuchungen zum Neuen Testament
ZNW	*Zeitschrift für die neutestamentliche Wissenschaft und die Kunde der älteren Kirche*
ZTK	*Zeitschrift für Theologie und Kirche*

INTRODUCTION

Second Corinthians is an extraordinary document that contains some of Paul's richest theological formulations. The letter offers a unique historical window into the complexity of an early church and the apostle's dealings with it, and also reveals his great passion and range of emotions. Most extraordinary, however, is the breathtakingly bold rhetoric Paul employs as counter-thrust to the Corinthian challenge to his authority.

The Corinthians, a reader quickly learns, have several reasons for doubting Paul. Changes in his travel plans have raised the issue of his trustworthiness. His weak appearance and unpolished speaking skills have disappointed a community familiar with the boldness of his letters. He has responded to a nasty incident (that cut short his previous visit) from the safety of distance, ordering punishment of the offending party via a letter. He suffers much, and evokes opposition from other missionaries/evangelists. And he raises suspicions of fraudulent dealings by ostentatiously refusing financial support from the Corinthians even as he cajoles them to give generously to his pet project, the Jerusalem collection. In short, the Corinthians feel entitled to challenge the apostle's character.

But Paul turns the tables on the Corinthians: It is the Corinthians' character, he argues, not his own, that is the pressing issue. In fact, in a remarkable rhetorical move at the very climax of the letter (2 Cor 13:5), Paul challenges the community to self-examination. The apostle employs a powerful strategy to make his case, using the story and character of Jesus in ways never before utilized. Paul's Greek is subtle and allusive. A particular sensitivity to this subtlety is necessary to understand his approach and techniques. Only with this sensitivity can the reader detect the underlying story of Jesus in the apostle's argument in 2 Corinthians. This is, in fact, the simple thesis of this study: that it is the character of Jesus that underlies the self-commendation of Paul's apostleship in 2 Corinthians, as well as his exhortations and challenge to the Corinthians to embody a particular manner of discipleship. By the character or *ethos* of Jesus, I mean the specific attitudes, virtues, and self-emptying mode of existence that Paul extrapolates from Jesus. The character of Jesus, I submit, serves as the linchpin to the apostle's presentation in this letter. In Part Two, I will argue my thesis in three steps: (1) Paul draws upon the story and character of Jesus in ways that previous scholarship has not fully appreciated (Chapter Four); (2) Paul commends his manner of being apostle through the *ethos* of Jesus; in other words, he claims that the story of Jesus continues in him (Chapter Five); and (3) the apostle challenges the Corinthians to participate in the story of Jesus by taking on the latter's characteristics (Chapter Six).

My proposal concerning the significance of Jesus' character for Paul in 2 Corinthians is unique (at least in its explicitness) and should prove to be provocative. Indeed, this letter has been used to support the opposite position, namely that the character of Jesus – especially as manifested in his humanity – is not important to Paul; rather, his concern (according to this position) is solely with the resurrected Christ. In 2 Cor 5:16 – "in one of the most arresting sentences of the New Testament"[1] – the apostle writes, "Therefore, from now on, we no longer regard anyone according to the flesh; even if we knew Christ according to the flesh, now we no longer know [him thus]."[2] Rudolf Bultmann, for instance, took this verse as evidence that the story and character of Jesus have little or no value for Paul.[3] This interpretation, I submit, both misreads the

---

[1]P.E. HUGHES, *Paul's Second Epistle to the Corinthians: The English Text with Introduction, Exposition and Notes*, NICNT (Grand Rapids, Mich.: Eerdmans, 1962) 198.

[2]All translations of Scripture, unless otherwise noted, are mine.

[3]"The Χριστὸς κατὰ σάρκα is Christ as he can be encountered in the world, before his death and resurrection. He should no longer be viewed as such. . . ." See R. BULTMANN, *The Second Letter to the Corinthians*, ed. E. DINKLER, trans. R.A. HARRISVILLE (Minneapolis: Augsburg, 1985) 155. Cf. the more general assessment of R.C. TANNEHILL: "Paul seldom concerns himself with the ethical quality of Jesus' life. Instead, he focuses his attention on the saving events of the cross and resurrection." See *Dying and Rising with Christ: A Study in Pauline Theology*, BZNW 32 (Berlin: Alfred Töppelmann, 1967) 26-27.

grammar of 2 Cor 5:16 and fails to recognize the subtle and allusive texture of the apostle's argument throughout the letter.

Before I can develop this thesis, however, I must attend to preliminary issues, issues which are the subject of Part One. The first is the history of interpretation of 2 Corinthians. The letter is a complex and, at times, convoluted document. The attempt to interpret it can be compared to a journey over rough and uncharted terrain. Exegetes have discerned inconsistencies, interruptions of narrative and logic, and bewilderingly sharp mood swings in the text as it has been handed down in its canonical form. Indeed, interpreters encounter several apparent forks in the road. These are the perceived "seams" in the text that have given scholars reason to pause before proceeding and that have caused many to take meandering routes. Most scholars over the past one hundred years have undertaken a historical-literary approach to the interpretation of 2 Corinthians. This method has taken two main forms, partition theories and readings based on the identification of Paul's so-called "opponents." Chapter One reviews the major contributions of the historical-literary analysis of 2 Corinthians. I contend that this approach has led the quest for understanding into several blind alleys.[4] More recent interpreters eschew this method, looking instead to rhetorical analysis to study 2 Corinthians. Such analysis involves a rigorous investigation of the text itself, either in its entirety or in part, within the conventions of Greco-Roman rhetorical theory. As Chapter Two demonstrates, rhetorical analysis has fundamentally advanced our understanding of Paul's compositional and argumentative techniques, and points us to the importance of the *ethos* dimension of the apostle's argument in 2 Corinthians. The presence of this dimension is crucial for my thesis.

The second preliminary issue deals with the larger question of New Testament (hereafter, NT) theology. Two recent developments in Pauline theology provide a vital foundation for my thesis, and serve as its starting point. First, the past two decades have seen a growth in understanding of the part that "the story of Jesus" plays in Paul's writings. Second, an increasing number of scholars have come to appreciate the critical role that Jesus' own faithfulness and obedience have in the apostle's thought. Chapter Three sets forth the significance of these two developments for my thesis.

---

[4]This metaphor, of course, was used by E. KÄSEMANN in a different context. See "Blind Alleys in the 'Jesus of History' Controversy," in *New Testament Questions of Today*, trans. W.J. MONTAGUE (Philadelphia: Fortress, 1969) 23-65.

Part One
Preliminary Issues

Chapter One
History of Interpretation I
Partition Theories and Opponent-Driven Readings

I. Partition Theories

Partition theories for 2 Corinthians emerge from a close, critical reading of the text itself. In particular, interpreters struggle with the logic and coherence, or perceived lack thereof, in Paul's presentation. Why, for instance, would the apostle, after emphasizing his reconciliation with the Corinthians and asking for their generous participation in his collection, proceed to harangue and threaten them (2 Cor 9:15//10:1)? Why does he seem to introduce the collection as a new topic when he has just given a lengthy exhortation concerning it (8:24//9:1)? Why does Paul suddenly interrupt his account of his anxious pursuit of news from Titus with an exclamation of thanksgiving (2:13//2:14)? And is it not odd that the apostle recounts, seemingly from out of the blue, his joyful reunion with Titus several chapters later (7:4//7:5)? What is one to make of the unusual phraseology and imagery in 6:14-7:1 which intrudes on two invitations from Paul to the Corinthians to open their hearts to him (6:13//6:14 and 7:1//7:2)? And does not the admonition to withdraw from the ἄπιστοι contradict what the apostle had said in 1 Cor 5:9-13? Indeed, the majority of scholars have concluded that one or more of these breaks or "seams" in the text gives evidence that canonical 2 Corinthians is a composite of two or more letters, or parts of letters, from Paul to the community (and, in the case of 2 Cor 6:14-7:1, from another hand).

In addition to detecting seams, partitionists observe that 2 Corinthians presents both a number of tantalizing clues as well as a series of problems for the historical reconstruction of Paul's career. The apostle intimates that he is about to visit the Corinthians for the third time (2 Cor 12:14 and 13:1). Was the first visit his founding of the community, and his second the so-called "painful visit" (2:1)? How is one to reconcile the change in Paul's travel plans (2 Cor 1:15-17; cf. 1 Cor 16:5-9)? Was there a visit about which we do not know? What was the content of the "painful letter" (2 Cor 2:4 and 7:8-12)? Is it no longer extant? Is it canonical 1 Corinthians? Or is it contained (at least in part) within the text of 2 Corinthians? Who was the "offender" (2:5-11 and 7:12), and what was the nature of the offense? Who was the victim: Paul, or one of his cohorts, or another member of the community? Is the offender to be identified with the man living in incest referred to in 1 Cor 5:1-5? What relationship was there, if any, between the offender and the opposition to Paul alluded to in 2 Cor 10:2, 10:10-11, and 11:13-23? Is the latter to be identified with or distinguished from the "superlative apostles" (11:5 and 12:11)? Are the opponents to Paul connected to judaizing (cf. 3:7-18), or to hellenizing or gnostic influences? Are they linked to the perceived rivalry with Cephas and Apollos (1 Cor 1:12)? How many visits did Titus make to Corinth (2 Cor 7:6-16; cf. 8:16-24 and 12:17-18)? How does one reconstruct the stages of the process implemented for taking up the collection, "the ministry unto the holy ones" in Jerusalem (2 Cor 8:10-12; cf. 1 Cor 16:1-4)? Is Paul's reference to "Achaia" (2 Cor 9:2) a synonymous term for the Corinthian church, or does it refer to another group of Christians?

Second Corinthians thus presents a number of literary and historical puzzles. It is no wonder that Johannes Weiss exclaimed, "How immensely fertile is this source, how complicated are the problems which it presents to us!"[5] The delicate interplay between historical reconstruction and literary hypothesis makes the historical-literary approach particularly challenging. As C. K. Barrett notes, it is easy to argue in a circular manner, that is, from historical reconstruction to literary hypothesis and vice-versa. He also candidly acknowledges that this line of interpretation "is one in which theories are more numerous than facts, and clear distinctions between the two are not always made."[6]

The key strategy for those who posit partitions is to ask the question, at any given point in the letter: Where are we in the story of Paul and his relationship with the Corinthians? This approach exerts pressure on some or all of the seams in the text in order to tease out separate letters or parts of letters. The pressure is applied to these points because of perceived literary problems with the text as it now stands, and/or because of difficulties in reconciling references to people and events in different parts of the text. Once the different

---

[5]J. WEISS, *Earliest Christianity: A History of the Period A.D. 30-150, Volume I*, trans. F.C. GRANT (New York: Harper & Row, 1959) 323. Weiss was speaking of the Corinthian correspondence as a whole.

[6]C.K. BARRETT, *The Second Epistle to the Corinthians*, BNTC 8 (London: A & C Black, 1973) 5.

pieces of the whole are separated and analyzed, the historical-literary approach then attempts to reconstruct the stages of Paul's dealings with the Corinthians, including the chronology of his correspondence. The goal is to give a plausible and coherent account of the historical events and persons that lay behind the text. The final step is to offer a reasonable explanation for why the text has been put into the final form which has been handed down.

Since the critical work of J.S. Semler over two centuries ago, partition theories have been the predominant method used to explain the complex character of 2 Corinthians.[7] Semler detected two seams in the text. The first is between chapters 8 and 9. Beginning at 2 Cor 9:1 Paul resumes the same subject matter with which he had been occupied throughout 8:1-24, namely, the collection for the church in Jerusalem. Although the wording and style of these two chapters differ, Semler held that the apostle's argument is essentially the same in both, which struck him as oddly redundant if 2 Corinthians were a single, unified letter. Thus, Semler surmised that chapter 9 was originally a separate letter which was sent not to Corinth but elsewhere in Achaia, and that it was later joined to the first eight chapters.[8] The second seam is between chapters 9 and 10. According to Semler, the tone and content of 10:1-13:10 do not fit with what preceded in the first nine chapters. Paul's polemics in the final four chapters belie the notes of reconciliation sounded at various points earlier in the text (e.g., 7:6-16). Furthermore, the apostle's recounting of accusations

---

[7]For a succinct account of the history of partition theories of 2 Cor, see H.D. BETZ, *2 Corinthians 8 and 9: A Commentary on Two Administrative Letters of the Apostle Paul*, Hermeneia (Philadelphia: Fortress, 1985) 3-36. Although Betz's focus in this monograph is 2 Cor 8:1-9:15, his historical survey takes into account all the partitions proffered except those involving 6:14-7:1. Cf. R. BIERINGER, "Teilungshypothesen zum 2. Korintherbrief: Ein Forschungsüberblick," in R. BIERINGER and J. LAMBRECHT, *Studies on 2 Corinthians*, BETL 112 (Leuven: Leuven University Press, 1994) 67-105. In addition, M.E. THRALL offers a good summary of the arguments for and against the various proposals of separating and reordering units of the text. See her *A Critical and Exegetical Commentary on The Second Epistle to the Corinthians*, 2 vols., ICC (Edinburgh: T. & T. Clark, 1994-2000) 1.3-49 (hereafter cited as *II Corinthians*).

[8]See J.S. SEMLER, *Paraphrasis II: Epistolae ad Corinthios* (Halle, 1776) 238, n. 264. The Latin text reads: "Res agitur eadem, ut fere tantum phrases different; itaque mirum omnino videri possit, in *eadem Epistola* idem argumentum fere repeti. . . . opinari et coniicere liceret, aliquas Epistolas serium demum sic quasi in unum corpus compositas fuisse. . ." (Semler's italics).

and calumnies against himself concerning the collection does not cohere well with his exhortation to the Corinthians in chapters 8 and 9 that they be generous in contributing.[9] Semler therefore concluded that the tone and content of the final four chapters make sense only if they formed a separate letter from the first letter (chapters 1-8), the latter of which must have aroused suspicions among the Corinthians.[10] In short, Semler proposed that 2 Corinthians is made up of three letters, in the following sequence: (1) 1:1-8:24 (+13:11-13); (2) 9:1-15; and (3) 10:1-13:10. With this hypothesis, Semler sought to explain the appearance of a redundant chapter, an incomprehensible mood shift, and a peculiar manner of soliciting funds.

H.D. Betz has observed that the significance of Semler's partition hypothesis lies not so much in its accuracy or inaccuracy, but rather in the very fact that he proposed it. That is, following Semler, "the dam had broken, releasing a mighty flood which swept scholars of all persuasions and schools into the debate on partition theories of 2 Corinthians. . . ."[11] Four major partition theories for interpreting and making sense of 2 Corinthians have arisen as a result. In what follows, for each theory, I (1) lay out what it claims to accomplish exegetically; (2) give the pertinent details of the historical reconstruction associated with it; (3) describe the compilation process hypothesized in connection with it; and (4) offer a brief critique. It should be noted in advance that this review does not claim to be exhaustive, but rather strives to be broadly illustrative.[12]

---

[9]Ibid., 310, n. 350. The Latin text reads: "Quomodo enim haec iam componi queant cum istis rebus et laudibus, quae Capite 7, 6-16 leguntur? . . . quomodo, *eadem* in hac epistola potest commemorare istas accusationes et calumnias in ipsum aut in Titum ab aliis spargi solitas?" (Semler's italics).

[10]Ibid.

[11]BETZ, *2 Corinthians 8 and 9*, 4.

[12]For a list of the various partition proposals and their advocates, see THRALL, *II Corinthians*, 1.47-49.

A. *Hausrath-Kennedy Proposal*

A century after the work of Semler, Adolf Hausrath and James H. Kennedy, working independently of one another, turned Semler's hypothesis on its head. That is, while Hausrath and Kennedy agreed with Semler that 2 Cor 10-13 constitutes a separate letter, they argued that it was written *before* the letter which is now contained in 2 Cor 1-9. Moreover, Hausrath identified the final four chapters as the painful letter (*Schmerzensbrief*) referred to in 2:4 and 7:8,[13] whereas Kennedy postulated more modestly that 2 Cor 10-13 is a portion of that letter.[14] This proposal, here dubbed "the Hausrath-Kennedy proposal," won several adherents in the earlier part of the twentieth century, most notably Alfred Plummer[15] and Kirsopp Lake.[16]

(1) In the main, proponents of this theory argue that it solves two puzzling characteristics of the canonical form of 2 Corinthians. First, it accounts for the "absolute break" between chapters 1-9 and 10-13. Whereas the tone of 2 Cor 1-9 is said to be joyful and to convey a sense of relief from great anxiety (e.g., 7:7-16), the final four chapters are filled with defensiveness, vituperation, and threats. Indeed, Lake confidently claimed that "if 2 Cor x.-xiii. had existed in a separate form, no one would ever have dreamt of suggesting that it was the continuation of 2 Cor i.-ix."[17] Like Semler's thesis, this proposal attempts to alleviate the "psychological maladroitness" of the text as it now

---

[13]See A. HAUSRATH, *Der Vier-Capitel-Brief des Paulus an die Korinther* (Heidelberg: Bassermann, 1870). For an even briefer statement of Hausrath's proposal, see his *A History of the New Testament Times: The Time of the Apostles*, vol. 4, trans. L. HUXLEY (London: Williams & Norgate, 1895) 55-67.

[14]See J.H. KENNEDY, *The Second and Third Epistles of St. Paul to the Corinthians* (London: Methuen, 1900). Kennedy's work (hereafter cited as *The Second and Third Epistles*) with the text of 2 Corinthians is more thorough and critical than Hausrath's.

[15]See A. PLUMMER, *A Critical and Exegetical Commentary on the Second Epistle of St. Paul to the Corinthians*, ICC (Edinburgh: T. & T. Clark, 1915) esp. xxvii-xxxvi (hereafter cited as *II Corinthians*).

[16]See K. LAKE, *The Earlier Epistles of St. Paul*, 2nd ed. (London: Rivingtons, 1914) esp. 144-75.

[17]Ibid., 157.

stands. That is, how could Paul in his right mind have thought that his overtures towards reconciliation and his request for the Corinthians' involvement in the collection would not be vitiated by the tone and content of 2 Cor 10-13?[18] Unlike Semler, however, these scholars see in the content of the last four chapters an apt candidate for the apostle's description of having written a letter "out of great affliction and anguish of heart" (2 Cor 2:4) which caused him moments of doubt and regret for having sent it (7:8). Thus, in their analysis of the two partitions, they claim that 2 Cor 10-13 is the earlier text, and identify it with the *Schmerzensbrief.*

This inversion explains, it is claimed, a second problematical feature of 2 Corinthians, namely, a series of apparent verbal cross-references.[19] Lake observed three "very striking" pairs in particular: 2 Cor 1:23 and 13:2; 2:3 and 13:10; and 2:9 and 10:6. The first pair illustrates his point well. In 13:2 Paul warns the Corinthians that if he comes again he will not spare them (ἐὰν ἔλθω εἰς τὸ πάλιν οὐ φείσομαι); in 1:23 he swears an oath that he did not come to Corinth in order to spare them (ὅτι φειδόμενος ὑμῶν οὐκέτι ἦλθον εἰς Κόρινθον). It is argued that these verses refer to the same event. What is striking is that 13:2 is in the present tense, whereas 1:23 reports what has already taken place. Now, this makes sense only if 13:2 were written prior to 1:23.[20] Similarly, Plummer pointed to other cross-references – such as 7:16 and 10:1; 8:22 and 10:2 – in which "Paul seems to be purposely repeating in a friendly sense an expression which in the former letter he had used in a stern and unpleasing sense."[21] Thus, whereas in 10:1 he writes, "I have confidence *against* you" (θαρρῶ εἰς ὑμᾶς), in 7:16 he states, "I have confidence *in* you"

---

[18]See PLUMMER, *II Corinthians*, xxix-xxx.

[19]See KENNEDY, *The Second and Third Epistles,* 80-86; LAKE, *The Earlier Epistles of St. Paul*, 159-62; and PLUMMER, *II Corinthians,* xxx-xxxiii. For Kennedy, these represent "the most important proofs, because they are of the nature of positive evidence." See *The Second and Third Epistles*, 80.

[20]See LAKE, *The Earlier Epistles of St. Paul*, 159-60. The same dynamic, it is claimed, is true of the other pairs. That is, in each pair the same event is referred to, and the passage from the final four chapters is in the present tense while that from the first nine chapters is in the past tense. Cf. KENNEDY, *The Second and Third Epistles*, 82-84.

[21]PLUMMER, *II Corinthians*, xxxi.

(θαρρῶ ἐν ὑμῖν). The point is that these cross references can best be harmonized if 2 Cor 10-13 was written before 2 Cor 1-9.[22]

(2) The Hausrath-Kennedy proposal entails the following historical reconstruction.[23] Upon receiving news that all was not well in Corinth, Paul paid an emergency visit there (the so-called "intermediate visit"), during which a nasty incident involving the apostle and an unnamed offender occurred. Paul then returned to Ephesus, where he wrote the painful letter to the Corinthians, part of which has been preserved in 2 Cor 10-13. At that point, Titus was sent to Corinth to deliver this letter and to foster healing. Paul, anxious to hear the result of Titus's mission, left first for Troas, and then crossed over to Macedonia. There the apostle encountered Titus, who recounted the success of his mission, including the decision by the community to punish the offender. Greatly relieved and overjoyed, Paul next penned what is now partly preserved in 2 Cor 1-9, and sent Titus back to Corinth to deliver it. In this letter, the apostle encouraged the Corinthians to forgive the offender and to resume their preparation for the collection for the church in Jerusalem. This basic account is sometimes elaborated with speculative elements, including psychological explanations.[24]

---

[22]KENNEDY thought that Paul's use of καύχ- language (καυχῶμαι, καύχησις, καύχημα) also shows the chronological priority of 2 Cor 10-13: "A comparison of the way in which the writer employs these words. . . in Chapters i.-ix., with his use of them in x.-xiii., reveals a contrast so delicate and so suggestive that, I think, it alone would convince me that he wrote Chapters i.-ix. with recollection of Chapters x.-xiii., and with the conviction that his readers recollected them also" (see *The Second and Third Epistles*, 88-89). Paul's use of self-commendation language is similarly explained.

[23]This account follows in the main that offered by LAKE, *The Earlier Epistles of St. Paul*, 173-75.

[24]For example, KENNEDY insisted that the "minority" (cf. 2:6), i.e., those who seemingly did not go along with the punishment of the offender as decided by the majority (ὑπὸ τῶν πλειόνων), have been maligned in the history of interpretation. Rather than identify the minority with adherents of Paul's opponents, Kennedy identified them as staunch supporters of the apostle who sought more stringent punishment. See *The Second and Third Epistles*, 102-9.

C.H. DODD, another proponent of identifying 2 Cor 10-13 with the painful letter, filled in the picture with certain psychological features. For instance, he cited 2 Cor 1:8 as evidence that Paul was ill when he wrote the painful letter, and that he had

(3) What explanation is offered, then, for the production of the "redacted" form of 2 Corinthians?[25] Unlike the document now known as 1 Corinthians, which was highly valued from the time it was written and received, neither the painful letter (2 Cor 10-13) nor Paul's "third letter" (i.e., 2 Cor 1-9) – viewed by Lake as nothing more than an expression of the apostle's gratitude for the favorable turn of events[26] – was intrinsically valued. It was only later, when Paul's writings generally began to be treasured because of their authorship, that the two subsequent letters aroused interest.[27] The scribes who copied the originals, which by that time must have been in poor shape, pieced together as best they could the various fragments into one document. It is further surmised that the beginning of the painful letter and the conclusion of the letter of gratitude were missing. Thus it came to be that the chronologically prior letter was attached at the end.

(4) The Hausrath-Kennedy proposal is deficient on several counts. First, the "absolute break" posited between 2 Cor 1-9 and 2 Cor 10-13 is greatly exaggerated. Like the latter, the former section contains examples of Paul's defensiveness (e.g., 2:17 and 4:2) and plaintiveness (e.g., 6:13 and 7:2). And the latter, like the former, describes his affection for the community (e.g., 10:1 and 12:14-15). The supposed chasm between them rests on oversimplified characterizations. For example, is 2 Cor 1-9 justly characterized as an extended "thank you" to the Corinthians? Moreover, adjudicating what is psychologically possible and appropriate for Paul is, at best, a subjective enterprise.[28]

---

nearly died. In 2 Cor 1-9 Dodd observed that the apostle "makes it plain that he has gone to the depths and made terms with the last realities." This served as a chastening spiritual crisis, which Dodd isolated "as a sort of second conversion." See his *New Testament Studies* (Manchester: Manchester University Press, 1953) 80-81.

[25]The following is a summary of LAKE, *The Earlier Epistles of St. Paul*, 163-64, who follows KENNEDY.

[26]See LAKE, *The Earlier Epistles of St. Paul*, 163.

[27]Clement's letter to the Corinthians is thought to be the catalyst. See *1 Clem.* 47:1-4.

[28]PLUMMER illustrates this well. In arguing against those who would separate 2 Cor 13:11-13 from its immediate context, he states: "To say that no one could write xiii. 10, and then immediately afterwards write *v.* 11, is a dogmatic assumption. The sudden change of tone, so far from being incredible, is natural, especially in one who was so full

Second, the claim that 2 Cor 10-13 is the *Schmerzensbrief* suffers from two fatal flaws. On the one hand, the offender, the major subject of the 'painful letter' (2:3-11 and 7:8-12), is mentioned nowhere in the final four chapters; on the other, when recounting the beneficial effects of the letter (7:5-16), Paul makes no allusion to the opponents with whom he is so occupied in 2 Cor 10-13. To argue that such references were included in the (now) lost sections of the two letters is to argue desperately from silence.

Third, the treatment of the cross-references is less than convincing, as the parallels are forced. To use the example cited above: The context of 2 Cor 13:2 is the apostle's announcement of a coming visit, whereas in 1:23 he expressly states that he had written to the Corinthians in order to *avoid* making a visit. Indeed, the attempt to find and harmonize cross-references is symptomatic of a mode of interpretation that views 2 Corinthians as a "problem" to be "solved." It also seems to presume that the story must have a "happy ending," an assumption that Paul's letter to the Galatians ought to dispel.

Finally, the proposal to splice the two letters is at best forced, if not downright fanciful. Indeed, there is no evidence from any manuscripts or patristic writings that canonical 2 Corinthians ever existed other than in its present form, a fact with which all partition theories must reckon.

B. Weiss's Proposal

Johannes Weiss, in the early years of the twentieth century, made the following observation concerning 1 and 2 Corinthians: ". . . the conviction forces itself upon me more and more that the old church tradition has collected in these two documents the remains of more than two letters, and that these several letters originated at different stages. . . ."[29] Indeed, Weiss pulled at *all* the perceived seams of 2 Corinthians. He suggested that the canonical form of the epistle is a compilation of three letters, in the following order: (1) 8:1-24;

of shifting emotions as St. Paul" (see *II Corinthians*, xxvii). But could not the same line of argument be used concerning the relation between 9:15 and 10:1? At what point does one determine when Paul's mood shifts cross the line from credible to incredible? More importantly, it is critical to analyze the apostle's *rhetorical* strategy, not his personality.

[29]WEISS *Earliest Christianity*, 324. For his analysis and partitioning of both 1 and 2 Cor, see pp. 323-57. For the present task, I limit myself to Weiss's treatment of 2 Cor (pp. 341-57).

(2) 2:14-6:13[30] + 7:2-4 + 10:1-13:13; and (3) 1:1-2:13 + 7:5-16 + 9:1-15. Although his reading has not won many adherents, he was followed by Bultmann in combining 2:14-7:4 with 10:1-13:13.[31]

(1) Weiss's proposal deals with four key exegetical issues. First, although he accepted the Hausrath-Kennedy proposal that 2 Cor 10-13 is part of the *Schmerzensbrief*, Weiss claimed that the hypothesis was insufficient. He noted that several passages in 2:14-7:4 (e.g., 2:17-3:1; 6:11-13) seem to have been written in the same mode of embattlement as 2 Cor 10-13. He therefore asserted that the painful letter consisted in the main of these two large sections.[32] Second, his proposal addresses the apparent interruption of Paul's account of waiting to hear news from Titus, which appears to be broken off at the moment of greatest tension at 2:13, only to be resumed at 7:5. Weiss argued that "[t]his separation of what belongs so closely together is unheard of and intolerable from a literary point of view, while 2:13 and 7:5 fit onto each other as neatly as the broken pieces of a ring."[33] Thus, 1:1-2:13 and 7:5-16 originally formed the heart of Paul's letter of reconciliation (*Versöhnungsbrief*) that followed upon the news that the Corinthians had responded favorably to the *Schmerzensbrief*. Third, Weiss noted that Paul's manner of bringing up the collection in 9:1 sounds like an introduction of the topic, and thus 9:1-15 was not originally connected to 8:1-24. Rather, he surmised that 9:1-15 had been attached to the *Versöhnungsbrief*. Fourth, his proposal attempts to explain anomalies regarding 8:1-24, now separated completely from its canonical context. Weiss held that

---

[30]WEISS contends that 2 Cor 6:14-7:1 was part of the very first letter sent by Paul to the Corinthians, the letter alluded to in 1 Cor 5:9. See *Earliest Christianity*, 325.

[31]See BULTMANN, *The Second Letter to the Corinthians*, 16-18. Bultmann regarded 6:14-7:1 as non-Pauline, and also included 9:1-15 with this longer letter. He held that the later letter of reconciliation consisted of 1:1-2:13 + 7:5-8:24.

[32]It is typical of WEISS that he foresees probable objections to his views. For instance, he recognizes that Paul's optimistic expression in 7:4 does not fit the tone and tenor of the *Schmerzensbrief*: "The last words sound joyous and confident, but one has the feeling about them that Paul has forcibly wrung them from himself." See *Earliest Christianity*, 349. Needless to say, such an appeal to "feeling" does not qualify as solid exegesis.

[33]Ibid.

the visit of representatives announced in 8:16-24 was the same one recounted in 12:17-18 as a past event. Because the latter passage is part of the painful letter, 8:1-24 must be part of a letter written at an earlier phase of the apostle's dealings with the Corinthians. In fact, Weiss argued that the confidence expressed in 8:7 gives evidence that this letter was written before the incident involving the offender occurred.[34]

(2) Weiss's proposal requires the following historical reconstruction.[35] At about the time Paul wrote 1 Corinthians from Ephesus, he received word from Macedonia that the churches there were eager to participate in the collection. In response, he dispatched Titus and two brothers (carrying 2 Cor 8:1-24) – first to Macedonia, and then to Corinth – to facilitate bringing the collection to completion. Before Titus arrived in Corinth, however, several things happened in quick succession: Timothy's visit to Corinth and his subsequent return to Paul with news that all was not well; the apostle's second visit to Corinth and the incident with the "offender"; and Paul's sending to the community the *Schmerzensbrief*. In the meantime, Titus was "in some way or other" informed that he had a new mission, namely, to ascertain the effects of the painful letter. Finally arrived in Corinth, Titus was met with "fear and trembling" (2 Cor 7:15) by the chastised community,[36] and he immediately returned to Paul to report their repentance and loyalty to him. The apostle then wrote the letter of reconciliation, which included a renewed exhortation to complete the collection, as well as a notice that the Macedonians had increased their contribution even more.

(3) Weiss did not hypothesize how the text has come into its present form.

(4) Admittedly ingenious in many respects, Weiss's proposal is nevertheless faulty. While he was correct in seeing much continuity between 2 Cor 2:14-7:4 and 10:1-13:13, thereby avoiding exaggerated differences

---

[34]Ibid., 353.

[35]For what follows, see WEISS, *Earliest Christianity*, 353-57.

[36]Here is a good illustration of WEISS'S astute, careful reading of the text. He challenges the assumption that Titus had delivered the *Schmerzensbrief* because "this is nowhere stated and it even seems to be excluded by II Cor. 7:15, for the insubordinate church cannot have felt 'fear and trembling' in the presence of the bearer of a letter even before they had read the letter." See *Earliest Christianity*, 345.

between them, his identification of the passages as the main parts of the painful letter is subject to the same critique directed to Hausrath-Kennedy. Moreover, he overstates the formal and material likeness between 2:12-13 and 7:5-6. To give but one example, Paul uses the singular first person pronoun in the former, and the plural in the latter. Weiss's removal of 8:1-24 from what precedes is unwarranted, as the apostle elaborates in this section on several themes and images established in earlier chapters. Weiss's reading rests on a very complex reconstruction of events centered around Titus, a reconstruction that goes well beyond what the textual data allows. For instance, there is no mention in 8:1-24 of Titus's being commissioned to go to Macedonia to complete the collection there, or even to go there first; rather, 8:6 expressly states that he is being sent to the Corinthians. In fact, it is hard to read 8:1-6 and not conclude that it was written from Macedonia, rather than from Ephesus. Weiss's reconstruction rests on too shaky a foundation – for instance, the assumption that Titus was delayed on a task (in Macedonia), guess work of which there is no evidence; and the unsupportable presupposition that he somehow received word that his mission to Corinth had been changed (from completing the collection to learning about the reception of the painful letter). However, the most telling criticism of Weiss's proposal is that he offered no account for how 2 Corinthians received its present "cut and paste" form.

C. Bornkamm's Proposal

Günther Bornkamm, like Weiss, pulls at all of the seams of 2 Corinthians. In his reading and reconstruction, however, the text is torn completely asunder. Bornkamm's interpretation rests on the premise that, in 2 Corinthians, "several fragments of letters written at various times to meet very different external and internal situations are set alongside one another, in an order not corresponding to the course of events."[37] Bornkamm's reading separates out portions of five letters: (1) 2:14-7:4 (minus 6:14-7:1); (2) 10:1-

---

[37]G. BORNKAMM, *Paul*, trans. D.M.G. STALKER (Minneapolis: Fortress, 1995) 244. Bornkamm's partition proposal is set forth in his *Die Vorgeschichte des sogenannten zweiten Korintherbriefes*, 2nd ed (Heidelberg: Carl Winter, 1965). For a resumé of the latter, see his "The History of the Origin of the So-Called Second Letter to the Corinthians," *NTS* 8 (1962) 258-64; and idem, *Paul*, 74-77 and 244-46.

13:13; (3) 1:1-2:13 + 7:5-16; (4) 8:1-24; and (5) 9:1-15. This proposal has been embraced and advanced by (among others) Dieter Georgi[38] and H.D. Betz.[39]

(1) Proponents of the Bornkamm partition theory seek to solve the following exegetical puzzles. While accepting that 2 Cor 10-13 is the *Schmerzensbrief*, they (like Weiss) are also sensitive to the fact that 2 Cor 2:14-7:4 does contain apologetic passages as well as allusions to opposition to Paul. This theory, however, notes a difference in tone. Because the apostle seems less desperate about the Corinthians' loyalty in the earlier chapters, the proposal holds that 2 Cor 2:14-7:4 represents an earlier phase of the controversy than 2 Cor 10-13. Thus, part of 2 Cor 1-9 must have been written *prior* to the painful letter. Similar to Weiss, Bornkamm is struck by the violent interruption of Paul's dramatic account of his looking for Titus (2:12-13), an account that is oddly not resumed until much later (7:5-16).[40] In addition, it is held that 6:11-13 + 7:2-4 bears all the marks of a letter conclusion,[41] and that 2:14-7:4 is "without any relationship whatsoever to what precedes (1:1-2:13) or what follows (7:5-16)."[42] Hence, 2:14-7:4, dubbed Paul's "great apology for the apostolic office," is taken for this earlier piece of correspondence. Sections 1:1-2:13 and 7:5-16 are then spliced together, forming the main part of the later fragment of correspondence, the fragment that relates the eventual reconciliation between the apostle and the community. This proposal further views 2 Cor 8-9 as two separate letters pertaining to the collection. Whereas Bornkamm considers the possibility that 2 Cor 8 could have been attached to the *Versöhnungsbrief*, Georgi holds that "ch. 7 does nothing to prepare for the collection for the Jerusalem church, which dominates ch. 8, and ch. 8 does not pick up the

---

[38]See D. GEORGI, *The Opponents of Paul in Second Corinthians: A Study of Religious Propaganda in Late Antiquity* (Edinburgh: T. & T. Clark, 1987) esp. 9-18; and idem, "Corinthians, Second Letter to the," in *IDBSup*, 183-86.

[39]See BETZ, *2 Corinthians 8 and 9*, and "Corinthians, Second Epistle to the," in *ABD*, 1.1148-54.

[40]". . . fast 7 Seiten des Nestle-Textes später!" See BORNKAMM, *Die Vorgeschichte des sogenannten zweiten Korintherbriefes*, 21.

[41]See BETZ, *ABD*, 1.1149.

[42]So BORNKAMM, *Paul*, 245.

reconciliation theme of ch. 7."[43] Thus, Georgi argues that 8:1-24 marks a subsequent piece of Paul's Corinthian correspondence, and 9:1-15 a still later one. Second Corinthians 6:14-7:1 is held to be a non-Pauline – or even an *anti-Pauline*[44] – interpolation.

(2) The Bornkamm proposal requires a much more elaborate reconstruction of events and a larger time frame.[45] Thus, shortly after writing 1 Corinthians, Paul dispatched Titus to Corinth from Ephesus to expedite the collection. Soon afterwards, rival missionaries arrived and agitated the community against the apostle. Paul responded by sending a letter (2 Cor 2:14-7:4) that defended his manner of being an apostle. This letter had little effect, however, and the apostle decided to pay a personal visit. He found the community in open rebellion against him, the incident with the "offender" occurring at this time. Paul returned to Ephesus, from where he sent the painful letter with its frontal assault (10:1-13:13). Titus carried this letter to Corinth, and was charged with trying to bring about reconciliation. After suffering a brief imprisonment, Paul sought news from Titus, and eventually encountered him in Macedonia. Titus reported the community's repentance and the departure of the opposition, and the apostle quickly sent the *Versöhnungsbrief* (1:1-2:13 and 7:5-16). Then, inspired by the Macedonians' enthusiasm for the collection, the apostle sent Titus a third time to Corinth in order to bring the collection to completion (8:1-24). He also sent a second brief letter to other churches in the province of Achaia in this connection (9:1-15).

(3) The real burden of this proposal is to offer a credible account of the process of the redaction and compilation of 2 Corinthians into its present form. Bornkamm is fully aware of the challenge: "It is first of all strange that the editor not only changed around the course of events in time, but also . . . destroyed the consolatory effect of his own collection" of texts.[46] How does one explain the redactor's insertion of 2 Cor 2:14-7:4 into the *Versöhnungsbrief*, and

---

[43]GEORGI, *IDBSup*, 184.

[44]See BETZ, "2 Cor 6:14-7:1: An Anti-Pauline Fragment?" *JBL* 92 (1973) 88-108.

[45]The following is taken from BORNKAMM, *Paul*, 76-77; and GEORGI, *The Opponents of Paul in Second Corinthians*, 16-18.

[46]BORNKAMM, "The History of the Origin of the So-Called Second Letter to the Corinthians," 261.

his choosing to place the *Schmerzensbrief* at the end?[47] According to Bornkamm, the letter of reconciliation was used as the foundation document for the redaction. Paul's rehearsal of his journey from Ephesus to Macedonia via Troas (2:12-13) in this document then seemed to the redactor an appropriate place to insert the fragment which speaks of the apostle's *Triumphzug* (cf. 2:14). This metaphor, Bornkamm suggests, was understood by the collator in light of Paul's success as apostle to the nations. The end of the account of Paul's reconciliation with the Corinthians was deemed a suitable point to place the two letters concerning the collection.[48] Finally, Bornkamm hypothesizes that the redactor added the fragment containing the painful letter at the end of the compilation in order to portray Paul's opponents as false prophets who portended the end times. That is, the redactor was following a "formal rule" of early Christian literature that presented apostolic figures as warning their flocks against heresies to come. There is no explanation for how 6:14-7:1 came to be inserted into the text – only the assertion that it is a later interpolation.

(4) Bornkamm's thesis is defective beyond the weaknesses it shares with the Hausrath-Kennedy proposal.[49] Its tendency to atomize the text betrays a failure to see various semantic and rhetorical connections between parts of the letter. For instance, 2 Cor 7:4 is replete with terms that Paul elaborates in 7:5-16.[50] And while there are few direct semantic connections between 2 Cor 7 and 8, the apostle's joy in rehearsing the community's reconciliation with him is certainly done with an eye to motivating the Corinthians to be generous in their

---

[47]What follows is a summary of BORNKAMM'S account in *Der Vorgeschichte des sogenannten zweiten Korintherbriefes*, 24-36.

[48]For the placement of 2 Cor 8-9 after the letter of reconciliation, see BORNKAMM, *Paul*, 245-46.

[49]BORNKAMM acknowledges that the omission of any mention of the offender in the *Schmerzensbrief* and of the opponents in the *Versöhnungsbrief* is problematic. His attempts to explain the redactor's reasons for these omissions, while clever, are still a resort to an argument from silence. See *Der Vorgeschichte des sogenannten zweiten Korintherbriefes*, 19-20.

[50]The notion of being consoled (παρακλη-) appears again in 7:6 (2x), 7:7 (2x), and 7:13 (2x); of boasting (καυχη-) in 7:14 (2x); of joy (χαρ/χαιρ-) in 7:7, 7:9, 7:13 (2x), and 7:16; and of affliction (θλιψ-) in 7:5.

contribution to the collection. Thus, Georgi's assessment concerning the lack of relationship between chapters 7 and 8 reveals a myopic reading of the text. In fact, proponents of the Bornkamm thesis tend to exaggerate the presence of distinct genres in 2 Corinthians.[51] Finally, Bornkamm's theory of compilation must be called into question. His explanation of the redactor's insertion of the first apology (2:14-7:4) after 2:13 is based on a misreading of Paul's use of the image of the triumphal procession. The apostle presents himself as the *object* of the procession, not the subject, and thus as one who has been conquered. In addition, 2:12-13 does not connote a sense of triumph, but great anxiety. Bornkamm's recourse to the redactor's adherence to a "formal rule" of warning against end time false prophets depends on a gross distortion of the content of 2 Cor 10-13. These chapters are *not* testamentary literature.

D. *Semler's Proposal Simplified*

The most popular partition theory today is the simplest one. Like the Hausrath-Kennedy proposal, it posits a single seam in the text between chapters 9 and 10. Like Semler, it regards 2 Cor 10-13 as written *after* 2 Cor 1-9. It thus holds that the *Schmerzensbrief* is no longer extant. Unlike Semler, it does not separate 2 Cor 9 from 2 Cor 1-8. Prominent among the advocates of this simplified partition theory are C.K. Barrett[52] and Victor P. Furnish.[53]

(1) Proponents of this simplified theory contend that it resolves two exegetical difficulties. First, like the other partition theories, it attempts to account for the "abrupt shift" in subject matter, mood, and style between 2 Cor 10-13 and 2 Cor 1-9, taking into account the fundamental differences and incongruities perceived between the two sections. Among the additional observations made by advocates of the simplified partition theory, two from

---

[51]For instance, GEORGI refers to each of the five "fragments" as a distinct genre. See *IDBSup*, 184. In *2 Corinthians 8 and 9*, BETZ sees two separate administrative letters in 2 Cor 8 and 9. For a critique of Betz's "micro reading" of 2 Cor 8 and 9, see S.K. STOWERS, "*PERI MEN GAR* and the Integrity of 2 Cor. 8 and 9," *NovT* 32 (1990) 340-48.

[52]See BARRETT, *The Second Epistle to the Corinthians*, esp. 1-25.

[53]See V.P. FURNISH, *II Corinthians*, AB 32A (New York: Doubleday, 1984) esp. 29-55.

Furnish will suffice for illustrative purposes. He observes that, whereas the first person plural is prevalent in 2 Cor 1-9, the final four chapters are marked by Paul's use of the first person singular.[54] In addition, Furnish finds it significant that the series of appeals in 5:20-9:15 emerge in the context of the apostle's announcement of an impending visit by his representatives. This, he argues, is an appropriate way to end a letter. It is difficult to reconcile the presence, in the same letter, of these appeals and announcement with the strikingly different appeals in 2 Cor 10-13 and the announcement there of *Paul's* own imminent visit.[55] In other words, there seem to be two endings to the text as it now stands.

Second, by positing 2 Cor 10-13 as a later writing, this simplified proposal claims to succeed in offering a coherent account of the various references to Titus and the collection. Proponents argue that 7:6-16 recounts Titus's first visit (see esp. 7:14) to the Corinthians, and there is no mention here of a companion. In 8:16-24 Paul announces a second visit by Titus, now accompanied by two brothers, for the purpose of bringing to completion the Corinthians' contribution to the collection. In 12:17-18, however, Paul refers to a past visit to the Corinthians by Titus and one brother. This can be harmonized only if 12:17-18 is part of a later letter that makes reference to Titus's second visit (as announced in 8:16-24).[56] In addition, this theory attempts to reconcile the tension between Paul's confidence expressed in 2 Cor 8-9 concerning the collection and his allusions in 12:14-18 to charges of fraud in connection with it. Indeed, Furnish asserts that the apostle's confidence in 2 Cor 8-9 "is as inconceivable in a letter which postdates chaps. 10-13 as it would be in the same letter with the remarks of 12:14-18."[57] Thus, it is argued that 2 Cor 10-13 must be part of a later letter than the contents contained in 2 Cor 1-9.

---

[54]See FURNISH, *II Corinthians*, 32.

[55]Ibid., 37.

[56]See FURNISH, *II Corinthians*, 31, 36, and 38; and BARRETT, *The Second Epistle to the Corinthians*, 20-21. For a more complete account of the importance of Titus for a historical reconstruction of the events behind 2 Cor, see BARRETT, "Titus," in *Essays on Paul* (Philadelphia: Westminster, 1982) 118-31.

[57]FURNISH, *II Corinthians*, 38.

(2) The historical reconstruction involved with this theory includes the following unique aspects. Titus's visit to the Corinthians in conjunction with the (now lost) painful letter, recounted in 2 Cor 7:6-16, also entailed his first involvement with the collection (see 8:6). Barrett sees this more clearly than Furnish, and insists that part of Titus's charge on this initial visit must have included dealing with the collection. Two important consequences follow from this insight: first, Paul's "sorrowful visit was not as sorrowful as is sometimes thought," since he felt comfortable asking for money in his follow-up letter; and second, the apostle's anxiety in waiting for Titus was due more to his worrying about Titus and the dangers that might befall him while carrying a large sum of money (and not to Paul's concern about how he stood vis-à-vis the Corinthians).[58] After Titus's reunion with him – according to Barrett, Titus had left Corinth before the collection was completed in order to assure the apostle of their loyalty – Paul wrote 2 Cor 1-9, and sent Titus back (probably carrying the letter) to complete the work on the collection. A little later, however, the apostle received a report that the situation had worsened in Corinth, for rival apostles had succeeded in turning the Corinthians against Paul. It is surmised that either Titus had misread the situation during his first visit, or that there was a sudden dramatic increase in the opposition against Paul. In response, the apostle wrote another letter, part of which is contained in 2 Cor 10-13.[59]

(3) The simplified partition theory has a lighter burden to bear in giving an account of the compilation process. It holds that the reception of *1 Clement* or the prior publication and distribution of 1 Corinthians led to increased interest in Paul's other correspondence to Corinth. Although some of the content of 2 Cor 10-13 was potentially embarrassing to the Corinthians, it was acknowledged that these chapters contained valuable information about the apostle. The uncomplimentary aspects, moreover, would be mitigated by their combination with 2 Cor 1-9, a natural appendation given that 2 Cor 1-9 and 2 Cor 10-13 dealt with similar topics. It made sense to attach the shorter to the longer letter, perhaps because this was remembered to be the case chronologically or because 2 Cor 1-9 contained a blessing period (1:3-7) that would parallel the thanksgiving section in 1 Cor 1:4-9. The ending of 2 Cor 1-9 and the beginning

---

[58]See BARRETT, *The Second Epistle to the Corinthians*, 8 and 20. The quotation is found on p. 20.

[59]BARRETT'S reconstruction is found in *The Second Epistle to the Corinthians*, 8-13 and 20-21; FURNISH'S in *II Corinthians*, 41-42, 44-46, and 54-55.

of 2 Cor 10-13 were then removed (if one was not lost already) to give canonical 2 Corinthians its present form.[60]

(4) The simplified proposal is an improvement over the previous three in that it avoids the problems of identifying 2 Cor 10-13 as the *Schmerzensbrief*. In contrast to Weiss's and Bornkamm's theories, it correctly recognizes the logic and coherence of Paul's presentation in 2 Cor 1-9. However, the simplified proposal has its own weaknesses. First, it argues from silence, since there is no reference in 2 Cor 10-13 to Paul's receiving a report concerning his rival missionaries/evangelists (cf. 1 Cor 1:11; 7:1; and 11:18 – where the apostle *does* indicate having received new information). Second, it downplays too much the various notices in 2 Cor 1-9 of the rivals' activities and insinuations (see, e.g., 2:17-3:1; 4:2; and 5:12). Third, this proposal still cannot completely resolve the issue of Titus, an issue that is critical to this construal. For instance, it can be argued that 8:16-24 and 12:17-18 refer to two different visits, for the former announces Titus's coming with *two* brothers, while the latter refers to a previous visit by Titus and *one* brother. Fourth, given the importance of the collection for Paul, it is odd that there is scant reference to it in 2 Cor 10-13 (if this were a separate letter). Moreover, the force of the argument that holds that the apostle would not write these scathing chapters immediately after asking for money can be turned on this theory as well. How motivated would the Corinthians be to give generously after receiving 2 Cor 10-13? Lastly – and this constitutes a major problem for all partition theories – there is no manuscript evidence that any partitions of 2 Corinthians ever existed independently.

E. Summary

This survey reveals an extraordinary diversity of opinion regarding the composition and compilation of 2 Corinthians, as well as the sequence and nature of events that lay behind the text. Furnish concludes his own survey of partitions by observing: "Anyone who reads carefully through the literature on the question of the literary integrity of 2 Cor is bound to be impressed with the complexity of the problem, with the ambiguity of much of the data, and with the

---

[60]This account takes elements from FURNISH, *II Corinthians*, 40-41, and THRALL, *II Corinthians*, 1.45-47. Although Thrall holds that 2 Cor is a composite of three letters (chapters 1-8, 9, and 10-13 – in that order), her compilation hypothesis coheres with that offered by proponents of the simplified proposal.

many different, reasonable interpretations of the data that are possible."[61] Certainly, the interpretation of 2 Corinthians is a complex undertaking, and much of the data is indeed ambiguous. But ought one to be impressed, or *depressed*, by such a lack of consensus among scholars using critical literary and historical hypotheses? From a logical standpoint, at most only one of these theories can be correct. Given the deficiencies of each outlined above, there is good reason to doubt the sufficiency of any one of them. In fact, there is a certain "all or nothing" quality to these partition theories. As Barrett aptly points out, "the literary and historical hypotheses stand or fall together."[62] I submit that none of the partition theories is able to withstand critical scrutiny.[63]

Interpretation of 2 Corinthians by means of partition theories is inevitably sidetracked by detours that lead to several dead ends. Indeed, it is typical of those whose principal concern is to reconstruct the historical career of Paul to divide the text into several fragments, thus raising the question of whether the historical quest drives the interpretation of the text (rather than vice versa). Even the simplest partition theory must resort to a historical reconstruction that raises as many questions as it gives answers. Now, my point here is not to challenge the validity of critical historical and literary inquiry of Scripture. I do, however, raise the question about its limitations for the interpretation of 2 Corinthians. That is, given the fact that "many different, reasonable interpretations of the data" are possible vis-à-vis partition theories,

---

[61]FURNISH, *II Corinthians*, 34.

[62]BARRETT, *The Second Epistle to the Corinthians*, 17.

[63]It is important to point out that those who argue for the literary unity of 2 Corinthians on literary-historical grounds must also rely on hypotheses that are not without problems. For instance, see W.G. KÜMMEL, *Introduction to the New Testament*, rev. ed., trans. H.C. KEE (Nashville: Abingdon, 1973) 281-93.

A. STEWART-SYKES has made an important contribution to the question of the plausibility of partition theories. Recognizing the various complexities involved in the compositional and (proposed) redactional processes, he proposes a new criterion for adjudicating partition theories, namely, the criterion of the *physical* possibility of producing the text. On the basis of such a criterion, he argues that the more complex partition theories become less tenable. See "Ancient Editors and Copyists and Modern Partition Theories: The Case of the Corinthian Correspondence," *JSNT* 61 (1996) 53-64.

it is fair to ask whether the historical-literary approach leads to more blind alleys than satisfactory readings of the text.

The judgment of the inadequacy of each of the partition theories is crucial to my thesis. I read 2 Corinthians as a single letter. Although one cannot make a conclusive case for its literary unity (or for any partition theory) by means of historical-literary analysis, I contend, and will argue below, that sensitivity to rhetorical features opens a plausible way of reading the text as it now stands.[64] The important point for the time being is that the major partition theories have been found wanting. Now I consider whether readings based on the identity of Paul's opponents – many of which are intricately connected to partition theories – yield the same conclusion.

II. Readings Based on the Identity of Paul's Opponents

The identity of Paul's rivals or opponents is one of the more vexing historical-critical issues in Pauline studies. Second Corinthians has been an important source for scholars investigating this problem. Several of the questions raised at the beginning of this chapter deal with the issue of the apostle's opponents. Barrett expresses the critical importance of this problem for several NT scholars: ". . . this opposition constitutes one of the crucial questions for the understanding of the New Testament. It is not too much to say that a full understanding both of New Testament history and of New Testament theology waits on the right answering of this question."[65] More important for the present study is the assumption that correct identification of Paul's rivals is the interpretive key that unlocks the meaning of 2 Corinthians. Jerry L. Sumney represents this assumption when he writes: ". . . one's identification of the opponents helps to provide the context of the letter, and thereby, *serves as a*

---

[64]Cf. the assessment of B. WITHERINGTON: "Part of the reason for the existence of [partition] theories is that most treatments of 2 Corinthians have not taken into account Paul's use of ancient rhetorical conventions." See *Conflict & Community in Corinth: A Socio-Rhetorical Commentary on 1 and 2 Corinthians* (Grand Rapids, Mich.: Eerdmans, 1995) 329.

[65]BARRETT, "Paul's Opponents in 2 Corinthians," in *Essays on Paul* (Philadelphia: Westminster, 1982) 60-86, here 60.

basis for interpreting the whole."[66] I contend that this assumption leads the interpretation of 2 Corinthians into still more blind alleys.

There are four major hypotheses concerning the identification of Paul's opponents: Gnostics, Divine Men, Judaizers, and Pneumatics.[67] A separate theory holds that the "superlative apostles" (2 Cor 11:5 and 12:11) represent a different group from the rivals whom Paul takes on in 2 Corinthians. I present each approach by (1) setting forth the basic hypothesis; (2) giving some examples of how it impacts the exegesis of 2 Corinthians; and (3) offering a brief critique. As with the partition theories, my purpose is to be broadly illustrative as I focus on one or two representative figures for each hypothesis. Sumney has made an important contribution to the issue of Paul's opponents with his incisive critique of the methodologies various scholars have utilized. I rely heavily on Sumney's work throughout this section. My concern, however, has more to do with the deleterious exegetical consequences of these hypotheses than with the methodologies employed.

A. Gnostics (Walter Schmithals)

(1) Walter Schmithals asserts that Paul's opponents are Jewish-Christian Gnostics. In *Gnosticism in Corinth*, he argues that 1 and 2 Corinthians must be interpreted in light of "the penetration of the Gnostics into the Corinthian community."[68] Schmithals begins his treatment by positing a system of *pre-*

---

[66] J.L. SUMNEY, *Identifying Paul's Opponents: The Question of Method in 2 Corinthians*, JSNTSup 40 (Sheffield: Sheffield Academic Press, 1990) 189-90 (italics added). Cf. D. OOSTENDORP'S comments on studies that attempt to uncover the nature of Paul's opponents in 2 Cor: "Any such study can only reach tentative results because of the incompleteness and ambiguity of the available evidence. However, it is necessary to make the attempt, *for the exact point of Paul's argument often depends on the nature of his opponents' position.*" See his *Another Jesus: A Gospel of Jewish-Christian Superiority in II Corinthians* (Kampen: J.H. Kok, 1967) 80 (italics added).

[67] For an insightful historical investigation of how scholars have treated the question of Paul's opponents at Corinth, see R. BIERINGER, "Die Gegner des Paulus im 2. Korintherbrief," in *Studies on 2 Corinthians*, 181-221. In addition, see THRALL, *II Corinthians*, 2.926-45.

[68] W. SCHMITHALS, *Gnosticism in Corinth: An Investigation of the Letters to the Corinthians*, 3rd ed., trans. J.E. STEELY (Nashville: Abingdon, 1971) 286.

Christian Gnosticism, a construction that is based on an anachronistic reading of texts dating from the second century CE and later. He defines Gnosticism as "that religious movement which teaches man to understand himself as a piece of divine substance."[69] Its major characteristics are cosmological and anthropological dualism, the myth of the fall and imprisonment of the divine substance into (some) human bodies, and redemption as the knowledge of this indwelling by those so possessed. Schmithals next offers a literary-critical analysis of 1 and 2 Corinthians, as well as a reconstruction of the events that lay behind them. According to him, canonical 1 and 2 Corinthians are composites of *six* separate letters from Paul written in a period of eight months.[70] This short time span is important for Schmithals because he posits a single front of opposition to the apostle in both 1 and 2 Corinthians. Schmithals then goes on to analyze various individual passages in light of his construction of Gnosticism and his partitioning of the letters. His concern is to set forth the theology of Paul's opponents. Crucial to his work is the assumption that, at several points, the apostle misunderstands his rivals.

(2) How does Schmithals's thesis impact his exegesis of 2 Corinthians? I limit myself to two examples. Second Corinthians 11:4 – with its reference to 'another Jesus, different spirit, different gospel' – is critical to his theory. According to Schmithals, the ἄλλος 'Ιησοῦς refers to the Gnostics' negative assessment of the man Jesus as the mere "sarkic" part of the redeemer. The πνεῦμα ἕτερον alludes to the Pneuma, the divine substance that is present in the "pneumatics" of the Gnostic myth. And the εὐαγγέλιον ἕτερον denotes the Gnosis itself, the redemptive knowledge of the pneumatic's true identity and destiny.[71] In addition, the references in 5:11-13 to φανερόομαι and ἐξίστημι,

---

[69]Ibid., 30. For his reconstruction of pre-Christian Gnosticism, see pp. 25-86.

[70]Ibid., 87-116. Schmithals's partitioning of 1 and 2 Cor is as follows: "Letter A" = 2 Cor 6:14-7:1 + 1 Cor 6:12-20 + 9:24-10:22 + 11:2-34 +15:1-58 +16:13-24; "B" = 1 Cor 1:1-6:11 + 7:1-9:23 + 10:23-11:1 + 12:1-14:40 + 16:1-12; "C" = 2 Cor 2:14-6:13 + 7:2-4; "D" = 2 Cor 10:1-13:13 (the *Schmerenzbrief*); "E" = 2 Cor 9:1-15; and "F" = 2 Cor 1:1-2:13 + 7:5-8:24. Of the partition theories treated above, his division of 2 Cor most resembles the Bornkamm proposal, and shares many of its inadequacies.

[71]SCHMITHALS, *Gnosticism in Corinth*, 124-41, esp. 132-35 and 167-69.

terms Schmithals equates one with the other, are important for his thesis that Paul responds to the Gnostics' demand for ecstatic manifestations of the Spirit.[72]

(3) Schmithals's proposal fails on several counts. First, his historical reconstruction assumes that later century documents pertaining to Gnosticism accurately reflect the first century situation. In doing so, he commits the "fallacy of presentism." Moreover, his hypostatized construction predetermines his selection and analysis of the texts.[73] Second, Schmithals's literary-critical analysis is arbitrary. His elaborate partitioning of the Corinthian epistles requires more substantial explanation for their current form than he provides.[74] Indeed, similar to his construction of the Gnostic system, Schmithals's partition theory governs his exegesis rather than the other way around. Third, in his major exegetical section, Schmithals's work reads more like a systematic, topic-by-topic treatment of Gnosticism supplemented by disparate Corinthian texts than a rigorous, contextual analysis of the letters themselves. This is due, in part, to his avowed concern to deal with the Gnostics' theology in Corinth.[75] Fourth, Schmithals's presumption that he knows the opponents better than Paul is untenable. As Sumney notes, "There is a great deal of difference between recognizing that an ancient author did not fully understand the situation s/he addresses and saying that a modern scholar understands better. The former is often a possibility, the latter is improbable."[76]

In addition, Schmithals's treatment of individual passages is problematic. His discussion of 2 Cor 11:4 never takes into account its immediate context. Rather, his assumptions about Gnosticism drive his interpretation. For instance, Schmithals's discussion of the ἄλλος Ἰησοῦς

---

[72]Ibid., 187-92, esp. 190.

[73]See SUMNEY, *Identifying Paul's Opponents*, 78 and 82.

[74]See, e.g., SCHMITHALS, *Gnosticism in Corinth*, 96 and 100.

[75]Observe SCHMITHALS'S treatment of 13:2b-5 in *Gnosticism in Corinth*, 196: "The idea of 13:2b-3 is continued in vs. 5, after *the nonessential theological comment of vs. 4*" (italics added). Surely, Paul's statements that (1) Christ was crucified out of weakness but lives out of the power of God, and (2) the apostle himself participates in this power, rank higher than "nonessential"!

[76]SUMNEY, *Identifying Paul's Opponents*, 84.

depends mostly upon his analysis of 1 Cor 12:3, where he proposes that ἀνάθεμα Ἰησοῦς refers to an ecstatic proclamation by Pneumatics in the community. Schmithals engages in similar Gnostic catchword exegesis in 2 Cor 5:11-13. Even if one grants him the dubious assumption that ἐξίστημι ("be ecstatic," 5:13) and φανερόομαι (5:11) are used synonymously, his linkage of the *passive* verb φανερόομαι to the phrase φανέρωσις τοῦ πνεύματος in 1 Cor 12:7 is objectionable as a grammatical matter. Even more intolerable is his assessment of the latter phrase as a fixed Gnostic expression: "Even though I am not acquainted with a parallel, I should nevertheless confidently assert that it, along with the abundance of concepts encountered in [1 Cor 12:]8 ff., is of Gnostic origin. . . ." Schmithals has at this point tossed aside all exegetical controls![77]

B. Divine Men (Dieter Georgi)

(1) In *The Opponents of Paul in Second Corinthians*, Dieter Georgi proposes that the rivals are Hellenistic-Jewish propagandists whose distinguishing characteristic is their θεῖος ἀνήρ ("divine man") christology. After some preliminary literary-critical remarks on 2 Corinthians, he starts with the opponents' "self-designations" of function and origin in 2 Cor 11:13 and 11:22-23.[78] According to Georgi, these self-designations are best understood within the context of Hellenistic-Jewish apologetics and mission. Citing various Hellenistic-Jewish texts – in particular, Josephus and Philo – he argues that "the Jewish mission" depicted legendary figures like Abraham and (especially) Moses as "divine men." This mission was marked by Hellenistic influences, including the allegorical interpretation of Scripture and powerful pneumatic manifestations. Its practitioners believed in a "synergistic process" in which God participates in the human and humans participate in the divine. Such transfiguration was true for the great θεῖοι ἄνδρες in the past, and was a

---

[77]SCHMITHALS'S approach to 2 Cor is so one-sided that he regards 3:17, 3:18b, and 5:16 as Gnostic glosses because they represent the *opponents'*, not Paul's, theology. Schmithals suggests that they were written on the margins of the original epistle (= Letter C), and thus transmitted in all copies. See *Gnosticism in Corinth*, 302-25.

[78]See GEORGI, *The Opponents of Paul in Second Corinthians*, 27-60. For his partition theory and reconstruction of the underlying events, see pp. 9-18. I have already offered a critique of his partition theory in my treatment of Bornkamm's proposal.

possibility for the missionaries as well. Georgi next posits that this Jewish θεῖος ἀνήρ theology exerted a strong influence on the early church's christology and understanding of apostleship, as is evident, for instance, in Acts. He concludes that Paul's rivals in Corinth were representatives of such a missionary movement, which was in actuality anything but a fringe movement in the early church.[79] With this historical reconstruction in place, Georgi returns to an analysis of texts in 2 Corinthians.

(2) Georgi's thesis exerts its strongest exegetical impact on his analysis of 2 Cor 3:7-18, a notoriously difficult passage. He contends that the core of this pericope represents the *rivals'* interpretation of Exod 34:29-35 (highlighting Moses as a θεῖος ἀνήρ). Georgi argues that the awkwardness of 2 Cor 3:7-18 stems from Paul's insertion of glosses into the opponents' "text." By means of these modifications, the apostle rebuts his opponents' claims.[80] In addition, Georgi asserts that the opponents' divine man christology lurks behind 4:5-11. He surmises that "[t]he phrase ζωὴ 'Ιησοῦ was probably one of their slogans. It referred to the sensational power of life demonstrated by the θεῖος ἀνήρ Jesus in the past, which could be reproduced by his messengers since."[81] Georgi then asserts that Paul counters his opponents by interpreting ζωὴ 'Ιησοῦ in light of the νέκρωσις 'Ιησοῦ. In other words, the apostle reinterprets ζωὴ 'Ιησοῦ as referring to the human Jesus' mode of existence which led to the cross, not one marked by pneumatic manifestations.

(3) Georgi's theory is highly problematic. First, he makes an unwarranted methodological leap. He begins by hypothesizing that the opponents' self-designations point to the world of Hellenistic-Jewish apologetics. Modest enough. When he comes back to 2 Corinthians, however, "*he proceeds as if he has proven* that the opponents' theology is dependent on these apologists. *He seems to assume that he has established* that the opponents are divine men with titles from 2 Corinthians 10-13 and thus, their connection to divine man theology."[82] Second, while Georgi rightly focuses on first century

---

[79]Ibid., 83-174.

[80]Ibid., 264-71. For Georgi's reconstruction of the opponents' text, see 270-71.

[81]GEORGI, *The Opponents of Paul in Second Corinthians*, 275. For his treatment of 4:5-11, see 273-76.

[82]SUMNEY, *Identifying Paul's Opponents*, 52 (italics added).

CE authors in his historical reconstruction of the Jewish mission, these sources yield a paucity of references to θεῖος ἀνήρ. In particular, as Carl R. Holladay has shown, this is true concerning Josephus and Philo, Georgi's main sources. Their use of this concept, moreover, differs significantly from his interpretation.[83] Third (and this stems immediately from the preceding) is the issue of the validity of Georgi's reconstruction of the Hellenistic-Jewish mission. The reconstruction rests on a meager foundation, one which certainly is not capable of bearing the weight of the elaborate structure Georgi creates. And as Sumney notes, when a reconstruction is found to be faulty, that on which it is based is bound to be inaccurate as well.[84]

Finally, although Georgi engages the text of 2 Corinthians more rigorously than Schmithals, he nevertheless allows his reconstruction to determine his reading. His (admittedly clever) interpretation of 2 Cor 3:7-18 rests entirely on speculation. Sound exegetical practice does not base analysis of a passage on a hypothetical text produced by hypothetically – and in this case, faultily – reconstructed opponents, especially when Paul gives no indication at

---

[83]See C.R. HOLLADAY, *Theios Aner in Hellenistic Judaism: A Critique of the Use of This Category in New Testament Christology*, SBLDS 40 (Missoula, Mont.: Scholars Press, 1977). Holladay points out that the term θεῖος ἀνήρ occurs only once in Josephus (*Ant*. 3.180) and only three times in Philo (*Virt*. 177; *Prov*. 2.39 and 2.48). Interestingly, Georgi appeals to only one of the texts from Philo, *Virt*. 177. For Holladay's treatment of θεῖος ἀνήρ in Josephus, see *Theios Aner in Hellenistic Judaism*, 47-102; for his discussion of θεῖος ἀνήρ in Philo, see pp. 173-98.

[84]See SUMNEY, *Identifying Paul's Opponents*, 55. HOLLADAY offers the following assessment in *Theios Aner in Hellenistic Judaism*, 239: "As to the question of missionary preaching, the question of the exact relationship between Hellenistic-Judaism, its sources, its theology, its sociological complexion, and early Christian missionary preaching is still unresolved. The first question is whether the *sources* are adequate enough to construct the picture of Hellenistic-Jewish missionary activity that Georgi does. To assemble all the references to supposed missionary activity within the mystery religions and add to them the occasional pieces of evidence for travelling Jews, from which is elaborated a detailed picture of Hellenistic-Jewish missionaries is a highly questionable method of approach" (Holladay's italics). Cf. D.L. TIEDE, *The Charismatic Figure as Miracle Worker*, SBLDS 1 (Missoula, Mont.: Scholars Press, 1972).

all that he is revising another document.[85] Moreover, Georgi's reading of 4:10-11 suffers from the same tendency. Instead of conjecturing that ζωὴ ᾿Ιησοῦ is a slogan of the opponents, his exegesis would be better served by investigating *Paul's* understanding of the phrase. Indeed, later on Georgi rightly recognizes that, in 2 Cor 13:4, "Paul speaks of ζωή here too, but here he means the resurrected and not the earthly Jesus."[86] A close look at Georgi's reading of 2 Corinthians reveals that divine man christology governs his reading more than the apostle's own exposition.

C. Judaizers (Derk Oostendorp)

(1) In *Another Jesus*, Derk Oostendorp claims that Paul's opponents are Judaizers. He argues that the Gnostic and Divine Man theories are not sufficient to overturn F.C. Baur's Judaizer thesis. Rather, Baur's thesis only needs to be modified to take more account of the role of the Spirit in 2 Corinthians.[87] According to Oostendorp, the opponents "taught that Jesus as the Christ had introduced a new era in which the primacy of Israel over the Gentiles was to be made manifest."[88] Consequently, the Mosaic law continued to be regarded as the supreme manifestation of God's will. Moreover, it was through obedience to the law that Christians were empowered by the Spirit. Thus, pneumatic gifts were evidence of fidelity to the law. Oostendorp asserts that the opponents chastised Paul because he refused to inculcate the Mosaic law among the

---

[85]For a reading of 2 Cor 3 that does not rely on the identity of Paul's opponents or on a reconstruction of their theology, see H. MARKS, "Pauline Typology and Revisionary Criticism," *JAAR* 52 (1984) 71-92, here 81-85.

[86]GEORGI, *The Opponents of Paul in Second Corinthians*, 279.

[87]See OOSTENDORP, *Another Jesus*, 4. For F.C. BAUR'S position, see his "Die Christuspartei in der korinthischen Gemeinde, der Gegensatz des petrinishen und paulinischen Christentum in der ältesten Kirche, der Apostel Petrus in Rom," *Tübingen Zeitschrift für Theologie* 4 (1831) 61-206; and idem, *Paul, The Apostle of Jesus Christ – His Life and Work, His Epistles and Doctrine: A Contribution to the Critical History of Primitive Christianity*, vol. 1, 2nd ed., trans. E. ZELLER (London: Williams & Norgate, 1876).

[88]OOSTENDORP, *Another Jesus*, 80.

Corinthians, and gave little evidence of possessing spiritual gifts.[89] Unlike Baur, Oostendorp offers no historical reconstruction of the rivals, nor does he enter into the debate over the unity of 2 Corinthians.[90]

(2) Second Corinthians 3:7-18 is central to Oostendorp's Judaizer theory, for it is here that Paul deals explicitly with Moses and the "old covenant." Oostendorp begins his treatment of this pericope by turning first to Galatians. His rationale is that the latter epistle contains several passages in which the Judaizers in Galatia associated the Spirit with law observance. Oostendorp then states that "it would be reasonable to assume that in Corinth, too, the opponents considered the Spirit to be inseparably linked with the law."[91] He goes on to analyze 2 Cor 3 with this assumption, and contends that Paul's strategy is to wrest Moses from his opponents. Moreover, Oostendorp argues from the apostle's references to the opponents in 11:15 as διάκονοι δικαιοσύνης ("servants of righteousness") and to their "pedigree" in 11:22 that they promote righteousness through law observance.[92] Oostendorp also claims that 4:10-12 is best understood in light of the apostle's "dealing with the problem of the relationship between Israel and the Christian." He contends that in these verses, "we" refers to Paul and his fellow Israelites, and "you" to the Gentiles. Citing Rom 11:11-15, Oostendorp holds that 2 Cor 4:10-12 points to Israel's rejection of the gospel and to the Gentiles' acceptance of it.[93]

(3) Oostendorp's thesis founders in many ways. First – and this is the embarrassment of all Judaizer hypotheses – there is no mention of νόμος or

---

[89]Ibid.

[90]See, e.g., OOSTENDORP, *Another Jesus*, 5: ". . . I would like to point out that accepting or challenging the unity of II Cor. makes very little difference for the results of this study."

[91]Ibid., 36. Oostendorp cites the following texts from Gal: 3:2-5; 5:14; 5:18; 5:23; and 6:2.

[92]Ibid., 11-13. Observe OOSTENDORP'S reasoning in *Another Jesus*, 5: "This emphasis on their Jewishness does not prove that keeping the commandments of the law played an important role in their gospel, but Israel and keeping the law are so united for all known Jewish contemporaries of Paul that it would be strange if keeping the law did not play a role in their theology." This is tantamount to begging the question.

[93]Ibid., 61-67. The quotation is from p. 63.

circumcision or dietary regulations in 2 Corinthians.[94] Second, his way of setting up his project is problematic. By assuming from the outset that the opponents are either Judaizers or Pneumatics, he excludes *a priori* all other hypotheses, as well as the possibility of significant overlap between the two groups he does propose. In fact, Oostendorp's own solution demonstrates that he posed the question in too facile a manner.[95] Third, he allows his hypothesis to determine and distort his reading of several passages. Fourth, Oostendorp resorts too often to other texts, especially Galatians and Romans, to adjudicate his interpretation of 2 Corinthians. Indeed, those holding to the Judaizer theory are often guilty of importing Galatians into their reading of 2 Corinthians.

Oostendorp's analysis of the passages cited above illustrate the last two points. His treatment of 2 Cor 3:7-18 is overly influenced by what he finds in Galatians concerning the relationship between law observance and the Spirit. In fact, his interpretation entails a troubling picture of Moses.[96] In addition, Oostendorp's Judaizer hypothesis leads him to read too much into the reference

---

[94]C.K. BARRETT, who also argues that the opponents are Judaizers, protests that the lack of reference to circumcision in 2 Cor is inconclusive: "There were Judaizers who did not call for circumcision, and one of them had most probably been in Corinth already before 1 Corinthians was written – Cephas. Without demanding circumcision he had attempted to impose a Judaic pattern of thought and religious life upon a Gentile community. . . ." See BARRETT, "Christianity in Corinth," in *Essays on Paul* (Philadelphia: Westminster, 1982) 1-27, here 21. It is incumbent upon Barrett, however, to adduce more evidence than to refer to T.W. MANSON'S "The Corinthian Correspondence (1)," in *Studies in the Gospels and Epistles*, ed. M. BLACK (Philadelphia: Westminster, 1962) 190-209. Where is there evidence in 2 Cor of "the concerted move to instill Palestinian piety and Palestinian orthodoxy into the Corinthian church" (see BARRETT, "Christianity in Corinth," 27, n. 103 – the quoted words are Manson's)? Indeed, it is telling that Barrett cites Manson's essay on *1 Cor*, not 2 Cor.

[95]See SUMNEY, *Identifying Paul's Opponents*, 81-82.

[96]According to OOSTENDORP, Paul claims that when Moses entered the tabernacle, he enjoyed freedom from the written code (which only leads to condemnation and death). This is how the apostle wrested Moses from those claiming that it was only through law observance that one received the Spirit. Oostendorp explains that Moses put on the veil when he communicated the written code to the Israelites in order to indicate that the Spirit is not efficacious where the law is proclaimed (see *Another Jesus*, 45-46). This explanation depicts Moses as indirect at best, and cynical at worst.

to δικαιοσύνη in 11:15. There is nothing in the context of this verse that speaks of law observance. Lastly, Oostendorp's explication of 4:10-12 reveals both of these tendencies. He forces Paul's meaning in Rom 11:11-15 onto this passage. And his presupposition of the Judaizers' theological *tendenz* leads him to conclude that the "we" and "you" in 2 Cor 4:10-12 refer to people other than the obvious sense in the text, namely, the apostle and his co-workers (= "we") and the Corinthians (= "you"). In sum, Oostendorp's theory results in some dubious exegesis.

D. ὑπερλίαν ἀπόστολοι *as Jerusalem Apostles (Barrett and Käsemann)*

(1) C.K. Barrett and Ernst Käsemann assert that the "superlative apostles" (2 Cor 11:5 and 12:11) are to be distinguished from the group whom Paul describes as "false apostles" (11:13) and 'Satan's servants' (11:15). They claim that the ὑπερλίαν ἀπόστολοι were the Jerusalem apostles, those referred to as "pillars" (Peter, James, and John) in Gal 2:9, and that the ψευδαπόστολοι were a delegation sent from the Jerusalem church (so Käsemann) or itinerant agents from Jerusalem who misrepresented their principals (so Barrett).[97] Only the itinerant preachers, not the Jerusalem apostles themselves, arrived in Corinth and wreaked havoc there (in the apostle's mind, at least). According to Käsemann and Barrett, Paul unleashes his strongest invective upon these agents. He settles for using irony against the "superlative apostles."

(2) Käsemann's chief argument focuses on the "jerky" (*sprunghaft*) transition between 2 Cor 11:4 and 11:5. He reads 11:4 (which refers to ὁ

---

[97]See E. KÄSEMANN, "Die Legitimät des Apostels: Eine Untersuchung zu II Korinther 10-13," *ZNW* 41 (1942) 33-71, here 46; and C.K. BARRETT, "Paul's Opponents in 2 Corinthians," 81. There, Barrett states that "[t]he precise relation between the two groups is far more difficult to establish than the fact that they existed." In "Die Legitimät des Apostels" (p. 40), Käsemann claims that the 'servants of Satan' are Pneumatics: "Aber von dem sporadischen Auftreten dieser einzelnen Daten ganz abgesehen – dominierend steht ja das "Amt" des Paulus im Vordergrund – läßt sich aus diesen Daten nicht mehr erheben, als daß die Gegner tatsächlich Pneumatiker sind und das selbst dem Apostel gegenüber betonen." As we have seen (n. 94), Barrett holds that the opponents are Judaizers. In addition, see BARRETT, *The Second Epistle to the Corinthians*, 6-7; and idem, "ΨΕΥΔΑΠΟΣΤΟΛΟΙ (2 Cor. 11.13)," in *Essays on Paul* (Philadelphia: Westminster, 1982) 87-107.

ἐρχόμενος who preaches 'another Jesus, spirit, and gospel') in light of 11:3 – and, *even more so*, in light of 11:13-15 – so that the referent is "Träger satanischen Truges." Käsemann then finds it odd that, in 11:5, Paul merely remarks that he is not inferior to such deceitful workers of Satan. Conversely, this dilemma is obviated by recognizing that 11:5 (which mentions οἱ ὑπερλίαν ἀπόστολοι) has a different referent.[98] Thus, Käsemann argues that 11:5 is a parenthetical remark between vv. 4 and 6, both of which refer to the itinerant agents.[99]

Barrett musters several more arguments. First, he observes that Paul raises the issue of apostolic support in close connection with "the superlative apostles" (cf. 2 Cor 11:7-11 and 12:13). Barrett further notes that Paul had explicitly mentioned "the other apostles and the brothers of the Lord and Cephas" in his discussion of the apostles' rights to financial support in 1 Cor 9:3-18. He concludes that this offers "a strong indication" that the ὑπερλίαν ἀπόστολοι were the Jerusalem apostles.[100] Second, Barrett interprets 2 Cor 10:12-18, where the apostle discusses his mission field, with reference to the mission agreement with the "pillars" recounted in Gal 2:9. That Paul would later mention the Jerusalem apostles in 2 Cor 11:5 and 12:11 is therefore not surprising, according to Barrett. In fact, he notes that just as the apostle referred ironically to "those reputed to be something" in Gal 2:6, so he now uses the ironic expression ὑπερλίαν ἀπόστολοι.[101] Third, Barrett argues that Paul shifts gears in 2 Cor 11:21b. With his reference there to τις, "Paul's thought has moved beyond his immediate rivals, the intruders . . . to those who stand

---

[98]See KÄSEMANN, "Die Legitimät des Apostels," 42: "Wie kann Paulus Irrlehrern gegenüber eine unüberbrückbare Kluft aufreisen, . . . um dann zu schließen, er sei nicht weniger als sie"; and p. 44: "Nur wo man sich diese diese Beobachtungen und Fragen vergegenwärtigt, wird man den *sprunghaften* Übergang von 11:4 zu 11:5 richtig erfassen" (italics added).

[99]Ibid., 44-48.

[100]See BARRETT, "Paul's Opponents in 2 Corinthians," 74.

[101]See BARRETT, "Christianity at Corinth," 17-20; cf. idem, *The Second Epistle to the Corinthians*, 278.

behind them . . . ."[102] This reading guards against the "unlikelihood" that the apostle would refer to the same group of people as Satan's servants (2 Cor 11:15) and "servants of Christ" (11:23).

(3) Käsemann's isolation of 2 Cor 11:5 as a parenthetical comment does not stand up under scrutiny. This verse is the last of a series of three reasons Paul offers to the Corinthians in support of his appeal in 11:1 to bear with his foolishness (cf. the three-fold γάρ in 11:2, 11:4, and 11:5). In addition, 11:6 *explains* the comparison made in 11:5; these two verses thus form a single integrated statement.[103] Bultmann argues, moreover, that the aorist verbs in 12:11-12 (ὑστέρησα and κατειργάσθη) show that the events pertaining to the superlative apostles took place in Corinth. Thus, this group must be identical to the "false apostles" and 'servants of Satan.'[104] The structure of Paul's "Fool's Speech" (11:1-12:13) corroborates this conclusion. Given that the ὑπερλίαν ἀπόστολοι are mentioned in the speech's introduction and conclusion, it is to be expected that they are the subject of the body of the speech. Indeed, the content of 11:7-12:11 makes it clear that the Jerusalem apostles are *not* the subject here.[105]

Barrett's arguments for identifying the ὑπερλίαν ἀπόστολοι as the Jerusalem apostles rest on faulty exegesis as well. His use of 1 Cor 9 to illuminate 2 Cor 11-12 is flawed. In 1 Cor 9 Paul sets himself forth as an example of giving up one's rights for the sake of others (in the context of a discussion on eating food offered to idols). In 2 Cor 11-12 the apostle *explicitly* defends his practice of not taking support from the Corinthians. That Paul happens to mention Peter and the other apostles in the former context has no bearing on the latter. Barrett is also guilty of inappropriately importing Gal 2 into his interpretation of 2 Cor 10:12-18. Just because Paul uses irony in connection with the Jerusalem apostles in Gal 2:6 does not mean that his ironic

---

[102]BARRETT, *The Second Epistle to the Corinthians*, 292.

[103]So, e.g., R. BULTMANN, *Exegetische Probleme des zweiten Korintherbriefes* (Darmstadt: Wissenschaftliche Buchgesellschaft, 1963) 27-28; and FURNISH, *II Corinthians*, 504; cf. M.E. THRALL, "Super-Apostles, Servants of Christ, and Servants of Satan," *JSNT* 6 (1980) 42-57, here 45-46.

[104]See BULTMANN, *Exegetische Probleme des zweiten Korintherbriefes*, 28.

[105]See SUMNEY, *Identifying Paul's Opponents*, 160.

use of ὑπερλίαν ἀπόστολοι in 2 Corinthians has the same referent. Barrett's arguments rely more on coincidental linkages between letters than on rigorous exegesis of the text. His interpretation of 2 Cor 11:21b is also problematic. The apostle has just used τις in 11:20 to refer to the false apostles. As Sumney points out, "It is unlikely that now in v. 21b, without warning, Paul would change the referent of his pronoun without some signal."[106] Barrett's insistence that the apostle would not call the same group of people "servants of Christ" and 'servants of Satan' is arbitrary. First of all, these references appear in different parts of Paul's argument; second, Barrett does not allow for the possibility that the apostle employs rhetorical effect.[107] In short, the thesis that the ὑπερλίαν ἀπόστολοι refer to the Jerusalem apostles fails.

E. Pneumatics (Jerry Sumney)

(1) In *Identifying Paul's Opponents*, Jerry Sumney contends that Paul's rivals are Pneumatics. He draws this conclusion after laying out his "proposal of a sound method" for identifying these adversaries. His method entails interpreting individually each letter in which opponents appear. Because Sumney holds to the simplified version of Semler's partition proposal, he analyzes 2 Cor 1-9 and 2 Cor 10-13 separately. He cautions against an uncritical use of parallel passages from the apostle's other letters. Parallels can, at most, *add* to the understanding of a passage. But the understanding must be derived from the text in which the passage is found. It is thus important, according to Sumney, to be able to assess various passages in terms of certainty of their reference and their reliability. Sumney argues that explicit statements and allusions, particularly those in didactic contexts, are the best sources for identifying Paul's opponents.[108] Having set forth his method, he goes on to analyze passages in 2 Cor 1-9 and 2 Cor 10-13.

(2) My interest here is in Sumney's exegetical *conclusions*. He argues that, in 2 Cor 1-9, the key issue between Paul and his opponents is "the proper

---

[106]SUMNEY, *Identifying Paul's Opponents*, 154.

[107]Cf. BULTMANN, *Exegetische Probleme des zweiten Korintherbriefes*, 26. Indeed, the synoptic evangelists have no problem relating Jesus' calling Simon Peter μακάριος in one breath, and Σατανᾶς in the next (see Matt 16:13-23 and parallels).

[108]For SUMNEY'S methodological proposals, see *Identifying Paul's Opponents*, 75-120.

manifestation of divine power in apostles' lives,"[109] a manifestation that involves both the possession of charisms and the exercise of authority. 2 Cor 1-9, however, is not sufficient to assert that the opponents are Pneumatics. According to Sumney, the "letter" contained in 2 Cor 10-13 provides the evidence to make this claim. After analyzing the allusions to the opponents in these chapters, he asserts that the proper manifestation of the *Spirit* is the point of contention in 2 Cor 10-13: "The most important thing we learn from the allusions is that the Spirit is important in the opponents' theology."[110] Indeed, the "Spirit-inspired way of life" underlies all the various claims made by Paul's rivals to legitimate their apostleship: their commanding presence and speaking abilities; their visions; their claims for financial support; and their performance of signs, wonders, and mighty works (cf. 12:12). Because in their estimation Paul lacks these "spiritual gifts," his rivals question his apostolic legitimacy. Thus, 2 Cor 10-13 confirms what 2 Cor 1-9 pointed to, namely, that the opponents are Pneumatics.[111]

(3) Given Sumney's insistence upon methodological caution, his confidence in knowing the opponents' Spirit-based theology is surprising. He claims to read 2 Cor 10-13 on its own terms. Yet, these chapters say very little explicitly about the Spirit. Paul mentions "another spirit" (πνεῦμα ἕτερον) in 11:4, but even Sumney concedes that "we cannot attach specialized significance" to this reference.[112] The next occurrence of πνεῦμα is in 12:18, where the apostle claims to have "walked in the same spirit" as Titus. The issue here is manner of conduct, not the divine Spirit. In fact, the only reference to *God's* Spirit in 2 Cor 10-13 is in the final blessing: "the fellowship of the Holy Spirit be with you" (13:13). This is a meager basis upon which to make such

---

[109]SUMNEY, *Identifying Paul's Opponents*, 147. For his treatment of 2 Cor 1-9, see pp. 127-47.

[110]Ibid., 172.

[111]For SUMNEY'S analysis of 2 Cor 10-13, see *Identifying Paul's Opponents*, 149-79. Cf. KÄSEMANN, "Die Legitimät des Apostels."

[112]See SUMNEY, *Identifying Paul's Opponents*, 170. What is not acceptable is Sumney's statement, made in connection with his analysis of 2 Cor 11:4, that "[w]e have seen some discussion of the Spirit in this letter" (ibid.). *Where* is that discussion in 2 Cor 10-13?

bold claims about Pneumatics. Moreover, neither the adjectival form (πνευματικός) nor the adverbial form (πνευματικῶς) appears anywhere in 2 Corinthians. One then wonders why Sumney speaks of "references to *spiritual gifts* in 10-13."[113] It seems that his own method does not guide his theory of the rivals' theology of the Spirit. Appeal to the criterion of "allusions" is loosed from firm moorings here. Granting Sumney his recourse to "allusions" (rather than explicit statements), because he takes 2 Cor 10-13 as a separate letter, there is little "context" in which to make sense of the proposed allusions.

The irony is that Paul *does* refer several times to God's Spirit in 2 Cor 1-9 (the "letter" in which Sumney finds only intimations that the Spirit is at issue).[114] Now, undoubtedly the Spirit and the workings of the Spirit *are* important topics throughout 2 Corinthians. While Sumney's critique of other scholars' attempts to identify Paul's opponents is cogent – indeed, it is a major contribution to Pauline scholarship – he goes well beyond his own methodological constraints in reconstructing the rivals' theology. What is more important, and more susceptible to methodological control, is *what the apostle says* concerning the Spirit.[115]

F. Summary

As was the case with the partition theories, there is a bewildering variety of opinions concerning the identity and theology of Paul's opponents in 2 Corinthians. Furnish identifies the critical issue when he observes "what varied conclusions can be drawn *from the limited evidence that is available*."[116] Although Sumney's methodological critiques are warranted, the major obstacle to identifying Paul's rivals in 2 Corinthians is the lack of sufficient data. The effort to identify them is thus doomed from the start. By seeking more than the

---

[113]Ibid., 183 (italics added).

[114]See 1:22; 3:3; 3:6 (2x); 3:8; 3:17 (2x); 3:18; 4:13; 5:5; and 6:6. Indeed, Sumney's case would be stronger if he regarded 2 Cor as a single letter.

[115]SUMNEY'S confidence in the opponents' identity in 2 Cor has not waned. See his *"Servants of Satan," "False Brothers" and Other Opponents of Paul*, JSNTSup 188 (Sheffield: Sheffield Academic Press, 1999) 79-133.

[116]FURNISH, *II Corinthians*, 49 (italics added).

data can yield, many scholars have misplaced – and in some cases, lost – the focus of the rich content of 2 Corinthians. This is particularly true when interpreters attempt to reconstruct the opponents' "theology" (an exercise that inevitably entails circular modes of argumentation[117]). The effort has led the quest to understand 2 Corinthians down blind alleys.

For example, the effort to identify Paul's opponents in 2 Corinthians has had a deleterious effect on the consideration of the letter's christology. In particular, 2 Cor 5:16b, where the apostle states that he no longer knows Christ according to the flesh, receives disproportionate emphasis. Schmithals regards this passage as a Gnostic gloss on Paul's text, a gloss that manifests Gnostic disdain for the "sarkic" aspect of Christ. Oostendorp claims that Paul here rejects his opponents' Jewish nationalistic conception of the Messiah. And Georgi holds that the apostle disavows his rivals' understanding of Jesus as a θεῖος ἀνήρ.[118] In all cases, it is the hypothesized opponents' christology that drives the interpretation. This is misguided. The issue of christology *is* important in 2 Corinthians. But it is *Paul's* christology, not the opponents', that is accessible to us. Investigating his christology is a more fruitful and promising enterprise than the construction of hypothetical rival christologies. As Chapter Four demonstrates, the apostle builds this letter around the character of Jesus.

Similarly, readings based on the identity of Paul's rivals manifest great diversity concerning the Spirit and its empowerment. Emphasis on the Spirit gets misplaced: Schmithals focuses on a Gnostic notion of πνεῦμα and its ecstatic manifestations; Oostendorp on the linking of the Spirit with adherence to Mosaic law; Georgi on the Spirit's association with allegorical interpretation of Scripture and powerful deeds; and Sumney on the Spirit's proper

---

[117]Cf. the following assessment of F. YOUNG and D.F. FORD: "Not only does the multiplication of reconstructions undermine confidence in the validity of any of them, but so often the argumentation is circular. The texts are used to make the reconstructions, and then they are interpreted in light of those conclusions." See their *Meaning and Truth in 2 Corinthians* (Grand Rapids, Mich.: Eerdmans, 1988) 119-20.

[118]See SCHMITHALS, *Gnosticism in Corinth*, 302-15; OOSTENDORP, *Another Jesus*, 54-55; and GEORGI, *The Opponents of Paul in Second Corinthians*, 252-53 and 276-78.

manifestation.[119] In each instance, the opponents' pneumatology provides the foil against which to understand what the apostle says about the Spirit. But again, it is *Paul's* understanding of the Spirit, and of the Spirit's power to transform people, that is available to us – not the opponents' formulations. And the apostle does in fact have much to say about the workings of the Spirit (cf., e.g., 2 Cor 1:21-22; 3:2-3; 3:18; and 4:13), as I show in Chapters Five and Six.

In fact, such opponent-driven interpretations of 2 Corinthians overstate the importance of the rivals. They are not the main concern of this letter, not even of 2 Cor 10-13.[120] Rather, the critical issue here, according to Paul, is whether or not the Corinthians are ἐν τῇ πίστει (13:5). In fact, the heart of the matter throughout 2 Corinthians is whether or not Paul and, even more, the Corinthians, are taking on the character of Christ. All that is known about the so-called opponents in this epistle is the apostle's *rhetoric* concerning them. This fact suggests that a more fruitful approach to 2 Corinthians is rhetorical analysis. Indeed, one of the noteworthy recent developments in biblical studies is the rediscovery of the extent to which Paul utilized rhetorical conventions in his writings.

In sum, attempts to interpret 2 Corinthians vis-à-vis the identity of the apostle's opponents fail to convince. Like the partition theories, readings based on the opponents' theology lead to detours and dead ends. For these reasons, critical historical-literary work on 2 Corinthians has yielded unsatisfactory results. This is not an indictment of historical-literary investigation *per se*. The preceding review does suggest, however, that the text of 2 Corinthians eludes such analysis, and that a different approach is needed. Rhetorical analysis provides this alternative mode of interpretation. It is this enterprise, together with its fruits and shortcomings, that is the subject of the next chapter.

---

[119]See SCHMITHALS, *Gnosticism in Corinth*, 167-69; OOSTENDORP, *Another Jesus*, 45-46; GEORGI, *The Opponents of Paul in Second Corinthians*, 264-71 and 279-80; and SUMNEY, *Identifying Paul's Opponents*, 171-72.

[120]J. MUNCK demonstrates commendable restraint in his treatment of the opponents in 2 Cor 10-13. He rightly recognizes that "[t]his section of the letter too deals with the church." See his *Paul and the Salvation of Mankind* (London: SCM, 1959) 175-77 (the quotation is found on p. 175).

Chapter Two
History of Interpretation II
The Use of Rhetorical Analysis and the Issue of *Ethos*

I. Readings of the Whole of 2 Corinthians through Rhetorical Analysis

The 1970s ushered in an extraordinary resurgence of interest in studying Paul's letters in light of ancient rhetorical theory and conventions.[121] Several scholars have utilized various forms of rhetorical analysis – via analysis of style, of rhetorical species, of invention and arrangement, etc. – in their investigation of 2 Corinthians. For the most part, these studies have focused on smaller units of the letter rather than on the text as a whole.[122]

---

[121]For a brief review, see B. FIORE, "NT Rhetoric and Rhetorical Criticism," in *ABD*, 5.715-19; R.D. ANDERSON, JR., *Ancient Rhetorical Theory and Paul*, CBET 18 (Kampen: Kok Pharos, 1996) 13-28; and B.K. PETERSON, *Eloquence and the Proclamation of the Gospel in Corinth*, SBLDS 163 (Atlanta: Scholars Press, 1998) 12-32. For a helpful treatment on rhetorical criticism, with particular sensitivity to its social and cultural implications, see V.K. ROBBINS, *The Tapestry of Early Christian Discourse: Rhetoric, Society and Ideology* (New York: Routledge, 1996).

[122]For the application of ancient rhetorical theory and conventions to study 2 Cor 10-13, see H.D. BETZ, *Der Apostel Paulus und die sokratische Tradition: Eine exegetische Untersuchung zu seiner "Apologie" 2 Korinther 10-13*, BHT 45 (Tübingen: Mohr Siebeck, 1972); C. FORBES, "Comparison, Self-Praise and Irony: Paul's Boasting and the Conventions of Hellenistic Rhetoric," *NTS* 32 (1986) 1-30; D. MARGUERAT, "2 Corinthiens 10-13: Paul et l'expérience de Dieu," *ETR* 63 (1988) 497-519; J.P. SAMPLEY, "Paul, His Opponents in 2 Corinthians 10-13, and the Rhetorical Handbooks," in *The Social World of Formative Christianity and Judaism: Essays in Tribute to Howard Clark Kee*, ed. J. NEUSNER et al. (Philadelphia: Fortress, 1988) 162-77; M.-A. CHEVALLIER, "L'argumentation de Paul dans II Corinthiens 10 à 13," *RHPR* 70 (1990) 3-15; F.W. DANKER, "Paul's Debt to the *De Corona* of Demosthenes: A Study of Rhetorical Techniques in Second Corinthians," in *Persuasive Artistry: Studies in New Testament Rhetoric in Honor of George A. Kennedy*, JSNTSup 50, ed. D.F. WATSON (Sheffield: Sheffield Academic Press, 1991) 262-80; J.T.

FITZGERALD, "Paul, the Ancient Epistolary Theorists, and 2 Corinthians 10-13: The Purpose and Literary Genre of a Pauline Letter," in *Greeks, Romans, and Christians: Essays in Honor of Abraham J. Malherbe*, ed. D.L. BALCH, E. FERGUSON and W.A. MEEKS (Minneapolis: Fortress, 1990) 190-200; G. HOLLAND, "Speaking Like a Fool: Irony in 2 Corinthians 10-13," in *Rhetoric and the New Testament: Essays from the 1992 Heidelberg Conference*, JSNTSup 90, ed. S.E. PORTER and T.H. OLBRICHT (Sheffield: JSOT Press, 1993) 250-64; H.-G. SUNDERMANN, *Der schwache Apostel und die Kraft der Rede: Eine rhetorische Analyse von 2 Kor 10-13*, Europäische Hochschulschriften, Reihe 23: Theologie 575 (Frankfurt: Lang, 1996); and B.K. PETERSON, *Eloquence and the Proclamation of the Gospel in Corinth*, 75-139; on 2 Cor 11-12, see M.M. MITCHELL, "A Patristic Perspective on Pauline περιαυτολογία," *NTS* 47 (2001) 354-71; and J. ZMIJEWSKI, *Der Stil der paulinischen "Narrenrede": Analyse der Sprachgestaltung in 2 Kor. 11,1-12,10 als Beitrag zur Methodik von Stiluntersuchungen neutestamentlicher Texte*, BBB 52 (Cologne and Bonn: Peter Hanstein, 1978); on 2 Cor 1-9, see D.A. DESILVA, "Measuring Penultimate against Ultimate Reality: An Investigation of the Integrity and Argumentation of 2 Corinthians," *JSNT* 52 (1993) 41-70; H.-W. WÜNSCH, *Der paulinische Brief 2 Kor 1-9 als kommunikative Handlung: Eine rhetorisch-literaturwissenschaftliche Untersuchung*, Theologie 4 (Münster: Lit, 1996); and K.YAMADA, "Epistolary Theoretical and Rhetorical Analyses of 2 Cor. 1-9," *AJBI* 24 (1998) 83-116; on 2 Cor 1-7, see G.A. KENNEDY, *New Testament Interpretation through Rhetorical Criticism* (Chapel Hill, N.C.: The University of North Carolina Press, 1984) 86-91; L.L. BELLEVILLE, "A Letter of Apologetic Self-Commendation: 2 Cor. 1:8-7:16," *NovT* 31 (1989) 142-63; and D.A. DESILVA, "Meeting the Exigency of a Complex Rhetorical Situation: Paul's Strategy in 2 Corinthians 1 through 7," *AUSS* 34 (1996) 5-22; on 2 Cor 1:1-2:13 + 7:5-16, see L.L. WELBORN, *Paul's Letter of Reconciliation in 2 Corinthians* (Ph.D. diss., University of Chicago, 1987); idem, "Like Broken Pieces of a Ring: 2 Cor 1:1-2:13; 7:5-16 and Ancient Theories of Literary Unity," *NTS* 42 (1996) 559-83; and idem, "Paul's Appeal to the Emotions in 2 Corinthians 1:1-2:13; 7:5-16," *JSNT* 82 (2001) 31-60; on 2 Cor 1:1-2:13 + 7:5-8:24, see F.W. HUGHES, "The Rhetoric of Reconciliation: 2. Corinthians 1:1-2:13 and 7:5-8:24," in *Persuasive Artistry: Studies in New Testament Rhetoric in Honor of George A. Kennedy*, 246-61; on 2 Cor 2:14-6:13 + 7:2-4, see idem, "Rhetorical Criticism and the Corinthian Correspondence," in *The Rhetorical Analysis of Scripture: Essays from the 1995 London Conference*, JSNTSup 146, ed. S.E. PORTER and T.H. OLBRICHT (Sheffield: Sheffield Academic Press, 1997) 336-50; on 2 Cor 2:14-7:1, see J.I.H. MCDONALD, "Paul and Preaching: A Reconsideration of 2 Corinthians 2:14-17 in its Context," *JSNT* 17 (1983) 35-50; on 2 Cor 6:14-7:1, see E. WALLER, "The Rhetorical Structure of II Cor. 6:14-7:1 – Is the So-called 'Non-Pauline Interpolation' a Clue to the Redactor of II Corinthians?," *Proceedings of the Eastern Great Lakes and Midwest*

While such investigations shed light on the apostle's particular modes of argumentation, many of them tend to lose the forest for the trees. Where the entire text and context of 2 Corinthians is not kept in mind, rhetorical analysis of particular passages can lead to distortions and misreadings.[123] In fact, it is striking how many of these studies adopt unquestioned the delineations proposed in the various partition theories, the inadequacies of which I have already treated. Such theories, whether arrived at through historical-literary or rhetorical readings, tend to presume, as J.D.H. Amador has pointed out, a hermeneutic by which Paul's letters are thought to exhibit "restricted coherence, focused consistency and unitary intentionality and context."[124] Both the complexity and the subtlety of Paul's presentation in 2 Corinthians give the lie to this assumption.

I focus on rhetorical analyses of the *whole* of 2 Corinthians. In the last fifteen years, Frances Young and David F. Ford, Frederick W. Danker, Ben Witherington III, Fredrick J. Long, and Jerry W. McCant have offered

---

Biblical Societies 10 (1990) 151-65; on 2 Cor 8-9 (as one rhetorical unit), see K.J. O'MAHONY, "The Rhetoric of Benefaction," PIBA 22 (1999) 9-40; and idem, *Pauline Persuasion: A Sounding in 2 Corinthians 8-9*, JSNTSup 199 (Sheffield: Sheffield Academic Press, 2000); on 2 Cor 8-9 (as separate administrative letters), see BETZ, *2 Corinthians 8 and 9*; and, on 2 Cor 8, see S.J. JOUBERT, "Behind the Mask of Rhetoric: 2 Corinthians 8 and the Intra-textual Relation between Paul and the Corinthians," *Neot* 26 (1992) 101-12.

[123]For instance, in his analysis of 2 Cor 8-9 as two separate administrative letters, BETZ claims to find a five-part rhetorical structure – *exordium*, *narratio*, *propositio*, *probatio*, and *peroratio* – in each epistle. While there is a certain seductive quality to his work, closer analysis shows how much he has to force this structure onto the text. In fact, he commits violence on Paul's grammar and syntax. To give one example: Betz claims that 9:5ab forms the conclusion of the *narratio* and that 9:5bc forms the *propositio*, the thesis statement, of 9:1-15. Yet, where Betz makes this division is right in the middle of a purpose clause (introduced by ἵνα); even worse, his analysis separates the verb ("they might arrange in advance" – part of the *narratio*) from its direct object ("your previously promised gift" – the first half of the *propositio*, the second half of which is a clause that is subordinated to 9:5a). If Betz is right, Paul certainly was obscure in making his thesis statement! See *2 Corinthians 8 and 9*, 88 and 95-97.

[124]J.D.H. AMADOR, "The Unity of 2 Corinthians: A Test Case for a Re-discovered and Re-invented Rhetoric," *Neot* 33 (1999) 411-32, here 411.

monograph-length treatments of the entire text of 2 Corinthians by some means of rhetorical analysis.[125] Additionally, in two recent articles, J.D.H. Amador has made the case for the unity of 2 Corinthians based on a "re-discovered and re-invented rhetoric."[126] After briefly setting forth each one's basic proposal, I offer a critique of the strengths and weaknesses of these readings as a group.[127]

A. Recent Proposals for Rhetorical Readings of 2 Corinthians as a Whole

Young and Ford argue that 2 Corinthians is best understood as a letter of self-defense, "an apologetic speech in epistolary form." They consider a

---

[125]See YOUNG and FORD, *Meaning and Truth in 2 Corinthians*; F.W. DANKER, *II Corinthians*, ACNT (Minneapolis: Augsburg, 1989); WITHERINGTON, *Conflict & Community in Corinth*; F.J. LONG, *"Have We Been Defending Ourselves to You?" (2 Cor 12:19): Forensic Rhetoric and the Rhetorical Unity of 2 Corinthians* (Ph.D. diss., Marquette University, 1999); and J.W. MCCANT *2 Corinthians* (Sheffield: Sheffield Academic Press, 1999).

[126]J.D.H. AMADOR, "The Unity of 2 Corinthians"; and "Revisiting 2 Corinthians: Rhetoric and the Case for Unity," *NTS* 46 (2000) 92-111.

[127]Three other recent works will not receive attention here, although at first blush they may appear to belong. First is J.A. CRAFTON'S *The Agency of the Apostle: A Dramatistic Analysis of Paul's Responses to Conflict in 2 Corinthians*, JSNTSup 51 (Sheffield: Sheffield Academic Press, 1991). While Crafton's analysis can be dubbed a type of rhetorical analysis, it does not refer to the canons of ancient rhetoric. Rather, he interprets 2 Cor using K. Burke's contemporary rhetorical-critical method known as "dramatism." Furthermore, Crafton accepts Bornkamm and Georgi's partitioning proposal and the latter's identification of the opponents as *theoi andres*. Second is P.W. BARNETT'S *The Second Epistle to the Corinthians*, NICNT (Grand Rapids, MI: Eerdmans, 1997). While Barnett mentions a four-fold rhetorical structure (*exordium*-narrative-proofs-peroration) to support his position of the unity of 2 Cor in his opening chapter (pp. 17-19), his exposition of the text does not develop this insight. In addition, he does not often engage Greco-Roman rhetorical sources. Third is S. WAN'S *Power in Weakness: Conflict and Rhetoric in Paul's Second Letter to the Corinthians*, NTC (Harrisburg, Pa.: Trinity International, 2000). Although he refers several times to Paul's "rhetorical strategy," he (like Barnett) rarely refers to ancient rhetorical theory. Moreover, he regards 2 Cor as a composite of four letters, and thus the canonical form is due to "an unknown compiler in the early church" who "took the trouble to stitch the different letters and fragments" (p. 11).

forensic letter attributed to Demosthenes, the so-called *Epistle 2*, to be the closest literary analogue to 2 Corinthians. Young and Ford submit that both works exhibit a four-part rhetorical structure. Both begin with an *exordium* in which the writer attempts to gain the audience's sympathy. Both continue by offering points for and against the author, as well as a response to charges leveled against him. These correspond to the "narrative" (*narratio*) and "proof" (*probatio*) of a forensic argument. Finally, both Demosthenes and Paul conclude with an emotional *peroratio* in which they recapitulate earlier proofs and arguments. According to Young and Ford, this genre of the written legal defense suggests an overall structure of the epistle, and would demonstrate its unity if correct. It also helps to account for how 2 Cor 10-13, understood as Paul's impassioned *peroratio*, fits into the flow and "logic" of what precedes.[128] Indeed, they insist upon the importance of genre for understanding all the various parts of 2 Corinthians: "As we try to understand the parts of a discourse in sequence, it is vital what conception we have of the whole."[129]

Danker interprets 2 Corinthians within the Greco-Roman cultural context, a context marked by benefaction, the system of reciprocity, and rhetoric. Making several references to both classical literature and inscriptional evidence, he maintains that "beneficence and reciprocity are dominant structural motifs" in 2 Corinthians.[130] In fact, Danker sees beneficence as the theme that links together the different parts of the letter: God is the Supreme Benefactor who has acted through Jesus; Paul casts himself as benefactor to the Corinthians in his role as their apostle; he appeals to the Corinthians to be benefactors to the poor in Jerusalem; and, in the final chapters, Paul chastizes the Corinthians for their ingratitude in light of his benefaction. Danker also insists upon the

---

[128]See YOUNG and FORD, *Meaning and Truth in 2 Corinthians*, 27-28 and 36-40. For the text of Demosthenes' letter, see *Démosthène: Lettres et Fragments*, ed. and trans. R. CLAVAUD (Paris: Société d'Edition "Les Belles Lettres," 1987) 97-104. It should be pointed out that, unlike the other works treated in this section, *Meaning and Truth in 2 Corinthians* is not a sequential commentary on 2 Cor, but a series of essays on the text.

[129]YOUNG and FORD, *Meaning and Truth in 2 Corinthians*, 145.

[130]See DANKER, *II Corinthians*, 116. For a more detailed analysis of the reciprocity system as background for the interpretation of various NT passages, see DANKER'S *Benefactor: Epigraphic Study of a Graeco-Roman Semantic Field* (St. Louis: Clayton, 1982).

importance of appreciating the apostle's utilization of rhetorical conventions: "[T]here are rhetorical considerations that have been overlooked in the history of interpretation of 2 Corinthians and these suggest that some cautions are in order against a too-ready adoption of partitionist hypotheses without some compelling modifications."[131]

Witherington contends, like Young and Ford, that "2 Corinthians taken as a compositional whole is an example of forensic or judicial rhetoric."[132] Unlike Young and Ford, however, Witherington offers a more detailed rhetorical disposition (or structure) of the letter: *exordium* (1:3-7); *narratio* (1:8-2:16); *propositio* (2:17); *probatio* and *refutatio* (3:1-13:4); and *peroratio* (13:5-10). The real innovative feature of his analysis is his judgment that 2:17 serves as the thesis statement of the entire epistle. Witherington regards Paul's self-presentation in this verse – that he does not peddle God's word; that he is sincere; and that, as one commissioned by God, he speaks in Christ – as that which the apostle sets out to demonstrate in the course of the letter. He thus considers 2 Corinthians to be Paul the defendant's response to "the basic charge that he is no *apostolos*."[133] For Witherington, then, the issue in this epistle is the apostle's past behavior.

Similarly, Long argues that "2 Corinthians is a unified letter of self-apology deliberately formed in conformity to forensic oratorical practice."[134] He submits that Paul himself offers an important genre clue in his "self-reflective" comment in 12:19a that this letter is a defense or apology (cf. ἀπολογούμεθα). Long proposes an even more elaborate rhetorical disposition grid for 2 Corinthians than Witherington. Second Corinthians 1:17-24 is the complex thesis statement or *partitio* which "contains several heads which outline the *probatio* in the same order. . . ."[135] Specifically, the apostle lists five headings in 1:17-24 which he then elaborates in the course of the letter: 1:17 is taken up in 2:1-11; 1:18-20 in 2:17-3:18; 1:21-22 in 4:1-5:10; 1:23 in 5:11-7:1; and 1:24

---

[131]DANKER, *II Corinthians*, 19-20.

[132]WITHERINGTON, *Conflict & Community in Corinth*, 333 (italics excluded).

[133]Ibid., 371.

[134]LONG, *"Have We Been Defending Ourselves to You?"*, 335.

[135]Ibid., 235.

in 8:1-9:15. 2 Cor 10-13 consists of Paul's *refutatio* of his opponents (10:1-11:15), a treatment concerning himself (11:16-12:10; cf. περὶ ἑαυτοῦ), and the *peroratio* (12:11-13:10). Long hypothesizes that the apostle is facing "a scrutiny trial of sorts," and that 2 Corinthians is his response to the charge that he had failed to visit the community as he had formerly promised (a charge that led to other charges, e.g., extortion concerning the collection). For Long, understanding the genre of forensic oratory, with its form and intentions, is the key to interpreting this letter.

McCant disputes the claim that Paul's goal in 2 Corinthians is self-defense. Like Long, McCant focuses on the apostle's comment in 2 Cor 12:19a: πάλαι δοκεῖτε ὅτι ὑμῖν ἀπολογούμεθα. Unlike Long, he interprets the apostle's statement as a *disavowal* of defense. In fact, McCant proposes that Paul's disclaimer in 12:19a, coming on the heels of what appears to be a sustained defense, "suggests that irony and parody are frolicking on every page" of 2 Corinthians.[136] He submits that, although this epistle takes the form of judicial rhetoric, the apostle uses parody throughout the text in order to subvert the Corinthians' expectations, to undermine their complaints, and to educate them concerning the ways of following Christ. McCant insists that "[t]here is no defense because Paul cannot and will not recognize the Corinthian body as a judicial body; only God can judge him."[137] Thus, he sets forth the apostle's "parody of defense" as follows: 2 Cor 1-7 is a parodic defense of his apostolic behavior; 2 Cor 8-9 is a parody of beneficence (in which Paul undermines the expectations of the patronage system); and 2 Cor 10-13 is a parodic defense of his apostolic authority. McCant maintains that an interpretation of 2 Corinthians must cut below the surface of the text to take into account this use of parody by the apostle.

Amador criticizes readings of 2 Corinthians that fail to take seriously "the complexity of argumentative and persuasive dynamics and situations" involved.[138] Historical-critical and even some rhetorical-critical readings (*à la* Betz) restrict the interpretive enterprise too narrowly by, for instance, seeking only to discover events and circumstances behind the text, imposing strict expectations on the possibilities of Paul's logic and moods, or identifying a

---

[136]MCCANT, *2 Corinthians*, 13.

[137]Ibid., 158.

[138]AMADOR, "Revisiting 2 Corinthians," 94.

single rhetorical species. Rather, Amador contends that it is vital to recognize "the freedom with which argumentative and persuasive communication is conceptualized and arranged in the face of the dizzying array of circumstances that can confront an author/rhetor."[139] Thus, Amador focuses on the importance of *inventio* – that is, "on how the individual pieces of the argument are used to create a persuasive whole"[140] – and not on some rigid rhetorical arrangement (*dispositio*) in his analysis of 2 Corinthians. He proposes a rhetorical outline that is "threaded" by the *narratio* (1:15-16; 2:12-13; 7:5; 8:1-2; 9:2; 11:9; and 12:14-18). Paying close attention to rhetorical units[141] and to shifts in the argumentative situation, he claims that the apostle carefully develops an argumentative groundwork for his later appeals to the community and for the assertion of his apostolic authority. Paul lays this groundwork by introducing various topics, by dissociating human from divine standards, and by drawing the Corinthians with him into the sphere of the "new creation."

B. Strengths of Proposed Rhetorical Readings of 2 Corinthians as a Whole

These proposals share several salutary features. In the first place, they offer many plausible arguments for *reading the text as a literary unity*. All of them effectively demonstrate the "interlinkage" and coherence of certain key terms, *topoi*, and themes, such as: παρακαλ-, καυχ- and δοκιμ- terminology; the topics of affliction and commendation; behavior termed κατὰ σάρκα; and the theme of God's power as manifested paradoxically through weakness.

---

[139]Ibid.

[140]The phraseology is that of S.J. KRAFTCHICK. See his *Ethos and Pathos Appeals in Galatians Five and Six: A Rhetorical Analysis* (Ph.D. diss., Emory University, 1985) 38-39.

[141]AMADOR submits the following rhetorical outline: 1:1-14 = introductory unit; 1:15-2:13 = unit 1 (plans for Corinth and Achaia as they relate to the past); 2:14-7:4 = unit 2 (purpose of the ministry as related to the present); 7:5-9:15 = unit 3 (plans for Corinth and Achaia for the future); 10:1-13:4 = Unit 4 (apostolic *apologia*); and 13:5-13 = concluding remarks. See "Revisiting 2 Corinthians," 110-11; cf. idem, "The Unity of 2 Corinthians," 414-16.

These terms, *topoi*, and themes appear in every part of the letter.[142] In addition, the proposals for literary and rhetorical unity show how Paul's argument *develops* in the course of the letter. For instance, the hardship list in 2 Cor 6:4-10 presupposes the list of tribulations in 4:8-9 and supplements it; moreover, 6:4-10 anticipates the more detailed hardship catalog in 11:23-29.[143]

Rhetorical readings of the whole of 2 Corinthians succeed in showing the argumentative relationships between various parts of the letter, including the "main suspects" in partition theories. One example is Young and Ford's evaluation of the references to Paul's reunion with Titus in 2:12-13 and 7:5-16. Instead of observing here "an inexplicable hiatus in the narrative," they show how each allusion functions within its immediate context. In the case of 2:12-13, the reference serves to express the extent of the apostle's concern for the Corinthians, thereby continuing a theme that he has sounded throughout 1:12-2:11. In the case of 7:5-16, it functions to encourage further reconciliation between Paul and the community (6:13 and 7:2) and to set up his request concerning the collection (8:1-9:15).[144] Another example is the rhetorical function of 6:14-7:1, which Danker captures well. After presenting himself as God's envoy inviting the Corinthians to reconciliation with God (5:20-6:2), the apostle describes himself as God's faithful servant (6:3-10) who begs the community to widen their hearts for him (6:11-13). Second Corinthians 6:14-7:1 follows naturally as Paul's personal appeal to the Corinthians to tend to their relationship with God with utmost seriousness. Then, in 7:2, the apostle resumes his plea that they open their hearts to him, God's envoy.[145]

---

[142]Another example is YOUNG and FORD'S analysis of economic metaphors and their prevalence throughout 2 Cor. See *Meaning and Truth in 2 Corinthians*, 166-85.

[143]See WITHERINGTON, *Community & Conflict in Corinth*, 398-99; and MCCANT, *2 Corinthians*, 55 and 102. Both cite J.T. FITZGERALD, *Cracks in an Earthen Vessel: An Examination of the Catalogue of Hardships in the Corinthian Correspondence*, SBLDS 99 (Atlanta: Scholars Press, 1988).

[144]See YOUNG and FORD, *Meaning and Truth in 2 Corinthians*, 19, 22, and 35.

[145]See DANKER, *II Corinthians*, 83-102. Cf. AMADOR, "Revisiting 2 Corinthians," 101-5. Amador sees 2 Cor 6:11-7:4 as one of many examples in which Paul uses a framing device (cf. Rom 5:18-21 and 8:1-2 framing 6:1-7:25; Gal 5:1 and 5:13-15 bracketing 5:2-12). In fact, Amador insists that taking 2 Cor 6:14-7:1 as an interpolation

In addition, each of the interpreters offers detailed explanations of how 2 Cor 10-13 functions to provide "an appropriate rhetorical climax" to 2 Cor 1-9.[146] It is beyond the scope of this section to go into detail here, so a few observations will have to suffice. First, Paul's insertion of a παρακαλῶ period in 10:1 (αὐτὸς δὲ ἐγὼ Παῦλος παρακαλῶ ὑμᾶς) immediately following his thanksgiving/doxology to God (9:15) is not in the least surprising, for he does it elsewhere.[147] Second, while there *is* an abrupt change starting in 10:1 (e.g., in tone, in the prevalence of first person pronouns, etc.), the apostle's argumentation in 2 Cor 1-9 has laid the foundation for his (admittedly) risky confrontational tone in 2 Cor 10-13. The risk involved, however, is calculated; he has prepared his audience for it. Indeed, Amador cogently argues that "to consider [these four chapters] as a separate source . . . would make it a *foolhardy* risk since it is to be taken without any previous argumentative preparation."[148]

---

leaves κατάκρισις in 7:3 without a referent.

[146]See, e.g., WITHERINGTON, *Community & Conflict in Corinth*, 429-76; LONG, *"Have We Been Defending Ourselves to You?"*, 262-89; MCCANT, *2 Corinthians*, 101-72; and AMADOR, "Revisiting 2 Corinthians," 98-100. The quotation is from DANKER, "Paul's Debt to the *De Corona* of Demosthenes," 280.

[147]Cf. Rom 11:33-12:1; 1 Cor 1:4-10; and 1 Thess 3:9-4:1 for other examples of the connection between thanksgivings/doxologies and παρακαλῶ periods. See WITHERINGTON, *Conflict & Community in Corinth*, 432; and MCCANT, *2 Corinthians*, 102, both of whom cite the analysis of C. J. BJERKELUND. For a more in-depth treatment of παρακαλῶ in 2 Cor, see BJERKELUND'S *PARAKALÔ: Form, Funktion und Sinn der parakalô-Sätze in den paulinishen Briefen* (Oslo: Universitetsforlaget, 1967) 147-55.

[148]AMADOR, "The Unity of 2 Corinthians," 428 (Amador's italics). In "Revisiting 2 Corinthians," Amador offers the following succinct account of how Paul has laid the groundwork for 2 Cor 10-13 in 2 Cor 1-9:

"Throughout the argument in chapters 10-13, frequent reference to the *topoi* of 'confidence' (cf. 1:23-2:11; 3:1-4:6), 'boasting,' (cf. 1:12-14; 7:6-16), 'obedience' with respect to 'testing' (cf. 1:23-2:11, esp. 2:9; 6:11; 9:13), 'building up' rather than 'tearing you down' (cf. 4:7-6:10), the catalog of 'afflictions' (cf. 1:3-11; 4:8-11; 5-6; 7:5; 8:2), being 'beside' oneself/beyond the limits (5:13), the argumentative presence of Satan (2:11; cf. 6:15), and love (2:4; 6:11-12; etc.) are made. Additionally, the argument functions upon the basis of the dissociation human vs. divine standards of judging the

Third, it is important to note that Paul's tone shifts just as dramatically between 10:18 and 11:1 as it does between 9:15 and 10:1. Yet nobody has proposed a separate partition beginning at 11:1.[149]

A second salutary feature of these interpretations is that they *avoid the pitfall of reading 2 Corinthians through the identity and theology of the so-called opponents*. For example, Young and Ford correctly understand that "Paul is more concerned to convey his own understanding of his own role and woo back the doubters, misled by others or not, than to attack any specifically identifiable 'opponents.'"[150] For the most part,[151] these readings recognize that

---

ministry and the *ethos* of Paul (cf. 4:17-6:10, esp. 5:12). Finally, it works within the Macedonia-Titus-'brother' *narratio*.

"Each of these aspects has deep argumentative roots in chapters 1-9, roots that are presupposed by and required for chapters 10-13 to function" (p. 99).

[149]See MCCANT, *2 Corinthians*, 22. It should be noted that DANKER exhibits a strange ambivalence concerning the question of the unity of 2 Cor. On the one hand, he states in his introduction to *II Corinthians* that "the probability is strong that 2 Corinthians was not written in its present form at one sitting, but consists of at least two letters" – minimally, 2 Cor 1-9 and 10-13 (p. 18). This judgment is made, it seems, on the basis of recent scholarship. On the other hand, in the course of his analysis, Danker observes that 6:14-7:1 functions as a digression to amplify the theme of fidelity; that the expression περὶ μὲν γάρ in 9:1 is a rhetorical ploy to develop further the strategy of "shaming" the Corinthians to generosity that was implicit in 8:24; and that 2 Cor 10-13 is an appropriate rhetorical climax to the apostle's utilization of the reciprocity system in 2 Cor 1-9. In each instance, his exegetical and rhetorical analysis points strongly in the direction of the letter's *unity*. But Danker then takes a desperate measure to resolve this tension: the editor responsible for the final form of the text must have been well-versed in the conventions of rhetoric in order to iron out the supposed seams (see pp. 18, 96, 134-135, and 147). Thus, Danker seems to allow more weight to his presuppositions about the text's composite nature than to the findings of his own exegetical investigation.

[150]YOUNG and FORD, *Meaning and Truth in 2 Corinthians*, 14-15. Cf. DANKER, *II Corinthians*, 177; LONG, *"Have We Been Defending Ourselves to You?"*, 208-10; and MCCANT, *2 Corinthians*, 17-18, 119, 130, and 150.

[151]It is interesting to observe how characterizations of the opponents at times infiltrates these readings, despite the restrained attitude concerning them. At one point YOUNG and FORD (*Meaning and Truth in 2 Corinthians*, 213-14) seem to accept Oostendorp's suggestion that Paul's opponents accused him of being a weak disciplinarian, and they

the rivals serve as foils for Paul and his manner of exercising apostleship, and that he resorts to stereotyped language in reference to them. The pursuit to identify them is therefore a red herring. Insofar as the apostle treats of and exhorts "problem people," he does so among the Corinthians themselves, and not outside agitators. Because 2 Corinthians is thus about Paul and the Corinthians – and *not* his so-called rivals – McCant's assessment that "[p]erhaps it is time to close the door on discussions about opponents at Corinth"[152] is apt.

A third beneficial aspect of these readings is their *sensitivity to Paul's utilization of rhetorical techniques*. All of the commentators excel in highlighting the apostle's use of rhetorical conventions such as digression, amplification, resumption, anaphora, pleonasm, paronomasia, *synkrisis*, irony, and satire. Amador is particularly effective in pointing out Paul's strategic use of *narratio*, which he employs as a threading device "by which argumentation is simultaneously driven forward and integrated."[153] One of McCant's strengths is his sensitivity to the apostle's utilization of *inclusio* for delimiting argumentative units. McCant also underscores Paul's employment of overlapping techniques and ring composition.[154] Additionally, both Long and

---

interpret 11:20 in terms of the opponents' harsh administration of discipline. WITHERINGTON (*Conflict & Community in Corinth*, 348-50) hypothesizes that the rivals are imbued with the values of the rising Sophistic movement. LONG (*"Have We Been Defending Ourselves to You?"*, e.g., 210) surmises that the opponents were those entrusted by the Corinthians to take their portion of the collection to the Jerusalem church. Even MCCANT (see e.g., *2 Corinthians*, 83) suggests the possibility that the rivals represented the wealthy minority in Corinth, led by the offender referred to in 2:5-9. Nevertheless, unlike the interpretations treated in Chapter One, Section II, these observations are peripheral and are not allowed to affect and distort the reading of the text.

[152]MCCANT, *2 Corinthians*, 18.

[153]AMADOR, "The Unity of 2 Corinthians," 420-425, here 421. Cf. DANKER, *II Corinthians*, 169-70.

[154]For Paul's use of *inclusio*, see, e.g., MCCANT, *2 Corinthians*, 103, 110, 114, and 116. For the apostle's employment of overlapping technique, where the same statement serves to conclude what precedes it and to introduce what follows, see MCCANT, *2 Corinthians* 38, 40, and 47; cf. LONG, *"Have We Been Defending Ourselves to You?"*, 324. For Paul's utilization of ring composition, where the conclusion reverts to earlier statements

McCant competently indicate the intricate texture of the apostle's mode of argumentation by paying careful attention to his use of the conjunctions γάρ (which most often has an explanatory function) and οὖν (which has an inferential function). Their analyses thus foster greater appreciation of the enthymemic quality of Paul's argumentation, and of the way in which he amplifies certain themes.[155] In sum, the rhetorical readings of 2 Corinthians successfully illustrate the apostle's use of rhetorical techniques on what might be called the "micro level."

Lastly, and most broadly speaking, these readings *effectively bring significant elements from the Greco-Roman world to bear on the interpretation of 2 Corinthians*. They accomplish this primarily in two ways. First, these readings place 2 Corinthians within the literary context of philosophers, moralists, rhetoricians, and other writers prior to and contemporary with Paul. Analysis of this epistle in light of the writings of figures such as Quintilian, Demosthenes, Plutarch and Epictetus sheds light on, among other things, the apostle's use of certain images and metaphors and his argumentative strategies. Second, these studies set 2 Corinthians within the socio-cultural context of Corinth and the Greco-Roman world of Paul's time. To read this letter against the background of status-consciousness, honor and shame, patron-client relationships, etc. is to illuminate it in important ways. As Danker notes throughout his commentary, it is essential to appreciate the apostle's adeptness at being "a Hellene among Hellenes."[156]

C. *Weaknesses of Proposed Rhetorical Readings of 2 Corinthians as a Whole*

Yet, these readings are also deficient in some important respects. First is the "shadow side" of the aforementioned strength, namely, that the interpretation of 2 Corinthians can become "too Hellenistic." That is, *the insights derived from Greco-Roman literature and culture can distort the exegesis of 2 Corinthians* if not used critically. One example is Danker's

---

and thus completes the circle of ideas, see MCCANT, *2 Corinthians*, 40.

[155]See LONG, *"Have We Been Defending Ourselves to You?"*, 103-9 and 322-29; and MCCANT, *2 Corinthians*, e.g., 48 and 67.

[156]DANKER, *II Corinthians*, e.g., 194.

reading too much contractual and bureaucratic language into Paul's formulations in 2 Cor 8:1-9:15. Instead of interpreting the apostle's reference to πίστις in 8:7 within its immediate context (which includes references to 'testing' "genuine love" and to the self-emptying examples of the Macedonians and Christ, cf. 8:1-9), Danker focuses on the Hellenic bureaucratic world of contractual obligations. He does the same with the expression ὑποταγῇ τῆς ὁμολογίας (9:13), thereby missing the convergence of terms pertaining to the notion of character in this passage.[157] A second example is McCant's assessment that Paul uses parody *throughout* 2 Corinthians. While his analysis of parody in 11:1-12:18 is suggestive, McCant's insistence upon finding parody elsewhere in 2 Corinthians is unconvincing. Indeed, he goes so far as to say, in the course of his treatment of 6:4-10, that "[p]arody is the only way to make sense of what [Paul] is saying."[158] I submit, instead, that the apostle's catalog of his sufferings as "God's servant" makes very good sense in light of his references to the sufferings of Christ (cf. 4:10-11; 5:14; and 5:21) and his claim to be an ambassador for Christ (ὑπὲρ Χριστοῦ, 5:20). Indeed, McCant's claim that invective is ubiquitous in 2 Corinthians is hard to reconcile with his statements that Paul's tone is pastoral and conciliatory.

The penchant to "overread" Greco-Roman elements in 2 Corinthians is evident from two other interpretive patterns. On the one hand, insofar as these readings address the question of Paul's *ethos*, they tend to turn to the rhetorical handbooks, as well as to philosophical and socio-cultural motifs, to explain how the apostle attempts to establish his *ethos*.[159] Such references do shed light on Paul's method, but they fail to illuminate the over-arching strategy which he employs. I will return to this point below. On the other hand, thorough-going

---

[157]See DANKER, *II Corinthians*, 124 and 146. Danker's reading of 2 Cor 8-9 follows closely upon BETZ'S in *2 Corinthians 8 and 9.* I will analyze these passages more thoroughly in Chapters Four and Six.

[158]MCCANT, *2 Corinthians*, 56.

[159]For example, WITHERINGTON tends to emphasize the motif of the "suffering sage." See *Conflict & Community in Corinth*, 388-89, 398-401, and 450-53. He also cites Quintilian's *Institutio Oratoria* in conjunction with establishing *ethos* in the *exordium* (p. 353). DANKER focuses on the notion of the "endangered benefactor," and often cites Plutarch's *On Inoffensive Self-Praise* in conjunction with *ethos*. See *II Corinthians*, 175, 180, 184, and 196-97.

rhetorical treatments like Long's, which make extensive use of actual apologetic speeches as well as the rhetorical handbooks, can become myopic. That is, the effort expended to demonstrate that Paul closely follows the conventions of forensic oratory leads Long to a remarkable omission. In commenting on 12:9-10 (where the apostle is told that the Lord's grace is sufficient for him), Long states: "This idea of Paul's suffering obviously unites the whole book from beginning to end."[160] Fair enough. But one is hard pressed to learn from Long's analysis *how* this 'obvious' notion unites the various parts of 2 Corinthians, not to mention why the apostle's suffering is ultimately significant. Instead, one reads about the numerous ways this epistle resembles a defense speech.

A second weakness of some of these readings, in a sense another manifestation of the first shortcoming, is that *they force rhetorical grids upon the text of 2 Corinthians*. Whereas the rhetorical readings succeed in demonstrating Paul's rhetorical acumen at the "micro level," they fail to give an adequate account at the "macro level" of the overall structure, the "rhetorical disposition," of the text. For instance, Young and Ford's search for an overarching four-part structure (*exordium*-narrative-proofs-*peroratio*) and genre leads them to assert too much concerning the analogy with Demosthenes's *Epistle 2*. It is surely incumbent upon them to substantiate their claim with more than the sketchy comparison they offer. In fact, Margaret E. Thrall has shown that 2 Cor 1-7 aligns better with the patterns of *Epistle 2* than does 2 Cor 1-13.[161]

Witherington's more detailed proposal is also deficient. In particular, his claim that 2 Cor 2:17 is the text's *propositio* or thesis statement is highly problematic. This is evident from both the content and function of 2:17. In terms of content, Witherington has to load this verse with more meaning than it can bear in order to justify his claim. That is, he asserts that 2:17 refers both to the "charge" that Paul is no apostle and to his opponents whom (according to Witherington) Paul classifies as "Sophists." But surely this imports too much into the apostle's actual words here. Besides, 2:17 functions as an *explanatory* continuation (cf. γάρ) of what precedes, namely, the thanksgiving period

[160]LONG, *"Have We Been Defending Ourselves to You?"*, 311.

[161]See THRALL, *II Corinthians*, 1.11-12.

beginning in 2:14, and not as a new premise or proposition.[162] A comparison with 1 Cor 1:10, the *propositio* of 1 Corinthians, is helpful. There Paul clearly asserts a new proposition, and, just as significantly, *follows* it with an explanatory γάρ clause.[163] In his quest to identify a *propositio* in 2 Corinthians, I suspect that Witherington is unduly influenced by the cleaner rhetorical schema he finds in 1 Corinthians. In spite of his efforts, however, 2 Corinthians does not yield such a neat rhetorical structure.[164]

Long's hypothesis is similarly untenable. Recall his argument that 2 Cor 1:17-24 is the *partitio* which consists of five "partition heads" that Paul takes up in sequence in 2:1-9:15. *Prima facie*, it is difficult to discern five distinct headings when reading 1:17-24. Long acknowledges this, but counters that the apostle here takes a "subtle approach to the presentation of the partition."[165] In support of this claim, Long quotes with approval Quintilian's advice: "Sometimes we shall even have to hoodwink the judge . . . so that he

---

[162]See my analysis of 2:14-17 in Chapter Five for an explanation of how 2:17 functions in connection with what precedes it. Indeed, WITHERINGTON shows elsewhere in his analysis his awareness of the linking function of γάρ with what precedes. See his comments on 2 Cor 4:14-5:10 (with its five-fold use of γάρ) and 9:10 in *Conflict & Community in Corinth*, 389 and 423, respectively.

[163]Cf. Rom 3:21-22, the *restatement* of the thesis in Paul's letter to the church in Rome, for a similar dynamic. Admittedly, the presence of the postpositive γάρ in 2 Cor 2:17 does not in and of itself preclude its being the *propositio*; in fact, cf. Rom 1:16-17 (the letter's thesis statement). But in the latter case, Paul begins what is tantamount to a new line of thought, expanding upon his wish to proclaim the gospel in Rome (1:10-15) to describe *the gospel as the power of God for salvation* (see Chapter Three).

[164]For WITHERINGTON'S treatment of 1 Cor, see *Character & Conflict in Corinth*, 69-324. There he follows closely the rhetorical analysis offered by M.M. MITCHELL set forth in her monumental *Paul and the Rhetoric of Reconciliation* (Tübingen: Mohr Siebeck, 1991). For another critique of Witherington's view of 2 Cor 2:17, see LONG, *"Have We Been Defending Ourselves to You?"*, 194-95.

[165]LONG, *"Have We Been Defending Ourselves to You?"*, 237.

may think that our aim is other than it is."[166] But does such 'hoodwinking' approach jibe well with what the apostle has just claimed in 1:12-13, namely that he has behaved toward the Corinthians with godly sincerity and that he writes (present tense!) nothing but what they can understand? Long seems more attuned here to Quintilian than to Paul! But grant to Long his thesis for a moment. Does 1:23 (the so-called fourth heading of the *partitio*) – "Now I call upon God as witness against my life that it was to spare you that I did not come to Corinth" – really introduce the content and argument of 5:11-7:1? In fact, as I will argue in Chapters Four and Five, 2 Cor 1:17-22 forms a single, coherent argument rather than the series of "discordant" verses that Long discerns.[167]

I have chosen to focus my critique of Witherington and Long on their respective analyses of the *propositio* (or *partitio*) because it serves as the linchpin to classical rhetorical arrangement (*exordium-narratio-propositio/partitio-probatio-peroratio*). That is, they understand Paul's thesis statement as the basic point(s) to be proven true or false, which is then developed in the course of the letter. But if the linchpin is faulty, the entire structure crumbles. And as I have just shown, Witherington's and Long's linchpins are defective. Thus, their proposals for the overall rhetorical structure fall to pieces. Indeed, I submit that Witherington and Long, as well as Young and Ford, are "guilty of overlaying a 'disposition grid'" onto the text of 2 Corinthians.[168] Moreover, they err in their identification of the rhetorical species of this letter, which leads to the following observations.

A third major weakness of many of these interpretations is that *they misidentify Paul's rhetoric in 2 Corinthians as judicial or forensic rhetoric*. On the contrary, I will argue in Chapter Six that 2 Corinthians is predominantly *deliberative* rhetoric. In 2 Cor 1:13b-14 Paul expresses his hope that the Corinthians will understand him fully and that they will be one another's

---

[166]LONG, *"Have We Been Defending Ourselves to You?"*, 237. Long's quotation from Quintilian is taken from *Inst. Ora.*, 4.5.5, cited from *The Institutio Oratoria of Quintilian*, vol. 2, trans. H.E. BUTLER, LCL (Cambridge, MA: Harvard University Press, 1960) 138-39.

[167]See LONG, *"Have We Been Defending Ourselves to You?"*, 239-40.

[168]The quotation is from LONG, *"Have We Been Defending Ourselves to You?"*, 275, in his assessment of B.K. PETERSON'S analysis of 2 Cor 10-13 in *Eloquence and the Proclamation of the Gospel in Corinth.*

"boast" on the day of the Lord. In 2:8 he begs them to forgive one of the members of their community. In 6:11-13 and 7:2-4 the apostle entreats the community to open their hearts to him. In 8:8, 8:24, and 9:13 he exhorts the Corinthians to be generous in giving to the collection. And, in 13:5, at the climax of the letter where Paul announces his impending visit, he challenges them to test themselves to see whether they are ἐν τῇ πίστει.

In fact, McCant rightly observes that "Paul's purpose in 2 Corinthians is to call [the Corinthians] to self-examination!"[169] The central issue in this letter is not the apostle's self-defense; rather, it is his challenge or test to the Corinthians to determine what kind of people they are, whether or not they take on the character of Jesus. This is not to deny that the Corinthians have raised doubts and concerns about Paul's character. Nevertheless, the apostle does not for a single moment submit to defending himself on their terms, as is clear from 2 Cor 13:1-5. Long is wrong to read 12:19 as Paul's admission that he has been defending himself throughout. This might be what the Corinthians were thinking and wanting (12:19a), but the apostle disabuses them of this notion immediately afterwards (12:19b): his concern is to 'speak in Christ' for the purpose of *their* upbuilding.[170]

To be fair, those who argue that 2 Corinthians is forensic rhetoric do acknowledge the deliberative elements in the letter. Witherington recognizes that Paul makes deliberative arguments in 2 Cor 8:1-9:15. Nevertheless, he claims that "they serve larger forensic purposes, both in Paul's defense and in his attack on the roots of the alienation of some of the Corinthian Christians from him."[171] This evaluation of purpose differs greatly, however, from the one that the apostle himself offers at the end of this section (9:12-15). Long also sees that this letter serves a deliberative purpose. Nevertheless, he insists that "in 2 Corinthians the emphasis rests upon the apologetic need, since Paul needs to clear himself of any wrong doing before" he can ask the community for their

---

[169]MCCANT, *2 Corinthians*, 164.

[170]Cf. 1 Cor 4:3-5 for Paul's thoughts about being judged by the Corinthians. For the apostle, ὁ κύριος is the only one who will judge Paul, a point to which he alludes in 2 Cor 5:10. Of the authors treated in this section, MCCANT is the one who understands most clearly that the apostle refuses to yield to the judgment of the Corinthians. See *2 Corinthians*, 13, 33, 36, 52, and 157-58.

[171]WITHERINGTON, *Conflict & Community in Corinth*, 412-13.

cooperation.[172] But does Paul, as Long claims, really apologize to the Corinthians in 12:13? Is he not being sarcastic here? And does the apostle, as Long claims, really admit to the appearance of wrongdoing in 13:7?[173] Reading 2 Corinthians through the lens of forensic rhetoric has distorted Long's interpretation of the text.

Given my preference for the literary unity of 2 Corinthians, as well as my positive assessment of the rhetorical analysis of it at the "micro level," what do *I* say concerning its rhetorical species? And can I propose a more satisfactory overarching rhetorical structure of the text? While I claim that this letter is largely deliberative in purpose, it is not helpful to delimit it exclusively as deliberative rhetoric, since there are apologetic passages in it as well. Nor is it beneficial to mine either the rhetorical handbooks or illustrative deliberative speeches in order to discern a structure of deliberative rhetoric into which to fit 2 Corinthians. Paul's presentation here is too complex and nuanced for such a rigid schema.[174] Nevertheless, I do contend that the apostle's mode of argumentation in this epistle is cumulative and coherent. Second Corinthians thus requires a rhetorical analytical approach "that discerns a multiplicity of argumentative threads running through it, causing it to cohere into a complex argumentative whole. . . ."[175]

I remind my readers that my aim is not to advance and defend a particular "disposition grid" for 2 Corinthians. My project is to set forth Paul's *ethos* strategy, a strategy that pervades the entire text. For my purposes, it is enough to accept (in the main) the rhetorical structural outline proposed by Amador, which consists of the following major argumentative units: 2 Cor 1:1-14 = the introductory unit; 1:15-2:13 = first unit; 2:14-7:4 = second unit; 7:5-9:15 = third unit; 10:1-13:10 = fourth unit; and 13:11-13 = concluding

---

[172]LONG, *"Have We Been Defending Ourselves to You?"*, 344-45.

[173]Ibid., 287-88.

[174]KRAFTCHICK'S comments about Gal are apposite concerning 2 Cor as well: ". . . we should not be restricted to interpreting the epistle as an example of a specific rhetorical genre. Instead we should allow fluidity its full force." See *Ethos and Pathos Appeals in Galatians Five and Six*, 40.

[175]AMADOR, "The Unity of 2 Corinthians," 412.

remarks.[176] Amador rightly claims that the apostle's argument is both aggregate and integrated. Whereas Amador sees the *narratio* as the rhetorical device which helps to thread the argument together, I submit that his structure also allows for what my thesis proposes, namely, that the character of Jesus is the linchpin to Paul's presentation in 2 Corinthians. Thus, the linchpin is not to be found in a single thesis statement; rather, it is located in the arena of *ethos*, which brings me to a fourth and final criticism.

In concentrating largely upon the rhetorical disposition of 2 Corinthians, the readings treated in this section *fail to give an adequate account of the apostle's* ethos *argument*. Because their rhetorical analyses tend to focus on structural components (e.g., *exordium*, *narratio*, etc.), they deal with the three so-called "artificial proofs" (πίστεις ἔντεχνοι) – *ethos*, *pathos*, and *logos*[177] – mostly in passing. And insofar as these scholars do treat the question of *ethos* in 2 Corinthians, they do so via rhetorical handbooks and various philosophical writings.[178] But does this strategy adequately capture what *Paul* is up to in 2 Corinthians?[179]

---

[176]See n. 141 above. In addition, see AMADOR, "The Unity of 2 Corinthians," 414-16 and 420-27, for his brief description of the dynamics and strategies involved in the course of Paul's argument. I have made one slight adjustment to Amador's schema, as I take 13:5-10 as the climax of the fourth unit and not as part of the apostle's concluding remarks.

[177]See Aristotle, *Rhet.*, 1.2.3-6. For Aristotle's text, see *The "Art" of Rhetoric*, trans. J.H. FREESE, LCL (Cambridge, Mass.: Harvard University Press, 1991) 16-17. All the quotations from Aristotle's *Rhetoric* in the next section are taken from this text and Freese's translation.

[178]See n. 159 above.

[179]Since writing this chapter, S.P. FULTON'S dissertation came to my attention. Fulton offers a rhetorical analysis of 2 Cor, arguing for the unity of the text, in *A Rhetorical Analysis of Second Corinthians with a View to the Unity Question* (Ph.D. diss., The Southern Baptist Theological Seminary, 1999). Fulton's work shares one of the strengths and several of the weaknesses of the monographs treated above. On the one hand, the strength of his dissertation lies in demonstrating how Paul develops certain themes throughout the course of the letter (see esp. pp. 145-54). On the other hand, Fulton misidentifies 2 Cor as forensic rhetoric, and imposes a rhetorical grid upon the text (pp. 64-65). For instance, he argues that 3:1-11 is the *propositio* of Paul's first argument (3:1-

II. The Question of *Ethos* in 2 Corinthians

Very few studies have analyzed Paul's writings methodologically from the vantage point of Aristotle's three proofs. As far as I can see, only Mario M. DiCicco has investigated 2 Corinthians in this manner, and his study is limited to 2 Cor 10-13.[180] This section consists of three parts. First, I offer a brief review and critique of DiCicco's study of Paul's use of ἦθος arguments. Second, I preview the particular ways in which I will argue that the apostle *does* summon the issue of character in 2 Corinthians. Third, I propose a brief theoretical justification for claiming my work as a type of rhetorical analysis, one that focuses exclusively on the question of *ethos*.

A. DiCicco on Paul's Utilization of Ethos *Arguments in 2 Cor 10-13*

In *Paul's Use of Ethos, Pathos, and Logos in 2 Corinthians 10-13*, DiCicco employs a historical-critical approach that "puts significant stress" on Aristotle's three-fold strategy of persuasion. My concern here is limited to his analysis of *ethos*. DiCicco consults the rhetorical handbooks and various ancient speeches and letters in order to assess what they say about the nature and

---

5:21). This is surely to attribute to Paul an unwieldy thesis statement! Fulton is also guilty at times of letting the rhetorical handbooks highjack his interpretation. For example, in his analysis of 1:17-22 (concerning Paul's change in travel plans), he claims that the apostle here follows the strategy advocated by Cicero of "shifting the blame," and that "Paul has shifted the question of guilt from himself to God" (p. 76). I submit that rigid adherence to rhetorical handbooks, rather than careful exegesis, has distorted Fulton's reading of this passage. Paul does not "blame" God here.

Near the beginning of his work, Fulton makes an important observation with which I agree wholeheartedly: "The position that I will take in the dissertation is that *rhetoric will describe what Paul is doing in his letters* but not that rhetoric determined how Paul arranged his letters" (p, 21, italics added). This is a critical insight. Fulton's own analysis, however, belies his disclaimer. It seems that rhetoric does determine how Fulton reads 2 Cor.

[180]See M.M. DICICCO, *Paul's Use of Ethos, Pathos, and Logos in 2 Corinthians 10-13*, MBPS 31 (Lewiston, N.Y.: Mellen Biblical, 1995). In addition, see KRAFTCHICK, *Ethos and Pathos Appeals in Galatians Five and Six*; and T.H. OLBRICHT and J.L. SUMNEY (eds.), *Paul and Pathos*, SBLSymS 16 (Atlanta: Society of Biblical Literature, 2001).

usages of *ethos*. In light of these findings, he then investigates Paul's utilization of *ethos* proofs to persuade the minds of the Corinthians.[181] Even though DiCicco's work deals only with 2 Cor 10-13, I choose to review his work for two reasons. First, he treats the issue of *ethos* in an engaged and sustained manner. Second, his work is representative of what I consider to be the strengths and the weaknesses of the references to *ethos* in the works treated in the previous section.

DiCicco's analysis of Paul's *ethos* arguments is particularly illuminating against the background of hardship catalogs and the conventions of benefaction and gratitude. DiCicco succeeds in showing the relevance of *peristasis* catalogs, especially from Stoic moralists, to 2 Cor 11:23-29. These lists functioned to prove the virtue and steadfastness of character of the one undergoing the enumerated trials and adversities. They also served to show that such hardships were paradoxically considered to be a sign of God's favor and love, that endurance gave witness to a divine calling.[182] In addition, DiCicco effectively brings the Greco-Roman *mores* of reciprocity to bear on his study of the apostle's mode of *ethos* argumentation. He states that "Paul's basic argument here is that he has an ἦθος which is filled with unmatched benevolence toward the Corinthians, a giving that is generous and selfless. This should be recommendation enough for their loyalty to him, their patron. . . ."[183] This cultural backdrop sheds light on the poignancy of passages such as 11:2-3 and 12:14-15.

DiCicco's investigation is also flawed in many ways. In his effort to show the value of analyzing 2 Cor 10-13 in light of Greco-Roman treatments of *ethos*, he allows the latter to distort his reading of the former. DiCicco's treatment of 2 Cor 12:1-8 illustrates this well. He claims that Paul's recounting his "rapture into paradise (12:1-6) functions as the second major example of his

---

[181]See DICICCO, *Paul's Use of Ethos, Pathos, and Logos in 2 Corinthians 10-13*, 36-77, for his treatment of the definition, nature, and use of ἦθος in ancient sources. For his analysis of Paul's use of ἦθος proofs in 2 Cor 10-13, see pp. 77-112.

[182]Ibid., 87-99. DICICCO makes ample and effective use of J.T. FITZGERALD'S *Cracks in an Earthen Vessel.*

[183]DICICCO, *Paul's Use of Ethos, Pathos, and Logos in 2 Corinthians 10-13*, 107-12. The quotation if found on p. 112. It is interesting to note that DiCicco refers throughout this section to the works of F.W. Danker.

argument from ἦθος."[184] DiCicco explains that the apostle's rhetorical purpose here is to offer "the argument from one's life, which Aristotle had said was the most powerful means of persuasion. . . ." It also serves to address what Aristotle recommended concerning the *topos* of removing prejudice.[185] DiCicco then goes on to interpret 12:7-8 in a peculiar way. His focus is on what he calls Paul's "casual asides": in 12:7, on the apostle's allusion to an "excess of revelations"; in 12:8, on the fact that he "talked to the Lord regularly." Their cumulative effect, according to DiCicco, is to show Paul as "a man long experienced in such visions."[186] But is this actually *Paul's* strategy here? Is not his purpose in 12:7 to emphasize the σκόλοψ that he had been given, rather than to accentuate his experience of an excess of revelations? Does not 12:8 refer to the apostle's three-fold prayer to the Lord to have it removed, and not to regular visionary experiences? And is not Paul being ironic in recounting a revelation which cannot be communicated to others (cf. 12:4)? It seems that DiCicco's efforts to show the apostle's adherence to the canons of *ethos* persuasion lead him to misinterpret the passage.

In fact, DiCicco's treatment gets sidetracked from the outset. At the beginning of his section "The Use of ἦθος in 2 Corinthians 10-13," he states that Paul secures the Corinthians' goodwill "from the four quarters discussed by Aristotle, Cicero, and other rhetorical theorists."[187] One of these quarters is "from the person of his opponents."[188] Although DiCicco insists that the identity of the opponents and their theological tenets are moot points, he nevertheless allows the specter of these rivals to exert much influence over his

---

[184]DICICCO, *Paul's Use of Ethos, Pathos, and Logos in 2 Corinthians 10-13*, 99. The first major example, according to DiCicco, is the *peristasis* catalog in 11:23-29.

[185]Ibid., 84-86. The quotation is from p. 86.

[186]Ibid., 102.

[187]Ibid., 78.

[188]The other three are from the rhetor's own person, from the persons of the audience, and from the case itself. See DICICCO, *Paul's Use of Ethos, Pathos, and Logos in 2 Corinthians 10-13*, 44-46. Cf. Aristotle, *Rhet.*, 3.14.17; and Cicero, *De inv.*, 1.16.22. For Cicero's text, see *Cicero: De Inventione: De Optimo Genere Oratorum: Topica*, trans. H.M. HUBBELL, LCL (Cambridge, Mass.: Harvard University, 1949) 2-345.

interpretation of 2 Cor 10-13. In fact, he lists 11 charges (!) that "were deliberately calculated to impugn Paul's reputation and his message."[189] (Note that, in DiCicco's treatment, it is this "slander" which gives the apostle justification for engaging in "self-praise" in accord with the handbooks.) Moreover, DiCicco draws a comparison between the situation of Paul and his opponents on the one hand, and the debate between Demosthenes and Aeschines recounted in *De Corona*[190] on the other. That is, he brings his investigation of *ethos* into the arena of forensic discourse. Thus, DiCicco's study is unduly influenced by two viewpoints that I have already shown to be problematic: opponents-driven interpretations, and readings of 2 Corinthians through the lens of judicial rhetoric.

Furthermore, I suggest that DiCicco's reliance upon the "four quarters" of the rhetorical theorists contributes to his failure to consider another possibility, namely, that Paul draws upon the *ethos* of a third party (other than the opponents). Although he recognizes the pivotal role that God's δύναμις plays in the apostle's self-presentation, DiCicco misses how Paul draws upon and aligns himself with the character of Jesus. Now, this might be the consequence of limiting his study to the final four chapters of 2 Corinthians, although the apostle draws upon Jesus' character there, too (10:1; 10:5; 11:3; and 13:4). At any rate, DiCicco would do well to heed the following warning issued by J. Paul Sampley: "... as is the case with everything that Paul co-opts from his culture, *Paul is no prisoner of the rhetorical conventions and practices of his time*.... // It is appropriate that Paul employs the rhetorical conventions only when they serve his purposes, because *his purposes are not identical to*

---

[189]DICICCO, *Paul's Use of Ethos, Pathos, and Logos in 2 Corinthians 10-13*, 81-82. The quotation is from p. 82.

[190]Demosthenes' *De Corona* is a key text for DiCicco in setting forth the use of ἦθος in ancient sources. See DICICCO, *Paul's Use of Ethos, Pathos, and Logos in 2 Corinthians 10-13*, 65-72. For Demosthenes' text, see *On the Crown (De Corona)*, trans. S. USHER, Greek Orators 5 (Warminster, England: Aris & Phillips, 1993).

those envisioned by the handbooks."[191] Indeed, in 2 Corinthians the apostle appeals to the notion of *ethos* in several special ways.

B. *Paul's Ways of Drawing upon the Issue of Character in 2 Corinthians*

The issue of character *is* central to the interpretation of 2 Corinthians. But it is pivotal in ways that differ from the discussion of ἦθος in the rhetorical handbooks. Paul's concern with character reveals itself in this letter through three unique features. First, 2 Corinthians contains several references to characteristics and attributes of Jesus. Second, the language of commendation and of self-commendation in particular appears throughout this epistle. Third, Paul employs several δοκιμ- cognates, which refer to the notions of "testing" and of "approved character." For the moment, I merely introduce these themes.

Paul refers to several characteristics and attributes of Jesus throughout 2 Corinthians. These qualities – πραΰτης (gentleness), ἐπιεικεία (forbearance), ὑπακοή (obedience), πίστις (faithfulness), ἀγάπη (love), μὴ γνῶναι ἁμαρτίαν (not knowing sin), χάρις (generosity), ἁπλότης (singleness of purpose), and ἀλήθεια (truth) – both resemble and differ in many respects from lists of virtues associated with *ethos* in the rhetorical handbooks.[192] Now, it is important to note that the apostle only alludes to these characteristics without defining them. Hence, it will be necessary to analyze carefully the texts in which the allusions occur in order to determine what Paul *presumes* about these qualities when referring to them, and thus what he presumes about the *ethos* of Jesus. This analysis is the task of Chapter Four. This task is crucial because the apostle draws upon and extrapolates from these same characteristics throughout 2 Corinthians in presenting his own *ethos* and in exhorting the Corinthians.

The issue of self-commendation is also very important in 2 Corinthians. Nine of Paul's fourteen usages of the verb συνίστημι occur here, as do seven of the eight instances in which he connects this verb with the reflexive pronoun.

---

[191]J.P. SAMPLEY "Paul, His Opponents in 2 Corinthians 10-13, and the Rhetorical Handbooks," 174 (italics added). Ironically, in this article Sampley, too, makes use of the "four quarters" from which to cultivate goodwill. His analysis thus suffers the same shortcoming as DiCicco's in that he fails to see how Jesus' *ethos* functions in the argument.

[192]Cf., e.g., Aristotle, *Rhet.*, 1.9.5.

Moreover, as John T. Fitzgerald has astutely pointed out, one must pay careful attention to the apostle's syntax when he joins together the notions of "self" and "commending." That is, when Paul writes positively about self-commendation, either his own or that of others, he places the verb before the pronoun. Conversely, when the apostle disparages self-commendation, he reverses the word order.[193] Obviously, the issue of self-commendation is connected to *ethos*, the presentation of one's character. And, as will be shown, the basis for Paul's positive self-commendation is the *ethos* of Jesus. Such is the argument presented in Chapter Five.

Similarly, the apostle's use of δοκιμ- cognates in 2 Corinthians is striking, both in terms of its frequency (compared with his other letters) and by virtue of its placement. Concerning the latter, the substantive, verbal, and adjectival forms of δοκιμ- all appear in the letter's climax (2 Cor 13:3-7). In addition, Paul employs δοκιμ- at several key points throughout his argument, usually in the context of challenging the Corinthians to action. Because δοκιμ-language denotes "testing" in order to ascertain one's "character," it obviously pertains to the issue of *ethos*. Indeed, DiCicco is correct when he claims that Paul attempts to inculcate his *ethos* among the Corinthians.[194] But it is the *ethos* of Jesus, the *ethos* the apostle himself claims to embody, that he wishes the Corinthians to incarnate. Chapter Six takes up this project.

Thus, Paul *is* concerned primarily with the subject of character in 2 Corinthians, but his manner and purpose are quite different from those of the classical rhetoricians. *How* the apostle utilizes *ethos* argumentation will be the focus of the exegetical analyses in Part Two.

C. *"Rhetorical Justification" of This Study*

It is now necessary to position the present study vis-à-vis the current body of rhetorical analysis of 2 Corinthians. My investigation does not involve

---

[193]See FITZGERALD, *Cracks in an Earthen Vessel*, 187 (esp. n. 192). Fitzgerald credits Henry Alford for making this observation concerning the placement of the reflexive pronoun. Cf. H. ALFORD, *The Greek New Testament*, vol. 2 (Grand Rapids, Mich.: Baker, 1980; reprint of rev. ed., 1871-75) 688. I will develop the distinction between self-*commendation* and *self*-commendation in greater detail at the beginning of Chapter Five.

[194]See DICICCO, *Paul's Use of Ethos, Pathos, and Logos in 2 Corinthians 10-13*, 96.

examining the text according to an overarching rhetorical structural grid. That is, I do not attempt to read 2 Corinthians in light of a single species of rhetoric nor according to a particular arrangement of textual units. Neither do I utilize the rhetorical handbooks as a thorough-going background and guide for interpretation. In these ways, my analysis differs greatly from the rhetorical analyses treated above. Nevertheless, because *ethos* is an essential part of the "rhetorical world," I do claim that my study is properly defined as a type of rhetorical analysis. Indeed, Aristotle makes four observations in his *Rhetoric* that are germane to my thesis concerning Paul's use of *ethos* arguments in 2 Corinthians. I submit that Aristotle's reflections, which are general in nature, offer a better background for insight into the apostle's *ethos* strategy in this letter than attempts like DiCicco's to bring several specific elements from different rhetorical handbooks to bear upon their interpretations.

First, Aristotle emphasized the crucial, indeed essential, importance of moral character: ". . . for it is not the case, as some writers of rhetorical treatises lay down in their 'Art,' that the worth of the orator in no way contributes to his powers of persuasion; on the contrary, moral character, so to say, constitutes the most effective means of proof."[195] In connection with this citation, Steven J. Kraftchick observes that the issue of *ethos* "is especially pertinent for arguments for which the logical evidence is strong on both sides."[196] That is, there are cases in which the external situation is ambiguous. Now, 2 Corinthians certainly exhibits ambiguity. What is one to make of Paul's change in travel plans? Of his tearful letter? Of his threats from afar compared to his more humble presence? Of his refusal to be remunerated combined with his plea for the collection? Of his suffering? Such questions can yield different answers, and thus different conclusions concerning Paul. The apostle's recourse, I submit, is to align himself with the *ethos* of Jesus, a strategy that "constitutes the most effective means of proof."

Second, Aristotle distinguished several aspects of ἦθος. In addition to the most common understanding, whereby the rhetor attempts to establish his

---

[195]*Rhet.*, 1.2.4. The Greek text reads: οὐ γὰρ ὥσπερ ἔνιοι τῶν τεχνολογούντων τιθέασιν ἐν τῇ τέχνῃ καὶ τὴν ἐπιείκειαν τοῦ λέγοντος ὡς οὐδὲν συμβαλλομένην πρὸς τὸ πιθανόν, ἀλλὰ σχεδὸν ὡς εἰπεῖν κυριωτάτην ἔχει πίστιν τὸ ἦθος.

[196]KRAFTCHICK, *Ethos and Pathos Appeals in Galatians Five and Six*, 103.

or her own moral character,[197] Aristotle referred to two other aspects of *ethos*. One is the *ethos* of the audience.[198] Here the rhetor must be aware of the character of the interlocutors so as to communicate with them effectively. This aspect of *ethos* also pertains to the rhetor's concern to persuade the audience, and thus (by implication) to inspire them to take on a certain character. Furthermore, Aristotle wrote about *ethos* in connection with the stylistic feature of *ethopoiia*, the portrayal of characters in a speech.[199] This second additional aspect of *ethos* involves reference to the character of a "third party" in the course of the rhetor's argument. Now, this threefold delineation of *ethos* fits well with my thesis that Paul deals with *ethos* on three levels. He certainly is concerned with confirming his own character (e.g., 2 Cor 7:2 and 12:18). He also alludes throughout the letter to Jesus and to certain of his characteristics (cf. Aristotle's *ethopoiia*), through which he validates his own character. In addition, he challenges the Corinthians, his "audience," to test themselves to determine whether they are taking on the character of Jesus (cf. 13:5).

Third, whereas the majority of rhetorical handbooks limited discussion concerning the presentation of character to the *exordium* and *peroratio*, Aristotle suggested that it ought to permeate all parts of a speech: "If you have proofs, then, your language must be both ethical and demonstrative; if you have no enthymemes, ethical only. In fact, it is more fitting that a virtuous man should show himself good than that his speech should be painfully exact."[200] This is very suggestive. Indeed, Paul alludes to characteristics of Jesus, raises the issue of self-commendation, and deals out challenges to the Corinthians to prove

---

[197]See, e.g., *Rhet.*, 1.2.3-4.

[198]See *Rhet.*, 2.12-27, esp. 2.13.16. Cf. 1.8.6.

[199]See *Rhet.*, 3.7.6 and 3.16.9. For more on these distinctions, see E.M. COPE, *An Introduction to Aristotle's Rhetoric* (London: Macmillan, 1867; repr. Dubuque, Iowa: Wm. C. Brown Reprint, 1966) 108-113. Cf. J. WISSE, *Ethos and Pathos from Aristotle to Cicero* (Amsterdam: Adolf M. Hakkert, 1989) 60-61; and DICICCO, *Paul's Use of Ethos, Pathos, and Logos in 2 Corinthians 10-13*, 39-43.

[200]*Rhet.*, 3.17.12. The Greek text reads: ἔχοντα μὲν οὖν ἀποδείξεις καὶ ἠθικῶς λεκτέον καὶ ἀποδεικτικῶς, ἐὰν δὲ μὴ ἔχῃς ἐνθυμήματα, ἠθικῶς· καὶ μᾶλλον τῷ ἐπιεικεῖ ἁρμόττει χρηστὸν φαίνεσθαι ἢ τὸν λόγον ἀκριβῆ. Cf. WISSE, *Ethos and Pathos from Aristotle to Cicero*, 15.

themselves – all of which pertain to *ethos* – *throughout* 2 Corinthians. That is, the issue of *ethos* pervades this letter, and is not simply relegated to the beginning and the end.

Fourth, Aristotle implied that *ethos* argumentation may be expressed by enthymemes: ". . . we have in like manner already established all the topics from which enthymemes may be derived on the subject of good or bad, fair or foul, just or unjust, characters, emotions and habits."[201] That is, he seems to have expanded the possibilities of enthymemic argumentation, rhetoric's form of the syllogism, beyond the arena of *logos* (logical demonstration) to include *ethos*. Again, this is suggestive. At several key points in Paul's presentation in 2 Corinthians, he employs a statement about Jesus Christ as an *explanation* for what precedes it (cf. 1:19; 5:14; 8:9; and 13:4). In each case, the apostle uses the construction γάρ + an allusion to the story and character of Jesus. Similarly, he utilizes γάρ in connection with the notions of self-commendation (10:18) and δοκιμή (2:9). This suggests that Paul's use of *ethos* is embedded within the very fabric of his argumentation.

Now, it is important to be clear that I am not suggesting that the apostle executed his *ethos* strategy in 2 Corinthians with one eye upon Aristotle's *Rhetoric*. Indeed, in the previous subsection, I argued that Paul's approach is unique and not a product of following the rhetorical handbooks. Nevertheless, I submit that the foregoing observations give some theoretical justification for my claim that the apostle is making what can properly be called an *ethos* argument in this letter.

Before concluding this introduction of *ethos*, it will be helpful to set forth a few definitions. First, when I refer in this work to "character" or *ethos* – whether that of Jesus, of Paul, or of the Corinthians – I mean the complex of attitudinal, behavioral, and ethical traits that mark a certain person in his or her individuality. In short, I take *ethos* as signifying "moral character."[202] Second,

---

[201]*Rhet.*, 2.22.16. The Greek text reads: . . . ἐξ ὧν δεῖ φέρειν τὰ ἐνθυμήματα τόπων περὶ ἀγαθοῦ ἢ κακοῦ ἢ καλοῦ ἢ αἰσχροῦ ἢ δικαίου ἢ ἀδίκου, καὶ περὶ τῶν ἠθῶν καὶ παθημάτων καὶ ἕξεων. . . . Cf. L. ARNHART, *Aristotle on Political Reasoning: A Commentary on the "Rhetoric"* (DeKalb, Ill.: Northern Illinois University Press, 1981) 51-53.

[202]Thus, my usage is similar to that of Aristotle. Cf. *Aristotle,* On Rhetoric*: A Theory of Civil Discourse*, trans. G.A. KENNEDY (New York: Oxford University Press, 1991) 37, n. 40.

by the phrase "*ethos* argument," I intend to connote any of the ways – whether through allusion, through argumentation, or through exhortation – by which the apostle attempts to inculcate a particular character, namely, the character of Jesus.

III. Summary

A survey of rhetorical analyses of 2 Corinthians reveals mixed results. On the positive side, analyses of the whole letter offer a tenable way of reading the text as a literary unity, thereby avoiding the problems associated with partition theories.[203] They do so chiefly by two means. First, they attend carefully to the interlinking and coherence of several terms, topics, and themes – many of which are seen more readily in the Greek text than in translations. Second, they show how various passages function vis-à-vis one another, and how Paul's argument develops over the course of the letter, with the earlier chapters laying the necessary groundwork for the final chapters. Rhetorical analyses also demonstrate the apostle's use of compositional techniques and rhetorical devices, particularly at the "micro level." In addition, the rhetorical readings reviewed above avoid the pitfalls associated with focusing on the so-called opponents and their theology.

On the negative side, several of the rhetorical analyses impose rigid structural grids upon the text, a process that leads to distorted readings. Attempts to ferret out a single *propositio* (thesis statement) or *partitio* fail because of the complexity of both the rhetorical situation of 2 Corinthians and the apostle's argumentative techniques. Furthermore, many of the readings examined above err in characterizing 2 Corinthians as forensic rhetoric, thereby missing the deliberative thrust of the apostle's strategy. In sum, these analyses tend to go awry when the emphasis falls upon "demonstrating" Paul's use of specific rhetorical guidelines culled from the handbooks. I submit that a more satisfactory approach is to allow the apostle's rhetorical strategies, both

---

[203]It is worth pointing out that several recent commentaries on 2 Cor have argued for the letter's unity *without* resorting to a thoroughgoing rhetorical analysis. See J.M. SCOTT, *2 Corinthians*, NIBC 8 (Peabody, Mass.: Hendrickson, 1998); D.E. GARLAND, *2 Corinthians*, NAC 29 (Nashville: Broadman & Holman, 1999); J. LAMBRECHT, *Second Corinthians*, SP 8 (Collegeville, Minn.: Liturgical, 1999); S.J. HAFEMANN, *2 Corinthians*, NIVAC (Grand Rapids, Mich.: Zondervan, 2000); and F.J. MATERA, *II Corinthians*, NTL (Louisville: Westminster John Knox, 2003).

conventional strategies and those that bear his unique stamp, to emerge from a careful reading of the text on its own terms.

The one feature of rhetorical studies that is singularly pertinent to my investigation is the analysis of ἦθος. Paul's employment of *ethos* arguments in 2 Corinthians has received insufficient attention. While the cultural background of beneficence and the comparison of certain passages in 2 Corinthians with various *peristasis* catalogs do yield important socio-cultural insights into the apostle's usage, they fail to capture the essence of his *ethos* strategy – namely, that he draws upon the *ethos* of Jesus throughout this letter. Before demonstrating this claim, however, it will be helpful to place my thesis within the context of two recent developments in Pauline theology.

Chapter Three
Recent Developments in Pauline Theology that Point to the Character of Jesus

The pursuit of understanding what Paul is up to in 2 Corinthians has taken many wrong turns and hit several dead ends, as the history of interpretation indicates. While rhetorical criticism has set the enterprise in the right general direction, attention to the apostle's concern for *character* opens up an even more promising avenue of exploration. Careful analysis of the *ethos* dimension of Paul's presentation – suggested by his constant allusions to Christ, his several references to "commendation," and his concentrated use of δοκιμ-cognates – provides a better path toward understanding the apostle's argument in this letter. Such is the conclusion suggested by the preceding analysis.

Can my thesis that the notion of character – and the character of Jesus in particular – is the linchpin to Paul's presentation in 2 Corinthians be supported from another perspective? Two recent developments in Pauline theology converge upon the theme of this study. First is the growing appreciation that Paul's arguments are rooted in the story of Jesus the Messiah, a story that remains mostly implicit in his letters. Second is the recognition of the pivotal role that Jesus' own faithfulness and obedience play in the apostle's thought. In the present chapter, I review current scholarship on the "story of Jesus" in Paul, and briefly examine key exegetical claims that highlight the centrality of Jesus' πίστις and ὑπακοή in Romans. I then conclude with a brief statement on the method that I will employ in the following exegetical chapters.

I. The "Story of Jesus" in Paul

Recognition of the importance of "the story of Jesus" for Paul has proved to be a significant development in Pauline scholarship over the last twenty years. Richard B. Hays, N.T. Wright, Ben Witherington III, and Stephen E. Fowl are key figures in the discussion. I offer a brief review of their work, with no pretense of exhaustive analysis. My discussion of each scholar is limited to two topics: a consideration of the role of the story of Jesus for Paul, and a critical look at the methodology employed. I also offer comments on how my investigation resembles and, more importantly, differs from their approaches.

A. Richard B. Hays

In *The Faith of Jesus Christ*, Richard B. Hays argues that Paul's theological exposition in the central section of Galatians (3:1-4:11) rests upon a narrative substructure, a "sacred story" which is a "story about Jesus Christ."[204] Hays emphasizes the notion of substructure because, he contends, the apostle wrote to the Galatians in a "mode of recapitulation"[205]: because Paul had already proclaimed the gospel to the community (cf. Gal 3:1), he could *presuppose* that the story of Jesus served as common ground between them. Hence, the apostle had merely to allude to aspects of that story in order to recall and evoke the whole narrative. Paul's purpose in writing was "to draw out the implications of this story for shaping the belief and practices of his infant churches."[206] His christological formulations and other allusions to the story of Jesus thus serve as warrants from which he could draw soteriological and exhortative inferences. What holds the apostle's treatment together, according to Hays, is neither a system of doctrines nor Paul's own religious experience. Rather, Hays claims that the cohesive element is the material unity of the "particular paradigmatic story about Jesus Christ."[207]

Hays demonstrates his thesis through an examination of the narrative christological formulations in Gal 3:1-4:11, namely, 3:13-14 and 4:3-6. At first glance, these two passages appear to view Jesus Christ from two vastly different perspectives: Galatians 3:13 focuses on Jesus' death as having redeeming significance, while Gal 4:4-5 highlights the redemptive consequence of the

---

[204]R.B. HAYS, *The Faith of Jesus Christ: The Narrative Substructure of Galatians 3:1-4:11*, 2nd ed. (Grand Rapids, Mich.: Eerdmans, 2002), 6. The second edition, a reprint of Hays's doctoral dissertation (Emory University, 1981), includes a new, extensive introduction (pp. xxi-lii). All references to *The Faith of Jesus Christ* in this study are from the second edition.

[205]Ibid., 29.

[206]Ibid., 6.

[207]Ibid., 20.

incarnation. However, utilizing a model derived from A.J. Greimas,[208] a model that involves "narrative sequences"[209] and "actantial roles,"[210] Hays argues that

---

[208]For A.J. GREIMAS'S work on structural narrative analysis, see both his *Sémantique structurale* (Paris: Librairie Larousse, 1966) and *Du Sens* (Paris: Seuil, 1970). For more accessible treatments of Greimas's theory and method, see D. PATTE, *What is Structural Exegesis?* (Philadelphia: Fortress, 1976); and J. CALLOUD, *Structural Analysis of Narrative*, Semeia Sup. 4, trans. D. PATTE (Philadelphia: Fortress, 1976).

[209]A basic narrative structure consists of three sequences. In the initial sequence, a protagonist is charged with a mission to carry out, but is hindered by some person or obstacle from doing so. This situation of an unfulfilled task is what gives rise to the narrative. In the next sequence, called the "topical sequence," a second protagonist is commissioned to carry out a different task that will enable the first protagonist to succeed. In this second sequence, the hero (i.e., the second protagonist) must engage in conflict with a dangerous foe in order to give the first protagonist the needed assistance. In the final sequence, the first protagonist, fortified with the necessary aid provided by the second hero's successful mission, is able to carry out the initial mandate. In the actual performance of narratives, it is the second sequence which is recounted most fully, for this is where the heart of the story is. The initial and final sequences are often only alluded to, and must be inferred by the reader/audience. See R.B. HAYS, *The Faith of Jesus Christ*, 82-90, for a fuller account. Of course, each sequence is capable of having a more complicated structure than this bare outline might suggest.

[210]Again following the work of Greimas, HAYS states that "any narrative sequence presupposes or manifests six actantial roles or positions. These may be occupied by human characters, but objects or abstract values or qualities may also fill actantial positions." See *The Faith of Jesus Christ*, 90-91. The six roles are: (1) the "Sender," the figure who establishes the mandate or mission; (2) the "Subject," the figure who receives the mandate (this is the protagonist/hero mentioned in n. 209); (3) the "Object," the thing or quality that the Sender desires to bestow on another through the Subject; (4) the "Receiver," the figure to whom the Sender wants to communicate the Object; (5) the "Opponent," the figure or force that strives to prevent the Subject from accomplishing the mission; and (6) the "Helper," the figure or force that assists the Subject. The following diagram illustrates the mutual relations among the six actants:

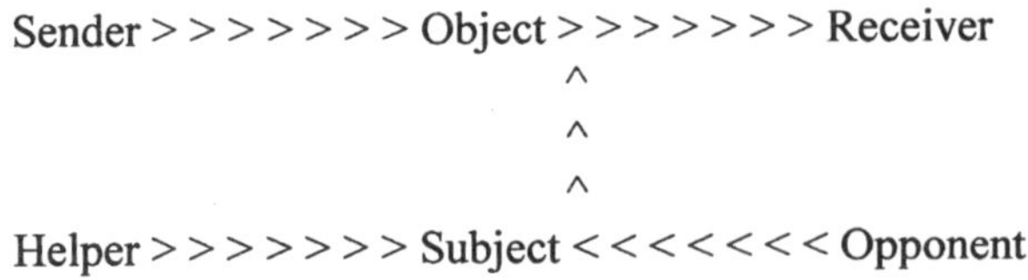

the various components alluded to in Gal 3:1-4:11 "cohere fitly" into "a single story-structure."[211] This story-structure is as follows: God responded to humanity's plight of enslavement to τὰ στοιχεῖα (associated with the Law, 4:3) by sending God's Son to redeem them and enable their adoption as God's children (4:4-5). Christ (= the Son) embarked upon this mission, as one born of woman and born under the law (4:4). He carried out his task by becoming a curse (i.e., by being crucified), thereby freeing those who had been under the enslaving curse (3:13). Moreover, it was through Christ that God bestowed the promised Spirit upon humanity (3:14), the Spirit who as the "Spirit of [God's] Son" is associated with their adoption as God's children (4:6). Lastly, the "power" or quality that allowed Jesus to carry out his mandate was his πίστις; that is, by means of his faithfulness, Jesus accomplished his mission.[212]

Hays's approach succeeds because he is careful not to claim too much. His model for analyzing narrative structure is a heuristic device that allows the *prima facie* puzzling allusions to "cohere fitly" into a single story. He recognizes, however, that this analysis does not stand alone; he goes on to show how his findings aid in illuminating the logic of the argument of the entire passage.[213] Hays is also clear that the story he has pieced together pertains specifically to Gal 3:1-4:11, and he does not universalize his findings. He rightly insists that the narrative structure "is *in* the text, and its shape and sequence were determined through the analysis of specific passages in Galatians 3 and 4."[214] Hays is therefore innocent of importing the story of Jesus into the apostle's argument.

Several features of Hays's treatment of the story of Jesus in Galatians merit attention because they help to bring my own project into clearer focus. First of all, Hays's approach is material and not formal. That is, he distinguishes

---

[211]HAYS, *The Faith of Jesus Christ*, 111.

[212]See *The Faith of Jesus Christ*, 95-117. Using the notions of narrative sequence (see n. 209 above) and actantial roles (n. 210), this sketch deals with the crucial topical (or main) sequence. The actantial roles are as follows: Sender = God; Subject = Jesus; Object = freedom/adoption/Spirit; Receivers = believers; Opponent = Law; and Helper = πίστις.

[213]HAYS does this in Chapter 5 of *The Faith of Jesus Christ*, 163-207.

[214]Ibid., 206 (Hays's italics).

his attempt to find the narrative substructure in Galatians, in which Paul's theological formulations derive their material unity, from rhetorical criticism, which seeks to demonstrate coherence through formal analysis. Hays does not apologize for the fact that his approach sheds little light on the text's formal structure. His method illuminates an underlying story that provides the apostle's argument with its material unity.[215] Nevertheless, he does recognize that his project can be complemented by those who approach Galatians using historical-critical and rhetorical critical methodologies.[216] Like Hays, in Part Two I focus more on material coherence than formal analysis. That is, I focus on the story and character of Jesus in 2 Corinthians, from which Paul both commends his manner of apostleship and exhorts the Corinthians. As was argued in Chapters One and Two, however, 2 Corinthians stubbornly resists analysis through formal rhetorical and purely historical approaches. I am less optimistic about their fruitful application to 2 Corinthians than Hays is about their viability in the study of Galatians.

In his treatment of "narrative logic," Hays discusses the "twin narrative properties" of sequence and shape.[217] Concerning sequence, he insists that it is important to ascertain which part of the story[218] Paul exploits at any given time: the plight of humans from which they need deliverance; God's saving intervention on humanity's behalf through Jesus; or the continuation of the story into the present through the building up of the body of Christ. Indeed, Paul appeals to the "logic" of sequence in his letter to the churches in Galatia. He contends that the Galatians' practice of observing "days and months and seasons and years" is tantamount to returning to the initial sequence of the story in which they had been enslaved by τὰ στοιχεῖα (Gal 4:8-11). The apostle exhorts them to recognize where they are in the story, in the final sequence,[219]

---

[215]Ibid., 194 and 206.

[216]Ibid., 227.

[217]Ibid., 194-96.

[218]It is pertinent to point out that, for HAYS, "story" refers "to the *ordered series of events* which forms the basis for various possible narrations." See *The Faith of Jesus Christ*, 18 (italics added).

[219]For "initial sequence" and "final sequence," see n. 209 above.

having been redeemed through Jesus' becoming a curse on their behalf. They must therefore follow the logic of the story and live in freedom, empowered by the Holy Spirit. In other words, they are the protagonist of the final chapter of the story, assisted in their task by the Spirit.[220] As I show in the following chapters, Paul appeals implicitly to the logic of sequence in 2 Corinthians.

Concerning the story's shape, Hays states that a "story posits *patterns* of order and value.... In the case of stories which become foundational stories for a community, these patterns may take on a prescriptive-ethical significance: the 'fittingness' of an action may be measured as a function of its correspondence to a particular narrative pattern."[221] According to Hays, Jesus' role in the crucial middle sequence of the story is not reducible to his freeing humanity from "the curse of the law" (Gal 3:13). Jesus' action also defines a pattern of living that Paul refers to as ἐκ πίστεως (3:22; cf. 2:16). Those who live in the story's final sequence, those who are "in Christ," are to live according to this pattern. Indeed, the πίστις of Jesus Christ is the distinguishing mark of the lives of the Spirit-empowered protagonists of the last sequence of the story.[222]

This logic of narrative shape is crucial to the present study. The "logic" of both the apostle's self-presentation and his exhortation to the Corinthians is grounded in the shape of life marked by Jesus. Paul's strategy in 2 Corinthians involves alluding to and appealing to the Christ-story in order to point the community to the *character* of Jesus. My approach therefore differs slightly from that of Hays: whereas Hays looks more to the story itself, I highlight the apostle's focus on the story's protagonists, Jesus and those who, through the Spirit, are "in him."[223]

---

[220]See HAYS, *The Faith of Jesus Christ*, 223-24 and 228-29. For a brief description of "subject," "helper," and the other actantial roles, see n. 210 above.

[221]HAYS, *The Faith of Jesus Christ*, 195.

[222]Ibid., 204 and 206-7.

[223]Given that, in *The Faith of Jesus Christ*, HAYS deals with Gal 3:1-4:11, a section marked by theological exposition more than paraenesis, it is not surprising that his emphasis is on the story rather than the character of Jesus. This is especially the case since Paul's argumentative strategy involves the Abraham story (3:6-18; cf. 4:21-31), which he takes up into the Christ story. In addition, Paul is concerned here with the

Hays raises another important issue concerning the nature of Paul's language. If the apostle presupposes the story of Jesus in Galatians (and, perhaps, in all his letters[224]), his language is neither self-contained nor purely referential. Rather, it is necessarily allusive, as Paul refers to and appeals to a story he presupposes as common ground between himself and his communities. Hays suggests that "perhaps Paul's language is less univocal and more 'poetic' than the Western theological tradition has usually supposed."[225] He proposes a certain degree of polyvalence in the apostle's writings. Interpreters should therefore avoid imposing a rigid univocity upon Paul's language; instead, they should be sensitive to its range of connotations.[226] Hays's observation is critically important. It pertains both to the interpretation of certain key terms (e.g., πίστις) and to the way in which the apostle *uses* language. I attempt to bring the same sensitivity to the text of 2 Corinthians. I am concerned to identify not only story fragments (i.e., allusions to the underlying gospel story), but also intratextual echoes and semantic connections, as well as intertextual allusions. It should be noted that several of these intratextual and intertextual connections are more apparent in the Greek text than in translations.

In his concluding chapter, Hays asks whether his detection of a narrative substructure in Galatians might be extended to other letters. He lists 1 Cor 15, Phil 2:6-11, and Rom 3:21-26 and 5:12-21 as possible pericopes which "presuppose and manifest, however fragmentarily, a narrative christology."[227]

Galatians' appreciation of the story's *sequence*. In a later article, Hays brings the story's *shape* to bear on his interpretation of Gal. See his "Christology and Ethics in Galatians: The Law of Christ," *CBQ* 49 (1987) 268-90, esp. 276-83.

[224]In his concluding chapter in *The Faith of Jesus Christ*, there are times when HAYS shifts from hypothesizing (e.g., pp. 209-10) to assuming (e.g., pp. 226-28) that his findings in Gal can be extended to Paul's other letters.

[225]Ibid., 227.

[226]Ibid., 228. In his "Introduction to the Second Edition" of *The Faith of Jesus Christ*, HAYS remarks, "My investigation of narrative substructure in Galatians is intended not only to expose the narrative roots of Paul's argument but also thereby to free up our reading of the text, to make our reading more supple, more witty, and therefore more responsive to the character of the rich language that confronts us in the letter" (p. xxxiv).

[227]Ibid., 210.

Conspicuously absent from this list is 2 Corinthians. However, as Frances Young and Dale F. Ford have remarked in passing, what Hays has done for Galatians could also be done for 2 Corinthians.[228] I agree. Paul indeed does allude several times in 2 Corinthians to the story of Jesus, and evokes Christ's *ethos* by referring to certain of his characteristics (the subject of the analysis in the next chapter).

In summary, Hays's treatment of the narrative substructure of Galatians serves as a springboard to the present study. In 2 Corinthians the story and (more specifically) the character of Jesus serve as the foundation of the apostle's self-commendation and paraenesis. In particular, my study builds on Hays's insights concerning Jesus' πίστις and its importance for Paul's presentation of the gospel, the focus on material rather than formal unity, the "logic" of narrative shape, and the character of the apostle's language as allusive and poetic.[229]

B. N.T. Wright

N.T. Wright is in basic agreement with Hays that Paul "knows the outline of the story of Jesus, and can use it as it stands, or, more frequently, as a substructure for theological argument."[230] Wright is more insistent, however, in placing the story of Jesus within the larger narrative of the story of God, Israel, and the whole world.[231] This larger story is a Jewish story, a story that

---

[228]See YOUNG and FORD, *Meaning and Truth in 2 Corinthians*, 261, n. 3.

[229]HAYS offers a precise summary reconstruction of the narrative framework presupposed and alluded to by Paul in 1 and 2 Thess, Phil, Gal, and Phlm in "Crucified with Christ: A Synthesis of the Theology of 1 and 2 Thessalonians, Philemon, Philippians, and Galatians," in *Pauline Theology. Volume I: Thessalonians, Philippians, Galatians, Philemon*, ed. J.M. BASSLER (Minneapolis: Fortress, 1991) 227-46, here 231-34.

[230]N.T. WRIGHT, *The New Testament and the People of God*, Christian Origins and the Question of God, Vol. 1 (London: SPCK, 1992) 409.

[231]To be fair to HAYS, he also recognizes that the story of Jesus does not exist in a vacuum for Paul. In *Echoes of Scripture in the Letters of Paul* (New Haven, Conn.: Yale University Press, 1989), Hays argues that Paul reads Scripture as a narrative of God's election and promise (p. 157; cf. pp. 53 and 105). In this work, Hays maintains

pivots on God's covenant with Israel. For Paul, the Jewish story now stands in a dialectical relationship with the story of Jesus. On the one hand, the apostle redraws the essentially Jewish story around Jesus, a redrawing that modifies and even subverts that story. On the other hand, the story of Jesus is interpreted within the wider Jewish narrative, especially under the themes of monotheism, election, and eschatology. While Wright insists that the story of Jesus is "the hinge upon which Paul's rereading of that larger story turned,"[232] he also identifies the story of Christ as Israel's story. Thus, when interpreting the apostle's writings, it is necessary to keep in view his presupposed story-world, and especially the symbolic universe that accompanies it. While this basic insight is correct enough, Wright's pursuit of it becomes problematic.

Wright goes to great pains to reconstruct what he calls "the authentic Jewish worldview," including its controlling story and belief structure.[233] As impressive as his reconstruction appears at first glance, however, it leaves one feeling uneasy that it has been accomplished at the expense of leveling the data. Although at several points Wright acknowledges the great diversity within Second Temple Judaism, he nevertheless produces a single monolithic grid upon which he maps Israel's story and symbols – in short, her self-understanding. One cannot help but suspect a "forced" quality in the project, even an artificiality. Moreover, the *manner* in which Wright utilizes this reconstructed Jewish worldview is problematic. Instead of serving as a heuristic device to illuminate texts, Wright's reproduction of Jewish presuppositions has the

---

that the apostle's hermeneutic is more "ecclesiocentric" than "christocentric," for Paul runs the biblical texts through the filter of his experience of what God has done in forming the church (p. 102). At first blush, this might be taken to contradict the claim made in *The Faith of Jesus Christ* concerning the centrality of the story of Jesus for Paul. Nevertheless, in *Echoes of Scripture in the Letters of Paul*, Hays still insists that christology is the presupposition and foundation of the apostle's ecclesiocentric interpretations. See *Echoes of Scripture in the Letters of Paul*, 120-21. Later, in his "Introduction to the Second Edition" of *The Faith of Jesus Christ*, Hays briefly discusses how the story of Jesus fits into the story of Israel (pp. xxxv-xxxviii). He concludes by stating: ". . . Paul finds in Scripture the story of Israel as a prefiguration of the story of Jesus the Messiah *and* of the church that he brings into being, 'the Israel of God' (Gal 6:16)." See *The Faith of Jesus Christ*, pp. xxxviii (Hays's italics).

[232]WRIGHT, *The New Testament and the People of God*, 407.

[233]Ibid., 149. Wright's detailed treatment can be found on pp. 145-338.

potential of becoming a rigid template to be imposed upon texts. There is at times a deductive quality to his interpretation. That is, his conclusions lead one to suspect that he extrapolates from certain texts what his reconstructed grid has already established.[234]

Wright's interpretation of Rom 5:12-21 and 8:3-4[235] serves as an apt illustration, especially as these are two passages where (he rightly claims) Paul draws upon the story of Jesus. Wright correctly focuses on the obedience of the human Jesus, his "obedience unto death." His interpretation of this obedience, however, is questionable. Wright fastens upon the phrase "where sin increased" (Rom 5:20b). He names Israel as the *locus* where sin abounds, and cites Rom 7:13-20 as evidence for this assertion.[236] He then looks ahead to the christological passage in Rom 8:3-4, where he argues that "the positive reason for the negative role of Torah" was to magnify and heap sin upon Israel so that it (sin) might be drawn upon Christ as Israel's representative and dealt with on the cross. Wright concludes that by his obedient act, Christ did for Israel what she could not do for herself. That is, Christ's obedience unto death remedied Israel's failure to obey.[237] How does Wright *connect* these passages so as to arrive at his conclusion? He appeals to "Paul's Jewish background," which "contained the idea that Abraham's family was to be the means of solving the

[234]It should be pointed out that in *The New Testament and the People of God*, Wright is setting up the later volumes of his projected five-volume series entitled "Christian Origins and the Question of God." In this first volume, he paints in broad brush strokes in his treatment of the NT writers. In a section dealing with Paul's use of story, Wright indicates that he will substantiate his claims in the forthcoming volume on Paul (see *The New Testament and the People of God*, 405, n. 108). Nevertheless, the criticism offered here is based on his more extended analysis of Pauline passages in his *The Climax and the Covenant: Christ and the Law in Pauline Theology* (Edinburgh: T. & T. Clark, 1991).

[235]See WRIGHT, *The Climax of the Covenant*, 18-40.

[236]Ibid., 39. In a later chapter, Wright declares without any explanation that the oft-repeated *first person singular* pronouns in Rom 7:7-25 refer to "Israel" (see p. 179). This is an unpersuasive exegetical maneuver.

[237]Ibid., 39.

problem posed by Adam's sin."[238] Thus, at the center of Wright's argument is an assumption, based on his constructed Jewish worldview, which Paul is supposed to have made. This has two deleterious ramifications. It posits what cannot be found anywhere in the apostle's writings, namely, that Israel was by her obedience to remedy the sin of Adam. And it assumes the theologically objectionable view that the gathering of sin *upon Israel* was part of God's plan.[239]

Nevertheless, Wright does appreciate the role that the story of Jesus plays in Paul's writings. In his treatment of 2 Cor 5:16 – where Paul states that "even if we knew Christ according to the flesh, now we no longer know [him thus]" – Wright correctly insists (against, e.g., Bultmann) on the possibility and relevance of the apostle's knowledge about the human Jesus. He asserts that Paul's argument in this section of 2 Corinthians rests upon "the pattern of the ministry of Jesus."[240] Indeed, citing Rom 15:7-9, Wright comments that at times the apostle refers explicitly to the ministry of Jesus without focusing on his death.[241] This is suggestive. As I will show in Chapter Four, Paul *does* allude to aspects of Jesus that cannot be reduced completely to his passion and death. In addition, Wright's treatment of the ongoing expression of the righteousness of God through the apostle's "Christ-shaped ministry"[242] will be brought to bear

---

[238]WRIGHT, *The Climax of the Covenant*, 59. For Wright's bringing this assumption to bear on the argument referred to here, see ibid., 36.

[239]For a similar criticism, see R.B. HAYS, "Adam, Israel, Christ: The Question of Covenant in the Theology of Romans: A Response to Leander E. Keck and N. T. Wright," in *Pauline Theology. Volume III: Romans*, ed. D.M. HAY and E.E. JOHNSON (Minneapolis: Fortress, 1995) 68-86, here 82. Hays is responding here to WRIGHT'S article "Romans and the Theology of Paul," pp. 30-67, in the same volume. Like Hays, I do not insinuate any anti-Jewish intent on the part of Wright. However, his interpretation leaves him with a problematic viewpoint.

[240]WRIGHT, *The New Testament and the People of God*, 408. Cf. BULTMANN, *The Second Letter to the Corinthians*, 155-56.

[241]See WRIGHT, *The New Testament and the People of God*, 408-9.

[242]See WRIGHT, "On Becoming the Righteousness of God: 2 Corinthians 5:21," in *Pauline Theology. Volume II: 1 & 2 Corinthians*, ed. D.M. HAY (Minneapolis: Fortress, 1993), 200-208.

on the analysis of 2 Cor 5:21 in Chapter Five. In these and other ways, I will draw with profit upon Wright's insights.

It will also be necessary to heed the warning implicit in my critique of Wright. Whereas Wright's project at times allows his reconstruction of the first century Jewish worldview to determine how he interprets certain passages and finds links between them, my approach is more inductive. I propose analyzing passages individually, within their immediate contexts, and linking passages via intratextual semantic and conceptual connections. The force of my argument is thus *cumulative* in nature. Moreover, whereas Wright seems to emphasize the story of Jesus in connection with what has preceded it,[243] the present study highlights the story of Jesus in connection with what follows upon it, namely, how Paul and the Corinthians are to take part in and continue the story.[244]

C. *Ben Witherington III*

Ben Witherington offers a full-length treatment of the narrative substructure of the apostle's writings in *Paul's Narrative Thought World.* Witherington is "convinced that *all* Paul's ideas, all his arguments, all his practical advice, all his social arrangements are ultimately grounded. . . . in a grand narrative and in a story that has continued to develop out of that narrative."[245] According to Witherington, the apostle refers to "four interrelated stories" which constitute the larger Story: (1) the story of the world gone wrong; (2) the story of Israel; (3) the story of Christ (which arises from the first

---

[243]Wright's interest centers on how the story of Jesus modifies and subverts the larger story. For example, in *The Climax of the Covenant*, 204-14, Wright's narrative analysis of Rom 8:3-4 – in which he uses the model Hays adapts from Greimas – focuses on the *initial* sequence in which the Torah is unable to give life to the people of God. This "backward glance" may be a function of Wright's working predominantly upon the text of Rom.

[244]Using the terminology from Greimas's model, my study will emphasize the topical and final sequences of the underlying narrative.

[245]B. WITHERINGTON, *Paul's Narrative Thought World: The Tapestry of Tragedy and Triumph* (Louisville: Westminster/John Knox, 1994) 2 (Witherington's italics). Witherington dedicates this monograph to Hays and Wright, whom he dubs "fellow followers of the Story,/ fellow diggers in the communal plot."

two stories, but also from the story of God as creator and redeemer); and (4) the story of Paul and Christians. The third story is pivotal: "Christ's story is the hinge, crucial turning point, and climax of the entire larger drama. . . ."[246] Witherington's project is to set forth these four stories in sequence and to show how they function in the apostle's writings. By far, the largest portion of his book is dedicated to the story of Christ[247] and to the ongoing story of Christians.

Methodologically, Witherington eschews an inductive approach to Paul's writings.[248] Rather, he contends that the apostle "has already provided us with hints and sometimes clear expressions of a fundamental Story out of which all his discourse arises. What is needed is to connect the exegetical details to the corresponding places in the plot they comment on or come from."[249] It is the overall plot which serves as the proper context, that is, the "*Pauline* context," from which to interpret individual texts. Such an approach is an improvement over Wright's imposition of the template of a reconstructed first century Jewish worldview. Witherington's method, however, raises a further question: from where does he derive this larger context? Should not the context be derived from a careful reading of the individual letters? In fact, Witherington offers no theoretical discussion concerning his approach. Although his presentation of the apostle is largely accurate, one cannot help but be suspicious that at certain points Witherington's own theological agenda intrudes upon his "larger picture."[250] As indicated above, my approach is more inductive, focused on the text of 2 Corinthians.

---

[246]Ibid., 5.

[247]Unlike Wright, Witherington does not identify the story of Christ as Israel's story.

[248]Such an inductive approach, as WITHERINGTON notes, was undertaken by the Society of Biblical Literature Pauline Theology Seminar from 1986 through 1995 (see *Paul's Narrative Thought World*, 3). It involved close exegetical work on each of the seven undisputed Pauline epistles with the intent of arriving at the theology (or theologies) of the individual letters before making any attempt to synthesize the findings into a broader "Pauline theology."

[249]Ibid., 4.

[250]For instance, WITHERINGTON'S treatment of how Jesus' death propitiates God's wrath seems driven by a theory of atonement that goes beyond what Paul actually says. See *Paul's Narrative Thought World*, 163-68.

Yet, despite this absence of an inductive approach, one aspect of Witherington's methodology does mark an advance over Hays. Witherington is willing to go beyond the "canon" of the seven so-called undisputed Pauline epistles.[251]

In his treatment of the story of Christ, Witherington properly notes the importance of the humanity of Jesus for Paul.[252] The key characteristics of the human Jesus, the "eschatological Adam," are his obedience, humility, and faithfulness. Moreover, Witherington understands the role that *imitatio Christi* plays in Paul's writings: "It is [Jesus'] *human career* . . . that is seen as some sort of pattern for behavior and belief."[253] While he rightly notes that the apostle's use of Jesus as ethical example focuses on his death, Witherington seems to collapse the whole of Jesus' character into the event of the cross. That is, while he can talk of Christians' "conformity to Christ's character," Witherington does not give much "flesh" to what this character looks like.[254] This may be due, in part, to the fact that he does not have a strategy for identifying Paul's more subtle allusions to the story and character of Jesus. My approach expressly draws on such allusions and shows what the apostle presumes about Christ's character in making them.

The outstanding feature of Witherington's work is his recognition of how the story of Jesus is to be taken up and enacted by Paul, indeed, by all Christians. According to Witherington, "the story of Christ is the basis, ground,

---

[251]WITHERINGTON accepts that Paul wrote Col and 2 Thess. He treats Eph and the so-called pastoral epistles "as later developments in the Pauline tradition, whether by Paul (which I would not rule out) or a later Paulinist." See *Paul's Narrative Thought World*, 6, n. 5. The fact that he places this information in a footnote is symptomatic of a need to be more explicit about methodology. It should be noted that Wright's "Pauline canon" extends beyond the seven to include Col.

[252]To be sure, Paul's christology viewed *in toto* has a "V pattern" of descent/ascent. That is, WITHERINGTON recognizes that Paul's christology includes Christ's pre-existence, his incarnation, his death and resurrection, his exaltation, and his role in the consummation of the story. See *Paul's Narrative Thought World*, 81-211.

[253]Ibid., 104 (Witherington's italics).

[254]One exception is WITHERINGTON'S treatment of ταπεινοφροσύνη ("humility"). See *Paul's Narrative Thought World*, 98. Yet even here the explanation is only one paragraph long.

and generating influence that both makes possible the Christian story and continues to make it a viable and ongoing drama."[255] Concerning the apostle, Witherington describes several ways in which Paul portrays his own Christian story: as a prisoner of Christ in a Roman triumphal procession; as a suffering servant; as a moral athlete; as a spiritual father or nurse; as an ambassador of Christ. Whatever role he plays, the apostle "takes it as axiomatic that he is called upon *to imitate Christ* to the extent that he can do so."[256] As to all Christians generally, Witherington holds that they too are called to greater "Christlikeness." He appreciates the importance of the ongoing process of sanctification for Paul, and the role that the Holy Spirit plays in this. One of the functions of the Spirit is illumination, which involves reproducing Christ's life and attitudes in Christians.[257] Commenting on the role of the Spirit in 2 Cor 3:18, Witherington suggests that the transformation into Christ's likeness "has likely to do with conformity to Christ's character."[258] This is an important insight. Chapters Five and Six of the present study take up a detailed analysis of its implications.[259]

Witherington uses the metaphor of "tapestry" to describe his approach to Paul's thought world. Just as a tapestry is appreciated best when one stands back and takes in the whole – thereby allowing one to see the overall drama portrayed in it – so, he maintains, it is with the apostle's writings. That is,

---

[255]Ibid., 245.

[256]WITHERINGTON, *Paul's Narrative Thought World*, 236 (italics added). Chapter Five will look in depth at how Paul continues the story of Jesus as his ambassador and as a righteous sufferer.

[257]Ibid., 283-84. In this connection, Witherington cites 1 Cor 2:6-16 and 12:3; and Eph 1:17-18. I will show that Paul refers to this process of illumination in 2 Cor 3:18 and 4:4-6.

[258]Ibid., 330.

[259]It is interesting to point out that WITHERINGTON notices the wordplay in 2 Cor 1:21 – "God is the One who establishes us with you in Christ (εἰς Χριστόν) and has anointed (χρίσας) us." See *Paul's Narrative Thought World*, 132. Moreover, he entitles his chapter on the continuation of the story of Jesus through the lives of Christians, "The Christening of the Believer." Yet, he does not bring out through textual analysis the full force of the "christing" that Paul refers to in this verse.

Witherington claims that Paul's thought world is best understood by considering it against the background of the entire Story from the creation and fall to the completion of redemption. He succeeds in highlighting the story of Jesus, and in showing its connection with and continuation in the stories of the apostle and all Christians. Witherington's work, however, is more like an impressionistic painting than a tapestry with its distinct story. True, one can get the general picture from his work. And the "impression" is accurate as far as it goes. Nevertheless, what is missing is an appreciation of the *manner* by which Paul brings together the stories of Jesus, the apostle (himself), and his churches. For example, despite his numerous references to 2 Cor 5:18-21, Witherington fails to show *that* – not to mention *how* – the apostle draws himself and the Corinthians into the story of God's work of reconciliation through Christ. The same is true of 2 Cor 8:9, another passage to which Witherington frequently alludes. By looking at a single letter, I propose to give sharper focus and more substantial, specific support to what Witherington rightly claims: "The story of the Christian and the Christian community was to be exegeted out of, indeed to live out of, the story of Christ."[260]

D. *Stephen E. Fowl*

In *The Story of Christ in the Ethics of Paul*, Stephen E. Fowl investigates the function of three hymnic passages about Christ: Phil 2:6-11, Col 1:15-20, and 1 Tim 3:16b. After establishing the distinctiveness and poetic quality of these hymns, he analyzes their content individually. Then, looking to the larger context, he seeks "to explore the role these distinct units play in the rhetoric of the epistle" in which each is found.[261] Thus, Fowl's approach, like Hays's, is inductive. According to Fowl, the apostle draws on these poetic descriptions of Christ's person and work in order to support certain ethical positions. Like Hays, Fowl correctly recognizes that, because the communities to which Paul writes were already founded on traditions and stories of Jesus' life, death, and resurrection, the apostle simply refers to aspects of these traditions in order to draw out particular implications for his churches. In short,

---

[260]Ibid., 319.

[261]S.E. FOWL, *The Story of Christ in the Ethics of Paul: An Analysis of the Function of the Hymnic Material in the Pauline Corpus*, JSNTSup 36 (Sheffield: Sheffield Academic Press, 1990) 36.

Paul's strategy in each case is to set forth a concrete portrayal of Christ alongside the particular situation of the community he addresses. He then shows how the story of Jesus calls for a particular response.[262] The underlying premise is this: "To be a part of this [i.e., the Christian] community is to share in this and/or other stories about Christ."[263] Thus, although he is dealing solely with hymnic materials, Fowl sees the apostle as drawing on a narrative substructure, namely the story of Jesus.

One important feature of Fowl's work is his notion of "exemplar," the term he uses to describe the function of Paul's references to the story of Jesus. For Fowl, there are two key characteristics in the use of exemplars. First, the exemplar itself is a concrete normative formulation. The apostle's allusions to Christ refer to certain of Jesus' activities or aspects of his character that are presented as having normative value for the churches. Second, the basic mode of reasoning involved is that of analogy.[264] That is, Fowl rightly notes that Paul does not see a one-for-one correspondence between Christ's activity and that of the communities founded upon his story. There are real differences between Christ and Christians.[265] Nevertheless, there are also real points of similarity between the story of Jesus and the situation of the churches. Fowl notes that "[i]t is up to Paul to note the similarities-in-difference between the story of Christ . . . and the particular situation of the church and to draw the appropriate analogies."[266] It is important to note that Fowl prefers the notion of exemplar to that of an example to be imitated. Throughout his discussion of exemplar, he

---

[262]Ibid., 202.

[263]Ibid., 130.

[264]See FOWL, *The Story of Christ in the Ethics of Paul*, 92-95. Fowl adapts his notion of exemplar from the work of T.S. KUHN on the role of exemplars in the learning and practice of science. See Kuhn's *The Structure of Scientific Revolutions*, 2nd rev. ed. (Chicago: University of Chicago Press, 1970) esp. 187-91.

[265]For instance, Christ's role in the work of reconciliation is unique, "once for all." Still, the reconciliation brought about through Christ makes particular demands upon those who have received this reconciliation. Another example, which will be taken up in greater detail below, concerns πίστις – there *is* a difference between Jesus' πίστις and that of Paul and other Christians.

[266]FOWL, *The Story of Christ in the Ethics of Paul*, 94-95.

has in mind Ernst Käsemann's critique of the concept of the imitation of Christ. While he recognizes that Käsemann caricatures the notion of imitation, Fowl seems inhibited, as we will see, in his vision of the full force of the apostle's reference to Jesus in Phil 2:6-11.[267]

Fowl understands that the "story in which Christ is the main character" has real consequences for those communities "founded on traditions about Christ."[268] In the course of his treatment of the hymnic passages about Jesus, Fowl provides three helpful criteria for determining *how* Paul connects the story of Jesus with the story of Christians.[269] The first involves an exhortation of application. For instance, the hymn in Phil 2:6-11 is preceded immediately by the apostle's admonition to the Philippians to conduct themselves in a way befitting the story of Jesus.[270] The second consists of "important verbal repetitions [found] elsewhere in the epistle."[271] That is, in other parts of the letter, Paul draws on particular words and images from the hymn in question in

---

[267]Ibid., 79-85. For KÄSEMANN'S critique of *imitatio Christi*, see "Kritische Analyse von Phil. 2.5-11," *ZTK* 47 (1950) 313-60; trans. by A. CARSE in *JTC* 5 (1968) 45-88.

[268]FOWL, *The Story of Christ in the Ethics of Paul*, 199. In a separate article, Fowl rejects the notion that Paul appeals to a *single* story of Jesus: "We should note, however, that Paul does not use the same story for all situations. Nor would it be adequate to claim that Paul has one large, coherent story which he applies differently in different situations, a sort of meta-gospel. Rather, the various stories of Christ Paul uses are, like his epistles in general, contingent interpretations of the traditions to which he is heir, made in the light of specific situations." See "Some Uses of Story in Moral Discourse," *Modern Theology* 4 (1987-88) 293-308, here 304.

[269]FOWL himself does not establish these as formal criteria. Rather, he differentiates the way he sees how 1 Tim 3:16b functions in comparison with Phil 2:6-11 and Col 1:15-20. I have extrapolated the criteria from his observations, as found in *The Story of Christ in the Ethics of Paul*, 175.

[270]While it is true that the syntax and structure of Phil 2:5 allow for flexibility in its translation and interpretation, it is clear that Paul wants the community's behavior to be influenced by ὃ καὶ ἐν Χριστῷ Ἰησοῦ – "what is also in Christ Jesus."

[271]FOWL, *The Story of Christ in the Ethics of Paul*, 175.

order to make a particular application of the story.[272] The third is more subtle. It entails focusing on how the reference to the story of Jesus functions in the logic of the passage in which it is found: What is being drawn from the story of Jesus that helps make sense of the passage, and the mode of argumentation therein, as a whole? This criterion relies "almost solely on inferences drawn from the context of the epistle rather than on explicit textual connections."[273] Although Fowl deals only with hymnic materials, I submit that his observations concerning the ways in which the apostle connects the story of Jesus with the story of the churches can be extended to non-hymnic allusions to the story and character of Christ.

Fowl attempts to reconstruct the situations to which Paul responded by referring to the story of Jesus. While it is valid and important to attempt to reconstruct the "rhetorical situation" of the apostle's letters, it is crucial not to squeeze more out of the data than the epistles can yield. Fowl's treatment of Phil 3 is an example of making claims that the text itself does not support. He sees in this chapter a different set of opponents than those referred to in Phil 1:28-30. Moreover, Fowl offers many details in his portrait of these opponents, whom he identifies as "Jewish-Christian missionaries who boasted of their spiritual attainments."[274] Through a dubious mirror-reading of Phil 3:4-12, Fowl comments on "the opponents' *claim* to have already fully appropriated the

---

[272]L.T. JOHNSON shows such sensitivity in his interpretation of Phil, as he notes several verbal and conceptual connections that link together what is said about Jesus in 2:6-8 and what the apostle says about himself in 3:4-11. Just as Jesus "was found" (εὑρεθείς, 2:7) to be in the form of a human being, so Paul wants to "be found" (εὑρεθῶ, 3:9) in Christ. Just as Jesus did not "regard" (ἡγήσατο, 2:6) equality with God as something to be taken advantage of, so the apostle now "regards" (ἡγοῦμαι, 3:7-8 [3x]) his former status and achievements as loss. And just as Jesus, though being in the "form" (μορφῇ, 2:6) of God, emptied himself and took on the "form of a slave" (μορφὴν δούλου, 2:7) and was "obedient unto death" (ὑπήκοος μέχρι θανάτου, 2:8), so now Paul seeks to share in Christ's sufferings and "be conformed" (συμμορφιζόμενος, 3:10) to his "death" (θανάτῳ, 3:10). See JOHNSON, *The Writings of the New Testament: An Interpretation*, rev. ed. (Minneapolis: Fortress, 1999) 377-78. For a similar reading of Phil, see W.S. KURZ, "Kenotic Imitation of Paul and of Christ," in *Discipleship in the New Testament*, ed. F.F. SEGOVIA (Philadelphia: Fortress, 1985) 103-26.

[273]FOWL, *The Story of Christ in the Ethics of Paul*, 175.

[274]Ibid., 99.

power of Christ's resurrection through fulfillment of the law," and states that "[*t*]*heir theology* can only accommodate the exalted Christ of 2.9-11."[275] Fowl even professes to know that τέλος (3:19) is "a catchword of Paul's opponents."[276] Indeed, his interpretation of Phil 3 seems driven more by appeals to the works of A.T. Lincoln and Helmut Koester than by a close reading of the text.[277] One negative effect of his interpretation is that Fowl misses the force of the apostle's presentation of himself in Phil 3:4-16 as an example of one who lives in the self-emptying pattern of Jesus described in 2:6-8.[278] This leads to a second, and related, criticism of Fowl's work.

While rightly recognizing the function of Jesus as exemplar in Phil 2:6-11, Fowl does not fully capture the texture of what Christ exemplifies. I suspect that Fowl's preoccupation with Käsemann's abhorrence of the notion of *imitatio Christi* is in part responsible. For Fowl, this passage gives an "account of Christ's activity of humiliation and God's vindication of that activity."[279] While this is true as far as it goes, Fowl fails to recognize that Paul's stress is on a mode of existence marked by self-emptying service and a commitment to putting the needs of others before one's own.[280] That this is the apostle's strategy can

---

[275]Ibid., 99-100 (italics added).

[276]Ibid., 100, n. 3.

[277]Fowl appeals several times to A.T. LINCOLN'S *Paradise Now and Not Yet*, SNTSMS 43 (Cambridge: Cambridge University Press, 1981), and to H. KOESTER'S "The Purpose of the Polemic of a Pauline Fragment," *NTS* 8 (1961-62) 317-32.

[278]L.T. JOHNSON points out that, rather than attempt to derive the identity of Paul's historical "opponents" in Phil 3:2-16, a more fruitful approach is to recognize the *literary function* of this passage. Here the apostle utilizes a "counter example" in order to highlight the positive model that he himself embodies after the manner of Jesus as set forth in Phil 2:6-8. See *The Writings of the New Testament*, 376-77.

[279]FOWL, *The Story of Christ in the Ethics of Paul*, 98.

[280]Elsewhere FOWL asserts that "the story of Christ's humiliation and exaltation in 2:6-11 supports Paul's position by providing a precedent for how God responds to the suffering of the righteous servant of God, not by providing a model of behaviour to be imitated." See "Some Uses of Story in Moral Discourse," 301. This way of construing the alternatives, however, is false. It is viable to maintain that Jesus' mode of self-

be seen by the way he follows his reference to Jesus' story with his own example ("even if I am being offered as a libation upon the sacrificial offering of your faith" – Phil 2:17a) and the examples of Timothy (2:19-24) and Epaphroditus (2:25-30). In each instance, the accent falls on seeking first the interest of others, even to the point of risking or offering one's life. It is telling that Fowl does not even mention Timothy and Epaphroditus in his exposition, but does bring his reconstruction of the opponents in Phil 3 to bear upon his interpretation of the function of Jesus as exemplar.[281]

In sum, I agree with Fowl that Paul draws upon the story of Jesus in order to draw implications for his readers. But whereas Fowl limits his work to three hymnic passages in three different epistles – note that, like Witherington, he is willing to go beyond the so-called "undisputed letters"[282] – I focus on all the references and allusions to Christ in a single epistle. Because 2 Corinthians does not contain an explicit exhortation of application to the story of Jesus (e.g.,

---

emptying service, the behavior Paul holds up for imitation, is *also vindicated by God.* Indeed, that is how 2:9-11, which refers to the story of Jesus' exaltation by God, is also applicable to the apostle and the Philippians. That is, Paul not only holds up the example of Jesus before the eyes of the Philippians; he also encourages them to trust in God to vindicate them in their living out the pattern of behavior modeled forth by Jesus.

[281]Cf. KURZ, "Kenotic Imitation of Paul and of Christ,"103-26. Kurz notes that the "[t]wo short sections on Timothy and Epaphroditus have their setting in the canonical letter between the exhortation based on Christ's example and that based on Paul's in 3:1-4:9. This setting seems to imply some carryover of Christ's example to Timothy and Epaphroditus and to prepare for Paul's presentation of his own example" (p.113). Kurz goes on to point out that, as Christ had taken on the form of a slave (μορφὴν δούλου, 2:7), so Timothy worked as a slave with Paul (σὺν ἐμοὶ ἐδούλευσεν, 2:22). And as Christ was obedient unto death (μέκρι θανάτου, 2:8), so Epaphroditus had come close to death (μέκρι θανάτου, 2:30) in doing the work of Christ. To be even-handed in critiquing Fowl, it should be noted that I am in general agreement with his treatment of Col 1:15-20 and 1 Tim 3:16b. In both cases, his re-creation of the rhetorical situation is grounded more solidly in his exposition of the texts themselves.

[282]FOWL does not make any definitive judgment about the authorship of Col and 1 Tim. The continuity he sees in the way the hymnic material functions in Phil, Col, and 1 Tim "may be just as attributable to a Pauline disciple, faithfully replicating Paul's style, as to Paul himself." See *The Story of Christ in the Ethics of Paul*, 210-11.

Phil 2:5),[283] this study looks for intratextual connections as well as pays particular attention to the context and mode of the apostle's argumentation in order to infer what he presumes about the character and activity of Jesus (the second and third criteria outlined above). While agreeing with Fowl that the story of Jesus stands in an analogous position vis-à-vis the story of Christians, I am less timid in speaking about *imitatio Christi*.[284] This study also exercises greater caution in reconstructing the rhetorical situation of 2 Corinthians in order to avoid interpreting passages on questionable bases and assumptions.

E. Summary

Hays, Wright, Witherington, and Fowl have made important contributions to an emerging appreciation of the importance of the story of Jesus for Paul. Hays was the first to take account of the centrality of this story in the apostle's argumentation. Whereas Wright connects the story of Messiah Jesus with what preceded it (namely, the story of Israel), Witherington emphasizes the continuation of the story of Jesus in Paul and the communities he founded. And Fowl highlights the ethical implications of the story for the apostle and his churches. These contributions, however, are appropriately reviewed collectively. Each author rightly recognizes that, in his letters, Paul refers to and draws on traditions narrating the life, death, and resurrection of Jesus. The apostle's communities were founded on his proclamation of the gospel that included at its heart the story of Messiah Jesus, which (with Hays) I take to signify the sequence of events in Jesus' life, death, and resurrection. Each scholar appreciates that a key component to Paul's strategy in writing to his communities is to set forth the *ongoing* implications of the story of Jesus. That is, the churches founded on this story are to continue the story, as the apostle does, by shaping their lives more and more to conform with that of the story's

---

[283]I will, however, argue that 2 Cor 13:5 serves in a similar capacity. See Chapter Six.

[284]For a succinct account of theological discomfort in general with the language of imitation, see J.B. WEBSTER, "Christology, Imitability and Ethics," *SJT* 39 (1986) 309-26, here 311-15.

protagonist, Jesus Christ. The present study situates itself within this manner of reading Paul.[285]

The notion of shaping lives in conformity with the life of Jesus presumes that something is known about his character. Indeed, my investigation of how the story of Jesus underlies Paul's presentation in 2 Corinthians shifts the focus from plot to character, as I show how, throughout this epistle, the apostle draws upon the *ethos* of Jesus. This approach raises an unavoidable question: Does Paul really say much, if anything, about the character of Jesus? More specifically, is there evidence that the apostle draws on the manner of living exhibited by *the human Jesus*?

II. The Character of Jesus in Romans

A growing number of scholars hold that the faithfulness and obedience of the human Jesus play a crucial role in Paul's understanding of the revelation of the righteousness of God. This is particularly evident in the apostle's letter to the church in Rome. In this section I set forth in brief the exegetical analyses of Douglas A. Campbell, Luke T. Johnson, and Michael Thompson of key texts in Romans. All three scholars highlight the importance of the character of Jesus for Paul in this epistle.

Before I do so, a brief three-fold explanation of my focus on selected passages in Romans is in order. First, Paul was not the founder of the church in Rome and had not taught there previously (cf. Rom 1:10). Because he did not

---

[285]Cf. the recent collection of critical essays on the narrative features of Paul's thought in B.W. LONGENECKER (ed.), *Narrative Dynamics in Paul: A Critical Assessment* (Louisville: Westminster John Knox, 2002). These essays deal with the question of Paul's use of story in Rom and Gal. For a summary of recent scholarship, see Longenecker's opening essay, "Narrative Interest in the Study of Paul: Retrospective and Prospective" (pp. 3-16), esp. pp. 5-11. In addition, see D.A. CAMPBELL, "The Story of Jesus in Romans and Galatians" (pp. 97-124), and G.N. STANTON'S critique, "'I Think, When I Read That Sweet Story of Old': A Response to Douglas Campbell" (pp. 125-32). In particular, note Stanton's question of whether Paul's initial proclamation may have included more of the story of Jesus *between* God's sending the Son and the suffering endured by Jesus (pp. 128-29). For critical questions and concerns raised against the use of "story" and "narrative" in the analysis of the apostle's writings, see J.D.G. DUNN, "The Narrative Approach to Paul: Whose Story?" (pp. 217-30), and F. WATSON, "Is There a Story in These Texts?" (pp. 231-39).

have a "shared history" with it (such as he had with the communities in Philippi, Thessalonika, and Corinth), it is to be expected that the apostle's exposition in Romans will have a straight-forward, non-recapitulative quality.[286] Second, Romans has a marked literary structure. In particular, several exegetes discern that 1:16-17 is the letter's thematic statement, and that 3:21-26 is a fuller re-statement and positive explanation of the thesis.[287] These pivotal passages receive extensive treatment below with an eye toward what Paul says in them about Jesus. Third, it is highly probable that Romans was written shortly after the composition of 2 Corinthians.[288] *Prima facie*, one might expect that the apostle wrote both letters within the same framework of recent experiences and of particular pastoral and theological reflections. I submit that the close proximity in time between the writing of these letters goes a long way toward explaining some of the structural and conceptual similarities in the two letters, similarities that will become apparent in the analyses below and in Part Two.

---

[286]Cf. R.B. HAYS, "ΠΙΣΤΙΣ and Pauline Christology," in *Pauline Theology. Volume IV: Looking Back, Pressing On*, ed. E. E. JOHNSON and D.M. HAY (Atlanta: Scholars Press, 1997) 35-60, here 40. For Paul's (more usual) manner of writing in the "mode of recapitulation," see the review of Hays in the preceding section.

[287]See, e.g., J.A. FITZMYER, *Romans: A New Translation with Introduction and Commentary*, AB 33 (New York: Doubleday, 1993) 98; D.J. MOO, *The Epistle to the Romans*, NICNT (Grand Rapids, Mich.: Eerdmans, 1996) 33 and 218; and L.T. JOHNSON, *Reading Romans: A Literal and Theological Commentary* (New York: Crossroad, 1997) 12-13.

[288]See, e.g., the dating of Paul's letters proposed by M.L. SOARDS, *The Apostle Paul: An Introduction to His Writings and Teachings* (New York: Paulist, 1987) 34-35; cf. J. MURPHY-O'CONNOR, *Paul: A Critical Life* (New York: Oxford University Press, 1996) 31 and 323. It should be noted that both Soards and Murphy-O'Connor regard the present form of 2 Cor as a compilation of letters. My position is that 2 Cor was composed in Macedonia. A short time later, Paul visited Corinth as previously promised (cf. 2 Cor 12:14 and 13:1), where he wrote his letter to the Romans (before embarking on his trip to Jerusalem with the money collected for the church there – cf. Rom 15:25-26). Indeed, as Fitzmyer rightly points out, Paul writes Rom as the house guest of Gaius (Rom 16:23a), who is most likely to be identified with the figure whom the apostle baptized in Corinth (1 Cor 1:14). Moreover, in Rom 16:23b Paul sends greetings from Erastus, the treasurer of Corinth (cf. 2 Tim 4:20). See FITZMYER, *Romans*, 85.

A. Douglas A. Campbell (Rom 1:16-17)

In a series of articles in the *Journal of Biblical Literature*, Douglas A. Campbell has argued that Jesus' πίστις is crucially important for Paul's articulation of the gospel.[289] For the purpose of this section, I limit my focus to Campbell's treatment of Rom 1:16-17, the letter's thesis statement. One striking feature of this *propositio* is the preponderance of πιστ- terminology contained in it:

> [1:16] For I am not ashamed of the gospel, for it is [the] power of God for salvation to everyone who has faith (τῷ πιστεύοντι), to the Jew first and also to the Greek. [1:17] For [the] righteousness of God has been revealed in it [i.e., the gospel] ἐκ πίστεως εἰς πίστιν, just as it is written, "The righteous one ἐκ πίστεως shall live."

A number of questions immediately emerges: What does the apostle signify by the unusual expression ἐκ πίστεως εἰς πίστιν? Is there a specific connection between the two instances of ἐκ πίστεως (the second of which occurs in Paul's first citation from Scripture in this epistle – from Hab 2:4)? If so, to whom does ἐκ πίστεως refer?

According to Campbell, Paul asserts in Rom 1:17a that the righteousness of God[290] has been revealed *within and by the gospel* (taking τὸ εὐαγγέλιον as the antecedent of the pronoun, and reading the prepositional phrase ἐν αὐτῷ as adverbial – as in my translation). Now, how does the apostle understand the term "gospel" here? In the immediately preceding verse (1:16) Paul explains what the gospel *is*,[291] namely "the power of God for salvation."

---

[289]See D.A. CAMPBELL, "The Meaning of ΠΙΣΤΙΣ and ΝΟΜΟΣ in Paul: A Linguistic and Structural Perspective," *JBL* 111 (1992) 91-103; "Romans 1:17 – A *Crux Interpretum* for the ΠΙΣΤΙΣ ΧΡΙΣΤΟΥ Debate," *JBL* 113 (1994) 265-85; and "False Presuppositions in the ΠΙΣΤΙΣ ΧΡΙΣΤΟΥ Debate: A Response to Brian Dodd," *JBL* 116 (1997) 713-19.

[290]For more on what Paul means by the expression δικαιοσύνη θεοῦ, see the treatment of 2 Cor 5:21 in Chapter Five, Section V.B.

[291]Note the inclusion of ἐστιν for emphasis in Rom 1:16.

Moreover, prior to this statement, the apostle has offered important clues concerning the *christological* substance of this gospel. For instance, at the very outset of the letter, Paul makes clear that "the gospel of God" (1:1) concerns "[God's] Son, who has descended from David according to the flesh and was designated Son of God in power according to the Spirit of holiness by resurrection from the dead" (1:3-4). And in his thanksgiving period, Paul again mentions τὸ εὐαγγέλιον τοῦ υἱοῦ αὐτοῦ – "the gospel concerning [God's] Son" (1:9). Thus, the apostle not only makes clear that the gospel is the expression of the saving power of God; its manifestation is also intimately connected with the person of God's Son, Jesus Christ.[292]

Paul then adds a further nuance to his understanding of how the righteousness of God has been revealed, namely within the gospel *ἐκ πίστεως* (Rom 1:17a). The question arises: Whose πίστις is referred to here? Campbell rightly dismisses the possibility that ἐκ πίστεως refers to the faith of human beings, for "[t]o make the eschatological disclosure of God's saving power conditional upon the believer's faith would be to press the role of anthropocentric faith too far."[293] Rather, given the accent upon God's power and righteousness in Rom 1:16-17, it would seem that ἐκ πίστεως likely refers to *God's* faithfulness (cf. Rom 3:3). Karl Barth, among others, read the text in this way.[294] Nevertheless, Campbell holds that there are weighty reasons for opting for a third referent of ἐκ πίστεως – Jesus, the one whom God's gospel concerns.

Campbell points out that Paul uses the phrase ἐκ πίστεως twenty-one times, and that his usage is limited to Romans (12 times) and Galatians (9 times). It is significant that it is only in these two letters that the apostle cites Hab 2:4 ("the righteous one shall live ἐκ πίστεως).[295] Now, given the

---

[292]See CAMPBELL, "Romans 1:17," 273-74.

[293]Ibid., 273.

[294]See K. BARTH, *The Epistle to the Romans*, trans. E.C. HOSKYNS from the 6th ed. (New York: Oxford University Press, 1968) 41-42. Cf., e.g., HAYS, "ΠΙΣΤΙΣ and Pauline Christology," 41.

[295]See CAMPBELL, "The Meaning of ΠΙΣΤΙΣ and ΝΟΜΟΣ in Paul," 99-102. Paul's use of ἐκ πίστεως appears in Rom 1:17 (2x); 3:26; 3:30; 4:16 (2x); 5:1; 9:30; 9:32; 10:6; and 14:23 (2x); as well as in Gal 2:16; 3:7; 3:8; 3:9; 3:11; 3:12; 3:22; 3:24; and

prominence of Rom 1:17 as part of Paul's thesis statement, it is striking that it contains his first use of ἐκ πίστεως in Romans, followed by the first scriptural citation (Hab 2:4) in this letter, a citation that also includes the phrase ἐκ πίστεως. Thus, Campbell insists that it is crucial to pay careful attention to the apostle's citation of Hab 2:4 in Rom 1:17b in order to understand the particular nuance he attaches to ἐκ πίστεως.

Romans 1:17b reads: καθὼς γέγραπται· ὁ δὲ δίκαιος ἐκ πίστεως ζήσεται. *Prima facie*, the notion that "the righteous one (or person) will live out of/on the basis of faith (or faithfulness)" does not appear to be an apt description of God.[296] Some interpreters attempt to get around the difficulty by denying that there is a close relationship between the two instances of ἐκ πίστεως in 1:17, saying that the first refers to God's faithfulness and the second to the individual believer's saving faith in the gospel.[297] Campbell rightly points out, however, that this reading fails to take into account the force of the introductory clause καθὼς γέγραπται ("*as* it is written"), which indicates that its function is to offer scriptural support for what has just been said. And because the citation does so with an identical phrase, it seems more than plausible that Paul intends an intimate relation between the two instances of ἐκ πίστεως.[298] Thus, given that the notion of the righteous one living ἐκ πίστεως undergirds the apostle's statement that "God's righteousness has been revealed *within the gospel* ἐκ πίστεως ," and given the clues in Rom 1:1-16 concerning the christological content of this gospel, it begins to appear that Jesus as the referent of ἐκ πίστεως provides the pivotal link to Paul's argument in Rom 1:17. Indeed, according to Campbell, the key to understanding the apostle's use

---

5:15.

[296]Indeed, as CAMPBELL points out, Paul's diatribe in Rom 3:1-9 makes clear that the idea of God's faithfulness was not a point of contention between the apostle and his audience. See "Romans 1:17," 278-79.

[297]Ibid., 278. Cf., e.g., T.W. MANSON, "Romans," in *PCB*, 40-53, here 42; and J.D.G. DUNN, *Romans 1-8*, WBC (Dallas: Word, 1988) 44-46. Both Manson and Dunn hold that the first instance of ἐκ πίστεως in 1:17 pertains to God's faithfulness, while the second instance involves an ambiguity that embraces both God's faithfulness and human faith.

[298]See CAMPBELL, "Romans 1:17," 278-79.

of Hab 2:4 is that he reads this text *as a messianic prophecy* brought to fulfillment through Jesus.

Paul's slight modification of the cited text also signals a messianic interpretation. Campbell points out that there is no extant textual variant that supports the apostle's rendering of Hab 2:4, which leaves ἐκ πίστεως unmodified. It is telling that Paul did not opt to cite the LXX tradition found in MSS S and B, where Hab 2:4 reads "the righteous one will live ἐκ πίστεως μου."[299] Here the personal pronoun "my" must refer to *God's* faithfulness. The apostle's rendering of Hab 2:4 also differs from the Masoretic text, which refers to any person who has faith (וצדיק באמונתו יחיה). Thus, given that Paul had options for rendering the text so that πίστις referred to God or to humans, it is telling that he chose a third alternative. That the apostle understands Hab 2:4 as a messianic prophecy is bolstered when it is observed that this is the first scriptural citation following his statement in Rom 1:2 that "the gospel concerning [God's] Son" had been "promised *previously* [προεπαγγέλλω] through [God's] prophets in the holy writings (ἐν γραφαῖς ἁγίαις)." Moreover, there is evidence that Hab 2:4 was understood in first century Judaism[300] and early Christianity[301] as a messianic text, and that ὁ δίκαιος was a common messianic title.[302]

Campbell submits that the evidence thus points to understanding Jesus as the referent of both instances of ἐκ πίστεως in Rom 1:17. God's righteousness has been revealed as a result of Jesus' faithfulness (1:17a), the faithfulness that was prefigured by the text in Habakkuk (1:17b). But what about the intervening phrase εἰς πίστιν (literally, "into faith" or "into

---

[299]Ibid., 279-80.

[300]See HAYS, *The Faith of Jesus Christ*, 134-41, and A. STROBEL, *Untersuchungen zum eschatologischen Verzögerungsproblem auf Grund der spätjüdisch-urchristlichen Geschichte von Habakuk 2,2ff* NovTSup 2 (Leiden: Brill, 1961) 47-66.

[301]See Heb 10:37-38.

[302]See Acts 3:14; 7:52; and 22:14; 1 Pet 3:18; and 1 John 2:1. In addition, cf. R.B. HAYS, "'The Righteous One' as Eschatological Deliverer: A Case Study in Paul's Apocalyptic Hermeneutics," in *Apocalyptic and the New Testament: Essays in Honor of J. Louis Martyn*, ed. J. MARCUS and M.L. SOARDS, JSNTSup 24 (Sheffield: JSOT Press, 1988) 191-215. Hays treats texts from 1 Enoch which refer to ὁ δίκαιος.

faithfulness")? By this phrase, Paul denotes both the goal and the implied recipient of God's eschatological action in and through Jesus. That is, εἰς πίστιν refers to the goal of faithfulness in those who accept the gospel. Thus, Campbell offers the following translation of 1:17a: "The eschatological saving righteousness of God is being revealed in the gospel by means of faithfulness (namely, the faithfulness of Christ), with the goal of faithfulness (in the Christian)."[303] Notice how this reinforces 1:16 – the gospel is God's power for salvation "to everyone who has faith (παντὶ τῷ πιστεύοντι)." In both cases, however, Paul's primary emphasis is on what God has done *in and through Jesus' faithfulness.*[304]

Now, if Campbell's interpretation is correct – and I think it is – we can expect to find that Paul refers to Jesus' πίστις in the re-statement and explanation of the *propositio* in Rom 3:21-26. The significance for my thesis is that the apostle is thereby drawing on the character of Jesus at the heart of his presentation of the gospel.

B. *Luke T. Johnson (Rom 3:21-26 and 5:15-21)*

Luke T. Johnson has made significant contributions to the literary analysis of Romans. Not only has he advanced the understanding of how Rom 3:21-26 functions as the re-statement of the letter's *propositio*; he also offers a cogent argument for reading 5:15-21 as Paul's demonstration of his thesis by means of *synkrisis* (comparison). The apostle himself, Johnson argues, interprets Jesus' faithfulness (at least in part) as *obedience.*[305]

Concerning the issue of Jesus' character, Johnson hones in on the three phrases in which Paul utilizes the term πίστις in Rom 3:21-26 (vv. 22, 25, and 26). In 3:22 the apostle writes: "[The] righteousness of God [has been

---

[303]CAMPBELL, "Romans 1:17," 281.

[304]That Jesus is the more likely referent of ὁ δίκαιος than humanity (i.e., 'the righteous person') is supported by the observation that Paul speaks of humanity in the following verses as guilty of ἀδικία (cf. Rom 1:18; 1:29; 2:8; and 3:5). See D.A. CAMPBELL, *The Rhetoric of Righteousness in Romans 3:21-26*, JSNTSup 65 (Sheffield: JSOT Press, 1992), 210.

[305]See L.T. JOHNSON, "Romans 3:21-26 and the Faith of Jesus," *CBQ* 44 (1982) 77-90; and *Reading Romans*, esp. 50-61 and 90-93.

manifested][306] διὰ πίστεως 'Ιησοῦ Χριστοῦ εἰς πάντες τοὺς πιστεύοντας. Noting that Paul is re-stating the thesis of 1:17, Johnson observes that two things follow from this simple but important observation. First, the apostle's emphasis here is on *God's* activity, namely "how God's way of making humans righteous is being revealed."[307] This emphasis on what God is doing[308] contrasts sharply with how Paul characterizes the "doings of humans" in 1:18-3:20. Indeed, the apostle has just demonstrated how Scripture bears testimony that *all* human beings up until "now" (cf. νυνί, 3:21) were "under the power of Sin" (3:9-18). The marks of humanity were "unfaithfulness" (ἀπιστία, 3:3) and "unrighteousness" (ἀδικία, 3:5). Not even the Law could "make righteous"; rather, it brought about "knowledge of Sin" (3:20). In 3:22, however, Paul recounts *in positive terms* how God's righteousness has now been made manifest – "through [the] πίστις of Jesus Christ." The contrast here is thus ultimately between Jesus' faithfulness and the unfaithfulness that marked humanity before the "now time." Johnson rightly notes that reading πίστις 'Ιησοῦ Χριστοῦ as a reference to Jesus' πίστις not only avoids redundancy in the following phrase (εἰς πάντες τοὺς πιστεύοντας); it also (and more importantly) maintains the proper emphasis on the gifted quality of *God's* action in and through Christ.[309]

---

[306]Supplying the verb πεφανέρωται from the preceding verse. Cf. S.K. WILLIAMS, "The 'Righteousness of God' in Romans," *JBL* 99 (1980) 241-90, here 271-72. Williams argues that extending the verb is justified because the particle δέ in 3:22 has "an intensifying, explanatory function" which introduces a more precise description of how the righteousness of God has been manifested in the "now time" (ἐν τῷ νῦν καιρῷ, 3:26).

[307]JOHNSON, "Romans 3:21-26 and the Faith of Jesus," 78.

[308]See JOHNSON, *Reading Romans*, 51: "God is the subject of this action, this good news. It is *God's* righteousness that is being manifested (3:21), *God* who is the giver of grace as a gift (3:23), *God* who puts forward Jesus as an expiation (3:25), *God's* righteousness that is shown by his forbearance of past sins (3:25) and the making of people righteous in the present (3:26). The good news, once more, is not simply a message *from* God but a message *about* God's work in the world" (Johnson's italics).

[309]In the interpretation of Rom 3:22, of course, one enters into the contentious fray of what Paul means by the disputed phrase πίστις 'Ιησοῦ Χριστοῦ. The phrase πίστις + the genitive form of "Christ" (or "Jesus Christ," "Jesus," or "the Son of God") occurs

The second implication of recognizing Rom 3:22 as the re-statement of 1:17, according to Johnson, is that it highlights the formal parallels between the two verses. Both passages have the same subject, δικαιοσύνη θεοῦ. Both passages utilize a verb in the passive voice that expresses the notion of divine disclosure (ἀποκαλύπτεται, 1:17; and πεφανέρωται, 3:22). And both passages convey the dynamic through which God's righteousness is revealed – "through/out of Jesus' faithfulness toward the goal of human faith (or faithfulness)." That is, the phrase ἐκ πίστεως in 1:17 corresponds to διὰ πίστεως 'Ιησοῦ Χριστοῦ in 3:22; and the phrase εἰς πίστιν in 1:17 corresponds to εἰς πάντες τοὺς πιστεύοντας in 3:22. In fact, Johnson sees the formal parallel here as "conclusive" for rendering 3:22 as a reference to Jesus' πίστις.[310]

I would add that Johnson's interpretation helps to account for Paul's use of the perfect tense of the verb φανερόω in Rom 3:22. Recall that the perfect tense indicates an action *in the past* that has continuing effects in the present.[311] Thus, the apostle's use of the perfect tense suggests that God's righteousness *has already been manifested* in the past, and that this manifestation has continuing ramifications for the present. Indeed, Paul spells this out a few verses later – God has already acted on behalf of humanity through Jesus' death, a death that is closely linked with his πίστις (3:25); moreover, God continues to act on behalf of all who are ἐκ πίστεως 'Ιησοῦ (3:26). In 3:22 the apostle indicates this dynamic of past-action-with-present-implications by referring to

---

eight times in the Pauline corpus: Rom 3:22 and 3:26; Gal 2:16 (2x), 2:20, and 3:22; Phil 3:9; and Eph 3:12. It is beyond the scope of my project to enter into this heated scholarly debate over the proper rendering of the genitive – whether as a subjective genitive (referring to Christ's own faithfulness) or as an objective genitive (referring to human beings' faith in Christ). For a balanced, concise review of the history of the πίστις Χριστοῦ debate, see P. POLLARD, "The 'Faith of Christ' in Current Discussion," *Concordia Journal* 23 (1997) 213-28. In addition, cf. the famous debate between R.B. HAYS [who argues for the subjective genitive reading in "ΠΙΣΤΙΣ and Pauline Christology," 35-60] and J.D.G. DUNN [who argues for the objective genitive reading in "Once More, ΠΙΣΤΙΣ ΧΡΙΣΤΟΥ," in *Pauline Theology. Volume IV: Looking Back, Pressing On*, ed. E. E. JOHNSON and D.M. HAY (Atlanta: Scholars Press, 1997) 61-81]. My own position is that the subjective genitive reading is the better interpretation.

[310]See JOHNSON, "Romans 3:21-26 and the Faith of Jesus," 79.

[311]See BDF, §§ 340 and 342.

the righteousness of God that was made manifest "through the faithfulness of Jesus," and that continues to be made manifest "for all those who are faithful (or have faith)."

The second πίστις-phrase analyzed by Johnson is in Rom 3:25, where Paul describes Jesus as the one whom God put forward as ἱλαστήριον διὰ τῆς πίστεως ἐν τῷ αὐτοῦ αἵματι – literally, as "an expiation through the faithfulness in his blood." To be sure, the phraseology and interpretation of 3:25 are notoriously difficult. Johnson challenges the RSV's translation ("an expiation by his blood, to be received by faith"). In particular, he sees the rendering of διὰ τῆς πίστεως as "to be received by faith" as "a desperation move."[312] A better approach is to read the phrase in question in light of what immediately precedes it – "expiation," which refers to Jesus – and what immediately follows – "in his blood," which also refers to Jesus. Reading 3:25 in this manner suggests that διὰ τῆς πίστεως likewise refers to Jesus. More specifically, because ἱλαστήριον and αἷμα point to Jesus' death on the cross, Johnson suggests that διὰ τῆς πίστεως alludes to Jesus' faithfulness in connection with the pouring out of his blood. Indeed, Bruce W. Longenecker provides an apt translation for 3:25: "whom God put forward as an atoning sacrifice, through (Jesus') faithfulness by means of his blood."[313] Notice how

---

[312]See JOHNSON, "Romans 3:21-26 and the Faith of Jesus," 79. Observe that in addition to inserting a significant element – the notion of (human) reception – the RSV changes the syntax, placing the phrase διὰ τῆς πίστεως at the end of the clause. Others, e.g., E. KÄSEMANN, posit an "insertion theory," claiming that Paul added this phrase to a pre-existing formula in order to put his characteristic stamp on it. See his *Commentary on Romans*, tran. and ed. G.W. BROMILEY (Grand Rapids, Mich.: Eerdmans, 1980) 97-98. Käsemann holds that διὰ τῆς πίστεως "should be treated as a parenthesis, in which Paul's reworking of the tradition can be seen" (p. 98). Like Johnson, I would characterize this hypothesis as a desperation move.

[313]See B.W. LONGENECKER, "ΠΙΣΤΙΣ in Romans 3:25: Neglected Evidence for the 'Faithfulness of Christ'?," *NTS* 39 (1993) 478-80, here 479. Longenecker's translation is, in my opinion, an improvement over Johnson's – "whom God put forward as an expiation: through faith, in the shedding of his blood" (taking the last two phrases as, in effect, a hendiadys). See JOHNSON, "Romans 3:21-26 and the Faith of Jesus," 80. W.D. ZORN observes that the phrases διὰ τῆς πίστεως and ἐν τῷ αὐτοῦ αἵματι express Jesus' faithfulness in two ways – by plain statement of fact, and the means or manner by which Jesus' πίστις was demonstrated. See ZORN, "The Messianic Use of Habakkuk 2:4a in Romans," *Stone-Campbell Journal* 1 (1998) 213-30, here 221.

this interpretation fleshes out in greater detail what the apostle says in 3:22 about God's righteousness having been manifested in the past through the faithfulness of Jesus Christ.

The third πίστις-phrase occurs in Rom 3:26, where Paul speaks of God's putting into right relationship τὸν ἐκ πίστεως 'Ιησοῦ – literally, "the one out of the faithfulness of Jesus." Johnson makes two observations here. First, he notes the formal parallel between τὸν ἐκ πίστεως 'Ιησοῦ and τῷ ἐκ πίστεως 'Αβραάμ in Rom 4:16. Similar to how the latter is almost universally understood to signify one who shares in Abraham's πίστις, Johnson argues that the former expression points to human participation in the πίστις of (the human) Jesus.[314] Second, Johnson contends that it is important to observe the apostle's use of Jesus' personal name here (i.e., without the titles "Christ" or "Lord"). Johnson notes that Paul "does not often speak of Jesus simply by name. When he does, his emphasis appears to fall on Jesus' *human* identity rather than on his messianic role. . . ."[315] Thus, in 3:26 the apostle claims that people can share in some way in the faithfulness of the human Jesus, a notion which the phrase εἰς πάντες τοὺς πιστεύοντας in 3:22 already suggested. As I will show in Chapters Five and Six, God's δικαιοσύνη continues to be made manifest through people (like Paul) who participate in Jesus' πίστις.[316]

---

[314]See JOHNSON, "Romans 3:21-26 and the Faith of Jesus," 80. Cf. S.K. STOWERS, "'Eκ πίστεως and διὰ τῆς πίστεως in Romans 3:30," *JBL* 108 (1989) 665-74. Stowers argues that the definite article + a prepositional phrase beginning with ἐκ was used in classical literature as a way to denote origins, participation, and membership. Thus, a plausible translation of τὸν ἐκ πίστεως 'Ιησοῦ is "the person who shares/participates in Jesus' faithfulness" (p. 672). Stowers regards the RSV's translation "him who has faith in Jesus" as "a gross mistranslation."

[315]JOHNSON, "Romans 3:21-26 and the Faith of Jesus," 80 (italics added). See also J.W. PRYOR, "Paul's Use of Iēsous – A Clue for the Translation of Romans 3:26?" *Colloq* 16 (1983) 31-45. This observation concerning Paul's use of the unadorned name "Jesus" will be significant for the analysis of 2 Cor 4:5-14 in Chapters Four and Five below. Cf. also Rom 8:11 and 1 Thess 1:10.

[316]It is important to point out that I consistently render Jesus' πίστις as "faithfulness" (unlike, e.g., Johnson and Hays, who speak of "the *faith* of Jesus"). Because of his unique and immediate relationship to God, Jesus' πίστις, even as a human being, forms a special category. My reason for translating Jesus' πίστις as "faithfulness" will become

Johnson then argues that Rom 5:15-21 is Paul's "demonstration" of his thesis through a comparison between Adam and ὁ ἄνθρωπος 'Ιησοῦς Χριστός – "the human being, Jesus Christ" (5:15). Johnson insists that it is crucial to observe "the resumptive force" of this passage vis-à-vis 3:21-26.[317] This resumptive quality is evident in three ways. First, in 5:15 the apostle refers to ἡ χάρις τοῦ θεοῦ καὶ ἡ δωρεὰ ἐν χάριτι τῇ τοῦ ἑνὸς ἀνθρώπου 'Ιησοῦ Χριστοῦ εἰς τοὺς πολλοὺς ἐπερίσσευσεν – "the grace of God and the gift in grace of the one human being, Jesus Christ, [have] abounded for the many." Notice how this language is parallel in form and meaning to that of 3:24 – δικαιούμενοι δωρεὰν τῇ αὐτοῦ χάριτι διὰ τῆς ἀπολυτρώσεως τῆς ἐν Χριστῷ 'Ιησου – where Paul highlights the 'gifted' and 'graced' quality of what God has done through Jesus. Second, the phrase εἰς τοὺς πολλούς in 5:15 echoes the expression εἰς πάντας τοὺς πιστεύοντας in 3:22. Third, 5:18-19 reveals the primacy of Jesus' human response of obedience, a response that corresponds to what the apostle says about Jesus' faithfulness in 3:22 and 3:25-26. This last point requires further demonstration.

In Rom 5:18 Paul writes: δι' ἑνὸς δικαιώματος εἰς πάντας ἀνθρώπους εἰς δικαίωσιν ζωῆς – "through the righteous deed of one [human being] [there is] a putting into right relationship [consisting] of life for all people." As Johnson rightly points out, what is noteworthy is that being-put-into-right-relationship is not connected here with the response of Christians to Christ or to the gospel; rather, the emphasis is on *Jesus' righteous deed*.[318] This theme is continued in 5:19, where the apostle contrasts Adam's disobedience and its consequence of making all people sinners with Jesus' obedience and its ramifications. Romans 5:19b reads: διὰ τῆς ὑπακοῆς τοῦ ἑνὸς δίκαιοι κατασταθήσονται οἱ πολλοι – "through the obedience of the one [human being] the many shall be established as righteous." Here Paul makes explicit that *Jesus' obedience* is the basis for the righteousness of others. Johnson summarizes this point well: ". . . it is on the basis of his [i.e., Jesus'] past act

---

clear in the analysis of 2 Cor 4:13 in the next chapter. In addition, I will explain (in Chapters Five and Six) both how human beings participate in Jesus' πίστις and how their own πίστις – which includes the notion of *believing* in the revelation of God in and through Jesus – *differs* from the πίστις of Jesus.

[317]See JOHNSON, "Romans 3:21-26 and the Faith of Jesus," 88.

[318]Ibid., 89.

that others will be established as righteous before God. The obedience of Jesus is God's way of saving other humans."[319]

The parallels between Rom 3:21-26 and 5:15-21 now become even more clear: (1) God intervened in the face of human faithlessness and unrighteousness in order to bring people into right relationship with God (cf. 3:21-22 and 5:15); (2) God's act was pure "gift" (δωρεά) and "grace" (χάρις – cf. 3:24 and 5:15); (3) God's gift was expressed through the human Jesus, whose agency was marked by faithfulness (3:22 and 3:25-26) and obedience (5:19); and (4) because of Jesus' agency, God's gift is now available to "all/the many " (cf. 3:22 and 3:26; plus 5:15 and 5:18-19). For Johnson, these formal and material parallels between the two passages suggest that Rom 5:15-21 "is the plain explication of Rom 3:21-26."[320] Thus, in 5:19 the apostle himself offers an interpretation of what is meant (at least in large part) by the faithfulness of Jesus, namely obedience.

This intimate connection between faithfulness and obedience is further suggested by Paul's use of the peculiar phrase ὑπακοὴ πίστεως in this letter. As Johnson observes, the fact that the apostle employs this phrase in both the opening (Rom 1:5) and closing of the letter (16:26) indicates that "the

---

[319]JOHNSON, "Romans 3:21-26 and the Faith of Jesus," 89. M. THOMPSON rightly observes that, while Jesus' obedience was expressed most eloquently in his self-giving on the cross, ". . . *this obedience includes the whole of his earthly life*, for otherwise his exaltation and the justification of sinners through his death would have been impossible . . . ." See THOMPSON, *Clothed with Christ: The Example and Teaching of Jesus in Romans 12.1-15.13* JSNTSup 59 (Sheffield: Sheffield Academic Press, 1991) 222 (italics added). I will take up Thompson's insight in my analysis of Jesus' obedience in 2 Cor.

[320]JOHNSON, "Romans 3:21-26 and the Faith of Jesus," 89. Moreover, as R.B. HAYS has pointed out, Johnson's "cogent argument" concerning Rom 5:15-21 "has never been seriously countered" (see "ΠΙΣΤΙΣ and Paul Christology," 49). V. KOPERSKY has challenged Johnson's reading of Jesus' πίστις in Rom 3:21-26, and objects to Johnson's equating Jesus' πίστις with his ὑπακοή. See her "The Meaning of *Pistis Christou* in Philippians 3:9," *LS* 18 (1993) 198-216. Kopersky, however, does not engage Johnson's exegesis of Rom 5:15-21. Her objection to Johnson's linking of πίστις and ὑπακοή comes down, in the end, to the fact that Paul does not *explicitly* equate the two. Such a reading, however, betrays a certain "tone deafness" to the apostle's presentation – particularly to its formal and material parallels.

expression is not casually chosen. . . ."[321] Indeed, the phrase functions as an *inclusio* that brackets the entire letter, thereby suggesting its thematic importance. In both instances, Paul claims that the purpose of his apostleship and preaching is to bring about ὑπακοὴ πίστεως. Johnson suggests that the genitive is epexegetical, thereby denoting the obedience which is faithfulness.[322] He argues that when Paul speaks of obedience, we get an insight into at least one important aspect of what the apostle intends by the term πίστις: faithfulness as "the fundamental responsive 'yes' to God."[323] Johnson's observations are pertinent to what I will present in Part Two. As we will see, Paul's first allusion to Jesus in the letter body of 2 Corinthians is to Jesus' "Yes" (2 Cor 1:19-20). Moreover, just as the apostle informs the church in Rome that, in his proclamation of the gospel, he strives to effectuate "the obedience which is faithfulness," so in 2 Corinthians he exhorts the community to take on various aspects of the character of Jesus.

One final observation: The relationship between Jesus' πίστις and ὑπακοή – so persuasively demonstrated by Johnson – sheds light on what Paul says in Rom 5:8: "God shows [God's] love for us, for while we were still sinners Christ died for us." Notice here the same elements found in 3:21-26 and 5:15-21: namely, God's action initiated in the face of human sinfulness + Jesus' agency. What is important to observe in 5:8 is that the apostle *presumes* the co-inherence of God's act and Jesus' demeanor. That is, as Leander E. Keck aptly comments, "Christ's dying can manifest God's love for us only if that dying expresses God's intent, if there is such congruence between them that the former

---

[321]JOHNSON, *Reading Romans*, 23.

[322]Ibid. I have taken the liberty of rendering the expression as "the obedience which is faithfulness," not as "the obedience which is faith" (as Johnson does – see n. 316). In addition, see A.B. DU TOIT, "Faith and Obedience in Paul," *Neot* 25 (1991) 65-74. Du Toit interprets ὑπακοή πίστεως as "a genitive of quality, which in fact can overlap with an epexegetical genitive provided that it has a *descriptive* rather than an identifying function. . ." (p. 67, italics added). Cf. R. BULTMANN, *The Theology of the New Testament*, 2 vols., trans. K. GROBEL (New York: Charles Scribner's Sons, 1951-55) 1.314. Bultmann also points out the parallelism between Rom 1:8 (πίστις) and 16:19 (ὑπακοή).

[323]JOHNSON, "Romans 3:21-26 and the Faith of Jesus," 86-87.

discloses the latter."[324] This insight suggests that, in addition to his πίστις and ὑπακοή, Jesus' *love* (ἀγάπη) is a crucial aspect of his character as presented by Paul in Romans. We will see that the same is the case in 2 Corinthians.

C. *Michael Thompson (Rom 15:1-3)*

In *Clothed with Christ*, Michael Thompson argues that, despite the fact that Paul seldom alludes explicitly to "Jesus tradition," he makes ample use of both Jesus' example and teaching to undergird the exhortations found in Rom 12:1-15:13. Thompson makes a valuable contribution to our understanding of how the apostle draws upon the teaching and, especially, the example of Christ in his ethical admonitions. I limit my focus here to Thompson's analysis of 15:1-3 and to one of his concluding theses.

In Rom 15:1-6 Paul summarizes the responsibility of bearing one another's burdens. The apostle emphasizes that the "strong" in the community are not to please themselves (μὴ ἑαυτοῖς ἀρέσκειν, 15:1), but rather are to seek to please their neighbors (15:2). Then in 15:3a he draws upon the example of Christ, who "did not please himself." Thompson rightly notes that, although there is no explicit exhortation to *imitatio Christi* (e.g., as found in 1 Cor 11:1), two textual clues indicate that such is Paul's intent. First is the parallel between the admonition ὀφείλομεν . . . μὴ ἑαυτοῖς ἀρέσκειν and the statement ὁ Χριστὸς οὐχ ἑαυτῷ ἤρεσεν. Second is the causal γάρ in Rom 15:3a, which introduces the rationale for the apostle's exhortation. Thompson expresses well Paul's logic: "Christians are not to please themselves but their neighbour, because Christ did not please himself. *The unspoken but assumed premise is*

---

[324]L.E. KECK, "'Jesus' in Romans," *JBL* 108 (1989) 443-60, here 458. F.J. MATERA makes a similar observation about the synergy between the love of Jesus and the love of God: "Noting that one would hardly die for a just person, although one might possibly die for a truly good person, Paul says that Christ died for us while we were still sinners (5:7-8). At this point, one might expect Paul to draw the conclusion that Christ's death manifested his love for us, much as Paul concluded in Gal 2:20. Instead, he writes: '*God* proves his love for us in that while we were still sinners Christ died for us' (5:8). This unexpected conclusion indicates the unique relationship between God and Jesus. The act of Jesus upon the cross becomes an act of God, so that the love Jesus manifests by dying for the ungodly is the love of God for sinful humanity." See MATERA, *New Testament Christology* (Louisville: Westminster John Knox, 1999) 117 (Matera's italics).

that they are to adopt his attitude."[325] What is noteworthy here is the apostle's mode of argumentation. We will see throughout 2 Corinthians that he employs "unspoken but assumed" premises.

In Rom 15:3b Paul goes on to offer scriptural support (καθὼς γέγραπται; cf. 1:17) for his statement about Christ's self-giving attitude: "The insults of those who insulted you have fallen upon me" (LXX Ps 68:10b, verbatim). Thompson makes two critical observations concerning the apostle's use of this citation. First, Paul makes *Christ* the speaker of the words of the psalm.[326] Second, Thompson insists that, in order to understand how the citation functions, it is necessary to examine *the broader context and story* of LXX Ps 68.[327] In particular, notice that the psalmist/Jesus encounters opposition and insults on account of God – ἕνεκα σοῦ ὑπήνεγκα ὀνειδισμόν (Ps 68:8a; the pronoun here refers to God, just as in 68:10b). Indeed, the psalmist/Jesus declares his zeal for God's house (68:10a), thereby indicating his deep desire to serve God. Thompson then draws out the significance of the citation: ". . . if Christ the righteous sufferer bore a burden of reproach as a result of seeking to please God, Christians all the more should be prepared to bear a burden (including abuse from others) when they seek to please (i.e. to serve) their

---

[325]M. THOMPSON, *Clothed with Christ*, 212 (italics added). Thompson later notes that the attitude of seeking what is best for others "was incarnate in Christ, whose earthly life climaxed in an ultimate act of self-giving on the cross for others" (p. 217). C.E.B. CRANFIELD offers a similar assessment: "The statement οὐχ ἑαυτῷ ἤρεσεν sums up with eloquent reticence both the meaning of the Incarnation and *the character of Christ's earthly life*." See his *A Critical and Exegetical Commentary on the Epistle to the Romans*, 2 vols., ICC (Edinburgh: T. & T. Clark, 1975-79) 2.732 (italics added). Cf. B. BYRNE, *Romans*, SP 6 (Collegeville, Minn.: Liturgical, 1996) 424.

[326]See THOMPSON, *Clothed with Christ*, 222. So, also, CRANFIELD: "Christ is addressing God, and saying that the reproaches with which men reproached God have fallen on Him (i.e., on Christ)." See *A Critical and Exegetical Commentary on the Epistle to the Romans*, 2.733.

[327]As noted by, e.g., B. BYRNE, LXX Ps 68 is a text frequently cited in the early Christian tradition in connection with the passion of Christ. See BYRNE, *Romans*, 425.

brethren – which ultimately is to please God."[328] I will bring these two points – that the apostle can portray Jesus as the speaker of a psalm, and that the broader context of the cited psalm must be kept in mind in order to understand how the citation functions – to bear on the interpretation of 2 Cor 4:13, where Paul quotes from LXX Ps 115:1.

At the end of his monograph, Thompson offers a series of conclusions in the form of theses. His thesis concerning the significance of the character of Jesus in Rom 12:1-15:13 deserves to be quoted in full:

> The example of Christ is not limited to the pre-existent or the risen Christ, but has at its focus *the character of Jesus*, seen most clearly in his death on the cross. Paul's use of Χριστός instead of Ἰησοῦς reflects his conviction that the man Jesus was the messiah, and does not imply any disregard for *his earthly life*. . . . The particular characteristics of Jesus that we see influencing Paul in general (there probably were others but we lack evidence) are shown at the cross: his humble-mindedness (ταπεινοφροσύνη), his meekness (πραΰτης), his gentleness (ἐπιεικεία), his love (ἀγάπη), his compassion (σπλάγχνα), his endurance (ὑπομονή) through suffering, his forgiving Spirit seen in receiving sinners (προσλαμβάνειν), and above all in his attitude as a servant (διάκονος, δοῦλος).[329]

Thompson's insistence on the importance for Paul of "the man Jesus" and of "his earthly life" is one that I share. Moreover, observe that Thompson claims that the apostle draws upon a considerable number of attributes of Jesus. When faithfulness (πίστις) and obedience (ὑπακοή) – the key characteristics of Christ drawn from 3:21-26 and 5:15-21 – are added to the list, a "character portrait" of Jesus begins to emerge, a portrait that is richer than most scholars

---

[328]M. THOMPSON, *Clothed with Christ*, 223. Thompson goes on to note that, in the context of the strong and weak, "the strong should be ready to please the weak and accommodate themselves to their scruples when necessary, even though that would mean exposing themselves to the same reproaches and ridicule from the world which the strong had formerly heaped upon the ἀδύνατοι" (ibid.).

[329]Ibid., 238-39 (italics added).

have grasped. We will find that a similarly rich portrait emerges from a careful reading of 2 Corinthians.[330]

D. *Summary*

Campbell, Johnson, and Thompson persuasively argue that the character of Jesus was critically important for Paul as he set forth his gospel to "all God's beloved in Rome" (Rom 1:7). Campbell and Johnson recognize the centrality in the letter's thematic statement – a statement laden with theological significance – of the human Jesus' faithfulness in the revelation of God's righteousness. Particularly significant is Johnson's understanding of the importance of Jesus' obedience. Thompson shows how the apostle draws upon the character of Christ in his exhortations to the community. He insists that Christ's example, which broadens Paul's portrait of Jesus, includes his willingness to put the interests of others before his own. Whereas Johnson's investigation hones in on intratextual connections in Romans (connections that are more often apparent in Greek than in translation), both Campbell and Thompson demonstrate the importance of intertextual interpretation. Sensitivity to the apostle's use of Scripture (e.g., Hab 2:4 and LXX Ps 68) reveals much about his perception of Jesus. We will discover similar dynamics and tendencies in the analysis of 2 Corinthians.

Thus, two current movements in Pauline theology have converged on the issue of Jesus' character. The recognition that the "story of Jesus" underlies Paul's writings has led to a greater appreciation of plot and of the protagonist's – Jesus' – role in that plot. More specifically, it has led to a clearer perception of the apostle's strategy of drawing out the ongoing significance of this story for the lives of his communities. So, too, recent scholarship on Romans points in the same direction, as it shows the importance of the character of Jesus in both Paul's theological formulations and his exhortations to the community. Concerning the latter, the apostle attempts to shape the lives of the Romans in conformity with the *ethos* of Jesus, a character made manifest especially in his humanity.

---

[330]Indeed, looking at the larger Pauline corpus, THOMPSON observes that significant work remains to be done on the allusions and echoes of the Jesus tradition in the Corinthian literature. See *Clothed with Christ*, 239.

So far I have refrained from defining with precision what Paul means when he refers to Jesus' πίστις, ὑπακοή, and other attributes. To this point, it has been sufficient to show that the apostle in fact alludes to such characteristics of Christ. Descriptions of these characteristics will be forthcoming in the more detailed exegetical analysis of 2 Corinthians in Part Two. Before turning to this investigation, a few words on my "methodology" are in order.

III. Methodological Considerations

I employ no sophisticated or specialized methodology to demonstrate my thesis. Rather, I undertake a rigorously "close reading" of the Greek text.[331] My reading involves the unglamorous task of wrestling with grammatical issues. It is sensitive to intratextual and semantic connections, as well as to intertextual echoes and allusions.[332] It also entails careful attention paid to the logic and texture of Paul's argument, including its epistolary and rhetorical features. I must beg my readers in advance for patience, as much of the force of my thesis is cumulative.

Chapter Four is a close, inductive analysis of Paul's references to Jesus in 2 Corinthians. These include explicit allusions to the story of Jesus, specific references to his life and character, and two intertextual allusions. In some cases (e.g., 2 Cor 10:5) it will first be necessary to argue that the apostle is even

---

[331]I concur wholeheartedly with the following observation by R.B. HAYS (in *The Faith of Jesus Christ*, xxvii): "The thing that matters is the message of the text, the story that it tells and interprets. Methodology is a secondary and instrumental concern." S.J. HAFEMANN'S description and rationale of his own "method" resonate very much with my own: "This study is not an attempt to apply a new method to a familiar text in order to discover something novel. Rather, *it is an attempt to start with the text itself without the assumption that its meaning has already been ascertained* and thus only needs to be reformulated or put within a new framework (e.g., literary, sociological, psychological, polemical, theological, etc.). My experience has been that *the Pauline texts themselves still remain to a great degree a foreign territory in need of discovery*." See HAFEMANN, *Suffering and Ministry in the Spirit: Paul's Defense of His Ministry in II Corinthians 2:14-3:3* (Grand Rapids, Mich.: Eerdmans, 1990) 2 (italics added).

[332]For more on intertextuality and on constraints for "hearing echoes," see HAYS, *Echoes of Scripture in the Letters of Paul*, 1-33.

referring to something about Jesus. In all instances my strategy is to show how these references and allusions *function* in Paul's mode of presentation and argumentation. That is, I seek to demonstrate what the apostle presumes and draws upon concerning Jesus in the course of writing 2 Corinthians.

Chapters Five and Six demonstrate, respectively, how Paul's self-commendation and his specific exhortations to the Corinthians are grounded in the portrait of Jesus that emerges from Chapter Four. In other words, I show how the apostle presents himself as continuing the story of Jesus, and how he calls the Corinthians to do the same. In these chapters I focus largely on intratextual echoes and semantic connections, as well as on conceptual linkages. Several of these connections are readily seen in the Greek text, but get lost in translations and interpretations of 2 Corinthians.

In all three exegetical chapters, I allow the text of 2 Corinthians to speak for itself as far as possible. Given all the problems with partitioning the text, I attempt to make sense of 2 Corinthians as it stands in its present canonical form. This includes taking seriously the sequence of presentation. Moreover, the primary source for understanding terms and referents contained therein is 2 Corinthians itself. Insofar as it is helpful, however, I do turn to other Pauline texts to illuminate how the apostle understands and uses certain words and concepts.

Lastly, a brief word about Pauline texts: By "Pauline texts" I include not only the so-called "undisputed texts" – Romans, 1 and 2 Corinthians, Galatians, Philippians, 1 Thessalonians, and Philemon – but also Ephesians, Colossians, and 2 Thessalonians (the so-called "deutero-Paulines), as well as 1 and 2 Timothy and Titus (the so-called "pastorals"). While acknowledging some real differences in style and content in the latter six, the arguments for considering them as later developments – and, in the case of some scholars, as aberrations – of Paul's theology are overstated and problematic. The position presumed here is that the thirteen canonical epistles attributed to Paul are all products of a "Pauline school," and were authorized by the apostle himself.[333]

---

[333]See L.T. JOHNSON'S brief treatment of the issue of authenticity in *The Writings of the New Testament*, 271-73. Johnson argues for the authenticity of 2 Thess on pp. 287-88; of Col on pp. 393-95; and of Eph on pp. 407-12. For a detailed discussion that challenges the conventional assumption that the pastorals were written well after Paul's life, see JOHNSON, *The First and Second Letters to Timothy: A New Translation with Introduction and Commentary*, AB 35A (New York: Doubleday, 2001) 55-97. In addition, see J.N.D. KELLY'S balanced discussion in *A Commentary on the Pastoral*

Those who find this presupposition suspect will take comfort in the fact that, after 2 Corinthians itself, the Pauline texts to which I refer most frequently are Romans, 1 Corinthians, Galatians, and Philippians. Indeed, as I have suggested in the previous section, there are some remarkable structural and conceptual confluences of 2 Corinthians and Romans.

Epistles, HNTC (New York: Harper & Row, 1963) 1-36; cf. G.D. FEE, *1 and 2 Timothy, Titus*, NIBC, rev. ed. (Peabody, Mass.: Hendrickson, 1988) 1-31. Fee's conclusion concerning the pastorals is one that I accept: "The best solution is that Paul used a different amanuensis for these letters than for earlier ones (or did he actually write these himself after having used amanuenses earlier?). . . . To say that Paul is the author of the [pastoral epistles] means that the letters ultimately come from him in the historical settings contained within them. It does not say *how* they came from him; the final answer to that question is not available to us" (p. 26).

It is interesting to observe that most scholars who question the authenticity of some of Paul's letters regard them as products of a *later* "Pauline school." What is rarely discussed or observed is that such a school would be more likely to exist in the apostle's lifetime than later.

Part Two
The Character of Jesus

Chapter Four
The Character of Jesus in 2 Corinthians

I. Introduction

My thesis in this work is straightforward: The character of Jesus – especially as manifested in his humanity – is the linchpin and heart of Paul's presentation in 2 Corinthians. Throughout the letter, the apostle refers to and draws upon the story and character of Jesus in ways that Pauline scholarship has failed to fully appreciate. In the present chapter, I analyze *all* the passages in which Paul alludes to some characteristic(s) of Christ. Such an analysis reveals what the apostle *presumes* about the *ethos* of Jesus.

I make two brief preliminary points as *prima facie* support for my thesis. While it is true that Paul offers no sustained treatment of the story of Jesus in 2 Corinthians, it was not necessary for him to do so. The Corinthians already knew about Jesus Christ prior to the composition of this epistle.[334] First Corinthians is helpful in this regard. There we learn that the apostle himself had earlier proclaimed among them "Jesus Christ and him crucified" (1 Cor 2:2). Indeed, it was "in Christ Jesus through the gospel" that Paul had begotten the community in the first place (4:15). His proclamation of the gospel must have included an account of the story of Jesus, as the apostle refers to specific traditions he had received and in turn delivered to the Corinthians. Paul directly cites the words of Jesus over the bread and wine "on the night on which he was handed over" (11:23-25), and makes reference to the traditions concerning Jesus' death and burial, his resurrection, and his appearances thereafter (15:3-

---

[334]Cf. L.L. BELLEVILLE, "Gospel and Kerygma in 2 Corinthians," in *Gospel in Paul: Studies on Corinthians, Galatians and Romans for Richard N. Longenecker*, JSNTSup 108, ed. L.A. JERVIS and P. RICHARDSON (Sheffield: Sheffield Academic Press, 1994) 134-164, esp. 140-141: "It is important, however, to remember that Paul's letters are not evangelistic tracts but occasional writings aimed at people who had already come to the Christian faith and *for whom the facts of Jesus' life and ministry needed no repeating*" (italics added). What Belleville says about Paul's letters in general is certainly apposite for 2 Cor.

8).[335] The text also indicates that the apostle is aware of at least some of the teachings of Jesus that are recounted in the synoptic gospels. Paul refers both to Jesus' proscription against divorce (7:10-11) and to his admonition that those who proclaim the gospel should be provided for (9:14).[336] In short, 1 Corinthians gives ample evidence that the community was already in possession of various aspects of the story of Jesus – including those pertaining to his earthly ministry.[337] In writing 2 Corinthians, therefore, it was not necessary for the apostle to retell this story. Instead, simple allusions and appeals to specific characteristics of Jesus were sufficient to evoke in the minds and hearts of the community what they already knew – the story and character of Jesus.

Second, I note the significance of Paul's initial allusion to the story of Christ in 2 Corinthians, immediately following the greeting. As is his typical practice, the apostle foreshadows the principal themes of his letter in the opening prayer period.[338] Here in the opening *berakah* (2 Cor 1:3-7) Paul raises "comfort/consolation" and "affliction" as two central themes that will run through the course of this epistle.[339] He blesses God for bestowing comfort

---

[335]Paul also alludes several times in 1 Cor to the cross and to Jesus' death. See 1:16; 1:23; 2:2; 5:7; 8:11; and 11:26.

[336]For Jesus' teaching about divorce, see Mark 10:11-12 and parallels. For his statement concerning support for missionaries, see Luke 10:7.

[337]Cf. F.J. MATERA, *New Testament Christology*, 92. Matera includes in the "story of Christ" – beyond his earthly ministry – Paul's description of Christ's parousia and the events to take place at the end of time (1 Cor 15:20-28 and 15:50-57), as well as intimations of his preexistence (8:6; 10:4; and 10:9).

I contend that 1 Cor makes clear that the appropriation of Jesus' character is important to Paul, for he reminds the Corinthians that "we have the mind of Christ" (2:16), and he exhorts them to "[b]ecome imitators of me, just as I am of Christ" (11:1). I will show in this and the following chapters that these two statements are, in effect, presupposed premises from which the apostle argues throughout 2 Cor.

[338]See P. SCHUBERT, *Form and Function of the Pauline Thanksgivings*, BZNW 20 (Berlin: A. Topelmann, 1939); and P.T. O'BRIEN, *Introductory Thanksgivings in the Letters of Paul*, NovTSup 49 (Leiden: E.J. Brill, 1977).

[339]Cf. 2 Cor 1:8; 2:4; 2:7-8; 4:8; 4:17; 5:20; 6:1; 6:4; 7:4-7; 7:13; 8:2; 8:4; 8:6; 8:13; 8:17; 9:5; 10:1; 12:8; 12:18; and 13:11.

upon those who are afflicted, and for empowering those thus comforted to bring comfort in turn to others (1:3-4). Then he immediately refers to τὰ παθήματα τοῦ Χριστοῦ – "the sufferings of Christ" (1:5) – which abound in the apostle and his companions, as does the fact that their being comforted abounds "through Christ." By alluding to the sufferings of Christ, Paul necessarily refers to Jesus in his humanity. This reference to the human Jesus at the very heart of the opening blessing is deeply significant. So, too, is the theme of the "pattern of interchange" that exists among Christ, Paul (and his co-workers), and the Corinthians. By means of this interchange, the apostle portrays his own experience of affliction and comfort for the sake of the Corinthians (1:6), who in turn share in these sufferings and comforts (1:7). To the degree 2 Corinthians reflects the form of Paul's other letters by anticipating key themes in the opening prayer period, we can expect Jesus' humanity and the pattern of interchange – and the resultant intimations of character – to play prominent roles in this epistle.[340]

Before proceeding, I anticipate two objections to my thesis concerning the *ethos* of Jesus. The first pertains to the issue of Christ's divinity and humanity. It will be objected that I "overread" Jesus' humanity into Paul's argument. For example, does not 2 Cor 8:9 – with its reference to "our Lord Jesus Christ" becoming poor in order to enrich others – refer to the incarnation of the pre-existent Christ rather than to his self-emptying mode of human existence? To be sure, the apostle was not himself concerned with distinguishing Jesus' human status from his divine status. That is, for Paul the story of Jesus Christ encompasses *all* of the following: his pre-existent (divine) status (Phil 2:6 – "in [the] form of God"); his incarnation (Phil 2:7 – "in [the] likeness of human beings"); his human life, which culminated with his death on the cross (Phil 2:8 – "becoming obedient unto death"); his being raised from the dead by God (cf. Rom 4:24 and 2 Cor 4:14); and his being exalted by God and given the name above every other name (Phil 2:9-11 – κύριος Ἰησοῦς Χριστός). Thus, when I speak of the story and character of Jesus in 2 Corinthians, this "big picture" must always be kept in mind. Let me be clear that the *ethos* of Jesus in his humanity is not something separate from the *ethos*

---

[340]Whereas O'Brien rightly recognizes that the theme of Christ's sufferings are sustained throughout 2 Cor 1-9 – especially as they relate to the apostle's sufferings – he fails to see how Jesus' character functions in Paul's argument. See O'BRIEN, *Introductory Thanksgivings in the Letters of Paul*, 247-57. Schubert deals only with 2 Cor 1:11 (because of the presence there of the verb εὐχαριστέω).

of "our Lord Jesus Christ." Jesus is one person (in his pre-existence, humanity, and exaltation), and thus has a single *ethos*. Nevertheless, while the apostle often draws upon all (cf. Phil 2:6-11) or much (cf. Rom 1:3-4) of the big picture in alluding to Jesus, there are times when he draws particular implications from the middle of the story, that part concerning ὁ ἄνθρωπος 'Ιησοῦς Χριστός (e.g., Rom 5:15-19).

The second anticipated objection concerns the rendering of the genitive Χριστοῦ. It will be objected that in some cases the genitive is objective rather than subjective. For instance, does not the expression ὑπακοή τοῦ Χριστοῦ in 2 Cor 10:5 refer to the obedience that is directed toward Christ (objective genitive) rather than to Jesus' own obedience (subjective genitive)? The force of this objection – as well as that of the first – can only be answered by the exegesis that follows.

I begin with the most obvious reference to Jesus' character in 2 Corinthians, namely his "gentleness and forbearance" (2 Cor 10:1). I then examine an allusion to Christ's obedience (10:5). Careful analysis of this passage shows that the traditional reading of 2 Corinthians does not do justice to the Greek text or to Paul's usage of obedience language elsewhere. After grounding the apostle's understanding of Christ's character in 10:1-5, I go back to the beginning of the letter body to work sequentially through the passages in which Paul draws upon the story and character of Jesus: his "Yes," which is an allusion to his obedience (1:19-20); his faithfulness (4:13); his love (5:14); his 'not knowing Sin' and 'being made "sin"' in his role in God's work of reconciliation (5:21); his graciousness (8:9; cf. 9:9); his integrity and innocence (11:3); and his 'being crucified because of weakness' (13:4). Again, I appeal to my readers' patience, as the force of my argument is cumulative in nature.

II. Christ's Gentleness and Forbearance (2 Cor 10:1)

After his exhortation to the Corinthians to contribute generously to the needs of the Jerusalem church (2 Cor 8:1-9:15), Paul seems to switch gears dramatically in subject matter and tone. He launches into 10:1 with great energy and passion. He presents himself as a trustworthy laborer sent by God to Corinth with the good news (10:13-16). He attacks the values and behavior of other (unnamed) missionaries/evangelists (see, e.g., 10:12, 11:12-15, and 11:20), while boasting in his own lowliness and weakness (11:30 and 12:10). And after informing the Corinthians of his impending third visit to them (12:14 and 13:1), he challenges them to prepare for it by testing themselves to see whether or not they are ἐν τῇ πίστει (13:5).

The apostle begins the section that extends from 2 Cor 10:1 to 13:10 with an emphatic appeal: "Now I, Paul myself, implore you" – αὐτὸς δὲ ἐγὼ Παῦλος παρακαλῶ ὑμᾶς. The apostle's insertion of a παρακαλῶ period immediately following an exclamation of thanksgiving to God (9:15) is not unusual, as he uses this construction elsewhere.[341] More to the issue at hand is the fact that Paul makes his appeal "through the πραΰτης and ἐπιείκεια of Christ" (10:1). The apostle's allusion to certain characteristics of Jesus at this point is in line with the encouragement he has just given the Corinthians to see their participation in the collection as a way of confessing "the gospel of Christ" (τὸ εὐαγγέλιον τοῦ Χριστοῦ, 9:13).

Before investigating the phrase διὰ τῆς πραΰτητος καὶ ἐπιεικείας τοῦ Χριστοῦ, it is important to point out that in this case the genitive Χριστοῦ can*not* be anything but subjective. On this point, all the commentators are in basic agreement.[342] Where scholars disagree is on the point of whether Paul here alludes to the kenotic act of Christ's incarnation, or to characteristics exhibited by Jesus during his life and ministry on earth. In order to answer this question, it is first necessary to examine what the apostle means by the terms πραΰτης and ἐπιείκεια, and then to analyze the placement, force, and function of the prepositional phrase.

What does Paul mean by the word πραΰτης? The term normally means "gentleness" or "humility,"[343] and the apostle certainly draws upon this general signification. His use of πραΰτης in other contexts enriches this basic understanding. In 1 Cor 4:21 Paul contrasts the possibility of his coming to the Corinthians "with a rod" (ἐν ῥάβδῳ) to that of his coming "in love with a spirit of gentleness" (ἐν ἀγάπῃ πνεύματι τε πραΰτητος). Notice that the apostle speaks here to the community as one who exercises authority over them as their

---

[341]Cf. esp. Rom 12:1; 1 Cor 1:10; and 1 Thess 4:1. See n. 147 above.

[342]See R. LEIVESTAD'S discussion in "'The Meekness and Gentleness of Christ' II Cor. X. 1," *NTS* 12 (1965-66) 156-64, esp. 156-57.

[343]See BDAG, s.v. πραΰτης.

"father."[344] Πραΰτης is thus linked with the exercise of power. It is associated with ἀγάπη and dissociated from the use of coercion and violence. In addition, in 2 Tim 2:25 Paul utilizes πραΰτης in his exhortation to Timothy in the latter's role as teacher. He instructs Timothy to correct (παιδεύω) "with gentleness" (ἐν πραΰτητι) those who opposed him. Once again, the apostle uses πραΰτης to denote "gentleness" in connection with the exercise of leadership.

Paul also refers to the quality of πραΰτης in his exhortations to the various communities he founded. After listing πραΰτης as one of the manifestations of the "fruit of the Spirit" in Gal 5:23, the apostle encourages the Galatians to "restore" (καταρτίζω) "in a spirit of gentleness" (ἐν πνεύματι πραΰτητος) any member overtaken in some trespass (Gal 6:1). This connection between gentleness and καταρτίζω is intriguing, for in his final instructions to the Corinthians Paul will exhort them to "be restored [to one another]" (καταρτίζεσθε, 2 Cor 13:11; cf. 13:9). In addressing the "Ephesians," the apostle begins his description of 'leading a life worthy of the calling' of Christ with the phrase "with all humility and gentleness" (μετὰ πάσης ταπεινοφροσύνης καὶ πραΰτητος, Eph 4:2). He also connects πραΰτης here with "forbearing one another (ἀνεχόμενοι ἀλλήλων) in love." Similarly, Paul counsels the Colossians to clothe themselves with πραΰτης (Col 3:12), which is again linked with "forbearing one another" (ἀνεχόμενοι ἀλλήλων, Col 3:13). What is pertinent here is that the apostle sees gentleness as constitutive of what it means to put on "the new person" (ὁ νέος ἄνθρωπος) who is renewed in knowledge "according to the image of the Creator" (κατ' εἰκόνα τοῦ κτίσαντος; see Col 3:9-10). We will see in Chapter Five how Paul employs these notions of transformation and Christ as the image (εἰκών) of God. For the time being, it is sufficient to note that, in addition to being a quality for leaders, the apostle considers "gentleness" (πραΰτης) as an essential mark of all Christians, a mark that is intimately coupled with forbearance.[345]

---

[344]See 1 Cor 4:15, where Paul writes ἐν Χριστῷ 'Ιησοῦ διὰ τοῦ εὐαγγελίου ἐγὼ ὑμᾶς ἐγέννησα ("in Christ Jesus I begot you through the good news").

[345]It is interesting to note that, of the four times the adjectival form πραΰς ("gentle, humble") appears in the NT, two describe Jesus. In Matt 11:29 Jesus says, "I am gentle and lowly in heart" (πραΰς εἰμι καὶ ταπεινὸς τῇ καρδίᾳ). In Matt 21:5 Jesus is described as entering Jerusalem "humble and mounted on a donkey" (πραΰς καὶ ἐπιβεβηκὼς ἐπὶ ὄνον, an allusion to Zech 9:9). In the latter Matthean passage, Jesus is presented as a king – and thus one who (like Paul in 1 Cor 4:21) exercises authority

This connection between πραΰτης and forbearance is present in 2 Cor 10:1. While ἐπιείκεια is similar in meaning to πραΰτης, it can also denote "clemency"and "forbearance."[346] Indeed, Paul highlights this latter denotation in his usage of the adjectival form ἐπιεικής. In Phil 4:5, after urging the Philippians to rejoice always, the apostle begins his final admonitions to the community by saying: "Let your τὸ ἐπιεικές be known to all people." Given that he has just finished exhorting two quarreling members of the community to "the same thinking in the Lord" (Phil 4:2-3), it makes sense that Paul has "forbearance" in mind.[347] In 1 Tim 3:3, in addressing the qualifications of an "overseer" (ἐπίσκοπος), the apostle urges that one be "not violent, but forbearing, not quarrelsome" (μὴ πλήκτην, ἀλλὰ ἐπιεική, ἄμαχον). Notice how ἐπιεικής is contrasted here with violence and quarreling. Moreover, in Titus 3:2 the apostle advises Titus to remind his congregation not to speak evil of others and to avoid quarreling; instead, they are to be "forbearing" (ἐπιεικεῖς) and to show forth "all gentleness" (πᾶσαν πραΰτητα) toward all people. Here, as in 2 Cor 10:1, Paul combines ἐπιείκεια and πραΰτης. Thus, given the apostle's usage elsewhere, I translate διὰ τῆς πραΰτητος καὶ ἐπιεικείας τοῦ Χριστοῦ as "through the gentleness and forbearance of Christ" – and not as "meekness and gentleness," which is the prevailing translation.

Analysis of the place, force, and function of this prepositional phrase sheds even more light on its meaning. In terms of placement, it is striking that immediately after the initial "I implore you" (2 Cor 10:1a), Paul offers no specific plea or request. Rather, παρακαλῶ ὑμᾶς is followed by the prepositional phrase in question and a long relative clause. Then, beginning with 2 Cor 10:2, the apostle takes up another appeal, using another finite indicative verb to do so – δέομαι ("I beg [of you]"). Rather than presume that

---

– who is gentle and humble. For an extended treatment of πραΰς in connection with Jesus, see D.J. GOOD, *The Meek King* (Harrisburg, Pa.: Trinity International, 1999). Good proposes that πραΰτης be understood as the virtue of "disciplined calmness," as opposed to, e.g., acting coercively out of anger and/or fear.

[346]See BDAG, s.v. ἐπιείκεια.

[347]R.P. MARTIN aptly translates τὸ ἐπιεικές in Phil 4:5 as "graciousness," "with the idea that Christians will have *a willingness to forgo retaliation* when threatened." See *2 Corinthians*, WBC (Waco, Tex.: Word, 1986) 302 (italics added).

Paul's grammar is careless, or that he changed his thought in mid-sentence,[348] I suggest that the apostle's initial appeal in 10:1 functions to cover all of the various components in the following four chapters.[349] That is, the clause "I, Paul myself, implore you through the gentleness and forbearance of Christ" introduces *all* that follows, up to the final exhortation and blessing (13:11-13). By its placement, the prepositional phrase διὰ τῆς πραΰτητος καὶ ἐπιεικείας τοῦ Χριστοῦ thus takes on great prominence, serving as the background against which to read and interpret all of 2 Cor 10-13.

Given its prominence of place, it is crucial to determine the force of the διά-phrase. The preposition διά, used in combination with παρακαλῶ, means "by reference to" or "by appeal to."[350] The object of this preposition, that to which Paul appeals, is best understood under two aspects. First, the reference to *Christ* serves to ground the apostle's appeal. That is, Paul utilizes a tactic he

---

[348]J. LAMBRECHT suggests that, originally, Paul intended to do at 2 Cor 10:1 what he does elsewhere (Rom 12:1 and 15:3), namely, formulate an exhortation to moral Christian life with reference to God or Christ as the grounds for the appeal. However, while writing διὰ τῆς πραΰτητος καὶ ἐπιεικείας τοῦ Χριστοῦ, Lambrecht proposes that the apostle's attention was diverted, and he recalled the slanders of his critics. This explains the break at 10:2. See LAMBRECHT, "Paul's Appeal and the Obedience to Christ: The Line of Thought in 2 Corinthians 10,1-6," *Bib* 77 (1996) 398-416, here 407-8. Lambrecht hypothesizes that 12:19-13:11 contains much of what Paul originally intended to exhort (see p. 415). I do not go so far as to surmise what the apostle's mental processes were in the course of his writing.

[349]So, too, H. CRUZ, *Christological Motives and Motivated Actions in Pauline Paraenesis*, EUS 23/396 (Frankfurt: Peter Lang, 1990) 245: "To understand this appeal and the motivated action, we have to keep in mind that these verses are the beginning of a section which is an unit all by itself. It consists of chapters 10-13."

[350]See R. BULTMANN, *The Second Letter to the Corinthians*, 182. LEIVESTAD'S position that διά "is most likely used in the same way as πρός (cf. Latin *per*) to introduce an invocation or an adjuration" is untenable (see "'The Meekness and Gentleness of Christ' II Cor. X. 1," 156). Cf. LAMBRECHT, "Paul's Appeal and the Obedience to Christ," 411, n. 34.

employs elsewhere,[351] one in which he indicates Jesus as the authority by whom he will implore the Corinthians, thereby making his appeal to them more persuasive and compelling. Second, the reference to Christ's *gentleness and forbearance* adds what Jan Lambrecht calls "a moral and exemplary nuance"[352] to the apostle's entreaty. That is, Paul gives texture to his authoritative appeal by referring to particular characteristics of Christ. This exemplary aspect of the apostle's reference to Christ becomes evident when one understands how διὰ τῆς πραΰτητος καὶ ἐπιεικείας τοῦ Χριστοῦ functions throughout 2 Cor 10-13.

Paul's allusion to Christ's gentleness and forbearance functions in relation to three parties: the apostle himself, the problematic elements within the church at Corinth (including the "superlative apostles" – see 2 Cor 11:5 and 12:11), and the Corinthian community as a whole. Paul aligns himself with Christ's gentleness and forbearance in his role as father to the community (see 12:14-15). As he announces his third visit to the Corinthians (12:14 and 13:1; cf. 10:2), the apostle intimates his continued preference for exercising his authority in a spirit of gentleness (cf. 1 Cor 4:21), as his purpose is to build up the community (2 Cor 10:8 and 13:10). Nevertheless, he will not spare the rod if necessary (13:2 and 13:10).[353] In addition, Paul's reference to Christ's gentleness/humility functions apologetically as well. That is, the apostle makes a virtue of his being "lowly" (ταπεινός, 10:1b and 11:7) and "weak" (ἀσθενής, 11:30 and 12:10) by aligning himself with Christ (cf. 13:3-4).[354] Paul's allusion to Christ's gentleness and forbearance also serves as a foil for

---

[351]See Rom 15:30: παρακαλῶ δὲ ὑμᾶς, ἀδελφοί, διὰ τοῦ κυρίου ἡμῶν 'Ιησοῦ Χριστοῦ; and 1 Cor 1:10: παρακαλῶ δὲ ὑμᾶς, ἀδελφοί, διὰ τοῦ ὀνοματος τοῦ κυρίου ἡμῶν 'Ιησοῦ Χριστοῦ. Cf. Rom 12:1.

[352]See LAMBRECHT, "Paul's Appeal and the Obedience to Christ," 407.

[353]To be sure, given the sarcastic and even vituperative tone throughout 2 Cor 10-13, it is debatable how much Paul himself actually succeeds in embodying gentleness and forbearance in these chapters.

[354]Cf. LEIVESTAD, "'The Meekness and Gentleness of Christ' II Cor X. 1," 161-64, esp. 163: "Those who deride the ταπεινότης of the apostle make a terrible mistake: they confuse flesh and spirit. They forget that God's power is made perfect in human weakness."

all that he rails against in 2 Cor 10-12: (negative) *self*-commendation and competitive comparisons (10:12); boasting in one's accomplishments (10:18); lording over others (11:20); placing high value in showy manifestations of power (12:12); and raising false suspicions (12:16-18). Indeed, such behavior represents the very antithesis of gentleness and forbearance.[355] Lastly, Paul holds up Christ's gentleness and forbearance to the Corinthians for emulation. He fears that he will find some whose conduct falls below the standard of Jesus (12:20). The apostle's allusion also encourages the community to be forbearing toward him rather than taking a confrontational stance (13:3), and to be restored in reconciliation to him and to one another (13:11; cf. Gal 6:1).

It is now possible to return to the question raised above: to what part of the story of Jesus does Paul allude with his reference to Christ's πραΰτης and ἐπιείκεια? Given that the apostle mentions "Christ" – not "Jesus" – and that he offers little information in his letters about the life of Jesus, many scholars argue that Paul refers in 2 Cor 10:1 to the kenosis of the pre-existent Christ.[356] I submit, however, that both the apostle's usage of the terms and the way they function in his argument require that he draw particularly upon characteristics of the human Jesus. Recall Paul's association of πραΰτης with

---

[355]Similarly, F.J. MATERA, *II Corinthians*, 220: ". . . some accuse Paul of being 'humble' (*tapeinos*) in the sense of 'base' or 'of no account' when in fact his humble bearing in their presence is a manifestation of Christ's meekness and clemency. Consequently to reject Paul as lowly and of no account is to reject the one whose life manifests the very meekness and clemency of Christ. Put another way, in misinterpreting Paul's humble bearing toward them, the Corinthians have misunderstood the gospel he has proclaimed to them."

In this connection, D.E. GARLAND makes an interesting observation. He observes that whereas many people today think of the apostle as being "pugnacious and uncompromising," many Corinthians apparently thought quite the opposite about him. Garland concludes: "The picture that some have of a combative, cantankerous Paul needs to be reevaluated." See his *2 Corinthians*, 433-34.

[356]See, e.g., LEIVESTAD, "'The Meekness and Gentleness of Christ' II Cor X. 1," 163: "Paul is not referring to the lenience and indulgence of the heavenly judge, *nor even to his mild and gracious attitude during his earthly life*; he is alluding to the fact of the kenosis, the literal weakness and lowliness of the Lord" (italics added). Cf. R. BULTMANN, *The Theology of the New Testament*, 1.294; and V.P. FURNISH, *II Corinthians*, 460: "It is much more likely that Paul is thinking of the pre-existent Lord who, in the gracious condescension of his incarnate life, became lowly, weak, and poor."

the exercise of power or authority. This is certainly congruent with the portrait of Jesus' earthly ministry in Matt 11:29 and 21:5.[357] Morever, the apostle uses the adjectival form of ἐπιείκεια to signify forbearance, an attribute more compatible with Jesus' human comportment than the act of incarnation itself.[358] And given the pervasive exemplary function of the phrase throughout 2 Cor 10-13, it makes more sense for Paul to appeal to a *human* example than to a divine example. The use of the title "Christ" is inconclusive, for we will see below that the apostle can use it to refer to the human Jesus as Messiah. In the end, the either/or quality of the question is probably misconceived, for as C.K. Barrett notes, the kenotic view is possible only if the human Jesus exhibited πραΰτης and ἐπιείκεια.[359] My point is that the apostle does draw upon "the manner in which Jesus acted and behaved during his life on earth, after birth and before death."[360]

The allusion to Christ in 2 Cor 10:1 thus evokes two interconnected aspects of the character of Jesus. First, πραΰτης refers to his quality of gentleness, exhibited especially in his role as teacher and master (cf. John 13:13-14), a gentleness marked by love and dissociated from the use of coercion. Second, ἐπιείκεια refers to Jesus' forbearance, manifested in particular by

---

[357]See n. 345 above.

[358]I suggest that the usual interpretation of πραΰτης and ἐπιείκεια as "meekness and gentleness" – thereby excluding forbearance (at least explicitly) – contributes to the interpretation of 2 Cor 10:1 as referring (exclusively) to the incarnation.

[359]See BARRETT, *The Second Epistle to the Corinthians*, 246: "There is something to be said about this view [i.e., that 10:1 refers to Christ's meekness and humility in accepting the conditions of earthly life at all], but it would have been impossible as theology had it been known that the behaviour of Jesus had been marked by arrogance and violence, and frigid if there had not been a tradition that depicted him as meek and gentle."

[360]J. LAMBRECHT, "Paul's Appeal and the Obedience to Christ," 414. J.D.G. DUNN also holds that 2 Cor 10:1 likely refers "not only to [Jesus'] self-giving death but also to the character of his ministry as a whole." See *The Theology of Paul the Apostle* (Grand Rapids, Mich.: Eerdmans, 1998) 193-94. I agree with the assessment of A. PLUMMER, *II Corinthians*, 273: "The appeal shows that St Paul must have instructed the Corinthians *as to the character* of the Redeemer, whose words and actions must therefore have been known to himself" (italics added).

patience, slowness to anger, non-retaliation, and his willingness to forgive – even his enemies and persecutors.[361] As we will see, the apostle makes another reference to Christ's character a few verses later.

III. Christ's Obedience (2 Cor 10:5)

Paul's specific reference to Christ's gentleness and forbearance indicates that the apostle has a particular character "portrait" of Jesus in mind. Strangely enough, Paul's imagery then changes dramatically in the next few verses (2 Cor 10:2-6). Here the apostle unabashedly uses metaphors of warfare as he confidently claims to "destroy strongholds" and "take captives." The paradox inherent in this approach – beginning an exhortation "through the gentleness and forbearance of Christ," then immediately launching into imagery connoting force and violence – is less substantive than it might first appear. In the first place, Paul's "weapons of warfare" are δυνατὰ τῷ θεῷ – "powerful because of God"[362] (10:4a). That is, the imagery of conquering in battle serves to metaphorically underscore *God's* power, not the apostle's (literal) power.[363] In the second place, that which Paul – as Christ's apostle "through God's will" (1:1) – attempts to bring about among the Corinthians is the ὑπακοὴ τοῦ Χριστοῦ (10:5b). It is to the interpretation of this expression that I now turn.

In 2 Cor 10:4-5 Paul writes, "For our weapons of warfare do not pertain to the realm of the flesh[364] but are powerful because of God for tearing down

---

[361]Cf. H. WINDISCH'S characterization of Christ's ἐπιείκεια: "ist herablassende Güte gegen die, die sie nicht verdient haben, die Verfolger und Feinde. . . ." See *Der zweite Korintherbrief*, KEK, repr. of 9th ed. [1924], ed. G. STRECKER (Göttingen: Vandenhoeck & Ruprecht, 1970) 292. For Paul's knowledge of the command to love one's enemies, see Rom 12:14-21 .

[362]Taking τῷ θεῷ as a dative of cause. See BDF, § 196.

[363]For the Cynic and Stoic background to Paul's use of military imagery in 2 Cor 10:3-6, see A.J. MALHERBE, "Antisthenes and Odysseus, and Paul at War," *HTR* 76 (1983) 143-73.

[364]I translate the adjective σαρκικά as "pertains to the realm of the flesh," that is, as that which *lacks the empowerment of God's Spirit.* See the discussion in Section VI concerning Paul's use of σαρκ- language in 2 Cor.

strongholds, as we tear down arguments and all pride raised up against the knowledge of God, καὶ αἰχμαλωτίζοντες πᾶν νόημα εἰς τὴν ὑπακοὴν τοῦ Χριστοῦ." The RSV translates the latter clause as "and [we] take every thought captive to obey Christ." Two aggressive aspects of this translation[365] are worth noting: first, it takes the liberty of rendering the substantive ὑπακοή as a verb; second, it interprets τοῦ Χριστοῦ as an objective genitive, thereby understanding Christ to be the *object* (or recipient) of obedience. Thus, the RSV – as well as the vast majority of commentators[366] – interprets Paul's "battle" as

---

[365]Similarly, MARTIN, *2 Corinthians*, 297: ". . . and we make every thought captive as it obeys Christ"; and S.J. KISTEMAKER, *New Testament Commentary: Exposition of the Second Epistle to the Corinthians* (Grand Rapids, Mich.: Baker, 1997) 335: "And we lead captive every thought to obey Christ"; cf. F.F. BRUCE, *1 and 2 Corinthians*, NCB (London: Oliphants, 1971) 230. MALHERBE also takes this verse as meaning "what is taken captive is every thought (νόημα), which is made to obey Christ" (See "Antisthenes and Odysseus, and Paul at War," 147). The NRSV has retained the RSV's translation.

[366]To my knowledge, only F. YOUNG/D.F. FORD, and S.K. WILLIAMS render ὑπακοὴ τοῦ Χριστοῦ in 2 Cor 10:5 exclusively as a subjective genitive – the "obedience of Christ." Young and Ford render the phrase thus in their translation without giving any explanation (see *Meaning and Truth in 2 Corinthians*, 239 and 271). Williams comments in a footnote that the Greek text in question "is subject to quite a different interpretation" than the objective genitive, and thinks it is likely that Paul sets forth here Christ's own obedience. See WILLIAMS, "Again *Pistis Christou*," *CBQ* 49 (1987) 431-47, here 435, n. 16. K. BARTH holds that the genitive in question is *both* subjective and objective, but this surely puts too much stress on the genitive. See *Church Dogmatics: Volume IV: The Doctrine of Reconciliation: Part 1*, ed. G.W. BROMILEY and T.F. TORRANCE, trans. G.W. BROMILEY (Edinburgh: T. & T. Clark, 1961) 194. Similarly, P.E. HUGHES, who translates the phrase "obedience of Christ," implies by his explanation that he takes Χριστοῦ both subjectively and objectively: "[Paul] earnestly desires that the members of the Corinthian church may learn what it means to bring both mind and will into complete submission to, and therefore harmony with, the mind and will of Christ." See *Paul's Second Epistle to the Corinthians,* 353. The last part of Hughes's comment, in my opinion, is right on the mark.

Conversely, the majority of commentators simply assume without explanation that the genitive is objective. See, e.g., J. LAMBRECHT, *Second Corinthians*, 155: "'Of Christ' is an objective genitive; so that they obey Christ." Cf. the similarly brief remark by FURNISH, *II Corinthians*, 458.

involving his attempt to bring the Corinthians to obey Christ. But is this what *the apostle* is really saying here?

Several factors suggest that this traditional understanding of ὑπακοὴ τοῦ Χριστοῦ in 2 Cor 10:5 should not be accepted uncritically:

1) As we have just seen, Paul begins this section of the letter with an appeal to Christ's gentleness and forbearance, an appeal that serves to contextualize all that follows. That is, the apostle has just alluded to the *ethos* of Jesus. Moreover, observe the formal parallelism between πραΰτης καὶ ἐπιείκεια τοῦ Χριστοῦ and ὑπακοὴ τοῦ Χριστοῦ. Given that the former phrase is universally recognized as a subjective genitive, why should the latter expression – which occurs only four verses later, and in the same paragraph – be considered an objective genitive?

2) Recall the discussion in the previous chapter of the importance of the character of Jesus in Romans. There I recounted Luke T. Johnson's argument for the subjective genitive reading of the phrase πίστις Χριστοῦ – as the "faithfulness of Christ" – in the interpretation of Rom 3:21-26. Moreover, recall Paul's statement in Rom 5:19: ". . . so, too, *by means of the one's obedience* (διὰ τῆς ὑπακοῆς τοῦ ἑνός) the many will be made righteous." The antecedent of τοῦ ἑνός is "the one human being, Jesus Christ" (ὁ εἷς ἄνθρωπος, Ἰησοῦς Χριστός; Rom 5:15). In fact, the apostle states that it is *through the human Jesus' obedience* that "grace reigns through righteousness to eternal life" (Rom 5:21). Thus, in a letter written shortly after 2 Corinthians, we are pointed to the importance of Jesus' faithfulness and obedience for Paul. Indeed, we saw that the apostle himself strongly suggests that what is meant (at least in part) by Jesus' faithfulness is his obedience.[367]

3) As we will see in Chapter Six, Paul exhorts the community throughout 2 Corinthians to tend to their own *ethos*. This strategy comes to a climax in 2 Cor 13:5, at the culmination of the apostle's presentation in 10:1-13:10, where he challenges the Corinthians to test themselves to see whether or not they are ἐν τῇ πίστει. The pertinent point to note here is that the very issue of *character* is prominent in this letter, especially in the latter chapters. Given this – and given that Paul explicitly alludes to Christ's *ethos* in 10:1 – is it not plausible that ὑπακοὴ τοῦ Χριστοῦ might refer to the *ethos* of Jesus?

---

[367]Recall JOHNSON'S argument that Rom 5:15-21 is "the plain explication" of Rom 3:21-26. See "Romans 3:21-26 and the Faith of Jesus," 89.

4) The apostle does not elsewhere signify obedience rendered to another person by using the genitive case. I will develop this point momentarily. For the time being, it is sufficient to observe that there are substantive reasons for positing that τοῦ Χριστοῦ should be read as a subjective genitive – namely, as "*Christ's* obedience."

To expand upon the fourth point: While it is grammatically possible to signify obedience to someone with the genitive of person,[368] Paul himself never utilizes this construction. Rather, he conveys the idea of obeying someone or something in one of two ways. First, the apostle uses the verb ὑπακούω + the *dative* case of the person or thing. He utilizes this construction eleven times in his writings. In five of these, a "thing" is the object of obedience: the body's passions (Rom 6:12); an unnamed object (Rom 6:16, the antecedent of the pronoun ᾧ is generic); the gospel (2x – Rom 10:16 and 2 Thess 1:8); and the message conveyed in Paul's letter (2 Thess 3:14). In the other six, a person or persons are the object of obedience: parents (Eph 6:1 and Col 3:20); earthly masters (Eph 6:5 and Col 3:22); Christ (Eph 6:5, verb implied); and Paul himself (Phil 2:12, object implied). The only time that Christ is mentioned as the object of obedience is in Eph 6:5: "Slaves, obey your earthly masters with fear and trembling, in singleness of heart, as [you obey] Christ (ὡς τῷ Χριστῷ)."[369]

Alternatively, the apostle uses the passive voice of the verb ὑποτάσσω ("subject oneself," "be subjected," and "obey")[370] + the *dative* case of the person or thing. He employs this expression (using the passive voice of the verb) eighteen times. In three of these, a "thing" is named as the object of one's submission or subjection: the law of God (Rom 8:7); futility (Rom 8:20); and

---

[368]Cf., e.g., *T. Gad* 8:3: τέκνα μου, ὑπακούσατε τοῦ πατρὸς ὑμῶν; and *Barn.* 9:1: εἰς ἀκοὴν ὠτίου ὑπήκουσάν μου [cf. LXX Ps 17:45 (Codex Alexandrinus)]. For the Greek text of *T. Gad*, see "Διαθήκη Γάδ," *The Greek Versions of the Testaments of the Twelve Patriarchs*, ed. R.H. CHARLES (London: Oxford University Press, 1908) 158-71. For the Greek text of the *Barn.*, see "ΒΑΡΝΑΒΑ ΕΠΙΣΤΟΛΗ," *Apostolic Fathers*, vol. 1, trans. K. LAKE, LCL (Cambridge, MA: Harvard University Press, 1985) 340-408. In addition, see BDAG, s.v. ὑπακούω, 1: DANKER notes that, in the LXX and papyri, the object of obedience is rendered in the genitive case more than in the dative.

[369]Paul's only other use of the verb ὑπακούω is in Rom 6:17. Here the object of obedience is rendered in the *accusative* – τύπον διδαχῆς ("standard of teaching").

[370]See BDAG, s.v. ὑποτάσσω, 1.b.β.

the righteousness of God (Rom 10:3). Among the persons listed as the object(s) of submission/obedience are: governing authorities (Rom 13:1; 13:5, object implied; and Titus 3:1); prophets (1 Cor 14:32); leaders in the community (1 Cor 16:16); fellow members of the community (Eph 5:21); husbands (1 Cor 14:34, object implied; Eph 5:22, verb implied; Eph 5:24; Col 3:18; and Titus 2:5); and masters (Titus 2:9). In addition, in 1 Cor 15:27-28 Paul says that, in the end (τὸ τέλος), all things will be subjected to Christ, who himself will then be subjected to God. Once again, only in Ephesians is Christ listed as the object of human submission: "As the church is subject to Christ (ὡς ἡ ἐκκλησία ὑποτάσσεται τῷ Χριστῷ), so also wives [are to be subject] to husbands in all things" (Eph 5:24). The point here is that the apostle uses the *dative* case to indicate the recipient or object of obedience/submission. Observe, too, that only *twice* does the apostle name Christ as the object of humans' obedience. Moreover, notice that both instances occur within the same Ephesian *haustafel*, and that obedience to Christ is mentioned both times in a subordinate clause as the standard for submission to another human being.

Even more to the point is Paul's use of the phrase ὑπακοή + the genitive of person. In Rom 15:8 the apostle speaks of the fact that Christ accomplishes through him the "obedience of [the] nations" (ὑπακοὴν ἐθνῶν). In Rom 16:19 Paul tells the church in Rome that "your obedience" (ἡ ὑμῶν ὑπακοή) is known to all. In 2 Cor 7:15 he recalls to the Corinthians Titus's joy at "the obedience of all of you" (τὴν πάντων ὑμῶν ὑπακοήν). In Phlm 21 the apostle expresses his confidence in Philemon's obedience to him (see τῇ ὑπακοῇ σου). And in 2 Cor 10:6 – in the immediate context of the phrase in question – Paul warns the Corinthians that he is ready to punish all disobedience when "your obedience" (ὑμῶν ἡ ὑπακοή) is complete. In all these instances, the genitive of person following ὑπακοή is incontestably subjective. And as noted above, the same is the case in Rom 5:19, *where the apostle refers to the obedience of the one human being, Jesus Christ.*

The crucial point here is that the evidence based on Paul's usage of obedience language is overwhelmingly in favor of reading ὑπακοὴ τοῦ Χριστοῦ as a subjective genitive.[371] Given this – and recalling the first three

[371]Thus, the following comment by R. BULTMANN misses the mark: "The εἰς τὴν ὑπακοὴν τοῦ Χριστοῦ is the equivalent of εἰς τὸ ὑπακούειν τῷ Χριστῷ" (*The Second Letter to the Corinthians*, 186). The very fact that Paul uses a different construction ought to alert us to the real possibility that he meant something different than the objective genitive that Bultmann assumed.

points mentioned above – I contend that the apostle refers in 2 Cor 10:5 to Christ's obedience, and that he summons the Corinthians to "complete" their obedience (10:6) by participating in the pattern of Jesus' obedience to God and to God's will. Indeed, in the next section I will demonstrate that Paul has already foreshadowed this allusion to Jesus' obedience. Before doing so, however, it is necessary to (1) offer a preliminary suggestion of what the apostle means by "Christ's obedience"; (2) indicate the function of Paul's allusion in 2 Cor 10:5; and (3) broach the issue of the "knowledge of God" raised in this passage, as well as the relationship of this knowledge to the *ethos* of Jesus.

To what does the expression "Christ's obedience" refer? Paul refers to Jesus' obedience in Phil 2:8 as well as in Rom 5:19. In Philippians he writes, "And having been found in human form [Christ Jesus] lowered himself, becoming obedient (ὑπήκοος) unto death, [the] death of a cross" (Phil 2:7b-8). Observe that Jesus' obedience was rendered to God, who in turn exalted him (Phil 2:9).[372] In this passage, the reference to Jesus' obedience follows directly upon the declaration of his becoming a human being (σχήματι εὑρεθεὶς ὡς ἄνθρωπος, Phil 2:7b). Thus, the apostle refers here to the human Jesus' obedience. He states that Jesus was obedient *unto death* – μέχρι θανάτου. The preposition μέχρι marks the degree or measure by which something is done, in the sense of "to the point of."[373] That is, Jesus' obedience to God was such that he was willing to be put to death. This preposition also marks the continuation of something in time, in the sense of "until."[374] I suggest that Paul intends this sense of the word as well. That is, Jesus was obedient *throughout*

---

[372]For in-depth discussion of the various exegetical issues in Phil 2:5-11 and of the different interpretations proffered, see R.P. MARTIN, *A Hymn of Christ: Philippians 2:5-11 in Recent Interpretation & in the Setting of Early Christian Worship* (Downers Grove, IL: Intervarsity Press, 1997) [originally published as *Carmen Christi: Philippians ii.5-11 in Recent Interpretation & in the Setting of Early Christian Worship* (London: Cambridge University Press, 1967)]. I will return to this passage in my analysis of 2 Cor 4:13 below.

[373]See BDAG, s.v. μέχρι, 3. Cf. 2 Tim 2:9: ἐν ᾧ κακοπαθῶ μέχρι δεσμῶν ὡς κακοῦργος ("for which I suffer even to the point [of wearing] fetters as a criminal"); and Phil 2:30.

[374]See BDAG, s.v. μέχρι, 2.a. Cf. Rom 5:14: ἐβασίλευσεν ὁ θάνατος ἀπὸ 'Αδὰμ μέχρι Μωϋσέως ("death reigned from Adam to Moses"); and 1 Tim 6:14.

his life "until death."[375] Thus, I propose that ὑπακοὴ τοῦ Χριστοῦ refers, in the first place, *to a habitual mode of human existence* lived in obedience to God. Moreover, according to Phil 2:8, Jesus' manner of living was marked by lowering himself (ἐταπείνωσεν ἑαυτόν), even to the point of offering his life for others. Further analysis of the apostle's references to Christ's *ethos* in 2 Corinthians – especially his ναί (1:19-20), his πίστις (4:13), his ἀγάπη (5:14), and his χάρις (8:9) – will substantiate these claims.

Returning to 2 Cor 10:5, how does the reference to Christ's obedience function in this passage? Paul states that he "take[s] captive every thought εἰς τὴν ὑπακοὴν τοῦ Χριστοῦ." The preposition εἰς here expresses the goal or result of the apostle's activity.[376] That is, he takes captive every thought in order to bring about a particular result among the Corinthians. Admittedly, in this instance we cannot take the phrase ὑπακοὴ τοῦ Χριστοῦ literally, for surely Paul does not mean that he intends to bring about Christ's obedience. What he does want to effect, however, is obedience *like* Christ's. Thus, I render 2 Cor 10:5b in this way: "and we take captive every thought unto 'Christ-obedience.'" The apostle seeks to bring about Christ-like obedience among the Corinthians. With these words, Paul encourages them to behave in a manner that reflects their possession of the νοῦς Χριστοῦ (cf. 1 Cor 2:16). As will be shown in Chapter Six, the apostle calls forth from the Corinthians a response of obedience throughout the epistle (2 Cor 2:9, 7:15, and 9:13 – indeed, note that the latter passage is located in the paragraph preceding 10:1-6). Now, near the close of the letter, Paul alludes to the obedience exhibited by Jesus. With this allusion

---

[375]This reading of Jesus' obedience is given support by E. KÄSEMANN in his analysis of the obedience of the "second Anthropos," Jesus. Käsemann observes that the statement in Rom 5:19 is *not* limited to the cross. Whereas Käsemann's emphasis is on the commencement of the end-time by the "second Anthropos," by implication he seems to recognize the *ongoing* aspect of Jesus' obedience. See *Commentary on Romans*, 157.

[376]See BDAG, s.v. εἰς, 4.e. Cf. 2 Cor 7:9: ἐλυπήθητε εἰς μετάνοιαν ("you were grieved into repentance"); Rom 6:16: [you are slaves] ἤτοι ἁμαρτίας εἰς θάνατον ἢ ὑπακοῆς εἰς δικαιοσύνην ("either of sin leading to death or of obedience leading to righteousness"); and Rom 8:15.

the apostle gives to the Corinthians a *standard* by which to gauge the completion of their own obedience (10:6).[377]

Lastly, it is important to observe the connection that Paul makes between right thinking, especially as it pertains to God, and the *ethos* of Jesus. At this point, I can only suggest a line of thought. Clearly the apostle is concerned with "right thinking" in 2 Cor 10:4-5. He claims that, with the help of God's power, he destroys *arguments* (λογισμούς, 10:4) and all pride lifted up "against the *knowledge* of God" (κατὰ τῆς γνώσεως τοῦ θεοῦ, 10:5). He also takes captive *every thought* (πᾶν νόημα) unto Christ-obedience. Earlier in the letter (as we will see in Chapter Five), Paul links "the *knowledge* of the glory of God" with the "πρόσωπον of Jesus Christ" (4:6).[378] Reference to Christ's πρόσωπον ("face") can also suggest the *entire person* of Jesus. Thus, the apostle intimates in 2 Cor 4:6 that knowledge of God is connected with what was revealed in the person of Jesus, including his *ethos*. In light of this, I submit that Paul's reference to destroying *all pride* (πᾶν ὕψωμα, 10:5a) erected against the knowledge of God is strategically placed in the midst of allusions to Jesus' gentleness, forbearance, and obedience. As will be observed throughout the present chapter, this relationship between right knowledge on the one hand, and the story and character of Jesus on the other, is a recurring theme.

---

[377]So, rightly, WILLIAMS, "Again *Pistis Christou*," 435, n. 16: "I think it likely that Paul is here setting forth Christ's own obedience, later emphasized in Romans 5, as the standard against which the Corinthian Christians should judge their own." I categorically disagree with KECK'S assessment in "'Jesus' in Romans," 459-60: "Given the difference between sin and death, Paul does not say that we participate in Christ's sin-breaking obedience; *nor does he urge us to imitate Christ's obedience*, for that would make it a requirement, a law" (italics added).

To argue negatively: What would "obedience *to* Christ" mean in this context? What would Christ be calling the Corinthians to obey? The traditional interpretation seems to presume that the answers to these questions are obvious. But are they?

[378]See Chapter Five, Section III. It might be argued that, in 2 Cor 10:5, the phrase γνῶσις τοῦ θεοῦ – rendered as an *objective* genitive (i.e., as "knowledge of God") – leads naturally to reading ὑπακοὴ τοῦ Χριστοῦ as an objective genitive. That is, it can be objected that interpreting the latter as subjective seems to be an arbitrary decision in light of what has just preceded. The force of this objection deteriorates, however, when one takes into account a similar move by Paul in 4:6. That is, following the phrase γνῶσις τῆς δόξης τοῦ θεοῦ (where δόξης is an objective genitive), the apostle refers to the πρόσωπον 'Ιησοῦ Χριστοῦ, a *subjective* genitive (pertaining to Jesus!).

It is now time to return to the claim made above that Paul foreshadows Jesus' obedience before his direct reference to it in 2 Cor 10:5. In fact, the apostle hints at "the obedience of Christ" in the opening chapter of 2 Corinthians.

IV. The "Yes" of Jesus Christ, the Son of God (2 Cor 1:19-20)

Paul's first reference to Jesus in the body of the letter occurs in 2 Cor 1:19-20, where he associates Jesus with the particle ναί ("Yes"). The immediate context is the apostle's attempt to explain a change that he had made in his travel plans, plans that involved a proposed visit to Corinth which he failed to make (1:15-17). Apparently, the Corinthians called his trustworthiness into question on the basis of this change in plans. After narrating what his original plans had been (1:15-16), Paul defends the change by suggesting that it was due to his following God's lead (1:17): "Was I acting with fickleness when I wanted [to visit you]? Or do I plan the things which I plan at the human level (κατὰ σάρκα), so that yes being yes and no being no is in my hands (παρ' ἐμοί – i.e., rests with me)?"[379] With these words, the apostle implies that he operates under the guidance of God, and that his original plans had to be changed in order to follow God's call. In 1:18, however, Paul quickly reassures the Corinthians that the gospel message (λόγος) which he and his co-workers Timothy and Silvanus had proclaimed to them is certain and trustworthy, not a

---

[379]I follow the reading proposed by F. YOUNG in "Note on 2 Corinthians 1:17b," *JTS* 37 (1986) 404-15. For a less detailed explanation, see YOUNG and FORD, *Meaning and Truth in 2 Corinthians*, 100-104. Young's reading takes seriously the presence of the definite article before the first instances of ναί and οὔ, and shows the syntactical parallel with Jas 5:12. She also counters the traditional assumption that Paul's use of ναί and οὔ is an explanation of what it means to act κατὰ σάρκα. The problem with the traditional assumption is that it involves inserting words into the text (cf., e.g., RSV – "*ready to say* yes and no *at once*"). Citing 2 Cor 1:12, Young suggests that κατὰ σάρκα refers to making plans in reliance on human wisdom rather than in reliance on God. Her reading also gives greater prominence to the phrase παρ' ἐμοί, which she takes as the predicate or complement after the verb ᾖ. (She then has to add an implied εἰμί following τὸ ναί and τὸ οὔ.) Young tellingly notes that John Chrysostom, whose first language was Greek, read the text in this manner.

For reading παρά + the dative as marking the connection of a quality or characteristic with a person – in the sense of "having something/nothing to do with" – see BDAG, s.v. παρά, B.4. Cf. Rom 2:11 and 9:14; and Eph 6:9.

matter of "yes and no." The apostle offers this assurance in two ways. First, he begins with an appeal to God's fidelity (πιστὸς δὲ ὁ θεός, 1:18a) as a warrant for what follows. Second, he grounds (cf. γάρ, 1:19a) the sureness of the gospel proclamation in the person of Jesus himself, "who did not become Yes and No, but in him the Yes has come to be" (1:19b). Moreover, concerning *all* God's promises, the Yes (τὸ ναί) has come to be in Christ (1:20a).[380] In alluding to God's promises and the Yes associated with Jesus, Paul draws upon the story and character of Jesus.

The question immediately arises: How is this Yes, which is so intimately connected with Jesus, to be understood? At first glance, the solemn reference to "the Son of God, Jesus Christ" (ὁ τοῦ θεοῦ υἱὸς Ἰησοῦς Χριστός, 2 Cor 1:19a) might be taken as a reference to the resurrected Lord on the basis of Rom 1:3-4.[381] I submit, however, that 2 Cor 1:19-20 offers a number of clues that Paul refers here primarily to Jesus in his humanity: the verb γίνομαι in 1:19b; the prepositional phrase ἐν αὐτῷ in 1:19b-1:20a; the particle ναί in 1:19b-1:20a; and the phrase τὸ ἀμήν that follows in 1:20b. Each of these clues requires closer examination.

The two main verbs in 2 Cor 1:19 are forms of γίνομαι. In skeletal form, this verse reads: Jesus Christ, the Son of God, *did not become* (ἐγένετο, aorist tense) Yes and No, but the Yes *has come to be* (γέγονεν, perfect tense) in him. To be sure, the verb γίνομαι can serve as a substitute or synonym for the verb "to be" (εἰμί), and several translators and commentators take it as such here.[382] But γίνομαι can also bear the stronger sense of "come to be," that is, "*become*." Moreover, with reference to persons or things, γίνομαι can be used

---

[380]Supplying γέγονεν from the preceding verse.

[381]"... [the gospel] concerning his Son who was descended from David according to [the] flesh and *who was designated 'Son of God' in power* according to [the] Spirit of holiness by [his] resurrection from the dead, *Jesus Christ our Lord*."

[382]See, e.g., RSV: The Son of God "was not Yes and No; but in him it is always Yes." Cf. MARTIN, *2 Corinthians*, 22-23; FURNISH, *II Corinthians*, 132; and P.W. BARNETT, *The Second Epistle to the Corinthians*, 103.

to indicate a change in nature or an entry into a new condition.[383] I propose that we take seriously Paul's choice of γίνομαι rather than εἰμί.[384] Note further that the subject of 1:19a is Jesus Christ, and thus Jesus is the *agent* of becoming. While 1:19a tells what Jesus did *not* become, 1:19b indicates what "in Jesus" (ἐν αὐτῷ) did come to be at some time in the past and still is[385] – namely, ναί. It is pertinent to note, too, that the apostle uses the verb γίνομαι elsewhere in connection with the story of Jesus' humanity.[386] The language of 2 Cor 1:19 thus strongly suggests that something in the past occurred in connection with the human Jesus that resulted in the entrance into a new condition which continues to have effects in the present.

The prepositional phrase ἐν αὐτῷ ("in him," referring to Jesus) is prominent in 2 Cor 1:19b-20a: ". . . but [the] Yes has come to be *in him*. For as many promises of God [there are], *in him* the Yes [has come to be]." While the preposition ἐν can denote a static locative sense, it can also serve as a marker of agency or cause. Used (as here) in conjunction with a person, it can

---

[383]See BDAG, s.v. γίνομαι, 5.a. Cf. Gal 3:13: Christ redeemed us from the curse of the law, γενόμενος ὑπὲρ ἡμῶν κατάρα ("having become a curse for us"); and Rom 4:18: Abraham hoped against hope, εἰς τὸ γενέσθαι αὐτὸν πατέρα πολλῶν ἐθνῶν ("that he might become father of many nations").

[384]M.E. THRALL (*II Corinthians*, 1.147, n. 147) hesitates to attach too much "theological weight" to γίνομαι in 2 Cor 1:19, although she concedes that the perfect tense "may be significant." On the contrary, I contend that we should take the "strong sense" of the verb into account. BULTMANN'S distinction between ἐγένετο as referring to Christ's mission and γέγονεν as referring to his presence in the kerygma or in the community is unfounded. See *The Second Letter to the Corinthians*, 40.

[385]See BDF, § 340: "The perfect [tense] combines in itself, so to speak, the present and the aorist in that it denotes the *continuance* of *completed action*" (italics in the text); cf. BDF, § 342.

[386]See Gal 4:4: "But when the fullness of time came, God sent his Son, born of woman (γενόμενον ἐκ γυναικός), born under [the] law (γενόμενον ὑπὸ νόμον); and Phil 2:8: "He lowered himself, having become obedient (γενόμενονς ὑπήκοος) unto death."

mean "with the help of" or "through."[387] Reading ἐν as a marker of agency in 1:19b-20a, I suggest, renders a better, more coherent reading of the text. Recall that Jesus Christ is the subject – that is, the *agent* – of the sentence beginning in 1:19a. And although Paul refers to "God's promises" at the outset of 1:20, the main clause of 1:20a reads "in [Jesus Christ] the Yes has come to be." That is, the apostle links the notion of ναί most intimately with Jesus, rather than with θεός.[388] It is Jesus Christ who did not become Yes and No. And it is "in him," in the sense of "through him," that the Yes has come to be.

This leads to Paul's employment of the particle ναί. This word can perform several functions. It can: (1) denote an affirmative response to a question; (2) serve to add emphasis (e.g., "yes, indeed") or give solemn assurance ("surely") to one's statement; (3) function to express agreement with a statement by another (in the sense of "certainly"); or (4) be part of a play on words used with οὔ ("no").[389] Now, which of these functions apply to the

---

[387]See BDAG, s.v. ἐν, 6. Cf. Rom 3:24: διὰ τῆς ἀπολυτρώσεως τῆς ἐν Χριστῷ Ἰησοῦ ("by means of the redemption that is through Christ Jesus"); and 1 Cor 6:2: εἰ ἐν ὑμῖν κρίνεται ὁ κόσμος ("if the world is to be judged by you"). Cf., *1 Apol.* 60:3: ἐὰν προσβλέπητε τῷ τύπῳ τούτῳ καὶ πιστεύητε ἐν αὐτῷ σωθήσεσθε ("if you gaze upon this type and believe, you will be saved through it" – referring to the "type of cross" Moses fashioned in the wilderness). For the Greek text of *1 Apol.*, see *Iustini Martyris: Apologiae pro Christianis*, ed. M. MARCOVICH, PTS 38 (New York: Walter de Gruyter, 1994) 31-133.

[388]*Pace* F.W. DANKER'S assessment (*II Corinthians*, 39): "As always, God is Paul's model. God does not talk out of both sides of the mouth, nor does Paul." THRALL rightly recognizes the shift in 1:19-20: ". . . in vv. 19-20 [Paul] emphasises *the reliability of Christ*, who puts all the divine promises into effect." See *II Corinthians*, 1.146 (italics added).

[389]See BDAG, s.v. ναί. For ναί in the sense of giving an affirmative response to a question, see, e.g., Matt 9:28 and John 21:15-16. For ναί in the sense of adding emphasis, see, e.g., Luke 10:21 and Phlm 20. For ναί in the sense of adding solemnity or assurance, see Rev 22:20. For ναί in the sense of expressing agreement with another's statement, see Rev 14:13 (ναί, λέγει τὸ πνεῦμα – "'Yes,' says the Spirit" – in response to a voice from heaven declaring the blessedness of those who die in the Lord) and Matt 15:27. Finally, for ναί in wordplay with οὔ, see Matt 5:37 and Jas 5:12. In addition, see P.S. MINEAR, "Yes or No: The Demand for Honesty in the Early Church," *NovT* 13 (1971) 1-13.

apostle's association *of Jesus* with τὸ ναί? The first and last do not. Jesus as Yes does not answer a question posed in the text. Neither is the apostle making a play on words. (The parallels with Matt 5:37 and Jas 5:12 are not as substantive as they may seem. Those texts pertain to oath-taking, which is not the issue concerning Jesus and τὸ ναί in 2 Cor 1:19-20.) The second function – giving solemn assurance to a statement – is a possibility, although Paul's solemn assurance rests primarily in *God's* faithfulness (πιστὸς δὲ ὁ θεός, 1:18a).

Now, it is important to recall that Paul has just associated "yes" and "no" with his own carrying out the will of God (2 Cor 1:17). This suggests that the third function of ναί – expressing agreement with another's word – is the one that most applies here. In 2 Cor 1:19-20a the apostle's focus on Yes is now in connection with Jesus (rather than his own ναί as in 1:17). Thus, I submit that Paul's allusion to Jesus' ναί connotes the latter's active response, his willingness to choose for someone and/or something. In this case, Jesus' ναί must be directed *to God*; the apostle alludes here to Jesus' consent *to obey God* and God's will for him (cf. Rom 5:19 and Phil 2:8).[390] Indeed, as Paul will make clear in 2 Cor 5:14-21, Jesus actively cooperated with God's plan of salvation for the world. In fact, notice that in the present passage, the apostle links Christ's Yes with God's faithfulness (1:18a) and God's promises (1:20a). Jesus' ναί also signifies that he *chose* to obey, a decision from which he did not waver – "he did not become Yes and No."[391] Such commitment marks, in effect, a new state of being. Moreover, Paul's use of the perfect tense of γέγονεν signifies that Jesus' ναί not only occurred in the past, but also has effected a state or

---

[390]Note also that Paul begins his opening prayer period by blessing "the God and Father of our Lord Jesus Christ" (1:3). Jesus is thus introduced in a "subordinate" manner vis-à-vis the Father – that is, the Father is also Jesus' God. Moreover, Paul introduces himself as "apostle of Christ Jesus *through the will of God*" (1:1). Hence, at the very outset of the letter, Paul gives primacy to God and God's will. MATERA rightly connects the ναί in 1:19-20a with "the faithfulness of Jesus Christ, the Son of God." Indeed, Matera interprets this faithfulness in terms of Jesus' perfect obedience to God. See *II Corinthians*, 55.

[391]Cf. J. MURPHY-O'CONNOR, *The Theology of the Second Letter to the Corinthians*, NTT (Cambridge: Cambridge University Press, 1991) 24: "He never wavered in his commitment, and his whole existence was the affirmative response that God expected . . . ."

condition that exists in the present time. Hence, I propose that the apostle's reference to ναί in 1:19-20 is an allusion to the *ethos* of Jesus – specifically to his obedience and (as will be seen) his faithfulness.[392]

Second Corinthians 1:20b provides another clue for understanding Paul's language about Jesus. This verse speaks of the salutary effects of Jesus' Yes. Translated literally, the apostle states: "Therefore, through him, [there is] the Amen to God for glory through us" (διὸ καὶ δι' αὐτοῦ τὸ ἀμήν τῷ θεῷ πρὸς δόξαν δι' ἡμῶν).[393] The phrase τὸ ἀμήν is often taken with reference to a liturgical formula.[394] For instance, the RSV translates 1:20b: "That is why *we utter* the Amen through [Jesus], to the glory of God" (italics added). This translation takes great syntactical, grammatical, and contextual liberties with the Greek text, adding as it does the verb "utter" and making "we" the subject of the clause. The first person plural pronoun (ἡμῶν) is the object of a preposition located at the end of the sentence. It is not a grammatical subject. The "Amen" is somehow directed *to* God (dative case), and the notion of "glory" is attached to this, rather than to a prayer "uttered" *for* the "glory of God" (which would require the phrase δόξα θεοῦ). Finally, there is nothing in the previous context that merits a liturgical inference. In 1:18-20 the apostle neither concludes a prayer or blessing with ἀμήν (as in, e.g., Rom 1:25, 9:5, 11:36, 15:33, and

---

[392]Arguing from different bases – esp. from a philological analysis of the particle ναί in relation to contracts and covenants – J. D.M. DERRETT arrives at a similar conclusion: "Christ is faithful and his Yes has not merely completed our entitlement to the promises of Abraham, but also *set an example of reliable behaviour* (on the part of his 'slaves,' i.e., the missionaries)." See DERRETT, "Ναί (2 Cor 1:19-20)," *Filología Neotestamentaria* 4 (1991) 205-9, here 208 (italics added).

[393]It is little wonder that A.T. HANSON characterized 2 Cor 1:20 as "perhaps the most compressed verse in the entire New Testament"! See *The Paradox of the Cross in the Thought of St Paul*, JSNTSup 17 (Sheffield: Sheffield Academic Press, 1987) 19.

[394]See, e.g., BDAG, s.v. ἀμήν, 1.a. In addition, cf. BARRETT, *The Second Epistle to the Corinthians*, 77-78: "Amen suggests a liturgical context. . . ; upon the words 'through Jesus Christ God's Son' (see verse 18), the congregation say *Amen*"; and PLUMMER, *II Corinthians*, 38: "This doubtless refers to the Amen in public worship . . . which the Church had taken over from the Synagogue." Cf., too, WINDISCH, *Der zweite Korintherbrief*, 69; BULTMANN, *The Second Letter to the Corinthians*, 41; FURNISH, *II Corinthians*, 147; MARTIN, *2 Corinthians*, 27; and BARNETT, *The Second Epistle to the Corinthians*, 109.

16:27), nor does he refer to prayer (as in 1 Cor 14:16). In short, the liturgical interpretation of 2 Cor 1:20b is suspect, presumed rather than demonstrated.

Another more plausible possibility is that Paul deliberately counterposes the "Amen" in 2 Cor 1:20b to πιστὸς ὁ θεός ("as God is *faithful*") in 1:18a. Observe that ἀμήν is the Greek transliteration of the Hebrew אמן, a term that denotes "faithfulness" when used in conjunction with God.[395] From the same root comes the more common noun אמונה, which means "steadfastness, fidelity." When used in the HB to describe *human* conduct – and more specifically, *human character* – אמונה is often associated with "righteousness" (צדק),[396] most notably in Hab 2:4 (וצדיק באמונתו יחיה – "and the righteous man lives by his faithfulness"). [Recall from the discussion of the character of Jesus in Romans how important Hab 2:4 is for Paul (cf. esp. Rom 1:17).] I suggest that, in 2 Cor 1:20b, the apostle draws upon this notion of human character and conduct, a notion that connotes steadfast and unwavering devotion and faithfulness in a life lived in accord with the dictates *and character* of God who is πιστός. Thus, Paul uses τὸ ἀμήν here to signify a mode of human existence, one marked by openness and fidelity to God and the ways of God. Jesus' ναί, then, *is* his ἀμήν to God (cf. τῷ θεῷ), a commitment to God and God's will that has resulted in the new condition (in the sense that it did not exist before Jesus' Yes) discussed above in conjunction with γίνομαι.

Notice, furthermore, that it is through the agency of Jesus (cf. διά αὐτοῦ) that there is "the Amen," which is directed "to God" (τῷ θεῷ) "for glory" (πρὸς δόξαν) "through us" (δι' ἡμῶν). In other words, Jesus empowers a steadfast response of fidelity to God, which redounds in glory (a key theme in 2 Cor 3:18-4:6) through Paul and others like him who have received the Spirit's "christing" and "sealing" action (1:21-22).[397] Presuming a likeness of effect to its cause, I submit that this resulting human fidelity to God

---

[395]Cf. HB Isa 65:16 (2x) – אלהי אמן ("God of faithfulness"). See BDBG, s.v. אמן.

[396]See BDBG, s.v. אמונה, and esp. 1 Sam 26:23 and Prov 12:17; cf. Isa 59:4.

[397]I will develop this point in greater detail in Chapter Five, Section II.

is grounded in Jesus' own faithfulness to God, the faithfulness that the apostle indicates by associating Jesus with ναί in 1:19b-20a.[398]

Second Corinthians 1:19-20 therefore yields a cogent, rich reading when one recognizes that the linchpin to Paul's argument is the *character* of Jesus – especially his obedience and faithfulness (as we saw in Romans). "Jesus Christ, the Son of God"[399] is after all the subject of 1:19a, and, in effect, of all that follows. Note the cumulative effect of reading γίνομαι as "become" in the sense of Jesus' entering into and bringing about a new state of being (i.e., human

---

[398]W.C. VAN UNNIK makes a much more radical proposal. He argues that the key to understanding 2 Cor 1:15-24 is to recognize Paul's word-play in these verses. That is, he asserts that this passage is held together by אמן and several cognates – the Aramaic equivalents of πιστός, γέγονεν, ναί, and ὁ βεβαιῶν. See "Reisepläne und Amen-Sagen, Zusammenhang und Gedankenfolge in 2. Korinther i 15-24," in *Sparsa Collecta: The Collected Essays of W.C. van Unnik*, Part 1 (Leiden: E.J. Brill, 1973) 144-59. Van Unnik pushes the semantic connections and etymologizing too far, however. For a critique, see J. BARR, *The Semantics of Biblical Language* (Oxford: Oxford University Press, 1961) 168-71.

I concur in the main with the following assessment by THRALL concerning the Yes brought about in Christ: ". . . it may mean also that *Christ himself, through his faithful obedience to God's purposes* (Phil 2.8), *has said Yes to God.* He has affirmed the will of God, said Amen to God's requirements. *He has also, potentially, set the human race off on a new path of obedience*, by reversing the disobedience of Adam (Rom 5.19). It is therefore through his agency, δι' αὐτοῦ, that *believers are themselves enabled to say Amen to the purposes of God* – an Amen expressed in the liturgy, but *expressed* also *in their whole existence.*" See *II Corinthians*, 1.150 (italics added). Cf. Rom 6:11: ζῶντας τῷ θεῷ ἐν Χριστῷ Ἰησοῦ ("living for God in Christ Jesus").

[399]I submit that any supposition, on the basis of Rom 1:3-4, that ὁ υἱὸς τοῦ θεοῦ is a title referring exclusively to the *resurrected* Jesus is erroneous. Cf. Gal 2:20, where Paul uses this title in connection with Christ's πίστις, which is extrapolated by the clause "who loved me and gave himself for me." That the apostle refers to Christ as God's Son in 2 Cor 1:19-20 is not surprising, since his obedience and faithfulness exhibit his *filial* devotion to God. For more on Paul's use of the title "Son of God," see W. KRAMER, *Christ, Lord, Son of God*, SBT 50, trans. B. HARDY (Naperville, Ill.: Alec R. Allenson, 1966) 183-94; and, M. HENGEL, *The Son of God: The Origin of Christology and the History of Jewish-Hellenistic Religion*, trans. J. BOWDEN (Philadelphia: Fortress, 1976) 7-15. I submit that it is too easy to draw quick inferences from Paul's use of christological titles. Careful exegesis in each instance must be the ultimate criterion for determining the apostle's meaning.

faithfulness to God); of taking ἐν αὐτῷ as signifying agency, meaning "through Jesus"; of understanding ναί as Jesus' active, willing response to the "word" (= will) of another (in this case, God's); and of interpreting τὸ ἀμήν as referring to human character and conduct marked by fidelity to God which comes about through Jesus. Such a reading also helps make sense of the apostle's use of the perfect tense of γίνομαι in 1:19b and 1:20a (implied). That is, Jesus' sustained Yes to God and to God's will, an assent that took place in the past, still has continuing effects: Not only is Jesus Christ now "Lord" (cf. 4:5), but he also continues to empower others to live in obedience and fidelity to God.[400]

Romans 3:21-26 (the re-statement of Paul's thesis concerning the gospel in 1:16-17) provides another perspective on 2 Cor 1:19-20. To be sure, the apostle's language in the two passages is different. Their structure and content, however, are remarkably similar. Both passages concern the working out of God's covenantal relationship with God's people – in Rom 3:21, "God's righteousness as borne witness to by the law and the prophets"; in 2 Cor 1:20, "all God's promises." Both passages emphasize God's faithfulness (cf. Rom 3:3[401]; 2 Cor 1:18). In both, Jesus plays the pivotal role in implementing God's plan – in Rom 3:22, "through the faithfulness of Jesus Christ," and in Rom 3:24, "by means of the redemption that is through Christ Jesus"; in 2 Cor 1:19, "in him the Yes [has come to be]." The main verb in each passage is in the perfect

---

[400]Cf. the following observations by M.D. HOOKER: "Christian faith is the response to God's faithfulness, but it is also a sharing in Christ's faithfulness. Believers share in Christ's faithfulness because, like him, they trust in God, and because they trust in God, who is faithfulness, they themselves stand firm." See "From God's Faithfulness to Ours: Another Look at 2 Corinthians 1:17-24," in *Paul and the Corinthians: Studies on a Community in Conflict. Essays in Honour of Margaret Thrall*, NovTSup 109, ed. T.J. BURKE and J.K. ELLIOTT (Leiden: Brill, 2003) 233-39 (here, 239). While I am sympathetic to Hooker's appraisal, great care must be exercised in setting forth the similarities – and dissimilarities – between Jesus' πίστις (ναί) and that of Christians. I will take this up in the following section.

In my exegesis of 2 Cor 1:21-22 in Chapter Five, I will indicate how 1:17-22 functions as an argumentative unit (*pace* LONG, who sees these verses as "discordant").

[401]R.B. HAYS argues persuasively that the expressions πίστις θεοῦ (Rom 3:3), θεοῦ δικαιοσύνη (3:5; cf. 3:21-22), and ἀλήθεια θεοῦ (3:7) are all subjective genitives which are, in effect, synonymous attributes of God. At issue in Rom 3 is God's faithfulness/righteousness/truth – in short, God's *integrity*. See HAYS, "Psalm 143 and the Logic of Romans 3," *JBL* 99 (1980) 107-15, esp. 110-11.

tense, signaling that what Jesus did continues to have effects – in Rom 3:21, πεφανέρωται; in 2 Cor 1:19, γέγονεν. Lastly, the continuing effects of Jesus' faithfulness are somehow communicated through the empowerment of his followers – in Rom 3:22, "for those who [in turn] are faithful"; in 2 Cor 1:20, "the Amen to God for glory [comes to be] through us." As in Romans, so too in 2 Corinthians, Paul alludes to the humanity of Jesus in terms of the latter's obedience and faithfulness. His shorthand for this in 2 Cor 1:19-20 is Jesus' Yes.

Thus, at the outset of 2 Corinthians, the apostle expressly engages the *ethos* of Jesus and its ongoing significance. He returns to this theme a few chapters later when he alludes to the faithfulness of Christ.

V. Jesus' Faithfulness (2 Cor 4:13)

How Paul embodies the character of Jesus is the topic of Chapter Five. For now, it is sufficient to observe the apostle's description of the paradoxical nature of this transformation in 2 Cor 4:7-15: Paul and his co-workers[402] endure many sufferings and hardships; indeed, death seems to be what is most at work in them. And yet, God's power to bring life to others is enacted through them. This much is clear. What is less straightforward is *how* the story and character of Jesus function here. I propose that the key to understanding this passage lies in the recognition of the apostle's appropriation and use of LXX Pss 114-115, psalms to which he alludes in 2 Cor 4:13. Paul draws upon a christological reading of these texts, a reading that unfolds a rich portrait of Jesus and his πίστις. Before demonstrating this claim, however, I will first draw attention to a peculiar characteristic of 2 Cor 4:5-14 – namely, Paul's use of the name "Jesus" – as well as to how the apostle points to the story and *ethos* of Jesus in 4:10 and 4:11.

One of the striking features of 2 Cor 4:5-14 is the concentrated use of Jesus' personal name. In fact, six of the eighteen instances of the unadorned name "Jesus" in Paul's writings occur in this brief span: once in 4:5 and 4:14; two times each in 4:10 and 4:11.[403] Ordinarily, the apostle associates the

---

[402]The context demands that the "we" of 2 Cor 4:7-15 refers to Paul and his associates.

[403]Cf. Rom 3:26; 8:11; and 10:9; 1 Cor 12:3 (2x); 2 Cor 11:4; Gal 6:17; Eph 4:21; Phil 2:10; and 1 Thess 1:10 and 4:14 (2x). In addition, there is strong manuscript evidence for reading *two* occurrences of "Jesus" in 2 Cor 4:14. See B.M. METZGER, *A Textual*

messianic title "Christ" and/or the title "Lord" with the name Jesus. When Paul does refer solely to the personal name Jesus – as was suggested in the review of Luke T. Johnson's analysis of Rom 3:21-26 – the emphasis is on Jesus' *human* identity.[404] For instance, in other letters the apostle names Jesus as the one whom God raised from the dead, just as he does in 2 Cor 4:14 (see Rom 8:11; and 1 Thess 1:10 and 4:14). Even more conspicuous are the allusions to the "faithfulness of Jesus" (πίστις 'Ιησοῦ) in Rom 3:26 and "the stigmata of Jesus" (τὰ στίγματα τοῦ 'Ιησοῦ) in Gal 6:17. Thus, the cluster of occurrences of Jesus' personal name in the present passage leads us to expect that Paul is evoking the story and *ethos* of Jesus here. Indeed, the discussion below will show this to be the case, although much care is needed to spell out what the apostle actually means by the expression ζωὴ τοῦ 'Ιησοῦ.

In 2 Cor 4:10a Paul states that he and his co-workers "are always carrying in the body τὴν νέκρωσιν τοῦ 'Ιησοῦ." Now, what does the apostle mean by referring here to Jesus' νέκρωσις? Some translations and prominent commentators render it as "death," taking it to signify Jesus' state of deadness (cf. Rom 4:19).[405] This word, however, can also denote the process of "putting to death,"[406] and it is this notion of process that yields a more cogent reading. Paul's grammar underscores this point. Notice the present tense of the participle

---

Commentary on the Greek New Testament, 2nd ed. (Stuttgart: Deutsche Bibelgesellschaft, 1994) 510-11.

[404]See, e.g., GEORGI, *The Opponents of Paul in Second Corinthians*, 271-72; PRYOR, "Paul's Use of Iēsous," 31-45; and JOHNSON, *Reading Romans*, 60. Cf. MARTIN, *2 Corinthians*, lx. MCCANT discusses the anaphoric effect of the repetition of the name Jesus in these verses. See MCCANT, *2 Corinthians*, 46.

[405]E.g., RSV ("always carrying in the body the *death* of Jesus" italics added); cf. NIV; JB. In addition, see E. GÜTTGEMANNS, *Der leidende Apostel und sein Herr: Studien zur paulinischen Christologie*, FRLANT 90 (Göttingen: Vandenhoeck & Ruprecht, 1966) 114-17; J.-F. COLLANGE, *Énigmes de la deuxième épître aux Corinthiens: Etude exégétique de 2 Cor. 2:14-7:4*, SNTSMS 18 (Cambridge: Cambridge University Press, 1972), 154-55; HANSON, *The Paradox of the Cross in the Thought of St Paul*, 49; and THRALL, *II Corinthians*, 1.331-32.

[406]See BDAG, s.v. νέκρωσις, 1.

περιφέροντες[407] and the prominent placement of the adverb πάντοτε ("always") at the beginning of the clause. The grammar indicates that the apostle discusses a present and ongoing phenomenon. It would be bizarre, to say the least, for Paul to claim that he always carried about Jesus' "state of being dead." Rather, the apostle asserts that "the putting to death of Jesus" is something that he constantly bears "in the body." As will be shown in Chapter Five, Paul uses the expression περιφέροντες τὴν νέκρωσιν τοῦ Ἰησοῦ to interpret and to metaphorically summarize the experiences named in 2 Cor 4:8-9: his being afflicted, confused, persecuted, and humiliated. The point here is that the apostle draws upon the story of Jesus – specifically, the graphic image of Jesus' being put to death – in order to recapitulate his own experience of travails and opposition. Moreover, the fact that Paul compares his ongoing experience with Jesus' νέκρωσις strongly suggests that he views "the putting to death" of Jesus more broadly in terms of Jesus' life as a whole – not the event of the crucifixion alone.[408]

---

[407]Used in conjunction with the main (governing) verb ἔχομεν (4:7 – also present tense).

[408]See FURNISH, *II Corinthians*, 283: "Thus in v. 10*a* Paul might be thinking of *the whole course of Jesus' life as a 'dying,'* a being given up to death, just as he is thinking of the whole of the apostolic life in that way" (italics added); and L.L. BELLEVILLE, *2 Corinthians*, IVPNTCS (Downers Grove, Ill.: InterVarsity, 1996) 122: "When we think of the 'dying' of Jesus, we tend to think of the cross. Paul, however, has in mind the hardships, troubles and frustrations that Jesus faced during his . . . ministry." In addition, cf. BARRETT, *The Second Epistle to the Corinthians*, 139-40; and PLUMMER, *II Corinthians*, 129-30. Plummer appositely remarks that this specific reference shows that "Paul taught his converts details in the history of Jesus, especially His sufferings ending in death. Here he assumes that they know" (p. 130).

R.C. TANNEHILL argues that Jesus' νέκρωσις refers to the way in which "the power of death" – one of the principal powers of the "old aeon" – has been brought into the service of the power of life in the new aeon. See *Dying and Rising with Christ*, 84-90, esp. pp. 85-86. Tannehill's reading, however, depends more on Rom 5:12-21 than on a reading of the immediate context of 2 Cor 4:10a. J.T. FITZGERALD takes a middle road of interpretation, arguing that νέκρωσις τοῦ Ἰησοῦ refers both to Jesus' death and to the process of his dying. See *Cracks in an Earthen Vessel*, 177-80.

For a thorough and balanced treatment of the expression νέκρωσις τοῦ Ἰησοῦ, see J. LAMBRECHT, "The Nekrōsis of Jesus: Ministry and Suffering in 2 Cor 4,7-15," in R. BIERINGER and J. LAMBRECHT, *Studies on 2 Corinthians*, BETL 112 (Leuven: Leuven University Press, 1994), 309-33.

The apostle continues the argument in 2 Cor 4:11a: "For we who live are constantly being handed over (παραδιδόμεθα) unto death διὰ Ἰησοῦν." There are many parallels between this clause and 4:10a: an adverb in prominent first position stressing the notion of "always"; a reference to Paul and his co-workers as tending toward "death"; and an allusion to the story of Jesus. Regarding the latter, the apostle's syntax is revealing. Observe the significant placement of the phrase διὰ Ἰησοῦν next to the verb παραδιδόμεθα.[409] Elsewhere Paul uses the passive voice of παραδίδωμι in connection with Jesus. The apostle has already told the Corinthians of Jesus' words over the bread and cup "on the night when he was handed over" (ἐν τῇ νυκτὶ ᾗ παρεδίδετο, 1 Cor 11:23). He recalls in Rom 4:25 the tradition that Jesus "was handed over for our trespasses" (παραδόθη διὰ τὰ παραπτώματα). While Paul does not identify the agent who handed over Jesus in either of these verses, he does in Rom 8:32: *God* is the one who did not spare God's Son, "but handed him over (παρέδωκεν) for us all." Thus, for the apostle, Jesus' being handed over involves the work and agency of God. But this is only one side of the coin.

The other side of the coin is Jesus' ναί to God and God's will (2 Cor 1:19-20). Paul also names Jesus as the subject of the active, reflexive sense of παραδίδωμι, that is, as the agent who "hands himself over." The apostle expresses this most succinctly in Eph 5:2: "Christ loved us and gave himself for our sake" (ὁ Χριστός ἠγάπησεν ἡμᾶς καὶ παρέδωκεν ἑαυτὸν ὑπὲρ ἡμῶν; cf. Eph 5:25). Here, Paul links Jesus' actively "giving himself" (= handing himself over) with an act of love. Indeed, the apostle uses the same words – 'Christ *loved* me and *gave himself up* for me' – in apposition to his reference to Jesus' faithfulness in Gal 2:20,[410] an apposition that serves to define how

---

[409]εἰς θάνατον παραδιδόμεθα διὰ Ἰησοῦν, *not* παραδιδόμεθα εἰς θάνατον διὰ Ἰησοῦν. BULTMANN points out that the phrase διὰ Ἰησοῦν defines "being handed over unto death" specifically in terms of Jesus' death. See *The Second Letter to the Corinthians*, 119.

[410]For rendering the phrase πίστει τῇ τοῦ υἱοῦ τοῦ θεοῦ as a subjective genitive – i.e., as a reference to *Jesus'* faithfulness – see F.J. MATERA, *Galatians*, SP 9 (Collegeville, Minn.: Liturgical, 1992) 101; J.L. MARTYN, *Galatians: A New Translation with Introduction and Commentary*, AB 33A (New York: Doubleday, 1997) 259; and R.B. HAYS, "The Letter to the Galatians: Introduction, Commentary, and Reflections," in *NIB*, 11.181-348, here 244.

Christ's πίστις was made manifest.[411] Thus, I suggest that Paul's juxtaposition of παραδιδόμεθα and διὰ 'Ιησοῦν in 2 Cor 4:11a not only draws upon the story of Jesus;[412] it also alludes to the latter's character, more specifically to his πίστις.

Paul claims in 2 Cor 4:11a that he is being handed over unto death διὰ 'Ιησοῦν. What is the force of this prepositional phrase? The preposition διά + accusative signifies the reason something exists or the reason something results. It is usually translated "for the sake of" or "because of."[413] I propose that both renderings apply here, but in a special way. Paul undergoes being handed over *for the sake of Jesus*, that is, in loyalty and service to the one whose apostle (2 Cor 1:1) and slave (Phil 1:1) he is.[414] In addition, he is handed over *because of* Jesus. Now, given the allusions to the story and character of Jesus in 2 Cor 4:10a and 4:11a, I submit that the apostle draws upon Jesus' manner and example in this prepositional phrase as well. Hence, I translate διὰ

---

[411]Gal 2:20: "And now [the life] which I live in [the] flesh I live in [the] faithfulness of the Son of God, *who loved me and gave himself for me* (τοῦ ἀγαπήσαντος με καὶ παραδόντος ἑαυτὸν ὑπὲρ ἐμοῦ)."

[412]Several commentators argue that Paul's use of the verb παραδίδωμι in 4:11a indicates that he is familiar with it as a technical word from the Jesus-tradition. See, e.g., BARRETT, *The Second Epistle to the Corinthians*, 140; THRALL, *II Corinthians*, 1.336; MCCANT, *2 Corinthians*, 45; and A.E. HARVEY, *Renewal through Suffering: A Study of 2 Corinthians* (Edinburgh: T & T Clark, 1996), 59-60. FURNISH does an unusual "about face" in this connection. After acknowledging Paul's knowledge and use of παραδίδωμι in connection with Jesus' passion (citing 1 Cor 11:23), Furnish immediately comments that "it is not necessary to suppose that [Paul] has chosen the word here in order to accentuate the relationship of apostolic hardships to Jesus' sufferings and death" (*II Corinthians*, 256). On the contrary, this is *exactly* what Paul is doing!

[413]See BDAG, s.v. διά, B.2.a. For διά in the sense of "for the sake of," see, e.g., Rom 4:23-24a and 11:28; 1 Cor 4:6 and 9:10; and 2 Cor 2:10; 4:15; and 8:9. For διά in the sense of "because of," see, e.g., Rom 4:25a; 6:19; 8:10; and 15:15; 2 Cor 3:7 and 9:14; Gal 4:13; Eph 2:4; and 1 Thess 5:13.

[414]Notice that this sense differs from ὑπέρ + the genitive, which denotes "for the sake of" in the sense of acting in another's best interest or even in place of another. See BDAG, s.v. ὑπέρ, A.1.

'Ιησοῦν as "because of Jesus" to connote Paul's activity in loyal service to Jesus, whose example he emulates.[415]

The apostle thus alludes to the story and *ethos* of Jesus in 2 Cor 4:10-11 with his reference to Jesus' νέκρωσις and by his juxtaposition of παραδίδωμι and the name "Jesus." There is one more phrase to be considered: "the life of Jesus" (ἡ ζωὴ τοῦ 'Ιησοῦ). Is this another reference to Jesus in his earthly existence? That is, does "the life of Jesus" here refer to the way of life exhibited by the human Jesus?[416] *Prima facie*, this might seem to be the case, given the

---

[415]For a similar view, see MURPHY-O'CONNOR, *The Theology of the Second Letter to the Corinthians*, 46: "Yet [Paul] persists 'on account of Jesus,' *not only because he has been called, but because he has been inspired and challenged by the ministry of Jesus*" (italics added). According to J.P. SAMPLEY, the phrase διὰ 'Ιησοῦν "specifies that it is not just any handing over that is being described. It is, instead, *a life lived in service of Jesus and in conformity to the gospel. . . .*" See "The Second Letter to the Corinthians: Introduction, Commentary, and Reflections," in *NIB*, 11.1-180, here 81 (italics added). BARNETT captures the sense succinctly: "like Master, like servant" (see *The Second Epistle to the Corinthians*, 237). Paul also utilizes this rich sense of διά + accusative in connection with Jesus in Phil 3:8; cf. Phil 2:30.

[416]Cf. MURPHY-O'CONNOR, who argues that Jesus' ζωή be understood "in the existential sense, i.e. as a mode of human existence (cf. Rom 6:13), which has been perfectly defined by Philo as loving God and living for him alone. . . . This is certainly an accurate description of the consistent attitude both of the historical Jesus and of Paul." See MURPHY-O'CONNOR, *The Theology of the Second Letter to the Corinthians*, 46-48 (the quotation is from p. 47), and idem, "Faith and Resurrection in 2 Cor 4:13-14," *RB* 95 (1988) 543-50, here 545-46. The problem with Murphy-O'Connor's analysis is that it pushes Paul's paradoxical expression too far. That is, he rightly notes that Jesus' νέκρωσις refers to Jesus' "whole ministry" and that "Paul viewed his own existence in the same perspective" (*The Theology of the Second Letter to the Corinthians*, 46). In other words, Murphy O'Connor seems to offer an existential interpretation of νέκρωσις (although he also remarks that 4:10a and 4:11a refer to death in the normal physical sense). But if Jesus' νέκρωσις refers to a human mode of self-emptying existence, the allusion to Jesus' ζωή must refer to something else. In addition, Murphy-O'Connor's criticism of the "eschatological" interpretation of ζωή – the one that will be offered here – is unbalanced. He reduces and limits the notion of eschatological life to a future reality. But Paul speaks of eschatological life both in terms of the future (e.g., in 2 Cor 4:14 and 5:1-10) and in terms of its present manifestation (e.g., in 2 Cor 1:20 and 3:18).

Similarly, GÜTTGEMANNS argues that Paul's paradoxical language be pushed to its full extent: the νέκρωσις *is* the epiphany of Jesus' ζωή. See *Der leidende Apostel*

unadorned use of Jesus' name and the formal parallel to νέκρωσις τοῦ 'Ιησοῦ (as well as to the expressions πραΰτης καὶ ἐπιείκεια τοῦ Χριστοῦ and ὑπακοὴ τοῦ Χριστοῦ). A closer look at 4:10-11, however, shows that ζωὴ τοῦ 'Ιησοῦ has a different referent than the mode of existence revealed by Jesus in his humanity.

In 2 Cor 4:10b and 4:11b Paul explains that the purpose (cf. ἵνα) for his "bearing the putting to death of Jesus" and his "being handed over because of Jesus" is that "the life of Jesus might be made manifest." It is true that the apostle *is* talking about a manner of living in these verses. As we will see in discussing 4:13, it is the way of life marked by loving, self-emptying service of others. It involves "lowering oneself" and enduring suffering so that others might benefit. But Paul's shorthand for this mode of existence – as exhibited by Jesus – takes form in the paradoxical expressions νέκρωσις τοῦ 'Ιησοῦ and παραδίδομαι διὰ 'Ιησοῦν, *not* ζωὴ τοῦ 'Ιησοῦ. The "life of Jesus" in 4:10b and 4:11b refers, instead, to *the power of the risen Jesus* that enables people (like Paul and his co-workers) to live as he lived. This power is what the apostle describes in 4:7 as "the superabundance of the power of God" (ἡ ὑπερβολὴ τῆς δυνάμεως τοῦ θεοῦ).[417] And it is this δύναμις that not only empowers a mode of human existence ἐν τῷ σώματι and ἐν τῇ σαρκί (4:10-11; cf. "in earthen vessels" in 4:7), but also sustains and preserves those (like Paul and his co-workers) who suffer afflictions and persecutions (4:8-9). Thus, ζωὴ τοῦ 'Ιησοῦ refers to the power of God that enables its recipients to live after the manner of Jesus, thereby manifesting *in the present* the power of resurrection life.[418] Recall that Paul has already alluded to this pattern of

---

und sein Herr, 94-126. But this also takes Paul's paradox too far. As LAMBRECHT rightly observes, "A paradox mentions only the antithesis and does not offer a complete presentation of the case. The paradox leads to reflection and by reflection the good listener or reader should find the way out." See "The Nekrōsis of Jesus," 320.

[417]So, rightly, TANNEHILL, *Dying and Rising with Christ*, 84-85; and LAMBRECHT, "The Nekrōsis of Jesus," 325. Cf. THRALL'S qualification in *II Corinthians*, 1.335.

[418]FURNISH'S précis of ζωὴ τοῦ 'Ιησοῦ is right on target: "The phrase as used here does not refer to the course of Jesus' earthly life and ministry, but *to the power of his resurrection life as that is manifested in the present*" (*II Corinthians*, 256, italics added). BARRETT'S assertion that "the primary reference here is to future resurrection" is mistaken (see *The Second Epistle to the Corinthians*, 140). Barrett is unduly influenced

interchange in 1:5 with his reference to sharing abundantly both in "the sufferings of Christ" and in comfort "through Christ." We will now see that the apostle refers to this power in another way in 4:13.[419]

It is helpful to begin the analysis of 2 Cor 4:13 with the full Greek text: ἔχοντες δὲ τὸ αὐτὸ πνεῦμα τῆς πίστεως κατὰ τὸ γεγραμμένον: *ἐπίστευσα, διὸ ἐλάλησα,* καὶ ἡμεῖς πιστεύομεν, διὸ καὶ λαλοῦμεν. This text presents at least five features that offer different interpretive possibilities. First is the circumstantial participle ἔχοντες: does it signify time, manner, cause, or some other nuance? Second is the particle δέ: does it indicate a connection or a contrast with what precedes it? Third is the adjective αὐτό, which modifies πνεῦμα: Paul has the "*same* πνεῦμα" as whom? Fourth is the substantive πνεῦμα: does it refer to a human attitude (i.e., a frame of mind) or to the Spirit of God? Fifth is the πιστ- terminology with which this verse is

---

by 4:14, and not the immediate context of 4:10-11 itself. For an excellent treatment of Paul's meaning here, see T.B. SAVAGE, *Power through Weakness: Paul's Understanding of the Christian Ministry in 2 Corinthians* (Cambridge: Cambridge University Press, 1996) 175-77.

Some commentators overload the phrase ζωὴ τοῦ 'Ιησοῦ with more meaning than it can possibly bear. For instance, M. CARREZ argues that three different aspects of "the life of Jesus" are inextricable: (1) Jesus' earthly life, which accomplished salvation and which continues through the apostolic ministry; (2) the resurrected life as it reveals itself presently in the community and renews its participants; and (3) the future resurrection; thus, there are past, present and future elements. See "Que Représente la Vie de Jésus pour l'Apôtre Paul?," *Revue d'Histoire* 68 (1988) 155-61. Similarly, BELLEVILLE (*2 Corinthians*, 123) questions whether there is a clear-cut distinction here between "a human mode of existence or the power of the risen Christ." These interpretations read the complexity of the whole of Paul's thought in 4:10-11 into the single phrase ζωὴ τοῦ 'Ιησοῦ, a phrase that functions in these verses as a specific element – namely, the power of the risen Christ – within that whole.

[419]The best commentary on 2 Cor 4:10-11 is Phil 3:10. Note that, in the latter passage, it is "the power of [Christ's] resurrection" (= ἡ ζωὴ τοῦ 'Ιησοῦ) that enables Paul to share Christ's sufferings, "becoming like him in his death." The apostle's use of the phrase ζωὴ τοῦ 'Ιησοῦ is a warning, on the one hand, that not all uses of the unadorned name refer to Jesus in his earthly life. On the other hand, as PLUMMER rightly observed, the repetition of the name Jesus in 4:10-11 reminds us that, for the apostle, the earthly Jesus and the glorified Christ both refer to the same Jesus. See *II Corinthians*, p.130.

suffused: does it denote the narrower notion of belief/believing or the broader sense of faithfulness/being faithful?

With these questions in mind,[420] consider the NRSV's translation of 2 Cor 4:13: "But just as we have the same spirit of faith that is in accordance with scripture – 'I believed, and so I spoke' – we also believe, and so we speak." Observe that the NRSV (1) renders the participle by adding, in effect, the conjunction καθώς ("just as"); (2) takes δέ as adversative; (3) understands "same" in connection with what is written in Scripture; (4) interprets πνεῦμα as referring to an attitude or disposition; and (5) translates the πιστ- language in terms of believing. I argue that the NRSV's translation is flawed in all five areas.

Paul cites LXX Ps 115:1 in 2 Cor 4:13: ἐπίστευσα, διὸ ἐλάλησα. This line is the middle verse of two psalms[421] that, taken together, tell the story of a righteous sufferer who cries out to God and is saved. That the apostle – in citing the line ἐπίστευσα, διὸ ἐλάλησα – has both psalms in mind is strongly suggested by the numerous verbal, conceptual, and thematic resonances of LXX Pss 114-115 found throughout the text of 2 Corinthians. The following table illustrates this point:

Table I
Comparison of LXX Psalms 114-115 with 2 Corinthians

LXX Psalms 114-115	*2 Corinthians*
ἠγάπησα – 114:1a (the first word)	ἀγάπη – 2:4; 2:8; 5:14; 6:6; 8:7; 8:8; 8:24; 13:11; 13:13 ἀγαπῶ – 9:7; 11:11; 12:15 (2x)
δέησις – 114:1b	δέησις – 1:11; 9:14 δέομαι – 5:20; 8:4; 10:2 **

[420]Another question raised is: What does Paul mean by the verb λαλέω? I will take up the answer to this question after discussing the five enumerated questions in reverse order.

[421]The editors of the HB regard as a single psalm (Ps 116) what the LXX divides into two: LXX Ps 114:1-9 = HB Ps 116:1-9; and LXX Ps 115:1-10 = HB Ps 116:10-19.

threat of + deliverance from θάνατος – 114:3a; 114:8a	threat of + deliverance from θάνατος – 1:9-10; 4:11; 6:9; 11:23
κίνδυνοι – 114:3b	κίνδυνοι – 11:26 (8x) ***
θλῖψις – 114:3c	θλῖψις – 1:4 (2x); 1:8; 2:4; 4:17; 6:4; 7:4; 8:2; 8:13 θλίβω – 1:6; 4:8; 7:5
ῥύομαι – 114:4b	ῥύομαι – 1:10 (3x)
ἐλεῶ – 114:5b; (cf. ἐλεήμων in 114:5a)	ἐλεῶ – 4:1
ταπεινῶ – 114:6b; 115:1b	ταπεινῶ – 11:7; 12:21 ** ταπεινός – 7:6; 10:1 **
ἐπιστρέφω – 114:7a	ἐπιστρέφω – 3:16
εὐαρεστῶ – 114:9	εὐάρεστος – 5:9
ἐναντίον κυρίου – 114:9; 115:6a	κατέναντι θεοῦ – 2:17; 12:19 ** ἐνώπιον τοῦ θεοῦ – 4:2; 7:12 ἐνώπιον κυρίου – 8:21
πιστεύω – 115:1a	πιστεύω – 4:13 (2x) πίστις – 1:24 (2x); 4:13; 5:7; 8:7; 10:15; 13:5 πιστός – 1:18; 6:15
"everyone is a liar" – 115:2b	intimations of deceit – 4:2; 7:2; 11:3; 11:13-15; 11:20; 12:16-18
σωτηρία – 115:4a	σωτηρία – 1:6; 6:2 (2x); 7:10
δοῦλος – 115:7a; 115:7b	δοῦλος – 4:5

***used by Paul only in 2 Corinthians
**at least half of Paul's usages of this term/expression occur in 2 Corinthians

One cannot help but be impressed by the sheer number of semantic and thematic resonances in the letter, as well as their distribution *throughout* the text. Indeed, these psalms seem to be in the air for Paul as he writes his epistle.[422]

Even more striking is the *story* told in LXX Pss 114-115. The psalmist identifies himself as God's "slave" – ὦ κύριε, ἐγὼ δοῦλος σός (Ps 115:7a). Twice he refers to his experience of "being brought low" (ταπεινόομαι, 114:6b and 115:1b), references that in effect bracket the line Paul cites. The psalmist describes his great affliction and pain in dramatic terms: the "throes of death encompassed" him, the "dangers of Hades found" him (114:3). In his dire need, he cried out to God, "Oh Lord, save my life!" (ὦ κύριε, ῥῦσαι τὴν ψυχήν μου, 114:4b). Moreover, the psalmist confesses that God – who is "merciful and righteous" (114:5a) – did save him (114:6b), delivering his life "from death" (ἐκ θανάτου, 114:8a). He now takes up "the cup of salvation" (ποτήριον σωτηρίου, 115:4a), calling on the name of the Lord, as well as declaring: "Precious before the Lord is the death of his holy ones" (115:6). And at the very heart of his recitation, the psalmist cries out, ἐπίστευσα, διὸ ἐλάλησα (115:1a). Now, how is the verb πιστεύω to be rendered here? The content of LXX Pss 114-115 suggests two things: first, the psalmist *trusted* in God to rescue him; second, he *has been faithful* to God whose slave he is. Thus, the psalmist speaks out because he has been faithful to and has trusted in God. God in turn vindicates God's "slave" who had been brought low, and saves him from death.

I submit that Paul has this entire story in mind as he cites LXX Pss 114-115 in 2 Cor 4:13.[423] Furthermore, he has this story in mind precisely because

---

[422]HARVEY rightly points out the significance of these two psalms in 2 Cor 1:3-11, where Paul draws upon their language and story. See *Renewal through Suffering*, 18 and 32. YOUNG and FORD cast the net wider, arguing that the apostle makes several allusions to LXX Pss 110-118 throughout 2 Cor, allusions that "seem to confirm the impression that this group of Psalms is far more deeply embedded in Paul's thought than the obvious allusions might suggest." See *Meaning and Truth in 2 Corinthians*, 63-69 (the quotation is from p. 67). I find the allusions to LXX Pss 114-115 (as well as to LXX Ps 111 – see Section VIII below) much more persuasive than Young and Ford's broader claims.

[423]*Pace* BARRETT and LAMBRECHT. According to Barrett, "Paul pays no heed to the context [of the psalms], but picks out the two significant words" (see *The Second Epistle to the Corinthians*, 143). Similarly, Lambrecht considers it "unlikely" that the apostle

it serves as an apt expression of the story of Jesus. That is, *for the apostle, LXX Pss 114-115 tells the story of Jesus*. Observe how the story of the righteous sufferer coalesces with the story of Jesus that Paul utilizes in Phil 2:6-11,[424] a story that portrays Jesus as one who emptied himself, taking on the "form of a slave" (μορφὴ δούλου, Phil 2:7); as one who, furthermore, "lowered himself" (ἐταπείνωσεν ἑαυτόν, 2:8), becoming obedient unto death (μέχρι θανάτου, 2:8); and, as one whose death God regarded as precious – "*Therefore* (διό) God highly exalted him. . ." (2:9).[425] In addition, the apostle's narration in 1 Cor

---

refers to the broader psalm context (see *Second Corinthians*, 74). Several commentators, however, rightly recognize that Paul draws upon the situation and story told in LXX Ps 115 (and, for some, LXX Ps 114 as well). See, e.g., P. BACHMANN, *Der zweite Brief des Paulus an die Korinther*, 4th ed., KNT 8 (Leipzig: A. Deichert, 1922) 202-4; PLUMMER, *II Corinthians*, 133; E.B. ALLO, *Seconde Épître aux Corinthiens*, 2nd ed. (Paris: Études bibliques, 1956) 116; HUHGES, *Paul's Second Epistle to the Corinthians*, 146-47; DANKER, *II Corinthians*, 68; THRALL, *II Corinthians*, 1.341; SAVAGE, *Power through Weakness*, 180; and MATERA, *II Corinthians*, 112. K.T. KLEINKNECHT also argues that Paul alludes more widely to LXX Ps 115, and furthermore correctly observes that the apostle makes the OT tradition of the suffering righteous one *christologically-centered.* Kleinknecht, however, fails to see the depth to which the apostle draws upon the story and character of Jesus in his analysis. See *Der leidende Gerechtfertigte: Die alttestamentlich-jüdische Tradition vom "leidenden Gerechten" und irhe Rezeption bei Paulus*, WUNT 2 (Tübingen: Mohr Siebeck, 1984) 260-61 and 277-78.

[424]Of course, the question of whether or not Paul is quoting an earlier composition has been hotly debated. For my purposes, it is enough to establish that, minimally, the apostle took over and appropriated the "Christ hymn," and in so doing, made it his own. For a brief but helpful discussion of the origin and background of the hymn – and of the ideas contained therein – see M.D. HOOKER, "The Letter to the Philippians: Introduction, Commentary, and Reflections," in *NIB*, 11.467-549, here 501-6.

[425]For studies arguing that Phil 2:6-11 is concerned primarily with the *human* existence of Jesus, see C.H. TALBERT, "The Problem of Pre-existence in Philippians 2:6-11," *JBL* 86 (1967) 141-53; J. MURPHY-O'CONNOR, "Christological Anthropology in Phil. II, 6-11," *RB* 83 (1976) 25-50; J.D.G. DUNN, *Christology in the Making: A New Testament Inquiry into the Origins of the Doctrine of the Incarnation* (Philadelphia: Westminster, 1980) 114-21; and G.E. HOWARD, "Phil 2:6-11 and the Human Christ," *CBQ* 40 (1978) 368-87. For studies that emphasize the exemplary function of this passage, see M.D. HOOKER, "Philippians 2:6-11," in *Jesus und Paulus*, ed. E.E. ELLIS

11:23-25 of Jesus taking (ἔλαβον)[426] "the cup" (τὸ ποτήριον) – now identified as "the new covenant in my blood" – echoes the reference in LXX Ps 115:4a to taking up (λαμβάνω) the "cup of salvation" (ποτήριον σωτηρίου). Recall, moreover, that this happened on the night when Jesus "was handed over" (cf. LXX Ps 115:1b, ἐταπεινώθην σφόδρα – "I was brought exceedingly low"). Thus, in alluding to LXX Pss 114-115, Paul evokes the story of Jesus' taking on the form of a slave, lowering himself (even more), and giving himself to others out of love – even to the point of giving his life in obedient response to God and God's will. As God's δοῦλος, it is thus *Jesus* who confesses, ἐπίστευσα – "I have been faithful."[427] In 2 Cor 4:13 the apostle cites the words which are, in his view, Jesus' testimony to his own πίστις.[428]

---

and E. GRÄSSER (Göttingen: Vandenhoeck & Ruprecht, 1975) 151-64; and L.W. HURTADO, "Jesus as Lordly Example in Philippians 2:5-11," in *From Jesus to Paul: Studies in Honour of Francis Wright Beare*, ed. P. RICHARDSON and J.C. HURD (Waterloo, Ontario: Wilfrid Laurier University Press, 1984) 113-26. See also N.T. WRIGHT, *The Climax of the Covenant*, 56-98. In addition to offering a helpful review of the history of interpretation, Wright proposes a reading in which he integrates Christ as Adam, as Servant, and as the Pre-existent One, while also suggesting the exemplary function of the passage.

[426]Supplying the verb from 1 Cor 11:23.

[427]Cf. the use of πιστός in connection with δοῦλος in Matt 25:21 and 25:23. I will explain below my translation of ἐπίστευσα as "I have been faithful."

[428]Cf. Rom 15:3 for another example of how Paul takes the words of a psalm (in that case, LXX Ps 68:10) as the words of Jesus. As we saw in Chapter Three, M. THOMPSON argues that, in order to appreciate fully the apostle's use of this verse, it is necessary to examine the wider context of the psalm, esp. v. 8. See *Clothed with Christ*, 221-25. Now, it may be objected that Rom 15:3 does not provide, for my purposes, a precise parallel to 2 Cor 4:13, given that in the former Paul explicitly names Christ before citing the words from LXX Ps 68:10. However, in the case of 2 Cor 4:13, the apostle has *already* set up Christ as the speaker of the psalm by alluding to Jesus' νέκρωσις (4:10) and to his "being handed over" (παραδίδομαι) διὰ Ἰησοῦν (4:11). Such explicit allusions to the story of Jesus do *not* occur in the verses preceding Rom 15:3.

To my knowledge, A.T. HANSON was the first to argue at any length that Paul reads LXX Ps 115 as expressing the words of Jesus. See HANSON, *The Paradox of the Cross in the Thought of St Paul*, 51-53, and idem, *Paul's Understanding of Jesus: Invention or Interpretation?* (Hull: University of Hull Press, 1963) 10-13. Following

At this point, I anticipate several possible objections to my interpretation. First, my interpretation of 2 Cor 4:13 makes Jesus the subject of the verb πιστεύω. *Prima facie*, this appears to be contrary to Paul's normal usage. For the apostle, Christians, prefigured by Abraham's act of faith, are the

---

the suggestion made by H.L. GOUDGE [in *The Second Epistle to the Corinthians* (London: Methuen, 1927) 41-42], Hanson's position is: "We have claimed that Paul read [HB] Psalm 116 as an utterance of the son to the Father, a prophecy of what would be his experience in the future when he came as man" (*Paul's Understanding of Jesus*, 12). While I agree that the apostle alludes to the wider context of the psalms, and that he sees here an apt description of Jesus, my interpretation differs from Hanson's in several respects. First, whereas he focuses on the content of LXX Ps 115, I take LXX Pss 114-115 as the underlying text. Second, we differ on the understanding of how Paul relates πιστ- language to Jesus. Hanson emphasizes that Jesus "still *believed* in God despite the deep humiliation of his days on earth, . . ." (see *The Paradox of the Cross in the Thought of St Paul*, 53 – italics added). I contend that Paul draws upon Jesus' *faithfulness* to God, exhibited in his mode of self-giving existence lived in obedience to God, and upon the trust that underlay this fidelity. Third, Hanson takes πνεῦμα (in 2 Cor 4:13) as referring to an attitude or disposition, while I take it as referring to the Holy Spirit (see below).

More recently, R.B. HAYS has proposed in outline a reading similar to what I offer. See his "Christ Prays the Psalms: Paul's Use of an Early Christian Exegetical Convention," in *The Future of Christology: Essays in Honor of Leander E. Keck*, ed. A.J. MALHERBE and W.A. MEEKS (Minneapolis: Fortress, 1993) 122-36, here 128-29. Hays, too, observes the similarity in vocabulary between LXX Ps 115 and Phil 2. He also notes that LXX Ps 115:4-6 can be read as a prefiguration of the Lord's Supper.

M.D. HOOKER tentatively submits that "perhaps it is 'Jesus'" whose faith is alluded to here. She understands Jesus' πίστις to be his confidence in the One who could raise him from the dead. See "Interchange and Suffering," in *Suffering and Martyrdom in the New Testament: Studies Presented to G.M. Styler by the Cambridge New Testament Seminar*, ed. W. HORBURY and B. MCNEIL (Cambridge: Cambridge University Press, 1981) 70-83, here 78-79. I do not share Hooker's tentativeness, and I extend her notion of Jesus' πίστις beyond that of "confidence" to the manner in which his trust was manifested by his self-emptying existence. Cf. HOOKER'S brief treatment of 2 Cor 4:13 in "ΠΙΣΤΙΣ ΧΡΙΣΤΟΥ," *NTS* 35 (1989) 321-42, here 335-36.

S.J. HAFEMANN comes close to my position when he states that Ps 116 [= LXX Pss 114-115] "provides an interpretive lens through which the apostle understands the significance of his experience in Christ, *the* suffering Righteous One." See *2 Corinthians*, 187 (Hafemann's italics).

typical subject of πιστεύω.[429] In fact, Jesus is not the subject of this verb anywhere else in the NT. This is a not an insubstantial objection.[430] I insist, however, that the key to interpreting 2 Cor 4:13 lies in an understanding of *how the allusion to LXX Ps 115:1 functions*. Paul's point is that he and his co-workers have τὸ αὐτὸ πνεῦμα τῆς πίστεως. The allusion functions to illuminate *this* phrase. I argue that the apostle's concern lies in the underlying story of LXX Pss 114-115 – a story that reverberates in the story of Jesus – and *not* in the subtleties or precision of specific theological formulations. This first anticipated objection gets "hung up," moreover, on the issue of whether or not Jesus *believed* (in God). In my opinion, this is a red herring – which leads me to anticipate a second objection.

My interpretation of 2 Cor 4:13 might evoke the following protest: Does not the verb πιστεύω denote "believe" rather than "be faithful"? To be sure, πιστεύω is most often rendered "believe." However, πιστ- terminology can also connote a more complete human response to God than is entailed by the act of belief.[431] In fact, as Rudolf Bultmann aptly observes, "[Paul] understands the *act* of faith as an *act* of obedience."[432] Indeed, we saw in the discussion of the character of Jesus in Romans how Christ's faithfulness and obedience are deeply intertwined. Thus, on the basis of *the apostle's usage* – rather than on the basis of preconceived theological notions (often derived elsewhere) – one need not presume that Paul signifies (only) "belief" when he employs πιστ-cognates. Indeed, the context of LXX Pss 114-115 calls such a presumption into question. This context suggests that the notions of faithful, obedient service (cf.

---

[429]Cf., e.g., V. KOPERSKY, "The Meaning of *Pistis Christou* in Philippians 3:9," 210: Paul "does not speak of Christ . . . as one who needs to believe in order to obtain righteousness."

[430]A. VANHOYE rightly criticizes M.D. HOOKER for minimizing the dogmatic issues involved here. See VANHOYE, "Πίστις Χριστοῦ: fede in Cristo o affidabilità di Cristo?" *Bib* 80 (1999) 1-21, here 13. Vanhoye is responding to HOOKER'S argument in "ΠΙΣΤΙΣ ΧΡΙΣΤΟΥ."

[431]See, e.g., JOHNSON, *Reading Romans*, 60.

[432]BULTMANN, *Theology of the New Testament*, 1.314 (italics added).

ὦ κύριε, ἐγὼ δοῦλος σός) and trust[433] undergird the words cited by the apostle in 2 Cor 4:13.

A third objection might be that my interpretation blurs the line between the πίστις of Jesus and the πίστις of Christians (e.g., of Paul and those to whom he ministered). Let me be clear: While there are similarities, there are also important differences. Thomas Aquinas's distinction between *fides quae* – concerning the content of one's faith – and *fides qua* – concerning one's self-commitment to God – can facilitate the comparison.[434] In terms of *fides quae*, the πίστις of Christians involves (minimally) believing what God has revealed through the life, death, and resurrection of Jesus. Obviously, the human Jesus' πίστις did not entail such "belief." In fact, Jesus' relationship with God was so immediate and unique that it is difficult to speak of the *fides quae* of Jesus.[435]

It is in terms of *fides qua* that we can speak of similarities. Indeed, I submit that when the apostle alludes to the πίστις of Jesus, it is in terms of the latter's *fides qua* (which is why I render Jesus' πίστις as *faithfulness*[436]): Christ's faithfulness involved his obedient commitment to God and God's will. Jesus manifested this faithfulness by his loving, self-giving mode of existence,

---

[433]See BDAG, s.v. πιστεύω, 2. Here, the notion of trust entails the "implication of total commitment to the one who is trusted."

[434]See *ST*, 2-2, q. 2, a. 2. G. O'COLLINS and D. KENDALL offer a helpful description of *fides quae* and *fides qua* in "The Faith of Jesus," *TS* 53 (1992) 403-23, here 405-7. For Aquinas's Latin text, see *Summa theologiae*, 5 vols. (Ottawa: Commissio Piana, 1953).

[435]Cf. O'COLLINS and KENDALL, "The Faith of Jesus," 421: ". . . [Jesus] *knew* and could not in the technical sense of the word confess the existence of God" (italics added). VANHOYE has good reason for taking HOOKER (see "ΠΙΣΤΙΣ ΧΡΙΣΤΟΥ," 329) to task for suggesting that Christ somehow shares Abraham's faith. See VANHOYE, "Πίστις Χριστοῦ," 14.

[436]Cf. VANHOYE'S criticism of HOOKER ("ΠΙΣΤΙΣ ΧΡΙΣΤΟΥ," 329) for 'passing surreptitiously' from speaking of πίστις in terms of fidelity (i.e., faithfulness) to speaking of it in terms of faith. See VANHOYE, "Πίστις Χριστοῦ," 15. Indeed, advocates of the subjective genitive reading of πίστις Χριστοῦ are often guilty of a lack of precision about what is meant by Christ's πίστις. Interestingly, O'COLLINS and KENDALL seem to suggest that, in 2 Cor 4:13, Paul alludes to Christ's πίστις. See "The Faith of Jesus," 417, n. 57.

even to the point of offering his life on the cross. Such faithfulness certainly entailed Jesus' trust in God. And, according to Paul, it is through Jesus' faithfulness (thus understood) that God's righteousness has been revealed (Rom 1:17 and 3:21-22). As a result, in light of what God has revealed through Jesus and in light of the gift of the Spirit (as we will see in Chapters Five and Six), Paul and all Christians are empowered to faithful obedience to God, faithful obedience they manifest by giving themselves in love for others. Nevertheless, the *fides qua* of Jesus also differs from that of Christians. In the first place, Jesus' *fides qua* makes possible the *fides qua* of Christians, and serves as its exemplar. In the second place, only Jesus manifested *perfect* obedience to God (as we will see in treating 2 Cor 5:21 below).

As a fourth possible objection to my interpretation of 2 Cor 4:13, it might be suggested that I too easily see semantic connections between the story of the righteous sufferer in LXX Pss 114-115 and the story of Jesus in Phil 2:6-11. For instance, the psalmist uses the verb ταπεινόω in the passive voice, whereas Paul uses the active, reflexive sense in Phil 2:8. Recall, however, the discussion above in connection with the verb παραδίδωμι. The apostle uses this word in both the active reflexive and passive voices in relation to Jesus in order to capture the same truth from two vantage points: on the one hand, *God* is the one who acts in and through Jesus; on the other hand, Jesus says ναί to God as an expression of his obedience and faithfulness. So too I propose it is with the verb ταπεινόω. Notice that in LXX Pss 114-115 the psalmist does not rail against *human* enemies as in other psalms (cf., e.g., LXX Pss 11:2-5; 34:1-3; and 40:6-10).[437] Rather the "throes of death" and "dangers of Hades" threaten the psalmist, who cries out in trust to God to save him and to vindicate his being God's faithful δοῦλος.

Indeed, the psalmist's cry (κύριε, ῥῦσαι τὴν ψυχήν μου) is another clue that Paul reads this story christologically. The apostle uses the same verb ῥύομαι three times in 2 Cor 1:10, where he describes himself and his fellows as being *rescued* from a deadly peril, and where he places his hope that God *will continue to rescue* them. Immediately preceding this verse, Paul claims that he has learned to place his reliance on τῷ θεῷ τῷ ἐγείροντι τοὺς νεκρούς –

---

[437]The only possible reference is "Everyone is a liar" in LXX Ps 115:2b. This, however, is not given as the explicit reason for the psalmist's being brought low. Moreover, it could serve as another pointer to the story of Jesus – the false witnesses against him on the night he was handed over (see Matt 26:59-61 and Mark 14:55-59).

"God who raises the dead" (1:9). Observe how, in the passage we are investigating (2 Cor 4:13), the apostle goes on to express his confidence "that *the one who raised the Lord Jesus* will also raise us with Jesus" (4:14). That is, Paul continues to draw upon the story of Jesus – now, the part where God vindicates Jesus by raising him from the dead. This is the divine response to Jesus' faithfulness to God and God's will, manifested in Christ's self-giving and suffering, even to the point of dying. And at the root of Jesus' πίστις was his trust in God – whom the apostle later describes in 7:6 as ὁ παρακαλῶν τοὺς ταπεινούς ("the one who comforts the lowly") – to bring the dead to life.

The story and character of Jesus, especially his faithfulness, are thus the key not only to understanding Paul's allusion in 2 Cor 4:13, but the entire argument of 4:7-15 as well. (As we will see in Chapter Five, after citing *Jesus'* words, the apostle makes them his own: καὶ ἡμεῖς πιστεύομεν, διὸ λαλοῦμεν.) At this point, I pull together Paul's argument by returning to the five interpretive questions raised earlier, but in reverse order.

The fifth question concerns the interpretation of the πιστ- terminology. The vast majority of translations and commentators render the two instances of πιστεύω in 2 Cor 4:13 as "believe," usually in the sense of having conviction/certainty concerning some content of faith.[438] Thus, the emphasis is on the cognitive sense of πιστεύω.[439] This exclusive focus on the cognitive aspect is problematic for two reasons. In the first place, it fails to do justice to the content of the verses which immediately precede it. There is no reference in 4:7-12 to any "belief content" to which one could give assent; rather, in these verses Paul discusses how he manifests *in action* the mode of human existence

---

[438]For understanding the πιστ- language in 2 Cor 4:13 as signifying "conviction," see, e.g., BELLEVILLE, *2 Corinthians*, 124-25; LAMBRECHT, *Second Corinthians*, 74; and SAMPLEY, *NIB*, 11.82. For understanding the πιστ- language as denoting "certainty," see BRUCE, *1 and 2 Corinthians*, 198. BULTMANN (*The Second Letter to the Corinthians*, 122) and BARNETT (*The Second Epistle to the Corinthians*, 241) argue that 4:14 describes the *content* of what Paul believes – namely, that God raises the dead to life. This way of interpreting 4:13 is captured well by HUGHES (*Paul's Second Epistle to the Corinthians*, 148): "Belief in the heart that God has raised Jesus from the dead . . . ." The problem with this line of interpretation is that *it misses the way Paul has been talking about faithfulness in 4:7-12.*

[439]See, e.g., BARRETT, *The Second Epistle to the Corinthians*, 143: "What [Paul] *believes* is the Gospel. . ." (italics added).

exhibited by Jesus – one marked by self-giving and suffering. In the second place, it fails to recognize the story of Jesus and his faithfulness to which the apostle alludes in 4:13 (as well as in 4:10-11).[440] Given that Paul offers no indication that he intends to change the subject here,[441] I submit that the verb πιστεύω in this verse is best rendered "be faithful" in the sense of living in constant fidelity and obedience to God's will (cf. *fides qua*). To be sure, such fidelity and obedience also entail trusting in God to vindicate one's faithfulness. Indeed, I suggest that it is *this* sense of trusting to which the apostle alludes in 4:14: *knowing* (εἰδότες) that God, who raised Jesus, will also raise him and others who have been faithful. Observe, however, that in 4:14 Paul uses a different verb, οἶδα – not πιστεύω.[442] I submit that he does so because he has just used πιστεύω in 4:13 to signify faithfulness as manifested (holistically) by a mode of existence characterized by self-giving.

The fourth question pertains to Paul's understanding of πνεῦμα. What does he mean by the phrase τὸ πνεῦμα τῆς πίστεως? In light of the discussion above, the phrase is best rendered "πνεῦμα *of faithfulness*." But this still leaves open whether "spirit" refers to a state of mind or disposition – the usual understanding of 2 Cor 4:13[443] – or to the Holy Spirit. I propose that the

---

[440]BULTMANN'S and KISTEMAKER'S observations in this connection are revealing. Bultmann claims that 4:13 can only refer to what follows "since there was yet no reference to the πνεῦμα τῆς πίστεως. . ." (see *The Second Letter to the Corinthians*, 121). Similarly, Kistemaker remarks, "*Paul has not spoken at all about faith* in the preceding chapters. He is not looking back but forward. . ." (see *The Second Epistle to the Corinthians*, 153 – italics added). In fact, Paul *has* alluded to πίστις – Jesus' as well as his own (and his co-workers') – by his references to ναί and τὸ ἀμήν in 1:19-20, and more immediately, by his allusions to the story and character of Jesus in 4:10-11. *Pace* Kistemaker, the apostle *is* looking backward (as well as preparing for 4:14).

[441]LAMBRECHT'S statement that "[t]he logical connection with what precedes is not evident" is symptomatic of the usual way of reading 4:13. See *Second Corinthians*, 74.

[442]LAMBRECHT (ibid.) rightly notes the importance of the distinction between the two verbs, although his reasons for doing so differ from mine.

[443]See, e.g., HUGHES, *Paul's Second Epistle to the Corinthians*, 147 ("disposition"); THRALL, *II Corinthians*, 1.339 ("spiritual state" or "disposition"); and BELLEVILLE, *2 Corinthians*, 124 ("attitude").

apostle refers to the latter here.[444] As we will see in the analysis of 3:18-4:6 (in Chapter Five) – the immediately preceding passage – Paul names the Spirit in 3:18 as the agent who transforms people into the likeness of Jesus, that is, as the one who empowers them to appropriate the *ethos* of Jesus and so to enter into his story. After describing the paradoxical nature of this transformation (4:7-12), the apostle again refers to the Spirit in connection with Jesus' prototypical mode of existence (as told in the story – κατὰ τὸ γεγραμμένον – of the righteous sufferer). Thus, the phrase τὸ πνεῦμα τῆς πίστεως refers to the Holy Spirit as the source of empowerment of the characteristic of *being* faithful (and trusting) as Jesus was.[445] In fact, I submit that this "Spirit of faithfulness" is intimately connected to, if not precisely synonymous with, the δύναμις of God (referred to in 4:7) and the ζωὴ τοῦ 'Ιησοῦ (mentioned in 4:10-11).[446]

The answer to the third question – what does Paul mean by having "the *same* (τὸ αὐτό) Spirit of faithfulness"? – now becomes clear. The *same Spirit* of faithfulness refers to the agent of transformation mentioned in 2 Cor 3:18, namely the "Spirit of the Lord." And the *same* Spirit of *faithfulness* refers to what the Spirit enables, namely Jesus' mode of self-emptying existence for others (alluded to in 4:10-11 by the expressions νέκρωσις τοῦ 'Ιησοῦ and

---

[444]So, too, do COLLANGE, *Énigmes de la deuxième épître aux Corinthiens*, 162; FURNISH, *II Corinthians*, 258 and 286; LAMBRECHT, "The Nekrōsis of Jesus," 316; SAVAGE, *Power through Weakness*, 180; and G.D. FEE, *God's Empowering Presence: The Holy Spirit in the Letters of Paul* (Peabody, Mass.: Hendrickson, 1994) 323-24. PLUMMER (*II Corinthians*, 133) remarks that this is how many of the church fathers understood πνεῦμα τῆς πίστεως. HUGHES (*Paul's Second Epistle to the Corinthians*, 147) makes a similar observation about "[m]any of the old commentators."

[445]SAVAGE articulates this well (*Power through Weakness*, 180): "Since it is the Spirit who conforms Paul to the image of Christ (cf. 2 Corinthians 3:18), it must also be the Spirit who produces Paul's Christ-shaped faith – thus we can read 'Spirit' (with a capital 'S')." Cf. HAFEMANN, *2 Corinthians*, 187: ". . . since it is the Spirit who creates faith and conforms one to Christ's faithfulness in the midst of adversity, the 'spirit' in view here is most likely the Holy Spirit as the source of faith. . . ."

[446]This interpretation will receive further support when I analyze 2 Cor 1:21-22 in Chapter Five. To anticipate that discussion for a moment: It is striking that, immediately after alluding to Jesus' ναί (1:19b-20a) and the holistic human response of faithfulness to God marked by the phrase τὸ ἀμήν (1:20b), Paul speaks of God's gift of the Spirit in terms of 'christing' him and his co-workers εἰς Χριστόν.

παραδίδομαι διὰ 'Ιησοῦν).[447] Indeed, the reference to the divine Spirit in 4:13 concludes the line of thought begun in 3:18: The Spirit-empowered transformation into the "same image" entails taking on more and more the mode of human existence manifested by Jesus – the εἰκὼν τοῦ θεοῦ, the new Adam (4:4). It will be important to retain this understanding of τὸ πνεῦμα τῆς πίστεως when looking at the apostle's dramatic, climactic challenge to the Corinthians to test themselves to see whether they are ἐν τῇ πίστει (13:5).[448]

The second and first questions – relating to the particle δέ and the circumstantial participle ἔχοντες – can be handled together. While it is grammatically possible to take δέ in an adversative sense, it can also have a linking function.[449] I submit that the linking function is operative here, as Paul *continues* in 2 Cor 4:13 his line of thought from the preceding verses.[450] Indeed, the apostle brings this discussion to its climactic conclusion in 4:13-15, as he gives the source and cause (= the Spirit) and alludes to the exemplar (= Jesus' πίστις) of his and his co-workers' faithfulness (καὶ ἡμεῖς πιστεύομεν), through which grace extends to more and more people and thanksgiving abounds

---

[447]Thus, the usual understanding of "same" as referring to 'the same spirit of faith that the psalmist had' (e.g., PLUMMER, *II Corinthians*, 133; and KISTEMAKER, *The Second Epistle to the Corinthians*, 153) is inadequate. So, too, is the interpretation 'the same faith which the Psalm describes' (e.g., BULTMANN, *The Second Letter to the Corinthians*, 121), unless one recognizes that, for Paul, this passage of Scripture speaks of Jesus' πίστις.

[448]In many respects, my interpretation mirrors that found in SAVAGE, *Power through Weakness*, 179-80.

[449]See BDF, §§ 442 and 447; and BDAG, s.v. δέ, 1 and 2. For examples of δέ used connectively in 2 Cor, see, e.g., 1:13; 2:10; 3:7; 3:17; 3:18; and 4:5. I argue in Chapter Five for the linking or connective use of δέ in 2 Cor 1:21.

[450]*Pace* BARNETT, who claims that Paul begins a new section in 4:13, and that this is "signaled by δέ." See *The Second Epistle to the Corinthians*, 240, n. 3. The presence of δέ by itself, however, is not sufficient to ground Barnett's claim. MARTIN also holds that the apostle begins a new section in 4:13, and translates δέ adversatively ("But. . ."). See *2 Corinthians*, 89. These interpretations fail to see that, as MURPHY-O'CONNOR notes, "there is every indication that [v. 13] is the continuation of Paul's reflection on his experience as described in vv. 7-12." See MURPHY-O'CONNOR, "Faith and Resurrection in 2 Cor 4:13-14," 548.

to God (4:15). Hence, I take ἔχοντες as a *causal* participle,[451] thus rendering ἔχοντες δέ as "Now, because. . . ."

Taking all of the foregoing into account, I propose the following translation of 2 Cor 4:13: "Now, because we have the same Spirit of faithfulness according to what has been written – 'I have been faithful, therefore I have spoken' – so also are we faithful, and therefore we also speak." Empowered by the Spirit, Paul and his co-workers are faithful to embodying the loving, self-giving mode of existence manifested by Jesus, God's faithful δοῦλος. This is the apostle's summary statement of his discussion 4:7-12. And because they have been faithful, they also "speak out" (καὶ λαλοῦμεν).

What Paul and his co-workers "speak out" precedes these verses in 2 Cor 4:5: "We proclaim not ourselves, but Jesus Christ as Lord ('Ιησοῦς Χριστὸς Κύριος); and [we proclaim] ourselves as your slaves (δούλους) because of Jesus (διὰ 'Ιησοῦν)." We can now appreciate more fully the apostle's claim here. That Paul proclaims "Jesus Christ is *Lord*" comes as no surprise, since this is the same proclamation found at the climax of the story of Jesus as told in Phil 2:6-11 (the story that, we have seen, the apostle evokes by his allusion to the story of the righteous sufferer in 4:13). Moreover, Paul proclaims that he is δοῦλος to the Corinthians.[452] That is, the way in which he proclaims Jesus' lordship most eloquently is by offering his life in loving, self-emptying service to the Corinthians. And, as is the case in 4:11a, the apostle does so "because of Jesus" – both *for the sake of Jesus*, whom Paul lovingly serves, and *because of Jesus*, who as δοῦλος himself, incarnated living and dying in love for others so that they might have life.[453] Thus, the apostle's

---

[451]So, too, do PLUMMER, *II Corinthians*, 133; FURNISH, *II Corinthians*, 257; and THRALL, *II Corinthians*, 1.338.

[452]DANKER (*II Corinthians*, 63) rightly insists that δοῦλος be rendered in the more poignant sense of "slave" – not "servant" (the latter is found in, e.g., RSV; BRUCE, *1 and 2 Corinthians*, 196; and KISTEMAKER, *The Second Epistle to the Corinthians*, 142).

[453]SAMPLEY captures well this sense of διὰ 'Ιησοῦν: Paul's depiction of himself as slave "accords with his picture of Christ and is, therefore, a Pauline imitation of Christ, who, as the *eikōn* ('image/reflection') of God (4:4), has just been mentioned as the focus of the gospel that Paul propounds. So Paul, like the Christ he proclaims at the heart of his gospel, takes the role of the servant/slave (cf. 'the form of a slave,' Phil 2:7) in his

earlier statement in 4:5 corroborates the interpretation proffered here for 4:10-11 and 4:13.

To summarize: Paul continues to draw upon the story and *ethos* of Jesus by aligning his own experience of suffering and self-giving in service to others with the νέκρωσις τοῦ 'Ιησοῦ (2 Cor 4:10a) and "being handed over" διὰ 'Ιησοῦν (4:11a). Even more, the apostle alludes to the story of Jesus' πίστις by the allusion to LXX Pss 114-115 in 2 Cor 4:13. One can fully appreciate the strategy and depth of Paul's argument only by understanding that he evokes the entire context of these two psalms, texts he understands as telling the story of Jesus. Indeed, the story told in these psalms begins with the psalmist's – or better, *Jesus'* – saying, ἠγάπησα ("I have loved," LXX Ps 114:1). This declaration of love contextualizes the entire story: Jesus as God's faithful δοῦλος; his experience of distress; his deliverance by God; and his expression of thanksgiving and loyalty to God. The story of Jesus' πίστις, therefore, is a story of his love (cf. Gal 2:20). As we see in the next section, the apostle further develops this notion of Christ's love.

VI. Christ's Love (2 Cor 5:14)

Paul's next allusion to the character of Jesus is in 2 Cor 5:14a, where he speaks of ἡ ἀγάπη τοῦ Χριστοῦ ("the love of Christ"). The immediate context of this reference is the apostle's statement that his own work is one of persuading people, as well as his expression of hope that the Corinthians will know him and gauge his activity rightly (cf. ἐν καρδίᾳ) rather than according to appearances (ἐν προσώπῳ, 5:11-12). Then, in 5:13 and 5:14-15, Paul offers two rationales (cf. γάρ) for his position. The apostle's allusion to the ἀγάπη τοῦ Χριστοῦ is thus made in connection with his self-understanding of the basis of his apostolic activity. In what follows, I argue that the genitive τοῦ Χριστοῦ is subjective. I then set forth the logic of Paul's statement in 5:14-15,

---

relation to the Corinthians" (see *NIB*, 11.74). In addition, see WINDISCH, *Der zweite Korintherbrief*, 138; MURPHY-O'CONNOR, *The Theology of the Second Letter to the Corinthians*, 43; BARNETT, *The Second Epistle to the Corinthians*, 222-23; LAMBRECHT, *Second Corinthians*, 66; and MATERA, *II Corinthians*, 103. BULTMANN'S disavowal of Paul's taking Jesus as a model is unwarranted (see *The Second Letter to the Corinthians*, 107), as is FURNISH'S statement that, by writing διὰ 'Ιησοῦν, there is "no indication that the historical career of Jesus is in mind, or even that his earthly humiliation is invoked particularly." See FURNISH, *II Corinthians*, 250.

paying particular attention to his use of the verb συνέχω and his grammar. Finally I analyze how the apostle draws out the consequences of Christ's love in 5:16-17.

What does Paul mean by the expression ἡ ἀγάπη τοῦ Χριστοῦ? Does he refer to Christ's love (subjective genitive), or to the love humans have for Christ (objective genitive)?[454] The apostle uses this expression in two other places. In Rom 8:35 he asks: "Who will separate us from the love of Christ (ἀπὸ τῆς ἀγάπης τοῦ Χριστοῦ)?" The reference here is clearly to the love that Christ has for us, as Rom 8:37 and 8:39 make evident.[455] And in Eph 3:19 Paul concludes a prayer with a petition that God grant the recipients of the letter the power "to know the love of Christ (τὴν ἀγάπην τοῦ Χριστοῦ) which surpasses knowledge." This expression is sandwiched between two others – "the breadth and length and height and depth" (3:18), and "all the fullness of God" (3:19) – that also connote something of tremendous measure. It is Christ's love for humanity, *not* a human love for Christ, that more aptly fits this context.[456] Hence, in the apostle's other usages of the phrase ἡ ἀγάπη τοῦ Χριστοῦ, the genitive τοῦ Χριστοῦ is subjective. Furthermore, in *all* other cases where Paul uses the substantive ἀγάπη + the genitive of person, the genitive is subjective.[457] When the apostle wants to express love *for* someone,

---

[454]While the majority of commentators take ἡ ἀγάπη τοῦ Χριστοῦ as a subjective genitive, J. HÉRING renders it as an objective genitive. See *The Second Epistle of Saint Paul to the Corinthians*, trans. A.W. HEATHCOTE and P.J. ALLCOCK (London: Epworth, 1967), 41-42. So, too, C. SPICQ submits that "the context (cf. v. 13) suggests an objective genitive, love for Christ." See *TLNT*, 3.341, n. 16.

[455]See FITZMYER, *Romans*, 533-34. In 8:37 Paul refers to τοῦ ἀγαπήσαντος ἡμᾶς ("the one [i.e., Christ] who loved us"); and in 8:39 the apostle asserts that nothing "will be able to separate us from the love of God [that is] in Christ Jesus our Lord."

[456]Cf. M.Y. MACDONALD, *Colossians and Ephesians*, SP 17 (Collegeville, Minn.: Liturgical, 2000) 278. After noting that the reference to "love" in Eph 3:17 is somewhat ambiguous, she remarks about 3:19: ". . . in this case there is no doubt concerning the type of love: it is the love of Christ, that is the love belonging to Christ, which he bestows on believers."

[457]This is true of ἡ ἀγάπη τοῦ θεοῦ as well. See Rom 5:5 and 8:39; 2 Cor 13:13; and 2 Thess 3:5 (plus those passages in which the possessive pronoun refers to God – Rom 5:8; Eph 2:4; and Col 1:13). It is also the case with ἡ ἀγάπη τοῦ πνεύματος in Rom

he uses the expression ἀγάπη + εἰς + the recipient.[458] Based on his usage elsewhere, therefore, we can expect that Paul employs a subjective genitive in 2 Cor 5:14a, an expectation that will be borne out by a deeper analysis of the passage.

After referring to Christ's love, Paul turns to that love's most dramatic manifestation: "[Christ] died for all" (ὑπὲρ πάντων ἀπέθανεν, 2 Cor 5:14b and 5:15a; cf. 5:15b). The preposition ὑπέρ is significant in this regard. In conjunction with the genitive, it signifies an activity undertaken in the interest of or on behalf of another. It can even denote something done in place of another[459] (a denotation I will take up below in the analysis of 2 Cor 5:21). For the time being, it is sufficient to take note of ὑπέρ as marking Jesus' dying on behalf of (or *for*) all. Recall from the previous section how the apostle elsewhere brings together the notions of Christ's love, his handing himself over, and his doing so *for* – ὑπέρ – others (see Eph 5:2 and 5:25; and esp. Gal 2:20, where Paul offers his précis of Jesus' πίστις). The apostle draws upon this same dynamic in 2 Cor 5:14-15 in terms of Jesus' act of dying. Recall, too (from the previous chapter), that Paul's argument in Rom 5:6-8 – where the apostle states that Christ died *for* (ὑπέρ) the "ungodly," *for* "sinners" in order to show forth God's love for all humanity – rests on the premise that Jesus' demeanor co-inheres with God's intent. Thus, the reference to Jesus' love is clearly connected to his dying on behalf of others. I submit that, for the apostle, Jesus' dying is a synecdoche of Christ's paradigmatic *living for others*. As we will see, the unfolding logic of 2 Cor 5:14-15 makes evident that the apostle here alludes to Jesus' mode of human existence.

The key to understanding this passage is the verb συνέχω. Paul states, "Christ's love συνέχει us." Several commentators understand the verb as having a negative or restraining function here: Christ's love "controls" or

---

15:30. In every single instance of ἀγάπη + the genitive personal pronoun, Paul signifies X's love, not love for X (see 1 Cor 16:24; 2 Cor 8:8 and 8:24; Phil 1:9; 1 Thess 3:6; 2 Thess 1:3; and Phlm 5 and 7).

[458]See Rom 5:8; 2 Cor 2:8; Eph 1:15; 1 Thess 3:12; and 2 Thess 1:3. Rom 5:8 illustrates well how the apostle expresses X's love for Y: συνίστησιν τὴν ἑαυτοῦ ἀγάπην εἰς ἡμᾶς ὁ θεός.

[459]See BDAG, s.v. ὑπέρ, A.1.

"constrains."[460] Admittedly, συνέχω has such a connotation in Phil 1:23, the apostle's only other use of this verb.[461] But does this constraining function of συνέχω capture what Paul is saying in 2 Cor 5:14-15? It is important to point out that συνέχω has several meanings.[462] It appears that the apostle exploits the richness of these meanings to convey the power of Jesus' love. The fundamental meaning of συνέχω is "hold together, sustain." The context of this usage is often one that is vast, even universal, in scope.[463] That Paul has such a global sense in mind is suggested by his use of πᾶς in the lines that follow – "one died for *all*" (5:14b and 5:15a); "*all* have died" (5:15a); and "those who are

---

[460]See, e.g., PLUMMER, *II Corinthians*, 173; BARRETT, *The Second Epistle to the Corinthians*, 167-68; THRALL, *II Corinthians*, 1.408; and MATERA, *II Corinthians*, 133.

[461]In Phil 1:23 Paul asserts that he is "hard pressed" or "held" as between the horns of a dilemma – on the one hand, he desires to depart this life and so be with Christ; on the other hand, he wishes to continue to be able to minister to the Philippians. J. LAMBRECHT asserts that the apostle appeals to the meaning of "constrain" in both of his usages of συνέχω. See "'Reconcile Yourselves. . .': A Reading of 2 Corinthians 5,11-21," in R. BIERINGER and J. LAMBRECHT, *Studies on 2 Corinthians*, BETL 112 (Leuven: Leuven University Press, 1994) 363-412, here 377, n. 30.

[462]See BDAG, s.v. συνέχω; and *TLNT*, 3.337-41. DANKER lists eight definitions, and SPICQ seven.

[463]See, e.g., Wis 1:7: πνεῦμα κυρίου πεπλήρωκεν τὴν οἰκουμένην, καὶ τὸ συνέχον τὰ πάντα γνῶσιν ἔχει φωνῆς ("[The] Spirit of [the] Lord has filled the universe, and that which holds together all things has knowledge of [its] sound"); *1 Clem.* 20:5: ἀβύσσων τε ἀνεξιχνίαστα καὶ νερτέρων ἀνεκδιήγητα κλίματα τοῖς αὐτοῖς συνέχεται προστάγμασιν ("The unsearchable places of the abysses and the unfathomable realms of the lower world are controlled by the same ordinances" [that is, by *God's* decrees that rule creation]); and *Diogn.* 6:7: ἐγκέκλειστται μὲν ἡ ψυχὴ τῷ σώματι, συνέχει δὲ αὐτὴ τὸ σῶμα· καὶ Χριστιανοὶ κατέχονται μὲν ὡς ἐν φρουρᾷ τῷ κόσμῳ, αὐτοὶ δὲ συνέχουσι τὸν κόσμον ("The soul has been shut up in the body, but itself sustains the body; and Christians are confined in the world as in a prison, but themselves sustain the world"). I have taken the latter two texts and translations from *The Apostolic Fathers*, vols. 1-2, trans. K. LAKE, LCL (Cambridge, MA: Harvard University Press, 1985-92). In addition, see *TLNT*, 3.338, n. 5 for more references from Philo and Plutarch.

living" (οἱ ζῶντες, 5:15b).[464] Hence, the apostle's association of Christ's love with συνέχω seems to be connected with something of universal anthropological significance. (In addition to alluding to the part of the story that refers specifically to Jesus' humanity, therefore, Paul here draws upon "the big picture" of the story of Jesus referred to at the beginning of this chapter.) Observe, moreover, that the object of συνέχω is the apostle,[465] who has made a particular determination (cf. κρίναντας). That which he has determined is described in the second half of 5:14.

Second Corinthians 5:14b reads: κρίναντας τοῦτο, ὅτι εἷς ὑπὲρ πάντων ἀπέθανεν, ἄρα οἱ πάντες ἀπέθανον ("*because* we have judged this – [since] one died for all, as a result all have died").[466] Paul's grammar offers subtle clues regarding his position that Jesus' death has brought into being a new possibility of existence for all people. The particle ἄρα is inferential, and here introduces an apodosis that emphasizes the *result* that follows from what immediately precedes (in this case, that "Jesus died for all").[467] Moreover, the placement of the definite article οἱ immediately before the pronominal adjective πάντες serves to highlight the contrast between the "one" and the "all."[468] Observe that this contrast is similar to the one the apostle makes in Rom 5:15-

---

[464]See, too, the cosmic language in 2 Cor 5:16-17, e.g., "new creation." It is interesting to note that V.P. FURNISH at one time chose to render συνέχω as "sustains," an interpretation that "best fits with Paul's view of God's love as the redeeming, reconciling, rightwising power for life." See *Theology and Ethics in Paul* (Nashville: Abingdon, 1968) 167. While not explicitly mentioning the universal or global connotation of this interpretive decision, his explanation seems to imply it. In *II Corinthians* (pp. 309-10), however, FURNISH changes his position and now renders the verb as "lay claim to."

[465]2 Cor 5:14-21 is notoriously difficult for tracing the referent of "we." I agree with THRALL that ἡμᾶς in 5:14 "refers simply to Paul himself: it is in line with the first plurals of vv. 11-13, which clearly have this reference." See *II Corinthians*, 1.409. LAMBRECHT also reads ἡμᾶς as "epistolary; Paul points to himself." See "'Reconcile Yourselves. . .'," 377.

[466]Reading the circumstantial participle κρίναντας as causal, as does THRALL, *II Corinthians*, 1.409, n. 1521; *pace* FURNISH, *II Corinthians*, 310.

[467]See BDAG, s.v. ἄρα, 2.a.. Cf. Gal 2:21 and 3:29.

[468]See BDF, § 275 (7).

21, in which he discusses what the obedience of "the one human being, Jesus Christ," the new Adam, has brought about for "the many."[469] That which the "one" – namely Jesus, who died as a manifestation of his love – has brought about for the "all" is initially expressed in 2 Cor 5:14b by the paradoxical formulation "all have died." Although Paul uses the verb ἀποθνῄσκω literally with regard to Jesus in 5:14b, surely he employs the same verb metaphorically with regard to οἱ πάντες. The apostle cannot mean that all people have physically expired. Rather, he suggests that something of extraordinary scope and proportion has "died."[470] As will become clear in 5:15 – where Paul expresses the *purpose* of Jesus' death – the converse of this metaphorical death is that an entirely new possibility for human existence has come about for all.[471] And it is in this new mode of existence that Christ's love now sustains "us."

The καί at the beginning of 2 Cor 5:15 is epexegetical, and is best rendered "that is to say."[472] Thus, this verse extrapolates from what comes before: "That is to say, [Jesus] died for all, *in order that* (ἵνα) those who are living might no longer live for themselves but for him who died for them and was raised." Observe that Jesus' 'dying for all' has a specific purpose. Again, careful analysis of Paul's grammar illuminates his meaning. Here the apostle uses the dative of *advantage*:[473] People are now to live not for their own

---

[469]Lambrecht, Martin, Furnish, and Thrall also note the connection between 2 Cor 5:14b and Rom 5. According to LAMBRECHT, the εἷς-πάντες antithesis indicates that "Paul must have been thinking of Christ as the new Adam" (see "'Reconcile Yourselves. . .'," 382). MARTIN remarks in this connection that, for the apostle, "Jesus is the progenitor of a new race, the representative of the new humanity" (see *2 Corinthians*, 131). FURNISH, in addition to seeing the connection with Rom 5:12-21, observes that "[t]his same notion has been accented in an earlier letter to this congregation. . ." in 1 Cor 15:22 (see *II Corinthians*, 326-27). Cf. THRALL, *II Corinthians*, 1.411. For more on Jesus as the "new Adam," see Chapter Five, Section III.

[470]See THRALL, *II Corinthians*, 1.409-11, for a review of six different interpretations.

[471]So, BARRETT, *The Second Epistle to the Corinthians*, 169: "Because Christ, being the person he was, died and was raised, there exists the universal possibility . . . of a new kind of human existence. . . ."

[472]See BDF, § 442 (9). So, too, FURNISH, *II Corinthians*, 310-11.

[473]See BDF, § 188 (2).

advantage, but for Jesus. Moreover, notice how Paul describes Christ at the end of the verse: The apostle reiterates for the *third* time in 5:14-15 that Jesus died *for* (ὑπέρ) others.[474] Paul thus implies that living for Jesus entails living as the latter lived[475] – not for his own advantage, but on behalf of, that is, *for the advantage of* others, even to the point of offering his own life. This offering is the supreme expression of love. Furthermore, I suggest that with these words the apostle exploits an additional sense of the verb συνέχω, that which signifies

---

[474]MARTIN points out that the active voice of the aorist participle ἀποθανόντι suggests "not only a historical fact, but that Jesus *voluntarily* laid down his life." See *2 Corinthians*, 132 (italics added).

[475]Cf. Rom 15:1-3 and 1 Cor 10:31-11:1. As we saw in Chapter Three, Paul insists in Rom 15:1-3 that the "strong" ought not to seek to please themselves, but rather to please their neighbor; that is, they are to seek their neighbor's good and edification. Then the apostle offers Christ as an example of one who did not please himself. In 1 Cor 10:31-11:1 Paul describes how he tries to please others in everything he does, not seeking his own advantage, but that of others. Then he offers to the Corinthians the pregnant exhortation: "Become imitators of me *just as I am of Christ*" – μιμηταί μου γίνεσθε καθὼς κἀγὼ Χριστοῦ.

MATERA'S commentary on 2 Cor 5:14-15 is illuminating: "... one might have expected Paul to write 'in order that the living might live no longer for themselves but *for others*.' Paul's reasoning, however, is christological. The purpose of life is to live *for* the one who died and rose *for* all (cf. Rom 14:7-9). Such a life necessarily includes living for others, since Christ has died for all. But instead of beginning with humanity, Paul starts with humanity's representative, so that life *for* Christ becomes the most profound kind of service to others." See *II Corinthians*, 135 (Matera's italics). In his comment on 2 Cor 5:14-15, MURPHY-O'CONNOR rightly notes that the apostle is alluding to the "altruism of Christ's existence culminating in his self-sacrifice." See *The Theology of the Second Letter to the Corinthians*, 57. HAFEMANN aptly concludes his treatment of 2 Cor 5:14-15 thus: "To live *for* Christ is to live *like* Christ." See *2 Corinthians*, 241 (Hafemann's italics).

"impel, urge on."[476] Christ's love has the power to impel others to live in such love.

The metaphorical sense of what Paul means by the expression "all have died" (2 Cor 5:14b) thus becomes clear. Jesus' death has brought into being the possibility of a new mode of human existence, namely living for the benefit of others. Things are not the same after Jesus' life, death, and resurrection. Elsewhere the apostle states that "Sin" and "Death"[477] reigned before the time of Christ (see Rom 5:12-14). On the level of human existence, the reign of Sin and Death is marked by selfishness, dissension, ruthless competition – in short, the breakdown of community.[478] It is the enslaving power of this mode of existence that now has "died" as a result of Jesus' death.[479]

Paul's reference to the ἀγάπη τοῦ Χριστοῦ thus has a rich signification. It evokes Jesus' love, manifested in his *living* for the benefit of

---

[476]See BDAG, s.v. συνέχω, 7. Cf. the Vulgate's "urget nos"; WINDISCH, *Der zweite Korintherbrief*, 181; and SAMPLEY, *NIB*, 11.92. P.B. DUFF argues that the richness of συνέχω sheds light on Paul's use of the verb θριαμβεύω in 2 Cor 2:14. In short, Duff contends that θριαμβεύω is also susceptible to a wide range of meanings, and that Paul might be referring to an epiphany procession of a deity (rather than solely to a military triumphal procession). See "Metaphor, Motif, and Meaning: The Rhetorical Strategy behind the Image 'Led in Triumph' in 2 Corinthians 2:14," *CBQ* 53 (1991) 79-92, esp. 86-87. My proposal concerning συνέχω is similar: Paul is exploiting "the semantic plenitude" of this verb.

[477]I capitalize "Sin" and "Death" to indicate that Paul understands these as cosmic forces. Cf. FITZMYER, *Romans*, 411-12: "*Hamartia* is the personified malevolent force, Sin (with capital S), hostile to God and alienating human beings from him; it strode upon the stage of human history at the time of Adam's transgression ([Rom] 6:12-14; 7:7-23; 1 Cor 15:56) and has dominated 'all human beings'" (p. 411). "'Death' is not merely physical, bodily death. . . . Death is thus a personified cosmic force ([Rom] 8:38; 1 Cor 3:22), the 'last enemy' to be vanquished (1 Cor 15:56)" (p.412).

[478]Cf., e.g., 2 Cor 12:20; and Gal 5:15 and 5:19-21.

[479]THRALL makes the intriguing suggestion that 2 Cor 5:14b is perhaps "a counter-statement to the assertion in Rom 5.12 that sin and death entered the cosmos through Adam, and that death became pervasive because all sinned." See *II Corinthians*, 1.411.

others,[480] even to the point of *dying* for them. In addition, the love of Christ refers to the ongoing power that (1) sustains the apostle and all those who are "in Christ" (ἐν Χριστῷ, cf. 2 Cor 5:17) within a new possibility of human existence, an existence marked by living not for oneself but for the sake of others, *and* (2) impels them to live in this manner.[481]

In 2 Cor 5:16-17 Paul goes on to describe the consequences of Jesus' powerful love, introducing both verses with the inferential conjunction ὥστε – "therefore, so."[482] It is helpful to look first at 5:17. In this verse the apostle claims that the power of Jesus' love is such as to bring about a *new creation*: "Therefore, if anyone is in Christ, [there is] a new creation (καινὴ κτίσις)! The old things have passed away; behold, new things have come to be (γέγονεν)!" Observe the cosmic language here, giving further support to the interpretation proffered above for συνέχω. The new creation to which Paul refers has its beginning point in Jesus, the new Adam, the εἰκὼν τοῦ θεοῦ (4:4) whose humanity, lived in love and service of others, radiates God's δόξα.[483] It

---

[480]Paul's appeal to Jesus' πραΰτης and ἐπιείκεια (2 Cor 10:1) takes on an even richer texture when these attributes are considered within the context of Christ's life lived for the advantage of others.

[481]Cf. J.W. FRASER'S assessment of the signification of ἀγάπη τοῦ Χριστοῦ: "In our context we read of 'the love of Christ,' a present reality, which cannot however be known apart from the way Christ once revealed that love, in His death for all. . . . 'Christ' cannot be considered apart from the historical Jesus." See FRASER, "Paul's Knowledge of Jesus: II Corinthians V. 16 Once More," *NTS* 17 (1971) 293-313, here 299. In addition, cf. the following observation by R. PICKETT: ". . . the self-giving love epitomized in Christ's death *impels the believer to live for others*. In these verses the self-giving love of Christ in his death for others is presented as a model for authentic Christian behaviour." See PICKETT, *The Cross in Corinth: The Social Significance of the Death of Jesus*, JSNTSup 143 (Sheffield: Sheffield Academic Press, 1997) 148 (italics added).

[482]See BDAG, s.v. ὥστε, 1.a. So, too, FURNISH, *II Corinthians*, 311 and 314.

[483]THRALL (*II Corinthians*, 1.426-29) rightly recognizes the new Adam motif in 2 Cor 5:17, as does HAFEMANN (*2 Corinthians*, 244), who observes: "Hence, whatever the 'new things' are in 5:17, they must certainly include a new life of growing obedience to God brought about by the Spirit. As the 'second Adam' reflecting the image of God, Christ brings his followers back to the glory associated with Adam before his fall into

is no coincidence that the apostle alludes in 2 Cor 5:17 to the language of LXX Isa 43:18-19, language that evokes images of new creation and new exodus. Jesus' self-giving life and death have broken the bonds of Sin and Death – to which Paul alludes in 2 Cor 5:21 (see the following section) – and brought about the possibility of a mode of existence that is truly life-giving.[484] Note, too, the perfect tense of the verb γέγονεν, which reminds the reader of 1:19b. Jesus' ναί – his self-giving in love and faithfulness to God's will – has brought about a condition that perdures "from now on" (ἀπὸ τοῦ νῦν,[485] 5:16a; cf. νυνί in Rom 3:21).

To be a new creation also entails a transformation of knowledge, especially as it pertains to the evaluation of others. This is the point of 2 Cor 5:16: ὥστε ἡμεῖς ἀπὸ τοῦ νῦν οὐδένα οἴδαμεν κατὰ σάρκα· εἰ καὶ ἐγνώκαμεν κατὰ σάρκα Χριστόν, ἀλλὰ νῦν οὐκετι γινώσκομεν ("Therefore, from now on we regard no one κατὰ σάρκα; even if we [once] understood Christ κατὰ σάρκα, we no longer understand [him so]"). This verse is, in the words of Walter Schmithals, "probably the hardest *crux interpretum* of II Corinthians, which is not poor in such *cruces*."[486] Here I limit my comments to discerning what Paul means by the phrase κατὰ σάρκα, and to probing his statements of how he now regards others, as well as how he once understood and now understands Christ.

---

disobedience." According to Hafemann, such obedience to God, as revealed by Christ, is manifested by living for others (*ibid.*, 243). MATERA (*II Corinthians*, 137) also sees the presence of the new Adam in 2 Cor 5:14-15. For more on Christ as the εἰκὼν τοῦ θεοῦ, and on the association of δόξα with the humanity of Jesus and the renewed humanity after the likeness of Christ, see Chapter Five, Section III.

[484]SAMPLEY brings Paul's reference to the "new creation" in Gal 6:15 – his only other use of this phrase – to bear with good effect upon the interpretation of 2 Cor 5:17. Sampley observes that Gal 6:15 is a "refinement" of Gal 5:6, and that the expressions "new creation" and "faith working through love" are mutually interpretive. See *NIB*, 11.93. Indeed, I submit that πίστις δι' ἀγάπης ἐνεργουμένη is, for the apostle, an apt summary of what Jesus revealed in his humanity and now empowers in others.

[485]TANNEHILL notes that this phrase refers "to the present age of the manifestation of God's righteousness, the time of salvation, in contrast to the time before God's decisive act." See *Dying and Rising with Christ*, 67.

[486]SCHMITHALS, *Gnosticism in Corinth*, 302.

The apostle's other usages of κατὰ σάρκα (literally, "according to [the] flesh") in 2 Corinthians are instructive. In 1:17 Paul refers to "planning" κατὰ σάρκα. Recall that the logic of this passage presumes that he contrasts making plans on the human level with following God's guidance.[487] In 10:2 the apostle warns that he will defend himself against the charge of conducting himself κατὰ σάρκα, while in 10:3 he denies that he "wages battle" κατὰ σάρκα. Then, in 10:4 he contrasts "weapons" that are σαρκικά with those that are "powerful because of God." Finally, in 11:18 Paul reluctantly gives in to boasting κατὰ σάρκα, even though by such boasting he is not speaking κατὰ κύριον ("according to [the] Lord," 11:17). Observe that in all of these cases, κατὰ σάρκα is used adverbially and has a strongly negative connotation. Moreover, the phrase is contrasted with acting or speaking in a manner that is influenced or empowered by God and God's ways – that is, κατὰ σάρκα is contrasted with that which is "according to the Lord." Now, are these characteristics true of the apostle's employment of κατὰ σάρκα in 5:16? I submit that they are.

The syntax of 2 Cor 5:16a indicates that the phrase is adverbial, modifying the verb οἴδαμεν.[488] Moreover, κατὰ σάρκα obviously has a negative connotation here. Paul states that he[489] *no longer* regards anyone in such a manner – that is, in a way that is *not* divinely influenced/empowered. But how can this be stated positively? The immediate context (5:14-15) suggests that, because Christ died for *all*, each and every person has value.[490] Indeed, in his previous correspondence to the Corinthians – in the context of the propriety of eating meat sacrificed to idols – the apostle has already drawn upon this idea: "For by your knowledge, the weak one is destroyed, *the brother for whom Christ*

---

[487]See Section IV, esp. n. 379.

[488]It is true that, when using the phrase adverbially, Paul usually places the phrase before the verb (e.g., Rom 8:4-5; and 2 Cor 1:17 and 10:2-3). But notice that in 2 Cor 11:18 he inserts it *after* the verb (as in 5:16a). Even more telling, as FURNISH observes, is the fact that "in no case where the phrase goes with a substantive does the verb intervene, as it does here . . ." (in 5:16a). See *II Corinthians*, 312.

[489]Taking ἡμεῖς to have the same referent as ἡμᾶς in 5:14a, and thus as epistolary. See n. 465 above. In addition, see LAMBRECHT, "'Reconcile Yourselves. . .'," 379; and THRALL, *II Corinthians*, 1.413.

[490]See SAMPLEY, *NIB*, 11.98.

died" (1 Cor 8:11). Paul makes a similar remark in Rom 14:15. In this passage, it is striking that the apostle contrasts acting out of a sense of superior knowledge (having little or no consideration for others) with conducting oneself κατὰ ἀγάπην ("according to *love*"!). Therefore, the converse of regarding others κατὰ σάρκα is to recognize their value in light of Christ's dying out of love for them, and thus to deal with them κατὰ ἀγάπην. Again, the immediate context of 2 Cor 5:15 spells out what this means: living not for one's own advantage, but for the advantage and benefit of others, as Jesus did.

What about 2 Cor 5:16b? Several prominent commentators have argued that κατὰ σάρκα is adjectival, modifying Christ.[491] This position, however, is belied not only by Paul's syntax, but also by the thrust of his statement. When the apostle uses κατὰ σάρκα adjectivally elsewhere, he normally places it *after* the substantive it modifies.[492] This is not the case here. More importantly, Paul's argument demands the adverbial interpretation. In 5:16b the apostle offers the example *par excellence* of the transformation of perception, a transformation that is the point of 5:16 as a whole.[493] Paul refers to his former way of understanding Christ apart from divine empowerment/influence. The

---

[491]E.g., F.C. BAUR held that the phrase Χριστὸς κατὰ σάρκα refers to the "Messiah" of Judaism (see "Die Christus Partei"); according to WINDISCH, it refers to "Jesus der Lehrer und Prophet," i.e., Jesus as he was before the passion (see *Der zweite Korintherbrief*, 188); according to BULTMANN, it refers to "Christ in his plainness, in his σχῆμα ὡς ἄνθρωπος, his μορφὴ δούλου" (see *The Second Letter to the Corinthians*, 155); according to GEORGI, it refers to the θεῖος ἀνήρ conception of Jesus held by Paul's opponents (see *The Opponents of Paul in Second Corinthians*, 276-77); and according to SCHMITHALS, the phrase in question was a gloss from the hand of gnostics, for whom Χριστὸς κατὰ σάρκα referred to the enfleshed, crucified Jesus (see *Gnosticism in Corinth*, 312-15).

[492]See Rom 1:3; 4:1; 9:3; and 9:5; and 1 Cor 10:18. The exceptions are Eph 6:5 and Col 3:22 – both of which refer to "[your] earthly masters" (τοῖς κατὰ σάρκα κυρίοις) – but these are clear examples of attributive adjectival usage. So too is the case with Rom 9:5, where κατὰ σάρκα does modify "Christ" (ὁ Χριστὸς τὸ κατὰ σάρκα). See the discussion in FURNISH, *II Corinthians*, 313. It is also pertinent to point out that, in 2 Cor, when Paul wants to convey "according to the flesh" adjectivally, he uses the adjective σαρκικός (see 1:12 and 10:4).

[493]Cf. LAMBRECHT, who maintains that, in relation to 2 Cor 5:16a, 5:16b "constitutes its confirmation and extreme illustration." See *Second Corinthians*, 95.

apostle does not elaborate upon this statement. It is highly probable that he alludes here to his former estimate of the crucified Jesus as cursed by God.[494] But "*now*" (ἀλλὰ νῦν) Paul has judged (κρίναντας, 5:14b) the true import of Jesus' death, and thus understands him aright. That is, when the apostle says that he no longer understands Christ κατὰ σάρκα, by implication he means that he now views him properly – as the εἰκὼν τοῦ θεοῦ who revealed what human existence can be in the new creation, and whose love empowers people to embody this mode of existence. Moreover, notice that, as in 2 Cor 10:4-5, we encounter the theme of the importance of right knowing (γινώσκω) in connection with Jesus.[495]

Thus, in explaining the basis for his apostolic activity in 2 Cor 5:14-17, Paul draws upon the *ethos* of Jesus by his reference to the latter's ἀγάπη. Jesus' love was manifested in his living for the advantage of others, which culminated in his giving his life for all. This has resulted in a new possibility for human existence – tantamount to a "new creation" – that entails both perceiving others in light of Christ's dying for all *and* living for their benefit, even to the point of giving one's own life. In the verses that immediately follow (5:18-21), the apostle continues to allude to the story of Jesus, offering two of his most conspicuous characterizations of Christ.

---

[494]See Gal 3:13; cf. Deut 21:23. For a similar view, see C. WOLFF, "True Apostolic Knowledge of Christ: Exegetical Reflections on 2 Corinthians 5:14ff," in *Paul and Jesus: Collected Essays*, JSNTSup 37, ed. A.J.M. WEDDERBURN (Sheffield: Sheffield Academic Press, 1989) 81-98, here 88. In addition, see PLUMMER, *II Corinthians*, 177; MURPHY-O'CONNOR, *The Theology of the Second Letter to the Corinthians*, 58; THRALL, *II Corinthians*, 1.416-17 and 420; SCOTT, *2 Corinthians*, 134; and HAFEMANN, *2 Corinthians*, 242.

[495]This reading of 5:16b takes εἰ και as introducing a real condition. For a discussion of the different interpretive possibilities, see THRALL, *II Corinthians*, 1.415-20. J.L. MARTYN correctly argues that the primary issue in 5:16 is epistemology, not christology. See "Epistemology at the Turn of the Ages," in *Theological Issues in the Letters of Paul* (Nashville: Abingdon, 1997) 89-110. Cf. FRASER, "Paul's Knowledge of Jesus," esp. p. 308. It is also true, as BARRETT remarks, that "the view, based on a false interpretation of this verse, that Paul had no interest in the Jesus of history, must be dismissed." See *The Second Epistle to the Corinthians*, 171. So also BRUCE, *1 and 2 Corinthians*, 208; and DUNN, *The Theology of Paul the Apostle*, 184-85.

VII. "The one who did not know Sin"/"The one whom God made [to be] 'sin'" (2 Cor 5:21)

Paul delineates another aspect of the "love of Christ" in 2 Cor 5:18-21 by means of the notion of reconciliation. A striking feature of this passage is that *God* comes to the fore in the apostle's discussion. God is named explicitly as the agent of reconciliation in 5:18-19, and is the subject of the main clause in 5:21. Indeed, at first glance, Jesus appears to play a greatly diminished role in this part of Paul's argument.[496] Closer analysis, however, reveals that the apostle continues to allude to the story of Jesus in these verses, and especially to his *ethos*. In what follows, I examine the prepositional phrases of which "Christ" is the object in 5:18-19, as well as the import of Paul's periphrastic construction in 5:19. Then I investigate what the apostle means by his enigmatic references to Jesus in 5:21 – namely, that he is the one "who did not know Sin," and that God made him "to be 'sin.'"

What is the force of the two prepositional phrases in 2 Cor 5:18-19 of which "Christ" is the object? In 5:18 Paul writes that God "reconciled us to [God's] self διὰ Χριστοῦ."[497] The force of διά + the genitive of person is to denote personal agency and mediation.[498] Although God is the ultimate agent of reconciliation between God and human beings, the apostle indicates here that Jesus as the Messiah (= ὁ Χριστός) played an active and personal role in this reconciliation as well. This allusion to Christ's agency sheds light on 5:19, where Paul states: "God was ἐν Χριστῷ reconciling the world to [God's] self." As is the case with 1:19-20, it is better to take the preposition ἐν as indicating agency – in the sense of "with the help of" or "through" – rather than in a static,

---

[496]Cf. LAMBRECHT, "'Reconcile Yourselves. . .'," 376: "In vv. 18-21 a shift occurs from Christology to theology. To be sure, Christ continues to be mentioned, but, with much emphasis, God is presented here as taking the initiative."

[497]For a fuller treatment of the theme of reconciliation in Paul, see J. DUPONT, *La réconciliation dans la théologie de Saint Paul*, ALBO II 32 (Louvain: Publications universitaires de Louvain, 1953) esp. pp. 8-10, 21-22 and 31-33; and R. P. MARTIN, *Reconciliation: A Study of Paul's Theology* (Atlanta: John Knox, 1981) esp. pp. 90-110.

[498]See BDAG, s.v. διά, A.4. Cf., e.g., Rom 5:9; 5:17; 5:19; 5:21; and 8:37; and 2 Cor 1:20.

locative sense.[499] Observe, moreover, the placement of the phrase ἐν Χριστῷ. Paul inserts it between the main verb ἦν and the remainder of the predicate. It is as if the apostle puts us on special notice that it is *with the help of Christ* that God was reconciling the world. In other words, as Leander Keck observes, what Paul formulates in 5:19 is "the co-inherence of God's act and Christ's demeanor."[500] In this way, the apostle draws upon the character of Jesus as one who sought to reconcile people to God.

Paul's employment of a periphrastic construction further bolsters the position that he refers to the agency and character of Christ in 2 Cor 5:19: "God was (ἦν, imperfect of εἰμί)... reconciling (καταλλάσσων, present participle) . . . ." I suggest that the apostle's use of the imperfect tense should be taken seriously.[501] It is true that in 5:18 Paul expresses God's act of reconciling with

---

[499]See n. 387 above. Indeed, several commentators agree that the phrase ἐν Χριστῷ in 5:19 is to be understood as parallel to διὰ Χριστοῦ in 5:18, thus having the sense of "through" or "by means of" Christ. See, e.g., PLUMMER, *II Corinthians*, 183; BULTMANN, *The Second Letter to the Corinthians*, 161; FURNISH, *II Corinthians*, 318; C.H. TALBERT, *Reading Corinthians: A Literary and Theological Commentary on 1 and 2 Corinthians* (New York: Crossroad, 1987) 166; BARNETT, *The Second Epistle to the Corinthians*, 306; and LAMBRECHT, *Second Corinthians*, 99. Lambrecht, however, also adds, "Yet the nuance of God's presence in Christ should not be overlooked" (ibid.). Cf. ALLO, *Seconde Épître aux Corinthiens*, 171. Indeed, 2 Cor 5:19 became one of the important scriptural sources for discerning the divine nature of Christ. For a good synopsis of the history of interpretation of this passage, including patristic interpretations, see R. BIERINGER, "2 Korinther 5,19a und die Versöhnung der Welt," in R. BIERINGER and J. LAMBRECHT, *Studies on 2 Corinthians*, BETL 112 (Leuven: Leuven University Press, 1994) 429-59, here 437-45. COLLANGE lays out four interpretive options for 5:19a. See *Énigmes de la deuxième épître aux Corinthiens*, 270-72.

[500]KECK, "'Jesus' in Romans," 458.

[501]So, BRUCE, who rightly notes: "The periphrastic construction emphasizes the imperfect or continuous aspect of the verb. . . ." See *1 and 2 Corinthians*, 209. I differ with Bruce, however, as to the significance of Paul's periphrastic imperfect. Bruce argues that the continuous aspect here implies that reconciliation is not completed without the response of faith. While the human response is indeed necessary, the apostle does not take up this response until 2 Cor 6:1, where he does so explicitly. THRALL wrongly takes ἦν καταλλάσσων as a "disguised aorist." See *II Corinthians*, 1.434.

an aorist participle (καταλλάξαντος). It is also true that elsewhere the apostle names the death of Jesus as the means by which humanity has been reconciled to God (cf. Rom 5:10). Nevertheless, the phrase ὡς ὅτι with which Paul begins 2 Cor 5:19 has an explicative function, in the sense of "because indeed."[502] In effect, the apostle offers a further commentary in 5:19 on God's act of reconciliation and Christ's role in it. By utilizing the imperfect tense of εἰμί, Paul suggests that there was a durative quality to God's act of reconciling, and thus *a durative quality to Jesus' agency*. In other words, while Jesus' death was central to God's work of reconciliation, 5:19 connotes that more was involved in Jesus' agency and help.[503] Thus, in 5:19 the apostle alludes both to Jesus' demeanor as reconciler and to the durative quality of his reconciling activity. This interpretation is borne out by the first reference to Christ in 5:21a.

The first half of 2 Cor 5:21a reads: τὸν μὴ γνόντα ἁμαρτίαν ὑπὲρ ἡμῶν ἁμαρτίαν ἐποίησεν ("[God][504] made the one who did not know Sin [to

---

[502]Reading with the Vulgate, *quoniam quidem*. The phrase ὡς ὅτι is unusual in the NT, appearing only two other times, both in Paul's writings (2 Cor 11:21 and 2 Thess 2:2). In these other instances, the Vulgate renders the phrase *quasi* ("as if"), a rendering that does not fit in the present case. ALLO points out that ὡς ὅτι has a causal sense in Esth 4:14 (see *Seconde Épître aux Corinthiens*, 169). BARRETT opts to give ὡς ὅτι in 2 Cor 5:19 a causal sense, although he does so with some hesitation (see *The Second Epistle to the Corinthians*, 176-77). LAMBRECHT says it has both a causal and comparative force (see *Second Corinthians*, 98). For a full discussion of the various ways this phrase has been construed, see FURNISH, *II Corinthians*, 317-18; and BIERINGER, "2 Korinther 5,19a und die Versöhnung der Welt," 433-37.

[503]Thus, the prepositional phrases διὰ Χριστοῦ and ἐν Χριστῷ ought not to be totally reduced to meaning, as BARNETT claims, "through that *death* by means of which God reconciled the world to himself" (see *The Second Epistle to the Corinthians*, 306 – Barnett's italics; cf. p. 302). BULTMANN (*The Second Letter to the Corinthians*, 158 and 161), FURNISH (*II Corinthians*, 317-18) and BELLEVILLE (*2 Corinthians*, 156) make this same reduction.

[504]The subject of 5:21 is not named explicitly. The immediately preceding context – καταλλάγητε τῷ θεῷ ("Be reconciled *to God*!") – makes clear, however, that "God" is carried over as the implied subject.

be] 'sin' for our sake").[505] This is a cryptic statement, but it is possible to explicate some of its implications. Jesus is identified as τὸν μὴ γνόντα ἁμαρτίαν, "the one who did not know Sin." Once again, Paul turns to the issue of knowing. As we have just seen, in 5:16 the apostle – using the verb γινώσκω twice and its synonym οἶδα once – describes the transformation of people's knowing in the new creation. Now, in 5:21, Paul says something about *Jesus'* knowing. Observe, moreover, the placement of the prepositional phrase ὑπὲρ ἡμῶν ("for our sake") immediately following τὸν μὴ γνόντα ἁμαρτίαν. Most commentators take this phrase as modifying "God made him [to be] 'sin.'" While this is certainly a grammatical possibility, so too is taking ὑπὲρ ἡμῶν as standing in connection with Jesus' 'not knowing Sin.' Given the role that Jesus' living for the advantage of others and dying for all plays in the argument beginning in 5:14, I propose that the apostle now alludes to another aspect of Jesus' character, one that is connected with knowing. And Jesus' *knowing*, like his living and dying for others, was "for our sake."

The key to understanding Paul's logic rests in the object of Jesus' knowing – or, more accurately here, of Jesus' *not* knowing. The object is "Sin" (ἁμαρτία). By referring to Jesus as the one who did not know Sin, the apostle implies that Jesus is the one human being who did not fall under the enslaving sphere of the cosmic power of Sin (cf. Rom 5:12-14). That is, Paul alludes to Jesus' not having a personal acquaintance with or experiential knowledge of Sin – in short, he alludes to Jesus' choosing not to sin.[506] The apostle thus refers to

---

[505]My reasons for translating the two instances of ἁμαρτία as Sin and "sin," respectively, will become evident below.

[506]For this connotation, see BDAG, s.v. γινώσκω, 1.a. Cf. esp. Rom 7:7. WOLFF aptly comments concerning this sense of γινώσκω in connection with Jesus: "The sense is then that Christ never practised sin; he did not fall victim to the power of sin." See "True Apostolic Knowledge of Christ," 96. Cf. THRALL, *II Corinthians*, 1.439: "It is the historical life of Jesus that Paul has in mind, not the sinlessness of the pre-existent Christ"; and MATERA, *II Corinthians*, 143: ". . . given the importance that Paul attributes to the perfect obedience of Christ, the new Adam, in Rom 5:12-21, he surely has in view the incarnate Christ who was the agent of reconciliation precisely because *he was perfectly obedient to God*" (italics added). The apostle's assessment of Jesus' sinlessness is shared elsewhere in the NT – see Heb 4:15 and 7:26; 1 Pet 2:22; and 1 John 3:5; cf. Matt 3:13-15; and John 7:18 and 8:46.

It should be observed that the aorist participle γνόντα is a *complexive* aorist, thereby indicating action "conceived as a whole irrespective of its duration." See BDF,

Christ's character, and specifically to his sinlessness. Jesus showed forth a different manner of living. Jesus' obedience, his ναί – which he enacted *throughout* his ministry[507] – was directed exclusively to God. His Yes was embodied in his living for the benefit of others and dying for them. In doing so, Jesus broke Sin's power and made possible a mode of human existence marked by freedom. Indeed, it is no accident that Paul – immediately before describing the Spirit-empowered transformation into Christ's image in 2 Cor 3:18 – remarks, οὗ τὸ πνεῦμα κυρίου, ἐλευθερία ("where the Spirit of [the] Lord [is], [there is] *freedom*," 3:17). And given the association of "knowing" with "truth," the apostle's reference to the one who did not know Sin suggests that this mode of human existence is also distinguished by the characteristic of ἀλήθεια. We will see that this is in fact the case.[508]

Paul continues in 2 Cor 5:21a by stating that God "made him [= Jesus, the one who did not know Sin] to be 'sin.'" The verb here is ποιέω, and the object complement is ἁμαρτίαν. What does the apostle mean by the odd expression ἁμαρτίαν ποιέω, especially considering the fact that God is the subject and Jesus the object of this action? Commentators have offered two basic lines of interpretation. One line reads the *whole* of 5:21 in terms of exchange or interchange of experience.[509] As in Gal 3:13 – where Paul writes that Christ became a curse in order to free those who were under the curse of the Law – there is an interchange of experience between Jesus and sinful humanity in 2 Cor 5:21. In this line, Christ is made the representative of sinful humanity, and sin is ascribed to him. According to C.K. Barrett, Christ "came to stand in that relation with God which normally is the result of sin, estranged from God

§ 318 (1).

[507]Observe how this ongoing aspect of Jesus' sinlessness confirms the interpretation of the imperfect tense in 2 Cor 5:19 as signaling the *durative* quality of his agency.

[508]I will discuss in greater detail both the Spirit-empowered transformation into the image of Christ and Paul's reference to ἀλήθεια Χριστοῦ (2 Cor 11:10) in Chapter Five.

[509]See, e.g., M. D. HOOKER, "Interchange in Christ," *JTS* 22 (1971) 349-61, esp. 352-53; BARRETT, *The Second Epistle to the Corinthians*, 179-81; THRALL, *II Corinthians*, 1.441-44; and MATERA, *II Corinthians*, 142-44.

and the object of wrath."[510] Jesus did so in order that human beings might become the righteousness of God (5:21b). As M.D. Hooker argues, however, this is not a straightforward interchange, "for we become the righteousness of God *in him.* If Christ has been made sin, he has also been made our righteousness."[511] This line of interpretation has some merit. First, it makes sense within the context of Paul's discussion of reconciliation because it focuses on the *relationship* between God and human beings. Second, it offers an explanation for the relationship between the two halves of 5:21, that is, between God's making Jesus to be sin and our becoming the righteousness of God.[512] Third, it takes up the pattern of interchange from the opening *berakah* (1:3-7). The major weakness of this position, however, is that it (somehow) ascribes sin to Jesus, something that the apostle's allusion to Christ's not knowing Sin belies.[513]

A second line of interpretation looks to the Jewish Scriptures for enlightenment. Here God's 'making Jesus to be sin' is understood in light of the "sin offering" (see Lev 4:1-5:13, esp. Lev 4:24) and/or the Isaian servant who bore the sins of others (Isa 53:4-11).[514] This line of thought argues that Paul

---

[510]BARRETT, *The Second Epistle to the Corinthians*, 180.

[511]HOOKER, "Interchange in Christ," 353 (Hooker's italics).

[512]I will argue in Chapter Five, however, that the understanding of "the righteousness of God" presumed in this line of thought – namely, that it signifies God's justification – is deficient.

[513]Indeed, MATERA – who supports the interchange interpretation – recognizes that it can be susceptible to suggesting that Christ committed sin. See *II Corinthians*, 143.

[514]See, e.g., BRUCE, *1 and 2 Corinthians*, 210; MARTIN, *2 Corinthians*, 157; TALBERT, *Reading Corinthians*, 167-68; BELLEVILLE, *2 Corinthians*, 159; DUNN, *The Theology of Paul the Apostle*, 212-23; and HAFEMANN, *2 Corinthians*, 247-48. In addition, see WRIGHT, *The Climax of the Covenant*, 220-25, where he argues persuasively that Paul refers in Rom 8:3 to God's sending Jesus as a sin offering. A common protest against this line of interpretation is that it requires different meanings for ἁμαρτία in the same verse. TALBERT calls this objection "a specious argument," citing LXX usage of ἁμαρτία, e.g., Lev 4:24 (see *Reading Corinthians*, 168). More telling is that Paul himself often utilizes the same term with different nuances in the same verse or passage. For instance, the apostle uses the term νόμος equivocally in Rom

utilizes *sacrificial* imagery and the notion of vicarious suffering from Jewish tradition in order to understand what God has done "in Christ." Taking the apostle's statement that "God made [Jesus] to be 'sin'" as referring to Jesus' sacrificial death ὑπὲρ ἡμῶν ("for our sake" – even, "in our place"[515]) has several virtues. First, it is consistent with what Paul says elsewhere concerning Jesus' death as a cultic sacrifice (e.g., Rom 3:25 and 8:3; and 1 Cor 5:7). Second, it explains what the apostle means by "sin" when he says that God made Jesus to be ἁμαρτία.[516] Third, it fits with Paul's allusion to Jesus' sinlessness.[517] Fourth, it helps to explain what the apostle says in 2 Cor 5:19 – namely, that God did not count people's "offenses" (παραπτώματα) against them.

For these reasons – especially the second and third – I contend that the sacrificial interpretation is the better explanation for Paul's statement in 2 Cor 5:21a. What is important for my purpose is the role that Jesus' *ethos* as sinless and innocent plays in the apostle's argument. Hence, although Paul certainly alludes to Jesus' death on the cross in 5:21a, this death is *the culmination of an entire life lived in faithful obedience* to God and God's will.[518]

3:27-28 (cf. ἔργα νόμου and νόμος πίστεως). In addition, see SAMPLEY'S discussion of Paul's multivalent use of the term χάρις in 2 Cor 8-9 in *NIB*, 11.119.

[515]Notice that, here, ὑπὲρ ἡμῶν is taken to modify 'God made him to be sin.'

[516]See, e.g., LXX Lev 4:24. There, after describing the process of laying hands on the head of a goat before slaughtering it, the text says simply: ἁμαρτίαν ἐστίν. This is understood as referring to the "sin offering."

[517]Cf. the various sacrificial animals "without blemish" (ἄμωμον – LXX Lev 4:3; 4:14; 4:23; 4:28; and 4:32), and the blamelessness of the Isaian servant (LXX Isa 53:7-9).

[518]Similarly, HOOKER remarks: "The Cross is of course vital – but it is the completion of *the obedience which characterizes the whole of Christ's life. . . .* The work of reconciliation between God and man is not achieved by the work of an outside Saviour (though, of course, it originates in the purpose of God), but is *the working-out of utter love and obedience in human nature.*" See "Interchange in Christ," 358 (italics added). SAMPLEY aptly states that "[i]n 2 Cor 5:21 Paul's chief interests in this particular recasting of the old story lie in getting the hearers to identify with Christ. . . " (see *NIB*, 11.96). In Chapter Five, where I analyze the second half of this verse, I will show that Sampley's observation is right on target.

Thus, the apostle continues to allude to the story and *ethos* of Jesus in 2 Cor 5:18-21. Paul's grammar in 5:18-19 indicates that he draws upon the reconciling character and agency of Jesus. In 5:21a the apostle makes two more references to Christ's *ethos*. As "the one who did not know Sin," Jesus broke Sin's death-dealing enslavement of humanity. By the very fact of his sinlessness, Jesus showed forth a new possibility of human existence in the sphere of freedom and truth. A life lived in freedom and truth led Jesus ultimately to offer that life – in obedience to God – "for our sake." Indeed, I submit that the phrase ὑπὲρ ἡμῶν – which the apostle strategically situates between the two unusual depictions of Jesus – serves a Janus-like function. It looks back to τὸν μὴ γνόντα ἁμαρτίαν (as I suggested earlier), thereby indicating that Jesus' sinlessness was "for us." But it also looks forward to ἁμαρτίαν ἐποίησεν, thereby signaling that Jesus' offering his life on the cross in obedience to God was "for us." I therefore offer the following translation for 2 Cor 5:21a: "[God] made the one who did not know Sin to be 'sin' [in the sense of a sin offering] – all this was for our sake."

VIII. Our Lord Jesus Christ's Graciousness (2 Cor 8:9 and 9:9)

Paul's next reference to the story and character of Jesus appears in 2 Cor 8:9. There the apostle writes: "For you know (γινώσκετε) the graciousness (χάριν) of our Lord Jesus Christ, that although he was rich he became poor for your sake, in order that by his poverty you might become rich." The broad context of this statement is the apostle's exhortation to the Corinthians to participate generously in the collection for the church in Jerusalem (8:1-9:15). In this section I argue first that Paul appeals in 8:9 to the mode of existence embodied by "our Lord Jesus Christ" – particularly (although not exclusively) in his humanity. Then I show, via 9:8-10, that the apostle also draws upon the notion of Jesus' radical trust in God. In doing so, I tentatively propose that Paul reads LXX Ps 111 – from which he cites two lines in 2 Cor 9:9 – through a christological lens.

Most commentators read 2 Cor 8:9 as an allusion to the descent of the pre-existent Christ.[519] Certainly, the apostle's use of the title κύριος ("Lord")

---

[519]THRALL aptly calls this "the traditional view," one she herself holds. See *II Corinthians*, 2.533-34. This view is summarized well by F.B. CRADDOCK: "The pattern used often by Paul for expressing the Christ-event is descent-ascent: The

connotes his divinity. Moreover, to what does the mention of Christ's "wealth" refer if not to his divine status?[520] Advocates of this interpretation, in support of their position, often refer to the story of Jesus told in Phil 2:6-11. They do so with good reason. Second Corinthians 8:9 seems to be a synopsis of the story told there.[521] Some prominent exegetes, however, read Phil 2:6-11 as referring primarily to Jesus in his human existence.[522] My own position is that Phil 2:6-11 refers to the *entire* story of Jesus.[523] Thus, it seems plausible that 2 Cor 8:9 also alludes to the *entire* story. While not denying the validity of the traditional interpretation, I propose a reading that also incorporates the role that Jesus'

---

preexistent Christ humbles himself, is killed, and is exalted in triumph over all created beings in the universe. This is the basic pattern of II Corinthians 8:9, although not as fully stated here as elsewhere. . . ." See "The Poverty of Christ: An Investigation of II Corinthians 8:9," *Int* 22 (1968) 158-70, here 166. In addition, see, e.g., PLUMMER, *II Corinthians*, 241; HÉRING, *The Second Epistle of Saint Paul to the Corinthians*, 60; BRUCE, *1 and 2 Corinthians*, 222; FURNISH, *II Corinthians*, 417; MARTIN, *2 Corinthians*, 263-64; BARNETT, *The Second Epistle to the Corinthians*, 408; and LAMBRECHT, *Second Corinthians*, 137 and 142-43.

[520]So, e.g., P. SEIDENSTICKER: ". . . Christ renounced *the riches of the glory of the divine world* in order to live within the narrow limits of earthly existence, deprived of that glory. . . ." See "St. Paul and Poverty," in *Gospel Poverty: Essays in Biblical Theology*, trans. M.D. GUINAN (Chicago: Franciscan Herald, 1977) 81-120, here 95 (italics added).

[521]See, e.g., SAMPLEY, *NIB*, 11.123: ". . . Paul reminds [the Corinthians] of the 'big story' in its most cursory form, this time told in categories of wealth and poverty. In Philippians, the same story had been told in grander, probably traditional form by Paul, and there cast in terms of loftiness and humility. . . . The story about grace in 2 Cor 8:9 is retrofitted into economic categories appropriate to the topic at hand: the collection." Similarly, HÉRING refers to 2 Cor 8:9 as "rather like a partial recapitulation" of Phil 2:6-11. See *The Second Epistle of Saint Paul to the Corinthians*, 60. ALLO rightly observes that Phil 2 is the best commentary on 2 Cor 8:9. See *Seconde Épître aux Corinthiens*, 217.

[522]See n. 425 for studies arguing that Phil 2:6-11 is concerned primarily with the human existence of Jesus.

[523]Phil 2:6-7c refers to Christ's pre-existence and incarnation; 2:7d-8 to his earthly existence and death; and 2:9-11 to his resurrection (implied) and exaltation.

humanity plays here. Indeed, observe Paul's use of the verb γινώσκω at the very outset of 8:9 ("For *you know* . . ."). We have continually seen that the apostle links cognitive terms with references to the character and story of the human Jesus throughout 2 Corinthians (10:5; 5:16; and 5:21). The linkage in 8:9 is suggestive.[524]

Paul's mode of argumentation throughout 2 Cor 8:1-9:15 seems to require that his appeal in 8:9 draw at least in part on Jesus' humanity. Observe that in 8:6-8 the apostle begins a direct challenge to the Corinthians to excel "in this gracious undertaking" (ἐν ταύτῃ τῃ χάριτι, 8:7), that is, in the collection. Then, as a rationale for his exhortation – note the use of the postpositive γάρ in 8:9 – Paul cites the example of the χάρις of Jesus.[525] *Prima facie*, it makes more sense for the apostle to appeal to the Corinthians to follow a *human* example than a divine example. In fact, Paul's other exhortative strategies in 8:1-9:15 involve very human elements. In 8:1-5 the apostle sets forth the example of the zeal and generosity of the churches of Macedonia. In 8:7 he appeals to the Corinthians' own pride in excelling. In 8:24 and 9:3-5 Paul warns of the potential shame that would result from their failure to contribute. And in 9:2 he appeals to a sense of competition between the Macedonian and Achaian churches. So too in 8:9, where he gives his first explicit rationale for the collection – which he pointedly calls "this χάρις" (8:7) – I argue that the apostle again appeals to the human level: in this instance, however, he appeals to the χάρις of Jesus, the new Adam.

If this is in fact the case, to what, then, does Paul allude when he says that Jesus "became poor" (ἐπτώχευσεν)? Obviously, the apostle speaks figuratively here, for there is no evidence of the human Jesus having financial largesse that he bestowed on others.[526] The term χάρις offers an important clue

---

[524]Cf. DUNN, *Christology in the Making*, 121: "Would it have been so obvious to Paul's readers that he was speaking of the incarnation or of Christ's descent from heaven?"

[525]BETZ (*2 Corinthians 8 and 9*, 61) and DANKER (*II Corinthians*, 126) – both of whom pay particular attention to Paul's rhetorical features – hold that 2 Cor 8:9 functions as an *exemplum*. *Pace* FURNISH, *II Corinthians*, 418.

[526]*Pace* G.W. BUCHANON, who attempts to argue for the possibility that Jesus was reared in the upper class of society and gave up his wealth *per* Jewish custom of entering a sectarian community (e.g., the Essenes). See "Jesus and the Upper Class," *NovT* 7 (1964/65) 195-209.

in this regard. In 2 Cor 8:9 χάρις denotes "gracious care or help," in the sense of a beneficent *disposition* toward others.[527] This notion of disposition suggests in turn that Paul is referring once again to the *ethos* of Jesus. Specifically, the apostle evokes aspects of Jesus' character that surfaced earlier in the text: his πίστις, which as God's δοῦλος (4:13 – recall the christological reading of LXX Pss 114-115) Jesus manifested by his mode of self-emptying existence for others (cf. 4:10-11); and his ἀγάπη, which Jesus revealed by his living and dying for the advantage of others (5:14-15; cf. 5:21).[528] Now, in 8:9, Paul aptly captures this disposition of self-emptying, gracious care in economic terms (recall the context of the collection): Jesus became poor so that others might be enriched. Indeed, the apostle appears to use ἐπτώχευσεν in this context as a synonym for ἐταπείνωσεν ἑαυτόν (cf. Phil 2:8).[529] As is the case with the latter expression, Paul's allusion in 2 Cor 8:9 is to Jesus' *pattern* of living. Thus, the reference here is to *ethos* as much as – if not more than – to *mythos*.[530] In fact, this interpretation of Christ's χάρις is corroborated by the apostle's usage elsewhere, notably in Rom 5:15 and 1 Tim 1:14.[531]

---

[527]See BDAG, s.v. χάρις, 2.a. Cf. Rom 5:15 and 1 Tim 1:14 (and n. 531 below).

[528]MURPHY-O'CONNOR – who argues against the traditional interpretation of 2 Cor 8:9 – rightly sees a similar connection between 5:21 and 8:9. See *The Theology of the Second Letter to the Corinthians*, 83. SCOTT aptly translates χάρις here as Jesus' "self-sacrificial giving." See *2 Corinthians*, 179.

[529]I thus take the verb ἐπτώχευσεν as a complexive aorist (indicating action conceived as a whole irrespective of its duration); see BDF, § 318 (1). In anticipation of an objection raised against my reading that it leaves no content for Jesus' "being rich," I would rejoin that Paul's language here is *metaphorical*, and is determined by the context of the collection. The real point is Christ's pattern of self-emptying existence that gives life to others.

[530]*Pace* BETZ, *2 Corinthians 8 and 9*, 61: "The statement presents in narrative form *a summary of the myth*" (italics added). Cf. DUNN, *The Theology of Paul the Apostle*, 290-92.

[531]In Rom 5:15 Paul refers to the χάρις "of *the one human being*, Jesus Christ," which he later associates with Jesus' ὑπακοή (Rom 5:19). In 1 Tim 1:14 the apostle relates the χάρις "of the Lord" (referring to Christ Jesus, cf. 1 Tim 1:12) with both Christ's πίστις and ἀγάπη.

Paul's evocation of Jesus' character in 2 Cor 8:9 thus functions to remind the Corinthians of their status and participation in the new creation. While the apostle does not call on them to become poor literally (8:13), he does exhort them to manifest caring in a practical manner by giving generously to the collection. Paul's evocation of Jesus' *ethos*, moreover, is not exhausted by the reference to his graciousness in 8:9. The apostle also implies that the Corinthians are to emulate Jesus in his *radical trust in God to provide*. Recall from the analysis of Paul's christological reading of LXX Pss 114-115 that Jesus' πίστις – understood in the broad sense of a holistic human response of loyalty and obedience to God and God's will – was rooted in his trust in God to vindicate that faithfulness (by raising him from the dead). Observe how, near the conclusion of his exhortation for the collection (2 Cor 9:8-10), the apostle refers to God's ability to supply and multiply the Corinthians' resources. Indeed, Paul points to God's power "to provide in abundance every benefaction" (πᾶσαν χάριν περισσεῦσαι, 9:8). It is trust in this generosity of God that allows him to command the Corinthians: "abound in this gracious undertaking" (ἐν ταύτῃ τῇ χάριτι περισσεύητε, 8:7). I propose that the apostle looks to Jesus' χάρις (8:9) – grounded in his radical trust in God to bring the dead to life – to serve as the paradigmatic example of generous caring *and* of trust in God.

That Paul implies Jesus' trust and "generosity" becomes more evident when one appreciates his strategy in citing LXX Ps 111:9ab in 2 Cor 9:9: "He scattered, he gave to the poor,/ his righteousness endures forever."[532] The apostle cites these lines immediately after his statement that God provides abundantly so that the Corinthians may in turn provide abundantly "for every good work" (9:8). Notice that Paul links the citation to what is said in 9:8 with the introductory formula, "just as it is written" (καθὼς γέγραπται). The key interpretive question is this: To whom does the unnamed subject of the citation refer in the context of 2 Cor 9:8-10? Some commentators, noting that God is the subject in 9:8 (explicitly) and 9:10 (implicitly), argue that God is the implied subject of 9:9. The apostle thus cites the lines from Scripture in order to refer to *God's* abundant provision of blessings.[533] The problem with this line of

---

[532]LXX Ps 111 = HB Ps 112. LXX Ps 111:9 contains a third line not cited by Paul: "His horn will be exalted in glory."

[533]So, BARNETT, *The Second Epistle to the Corinthians*, 440. Similarly, BETZ, *2 Corinthians 8 and 9*, 111; DANKER, *II Corinthians*, 140-41; MURPHY-O'CONNOR, *The Theology of the Second Letter to the Corinthians*, 92; and SAMPLEY, *NIB*, 11.130.

reasoning, however, is that the subject of the psalm is a righteous, God-fearing *man* (ἀνήρ) who is generous in giving alms. Other commentators, observing that the end of 9:8 refers to the Corinthians, propose that the referent is "the representative Corinthian contributor."[534] While this understanding avoids the pitfall of the first interpretation, it creates a new problem: namely, it attributes δικαιοσύνη – described here as enduring *forever* – to the Corinthians. Such enduring righteousness, however, seems to apply more appropriately to God than to the Corinthians. It is true that Paul *does* connect "righteousness" with the Corinthians in 9:10. But, as will be shown in the next chapter, when the apostle links human beings explicitly with δικαιοσύνη θεοῦ (5:21b), he names *Jesus* as the mediating agent of this righteousness.

Thus, I suggest another possible interpretation. I tentatively propose that Jesus is the implied subject of the lines cited in 2 Cor 9:9, and that Paul reads the *entire* psalm christologically, as he read LXX Pss 114-115 in 2 Cor 4:13. As was the case with LXX Pss 114-115, there are several verbal, conceptual, and thematic links between LXX Ps 111 and the text of 2 Corinthians, as the following table illustrates:

---

[534]So, THRALL, *II Corinthians*, 2.580-83 (the quoted words are from p. 583). Similarly, PLUMMER, *II Corinthians*, 261; ALLO, *Seconde Épître aux Corinthiens*, 234-35; BARRETT, *The Second Epistle to the Corinthians*, 238; BELLEVILLE, *2 Corinthians*, 239-40; LAMBRECHT, *Second Corinthians*, 147; and MCCANT, *2 Corinthians*, 95.

D. GEORGI offers another alternative, one that in effect combines the first two. Georgi acknowledges that the subject of LXX Ps 111 is a pious person. He claims, however, that this psalm should be read in conjunction with LXX Ps 110, whose subject is God. Georgi points out several parallels between these psalms, including the description of the subject as merciful and compassionate, the subject's provision for others, and the subject's enduring righteousness. In light of the "peculiar bond" that exists between LXX Pss 110 and 111, Georgi argues that ". . . the deliberate vagueness of the way the quotation is incorporated into the Pauline context necessarily leads one to realize that God is the true origin of human compassion and that his righteousness is the true source of our righteousness." See GEORGI, *Remembering the Poor: The History of Paul's Collection for Jerusalem* (Nashville: Abingdon, 1992) 98-99 (the quotations are from p. 99). For a similar interpretation, see FURNISH, *II Corinthians*, 449; and KISTEMAKER, *The Second Epistle to the Corinthians*, 314-15.

Table II
Comparison of LXX Psalm 111 with 2 Corinthians

LXX Psalm 111	*2 Corinthians*
ὁ φοβούμενος τὸν κύριον – 111:1a	φόβος τοῦ κυρίου – 5:11 *** φόβος θεοῦ – 7:1 **
δόξα – 111:3a; 111:9c	δόξα – 1:20; 3:7 (2x); 3:8; 3:9 (2x); 3:10; 3:11 (2x); 3:18 (3x); 4:4; 4:6; 4:15; 4:17; 6:8; 8:19; 8:23
πλοῦτος – 111:3a	πλοῦτος – 8:2 πλούσιος – 8:9 πλουτέω – 8:9 πλουτίζω – 6:10; 9:11 **
δικαιοσύνη – 111:3b; 111:9b	δικαιοσύνη – 3:9; 5:21; 6:7; 6:14; 9:9; 9:10; 11:15
ἐξανέτειλεν ἐν σκότει φῶς – 111:4a	ἐκ σκότους φῶς λάμψει – 4:6 ***! κοινωνία φωτὶ πρὸς σκότος – 6:14 **!
ἐλεήμων – 111:4b	ἐλεέω – 4:1
οἰκτίρμων – 111:4b οἰκτείρω – 111:5a	οἰκτιρμός – 1:3
χρηστός – 111:5a	χρηστότης – 6:6
ἐλπίζειν ἐπὶ κύριον – 111:7b	εἰς [θεὸν] ἐλπίζω – 1:10
confidence in face of enemies – 111:8	confidence in face of opposition – chh. 10-12
ὑψόω – 111:9c	ὑψόω – 11:7 ***

*** used by Paul only in 2 Corinthians
** at least half of Paul's usages of this term/expression occur in 2 Corinthian
! indicates that the terms σκότος/φῶς occur in the same clause

Again, the number of semantic and thematic resonances is striking. The sheer volume suggests that the apostle appropriated the content of this psalm in writing 2 Corinthians.

The lines from LXX Ps 111 cited in 2 Cor 9:9 – "He scattered, he gave to the poor,/ his righteousness endures forever" – harmonize with what Paul implies by "the χάρις of our Lord Jesus Christ" in 8:9, namely his self-giving mode of existence. In addition, notice how well several elements of LXX Ps 111 correspond with the apostle's portrait of Jesus. The ἀνήρ depicted in this psalm fears the Lord and takes pleasure in God's commandments (LXX Ps 111:1); so, too, Jesus' obedience (2 Cor 10:5) was embodied in his ναί/ἀμήν to God (1:19-20). The ἀνήρ is described as "merciful" (ἐλεήμων), "compassionate" (οἰκτίρμων), and "righteous" (δίκαιος, LXX Ps 111:4b); similarly, Paul refers to Jesus' gentleness and forbearance (2 Cor 10:1), and intimates elsewhere that Jesus was δίκαιος (see Rom 1:17[535]). The ἀνήρ is strengthened to hope in the Lord, and thus he does not fear (LXX Ps 111:7b-8a); likewise, Jesus' faithfulness was grounded in his trust in God to raise the dead (2 Cor 4:13-14). Finally, the horn of the ἀνήρ "will be exalted in glory" (ὑψωθήσεται ἐν δόξῃ, LXX Ps 111:9c); so, too, in Phil 2:9-11 the apostle states that God "highly exalted" (ὑπερύψωσεν) Jesus and bestowed on him the name above all other names unto the "glory of God." Hence, in citing LXX Ps 111:9 in 2 Cor 9:9, I suggest that Paul recalls his reference in 8:9 to Jesus' graciousness, as well as the latter's trust in God which underlay that χάρις. The apostle sees in the lines cited – indeed, in the entire psalm – an apt description of Jesus, "the righteous one," whose πίστις has manifested the righteousness of God (Rom 1:17 and 3:22).[536]

---

[535]Recall the discussion of Rom 1:17 in Chapter Three, esp. the messianic interpretation of Hab 2:4 and the use of ὁ δίκαιος as a messianic title.

[536]A.T. HANSON, with some hesitation, also argues that the citation in 2 Cor 9:9 has a christocentric reference. Like my interpretation, he appeals to LXX Ps 111:4b and 111:9c. He also surmises, in reference to 111:4a ("a light sprang up in darkness"), that "Paul might interpret the light rising of either the appearance of the Messiah in the flesh or of his resurrection." In sum, Hanson's position is analogous to Georgi's (n. 534 above) in that the former holds that Paul saw LXX Ps 111 ". . . as applying first to Christ, and secondarily to Christians in Christ." See HANSON, *Studies in Paul's Technique and Theology* (London: SPCK, 1974) 179-181 (the quotations are from p. 180). In addition to seeing more connections between LXX Ps 111 and the story of Jesus, I differ from

Thus, in his exhortation concerning the collection Paul continues to draw upon the *ethos* of Jesus. He does so explicitly in 2 Cor 8:9, recalling for the Corinthians Jesus' χάρις, understood as the pattern of his self-giving in love for others. Moreover, I suggest that the apostle implicitly evokes Jesus' character in 9:9 through a christological reading of LXX Ps 111. In doing so, he alludes to Jesus' trust and gracious generosity, characteristics manifested in his practice of lowering himself for the benefit of others.

IX. Christ's Integrity and Innocence (2 Cor 11:3)

In 2 Cor 11:3, near the beginning of his so-called "fool's speech," Paul associates ἁπλότης and ἁγνότης with Christ. In this verse, the apostle expresses his fear that, just as the serpent deceived Eve by his cunning, so now "[the Corinthians'] thoughts (τὰ νοήματα) might be seduced/led astray (φθαρῇ) ἀπὸ τῆς ἁπλότητος καὶ τῆς ἁγνότητος τῆς εἰς τὸν Χριστόν."[537] Does Paul refer here to ἁπλότης and ἁγνότης as something that the Corinthians ought to direct toward Christ? Or does the apostle allude to ἁπλότης and ἁγνότης as characteristics or attributes of Jesus, as he does to Christ's love (5:14) and gentleness and forbearance (10:1)? Practically all the translations and commentators opt for the former.[538] The RSV's rendering is

---

Hanson in that I read 2 Cor 9:9 to be a reference to Christ alone – and not as a conflated reference to both Christ and the Corinthians. It is true that Paul draws the Corinthians into the story of Christ's righteousness, but observe that the apostle only does so in the following verse, 9:10. (For more on the apostle's strategy of exhorting the Corinthians here, see Chapter Six.) My interpretation of 2 Cor 9:9 thus parallels Campbell's interpretation of Rom 1:17 analyzed in Chapter Three, Section II.A (in connection with the citation from Hab 2:4). That is, in both instances, the lines cited from Scripture are best understood as referring not to God or to a human being, *but to Jesus*.

[537]There are several textual variants involving the syntax of ἁπλότης and ἁγνότης, as well as the omission of one or the other element. In deference to the age and character of the textual witnesses to the longer reading (as cited), I opt for it. For a full discussion, see METZGER, *A Textual Commentary on the Greek New Testament*, 514-15, and A.J. MALHERBE, "Through the Eye of the Needle: Simplicity or Singleness?" *ResQ* 5 (1961) 119-29, here 119-21.

[538]One notable exception is the KJV: "from the simplicity that is in Christ."

representative: Paul fears that the Corinthians' "thoughts will be led astray *from a sincere and pure devotion to Christ*" (italics added).

This traditional understanding of 2 Cor 11:3 seems to be demanded by the immediately preceding context. In 11:2 Paul claims to have "betrothed" (ἀρόζομαι) the Corinthians as a "pure virgin" (παρθένος ἁγνή) to Christ. Yet, just as Eve was deceived, so now the apostle fears that the Corinthians are being corrupted.[539] Thus, Paul's line of argument seems clear cut: he fears that the Corinthians are being "seduced/led astray" from their singular, exclusive commitment to Christ. This interpretation is further enhanced by the fact that the preposition εἰς in the modifying attributive phrase τῆς εἰς τὸν Χριστόν can indicate the goal into which or toward which someone or something moves – in this case, *to* or *toward* Christ.[540] Besides, if the apostle intended to refer to attributes of Jesus here, would he not use a genitive construction, such as ἁπλότης καὶ ἁγνότης τοῦ Χριστοῦ? The traditional rendering of 11:3 would seem to have a solid basis.

Nevertheless, several factors call this traditional interpretation into question. Note that the translation on which this interpretation is based renders the articular substantives ἁπλότης and ἁγνότης as *anarthrous adjectives*, while *inserting* something that is *not* present in the Greek text – in the case of

---

[539]See Gen 3:1-24. As THRALL indicates, several commentators point out that Paul may have been influenced by legendary interpretations of this passage. In one line of interpretation, it was the devil who entered the garden and corrupted Eve (*2 En.* 31:6 [see J.H. CHARLESWORTH, ed., *The Old Testament Pseudepigrapha: Volume 1: Apocalyptic Literature & Testaments*, ABRL (New York: Doubleday, 1983) 154]; cf. Wis 2:24). Paul's characterization of his rivals as Satan's servants disguised as servants of righteousness (2 Cor 11:13-15) may reflect this myth. In another tradition, the serpent is understood to have seduced Eve sexually (see, e.g., 4 Macc 18:7-8). The phrase παρθένος ἁγνή in 2 Cor 11:2 and the verb φθείρω in 11:3, a term that can refer to sexual seduction, may indicate that the apostle has this second version in mind. See THRALL, *II Corinthians*, 2.662-63. BULTMANN (*The Second Letter to the Corinthians*, 201) and FURNISH (*II Corinthians*, 500) argue that the apostle draws upon this second line of interpretation. Furnish provides several more references to rabbinic writings.

[540]See BDAG, s.v. εἰς, 1 and 4.

the RSV, the element of devotion.[541] Are these modifications – which admittedly yield a smooth translation – fitting, or do they in fact distort what Paul actually says? Observe that the term ἁπλότης, used in connection with persons, signifies "sincerity, uprightness,"[542] whereas ἁγνότης denotes "purity."[543] Thus, a literal rendering of ἀπὸ τῆς ἁπλότητος καὶ τῆς ἁγνότητος τῆς εἰς τὸν Χριστόν is: "from the sincerity/uprightness and the purity that are εἰς τὸν Χριστόν."[544] It is understandable why commentators should add the idea of commitment or devotion here. The notion of '*the* sincerity/uprightness that is *toward* Christ' (as a goal?) and, especially, the notion of '*the* purity that is *toward* Christ' are awkward, to say the least.[545] But is this awkwardness best resolved by removing definite articles, translating nouns as adjectives, and inserting an element into the text that Paul himself does not include?

541THRALL similarly translates ἀπὸ τῆς ἁπλότητος καὶ τῆς ἁγνότητος thus: "from single-minded (and pure) *devotion*" (see *II Corinthians*, 2.656 – italics added). FURNISH renders the phrase "from a total and a pure *commitment*" (see *II Corinthians*, 484 – italics added). Other commentators make further additions. See, e.g., PLUMMER, *II Corinthians*, 292: "from the single-minded devotion and pure fidelity which *should be preserved* towards Christ" (italics added); and BARNETT, *The Second Epistle to the Corinthians*, 496: "from *your* sincere and pure devotion to Christ" (italics added).

542See BDAG, s.v. ἁπλότης, 1. The term also shades into meaning "generosity, liberality" (see BDAG, s.v. ἁπλότης, 2). The context in 11:3 demands the primary sense. I will treat Paul's use of ἁπλότης more extensively in Chapters Five and Six.

543See BDAG, s.v. ἁγνότης.

544Cf. MATERA, who notes that, if translated literally, the phrase in question in 2 Cor 11:3 would read "the sincerity and purity that are in (or toward) Christ." See *II Corinthians*, 239.

545Indeed, FURNISH senses this awkwardness and explains, "The word *commitment* has been supplied for purposes of translation." See *II Corinthians*, 488 (Furnish's italics).

Furthermore, neither the LXX nor the NT contains a single instance of ἁπλότης being directed toward a person or thing.[546] In fact, when ἁπλότης is associated with a person, it is always as an attribute belonging to that person, indicated by the genitive personal pronoun.[547] While it is true that there is no possessive genitive in 2 Cor 11:3, these observations give cause to hesitate before reading this verse as the only instance in Scripture where ἁπλότης is rendered explicitly *to* someone. It is also significant to note that five of the eight occurrences of ἁπλότης in Paul's writings appear in 2 Corinthians, as does the only other instance of ἁγνότης (6:6). In fact, as we will see in the following chapters, the apostle refers to his own ἁπλότης in order to attest to his good character. And he connects the ἁπλότης of the Corinthians (in regard to the collection) with a test of their character. This suggests that, in 2 Corinthians at least, Paul associates ἁπλότης with the issue of character. Does he link it with the *ethos* of Jesus in 11:3?

I propose that the apostle does not allude in 2 Cor 11:3 to the sincerity/uprightness and purity that are directed toward Christ, but rather to the ἁπλότης and ἁγνότης which are *in Christ*. That this is the case becomes more plausible when one considers the following: (1) the relationship between 2 Cor 11:3 and 11:4; (2) another possible meaning of εἰς in the attributive phrase τῆς εἰς τὸν Χριστόν; and (3) the grammatical subject of the second half of 11:3.

First of all, it is necessary to attend to the logic of Paul's argument as it develops in 2 Cor 11:4. The traditional reading focuses so narrowly upon the preceding context (11:2) that it fails to take adequa`te account of what follows. In 11:4 the apostle gives the rationale – note the postpositive γάρ – for the fear he expresses in 11:3.[548] Specifically, Paul is concerned that when someone

---

[546]Cf. LXX 2 Sam 15:11; 1 Chr 29:17; 1 Macc 2:37 and 2:60; 3 Macc 3:21; Wis 1:1; and Sus 1:63 (OG); as well as Rom 12:8; 2 Cor 1:12; 8:2; 9:11; and 9:13; Eph 6:5; and Col 3:22.

[547]LXX 2 Sam 15:11; 1 Macc 2:37 and 2:60; and Sus 1:63 (OG); also, 2 Cor 8:2.

[548]So, KISTEMAKER, *The Second Epistle to the Corinthians*, 361. Even those commentators who contend that the three-fold use of γάρ in 2 Cor 11:2, 11:4, and 11:5 functions to give the grounds for Paul's statement in 11:1 agree that 11:4 also explains the apostle's fear expressed in 11:3. See, e.g., BARRETT, *The Second Epistle to the Corinthians*, 274; FURNISH, *II Corinthians*, 488; and THRALL, *II Corinthians*, 2.664.

MATERA argues that 11:1-4 is a unit consisting of two parts. The first part is

comes preaching (κηρύσσω) "*another* Jesus" (ἄλλος Ἰησοῦς), the Corinthians readily submit to that preaching. Observe that the apostle's concern here is *not* that the community is abandoning their singular devotion to Christ. Rather, the issue seems to be *which* Jesus is being preached and *which* gospel is being accepted by them. Recall that Paul has already reminded the Corinthians of what had been proclaimed (κηρυχθείς) to them – namely "the Son of God, Jesus Christ." With this reminder, the apostle has already alluded to the story of Jesus and to his obedience and faithfulness (ναί/ἀμήν) to God in fulfillment of the divine promises (1:19-20). Thus, for Paul, the story and *ethos* of Jesus are intimately connected with proclamation. What the rhetoric in 11:4 implies is that any deviation from what the apostle has revealed and taught to the Corinthians is tantamount to following another gospel, and thus "another Jesus." Paul, who claims that he is "of Christ" (10:8) and – even more strikingly – that "Christ's truth" (11:10) is in him, insists upon a particular portrayal of Jesus.[549] I suggest that this portrayal includes Christ's ἁπλότης and ἁγνότης.

Second, the dynamic sense of the preposition εἰς – marking the goal toward which one looks or moves – ought not to be pushed too hard in 2 Cor 11:3. A more natural way to express Christ as the object of devotion would be

---

11:1-2, where Paul requests that the Corinthians bear with him, a request that he grounds in his Godlike jealousy for them. The second part is 11:3-4, where the apostle expresses his anxiety that the community is in danger of being corrupted by the intruding missionaries; he then grounds his anxiety in the willingness of the Corinthians to bear with the preaching of another Jesus. See *II Corinthians*, 240. I suggest that this way of structuring the text strengthens my claim that 11:3 should be interpreted primarily in terms of what follows in 11:4.

[549] J. MURPHY-O'CONNOR focuses on the fact that, in 2 Cor 11:4, Paul is the grammatical subject of 'preaching Jesus,' whereas the Corinthians are the grammatical subject of 'receiving the Spirit and gospel.' Since all the verbs are aorist tense, he argues that they refer to the time when the apostle evangelized the Corinthians. Thus, Murphy-O'Connor reasons, "The key element in 11:4, therefore, is 'Jesus'; the other two are dependent on it. If 'Jesus' is preached correctly, then the Corinthians' perception of 'Spirit' and 'Gospel' will be authentic." See MURPHY-O'CONNOR, "Another Jesus (2 Cor 11:4)," *RB* 97 (1990) 238-51, here 239-40. The quotation is from p. 240.

with the dative Χριστῷ or with the construction πρός + accusative.[550] Moreover, εἰς is employed at times where ἐν would be expected to express location.[551] It can thus signify the *place* where something exists. In this case, I propose that the apostle refers to the ἁπλότης and ἁγνότης which were *in* Christ, which Jesus himself possessed and manifested. Notice how this interpretation maintains the sense of the articular substantives, as well as the attributive quality of the phrase τῆς εἰς τὸν Χριστόν.[552]

Third, it is crucial to note that the grammatical subject of the second half of 2 Cor 11:3 is τὰ νοήματα ὑμῶν ("your [the Corinthians'] *thoughts*"). Once again, we encounter Paul's use of cognitive terms in conjunction with the character of Jesus. Recall the interpretation of 10:5 offered above: the apostle strives hard to bring "every thought" (πᾶν νόημα) to "Christ-obedience."[553] I submit that in 11:3 Paul expresses his fear that the Corinthians' thoughts are

---

[550]For πρός as denoting orientation or movement toward someone/something, see BDAG, s.v. πρός, 3.d.β. Cf. 2 Cor 3:4: πεποίθησιν δὲ τοιαύτην ἔχομεν διὰ τοῦ Χριστοῦ πρὸς τὸν θεόν; and Phlm 5: . . . τὴν ἀγάπην καὶ τὴν πίστιν, ἣν ἔχεις πρὸς τὸν κύριον 'Ιησοῦν.

[551]See BDF, § 205: "No NT writer except Matthew is entirely free from the replacement of ἐν by εἰς in a local sense. . . ." See 2 Cor 10:16 (εἰς τὰ ὑπερέκεινα ὑμῶν εὐαγγελίσασθαι); Rom 16:26; and 1 Cor 15:10 (see the following note). In addition, cf. 2 Cor 13:3b – ὃς εἰς ὑμᾶς οὐκ ἀσθενεῖ ἀλλὰ δυνατεῖ ἐν ὑμῖν – where εἰς and ἐν are used interchangeably. BULTMANN notes that in this verse there is "a rhetorical alternation of prepositions so dear to Paul." See *The Second Letter to the Corinthians*, 242.

[552]Cf. 1 Cor 15:10: χάριτι δὲ θεοῦ εἰμι ὅ εἰμι, καί ἡ χάρις αὐτοῦ ἡ εἰς ἐμέ. . . . One difference between 1 Cor 15:10 and 2 Cor 11:3 is that, in the former, it is *God's* grace that is in Paul, whereas in the latter, it is Christ's own sincerity and purity that are in him [i.e., Jesus], not those of the Corinthians. LAMBRECHT recognizes the challenge of respecting the attributive construction here. His solution, however, is less than satisfactory, as he inserts "you have" into the text – "from the sincerity and purity (you have) toward Christ." See *Second Corinthians*, 174.

[553]For my interpretation of 2 Cor 10:5, see Section III above. Cf. 4:4, where Paul refers to the blinding of the νοήματα of the ἄπιστοι, a blinding that keeps them from seeing "the enlightenment of the gospel of the glory of Christ, who is the image of God."

being led away *from* (ἀπό)[554] an understanding of important attributes that were present in Christ, namely his ἁπλότης and ἁγνότης. Hence, the apostle fears that the Corinthians are failing to appropriate these characteristics. Indeed, while the verb φθείρω can denote "seducing" a virgin,[555] it can also refer to "corrupting" people by leading them astray through false teaching.[556] Paul's disparaging reference in 11:5 to "superlative apostles" (ὑπερλίαν ἀπόστολοι, cf. 11:13) indicates, at least in his mind, a possible source of such erroneous teaching. That the apostle defends his own γνῶσις in 11:6 is also suggestive. Thus, I propose that Paul's concern in 11:3 involves the Corinthians' being led astray, away from the true understanding of Jesus and thus from the capacity to take on for themselves the ἁπλότης and ἁγνότης that he manifested. In other words, the apostle fears that they are in danger of abandoning possession of the νοῦς Χριστοῦ (cf. 1 Cor 2:16).

What, then, does Paul mean by the ἁπλότης and ἁγνότης that are in Christ? As mentioned earlier, ἁπλότης signifies sincerity and uprightness.

---

[554]Cf. Rom 8:35 for a similar usage of the preposition ἀπό to signify separation or alienation (see BDF, § 211) from an attribute of Christ: "Who will separate us *from the love of Christ* (ἀπὸ τῆς ἀγάπης τοῦ Χριστοῦ)?" In addition, see PLUMMER, *II Corinthians*, 296; and MARTIN, *2 Corinthians*, 333.

[555]See BDAG, s.v. φθείρω, 1.c. Cf. *Ant*. 4.252, for Moses's teaching that a man who corrupts (ὁ φθείρας) an unwed virgin must marry her, or pay her father the price for her virginity. In addition, cf. *Diogn*. 12:8, where φθείρεται is used in connection with Eve. For Josephus's text, see *Flavii Iosephi Opera*, Vol. 1: *Antiquitatum Iudaicarum*, Libri I-V, ed. B. Niese (Berlin: Weidmannsche Verlagsbuchhandlung, 1955). Commentators who contend that Paul draws upon the legend of the serpent's sexual seduction of Eve argue that this sense of φθείρω is operative here. See n. 539 above.

[556]See BDAG, s.v. φθείρω, 2. In his letter to the Ephesians, Ignatius of Antioch alludes to the possibility of being corrupted (φρείρῃ) "by false teaching" (ἐν κακῇ διδασκαλίᾳ). See Ign. *Eph*. 16:2. Cf. *J.W*. 4.510, where Josephus describes how "many powerful men" (πολλοὶ δυνατοί) "were corrupted" (ἐφείροντο) by Simon, son of Gioras, an outsider who gained great influence and power. For Ignatius's text, see *The Apostolic Fathers*, vol. 1, 172-97; for Josephus's text, see *Josephus: The Jewish War, Books III-IV*, trans. H. St. J. Thackeray, LCL (Cambridge, Mass.: Harvard University Press, 1997).

More fundamentally, it denotes *personal integrity*.[557] The opposite of διψυχία ("double-mindedness"), ἁπλότης refers to a singleness of mind and purpose. Given the apostle's allusions concerning Jesus' ναί (2 Cor 1:19-20), πίστις (4:13), and ὑπακοή (10:5), I propose that the ἁπλότης that was in Christ refers to his single-minded disposition to love and serve God, as well as to his manner of living that expressed this disposition.[558] Concerning the ἁγνότης that is in Christ, it is helpful to look at Paul's use of the adjective ἁγνός elsewhere. In the preceding verse (11:2) the word has the (metaphorical) meaning of "pure" or "chaste" (cf. Titus 2:5). In 2 Cor 7:11 it means "innocent," while in Phil 4:8 it connotes general moral goodness.[559] Finally, in 1 Tim 5:22 the apostle exhorts Timothy to be ἁγνός immediately after admonishing him not to participate in others' sins. This last usage is particularly suggestive. I submit that the ἁγνότης that is in Christ refers to his purity and innocence (recall τὸν μὴ γνόντα ἁμαρτίαν in 2 Cor 5:21). In effect, ἁπλότης and ἁγνότης form a hendiadys denoting Jesus' integrity and innocence. Paul's reference to this quality of Jesus suits well a context in which the apostle's own integrity has been called into question (see 2 Cor 10:10; cf. 11:7-12), in which he impugns the integrity of other missionaries/evangelists (10:12-16; cf. 11:5 and 11:13-15), and in which he fears that the Corinthians are veering toward insalubrious influences (11:4; cf. 11:20).

We are now in a position to understand more precisely how Paul's reference to Christ's character functions in 2 Cor 11:3. While it is true that the apostle begins in 11:2 with the marriage metaphor of presenting the Corinthian community as a bride to Christ, I suggest that the logic of his argument shifts in 11:3. The key interpretive question here is this: To what does Paul refer when he alludes to the story of Eve and the serpent? As noted above, some advocates

---

[557]See BDAG, s.v. ἁπλότης, 1.

[558]SPICQ captures well this meaning of ἁπλότης: "This is not just a dictionary entry but *an entire spirituality*" (italics added). See *TLNT*, 1.169. This single-minded pursuit of fidelity to God's will is exemplified in 1 Macc 3:27 by the willingness of the faithful Jews to be martyred: ἀποθάνωμεν πάντες ἐν τῇ ἁπλότητι ἡμῶν. For ἁπλότης as "singleness" or "undivided loyalty," see MALHERBE, "Through the Eye of the Needle,"123-25. Malherbe considers the term in light of the Jewish background.

[559]Cf. the discussion in FURNISH, *II Corinthians*, 344. Furnish renders ἁγνότης in 2 Cor 6:6 – Paul's only other usage – as "probity."

of the traditional reading argue that the apostle is drawing on an interpretation of Gen 3 in which Eve was sexually seduced by the serpent.[560] But is it not just as possible, if not more likely, that Paul utilizes a less tendentious reading of Gen 3? I propose that he alludes to this story in order to highlight the fundamental issue of faithfulness to God and God's commands (cf. Gen 3:2-3).[561] And just as the serpent "deceived" Eve, which led her (and Adam) to break God's commandment concerning the fruit of the tree in the middle of the garden, so now the apostle fears that the Corinthians are being led away from what Jesus, the new Adam (!), revealed by his ἁπλότης and ἁγνότης – namely, single-minded devotion to God and God's will. Thus, the element of devotion is present in 2 Cor 11:3, but the devotion is *to God.* Paul's reference to Christ is an implicit exhortation to the Corinthians to conform themselves to Jesus, who – as the model of authentic human existence – showed forth innocence and single-minded faithfulness to God.[562] Indeed, a few verses later (11:7), the apostle shows that he himself conforms to Christ's *ethos* by 'lowering himself' (ἑαυτὸν ταπεινοῦν, cf. Phil 2:8).[563]

In sum, I differ from the traditional interpretation of 2 Cor 11:2-4. Paul fears that the Corinthians are being led astray. But what they are being led away from is an essential attribute that was present in Jesus, namely his single-minded integrity in being faithful to God and God's will. It is *the gospel of God* (τὸ τοῦ θεοῦ εὐαγγέλιον) that the apostle preaches (11:7). Ultimately, therefore, it is devotion to God and to what God has revealed in and through Jesus that is at issue here. In the end, my interpretation does not entirely contradict the

---

[560]See n. 539.

[561]So, KISTEMAKER, *The Second Epistle to the Corinthians*, 361: "Paul's purpose in supplying the illustration of Eve's deception is *to emphasize the necessity of unblemished spiritual fidelity to God*" (italics added).

[562]Cf. MURPHY-O'CONNOR, *The Theology of the Second Letter to the Corinthians*, 109. The Corinthians will conform themselves to God and God's will by heeding God's messenger to them, namely Paul (cf. 2 Cor 10:13-16).

[563]I will develop this point in Chapter Five.

traditional understanding.[564] But it does add the important nuance of the character of Jesus and the role this plays in Paul's argument.

X. "Crucified out of weakness" (2 Cor 13:4)

Paul's final allusion to the story and *ethos* of Jesus appears in 2 Cor 13:4, at the climax of the letter. The context is one of admonition and challenge. After announcing his upcoming third visit to the Corinthians (13:1), the apostle warns that he will not be lenient in the face of opposition to him (13:2). Then in 13:3 he refers to the fact that the Corinthians seek "proof" (δοκιμή) that Christ speaks 'in him.' Paul has been challenged to give evidence that he is an authentic envoy of Jesus. In 13:5, however, the apostle throws the challenge right back at the Corinthians – they are to test themselves (δοκιμάζω ἑαυτούς) to ascertain whether or not they are ἐν τῇ πίστει. Within the bracket of these challenges, Paul refers to the story and character of Jesus: "he was crucified ἐξ ἀσθενείας, but he lives ἐκ δυνάμεως θεοῦ" (13:4a). In order to elucidate the meaning of 2 Cor 13:3b-4, it is necessary to pay careful attention to (1) the terms signifying "weakness" (ἀσθεν- terminology) and "power" (δυναμ/τ- terminology); (2) the force of the various prepositional phrases; and (3) the way the apostle uses the conjunction ἀλλά.

"Weakness" and "power" appear in tension three times in 2 Cor 13:3b-4. The first instance occurs in the relative clause used to describe Christ in 13:3b: ὃς εἰς ὑμᾶς οὐκ ἀσθενεῖ ἀλλὰ δυνατεῖ ἐν ὑμῖν. Grammatically, this clause is disjunctive[565] – Christ is not weak, *but rather* (ἀλλά) is powerful. Here 'being weak' and 'being powerful' are used, in effect, simply as antonyms.[566] Observe that both verbs are in the present tense, and that the Corinthians are the object of both prepositions. Thus, Paul is making a statement about Christ's being powerful *in the here and now* with respect to the

---

[564]Cf. BARRETT, who states that "disobedience to God and unfaithfulness to the bridegroom (Christ) are one and the same thing." See *The Second Epistle to the Corinthians*, 274.

[565]See BDAG, s.v. ἀλλά, 1.

[566]The ἀσθεν- word group can denote "sickness, disease" as well as "weakness." The context of 2 Cor 13:3b-4 demands the latter signification. See BDAG, s.v. ἀσθένεια, 1 and 2.

Corinthians.[567] Earlier in 2 Corinthians, the apostle has associated δύναμις explicitly with God (4:7 and 6:7; cf. 10:4, where the adjective δυνατά is modified by τῷ θεῷ). Moreover, Paul's only other use of the verb δυνατέω in this letter confirms this connection: "*God* is powerful (δυνατεῖ) to make abundant every gift with respect to you" (9:8).[568] This suggests that Christ's being powerful among the Corinthians is another way of saying that *divine* power is at work (a point to which I will return).

In 2 Cor 13:4 Paul offers the grounding for this power at work among the Corinthians, a grounding that is described in two steps (note the two-fold use of γάρ).[569] The first step is 13:4a, where the apostle appeals to the story and character of Jesus: καὶ γὰρ ἐσταυρώθη ἐξ ἀσθενείας, ἀλλὰ ζῇ ἐκ δυνάμεως θεοῦ. The initial καί is exepegetical, and is best rendered "that is to say." Hence, 13:4 (the whole verse) serves to explain how Christ is powerful among the Corinthians in the here and now. The conjunction ἀλλά appears again, but now with a different sense than in 13:3b. In 13:4a ἀλλά functions to introduce the apodosis of a concessive clause.[570] What Paul "concedes" in the

---

[567]I read the prepositional phrases εἰς ὑμᾶς and ἐν ὑμῖν as synonymous. See BDAG, s.v. εἰς, 5, for the sense of "with respect to, with reference to"; cf. Rom 8:28 and 2 Cor 9:8. In addition, see BDAG, s.v. ἐν, 8, for the meaning "in connection with"; cf. 1 Cor 4:2 and 14:11. See BULTMANN, *The Second Letter to the Corinthians,* 242. LAMBRECHT captures well the sense of 2 Cor 13:3b: "In it Christ's powerful relation to the Corinthians is twice expressed, first negatively then positively." See "Philological and Exegetical Notes on 2 Corinthians 13,4," in R. BIERINGER and J. LAMBRECHT, *Studies on 2 Corinthians*, BETL 112 (Leuven: Leuven University Press, 1994) 589-98, here 589.

[568]PLUMMER points out that the verb δυνατέω is peculiar to Paul in biblical Greek, and that he uses it exclusively in conjunction with *divine* power. See *II Corinthians*, 374. In addition, see MARTIN, *2 Corinthians*, 474.

[569]BULTMANN (*The Second Letter to the Corinthians*, 243) rightly recognizes that both instances of γάρ in 2 Cor 13:4 are to be construed as giving the reason for 13:3. In addition, see LAMBRECHT, *Second Corinthians*, 224; and SAMPLEY, *NIB*, 11.176.

[570]See BDF, § 448 (5) and § 457. Cf. 1 Cor 4:15: ἐὰν γὰρ μυρίους παιδαγωγοὺς ἔχητε ἐν Χριστῷ ἀλλ' οὐ πολλοὺς πατέρας.

protasis[571] is that Jesus "was crucified out of weakness." This is obviously a reference to the story of Jesus. But what does the apostle mean when he states that Christ was crucified ἐξ ἀσθενείας? Given that Paul has just stated that Christ is *not* weak with respect to the Corinthians, he must be using the term ἀσθένεια in a specialized sense in 13:4a. Indeed, the apostle uses it to convey something about Jesus' character.

Second Corinthians 10:1-12:13 offers two clues to what Paul means by the expression ἐξ ἀσθενείας. First, the apostle uses the notion of weakness as a foil to certain values and behavior that he opposes. In 10:10 we learn that some of the Corinthians hold Paul in contempt because his bodily appearance is "weak" (ἀσθενής) and his speech despicable. In 11:21 the apostle sarcastically "confesses" that he and his co-workers have been "too weak" (note the perfect tense ἠσθενήκαμεν) to exploit and lord over the Corinthians (see 11:20). Thus, "weakness" seems to connote for Paul a manner of appearance, speech, and behavior antithetical to that which he sees as valued by rival missionaries/evangelists and those adhering to them.[572] Second, the apostle employs the concept of weakness to signify a way of life marked by suffering and giving oneself up for others. In 11:30, in the context of listing the many hardships and humiliations he has endured in the process of giving himself to his ministry, Paul speaks of boasting only of "the things [that show] my weakness" (τὰ τῆς ἀσθενείας μου; cf. 12:5).

Returning to 2 Cor 13:4a, I propose that the idiom ἐξ ἀσθενείας refers to a mode of human existence marked by gentleness and humility, and by the willingness to endure suffering and hardship in giving oneself in service to others. Used here in connection with Jesus at the end of the letter, the phrase serves to encapsulate all that Paul has said concerning Jesus' character throughout the epistle. Indeed, the force of the preposition ἐξ supports this

---

[571]Note the textual support for the insertion of εἰ before ἐσταυρώθη. LAMBRECHT'S translation of 13:4 (see *Second Corinthians*, 220) rightly captures this concessive quality: "... *although* he was crucified in weakness.... *although* we too are weak in him ..." (italics added).

[572]Cf. 2 Cor 5:12, where Paul contrasts 'boasting in appearances' (ἐν προσώπῳ καυχάομαι) with valuing what is "in [the] heart" (ἐν καρδίᾳ).

interpretation. Here it signifies "by reason of, as a result of."[573] Thus, when the apostle states that Jesus was crucified "as a result of weakness," he means that the latter's death was *the culmination of a life lived for the sake of others*, a life characterized by humility and suffering.[574]

Yet – this is the sense of ἀλλά in a concessive clause – Christ "lives by the power of God." Note the present tense of the verb ζάω. Jesus, the one who was crucified, lives now, and he does so ἐκ δυνάμεως θεοῦ. Here the preposition ἐκ specifies the *source*[575] from which something flows. Jesus lives now because of the power of God, whom Paul earlier named as ὁ ἐγείρας τὸν κύριον ᾿Ιησοῦν ("the one who raised the Lord Jesus," 2 Cor 4:14). Hence, the apostle refers here (i.e., in the first step) to the power of God in connection with the resurrection of Jesus. This evokes Paul's use of the expression ἡ ζωὴ τοῦ ᾿Ιησοῦ in 2 Cor 4:10-11 (cf. 4:7). Recall that by this phrase the apostle refers to the power of God that enables its recipients to live after the manner of the human Jesus, thereby manifesting *in the present* the power of resurrection life. Indeed, Paul goes on to describe this very effect in 13:4b, the second step by which Christ is presently powerful with respect to the Corinthians.

The apostle explains this second step as follows: καὶ γὰρ ἡμεῖς ἀσθενοῦμεν ἐν αὐτῷ, ἀλλὰ ζήσομεν σὺν αὐτῷ ἐκ δυνάμεως θεοῦ εἰς ὑμᾶς. Observe that the formal structure of 2 Cor 13:4b is the same as that of 13:4a. Thus, once again, the conjunction ἀλλά introduces the apodosis of a concessive clause. That which Paul "concedes" (in the protasis) is that he is

---

[573]See BDAG, s.v. ἐκ, 3.e. Cf. Gal 3:5: ὁ οὖν ἐπιχορηγῶν ὑμῖν τὸ πνεῦμα καὶ ἐνεργῶν δυνάμεις ἐν ὑμῖν, ἐξ ἔργων νόμου ἢ ἐξ ἀκοῆς πίστεως; (cf. also Rom 11:6 and Gal 3:2). See MARTIN, *2 Corinthians*, 452. *Pace* BULTMANN, *The Second Letter to the Corinthians*, 243. Bultmann states that "ἐξ ἀσθενείας is scarcely meant in a causal sense . . .", and opines that Paul chose ἐκ here merely for its rhetorical correspondence to ἐκ δυνάμεως θεοῦ.

[574]Cf. BARRETT, *The Second Epistle to the Corinthians*, 335-36; MARTIN, *2 Corinthians*, 475; KISTEMAKER, *The Second Epistle to the Corinthians*, 448. *Pace* THRALL, who holds that Christ's death ἐξ ἀσθενείας was "due to, or made possible by, the essential weakness of humanity's earthly-bodily existence." See *II Corinthians*, 2.884; cf. BELLEVILLE, *2 Corinthians*, 329.

[575]See BDAG, s.v. ἐκ, 3.g. Cf. 1 Cor 9:14: οὕτως καὶ ὁ κύριος διέταξεν τοῖς τὸ εὐαγγέλιον καταγγέλλουσιν ἐκ τοῦ εὐαγγελίου ζῆν. In addition, see PLUMMER, *II Corinthians*, 375.

"likewise[576] weak in [Christ[577]]. . . ." Here the apostle aligns himself[578] – observe the addition of the nominative pronoun ἡμεῖς for emphasis[579] – with the mode of self-emptying existence signified by the phrase ἐξ ἀσθενείας.[580] That Paul points to his own inclusion in the story and character of Jesus is also indicated by the phrase ἐν αὐτῷ. The preposition ἐν here denotes cause or reason.[581] Thus, it is because of the apostle's intimate relationship with Jesus that he embodies the same mode of human existence as the latter.[582]

Yet, Paul claims that he "shall live with [Christ] by the power of God for [the Corinthians]." Although there is formal parallelism between 2 Cor 13:4a and 13:4b, the material parallelism breaks down in the second half of 13:4b. *Prima facie*, it appears that the apostle refers here to his future resurrection. Paul employs the same verb (ζάω) that he used in reference to Christ's resurrection in 13:4a. Moreover, ζήσομεν is future tense and is used in conjunction with the phrase σὺν αὐτῷ (cf. 4:14, where this construction refers

---

[576]Reading καί in the adverbial sense of "also, likewise." See BDAG, s.v. καί, 2.

[577]Although "God" is the most immediate antecedent, both the sense of 13:3-4 and the repetition of the phrase ἐκ δυνάμεως *θεοῦ* in 13:4b lead me to take Christ as the antecedent of the two instances of the dative pronoun αὐτῷ.

[578]BARRETT correctly observes that ἡμεῖς refers primarily to Paul himself. This is indicated by the phrase εἰς ὑμᾶς, which alludes to his impending visit (cf. 2 Cor 13:1: τρίτον τοῦτο *ἔρχομαι* πρὸς ὑμᾶς). See *The Second Epistle to the Corinthians*, 337. SAMPLEY'S characterization (*NIB*, 11.176) of ἡμεῖς as including "the collegiality of all those who have shared weakness in Christ's death and been adorned with God's power in the new life that has resulted" is too expansive, given the context of 13:1-4.

[579]As noted, e.g., by FURNISH, *II Corinthians*, 571.

[580]THRALL rightly connects Paul's statement here with what he says in 2 Cor 4:7-14; 11:23-27; and 12:9-10. See *II Corinthians*, 2.885.

[581]See BDAG, s.v. ἐν, 9.a. Cf. 1 Cor 7:14: ἡγίασται γὰρ ὁ ἀνὲρ ὁ ἄπιστος ἐν τῇ γυναικὶ καὶ ἡγίασται ἡ γυνὴ ἡ ἄπιστος ἐν τῷ ἀδελφῷ.

[582]SAVAGE captures this sense well: ". . . to be weak in Christ means to share in his un-self-striving, self-negating, servant-like, God-centered faith." See *Power through Weakness*, 174-75.

to the eschatological future). Nevertheless, both the context – the apostle's impending visit and his threat not to spare – and the final prepositional phrase, εἰς ὑμᾶς, demand that the reference is to what will happen when Paul arrives in Corinth.[583] So, what does the apostle claim in the second half of 13:4b?

The key to understanding what Paul means in 2 Cor 13:4b lies in its three consecutive prepositional phrases. All three modify the verb ζήσομεν. First, the apostle says that he will live σὺν αὐτῷ, referring to Christ. The preposition σύν here denotes "association in activity"; Paul associates his coming appearance in Corinth with the power of the risen life of Christ.[584] The phrase ἐκ δυνάμεως θεοῦ has the same sense as in 13:4a, namely, "because of God's power" (referring to God as the *source* of this power). Thus, the first two phrases refer, in effect, to one and the same thing. Finally, the apostle says that he shall live εἰς ὑμᾶς (referring to the Corinthians). In this case, the preposition εἰς expresses the equivalent of the dative *of advantage*. His activity is for the Corinthians' benefit.[585] Hence, Paul intimates that, empowered by God through the risen Christ, he will continue to pour himself out in love and service for the sake and advantage of the Corinthians (see 12:15), even if that means that he

---

[583]LAMBRECHT sums up well the position of the vast majority of commentators: "Although the language used in this verse is certainly that of resurrection life of all Christians alike, because of the specific context of 13,1-4 and of the striking addition of εἰς ὑμᾶς, we may assume that Paul has in mind here concretely his future powerful action in Corinth." See "Philological and Exegetical Notes on 2 Corinthians 13,4," 598. On the other hand, BARRETT (*The Second Epistle to the Corinthians*, 337) and DUNN (*The Theology of Paul the Apostle*, 401-2) seem to imply that the apostle's primary reference here is to the future resurrection (and only derivatively to the effects of the resurrection life in the present).

[584]See BDAG, s.v. σύν, 1.b. Cf. 1 Thess 5:10: ἵνα εἴτε γρηγορῶμεν εἴτε καθεύδωμεν ἅμα σὺν αὐτῷ ζήσωμεν. Cf. TANNEHILL, who states that σὺν αὐτῷ indicates "that Paul's weakness and life from God's power are not independent of Christ but are manifestations of his participation in Christ." See *Dying and Rising with Christ*, 99. For an extended study of Paul's use of the phrase "with Christ," see J. DUPONT, *ΣΥΝ ΧΡΙΣΤΩΙ: L'union avec le Christ suivant Saint Paul* (Bruges: Éditions de L'abbaye de Saint-André, 1952).

[585]See BDAG, s.v. εἰς, 4.g. Cf. Rom 10:12: ὁ γὰρ αὐτὸς κύριος πάντων, πλουτῶν εἰς πάντας τοὺς ἐπικαλουμένους αὐτόν. In addition, cf. 2 Cor 8:1; 9:1; and 9:13 (concerning ἡ διακονία ἡ ἐις τοὺς ἁγίους).

must come ἐν ῥάβδῳ (13:2; cf. 1 Cor 4:21). Or, to use the language and imagery of 2 Cor 4:10, the apostle will continue to bear the νέκρωσις τοῦ Ἰησοῦ in order that the ζωὴ τοῦ Ἰησοῦ might be manifested. This explains *how* Christ "is powerful" among the Corinthians in the present (13:3b).

Therefore, Paul's final reference to the character of Jesus in 2 Cor 13:3b-4 – which serves as a summary statement of the references that have preceded it – focuses on the paradoxical relationship of "weakness" and "power." The apostle states that Christ was crucified ἐξ ἀσθενείας, by which he means that Jesus' death was the climactic consummation of a life lived in love and service of others in obedience to God and God' will. Yet, Christ now lives by the power of God. Paul claims to participate in the same pattern of existence. And it is through the apostle's fidelity to such a self-emptying way of life that the Lord Jesus continues to exercise power among the Corinthians. The paradox is that δύναμις works through ἀσθένεια (understood in the specifically Pauline sense). As we will see in greater detail in the following chapter, this is the "proof" that Christ is speaking in Paul (13:3a).

XI. Summary

The foregoing analysis demonstrates that Paul draws extensively upon the story and character of Jesus in 2 Corinthians. The apostle's evocation and use of the story and *ethos* of Christ entail much more than the skeletal descent-ascent version often attributed to him – the version in which the preexistent Christ humbled himself by becoming human, was put to death, and is now exalted above all creation. Paul evokes a much richer and detailed portrait of Jesus.

This portrait features Jesus as the new Adam, the εἰκὼν τοῦ θεοῦ (cf. 2 Cor 4:4), the prototype of a new mode of human existence. As the new Adam, Jesus is the "one who did not know Sin" (5:21; cf. ἀγνότης as "innocence" in 11:3), and who thus broke the power of Sin and Death. His life was marked by obedience (10:5) – a continuous ναί and ἀμήν (1:19-20) to God and to God's will – as well as by faithfulness (4:13). As God's δοῦλος (cf. 4:13), Jesus showed forth both God's love and his own love (5:14) for all people by living and dying for their advantage. Christ's mode of self-emptying existence for others (4:10-11; 5:21; 8:9; and 13:4) was grounded in his deep-seated trust in God (4:13; cf 9:9) to bring the dead to life. Concerning his way of relating to other people, Jesus' manner was distinguished by his gentleness and forbearance (10:1). In short, the apostle alludes throughout 2 Corinthians to Christ's ἁπλότης (11:3) – to his single-minded disposition to love and serve God and others, as well as to the way his life manifested this disposition.

Paul consistently evokes the *ethos* of Jesus in 2 Corinthians. This letter, however, is not an encomium to Christ. The apostle's strategy in alluding to the story and character of Jesus is instrumental, an attempt to recall the "image" into which the Spirit transforms people (see 3:18). Indeed, Paul's purpose in summoning Jesus' *ethos* is two-fold. He commends his own mode of apostleship by aligning himself with Jesus' character and story. And he challenges the Corinthians to enter more fully into the story of Jesus by more faithfully embodying his character. I now turn my attention to the apostle's self-commendation.

Chapter Five
Paul Embodies the Character of Jesus

I. Introduction

Several commentators claim, as we saw in Chapter Two, that Paul's chief purpose in writing 2 Corinthians is to offer an *apologia* for his apostleship and authority. They contend that this epistle is an example of forensic rhetoric. Yet, it is striking that the apostle makes practically no use of the substantive ἀπολογία ("defense")[586] or the verb ἀπολογέομαι ("defend oneself")[587] in this letter. Rather, throughout 2 Corinthians Paul employs the verb συνίστημι with the reflexive pronoun to indicate the notion of self-commendation. Indeed, instead of referring to this letter as his self-defense, it would be more accurate to say that 2 Corinthians is – at least in part – the apostle's self-commendation.[588] I argue that Paul offers a unique form of self-commendation, one based on his sharing the *ethos* of Jesus. The apostle can commend himself to the Corinthians precisely because he embodies the pattern of loving, self-giving existence manifested by Jesus. In order to substantiate this claim, it is

---

[586]Only in 7:11, where Paul refers to the *Corinthians*' self-defense, not his own.

[587]Only in 12:19, where the apostle states: πάλαι δοκεῖτε ὅτι ὑμῖν ἀπολογούμεθα ("You think all this time that we are defending ourselves to you"). MCCANT rightly observes Paul's use of irony and diatribe here. In fact, throughout the Corinthian correspondence, the apostle insists that only God or Christ can judge him (1 Cor 4:3-5 and 2 Cor 5:10). See MCCANT, *2 Corinthians*, 157-58, as well as n. 170 above. *Pace* LONG (see *"Have We Been Defending Ourselves to You?"*, ii and 182), for whom 2 Cor 12:19 is Paul's self-reflective comment concerning the genre of 2 Corinthians.

[588]Cf. BELLEVILLE, who argues that, in 2 Cor 1-7, Paul creates "an official letter of apologetic self-commendation." See "A Letter of Apologetic Self-Commendation: 2 Cor. 1:8-7:16," 142-63. Her treatment, however, is deficient because it fails to take into account the letter as a whole, including the important paragraph on self-commendation in 10:12-18. Moreover, as I will argue in Chapter Six, while it is more accurate to regard 2 Cor as self-commendation than as *apologia*, the fundamental thrust of this letter is deliberative.

necessary first to take a closer look at how Paul uses the verb συνίστημι in 2 Corinthians.

The very number of occurrences of this verb immediately catches our attention. Nine of the fourteen instances of συνίστημι in the Pauline writings occur in 2 Corinthians, as do seven of the eight instances of συνίστημι + the reflexive pronoun.[589] Comparison with Paul's usage of συνίστημι in his other letters makes clear that this word has a particular nuance in 2 Corinthians.

In general, συνίστημι has a wide range of meanings. Its root meaning is "bring together" (transitive) or "hold together" (intransitive).[590] The apostle draws upon this sense in Col 1:17, where he states that all things "hold together" (συνέστηκεν, perfect tense), that is, continue to exist in Christ. The verb can also be read as "demonstrate, show, bring out."[591] Paul makes use of this signification in Rom 3:5: "Now if our unrighteousness [functions] *to show* God's righteousness, what shall we say?"; in Rom 5:8: "God *demonstrates* [God's] own love for us in that while we were still sinners Christ died for us"; and in Gal 2:18: "For if I build up again those things which I tore down, I *show myself* to be a transgressor." Finally, συνίστημι can denote "commend, recommend."[592] The apostle uses this meaning in Rom 16:1, where he introduces and commends the deaconess Phoebe to the followers of Christ in Rome.

When using συνίστημι in 2 Corinthians, Paul draws almost exclusively on the notion of commendation.[593] More specifically, the apostle is concerned with the self-commendation (συνίστημι + reflexive pronoun) of himself and

---

[589]This verb occurs in 2 Cor in 3:1; 4:2; 5:12; 6:4; 7:11; 10:12; 10:18 (2x); and 12:11. In the first seven instances, it is used in conjunction with the reflexive pronoun. Elsewhere Paul uses συνίστημι in Rom 3:5; 5:8; and 16:1; Gal 2:18 (where it is paired with the reflexive pronoun); and Col 1:17.

[590]See BDAG, s.v. συνίστημι, A.1 and B.3.

[591]See BDAG, s.v. συνίστημι, A.3.

[592]See BDAG, s.v. συνίστημι, A.2.

[593]The sole exception is 2 Cor 7:11, where Paul gladly relates how the Corinthians *showed* or *proved themselves* to be innocent in the matter involving the punishment of "the offender" (see 2:5-8 and 7:12).

of others. As was suggested in Chapter Two, it is critically important to pay close attention to his syntax. In this letter self-commendation has both negative and positive connotations.[594]

When Paul places the reflexive pronoun *before* the verb, the sense of self-commendation is negative. For example, immediately after distancing himself[595] from those who "peddle" God's message (2 Cor 2:17), the apostle asks in 3:1: "Are we beginning to commend ourselves (ἑαυτοὺς συνιστάνειν) again?" That Paul intends a negative answer to this question is evident from his follow-up question: "Or do we need, as some [do], letters of recommendation to you or from you?" The negative particle μή at the beginning of this second question indicates that the apostle expects a negative answer. Thus, in this instance, Paul denies that he commends himself. Likewise, in 5:12, after explaining that the endurance of suffering is involved in manifesting the life of (the risen) Jesus (4:7-5:10), the apostle asserts that he and his co-workers "are not again commending ourselves (ἑαυτοὺς συνιστάνομεν) to you."

Paul indicates in 2 Cor 10:12 what he means by this negative notion of self-commendation, signified by the syntax of ἑαυτὸν συνιστάνειν. After noting that he has been criticized for writing strong letters from afar and for making an unimpressive appearance in person (10:9-10), the apostle asserts in 10:12a: "For we do not dare to classify or compare ourselves with some of those who commend themselves (τῶν ἑαυτοὺς συνιστανόντων)." He then goes on to explain in 10:12b what ἑαυτὸν συνιστάνειν entails: a "measuring" (μετρέω) of oneself against others, and a "comparing" (συγκρίνω) of oneself with others. That is, ἑαυτὸν συνιστάνειν means being competitive and seeking one's own good reputation. Paul speaks of it as "boasting" (καυχάομαι) in one's own self and one's own accomplishments – even to the point of claiming the labors of others as one's own (see 10:13-17). Most

---

[594]The following analysis has its starting point in J.T. FITZGERALD'S observation that "[t]he difference in the placement of the pronoun [ἑαυτούς] is crucial. Every time in 2 Corinthians that Paul wishes to make a negative comment about self-commendation he places the pronoun before the verb.... When he speaks positively, ... he places it after the verb." See *Cracks in an Earthen Vessel*, 187.

[595]The pronoun here is actually plural. As will become evident, one of the recurring difficulties in interpreting 2 Cor is determining the specific referent of the first person plural pronouns. See n. 600 below for a brief discussion. In addition, see n. 713 for an explanation for interpreting *Paul* as the referent of the pronoun in 2:17.

significantly, it excludes any acknowledgment that *God* is the source of empowerment. The apostle concludes that "the one who commends himself" (ὁ ἑαυτὸν συνιστάνων) is *not* "approved" (δόκιμος) by the Lord (10:18).

The best translation of ἑαυτὸν συνιστάνειν, therefore, is "*self*-commend," with the emphasis on "self." To *self*-commend is to exalt oneself at the expense of others and at the expense of the truth. The critical truth dispensed with by this act is that *God* is the source of all that is good, and that the only legitimate boasting is 'boasting in the Lord' (2 Cor 10:17). Moreover, Paul stresses that those who *self*-commend "do not understand" (οὐ συνιᾶσιν, 10:12b). *What* they fail to understand is the basis for what the apostle regards as legitimate and positive self-commendation. Notice that once again we encounter cognitive terminology in 2 Corinthians. As we saw throughout Chapter Four – and will see below in the analysis of 3:18-4:6 – Paul utilizes the language of proper knowing in close conjunction with the story and character of Jesus. Thus, *prima facie*, I submit that we can expect that the positive concept of self-commendation is linked with the *ethos* of Jesus. This is borne out by the apostle's own discussion of the concept.

Paul expresses the notion of positive self-commendation by placing the reflexive pronoun *after* the verb συνίστημι. The first instance occurs in 2 Cor 4:2. The apostle has just made clear that he is a minister of the new covenant (see 3:6) by the mercy of God (4:1). Therefore, he has renounced hidden, shameful things, as he refuses to conduct himself in deceit or to falsify God's message. Rather, Paul and his co-workers are those who "commend [them]selves (συνιστάνοντες ἑαυτούς) to every person's conscience before God." It is important to take note of the *means* by which they do so: "by the revelation of the truth" (τῇ φανερώσει τῆς ἀληθείας). Given that the apostle contrasts this revelation of truth with deceitful conduct (cf. περιπατέω ἐν πανουργίᾳ), positive self-commendation is grounded in *conduct* that manifests "truth." What this conduct entails becomes clear in his next use of συνιστάνειν ἑαυτόν.

After denying that he and his co-workers give any cause for offense (2 Cor 6:3), Paul declares that "in every way we commend ourselves (συνιστάντες ἑαυτούς) as servants of God" (6:4). Observe that the positive sense of self-commendation is intimately connected here with being *servants of God* (διάκονοι θεοῦ). The apostle then outlines in 6:4-10 what being in God's service entails: bearing hardships (6:4b-5; cf. 4:10a); manifesting qualities such as innocence (ἁγνότης, 6:6a; cf. 11:3), forbearance (μακροθυμία, 6:6a; cf. 10:1), genuine love (ἀγάπη ἀνυπόκριτος; 6:6b; cf. 5:14), and truthful speech (λόγος ἀληθείας, 6:7a; cf. 11:10); and living for the sake of others – "as poor, but we enrich many" (ὡς πτωχοὶ πολλοὺς δὲ πλουτίζοντες, 6:10; cf. 8:9). In short, being God's servants means incarnating the mode of existence revealed by Jesus, a way of life that is empowered by God (ἐν δυνάμει θεοῦ, 6:7a; cf. 4:7)[596] *through* the Holy Spirit (ἐν πνεύματι ἁγίῳ, 6:6b; cf. 4:13),[597] a point upon which I will expand in the following section.

The expression συνιστάνειν ἑαυτόν, therefore, is best rendered "self-*commend*," with the emphasis on commendation – not on one's self. That which is commended is the mode of existence made manifest by Jesus, the εἰκὼν τοῦ θεοῦ (2 Cor 4:4), who revealed what it means to be truly and fully human. Such a way of life entails self-giving, not self-seeking; living for others and their needs, not for one's own glory; and boasting in the Lord, not in one's own accomplishments (see 10:17). The one who lives in this manner, according to Paul, is the one who is truly "approved" (δόκιμος, 10:18). Such a person is "one whom the Lord commends" (ὃν ὁ κύριος συνίστησιν). The apostle confidently engages in this positive self-commendation because he embodies Jesus' loving, self-emptying existence for others.[598] As we will eventually see, such a mode of existence is his "proof" that Christ is speaking in him (13:3).

In what follows, I show how Paul presents himself throughout 2 Corinthians as embodying the values, attitude, and behavior – in short, the *ethos* – of Jesus. First, I discuss the apostle's characterization of the effects of God's gift of the Spirit (1:21-22). Then I analyze how Paul describes being transformed into the image of Christ (3:18-4:6, with special emphasis on 3:18, 4:4, and 4:6). I will at that point be in a position to examine *how* the apostle depicts himself as participating in the story of Jesus by embodying the latter's character. This analysis takes place under three main headings: Paul's

---

596Reading ἐν in this instance as marking cause or reason (see BDAG, s.v. ἐν, 9.a). See 2 Cor 13:4 and n. 581.

597Reading ἐν here as denoting agency (see BDAG, s.v. ἐν, 6). See 2 Cor 1:19-20 and n. 387.

598That Paul regards himself as following in the way of Christ is evident from his exhortation to the Corinthians in 1 Cor 11:1: μιμηταί μου γίνεσθε καθὼς κἀγὼ Χριστοῦ ("Become imitators of me, just as I am of Christ"). The apostle offers this counsel in the context of presenting himself as one who does not seek his own advantage (10:33).

manifestation of the "Spirit of faithfulness" (see 4:13); his role in continuing the ministry of reconciliation (5:20-6:2); and his claim to act toward the Corinthians with ἁπλότης and ἀγάπη (1:12 and 12:14-15).

Thus, while the apostle does engage in the rhetorical strategy of establishing his own integrity and trustworthiness – that is, his *ethos* – he does so in a unique manner. Paul commends himself (i.e., self-*commends*) only insofar as he incarnates faithfully the *ethos* revealed by Jesus. In this way the story of Jesus continues. It is the development and continuation of Christ's character in the apostle, as well as the source of his empowerment – namely, the Holy Spirit – that are the focus of the next section.

II. The "Christing" of Paul through the "Sealing" of the Spirit (2 Cor 1:21-22)

After his allusion to Jesus' ναί in 2 Cor 1:19-20a, Paul concludes by stating in 1:20b: διὸ καὶ δι' αὐτοῦ τὸ ἀμὴν τῷ θεῷ πρὸς δόξαν δι' ἡμῶν ("Therefore, also through him, the Amen [comes to be][599] to God for glory through us"). Recall that in Chapter Four I argued that the phrase τὸ ἀμήν τῷ θεῷ signifies human faithfulness in living in accord with the dictates and character of God (cf. πιστὸς ὁ θεός, 1:18a). In effect, Jesus' Yes was his Amen to God. Recall, too, that the liturgical interpretation of 1:20b does not fit the context or content of the passage. Rather, the apostle draws an explicit connection between Jesus' ναί, which happened in the past, and τὸ ἀμήν, which continues in the present through Paul and his co-workers.[600] The source

---

[599]As was the case in 2 Cor 1:20a (see n. 380), so too in 1:20b the verb must be supplied. Given that γίνομαι is the main verb of the two independent clauses in 1:19, and given that supplying γέγονεν in 1:20a makes good sense of that half verse, it seems that the logical choice for the implied verb of 1:20b is γίνεται.

[600]Taking Paul, Silvanus, and Timothy (1:19) as the antecedents of "us" (ἡμῶν). One of the vexing problems in translating and interpreting 2 Cor is determining the precise referent of Paul's first person plural pronouns (of which there are 220!). For an insightful study of this issue, see D. FILBECK, "Problems in Translating First Person Plural Pronouns in 2 Corinthians," *BT* 45 (1994) 401-9. Filbeck discusses his experience of participating in the translation of 2 Cor into Mal (a Mon-Khmer language spoken in northern Thailand). In addition to heeding the immediate context in determining the referent, Filbeck looks for what he calls "discourse markers" (e.g., an explicit 'we/you'

of this connection is indicated by the phrase δι᾽ αὐτοῦ, that is, 'through Jesus.' Here, in addition to denoting personal agency, the preposition διά + genitive signifies the originator of an action.[601] In other words, Jesus' faithfulness to God has created the possibility that others might live in faithful obedience to God. What is most pertinent here is that the apostle emphasizes that he himself is now an agent of faithfulness to God.[602] That Paul highlights the continuation of Jesus' character and faithfulness through him and his co-workers is further suggested by the way 1:20b is bracketed by the prepositional phrase διά + personal pronoun ('through Jesus, . . . through us').[603] This bracketing implies a synergism between Jesus and the apostle.

Paul goes on to explain in 2 Cor 1:21-22 *how* this synergism comes about. First of all, it is important to note that the postpositive particle δέ (1:21a) serves a linking function. (That the apostle intends no contrast between 1:21-22 and what immediately precedes it will become clear in the analysis to follow.) As he does elsewhere, Paul utilizes δέ here to insert an explanation.[604] Thus, 1:21-22 is best translated: "*That is*, the one who establishes (βεβαιῶν) us with

---

contrast). He also invokes theological considerations, including: "Did the verse under consideration and containing a first person plural pronoun refer to *a general theological principle* that was (and is) inclusive of (applicable to) every believer regardless of special gifts (or lack thereof) in Christian service? If the answer was 'Yes', then the first person plural pronoun should probably be translated as inclusive" [indicating the speaker and *all* listeners] (see p. 407, Filbeck's italics). For another helpful study on this issue, see M. CARREZ, "Le 'Nous' en 2 Corinthiens," *NTS* 26 (1980) 474-86.

[601]See BDAG, s.v. διά, A.4.b.β. Cf. esp. Rom 1:5: δι᾽ οὗ ἐλάβομεν χάριν καὶ ἀποστολὴν εἰς ὑπακοὴν πίστεως . . . ("through whom we have received grace and apostleship to bring about obedience of faith. . ."). In addition, cf. Rom 5:17 and 5:21.

[602]Cf. MATERA, *II Corinthians*, 55: "In effect, Paul forges a chain of faithfulness that extends from God to Christ, from Christ to Paul, and from Paul to the Christian community. The faithfulness of God is manifested in the faithfulness of Christ, in whom Paul's apostolic ministry is rooted. This is why the community can, should, and must trust him."

[603]The phrase δι᾽ ἡμῶν also denotes personal agency. See BDAG, s.v. διά, A.4.

[604]See BDAG, s.v. δέ, 2. Cf. Rom 3:22 and 9:30; 1 Cor 10:11; and Phil 2:8. *Pace*, e.g., RSV and NAB, which read δέ in 2 Cor 1:21 as indicating contrast ("*But*. . . ").

you in Christ (εἰς Χριστόν) and has anointed us (χρίσας) is God, and [God is the one who] has sealed (σφραγισάμενος) us and given (δούς) us the first installment (τὸν ἀρραβῶνα) of the Spirit in our hearts." The apostle now deliberately shifts the focus to *God* as the source of empowerment. This does not, however, contravene what Paul has just said about the role of Jesus. God's faithfulness (1:18a) was revealed in a unique and unsurpassable way in Jesus' fulfillment of all God's promises (1:20a). Nevertheless, God's fidelity *continues* to be made manifest through the gift of the Spirit that is bestowed on the apostle (and his co-workers).[605] In order to fully appreciate Paul's understanding of God's action expressed in 1:21-22, it is necessary to examine more closely each of the four participles – βεβαιῶν, χρίσας, σφραγισάμενος, and δούς – as well as the term ἀρραβών.

What does the apostle mean by the statement: ὁ βεβαιῶν ἡμᾶς σὺν ὑμῖν εἰς Χριστὸν . . . θεός (2 Cor 1:21a)? The verb βεβαιόω means "confirm, establish, strengthen."[606] Paul's use of βεβαιόω elsewhere suggests

---

[605]Although there is no indication of a change of referent of the first person plural pronoun between 2 Cor 1:20 and 1:21, and although Paul uses the prepositional phrase σὺν ὑμῖν ("with you," referring to the Corinthians) in 1:21a, thereby distinguishing himself (along with Timothy and Silvanus) from the community, I hold that the pronouns in 1:21b-22 are fully inclusive. So, too, does FURNISH, who correctly points out that the apostle makes the distinction in 1:21a in order to emphasize that God is establishing *all* of them – himself and the Corinthians – in Christ. See *II Corinthians*, 136-37. L.L. BELLEVILLE makes a similar observation, paying careful attention to the tenses of the participles: ". . . there is no grammatical warrant for understanding, as some do, God's stabilizing activity as including the Corinthians but the anointing, sealing, and giving of the Spirit as excluding them. God's continuing activity in the church is dependent on his past work through the deposit of the Spirit in the human heart." See "Paul's Polemic and Theology of the Spirit in Second Corinthians," *CBQ* 58 (1996) 281-304, here 284 (plus n. 13). *Pace*, e.g., J.J. KIJNE, who argues that the pronouns in 1:21b-22 refer exclusively to Paul and his co-workers. See "We, Us and Our in I and II Corinthians," *NovT* 8 (1966) 171-79, here 176-77. YOUNG and FORD'S reading – in which they take the pronouns in 1:21 as referring to God's guaranteeing the apostleship of Paul and his companions, and those in 1:22 as referring to all believers – involves an unwarranted switch in the pronoun's referent between these two verses. See *Meaning and Truth in 2 Corinthians*, 103. I focus on the Spirit's empowerment of *Paul* in this chapter, and will take up the transformation of the Corinthians in the next chapter.

[606]See BDAG, s.v. βεβαιόω, 1.

intriguing connections here, connections that allow for greater precision in our understanding of the passage in question.[607] In Rom 15:8 the apostle says that Christ "became a servant" (διάκονον γεγενῆσθαι) to the Jews to manifest God's truthfulness "in order to confirm (τὸ βεβαιῶσαι) the promises (τὰς ἐπαγγελίας) made to the patriarchs." Observe the convergence here of several themes that are present in 2 Cor 1:18-20a. The perfect tense of the infinitive γεγενῆσθαι denotes Christ's becoming something in the past – namely, a servant – that has continuing effects in the present. This recalls the perfect tense of γέγονεν with reference to Jesus' ναί in 2 Cor 1:19. Christ's becoming a servant to reveal God's truthfulness evokes Jesus' Yes (2 Cor 1:19b-20a), which is a manifestation of God's fidelity (1:18a). And Christ's confirming God's promises is similar to Paul's saying that all God's promises find their Yes in Jesus (2 Cor 1:20a). What is important to recognize is that the apostle utilizes βεβαιόω in Rom 15:8 in close association with the story and character of Jesus.

Paul also uses βεβαιόω in connection with the *continuation* of the story and character of Jesus *in others*. In the opening thanksgiving period in 1 Corinthians, the apostle reminds the community that "Christ's testimony (τὸ μαρτύριον τοῦ Χριστοῦ) was established (ἐβεβαιώθη)" among them (1 Cor 1:6).[608] Paul makes this statement in the context of thanking God for the ways

---

[607]Several commentators cite the technical use of βεβαιόω in legal and commercial contexts, and claim that Paul utilizes a commercial metaphor here, as well as throughout 1:21-22 (citing evidence for the use of βεβαιόω, σφραγίζω, and ἀρραβών in the spheres of law and commerce). See, e.g., BARRETT, *The Second Epistle to the Corinthians*, 79-80; FEE, *God's Empowering Presence*, 290-93; and BELLEVILLE, "Paul's Polemic and the Theology of the Spirit in Second Corinthians," 284-86. For the use of βεβαίωσις and cognates as legal and commercial terms, see THRALL, *II Corinthians*, 1.153-54.

I share BULTMANN'S hesitation in applying these spheres to Paul's use of βεβαιόω in 1:21a since "it is not a purchase which is validated here but rather persons who are 'established.'" See *The Second Letter to the Corinthians*, 41. Thus, I submit that the best way to adjudicate the apostle's usage here is to look at how he uses the term elsewhere. THRALL seems to agree, but limits herself too narrowly by looking only at 1 Cor 1:8-9 (see *II Corinthians*, 1.159).

[608]Reading Χριστοῦ as a subjective genitive, indicating that which Jesus revealed through his own ministry, including his teaching and, especially, his manner of living. If it is objected that Χριστοῦ ought to be rendered as an objective genitive – that is, as "the testimony *about* Christ" – the sense of Paul's line of thought in 1 Cor 1:4-9 would

in which God has enriched the Corinthians through Christ. This enrichment includes knowledge (γνῶσις, 1:5), a knowledge that involves what Jesus himself revealed (or what was revealed about Jesus). Then, in 1:8, the apostle goes on to say that our Lord Jesus Christ "will strengthen (βεβαιώσει) you to the end." It is striking that Paul makes this claim in the immediate context of mentioning spiritual gifts (χαρίσματα, 1:7), God's fidelity (πιστὸς ὁ θεός, 1:9), and God's call to the Corinthians to enter into fellowship (κοινωνία, 1:9) with Jesus Christ. Moreover, in an exhortation to the Colossians (in Col 2:7), the apostle encourages the community in Colossae to walk in the ways of Christ, as they are "rooted and built up in him, and established in faithfulness (βεβαιούμενοι ἐν πίστει)." As in Rom 15:8, several key themes conspicuously configure around the verb βεβαιόω in 1 Cor 1:4-9 and Col 2:7: God's fidelity; the testimony of (or concerning) Christ; knowledge of this testimony; the bestowal of spiritual gifts; communion with Jesus Christ; and walking in Christ's ways, which is associated with πίστις.

I submit that in 2 Cor 1:21a Paul continues to link the verb βεβαιόω with the story and character of Jesus, and with the ongoing realization of that story in people's lives. We are certainly prepared for such a linkage by the immediately preceding context (1:18-20). More importantly, the connection of βεβαιόω with Jesus' story and character is further suggested by the force of the prepositional phrase εἰς Χριστόν. The apostle says that God establishes/strengthens him, literally, "into Christ." The preposition εἰς can indicate movement toward a goal; more specifically, it can express the *result* intended by an action.[609] Here Paul claims that God is doing something in order to move him toward a goal, namely Christ. God's action, moreover, is for the purpose of bringing about a result. This intended "result," I suggest, is that the apostle become more and more Christ-like, that is, that he embody more and more the character of Jesus.[610] Indeed, βεβαιόω can have the connotation of

---

not differ much.

[609]See n. 376.

[610]Cf. J.D.G. DUNN, *Baptism in the Holy Spirit: A Re-examination of the New Testament Teaching on the Gift of the Spirit in Relation to Pentecostalism Today*, SBT II.15 (Naperville, Ill.: Alec R. Allenson, 1970) 132: "This process εἰς Χριστόν is best understood in terms of a growing likeness to Christ (Gal. 4.19; II Cor. 3.18)." Dunn's reading here is to be preferred to his later assessment of the preposition εἰς in 2 Cor

making a person firm in one's commitment,[611] a connotation that is appropriate to the establishment of *ethos*. Observe, too, that the participle βεβαιῶν is in the present tense, thereby indicating that God's action is ongoing.[612] Hence, I submit that, in 2 Cor 1:21a, Paul refers to a process of God's establishing/strengthening him to take on Christ's character. Then, in 1:21b-22, the apostle goes on to employ three aorist tense participles to express metaphorically what God has done for him in the past that grounds his experience of continually being strengthened to become more and more like Christ.[613]

In 2 Cor 1:21b Paul begins his description of how God has acted upon him in the past: God is the one "who has anointed (χρίσας) us." The verb χρίω ("anoint") occurs only five times in the NT, and the apostle's only usage

---

1:21a as indicating a more general sense of "towards, in reference to, for" (see *The Theology of Paul the Apostle*, 405).

[611]See BDAG, s.v. βεβαιόω, 2.

[612]So, too, HUGHES, *Paul's Second Epistle to the Corinthians*, 39: ". . . the present tense showing that this is a *constant* experience, and the graphic 'into' that it is a *progressive* experience: in the purpose of God the stability is not only continuous, but is ever being intensified" (Hughes's italics). In addition, see DUNN, *Baptism in the Holy Spirit*, 132; and LAMBRECHT, *Second Corinthians*, 29. While some commentators take the expression βεβαιῶν εἰς Χριστόν to signify incorporation into the body of Christ [e.g., PLUMMER, *II Corinthians*, 40; and FURNISH, *II Corinthians*, 137], THRALL rightly points out that this interpretation is questionable: "One would expect either a past participle, referring to the moment of entry *into* the body of Christ, or else, with the present participle, reference to the confirmation of the believer's existing situation *in* Christ." See *II Corinthians*, 1.151-52 (Thrall's italics). She also holds that εἰς makes the commercial/legal interpretation of βεβαιόω unlikely. Indeed, the following parenthetical remark by BARRETT illustrates the difficulty of pushing the commercial metaphor too hard: ". . . that Paul here writes 'into Christ', εἰς Χριστόν, not 'in Christ', ἐν Χριστῷ, may be due to the commercial metaphor; we are, as it were, 'entered into Christ's account.'" See BARRETT, *The Second Epistle to the Corinthians*, 79. I submit that the apostle would more likely speak about taking on Christ's character than about being entered into Christ's account of property or merchandise! See n. 636 below.

[613]For a similar understanding of the significance of the tenses of the participles in 2 Cor 1:21-22, see GARLAND, *2 Corinthians*, 105.

is here. Elsewhere in the NT, χρίω is used exclusively with reference to Jesus. In Luke 4:18 Jesus reads from the scroll of the prophet Isaiah: "The Spirit of the Lord is upon me, because he has anointed (ἔχρισεν) me" (see LXX Isa 61:1). In the Isaian text – which Jesus continues to cite – this anointing empowers the recipient to proclaim good news, and to bring about healing as well as freedom from oppression. A few verses later, Jesus appropriates this text in reference to himself (Luke 4:21). Moreover, in Acts 10:38 Peter describes God as having anointed (ἔχρισεν) Jesus of Nazareth "with [the] Holy Spirit and with power" (πνεύματι ἁγίῳ καὶ δυνάμει). Thus anointed, Jesus is depicted as one who went about doing good and bringing about healing.[614] Two observations are pertinent to our discussion. First, Jesus is the recipient of the action of anointing, an anointing that is intimately linked with the gift of the Holy Spirit. Second, as "the anointed one" [= "the messiah" (ὁ Χριστός)], Jesus is empowered to do the work set forth for him by God.

Admittedly, Paul often seems to use Χριστός as, in effect, a personal name for Jesus – not as an appellative denoting "messiah."[615] It is also true that the apostle does not explicitly cite the tradition referred to in Acts 10:38 of the anointing of "Jesus of Nazareth" (the human Jesus), an anointing that empowered the latter to do God's work.[616] Nevertheless, Paul's placement of the participle χρίσας next to the phrase εἰς Χριστὸν in 2 Cor 1:21 is striking, and gives one reason to pause.[617] In fact, the apostle *does* at times use Χριστός

---

[614]Acts 4:27 and Heb 1:9 are the other two NT texts containing the verb χρίω.

[615]Cf. BULTMANN, *The Theology of the New Testament*, 1.80: "Only rarely does Paul use [Christ] as a title. Peculiar to him is 'Christ Jesus,' in addition to which he less frequently uses 'Jesus Christ.' But in either order, 'Christ' is a proper name, as his frequent expression 'our Lord Jesus Christ' shows. For Paul, 'Lord' and not 'Christ' is Jesus' title." As we will see, Bultmann's position is overstated.

[616]Cf., however, DUNN, who, in reference to Paul's only use of χρίω, says that: ". . . there may indeed be a further echo of the claim that Jesus himself had been anointed by the Spirit." See *The Theology of Paul the Apostle*, 453. I am sympathetic to Dunn's guarded assessment.

[617]Indeed, recall how Paul names Jesus as "the Son of God, Jesus Christ" in 2 Cor 1:19a. THRALL notes that "Son of God" may have been a messianic title in early Christian circles, and that the apostle may have been familiar with this. See *II Corinthians*, 1.146.

to refer to Jesus as messiah (e.g., throughout his argument in Rom 9-10).[618] And we have seen in the previous chapter how Paul alludes throughout 2 Corinthians to the story and character of Jesus (including his humanity). In light of these observations, I submit that, with the participle χρίσας, the apostle plays on the designation of Jesus as "the anointed one" and, more specifically, draws on the mode of self-emptying existence exhibited by Christ for the purpose of 'doing good.' Literally, Paul says that God "has *christed*" him. God has done something in the past to the apostle that has empowered him to be more like Messiah Jesus – to be, in effect, "another christ."[619] As we will see shortly, that which God has done is bestow the gift of the Spirit upon Paul (2 Cor 1:22b). This is the same Spirit with which Jesus was anointed,[620] and which is now involved in the "christing" of the apostle.

Paul offers a further description of God's action on him in the past: God is the one "who has sealed (σφραγισάμενος) us" (2 Cor 1:22a). It is important to note that the apostle elsewhere associates the verb σφραγίζω – which means "seal" or "mark with a seal" – with the Spirit. In Eph 1:13 Paul reminds his readers that it was in Christ that "you were sealed with the promised Holy Spirit" (ἐσφραγίσθητε τῷ πνεύματι τῆς ἐπαγγελίας τῷ ἁγίῳ). Observe once more the notion of "promise" (cf. 2 Cor 1:20a), this time linked with the bestowal of the Spirit. In Eph 4:30 the apostle warns against grieving the Holy Spirit, "in whom you were sealed (ἐσφραγίσθητε) for the day of redemption." In both passages in Ephesians, Paul's use of the passive voice

---

[618]For a reading of Rom 9-10 that highlights the messianic key to Paul's argument there, see JOHNSON, *Reading Romans*, 146-48 and 158-63; and idem, "Isaiah the Evangelist," *Mils* 48 (2001) 88-105, esp. 98-103. In addition, WRIGHT argues that the apostle makes extensive use of Χριστός as referring to "messiah." See *The Climax of the Covenant*, 41-49, and esp. 137-74. In the latter, Wright shows the importance of Paul's understanding of Jesus as Messiah in Gal 3.

[619]So, too, MURPHY-O'CONNOR: "To bring out [Paul's] play on words the phrase should be translated: God 'christed' Paul. . . . God has made Paul another Christ. . . ." See *The Theology of the Second Letter to the Corinthians*, 24. HUGHES'S interpretation rightly emphasizes the subordinate and derivative sense in which those who follow Christ are to be regarded: ". . . it is possible to speak of them as God's 'messiahs' or 'christs' = 'anointed ones.'" See *Paul's Second Epistle to the Corinthians*, 40.

[620]So, too, MATERA, *II Corinthians*, 56, who also remarks that the effect of God's anointing is to conform its recipients to Jesus. Cf. SCOTT, *2 Corinthians*, 41.

suggests that it is *God* who is the agent who performs the act of sealing. Returning to 2 Cor 1:22, it comes as little surprise to see that the apostle juxtaposes God's act of sealing with God's bestowal of the Spirit.[621]

What exactly does Paul mean when he says that God has sealed him? The verb σφραγίζω has a wide range of meaning,[622] and it appears that the apostle exploits its full, rich metaphorical potential. This term can have the connotation of marking someone or something as a means of identification. The act of marking in this sense denotes both one's ownership and protection of that which is so marked.[623] For example, Rev 7:3 refers to the marking of "the slaves of God" (οἱ δοῦλοι τοῦ θεοῦ), a marking that would serve to provide identity and protection.[624] This use of σφραγίζω is suggestive. That Paul intends God's sealing of him to indicate that he is God's "slave" is quite plausible in light of Rom 6:15-23. There, writing to those in Rome who were "called to be holy" (see Rom 1:7), the apostle employs the imagery of slavery to describe both their former plight – as "slaves of sin" (δοῦλοι τῆς ἁμαρτίας, Rom 6:17) – as well as the new condition granted them by God's mercy – "now . . . you have become slaves of God" (νυνὶ . . . δουλωθέντες τῷ θεῷ, 6:22). Indeed, Paul grounds his own call to be an apostle in the fact that he is a δοῦλος of Jesus (cf. Rom 1:1 and Phil 1:1) and of God (Titus 1:1). Morever, as we will see below in the analysis of 2 Cor 4:13, Paul includes himself in the story of God's faithful δοῦλος, Jesus. Thus, I propose that the apostle uses σφραγίζω to indicate that

---

[621]The only other instance of the verb σφραγίζω in Paul's writings is Rom 15:28, used in reference to the collection for the church in Jerusalem. FURNISH correctly sees the relevance of the passages from Eph – and *not* Paul's use of σφραγίζω in Rom 15:28 or his employment of σφραγίς in Rom 4:11 and 1 Cor 9:2 – for the interpretation of 2 Cor 1:22a. See *II Corinthians*, 137.

[622]See E. WOODCOCK, "The Seal of the Holy Spirit," *Bsac* 155 (1998) 139-63, here 139-47.

[623]See BDAG, s.v. σφραγίζω, 3, and the references given there.

[624]Rev 7:3 reads: "Do not harm the earth or the sea or the trees, ἄχρι σφραγίσωμεν τοὺς δούλους τοῦ θεοῦ ἡμῶν ἐπὶ τῶν μετώπων αὐτῶν (until we have sealed the slaves of our God upon their foreheads)." The seal used is identified in the previous verse as the σφραγίς θεοῦ (Rev 7:2).

he has been metaphorically "marked" – indeed, "branded" – as a slave in service to God, whose protection he now enjoys.[625]

A second meaning of the verb σφραγίζω involves the use of a signet or seal to inscribe something or to cause an impression upon a malleable material (e.g., wax or clay). The substantive σφραγίς is used to denote both the object used for sealing as well as the mark that is impressed or inscribed.[626] In LXX 1 Kings 20:8, for instance, King Ahab's wife Jezebel wrote letters in his name and "sealed [them] with [his] seal" (ἐσφραγίσατο τῇ σφραγίδι).[627] More importantly, Paul himself draws on this sense of impressing/inscribing in 2 Tim 2:19. There the apostle speaks metaphorically of a house's foundation bearing an inscription (σφραγίς).[628] It is this action of impressing/inscribing that is pertinent for the present discussion. I submit that the "sealing" of Paul also entailed God's "impressing" or "inscribing" the character of Jesus upon him. That is, the apostle alludes here to the beginning of the process of what today is called "character formation." God has acted upon Paul in such a way

---

[625]Several commentators (e.g., BARRETT, *The Second Epistle to the Corinthians*, 79; and MARTIN, *2 Corinthians*, 28) cite the work of G.A. DEISSMANN on papyri and inscriptions [*Bible Studies*, trans. A. GRIEVE (Edinburgh: T. & T. Clark, 1901) esp. 238-39] in their assertion that Paul uses σφραγίζω to denote the claiming of property as belonging to a rightful owner. In doing so, Martin dismisses the relevance of Rev 7:2-3 for the interpretation of 2 Cor 1:22a, stating that the apostle does not use σφραγίζω in the latter passage in an eschatological sense. Without quibbling over what is meant by "an eschatological sense," I maintain that the reference to marking "God's slaves" – an act that entails a claim of "ownership"! – *is* relevant for understanding the text in question.

[626]See BDAG, s.v. σφραγίς, 1 and 3.

[627]See also LXX Esth 3:10; 8:8; and 8:10.

[628]It is significant that the inscription or seal in 2 Tim 2:19 includes both God's making a claim on people – "The Lord knows those who are his" – as well as a resulting duty placed on those so claimed – "Let everyone who names the name of the Lord depart from iniquity." For more on this verse and on Paul's use of the term σφραγίς, see JOHNSON, *The First and Second Letters to Timothy*, 387 and 396-97.

as to "carve" the values, attitude, and ways of Jesus upon him.[629] As God's promises found fulfillment in Jesus' ναί (cf. 2 Cor 1:20a), so now God's act of sealing with the promised Holy Spirit (Eph 1:13) empowers the apostle to appropriate and embody the character of Messiah Jesus.

Paul makes explicit this role of the Spirit in 2 Cor 1:22b: God is the one "who has given the first installment of the Spirit in our hearts" (δοὺς τὸν ἀρραβῶνα τοῦ πνεύματος ἐν ταῖς καρδίαις ἡμῶν). Once again, the apostle refers to an action that God has done in the past on his behalf. Observe that, when God is the subject of δίδωμι, the verb can denote the bestowal of a gift by formal action.[630] This quality of formal gift-giving is enhanced by the object named, "the ἀρραβών of the Spirit."[631] The term ἀρραβών denotes "a first installment, deposit, pledge." It is a technical legal and commercial term for an advance payment that secured a claim on that which was purchased. (Notice how this denotation coheres with the understanding of σφραγίζω as indicating a mark of possession – in this case, Paul marked as God's δοῦλος.) Moreover, the payment of an ἀρραβών committed the contracting party to make further payments.[632] Indeed, the apostle alludes to this ongoing aspect of ἀρραβών in Eph 1:14, where he describes the Holy Spirit as the "ἀρραβών of our inheritance *until* [the] setting free of the property." The point is that ἀρραβών – here, God's gift of the Spirit – has two aspects: the act of paying an initial installment, and the ongoing obligation to make further payments.

---

[629]Cf. HUGHES, who makes a similar claim: ". . . as a sealing with the Holy Spirit of God, it is a stamping of the divine character upon the human personality, a fresh and indestructible communication to the believer of the image of God which was defaced through the fall (cf. 3:18)." See *Paul's Second Epistle to the Corinthians*, 41. I would modify Hughes's statement to make more explicit the role that the humanity and character of Jesus play in making manifest the image of God. I take up this theme in the following section.

[630]See BDAG, s.v. δίδωμι, 13 and 17.b. Cf. 2 Cor 13:10. For a brief discussion of the nature of the "formal action," see n. 637 below.

[631]Reading "of the Spirit" in τὸν ἀρραβῶνα τοῦ πνεύματος as an appositional genitive. So, too, do PLUMMER, *II Corinthians*, 41; BARRETT, *The Second Epistle to the Corinthians*, 80; FURNISH, *II Corinthians*, 137; and FEE, *God's Empowering Presence*, 293.

[632]See BDAG, s.v. ἀρραβών, and the references listed there.

I submit that Paul draws metaphorically upon both of these aspects. The prepositional phrase ἐν ταῖς καρδίαις ἡμῶν offers an important clue to what the apostle intends by the *initial* gift – the first installment, as it were – of the Spirit. To anticipate for a moment the analysis in the following section: In 2 Cor 4:6 Paul writes, "For it is God who said, 'Out of darkness light will shine,' who has shone *in our hearts* (ἐν ταῖς καρδίαις ἡμῶν) for [the] enlightenment of the knowledge of the glory of God in [the] πρόσωπον of Jesus Christ." This is a rich statement that will require careful analysis. For the time being, it is sufficient to observe that God is described as having brought about (see ἔλαμψεν, aorist tense) an enlightenment (φωτισμός) that involves the πρόσωπον of Jesus. As I will argue below, this illumination entails grasping the character – including the values, attitude, and behavior – of Jesus. Thus, an essential feature of the initial gift of the Spirit is an enlightenment that involves recognizing and appropriating the mode of loving, self-emptying existence as revealed by Christ, the "image of God" (4:4). Observe how this concept of enlightenment – which is tantamount to an act of creation[633] – parallels the notion of the production of an image caused by impressing a signet, as discussed above in connection with the participle σφραγισάμενος. I suggest that this enlightenment is an indispensable part of the "christing" alluded to by the participle χρίσας.

In fact, Paul has already adverted to this empowerment by the Spirit in 1 Corinthians. In the context of distinguishing between the "wisdom of this age" (σοφία τοῦ αἰῶνος τούτου, 1 Cor 2:6) and the "wisdom of God" (θεοῦ σοφία, 2:7), the apostle emphasizes the role of the Spirit (2:10). In particular, the Spirit aids its recipients in understanding τὰ ὑπὸ τοῦ θεοῦ χαρισθέντα ("the [gifts] bestowed by God," 2:12). Paul then goes on to mention the gift *par excellence*, the bestowal of the νοῦς Χριστοῦ ("mind of Christ," 2:16). With this phrase the apostle refers to Christ's way of thinking, perceiving, and valuing – in short, to the totality of his interior and moral state of being.[634] Hence, Paul speaks in 1 Cor 2:6-16 of the Spirit's role in inculcating the νοῦς Χριστοῦ. Returning to 2 Corinthians, the apostle points to the internal disposition and freedom of people like himself when he speaks of the Spirit's action ἐν ταῖς

---

[633]Note the allusion to Gen 1:3 in 2 Cor 4:6. In addition, cf. 2 Cor 5:17.

[634]See BDAG, s.v. νοῦς, 2.

καρδίαις ἡμῶν. I submit that the use of the marking/inscribing metaphor thus attempts to capture what the Spirit empowers in one's inner life.

God's gift of the Spirit is more than a one-time infusion of enlightenment, however. The term ἀρραβών signals further payments as well, with the work of the Spirit as an ongoing and progressive empowerment. Again, to anticipate a point in the following section: In 2 Cor 3:18 Paul describes the process of being transformed into the image of Christ. That this involves an ongoing process is indicated by the present tense of the participle κατοπτριζόμενοι ("while we gaze") and of the main verb μεταμορφούμεθα ("we are being transformed"). This ongoing aspect is not surprising given the notion of character formation, which connotes a sense of development and growth. Observe, moreover, that the apostle names this process as coming ἀπὸ κυρίου πνεύματος – "from [the] Lord, [who is the] Spirit" (3:18).[635]

Paul's letter to the Galatians sheds more light on the two-fold aspect of the Spirit as ἀρραβών. There the apostle writes: "God has sent the Spirit of [God's] Son (τὸ πνεῦμα τοῦ υἱοῦ αὐτοῦ) into our hearts" (Gal 4:6). The aorist tense of the verb ἐξαπέστειλεν signifies an action that occurred in the past. Observe, too, that the Spirit is here intimately connected with Jesus, and that the locus of the gift is "our hearts" (καρδίαι). But Paul also indicates that the work of the Spirit continues in the present. When he exhorts the Galatians to "walk by the Spirit" (πνεύματι περιπατεῖτε, 5:16) and poses the possibility of "being led by the Spirit" (εἰ πνεύματι ἄγεσθε, 5:18), the apostle uses verbs in the present tense, thereby indicating that the Spirit's work is ongoing. Moreover, Paul's description of the Spirit's ongoing role is revealing: The Spirit empowers people to embody such characteristics as love (ἀγάπη), faithfulness (πίστις), and gentleness (πραΰτης, 5:22-23). Recall that these are among the characteristics of Jesus to which the apostle alludes throughout 2 Corinthians. Thus, in Galatians Paul refers not only to the initial gift of the Spirit (4:6; cf. 3:2), but also to the Spirit's ongoing work in those upon whom it has been bestowed. This ongoing work includes the empowerment to

---

[635]Indeed, I suggest that Paul alludes to the Spirit's ongoing work again in 2 Cor 4:16: "our inner nature is being renewed day by day" – ὁ ἔσω ἡμῶν ἀνακαινοῦται ἡμέρᾳ καὶ ἡμέρᾳ. For more on the relationship between "Lord" and "Spirit" in 3:18, see n. 640 below.

incarnate the characteristics of Jesus[636] – an ongoing empowerment that, I submit, is what the apostle signifies by the present tense participle βεβαιῶν in 2 Cor 1:21a. And all this is a manifestation of the fidelity (2 Cor 1:18a) and the love of God: "God's love has been poured out (ἐκκέχυται, perfect tense!) in our hearts through the Holy Spirit which has been given to us" (Rom 5:5).[637]

---

[636]This ongoing empowerment, of course, does not exhaust the continuing work of the Spirit. Indeed, Paul's other reference in 2 Cor to the ἀρραβών of the Spirit (5:5) is helpful in this regard. There the apostle argues that the 'full payment' will come ultimately in eternal life in heaven (5:1-4). See, e.g., HUGHES, *Paul's Second Epistle to the Corinthians*, 42; FURNISH, *II Corinthians*, 149; FEE, *God's Empowering Presence*, 293-94; and THRALL, *II Corinthians*, 1.158.

A.J. KERR has pointed out that the reception of an ἀρραβών also laid obligations upon the recipient. He thus criticizes interpretations of 2 Cor 1:22 that emphasize in a one-sided manner God's gift. See "'ΑΡΡΑΒΩΝ," *JTS* 39 (1988) 92-97. FEE rightly counters that Paul's emphasis here is "on God's part in giving it, not on ours in receiving" (see *God's Empowering Presence*, 293, n. 33). Nevertheless, it certainly fits within the apostle's overall presentation in 2 Cor – not to mention, his writings as a whole – that the recipients of God's gift of the Spirit *are* obligated to follow the Spirit's lead and empowerment. Those who receive the πνεῦμα τῆς πίστεως (4:13) are to be ἐν τῇ πίστει (13:5) – that is, people who manifest the story and character of Jesus in their lives (see Chapter Six).

While it is true that Paul does draw upon terms having commercial and legal uses (esp. the terms σφραγίζω and ἀρραβών), reading the "commercial metaphor" as the linchpin to understanding 1:21-22 distorts the apostle's meaning. BELLEVILLE'S summary is illustrative: "To sum up, the Spirit's work in 2 Cor 1:21-22 is that of a down payment in the life of the congregation that guarantees God's indisputable relationship, commissions and equips for service, secures against falsification or tampering, and preserves the 'goods' of this relationship until the day of redemption" (see "Paul's Polemic and the Theology of the Spirit," 286). But does this fully capture *the apostle's* thought? The absence of any reference to Christ is telling. I submit that a better reading of this passage results from keeping Christ's character as the linchpin, and allowing the commercial metaphor a subsidiary role in shedding light upon – rather than co-opting – the interpretation.

[637]The aorist participles χρίσας, σφραγισάμενος, and δούς, as we have seen, indicate that God has done something for Paul at a time in the past. It is beyond the scope of this study to address in detail the important question of what that "moment" (i.e., the specific time in the past) of God's anointing, sealing, and giving of the Spirit involved. It seems to me that two extreme positions ought to be avoided. The first is an overly precise

To summarize: In 2 Cor 1:20b-22 Paul draws the connection between Jesus' ναί and the apostle's being empowered to embody Jesus' faithfulness to God's character and ways. Paul claims that God *establishes* (= *strengthens*) him, using a verb (βεβαιόω) that he elsewhere associates closely with God's fidelity – a fidelity manifested both in Jesus' fulfillment of God's promises and in the gift of the Holy Spirit, who empowers people to walk in the ways of Jesus. The apostle alludes to this empowerment when he says that he has been *anointed* – literally, "*christed*." Paul also claims to have been *sealed*, a term rich with multiple connotations: He has been marked as God's δοῦλος, and "imprinted"/"inscribed" with the very character of Jesus. Lastly, the apostle speaks of having been *given* the Holy Spirit, described as ἀρραβών. The latter term denotes both a "first installment" – which Paul describes (at least in part) in 4:6 as an enlightenment involving the πρόσωπον of Jesus Christ – and

---

sacramental reading of 2 Cor 1:21-22 – such as seeing there a sequence of a prebaptismal arousal of faith through the hearing of the gospel followed by baptism [so, I. DE LA POTTERIE, "L'onction du chrétien par la foi," *Bib* 40 (1959) 12-69]; a precise, step-by-step description of the baptismal ceremony [so, E. DINKLER, "Die Taufterminologie in 2 Kor. I 21 f.," in *Neotestamentica et Patristica: Eine Freundesgabe, Herrn Professor Dr. Oscar Cullmann zu seinem 60. Geburtstag überreicht*, NovTSup 6, ed. W.C. van Unnik (Leiden: E.J. Brill, 1962) 173-91]; or a sequence of baptism and confirmation [so, ALLO, *Seconde Épître aux Corinthiens*, 29-30]. The second extreme is to reject out of hand any possible reference to baptism (see, e.g., FEE, *God's Empowering Presence*, 294-96).

My position is that Paul *does* allude in 2 Cor 1:21b-22, at least in part, to what happens at baptism. In fact, in his earlier letter to the Corinthians he associated baptism with the Spirit: "For also in one Spirit we all were baptized into one body – whether Jews or Greeks, whether slaves or free – and all were made to drink in one Spirit" (1 Cor 12:3). The action of baptism, however, is not to be understood as occurring in a vacuum. Rather, it is the culmination of an action that includes as an indispensable element the proclamation and reception of the "message of truth" and "gospel of salvation" (see Eph 1:13), a message that includes the story and character of Jesus. Indeed, in 2 Cor 1:19 – immediately before the passage in question – Paul recalls his proclaiming Christ among the Corinthians. Gal 3:1-4:7 may be of help here. There the apostle reminds the Galatians both of their initial hearing of the gospel in faith (3:1-5) and of their baptism into Christ (3:27-4:7). *Both* experiences are connected with their reception of the Spirit.

In the end, I agree with FURNISH that Paul has baptism in view in 2 Cor 1:21-22, as well as with his assessment that the apostle's "multiplication of participles has resulted . . . from a rhetorical impulse, and not from an interest in specifying several discrete steps in Christian initiation" (see *II Corinthians*, 149).

"further payments" – which include the ongoing work of the Spirit in transforming people to manifest the character of Jesus (his attitude, values, and manner of existence).[638] It is to the apostle's further elaboration of these themes in 3:18-4:6 that I now turn.

III. Being Transformed into Christ, the "Image of God" (2 Cor 3:18; 4:4; and 4:6)

At the beginning of 2 Cor 3, Paul raises two interrelated themes. First is the theme of commendation (3:1-3), one we have seen to be crucial throughout this letter. Second is the theme of competence (ἱκανότης) to be a minister of the new covenant (3:4-6). In both instances, the apostle concludes with a reference to the Holy Spirit (3:3 and 3:6). Paul then proceeds to undertake a lengthy and difficult *synkrisis* between the "new covenant" and the Mosaic covenant in 3:7-18.[639] The apostle concludes this comparison with a remarkable claim: τὴν δόξαν κυρίου κατοπτριζόμενοι τὴν αὐτὴν εἰκόνα

---

[638]At this point, it is helpful to reiterate in succinct fashion the logic of 2 Cor 1:17-22. After describing his travel plans (1:15-16), Paul intimates that he changed his plans in obedience to God's directive (1:17). After invoking God's fidelity (1:18a), the apostle insists that the gospel message proclaimed in Corinth by himself, Timothy, and Silvanus is reliable (1:18b-19a). This message is reliable because all of God's promises have been fulfilled in Jesus' obedience and faithfulness, his ναί/ἀμήν (1:19b-20a). Moreover, through Jesus, Paul has been empowered now to live in faithfulness to God (1:20b). The apostle goes on to describe how God brings about this empowerment through the gift of the Holy Spirit (1:21-22). Thus, it is wrong to regard 1:17-22 as a series of discordant verses. *Pace* LONG, *"Have We Been Defending Ourselves to You?"*, 239-40.

[639]The argument in 2 Cor 3 is notoriously complex and difficult. See, e.g., C.K. STOCKHAUSEN, *Moses' Veil and the Glory of the New Covenant: The Exegetical Substructure of II Cor. 3,1-4,6*, AnBib 116 (Rome: Editrice Pontificio Istituto Biblico, 1989); L.L. BELLEVILLE, *Reflections of Glory: Paul's Polemical Use of the Moses-Doxa Tradition in 2 Corinthians 3.1-18*, JSNTSup 52 (Sheffield: JSOT Press, 1991); S.J. HAFEMANN, *Paul, Moses, and the History of Israel: The Letter/Spirit Contrast and the Argument from Scripture in 2 Corinthians 3*, WUNT 81 (Tübingen: J.C.B. Mohr/Paul Siebeck, 1995); and the bibliographies supplied therein. Of particular note, see W.C. VAN UNNIK, "'With Unveiled Face,' An Exegesis of 2 Corinthians iii 12-18," *NovT* 6 (1963) 153-69; and H. MARKS, "Pauline Typology and Revisionary Criticism," 81-86.

μεταμορφούμεθα ἀπὸ δόξης εἰς δόξαν ("while gazing upon the glory of the Lord, we are being transformed into the same image from glory into glory," 3:18). And at the very end Paul adds καθάπερ ἀπὸ κυρίου πνεύματος ("as from the Lord, that is, the Spirit"[640]). Significantly, once again, the apostle alludes to the work of the Spirit. Here the Spirit is named as the source of empowerment[641] in a process of transformation. Thus, Paul brings the discussion that began with the issues of commendation and competency to a climax in 3:18 by alluding to a Spirit-empowered transformation. I propose that what the apostle refers to here is a process whereby he and others are enabled by the Spirit to embody the character of Jesus.

An analysis of the content of 2 Cor 3:18 supports this claim. Paul's language and imagery in this verse are dense, to say the least, and careful exegesis is therefore required. Fortunately, in 4:4 and 4:6 the apostle himself provides several interpretive clues concerning the terms he employs in 3:18.[642] In 4:4 Paul speaks of "the enlightenment of the gospel of the glory of Christ, who is the image of God." I argue that the apostle supplies in this verse the referent of "gazing upon the glory of the Lord" (3:18). That is, "gazing upon the

---

[640]The referent of "Lord" in connection with "Spirit" in 2 Cor 3:17-18 is, of course, a hotly debated issue. For a helpful summary of interpretive options, see COLLANGE, *Énigmes de la deuxième épître aux Corinthiens*, 107-10. In addition, see BELLEVILLE, *Reflections of Glory*, 256-57. For my purposes, it is sufficient to establish that Paul attributes what he describes in 3:18 to the Spirit. While it is beyond the scope of this study to enter into a detailed discussion about how the apostle draws upon the story of LXX Exod 34:29-35 (to which he alludes throughout 2 Cor 3:13-18), I refer my readers to Belleville's discussion in *Reflections of Glory*, 263-67.

[641]Taking the preposition ἀπό as indicating the cause of something, and more specifically, the originator of an action. See BDAG, s.v. ἀπό, 5.d. Cf. Rom 1:7; 1 Cor 1:3; and 2 Cor 1:2 (χάρις καὶ εἰρήνη ἀπὸ θεοῦ πατρός); in addition, cf. Phil 1:28: ἥτις ἐστὶν αὐτοῖς ἔνδειξις ἀπωλείας, ὑμῶν δὲ σωτηρίας, καὶ τοῦτο ἀπὸ θεοῦ ("This is evidence to them of [their] destruction, but of your salvation, and this from God"). To bring out this force of ἀπό in 2 Cor 3:18, it is necessary to add the demonstrative "this" (referring to the process of transformation) and the verb "comes." Thus: "as [this comes] from the Lord, that is, the Spirit."

[642]FEE also notes that 2 Cor 4:3-6 – in which he finds Paul's application of the imagery of 3:18 – is the key to resolving many of the difficulties in the text. See *God's Empowering Presence*, 317.

glory of the Lord" is intimately connected with receiving "enlightenment" from the gospel. Furthermore, Paul identifies the "glory of the Lord" (3:18) as the "glory of Christ" in 4:4. And the apostle names Christ, "who is the image of God" (4:4), as the "image" into which he (Paul) and others are being transformed (3:18). Moreover, alluding to God's act of creation ("let light shine out of darkness" – cf. Gen 1:3) in 2 Cor 4:6, Paul describes God's *new* act of creation: "[God] has shone in our hearts for [the] enlightenment of the knowledge of the glory of God in [the] face of Jesus Christ." In this verse, the apostle (literally!) puts a face onto the "glory" about which he has been writing since 3:7 – namely the face of Jesus.

What can we learn about Paul's understanding of the Spirit-empowered process of transformation into "the same image" (2 Cor 3:18), that is, into Christ, "who is the image of God" (4:4)? I analyze the following elements to plumb this understanding: (1) the apostle's use of the phrase εἰκὼν τοῦ θεοῦ ("image of God"); (2) the expression πρόσωπον Ἰησοῦ Χριστοῦ; (3) the verbs μεταμορφόω and κατοπτρίζω; (4) the cognitive aspect of the process described here; and (5) the prevalence of the term δόξα ("glory") in these verses.

Paul's *imago Dei* anthropology and new Adam christology are evident elsewhere in his writings.[643] The apostle takes seriously the teaching in Gen 1:26-27 that human beings are created in God's image – κατ' εἰκόνα θεοῦ [ὁ θεὸς] ἐποίησεν [ἄνθρωπον]. In his previous letter to the Corinthians, Paul argued from the premise that "man" (ἀνήρ) is the "image and glory of God" (εἰκὼν καὶ δόξα θεοῦ, 1 Cor 11:7).[644] Now, in 2 Corinthians, the apostle

---

[643]For *imago Dei* in Paul, see J. JERVELL, *Imago Dei: Gen 1,26 f. im Spätjudentum, in der Gnosis und in den paulinischen Briefen*, FRLANT 58 (Göttingen: Vandenhoeck & Ruprecht, 1960). For Adam christology in Paul, see R. SCROGGS, *The Last Adam: A Study in Pauline Anthropology* (Philadelphia: Fortress, 1966); and DUNN, *Christology in the Making*, esp. 98-128. And for Adam christology in 2 Cor, see C.M. PATE, *Adam Christology as the Exegetical & Theological Substructure of 2 Corinthians 4:7-5:21* (Lanham, Md.: University Press of America, 1991).

[644]Cf. Gal 3:28 – "there is neither male nor female" for those who are "in Christ" – which N.A. DAHL rightly takes as another allusion to Gen 1:26-27. See "Promise and Fulfillment," in *Studies in Paul: Theology for the Early Christian Mission* (Minneapolis: Augsburg, 1977) 121-36, here 133. In addition, see W.A. MEEKS, "Image of the Androgyne: Some Uses of a Symbol in Earliest Christianity," *HR* 13 (1974) 165-208.

explicitly names "Christ" as the "image of God" (εἰκὼν τοῦ θεοῦ, 2 Cor 4:4). Moreover, Paul closely links "Christ's glory" (δόξα τοῦ Χριστοῦ) with his being the "image of God." Thus, the apostle offers the same juxtaposition of "image" and "glory" in connection with Christ in 2 Cor 4:4 as he did with ἀνήρ in 1 Cor 11:7. In addition, Paul closely associates creation language with "the glory of God in the face of Jesus Christ" in 2 Cor 4:6. And in 2 Cor 5:17 the apostle draws the conclusion, "Therefore, if anyone is in Christ, [there is] a new creation (καινὴ κτίσις)!" For Paul, it appears, Jesus Christ is the new human prototype, the new or second Adam, who fully reflects God's image and glory. Indeed, the portrayal of Christ in Rom 5:15-21 corroborates this, as the apostle discusses "the human being, Jesus Christ" (ὁ ἄνθρωπος Ἰησοῦς Χριστός, Rom 5:15), whose "type" (τύπος) was Adam (Rom 5:14).[645] In the latter passage, it is significant to note that, with reference to Jesus as the new Adam, Paul highlights his "righteous act" (δικαίωμα) and "obedience" (ὑπακοή). The pertinent point here is that the apostle draws on the *humanity* of Jesus in his portrayal of the true εἰκὼν τοῦ θεοῦ, the new Adam.[646]

VAN UNNIK also notes the relevance of the connection between 2 Cor 3:18 and 1 Cor 11:7. See "'With Unveiled Face,' An Exegesis of 2 Corinthians iii 12-18," 167-68.

[645]Cf. 1 Cor 15:21-22, where Paul offers a briefer treatment of the "human being" Adam and the "human being" Jesus. The apostle's depiction of Jesus as ἄνθρωπος in Rom 5:14-21 and 1 Cor 15:21-22 – and *not* as ἀνήρ – echoes the language of Gen 1:26-27a, where the initial emphasis is on God's creation of ἄνθρωπος. It is only in Gen 1:27b that the distinction between male and female is noted.

[646]As will be shown in the following paragraphs, the logic of Paul's argument in 2 Cor 3:18-4:6 presumes that he is drawing in large part upon what the humanity of Jesus reveals. HAFEMANN expresses this well: "Such an interpretation is confirmed by the background of Gen. 1:26-27, from which the concept of the 'image of God' introduced in 3:18 and 4:4 no doubt derives. In its original context, the 'image of God' is primarily a functional description of mankind's role in relationship to their sovereign Creator. Hence, just as Adam related to God in dependence and obedience before the Fall (cf. Gen. 1:28-30 with 2:15, 19 f.), Christ, as the 'second Adam,' was in the 'image of God' in his faithful obedience to God, even to the point of his death on the cross (cf. Rom. 5:19; Phil. 2:8). *It is this 'image of God' into which believers are being transformed* as a result of encountering the glory of God on the face of Christ." See HAFEMANN, *Paul, Moses, and the History of Israel*, 424 (italics added). In addition, see HUGHES, *Paul's Second Epistle to the Corinthians*, 130; BARRETT, *The Second Epistle to the*

Paul's allusion to the "πρόσωπον of Jesus Christ" in 2 Cor 4:6 is another clue that he evokes the story and, especially, the character of Jesus in these verses. In order to fully appreciate how this allusion to Jesus' πρόσωπον functions in the apostle's argument, it is necessary to note the parallel phrase "the face of Moses" (τὸ πρόσωπον Μωϋσέως) in 3:7. At one level, Paul's use of the face motif is straightforward and simple: Whereas Moses's face once radiated glory, so now "the glory of God" has shone in a surpassing way in the face of Jesus.[647] But there is, I submit, a deeper connotation. Just as the

---

Corinthians, 125; and MURPHY-O'CONNOR, *The Theology of the Second Letter to the Corinthians*, 43.

This is *not* to claim, however, that Paul – in alluding to Jesus as "the image of God" – understands Jesus *exclusively* as the prototype of the new humanity. The apostle also regards Jesus as the embodiment of Sophia (cf. Wis 7:26), who has a mediating role in creation (see, e.g., Col 1:15). In addition, Paul uses Adam typology in the context of discussing the resurrection body in order to emphasize that Christians one day will bear the image of "the second human being," the "heavenly one" (1 Cor 15:45-49). The apostle's use of *imago Dei* and Adam typology is rich and varied.

[647]Cf. BELLEVILLE, *2 Corinthians*, 119: "Paul is undoubtedly thinking of the Incarnation. The *face* is the image that we present in public. Christ's *face*, then, is what he presented during his earthly ministry" (Belleville's italics). While Belleville overstates the case, her insight is important – namely, that Paul's allusion to Christ's πρόσωπον evokes not only the fact of his being alive as risen Lord, but also his taking on flesh and living and dying for all. It is wrong, therefore, to associate the expressions "glory of Christ" (3:18; 4:4) and "face of Christ" (4:6) exclusively with a notion of 'Christ in risen glory.' For instance, the following assessment of WINDISCH concerning 2 Cor 4:4 is too narrow: "Auffallend ist, wie P. hier völlig absieht von dem ganz der δόξα entbehrenden X. ἐσταυρωμένος. . . ." See *Der zweite Korintherbrief*, 136-37). The risen Christ for Paul is always one with Christ crucified. PLUMMER hesitates in seeing an allusion to the story of Jesus in 3:18: "It is inadequate to interpret this of Christ's moral grandeur and beneficence during the life of His humiliation." See *II Corinthians*, 105. I would counter that it is only inadequate if it is denied that Christ is also risen. Plummer is more on target in his comment on 2 Cor 4:4: "St Paul may have in his mind the εἰκόνα Θεοῦ (Gen i. 27), the image of God, marred in Adam and restored in Christ" (ibid., 106).

It might be objected that the expression in 2 Cor 4:6 is better interpreted in light of the phrase ἐν προσώπῳ Χριστοῦ in 2 Cor 2:10. The context of 2:5-11, however, demands that the phrase be understood figuratively – "in the presence of Christ" (so, rightly, RSV).

reference to Moses's πρόσωπον serves to evoke the story of the man Moses (2 Cor 3:13-16; cf. Exod 34:29-35), so too the allusion to Christ's πρόσωπον serves to evoke the story of Jesus, the one in whom the promises of God have come to fulfillment (2 Cor 1:19b-20a) in the "new covenant" of the Spirit (3:6). Observe, moreover, that besides signifying "face," the term πρόσωπον can indicate *the entire person.*[648] Thus, in addition to suggesting the story's "plot," the apostle's allusion to Christ's πρόσωπον evokes all that is connected with the person of Jesus, including his character. Indeed, I argued in Chapter Four that Jesus' character is central to Paul's proclamation of the "gospel of the glory of Christ" (4:4). Furthermore, note that the pivotal point in the apostle's *synkrisis* is that the counterpart to the reading of "the old covenant" (3:14)/"Moses" (3:15) is the Spirit-empowered transformation (3:18) and enlightenment "in our hearts" (4:6). Reference to the *person* of Jesus in 4:6 intimates that this transformation/enlightenment somehow involves Christ's character.

That Paul – in the course of describing the Spirit-empowered process involving himself and others – draws upon Jesus as the human prototype is further suggested when one looks closely at his utilization of the verbs μεταμορφόω and κατοπτρίζω in 2 Cor 3:18. In the main clause of the verse, the apostle states that "we[649] *are being transformed* (μεταμορφούμεθα) into the same image." Now, there are several things to note about the verb

---

[648]See BDAG, s.v. πρόσωπον, 2.

[649]Once again, the precise referent of "we" is disputed. On the one hand, the addition of πάντες to ἡμεῖς – "we *all*" – at the beginning of 2 Cor 3:18 has led several commentators to conclude that Paul has *all Christians* in mind. See, e.g., FURNISH, *II Corinthians*, 213; THRALL, *II Corinthians*, 1.282; and LAMBRECHT, *Second Corinthians*, 55. On the other hand, BELLEVILLE limits the phrase πάντες ἡμεῖς to Paul and to "all true gospel ministers without exception" (see *Reflections of Glory*, 276). FEE submits a third alternative which is, in my opinion, the correct one: ". . . Paul here deliberately returns to the beginning of his argument [3:1] and includes the Corinthians in the experience of glory that the Spirit provides." See *God's Empowering Presence*, 314. Thus, the apostle refers here to himself, his co-workers, and the Corinthians. (Of course, what Paul says here can easily be extrapolated to include all Christians.) For the purpose of the present chapter, I focus on the Spirit's empowerment of *Paul* in this section (returning to the empowerment of the Corinthians in Chapter Six). As was the case in 1:21-22, I presume that what the apostle says about himself and his co-workers as a group pertains to Paul as an individual.

μεταμορφούμεθα. The verb is in the passive voice, indicating that another agent is at work in Paul. As we have seen, the apostle identifies this agent as the Spirit at the end of 3:18. In addition, Paul uses the present tense, signifying thereby that this transformation is taking place here and now, and is ongoing.[650] Observe, too, that this is a process that is happening in human beings, and that the *telos* of this transformation is "the same image" (τὴν αὐτὴν εἰκόνα), that is, "the glory of the Lord" – the glory that the apostle links in 4:4 with "Christ, who is the image of God."[651] Thus, the logic of 3:18 appears to depend on Paul's referring to *a present, ongoing transformation of human existence, a transformation that reflects more and more the prototype of humanity embodied by Jesus*, the εἰκὼν τοῦ θεοῦ.[652] It is significant to note that the apostle connects this process of human transformation with an increase in glory (ἀπὸ δόξης εἰς δόξαν), a point to which I will return.

This process of Spirit-empowered transformation does not occur in a vacuum. Paul's description in 2 Cor 3:18 suggests an element of human participation as well. That is, the apostle describes this transformation as taking place "with unveiled face, while we gaze upon the glory of the Lord." The verb κατοπτρίζω is a *hapax legomenon* in the NT. The middle voice of the verb has the connotation of "look at oneself in a mirror."[653] In 3:18, however, Paul refers to himself as gazing with unveiled face, not into a mirror, but rather at

---

[650]Cf. DUNN, *The Theology of Paul the Apostle*, 468. Dunn takes note of both the ongoing sense of transformation and the presence of Adam christology in 2 Cor 3:18.

[651]BULTMANN correctly emphasizes the "eschatological present" in connection with 2 Cor 3:18. This transformation occurs "as the divine power's coming into effect in the historical life of the believer. . . ." See *The Second Letter to the Corinthians*, 95. This is not to deny, however, that Paul writes elsewhere of a *future* transformation. Cf., e.g., 1 Cor 13:12 and Phil 3:20-21.

[652]HAFEMANN rightly observes that the Spirit's empowerment involves a progressive growth in freedom to obey God's will. See *2 Corinthians*, 161. Indeed, it is such obedience to the will of God that marked Jesus' human mode of existence.

[653]See BDAG, s.v. κατοπτρίζω. For a helpful excursus on "mirror-vision and transformation," see THRALL, *II Corinthians*, 1.290-95.

"the glory of the Lord."[654] But what does it mean to gaze at the Lord's glory? Recall how, a few verses later, the apostle associates "the glory of Christ" with "the gospel" – τὸ εὐαγγέλιον τῆς δόξης τοῦ Χριστοῦ (4:4). This association suggests that what is being gazed at in 3:18 is, in broad terms, the gospel, and more specifically, the *content* of the gospel.[655] And what is this content? We saw above that Paul reminded the Corinthians of what had been proclaimed (κηρυχθείς) to them – namely, "the Son of God, Jesus Christ." In the course of this reminder, the apostle alluded to the character of Jesus, to his obedience and faithfulness (ναί/ἀμήν) to God in fulfillment of the divine promises (1:19-20).[656] Thus, I submit that, in addition to the Spirit's

---

[654]LAMBRECHT notes that κατοπριζόμενοι in 2 Cor 3:18 is deponent, and thus active in sense. It is also transitive (the direct object is "the glory of the Lord"). See LAMBRECHT, "Transformation in 2 Corinthians 3,18," in R. BIERINGER and J. LAMBRECHT, *Studies on 2 Corinthians*, BETL 112 (Leuven: Leuven University Press, 1994) 295-307, here 297.

Some commentators (e.g., FURNISH, *II Corinthians*, 214; and THRALL, *II Corinthians*, 1.283) take "Lord" in the phrase "the glory of the Lord" as referring to God – and not to Jesus – citing the frequency of the phrase "glory of the Lord" in the LXX, as well as the allusion to the Tent of Meeting in the previous verses. Nevertheless, understanding "Lord" as Christ offers a more coherent reading of 3:18. In addition, observe how the expressions that follow in 4:4 (τὴν δόξαν τοῦ Χριστοῦ) and 4:5 (Ἰησοῦν Χριστὸν κύριον) suggest that Christ is the referent of "Lord." Cf. LAMBRECHT, "Transformation in 2 Corinthians 3,18," 297, n. 8.

[655]Cf. R.W. SCHOLLA, "Into the Image of God: Pauline Eschatology and the Transformation of Believers," *Greg* 78 (1997) 33-54, here 50: "Here, 'seeing the glory of the Lord' (3:18) comes very close to meaning, receiving the gospel of God (the gospel of Christ)." In addition, cf. FURNISH, *II Corinthians*, 242.

[656]Moreover, observe that in 2 Cor 11:4 Paul refers to '*Jesus* whom he proclaimed' (κηρύσσω), a proclamation that is linked closely with 'receiving the gospel' (δέχομαι εὐαγγέλιον) and 'obtaining the Spirit' (λαμβάνω πνεῦμα). Moreover, this notice of Jesus follows immediately upon a reference to his character – namely to his ἁπλότης and ἁγνότης (11:3).

empowerment, Paul refers in 3:18 to "looking" in some special manner at the *ethos* of Jesus.[657]

Although κατοπτρίζω is a NT *hapax legomenon*, Jas 1:22-25 provides an illuminating parallel. Luke T. Johnson has argued persuasively that in this passage James employs a *topos* from paraenetic literature, namely, the metaphor of the mirror (cf. ἐν ἐσόπτρῳ, Jas 1:23). As a rhetorical device, this *topos* was susceptible to a range of usages, one of which involved setting forth an *exemplum* – including an ideal one – as a model for living. Essential to the mirror *topos* was the role played by memory, that is, by the recollection of the model to be imitated.[658] I submit that Paul's use of κατοπτριζόμενοι invites an interpretation similar to the employment of the mirror *topos*. The apostle sets forth Jesus as the εἰκὼν τοῦ θεοῦ, the ideal or prototype of humanity, for his (and others') emulation.[659] Observe, moreover, that the participle is in the present tense, indicating that the act of gazing happens simultaneously with that of the main verb μεταμορφούμεθα, and thus too is ongoing. Hence, while the Spirit's empowerment in the work of transformation is primary, Paul's continued active contemplation[660] of the story and (especially) the *ethos* of Jesus

---

[657]Cf. LAMBRECHT, "Transformation in 2 Corinthians 3,18," 303: "We see Christ, as in a mirror, in the gospel and in *that specific Christian way of life the gospel inspires*" (italics added).

[658]See L.T. JOHNSON, "The Mirror of Remembrance (James 1:22-25)," *CBQ* 50 (1988) 632-45. In a footnote in this article, Johnson points to the application of this *topos* in 2 Cor 3:18 (see p. 638, n. 19).

[659]For Paul's use elsewhere of the motifs of models, memory, and imitation, see L.T. JOHNSON, "II Timothy and the Polemic Against False Teachers: A Reexamination," *JRelS* 6/7 (1978/79) 1-26. SAMPLEY'S comment on 2 Cor 3:18 is apropos in this regard: "Imitation of Christ is a theme of massive proportions in the Pauline letters and is evinced here." See *NIB*, 11.70.

[660]BULTMANN suggests that "the moment of beholding is primarily Christian worship, in which the gospel is proclaimed." See *The Second Letter to the Corinthians*, 96.

There are a number of interpreters who take κατοπτριζόμενοι in the sense of "reflecting." See, e.g., PLUMMER, *II Corinthians*, 105-6; HÉRING, *The Second Epistle of Saint Paul to the Corinthians*, 27; and BELLEVILLE, *2 Corinthians*, 112. The problem with this understanding of 2 Cor 3:18 is that it misses the thrust of Paul's argument. It is only through the Spirit-empowered transformation and accompanying

is also involved. Through his use of κατοπτριζόμενοι, the apostle alludes to the human response that accompanies the Spirit's empowerment, a response that entails an important cognitive component – namely, recalling and appropriating Jesus' paradigmatic character.[661]

This understanding is further strengthened by Paul's use of cognitive terms in 2 Cor 4:4 and 4:6. Indeed, throughout my treatment of the character of Jesus in Chapter Four, I pointed to the ways in which the apostle links cognitive terminology with references to the story and *ethos* of Jesus: the new way of knowing brought about by Jesus' dying out of love for all (5:16); Jesus' not knowing Sin (5:21a); Paul's reminding the Corinthians of what they know concerning the χάρις of Christ (8:9); the apostle's destroying arguments raised against the knowledge of God, and taking captive thoughts unto "Christ-obedience" (10:4-5); Paul's fear that the Corinthians' thoughts are being led astray from Jesus' ἁπλότης (11:3); and the apostle's defense of his own γνῶσις, a knowledge manifested in the proclamation of the gospel. (11:4-6).[662] In 2 Cor 4:4 Paul explains why some have not responded favorably to the gospel

---

contemplation/appropriation of the gospel – especially of the story and *ethos* of Jesus – that Christians *become* more like Christ. Then, and only then, can they be in a position to be *exempla* themselves, that is, people who reflect Christ's image. Thus, WRIGHT'S suggestion (in *The Climax of the Covenant*, 185-89) – namely, that the mirror in which Christians see reflected the glory of the Lord is "one another" – puts the cart before the horse. In 3:18 *Paul is talking about the process that yields the result* of people reflecting Christ.

[661]Thus, I take the participle κατοπτριζόμενοι to indicate attendant circumstance. In effect, active recollection and contemplation are a necessary – thought not sufficient – condition for transformation. The *sine qua non* is, of course, the Spirit's transforming empowerment.

DANKER also translates κατοπτριζόμενοι as "contemplating" or "beholding." In addition, he rightly recognizes that what is contemplated is "the Lord's character and personality." See *II Corinthians*, 58. But Danker considers the object of contemplation to be one's inner self, which because of the Spirit's activity, reflects this character. This understanding, however, takes the mirror metaphor too literally, and suffers from the same criticism offered above (n. 660).

[662]In addition, we will see in the following section that Paul refers to 'the knowledge concerning Christ' in 2 Cor 2:14. As will be shown, the apostle disseminates this knowledge by embodying Jesus' mode of self-emptying existence.

message: Their thoughts have been blinded "so that they do not look upon the enlightenment (τὸν φωτισμόν) of the gospel of the glory of Christ, who is the image of God." In this verse the apostle links the gospel with the enlightenment of thoughts (νοήματα), an enlightenment that centers upon Christ as the εἰκὼν τοῦ θεοῦ. Paul goes on to describe this enlightenment in greater detail in 4:6: God "has shone in our hearts for [the] enlightenment (φωτισμόν) of the knowledge of the glory of God in the πρόσωπον of Jesus Christ." Here the apostle connects enlightenment with the knowledge (γνῶσις) of God's glory, the manifestation of which involves the face – and even more, the person – of Jesus Christ.

The passages in 2 Corinthians that link cognitive terms with references to Jesus have an impressive cumulative effect.[663] It is crucial to recognize beyond their number what underlies and connects them all. Throughout this letter Paul's logic rests on the premise that *the Spirit endows its recipients with the gift of the νοῦς Χριστοῦ* (cf. 1 Cor 2:16). I suggest that the apostle's working assumption here is this: The Spirit *empowers* its recipients to take on more and more Jesus' way of thinking, perceiving, and valuing, and thus to embody more and more his character. To be sure, Paul is not concerned with γνῶσις for its own sake. Rather, as we will see in the next section, his concern is with how right thinking is manifested (φανερόω) in living for the sake of others (2 Cor 4:10-11; cf. 2:14-16). In his own unique way, then, the apostle shares the logic of the ancient moralists who held that moral behavior follows upon correct perception. In Paul's case, proper moral behavior entails continuing the story of Jesus by taking on the latter's *ethos*. The right thinking that underlies this behavior results from possession of the νοῦς Χριστοῦ. And it is the Spirit who bestows on the apostle (and others) the mind of Christ, thereby empowering him to embody the *ethos* of Jesus.

Paul's only other use of the verb μεταμορφόω supports this interpretation. In Rom 12:2 he exhorts his readers: "Be transformed (μεταμορφοῦσθε) by the renewal of your mind so that you might discerningly approve what is the will of God, [namely, what is] good and pleasing and perfect." Once again, the apostle uses the present tense and passive voice of

---

[663]Cf. V. KOPERSKY, "Knowledge of Christ and Knowledge of God in the Corinthian Correspondence," in *The Corinthian Correpondence*, BETL 125, ed. R. BIERINGER (Leuven: Leuven University Press, 1996) 377-96. Regarding 2 Cor, Kopersky discusses 2:14; 4:6; and 5:16. It should be obvious that I regard 2 Cor as an even richer source for such a treatment.

μεταμορφόω. Thus he sees this as an ongoing process, one that is empowered by another's agency. Observe that "the renewal of the *mind*" (τῇ ἀνακαινώσει τοῦ νοός) is the means of this transformation. Such renewal of the mind entails, I submit, the reception and appropriation of the νοῦς Χριστοῦ, a reception and appropriation that allow one to take on Jesus' values, attitudes, and behavior – in short, his character (see, e.g., Rom 15:3). The purpose of this renewal is to aid the community to "discerningly approve" or "test" (δοκιμάζω)[664] what the will of God is, and to act accordingly. This is how Paul understands 'offering oneself as holy and acceptable to God' (Rom 12:1; cf. the dynamic described above in connection with τὸ ἀμήν in 2 Cor 1:20).

I suggest that this same dynamic underlies the apostle's earlier statement in Rom 8:29 about being "conformed into the image of [God's] Son (συμμόρφους τῆς εἰκόνος τοῦ υἱοῦ αὐτοῦ), in order that he might be the first-born among many brothers and sisters." It is important to note that Paul has just described the *Spirit's* role in Christians' appropriation of their status as children of God (Rom 8:14-16), as well as the *Spirit's* role in reproducing in them the pattern of Jesus' dying and rising (8:11). Indeed, the apostle's letter to the Romans (especially chapters eight and twelve) offers impressive support for my interpretation of 2 Cor 3:18.[665]

---

[664]The verb δοκιμάζω and its cognates δοκιμή and δόκιμος are, as we will see in Chapter Six, crucially important to Paul in 2 Cor.

[665]Cf. L.T. JOHNSON, "Transformation of the Mind and Moral Discernment in Paul," in *Early Christianity and Classical Culture: Comparative Studies in Honor of Abraham J. Malherbe*, ed. J.T. FITZGERALD, T.H. OLBRICHT, and L.M. WHITE (Leiden: Brill, 2003) 215-36. Johnson captures well the dynamic of transformation: "In a shorthand that is anachronistic but also useful, the Holy Spirit may be seen as the effective cause of this transformation, and the messianic pattern as the formal cause" (p. 231). Cf. THOMPSON: ". . . the meaning of 'putting on Christ' . . . surely points to adoption of his mind, character and conduct. . . . By donning the characteristics of the second Adam, Christians reflect the true image of God and are changed into his likeness from one degree of glory to another in anticipation of the final glory of resurrection life (2 Cor 3.18)." See THOMPSON, *Clothed with Christ*, 158. In addition, see THRALL, *II Corinthians*, 1.285: ". . . assimilation to Christ as the image of God produces a visibly Christ-like character, so that the divine image becomes visible in the believer's manner of life"; and GARLAND, *2 Corinthians*, 201: ". . . Paul's point is that through the Spirit we are able now to live a more Christ-like life. . . ."

At this point, I anticipate the objection that I overread the story and character of Jesus – especially as the human prototype – into 2 Cor 3:18-4:6. Did not Paul encounter the *risen* Lord (cf. Gal 1:16 and 1 Cor 9:1)? Do not the expressions "glory of the Lord" (2 Cor 3:18), "glory of Christ" (4:4), and "God's glory on the face of Jesus Christ" (4:6) evoke the resurrection and exaltation of Jesus? Does not the apostle refer to Jesus as the new or second Adam, the *imago Dei*, in connection with the resurrection in 1 Cor 15:45-49? In short, it might be objected that my emphasis on Jesus as the *exemplum* of human existence leads to a *mis*reading of the text.

In no way do I want to suggest that in 2 Cor 3:18-4:6 Paul has no regard for Jesus as risen Lord. Indeed, in 4:5 the apostle makes clear that he proclaims "Jesus Christ is Lord" (cf. Phil 2:11). But as we saw in the previous chapter, the resurrection and exaltation of Jesus are the climax of the story of Jesus as God's faithful δοῦλος. The risen, glorified Lord *is* the crucified one and vice versa. The πρόσωπον 'Ιησοῦ Χριστοῦ reflecting God's glory thus evokes the *whole* story and character of Jesus.[666] I emphasize the importance of Jesus' humanity and *ethos* in these verses because I take seriously Paul's use of present tense verbs in 2 Cor 3:18, as well as what he says about the empowering gift of the Spirit in 1:21-22. Unlike 1 Cor 15:42-50 and 2 Cor 5:1-10 – where he speaks explicitly about the future fruits of the resurrection[667] – the apostle's concern in 2 Cor 3:18-4:13 is *the present manifestation* of the power of Christ's resurrection.[668] This manifestation entails embodying the character of Jesus, a

[666]See my comments in the introductory section of Chapter Four.

[667]Cf. 1 Cor 15:49: "And just as we have borne the image of the earthly human being, we shall also bear [φορέσομεν, future tense!] the image of the heavenly human being." In addition, cf. 2 Cor 5:4: ". . . in order that what is mortal may be swallowed up by life"; and 2 Cor 5:10: "It is necessary that all of us appear before the judgment seat of Christ. . . ." Indeed, 2 Cor 3:18-5:10 seems to move from a discussion about the transformation into Christ-like existence in the here and now (3:18-4:13) to a discussion about the future (and full) transformation of the resurrection (5:1-10). The transition point is 4:14-18, where Paul refers to the Lord Jesus' being raised, to the future raising of Paul and the Corinthians, and to the day by day renewal of their inner nature preparing them for what is eternal.

[668]HAFEMANN offers two apposite comments in this regard. The first is: "But this process of transformation into 'God's image' *in the present* does not entail living the resurrection mode of life on earth. The proof of this was Paul's demonstration of the

process of human transformation in the here and now. Recall from Chapter Four that it is the ζωὴ τοῦ 'Ιησοῦ – understood as the power of the risen Jesus – that enables Paul and others to live now in Jesus' self-emptying mode of human existence, a mode of existence that the apostle calls the νέκρωσις τοῦ 'Ιησοῦ (4:10-11; see the following section). So, too, this same dynamic is at work in 3:18-4:6.

This interpretation sheds light on the issues of commendation and competence raised in 2 Cor 3:1-6. In 4:2 Paul self-*commends* (the positive notion of self-commendation) by means of "the manifestation (φανέρωσις) of the truth." The apostle's use of φανερο- terminology is hardly accidental. We will see in the following section that he "manifests" (φανερόω) the power of the risen Christ by embodying Jesus' mode of self-giving existence. Moreover, it is the Spirit-empowered transformation of Paul – by means of which the apostle takes on more and more the *ethos* of Jesus, who himself became διάκονος (cf. Rom 15:8) – that makes him competent to be a διάκονος καινῆς διαθήκης ("minister of [the] new covenant," 2 Cor 3:6).

Before concluding this section, it is important to observe Paul's use of the term δόξα ("glory") in 2 Cor 3:18-4:6. The apostle relates δόξα to each one of the features just analyzed: *imago Dei*, the verbs μεταμορφόω and κατοπτρίζω, the allusion to the πρόσωπον of Jesus Christ, and the use of cognitive terms. In 4:4 Paul relates the content of the gospel to "the *glory* of Christ, who is the image of God." In 3:18 the apostle gazes upon "the *glory* of the Lord," and in doing so is transformed into the same image "from *glory* into *glory*." And in 4:6 Paul locates the "knowledge of the *glory* of God in the πρόσωπον of Jesus Christ." What does the apostle mean by this repeated use of δόξα? Recall what I argued above in connection with 1:20b: through Jesus, human faithfulness to God and God's ways – the proffered interpretation of τὸ ἀμήν – redounds to God "for glory" (πρὸς δόξαν). I submit that this reading sheds light on Paul's references to glory in 3:18, 4:4, and 4:6. At the heart of the proclamation of 'the gospel of glory' is the story of Jesus, the human prototype in the new creation (4:4). This Jesus is the *locus* where "the

---

Spirit and resurrection power of Christ *in the midst of and by means of* his own weakness and suffering." See *Paul, Moses, and the History of Israel*, 220 (Hafemann's italics). The second is: "For to Paul, the process of 'being transformed into the image and glory of God' (3:18), as revealed in Christ (4:4, 6) and as a result of the work of the Spirit in one's life (3:3, 6, 8, 17), is to take on those attitudes and actions which correspond to the way in which Christ himself lived as the 'second Adam'" (ibid., 222).

knowledge of the glory of God" is found (4:6). And it is through the Spirit's gift of the νοῦς Χριστοῦ that Paul (along with others) is being transformed into "the same image," a transformation that is strikingly described as an increase in glory (literally, "from glory into glory," 3:18).[669] Thus, the apostle closely associates δόξα with Jesus, and with human beings who are renewed (in the here and now) after Christ's likeness.[670]

To summarize: An appreciation of the role that the story and *ethos* of Jesus play in 2 Cor 3:18, 4:4, and 4:6 helps "unpack" the dense language in these verses. Paul refers to a process of Spirit-empowered transformation of people like himself into the image of Christ. Next, in the verses which immediately follow (4:7-14), the apostle describes vividly how the Spirit empowers him to continue the story of Jesus' πίστις.

IV. Paul Embodies the Faithfulness of Christ

Paul refers again to the empowering Spirit in 2 Cor 4:13: "Now, because we have the same Spirit of faithfulness according to what is written – 'I have been faithful, therefore I have spoken' – so also are we faithful, and

---

[669]Both THRALL (*II Corinthians*, 1.286) and BULTMANN (*The Second Letter to the Corinthians*, 95) rightly interpret ἀπὸ δόξης εἰς δόξαν as referring to the progressive attainment of glory in the present life. COLLANGE (*Énigmes de la deuxième épître aux Corinthiens*, 122-23) misses the focus on the here and now, and wrongly interprets εἰς δόξαν as the final state of glory.

[670]Cf. 2 Cor 8:23, where Paul refers to two unnamed brothers whom he commends to the Corinthian church. There he describes them as δόξα Χριστοῦ. It is pertinent to note that, in his commendation of one of these brothers, the apostle mentions that the brother has been *tested* (δοκιμάζω) often (8:22). As we will see in Chapter Six, Paul uses δοκιμ- language throughout this letter in order to test the Corinthians' character, a testing that culminates with his final challenge to the community to test the quality of their πίστις (13:5). And we will see that the standard of this test is the faithfulness of Christ. Thus, in vouching for the tested brother, the apostle implies that the former embodies the *ethos* of Jesus.

In connection with 2 Cor 3:18, MURPHY-O'CONNOR writes, "As applied to human beings 'glory of God' implies the ability to give glory to God, and is the equivalent of righteousness (cf. Rom. 3:23)." See *The Theology of the Second Letter to the Corinthians*, 40. This is suggestive, as will be seen in the treatment of 2 Cor 5:21 below.

therefore we also speak."[671] We are now in position to appreciate more fully what the apostle means by the phrase τὸ αὐτὸ πνεῦμα τῆς πίστεως ("the *same* Spirit of faithfulness"). This is the same Spirit mentioned in 3:18, the Spirit who empowers the transformation of Paul (as well as his co-workers and the Corinthians). This transformation involves a progressive incorporation of the character of Jesus, whose πίστις is recalled by the apostle's allusion in 4:13 to LXX Pss 114-115 (ἐπίστευσα, διὸ ἐλάλησα). As we saw in Chapter Four, Paul reads these psalms christologically, seeing in them an apt depiction of the story of Jesus – the story of God's faithful δοῦλος who gave his life out of love for the advantage of others, whom God has vindicated by raising him from the dead. Observe how, at the end of 4:13, the apostle now *explicitly* claims to continue this story when he asserts that he too is faithful and therefore he too speaks out (a point to which I will return in the analysis of 4:7-14).

That Paul sees himself continuing the story of Jesus told in LXX Pss 114-115 is also evident from several lexical and thematic connections between these psalms and the apostle's self-presentation throughout 2 Corinthians. Just as the psalmist (= Jesus) found himself in "affliction" (θλῖψις, Ps 114:3c) and "dangers" (κίνδυνοι, 114:3b), so too does Paul experience "afflictions"/"being afflicted" (2 Cor 1:4, 1:6, 1:8, 2:4, 4:8, 4:17, 6:4, 7:4, and 7:5) and several "dangers" (11:26). Just as the psalmist (= Jesus) was beset by "liars" (πᾶς ἄνθρωπος ψεύστης, Ps 115:2b), so too does the apostle find himself misunderstood and even wrongly accused (2 Cor 7:2, 11:7-11, and 12:16-18). Just as the psalmist "was brought low" (ταπεινόω, Pss 114:6b and 115:1b), so too Paul "lowers himself" (2 Cor 11:7) and is regarded as "lowly" (ταπεινός, 10:1b). Just as the psalmist cried out, "O Lord, save (ῥῦσαι) my life" (Ps 114:4b), and experienced being saved "from death" (ἐκ θανάτοῦ, 114:8b), so too does the apostle know the crucible of danger and God's deliverance (ἐκ τηλικούτου θανάτοῦ ἐρρύσατο, 2 Cor 1:10). Just as the psalmist confesses that "our God shows mercy" (ἐλεέω, Ps 114:5b), so too does Paul claim that "we have received mercy" (ἠλεήθημεν, 2 Cor 4:1). And just as the psalmist (= Jesus) regards himself as God's "slave" (δοῦλος, Ps 115:7ab), so too does the apostle – in announcing the lordship of Jesus – proclaim himself to be a "slave" διὰ Ἰησοῦν (2 Cor 4:5). Thus, in addition to his explicit statement in 2 Cor 4:13, Paul *alludes* several times throughout this letter to his participation

[671]See Chapter Four, Section V for the explanation and defense of this translation.

in the story and character of Jesus, the faithful one (ἐπίστευσα, Ps 115:1a; 2 Cor 4:13).[672]

In this section I analyze three passages in which the apostle aligns himself with the faithfulness of Jesus: the conspicuous connection, in 2 Cor 4:7-14, of Paul with the story of God's faithful δοῦλος, Jesus; the apostle's expression of his trust and hope in God in 1:8-10, trust and hope that serve as the basis for his own πίστις; and Paul's use of triumphal procession and fragrant sacrifice imagery in 2:14-17 to indicate how he manifests knowledge concerning Christ. I then summarize my findings by referring to 12:9-10, the verses in which the apostle concludes his "fool's boast" by narrating the risen Lord's revelation to him that power is perfected in weakness.

A. Paul's Explicit Inclusion in the Story of Jesus' Faithfulness (2 Cor 4:7-14)[673]

Paul begins his description of the paradoxical nature of the Spirit-empowered transformation into the likeness of Christ in 2 Cor 4:7: "Now, we[674] have this treasure (τὸν θησαυρὸν τοῦτον) in earthen vessels." The demonstrative pronoun "this" raises a question: To *which* treasure does the apostle refer?[675] The context suggests that the antecedent is the "enlightenment"

---

[672]Taking the aorist ἐπίστευσα as a *complexive* aorist, thereby indicating action "conceived as a whole irrespective of its duration." See BDF, § 318 (1). Cf. 2 Cor 5:21a (γνόντα) and 8:9 (ἐπτώχευσεν) for other complexive aorists used in connection with Jesus.

[673]I have already analyzed and treated several of the exegetical issues in this passage – especially those in 4:10-11 and 4:13 – in Chapter Four, Section V. In the paragraphs that follow, I draw upon several of the exegetical decisions previously made without repeating the arguments.

[674]That "we" refers to Paul and his co-workers is clear from both 2 Cor 4:5 and 4:12, where "we" is in contrast to "you" (referring to the Corinthians). Again, my emphasis in this chapter is on *Paul*.

[675]FITZGERALD sets forth five interpretive possibilities. See *Cracks in an Earthen Vessel*, 168, n. 145. In addition, see SAVAGE, *Power through Weakness*, 164. SCOTT suggests that the metaphor of the earthen vessel/clay jar echoes Gen 2:7, where God forms "man" (אדם) from the "earth" (אדמה). See *2 Corinthians*, 103. This is an

(4:6) which God has shone in human hearts. "This treasure" would therefore entail the enlightenment that is described in 4:4 as "the enlightenment of the gospel of the glory of Christ."[676] As argued in the previous section, this is an allusion to the Spirit-bestowed gift of the "mind of Christ," the νοῦς Χριστοῦ. By this reference, Paul speaks of having or possessing what empowers him to take on the character of Jesus to continue the latter's story. The *locus* of this treasure is "in earthen vessels" (ἐν ὀστρακίνοις σκεύεσιν), a metaphorical expression by which the apostle signifies enfleshed humanity. Parallel expressions in 4:10b ("in our body" – ἐν τῷ σώματι ἡμῶν) and 4:11b ("in our mortal flesh" – ἐν τῇ θνητῇ σαρκὶ ἡμῶν) underscore the enfleshment metaphor.[677] Notice how Paul literally uses "body language" in these verses. That is, the apostle intimates that his experience and actions – played out in his embodied existence – reveal and thus proclaim Christ.

Paul next describes graphically in 2 Cor 4:8-9 *how* this embodied revelation takes place through a series of participial clauses of manner: ἐν παντὶ θλιβόμενοι ἀλλ' οὐ στενοχωρούμενοι, ἀπορούμενοι ἀλλ' οὐκ ἐξαπορούμενοι, διωκόμενοι ἀλλ' οὐκ ἐγκαταλειπόμενοι, καταβαλλόμενοι ἀλλ' οὐκ ἀπολλύμενοι ("as we are afflicted in every way, but not crushed; (as we are) left in doubt, but not to the point of despairing; persecuted, but not abandoned; thrown down, but not destroyed").[678] The

---

intriguing suggestion, for it might be another clue that Paul continues to draw on a new or second Adam christology in this and the following verses.

[676]So, also, BACHMANN, *Der zweite Brief des Paulus an die Korinther*,193; and WINDISCH, *Der zweite Korintherbrief*, 141-42.

[677]See LAMBRECHT, "The Nekrōsis of Jesus," 314.

[678]It is important to note that 2 Cor 4:7-10 is one long sentence in the Greek text. The main clause is 4:7a – "We have this treasure in earthen vessels" – followed by a purpose clause introduced by ἵνα in 4:7b, a series of five participial clauses of manner in 4:8-10a, and another purpose clause introduced by ἵνα in 4:10b.

2 Cor 4:8-9 is the first instance of a peristasis catalog (catalog of hardships) in this letter. For more on Paul's use of such catalogs (in addition to FITZGERALD, *Cracks in an Earthen Vessel*), see W. SCHRAGE, "Leid, Kreuz und Eschaton: Die Peristasenkataloge als Merkmale paulinischer theologia crucis und Eschatologie," *EvT* 34 (1974) 141-75; and R. HODGSON, "Paul the Apostle and First Century Tribulation Lists," *ZNW* 74 (1983) 59-89. SAVAGE rightly comments that, whereas the apostle

transformation into the likeness of Christ entails for him the experience of sufferings and hardships. Observe, furthermore, the apostle's employment of present tense participles in these verses. Used in conjunction with the present tense of the governing verb, ἔχομεν (4:7), these participles indicate that his experience of suffering travails and opposition is one that is ongoing.[679] Then, in 4:10a, Paul renders a climactic participial clause that functions as a summary and interpretation of this experience: πάντοτε τὴν νέκρωσιν τοῦ 'Ιησοῦ ἐν τῷ σώματι περιφέροντες ("as we always carry in the body the putting to death of Jesus)." Here the apostle makes clear that he understands his present and ongoing experience of suffering in light of – and *as a continuation of* – the story of Jesus.[680]

Next, in 2 Cor 4:10b, Paul describes the *purpose* (cf. ἵνα) of his suffering: "in order that the life of Jesus (ζωὴ τοῦ 'Ιησοῦ) might also be manifested in our body." Recall that the phrase ζωὴ τοῦ 'Ιησοῦ signifies the power of the risen Jesus, here at work in the apostle. Two brief observations are in order. First, the purpose clause in 4:10b corresponds to the one in 4:7b – "in order that the extraordinary quality of the power might be [recognized as coming] from God and not from us." I propose that the power of the risen Jesus (ζωὴ τοῦ 'Ιησοῦ) is synonymous with the ὑπερβολὴ τῆς δυνάμεως τοῦ θεοῦ, a power that is an apt description of the transforming agency of the Spirit in 3:18. Second, Paul indicates that this power of the risen Christ is made manifest (φανερόω) in the former's embodied existence. How does the apostle make the ζωὴ τοῦ 'Ιησοῦ manifest? At one level, 4:8-9 indicates that, whereas Paul continually experiences affliction, confusion, persecution, and humiliation, he is nevertheless *not* crushed, *not* left in despair, *not* abandoned – and in the

---

speaks in general terms in 4:8-9, he offers more specific details later in 6:5 and 11:23-27. See *Power through Weakness*, 171.

[679]S.J. KRAFTCHICK captures this well: "... the adversities are understood as a typical and constant part of Paul's ministry, not exceptions or anomalies." See "Death in Us, Life in You: The Apostolic Medium," in *Pauline Theology. Volume II: 1 & 2 Corinthians*, ed. D.M. HAY (Minneapolis: Fortress, 1993) 156-81, here 173.

[680]LAMBRECHT aptly remarks that 2 Cor 4:10a "summarizes and qualifies in a christological way" what is expressed in 4:8-9. See "The Nekrōsis of Jesus," 325. Cf. 2 Cor 1:5, where Paul speaks of "the sufferings of Christ" (τὰ παθήματα τοῦ Χριστοῦ) abounding in him.

end, *not* destroyed.[681] Thus, the fact that the apostle has endured and persevered in the face of tremendous hardships gives evidence of the power of the risen Christ within him.[682] At a deeper level, however, the language and logic in 4:11-12 suggest something more than Paul's survival of various travails. In these verses the apostle intimates that the ζωὴ τοῦ Ἰησοῦ is made manifest by his incarnating Jesus' self-emptying mode of existence, a manner of living that brings life to others.[683]

It is essential to recognize how 2 Cor 4:11 and 4:12 *function* in Paul's argument. The postpositive γάρ in 4:11 signifies that the apostle offers the reason or grounds for what he has claimed in 4:10 – and, indeed, throughout the

---

[681]FITZGERALD points out that Paul's "four-fold use of οὐ with the participle, rather than the customary μή, serves to make his assertions of victory all the more emphatic." See *Cracks in an Earthen Vessel*, 166. Cf. ALLO, *Seconde Épître aux Corinthiens*, 113. SAVAGE attempts to bring out this emphatic quality of οὐ with the participle by translating it "*by no means*." See *Power through Weakness*, 171.

[682]Cf. 2 Cor 6:9, where Paul states that he and his fellow ministers are regarded "as dying, yet behold, we live; as punished, yet not killed" (ὡς ἀποθνῄσκοντες καὶ ἰδοῦ ζῶμεν, ὡς παιδευόμενοι καὶ μὴ θανατούμενοι). Concerning 4:10b, THRALL remarks: "[Paul] is thinking of the constant occasions of deliverance from mortal peril he has experienced, and in general of the power by which he is enabled to suffer without being totally overcome by suffering." See *II Corinthians*, 1.335. *Pace* GÜTTGEMANNS, who reduces the manifestation of Jesus' ζωή entirely to Paul's suffering itself, and not his deliverance from travails (see *Der leidende Apostel und sein Herr*, 94-126); and P. B. DUFF, who makes a similar claim in "Apostolic Suffering and the Language of Processions in 2 Corinthians 4:7-10," *BTB* 21 (1991) 158-65, esp. 163: ". . . Paul's suffering has come to function as a visual counterpart to the oral proclamation of the gospel."

[683]Whereas most commentators focus exclusively on Paul's being delivered in spite of such travails and adversities, HÉRING correctly observes that, in 2 Cor 4:11-12, the apostle suggests that the manifestation of the ζωὴ τοῦ Ἰησοῦ takes place in *two* ways: "On the one hand, God has preserved him from utter disaster, so that the new life is manifest by his mere physical existence . . .; and, on the other, he is a bearer of life to others." See *The Second Epistle of Saint Paul to the Corinthians*, 32. BARRETT makes a similar observation. He notes that 4:11 not only refers to Paul's "literal sufferings" but also points "to faith which conforms itself to the pattern of existence provided in Jesus." See *The Second Epistle to the Corinthians*, 140. I submit that Héring and Barrett are on the right track, although neither one reaps the full benefit of his insight.

compound-complex statement in 4:7-10.[684] His experience of being preserved amid sufferings and afflictions is grounded in the following: "*For* we, while living, are continually being *handed over* (παραδιδόμεθα) *unto death* (εἰς θάνατον) *because of Jesus* (διὰ 'Ιησοῦν) in order that the life of Jesus might also be manifested in our mortal flesh." While at first glance 4:11 appears to be a simple restatement of 4:10, the highlighted Greek terms and phrases suggest more than Paul's endurance of sufferings. So, too, does his statement in 4:12. Here the apostle reiterates the consequence or result of 'continually being handed over because of Jesus,' a result that is marked by ὥστε:[685] "*Consequently*, death is at work in us, but life [is at work] in you." Observe how Paul reminds the Corinthians that they are beneficiaries of his (and his co-workers') being handed over. In other words, the apostle alludes to something in 4:11 that results in the Corinthians' benefit.[686]

With this sense of how 2 Cor 4:11 and 4:12 function, we can more easily grasp Paul's allusive terminology, particularly his distinctive use of the language of "death" in these verses. In 4:11a the apostle claims that he is *continually* (ἀεί) being handed over εἰς θάνατον (literally, "into death"). And in 4:12 he asserts that θάνατος is at work in him, a process that is somehow connected to the Corinthians' experiencing "life" (ζωή). Certainly, Paul must intend a metaphorical meaning of death in these verses. Fortunately, the apostle himself provides the key to what he intends by his use of the passive voice of παραδίδωμι and the prepositional phrase διὰ 'Ιησοῦν in 4:11a.

Paul's use of παραδιδόμεθα (passive voice) is striking. Elsewhere he employs "being handed over" with reference to *Jesus* (see Rom 4:25 and 1 Cor

---

[684]Cf. BULTMANN, *The Second Letter to the Corinthians*, 119; FURNISH, *II Corinthians*, 256; and LAMBRECHT, "The Nekrōsis of Jesus," 325. All three recognize that 2 Cor 4:11 provides the basis for what has preceded it. Yet, commentators tend to focus too quickly on the structural and material similarities between 4:10 and 4:11, as well as to lose sight of the fact that 4:11 is, grammatically speaking, an independent statement. Moreover, given that 4:11 is a γάρ-statement – offering the reason or grounds for what precedes it – careful attention must be paid to ascertain what it says on its own terms, rather than interpreting it too narrowly in light of 4:10.

[685]As noted by, e.g., FURNISH, *II Corinthians*, 257; and SAVAGE, *Power through Weakness*, 178, n. 77.

[686]MARTIN aptly notes that ἐν ὑμῖν is a dative of advantage. See *2 Corinthians*, 89.

11:23).[687] Thus, in appropriating the term to describe his own experience, the apostle places himself within the framework of the story of Jesus – ὃς παρεδόθη διὰ τὰ παραπτώματα ἡμῶν ("who was handed over on account of our trespasses"; Rom 4:25). But Paul also knows that Jesus' ναί is part of the story, which thus evokes the latter's *ethos* as well. That is, Christ freely gave himself (cf. the active, reflexive sense of παραδίδωμι) out of love for the sake of others (see Eph 5:2 and 5:25). In fact, for the apostle this serves as the concise description of Jesus' πίστις (Gal 2:20). By stating that he is *continually* (ἀεί) being handed over, Paul suggests that he participates in the pattern of Jesus' giving himself in love for the sake of others, for their benefit and advantage. Hence, by his own ongoing ἀμήν to God, the apostle embodies Christ's faithfulness.[688]

The placement and use of the prepositional phrase διὰ Ἰησοῦν confirm this interpretation. Recall the peculiar syntax in 2 Cor 4:11a whereby Paul both juxtaposes this phrase with the verb παραδιδόμεθα and places it in the prominent end position of the clause.[689] The juxtaposition of διὰ Ἰησοῦν with the verb serves to reinforce that the apostle's constant "being handed over" is *because of Jesus*, in the sense of following the example of Christ, who

---

[687]Paul's only other use of the passive voice of παραδίδωμι is Rom 6:17, where it refers to the handing over of the "standard of teaching" (τύπος διδαχῆς).

[688]FITZGERALD makes an intriguing suggestion concerning the translation of παραδιδόμεθα. He proposes that it be read not as passive but as *middle* voice, meaning "we are always giving ourselves up" to death for Jesus' sake. See *Cracks in an Earthen Vessel*, 180. Fitzgerald is on the right track, although his middle voice reading of παραδίδωμι is not sustainable. Paul's other uses of this verb with middle/passive endings are best rendered in the passive voice (Rom 4:25 and 6:17; and 1 Cor 11:23). Moreover, the apostle *does* express the notion of "giving oneself up" with an active voice form of παραδίδωμι + the reflexive pronoun (Gal 2:20; and Eph 5:2 and 5:25). Fitzgerald's attempt to render a middle voice of παραδίδωμι thus fails. Yet, what he wants to convey – namely, that there *is* a sense in which Paul does actively give himself up – is tenable. As we will see in the analysis of 12:14-15 in Section VI below, the apostle expresses both the dynamic of being handed over (with God as the implied agent) and the dynamic of giving himself in love to others (which is his Yes to God). These dynamics are two sides of the same coin.

[689]εἰς θάνατον παραδιδόμεθα διὰ Ἰησοῦν, and *not* παραδιδόμεθα εἰς θάνατον διὰ Ἰησοῦν or διὰ Ἰησοῦν παραδιδόμεθα εἰς θάνατον.

incarnated living and dying in love for others so that they might have life. Furthermore, the phrase signifies that Paul is handed over *for the sake of Jesus*, in loyal service to the one whose apostle he is (cf. 1:1), to the one who himself was δοῦλος in loyal service to God (cf. LXX Ps 115:7ab).[690] Thus, as we saw in the previous chapter, the apostle's paradoxical expression παραδιδόμεθα διὰ Ἰησοῦν is his shorthand for the mode of existence revealed by Jesus.

We are now able to appreciate the full impact of Paul's purpose clause in 2 Cor 4:11b. The risen life of Jesus, the ζωὴ τοῦ Ἰησοῦ, is made manifest in the apostle's mortal flesh by his embodying the pattern of Jesus' loving, self-giving existence for the sake of others. To be sure, this manner of existence *does* involve suffering and hardships, as indicated in 4:8-9. What is more fundamental for Paul, however, is that he is empowered to live for the benefit and advantage of others (remember that his statement in 4:11 *grounds* what he says in 4:7-10). That the apostle is talking about more than being preserved in the midst of persecution and suffering is evident from the *consequence* of his way of existence: "life is at work among you [Corinthians]" (4:12b). Paul's ongoing experience of being-preserved-in-the-midst-of-suffering in and of itself does not benefit the Corinthians. What does benefit them is his embodying Jesus' love and self-emptying mode of existence for their sake.[691] Hence, 4:7-12 is more than a statement about the apostle's endurance of sufferings. In this passage he relates that the treasure of the νοῦς Χριστοῦ is made manifest most clearly by his incarnating the character of Christ in his own mortal flesh.[692]

---

[690]See nn. 413 and 453 for the explanation of this pregnant reading of διὰ Ἰησοῦν.

[691]Cf. GARLAND, who captures well the apostle's sense in 4:12: "[Paul] lives out his new life in Christ and the paradox of gaining life by giving it for others. He is . . . self-emptying like Christ." See *2 Corinthians*, 234.

[692]It might be objected that I make too strong a distinction between Paul's experience of sufferings and his embodying a self-giving mode of existence. Indeed, several commentators place exclusive focus on the apostle's sufferings in these verses. For instance, KRAFTCHICK offers the following assessment: "Thus, in this section of the letter [4:7-15] Paul's conviction about the death and resurrection of Christ is used metaphorically to reconstitute his adversity-filled life by means of the death/resurrection life structure; his adversities are to be understood as a dying which brings life" (see "Death in Us, Life in You," 177). Cf. FURNISH, *II Corinthians*, 287; and LAMBRECHT, *Second Corinthians*, 74. Admittedly, there is an apologetic tone in 4:7-10, an indication that Paul felt the need to explain and defend his "adversity-filled life."

The logic of Paul's statement in 2 Cor 4:13 thus becomes clear. He claims to possess "the same Spirit of faithfulness" as Jesus, "the anointed one" (ὁ Χριστός), to whose story the apostle alludes by citing LXX Pss 114-115. This is the same 'christing' Spirit (2 Cor 1:21b) who transforms Paul into the likeness of Christ (3:18), the image of God (4:4). Empowered by this πνεῦμα πίστεως, the apostle makes his own the words he attributes to Jesus: ἐπίστευσα, διὸ ἐλάλησα. Paul states here that *he*[693] (along with his co-workers) too is faithful, and that therefore he too speaks out (καὶ ἡμεῖς πιστεύομεν, διὸ καὶ λαλοῦμεν). When the apostle says that he is faithful (πιστεύω), he refers both to his experience of persevering in suffering *and* – more importantly – to his living in the same pattern of loving, self-giving existence as manifested by Christ.[694] In short, Paul encapsulates in 4:13 what he has been describing in 4:7-12. Furthermore, by appropriating to himself the words of Scripture, the apostle boldly claims to have taken on the very character of Jesus, especially his πίστις.

As a matter of fact, this does seem to be the best explanation for the presence of 4:8-9. But observe that the apostle does not connect his experience to the Corinthians in these two verses. Paul does, however, frame these verses with the notice that he proclaims himself as their slave (4:5), and with the statement that life is at work in them as a result of "death" being at work in him (4:12). The latter statement comes only after the apostle has alluded to, and included himself in, the story of Jesus' giving himself in love for the sake of others. Moreover, in Paul's more expansive *peristasis* catalogs later in the letter (6:4-10 and 11:23-33), he lists *afflictions which he has imposed upon himself* in order to bring the gospel to others (see esp. 6:5b and 11:27). That is, the apostle chooses to labor with his hands and to forgo meals and sleep in his commitment to be a *slave* to others διὰ 'Ιησοῦν (4:5). In the end, the distinction I propose goes hand-in-hand with my argument that Paul reads LXX Pss 114-115 as the story of the (active!) πίστις of Jesus, and not merely as the story of an unnamed or unknown (passive) sufferer who is rescued by God.

[693]Note the addition of the personal pronoun (ἡμεῖς) for emphasis.

[694]Cf. 2 Cor 5:7, where Paul states that he "walks" (= "conducts himself" – περιπατέω) *by means of faithfulness* (διὰ πίστεως). That the apostle here connotes by the term πίστις more than belief and/or trust is evident by what he says in 5:10 – namely, that the criterion for judgment is what one has done (πράσσω) "through the body" (διὰ τοῦ σώματος). See the Excursus on πίστις in Chapter Six.

Paul also says in 2 Cor 4:13 that he "speaks out" (λαλέω). Just as he understands LXX Pss 114-115 as expressing Jesus' testimony to his own (i.e., Christ's) story, so now the apostle speaks out about the same story. Because 2 Cor 4:13 is, in effect, a summarizing statement, we can be confident in looking to the preceding verses to find the content and manner of Paul's speaking. As is evident from 4:5, his speaking entails *verbal* proclamation: "we proclaim Jesus Christ as Lord" (κηρύσσομεν 'Ιησοῦν Χριστὸν κύριον). As was pointed out in the previous chapter, this is the climax of the story of Jesus (cf. Phil 2:11). Thus, the apostle proclaims in words the story of Jesus. In addition, Paul's "speaking" involves *embodied* proclamation. That is, in 4:5 he also proclaims himself as δοῦλος to the community. This suggests that the apostle lives for the Corinthians' benefit and advantage. Moreover, he does so διὰ 'Ιησοῦν – "because of Jesus" – a phrase that links him to the example and manner of Christ.[695] Indeed, 4:7-12 is Paul's vivid testimony that his whole manner of life is a proclamation.[696] By embodying the character of Jesus, the apostle proclaims with great eloquence the story of Jesus (see the treatment of 2:14-17 below).

---

[695]Cf. GARLAND, *2 Corinthians*, 215: "If Christ took the form of a slave, then those who follow him must be willing to give themselves over to serve others."

[696]BULTMANN was troubled by Paul's grammar in 4:5 because, by proclaiming himself a slave to the Corinthians, the apostle seems to include himself in the content of the gospel. Bultmann overcame this perceived difficulty by interpreting the apostle as saying that "in such proclamation we are only your slaves." See *The Second Letter to the Corinthians*, 107. KRAFTCHICK rightly observes that Paul's assertion ("we proclaim ourselves as your slaves because of Jesus") is a statement about his *behavior* with the Corinthians. Kraftchick aptly remarks: "Thus the gospel is presented in *both* the speech and bearing of the apostle who labors for the Lord and the benefit of the Corinthians." See "Death in Us, Life in You," 170 and n. 33 (italics added). Similarly, B.R. GAVENTA comments: ". . . the connection of 4:5c with the proclamation of Jesus' lordship is astonishing. The enslavement of the apostle to the churches stands alongside the gospel itself." See "Apostle and Church in 2 Corinthians: A Response to David M. Hay and Steven J. Kraftchick," in *Pauline Theology. Volume II: 1 & 2 Corinthians*, ed. D.M. HAY (Minneapolis: Fortress, 1993) 182-99, here 196. I would amend Gaventa's comment in this way: The enslavement of Paul to the churches is the embodied manner in which he *proclaims* – in addition to verbal proclamation – the gospel.

Finally, in 2 Cor 4:14, Paul articulates the element of trust and belief that lies at the heart of his faithfulness: "because we know[697] that the one who raised the Lord Jesus will also raise us with Jesus." Here the apostle alludes to God's vindication of Jesus' faithfulness and obedience unto death. Central to Christ's ἀμήν to God was his confidence in God to bring the dead to life. So too Paul grounds his ongoing experience of "being handed over" in his own trust in God to raise him to life with Jesus.[698] Notice the apostle's use of cognitive terminology (οἶδα) here in connection with the story of Jesus. Once again, immersion in this story is crucial, an immersion that is deeply intertwined in 4:14 with the notion of trust.[699] Indeed, immediately following the letter's opening *berakah* (1:3-7), Paul recounts an incident that profoundly deepened his trust and hope in God, the trust and hope that are the basis of his πίστις. It is to the apostle's statement in 1:8-10 that I now turn.

B. *The Basis of Paul's Faithfulness: Trust and Hope in God (2 Cor 1:8-10)*

Paul speaks dramatically in 2 Cor 1:8-10 of placing his reliance on God. It is striking that the apostle here characterizes God as "God who raises the dead" (ὁ θεὸς ὁ ἐγείρων τοὺς νεκρούς, 1:9), a depiction that foreshadows his reference in 4:14 to "the one who raised the Lord Jesus" (ὁ ἐγείρας τὸν κύριον Ἰησοῦν). Paul's testimony to his reliance on God is not surprising, given that he has just blessed God for comforting him in all his afflictions (1:3-4). In 1:8 the apostle begins to illustrate God's action on his behalf with a

---

[697]Reading the circumstantial participle εἰδότες as causal.

[698]Paul refers here to his own *future* resurrection from the dead. That is, just as God has raised (ἐγείρας, aorist participle) Jesus in the past, so the apostle trusts that God *will* raise (ἐγειρεῖ, future indicative) him. *Pace* N. BAUMERT and MURPHY-O'CONNOR, who argue that ἐγειρεῖ should be interpreted existentially – in a non-eschatological, "this life" sense (i.e., God will continue to raise him, again and again). See BAUMERT, *Täglich sterben und auferstehen: Der Literalsinn von 2 Kor 4, 12-5, 10*, SANT 34 (München: Kösel-Verlag, 1973) 88-94; and MURPHY-O'CONNOR, "Faith and Resurrection in 2 Cor 4:13-14," 543-50.

[699]Immersion in the story requires consciousness of the fact that one participates in the story.

reference to an affliction he experienced in Asia. Paul's description is both dramatic and opaque. The apostle says that he (along with Timothy)[700] was "weighed down" (ἐβαρήθημεν) to such an extent (note the redundant καθ' ὑπερβολὴν ὑπὲρ δύναμιν) that he "despaired" (ἐξαπορηθῆναι) even of living. Yet Paul offers no details of what this affliction entailed. It is necessary, therefore, to exercise a certain restraint in interpreting 1:8.[701] For my purposes, it is sufficient to focus on what the apostle says in 1:9-10 about his trust and hope in God.

In 2 Cor 1:9a Paul declares: ἀλλὰ αὐτοὶ ἐν ἑαυτοῖς τὸ ἀπόκριμα τοῦ θανάτου ἐσχήκαμεν. Most commentators take this statement as a continuation and reinforcement of what has just been said,[702] viewing the incident referred to in 1:8 as tantamount to a "sentence of death" (ἀπόκριμα τοῦ θανάτου) for the apostle. Several features in the text, however, indicate that Paul might intend something more by 1:9a. First, the conjunction ἀλλά – with which this clause begins – usually serves an *adversative* function, and thus calls into question the assumption that 1:9a merely continues 1:8. Second, the verb ἐσχήκαμεν is in the *perfect* tense. Although the apostle does, at times, use

---

[700]I take Paul's first person plural pronouns here as referring to himself and Timothy, the co-sender of this letter. There is nothing between 2 Cor 1:1 to 1:8 to suggest that the apostle has changed or broadened the referent of "we."

[701]Commentators have speculated about what Paul's affliction in Asia involved. The main hypotheses are: (1) a serious illness (so, e.g., ALLO, *Seconde Épître aux Corinthiens*, 15-19; and BARRETT, *The Second Epistle to the Corinthians*, 64); (2) an imprisonment in Ephesus (so, FURNISH, *II Corinthians*, 123); and (3) the riot in Ephesus recounted in Acts 19:23-20:1 (so, BARNETT, *The Second Epistle to the Corinthians*, 83-84). For HARVEY – who holds that 2 Cor 1:8 refers to some debilitating, life-threatening illness or disability – this experience, as well as Paul's reflection upon it, holds the key to understanding the entire epistle. See HARVEY, *Renewal through Suffering*. I, however, agree with LAMBRECHT'S cautious admonition: "Notwithstanding the general indication of the place of this misfortune and the emphasis on its magnitude, it is no longer possible for us to know what Paul is referring to, exactly what happened to him, and precisely where and when it happened." See *Second Corinthians*, 20.

[702]E.g., FURNISH, *II Corinthians*, 113; MARTIN, *2 Corinthians*, 12; and LAMBRECHT, *Second Corinthians*, 20. All three take the conjunction ἀλλά as supporting what was said in 1:8.

the perfect tense of ἔχω as the equivalent of an aorist (e.g., 2 Cor 2:13 and 7:5), what happens if we take his use of the verb here as a true perfect? Third, the meaning of τὸ ἀπόκριμα τοῦ θανάτου is far from clear. The term ἀπόκριμα occurs only here in the entire NT. It has the sense of "official report, decision."[703] But observe that Paul himself does not go into detail concerning his affliction in Asia; moreover, there is no evidence elsewhere of the apostle's having received any "sentence of death" there.

I propose, instead, that we read ἐσχήκαμεν as a true perfect so that Paul refers here to something that he received in the past (and thus now "has" or "possesses") that has ongoing ramifications in the present.[704] In addition, I submit that we understand τὸ ἀπόκριμα τοῦ θανάτου in light of 2 Cor 1:1-7, and not in light of the apostle's unclear statement in 1:8. In 1:1 he has introduced himself as an "apostle of Jesus Christ through God's will," and in 1:5 he has alluded to the "sufferings of Christ" that abound in him. Therefore, with the expression τὸ ἀπόκριμα τοῦ θανάτου – the graphic quality of which may have been influenced by the dramatic language of 1:8 – I suggest that Paul refers to the reality of his life as one chosen by God to be an apostle of Christ. This reality entails both suffering and embodying Jesus' self-emptying mode of existence. Thus, in 1:9a the apostle broadens the scope of the reference in 1:8 from an account of some singular incident in Asia to the larger reality of his apostolic existence.[705]

---

[703]See BDAG, s.v. ἀπόκριμα. C.J. HEMER has shown that this word was used in contemporary writings as a technical term for "an official decision in answer to the petition of an embassy." See "A Note on 2 Corinthians 1:9," *TynBul* 23 (1972) 103-7, here 106. Hemer's study has the virtue of calling into question the forensic connotations of some interpretations (e.g., 1:9 refers to a judicial "death sentence"). His own interpretation, however – namely, that Paul found himself in great peril, and presented a petition to God; the answer was "death," that is, the apostle would not live until the Parousia – does not do justice to the immediate context.

[704]So, too, BDF, § 343 (2). Cf. Rom 5:2. BELLEVILLE captures well the sense of ἐσχήκαμεν in 2 Cor 1:9: "we received and still experience." See *2 Corinthians*, 58.

[705]Thus, I translate ἀπόκριμα τοῦ θανάτου as "death sentence," but understood metaphorically and not as an actual judicial decision rendered against Paul by authorities (e.g., in Ephesus).

Whether Paul refers in 2 Cor 1:9a to a specific incident in Asia or more broadly to what his apostolic call involves, his main point is expressed 1:9b:[706] "so that[707] we might be reliant (πεποιθότες), not on ourselves, but on God who raises the dead." This is the apostle's key insight, and the foundation of his commitment to embody the faithfulness of Jesus. The perfect tense of πείθω denotes "depend on, trust in."[708] Paul makes clear that he can fulfill his apostolic calling – which involves both suffering and giving himself in love for the sake of others – only *with the help of God.* His ongoing experience of being an apostle has taught him to trust in God to empower him, to preserve him, and, finally, to raise him from the dead. Paul's characterization of God as "the One who raises the dead" recalls the story of Jesus. Indeed, later in 4:14 the apostle expressly refers to God's raising Jesus from the dead, a reference that fits well with Paul's christological reading of LXX Pss 114-115 (to which he has just alluded in 4:13). Just as Jesus, God's faithful δοῦλος, trusted in God and was vindicated, so too the apostle places his trust in God to sustain him and, ultimately, to vindicate him.[709]

That Paul has in mind in these early verses the story of Jesus as told in LXX Pss 114-115 is further suggested by the apostle's three-fold use of ῥύομαι in 2 Cor 1:10.[710] This verse consists of two relative clauses that supplement Paul's description of God. That is, the "One who raises the dead" (1:9) is also the One "who delivered (ἐρρύσατο) us from such terrible dangers of death and will deliver (ῥύσεται) [us]; in whom we have placed our hope that [God] will

---

[706]So, too, FURNISH, *II Corinthians*, 123; and THRALL, *II Corinthians*, 1.117-18.

[707]Taking ἵνα to mark result. See BDAG, s.v. ἵνα, 3. Cf. 2 Cor 1:17 and 1 Thess 5:4

[708]See BDAG, s.v. πείθω, 2.a. Cf. Phil 3:3-11 (esp. vv. 3-4).

[709]Cf. Rom 4:17, where the apostle describes Abraham's πίστις (cf. 4:16) as directed to God, "who gives life to the dead and calls into being the things that do not exist." In commenting on 2 Cor 1:9, SAMPLEY rightly states that Paul ". . . counted on God, on God's power, a power demonstrated and warranted in Christ's having been raised." See *NIB*, 11.42.

[710]I am not alone in hearing Paul echo the language of LXX Ps 114 in 2 Cor 2:10. See THRALL, *II Corinthians*, 1.119-20; HARVEY, *Renewal through Suffering*, 18; and BARNETT, *The Second Epistle to the Corinthians*, 87, n. 37.

deliver (ῥύσεται) [us] yet again."[711] The apostle thus implicates himself in the story told in LXX Pss 114-115 at the point where the psalmist (= Jesus) cries out, "O Lord, save (ῥῦσαι) my life" (Ps 114:4b), and at the point where he later reports that God "has saved my life from death (ἐκ θανάτου, 114:8a)." In 2 Cor 1:10 Paul makes clear that God has delivered him in the past, and will continue to do so in the future. Indeed, the apostle's trust in God is such that he has set his hope (note the perfect tense of ἠλπίκαμεν) in God to deliver him *yet again* (referring to the resurrection?).[712] The point here is that the basis of Paul's πίστις is his reliance on and hope in God to preserve him in his apostolic existence and to ultimately vindicate him in the resurrection. In possessing this trust and hope in God, the apostle both emulates Jesus' trust and hope, and is emboldened to embody the latter's manner of self-emptying existence, to which he alludes in 2:14-17.

C. *How Paul, the Slave of God, Emits the "Aroma of Christ" (2 Cor 2:14-17)*

In the course of recounting to the Corinthians his anxiety as he awaited news from Titus concerning their reception of the tearful letter (2 Cor 2:12-13; cf. 7:5-13a), Paul suddenly, in 2:14, breaks into thanksgiving. The apostle

---

[711]See METZGER, *A Textual Commentary on the Greek New Testament*, 506-7, for a discussion of the different textual variants in 2 Cor 1:10. My reading takes as original the plural τηλικούτων θανάτων (translated "such terrible dangers of death") instead of the singular τηλικούτου θανάτου. The former is the more difficult reading, and is attested to by the oldest manuscript, P[46]. FURNISH (*II Corinthians*, 114) and THRALL, (*II Corinthians*, 1.120-21) also read the text thus. Observe how this reading strengthens my interpretation of 1:9a (involving Paul's *ongoing* apostolic existence). My reading also takes ὅτι καὶ ἔτι as the original, rather than καὶ ἔτι. I agree with THRALL that the longer form accounts for the emergence of other readings, for why would the word ὅτι be added if it were originally absent? See *II Corinthians*, 1.121-22.

[712]BARNETT, who argues that the second use of ῥύσεται (future tense) refers to God's raising Paul from the dead, may very well be right: "Since by his nature God is and will always be a rescuer or redeemer ('God, who *raises* the dead'), he 'also will deliver' Paul from other 'afflictions'. . .and he will yet deliver Paul, ultimately, from death itself. . . ." See *The Second Epistle to the Corinthians*, 88 (Barnett's italics). BARNETT (ibid., 88-89) also astutely observes the correspondence between the perfect tense verbs ἐσχήκαμεν (1:9) and ἠλπίκαμεν (1:10).

employs two striking metaphors in expressing his gratitude to God. The first metaphor appears immediately: "Thanks be to God who always θριαμβεύοντι us in Christ" (2:14a). Now, what is meant by the verb θριαμβεύω, the subject of which is God and the object of which is Paul?[713] The verb evokes the Roman triumphal procession, a massive celebration of victory in war. The purpose of the celebration was to render thanksgiving to the deity, and to give honor to the conquering general. As Scott J. Hafemann has shown, part of the procession involved parading prisoners of war on the way to their execution. Thus, with his use of θριαμβεύω, the apostle gives thanks to God, who "leads [Paul] in [God's] triumphal procession." What is noteworthy is that this metaphor places the apostle – as the object of the verb – in the role of a captured *prisoner* or *slave* being led to death.[714]

---

[713]Again, the first person plural referent is debated here. Like HAFEMANN (see *Suffering and Ministry in the Spirit*, 12-16), I take ἡμᾶς as epistolary, and thus as referring to Paul. Cf. THRALL (*II Corinthians*, 1.195-96): "The ἡμᾶς refers primarily to Paul himself, since it is his own conception of apostleship that he expounds upon in what follows. . . ."

[714]See HAFEMANN, *Suffering and Ministry in the Spirit*, 16-34, and the evidence that he provides from relevant Greek sources from the first century BCE and the first century CE. Hafemann concludes his analysis thus: ". . . all the evidence points to the conclusion that there is only *one* basic and common meaning for [θριαμβεύω] available in the time of Paul, namely, that of the triumphal procession in which the conquered enemies were usually led as slaves to death, being spared this death only by an act of grace on the part of the one celebrating the triumph" (ibid., 33; Hafemann's italics). Hafemann's analysis picks up and expands upon that of L.WILLIAMSON, "Led in Triumph: Paul's Use of Thriambeuō," *Int* 22 (1968) 317-32. Cf. P. MARSHALL ["A Metaphor of Social Shame: ΘΡΙΑΜΒΕΥΕΙΝ in 2 Cor. 2:14," *NovT* 25 (1983) 302-17], who proposes that the apostle draws upon the social aspect of shame in the motif "led captive in triumph"; P.B. DUFF ["Metaphor, Motif, and Meaning," 79-92], who argues that Paul begins with the image of the triumphal procession in 2:14, but then subtly redefines it in the course of the epistle to encompass an epiphany procession; and C. BREYTENBACH ["Paul's Proclamation and God's 'Thriambos' (Notes on 2 Corinthians 2:14-16b)," *Neot* 24 (1990) 257-71], who contends that Paul does not portray himself as a captured prisoner, but rather that God celebrates God's "victory" over the apostle in and through the latter's missionary journeys.

This is a shocking image, the intensity of which several commentators and translations seek to mitigate.[715] Yet Paul's portrayal of himself as God's captured slave is not so jarring when one recalls the story of Jesus as God's faithful δοῦλος.[716] Indeed, observe how the apostle attaches the phrase ἐν τῷ Χριστῷ (literally, "in *the* Christ") to his description in 2 Cor 2:14a. Paul's placement of this phrase in the prominent end position of the clause is significant. So too is his use of the article before Χριστός. Moreover, observe that the preposition ἐν here signifies "in close association with, under the

---

[715]See, e.g., BRUCE'S comment (*1 and 2 Corinthians*, 187): ". . . the apostles are joyful participants in their commander's triumphal procession, not . . . the unwilling captives . . . . " Cf. HÉRING, *The Second Epistle of Saint Paul to the Corinithians*, 18. J.H. SCHÜTZ remarks without further explanation: "The verb is here best translated without any reference to its possible derisive overtones." See *Paul and the Anatomy of Apostolic Authority*, SNTSMS 26 (Cambridge: Cambridge University Press, 1975) 210. The KJV offers the following translation of 2:14a: "Now, thanks be unto God, which always causeth us to triumph in Christ." BARRETT translates the passage in question: "But thanks be to God, who goes always at our head in a triumphal progress in Christ" (see *The Second Epistle to the Corinthians*, 95). R.B. EGAN argues against the use of the triumph interpretation altogether, proposing instead that the verb θριαμβεύω means "make known, display, manifest, etc." See "Lexical Evidence on Two Pauline Passages," *NovT* 19 (1977) 34-62, esp. 40-52. Egan's argument, however, attaches too much weight to the meaning of ἐκθριαμβίζω for illuminating θριαμβεύω. Moreover, he appears overly concerned to harmonize 2:14a with 2:14b (and the verb φανερόω). J.I.H. MCDONALD questions whether Paul would have compared God's activity with that of a pagan general leading a triumph. See "Paul and the Preaching Ministry: A Reconsideration of 2 Cor. 2:14-17 in Its Context," *JSNT* 17 (1983) 35-50, esp. 37. This objection, however, seems to rest more on McDonald's own sense of theological appropriateness than on the text itself.

[716]WILLIAMSON remarks that Paul's imagery in 2 Cor 2:14a is not surprising, given how he refers elsewhere to himself as Christ's slave. See "Led in Triumph," 324. This is true, although here *God* – not Christ – is portrayed as the conquering figure. A better point of comparison is Titus 1:1, where Paul describes himself as δοῦλος θεοῦ, and *apostle* of Christ. It is striking, moreover, that Paul goes on in the same verse to describe his purpose as "God's slave" – to enhance the "faithfulness" (πίστις) and the "knowledge of truth" (ἐπίγνωσις ἀληθείας) among God's elect. As we will see in the paragraphs to follow, Paul's embodying Jesus' πίστις is how God spreads the knowledge of Christ in 2 Cor 2:14b. In addition, see 1 Cor 9:16-17, where Paul intimates that his preaching the gospel is a "necessity" laid upon him, a "task" entrusted to him.

influence of."[717] Hence, in 2:14a the apostle claims that God is always leading him as a prisoner or slave in close association with the Christ, that is, *in close association with Jesus, the anointed One*.[718]

A second conspicuous metaphor, that of fragrance (ὀσμή) being spread, emerges in 2 Cor 2:14b. In the course of continuing his thanksgiving, Paul depicts God as the One "who makes manifest through us the fragrance of the knowledge of [Christ] in every place." A few preliminary observations shed light on the apostle's use of this metaphor. First, the verb employed to describe God's action is φανερόω, the same verb Paul uses in 4:10-11 (cf. 4:2) to indicate how in his embodied existence the ζωὴ τοῦ 'Ιησοῦ is made manifest. Although God is the subject of φανερόω in 2:14b, that which God makes manifest occurs *through* (διά) the very being of the apostle. Second, the present tense participles (θριαμβεύοντι and φανεροῦντι) and adverbial modifiers ("always" and "in every place") indicate that God's revelation takes place through Paul's *ongoing* embodied experience. Third, that which God reveals through the apostle – here called "fragrance" – is intimately connected with the knowledge about Christ (ἡ ὀσμὴ τῆς γνώσεως αὐτοῦ).[719] Returning to the question of what Paul means to evoke by the metaphor of a fragrance being spread, there is a clear sense that the apostle's very existence is somehow revelatory of Christ.[720] The following verse confirms this supposition.

---

[717]See BDAG, s.v. ἐν, 4.c. Cf. Gal 2:20 and Phil 3:9.

[718]BARNETT rightly sees that the image of the captive-slave – modified by 'in Christ' – shows the "continuity of suffering shared by the obedient Christ and his faithful servant." See *The Second Epistle to the Corinthians*, 150.

[719]Most commentators take the pronoun αὐτοῦ as referring to God, not to Christ. As PLUMMER points out, however, "the preceding ἐν τῷ Χριστῷ and the Χριστοῦ εὐωδία which follows make the reference to Christ more probable." See *II Corinthians*, 70. In addition, see HUGHES, *Paul's Second Epistle to the Corinthians*, 79, n. 11; and BREYTENBACH, "Paul's Proclamation and God's 'Thriambos,'" 259. As the apostle himself points out in 2 Cor 4:6, knowledge of God is attained in and through Christ. In addition, PLUMMER appropriately regards the genitive "of the knowledge [of Christ]" as appositional to "fragrance" (see *II Corinthians*, 70).

[720]*Pace* those commentators (e.g., MCDONALD, "Paul and the Preaching Ministry," 42 and 48; and KISTEMAKER, *The Second Epistle to the Corinthians*, 90) who hold that Paul refers to the (verbal) preaching of the gospel in 2:14. The apostle *does* mention his

Second Corinthians 2:15 serves to ground Paul's statement about fragrance: "For[721] we are the aroma of Christ to God" (ὅτι Χριστοῦ εὐωδία ἐσμὲν τῷ θεῷ). Observe that the apostle here uses a synonym for ὀσμή, namely εὐωδία. It is instructive to see how he uses these two terms elsewhere. Besides 2 Cor 2:14-16, the words occur only in Phil 4:18 and Eph 5:2. In these latter texts, Paul places the terms in juxtaposition, ὀσμὴ εὐωδίας, a phrase that has the connotation of "fragrant offering."[722] In addition, in these passages the ὀσμὴ εὐωδίας is closely connected with the notion of "sacrifice" (θυσία) offered "to God" (τῷ θεῷ). Finally, and most significantly, the apostle explicitly links the ὀσμὴ εὐωδίας to the character and story of Jesus in Eph 5:2: "Conduct yourselves in [the way of] love, just as Christ loved us and gave himself up for us, an offering and sacrifice to God for a fragrant offering (ὀσμὴν εὐωδίας)." Here Paul explicitly depicts Jesus' self-giving existence out of love for the sake of others in terms of the sacrificial cult. The sacrifice offered to God as ὀσμὴ εὐωδίας *is* Jesus' entire mode of existence (culminating on the cross) – a way of living that the apostle elsewhere (Gal 2:20) encapsulates by reference to Christ's πίστις.

Returning to 2 Cor 2:15, I propose that Paul uses the spreading fragrance metaphor to signify his embodiment of Jesus' character and mode of self-emptying existence. Indeed, the apostle states that he is the aroma *of Christ*.[723] Paul's manner of loving and serving others follows after the pattern of Jesus, and is offered τῷ θεῷ, "to God." This is why the apostle says in 2:14b

---

proclaiming (in the sense of *verbal* proclamation) the word of God in this passage, but not until 2:17b (see below).

[721]Taking ὅτι as marking causality, as do PLUMMER, *II Corinthians*, 70; BARNETT, *The Second Epistle to the Corinthians*, 152, n. 26; and KISTEMAKER, *The Second Epistle to the Corinthians*, 90. See BDAG, s.v. ὅτι, 4.b. Cf. 2 Cor 4:6; 7:8; and 7:14.

[722]See both BARRETT (*The Second Epistle to the Corinthians*, 99) and HAFEMANN (*Suffering and Ministry in the Spirit*, 41-42, n. 17) for several LXX texts containing the phrase ὀσμὴ εὐωδίας as a technical term that translates ריח ניחח – signifying a soothing odor of sacrifices acceptable to YHWH. Cf. BDBG, s.v. ניחח and ריח.

[723]Several commentators correctly observe that Paul's placement of Χριστοῦ in first position is emphatic. See, e.g., PLUMMER, *II Corinthians*, 70; HUGHES, *Paul's Second Epistle to the Corinthians*, 79, n. 12; and LAMBRECHT, *Second Corinthians*, 37.

that it is through himself that God spreads the fragrance of the knowledge of Christ. In observing the self-giving manner of Paul, people can come to know something about the story and character of Jesus. Thus, the apostle draws upon the imagery of the sacrificial cult to describe his own way of embodying Jesus' faithfulness.[724] Notice how this is similar to Paul's presentation in 1:20b, where he uses the language of liturgy to express how human faithfulness (τὸ ἀμήν) – the faithfulness of Jesus, and that of the apostle and his co-workers – is directed to God (τῷ θεῷ) for glory.

The relationship between the two metaphors in 2 Cor 2:14 – triumphal procession and fragrance – now becomes clear. The imagery of God's leading Paul as a captured slave in a triumphal procession ἐν τῷ Χριστῷ connotes the apostle's being, like the faithful Jesus, God's δοῦλος who lives in obedience to God. The sacrificial interpretation of the fragrance/aroma metaphor intimates Paul's self-giving existence out of love for others, following in the pattern of Jesus.[725] Both metaphors speak of the same reality,[726] the reality that the apostle describes in 4:10-11 with another twofold pattern: the reality of always carrying

---

[724]As he does elsewhere, e.g., Phil 2:17: "Even if I am poured out as a libation upon the sacrifice and offering of your faith, . . ." Some commentators (e.g., PLUMMER, *II Corinthians*, 71; and FURNISH, *II Corinthians*, 177) deny that Paul uses the idea of sacrifice in 2 Cor 2:15. Indeed, it is true that the specific phrase ὀσμὴ εὐωδίας does not occur in 2:14b-15. However, as others (e.g., COLLANGE, *Énigmes de la deuxième épître aux Corinthiens*, 30; and THRALL, *II Corinthians*, 1.201) point out, the close juxtaposition of the words ὀσμή and εὐωδία strongly evokes the ὀσμὴ εὐωδίας of the OT sacrificial system.

[725]Cf. GARLAND, *2 Corinthians*, 146: "Paul has incarnated his apostolic message of the cross of Christ. *The cross determines* both his message and *his style of ministry*, and those who preach Christ crucified cannot expect to be crowned with glory by the world which crucified him" (italics added).

[726]Some commentators (e.g., WINDISCH, *Der zweite Korintherbrief*, 97-98; and HUGHES, *Paul's Second Epistle to the Corinthians*, 78-79) hold that the metaphor of the Roman triumph extends to the fragrance metaphor, since the burning of incense was also part of the triumphal procession. But the metaphor is not to be stretched too far, as THRALL (*II Corinthians*, 1.200) correctly observes: "Paul can scarcely be seen both as the captive who exhibits the victor's power and the burning incense which indicates the victor's arrival."

about the νέκρωσις τοῦ 'Ιησοῦ, and the constant "being handed over" διὰ 'Ιησοῦν.

Finally, after describing the different reactions to his manner of being apostle, along with the consequences of those reactions (2 Cor 2:15b-2:16a), Paul raises the question of sufficiency (2:16b), turning to the issue of verbal proclamation (2:17). In 2 Cor 2:17b the apostle insists that, as one who is ἐκ θεοῦ and κατέναντι θεοῦ, he speaks "in Christ" (ἐν Χριστῷ). I submit that the two metaphors in 2:14 illuminate the meaning of the phrases ἐκ θεοῦ and κατέναντι θεοῦ. The preposition ἐκ here signifies the *source,*[727] which evokes Paul's metaphor of spreading fragrance. *God* is the one who makes the fragrance of the knowledge of Christ manifest through the apostle's self-emptying mode of existence. The preposition κατέναντι marks one's position relative to another who is viewed as having jurisdiction.[728] This evokes Paul's metaphor of being led captive by God. *God* is the "overlord" whom the apostle, as slave, serves and obeys. Thus, Paul's sufficiency derives from his faithfulness to God in embodying Jesus' character and mode of existence. It is for this reason that the apostle is qualified to speak (λαλέω) – "in Christ" – the word of God, that is, the gospel. In fact, the logical progression of 2:14-17 sheds light on the citation in 4:13 from LXX Ps 115:1a (ἐπίστευσα, διὸ ἐλάλησα). It is *because* Paul is faithful in embodying Jesus' πίστις that he *therefore* speaks out by proclaiming the gospel.[729] Observe, furthermore, how the phrase ἐν Χριστῷ brackets 2 Cor 2:14-17. As one who has been "christed" (1:21b) by the Spirit, the apostle both lives and speaks as one "in close association with" Christ.

---

[727]See BDAG, s.v. ἐκ, 3.g. Cf. Rom 14:23.

[728]See BDAG, s.v. κατέναντι, 1. Cf. Sir 50:19 (where the "merciful Lord" is overlord); and Jdt 12:15 and 12:19 (where the overlord is Holofernes, the chief general of the Assyrian army). In addition, cf. 2 Cor 12:19.

[729]HAFEMANN, in previewing 2 Cor 2:14-3:3, appropriately remarks: ". . . Paul views himself in his apostolic calling not only as one who *preaches* the message of the good news to the world, but equally important, as one ordained by God to be an *embodiment* of that gospel, called to reveal the knowledge of God by and through his very life." See *Suffering and Ministry in the Spirit*, 16 (his italics). I would amend Hafemann's observation by insisting that the apostle's self-giving existence reveals knowledge of *Christ*. Cf. SCHÜTZ, *Paul and the Anatomy of Apostolic Authority*, 211.

D. *Summarizing Paul's Faithfulness after the Pattern of Jesus (2 Cor 12:9-10)*

As a way of reviewing how Paul incarnates Christ's faithfulness, I turn now to 2 Cor 12:9-10. My intention is not to give a thoroughgoing exegesis of this passage,[730] but to use it as an epitome to summarize this section. The apostle has just referred to some unnamed affliction, a σκόλοψ, that he bears in the flesh in order to keep him from becoming too inflated (12:7). Paul next recounts how he prayed to Christ the risen Lord to relieve him of his affliction (12:8). Then, in 12:9-10, the apostle narrates the Lord's response to his prayer, as well as his own reaction to this response. These verses, I submit, encapsulate well three dynamics that we have observed in the course of analyzing 4:7-14, 1:8-10, and 2:14-17.

First, there is the dynamic of Paul's posture of trust. The risen Lord's response to the apostle's prayer was: "My grace is sufficient for you, for power is made perfect in weakness" (2 Cor 12:9a). The perfect tense of the verb εἴρηκεν suggests that the risen Lord's answer to Paul's prayer has ongoing validity and force.[731] Thus, although his affliction is not removed, the apostle is promised the Lord's χάρις – his continual "gracious care/help."[732] More to

[730]For a more extensive treatment of 2 Cor 12:9-10 – including both the key exegetical issues and a summary of the interpretations offered by, e.g., Bultmann, Käsemann, Windisch, and Betz – see G.G. O'COLLINS, "Power Made Perfect in Weakness: 2 Cor 12:9-10," *CBQ* 33 (1971) 528-37.

[731]So too, THRALL, *II Corinthians*, 2.821.

[732]For this understanding of χάρις, see Chapter Four, Section VIII (including nn. 527 and 531). It might be objected that, whereas I have argued above that Paul places his trust *in God*, in 2 Cor 12:9-10 the apostle puts his trust *in the promise of Christ the risen Lord*. To be sure, this passage shows that Paul regards the risen and glorified Lord as possessing divine status (cf. Phil 2:9-11). Indeed, as we have seen, the conferral of the name "Lord" is the climax of the story of Jesus. But whether Paul's confidence is placed in God the Father or in the glorified Christ, the crucial point is that *the apostle relies upon the divine power to sustain him*. In addition, the reference to the χάρις of the risen Lord serves to remind us that the person of Jesus is one, and thus that he has a single *ethos*. Indeed, I argued in the previous chapter that the reference in 8:9 to "the χάρις of our Lord Jesus Christ" – while certainly pertaining to his humanity – encompasses the entire story of Jesus.

the point, observe Paul's reaction to this promise. The apostle now boasts "all the more gladly" (ἥδιστα μᾶλλον) of his weaknesses (12:9b); he even "considers it a good thing" (εὐδοκέω) that he experiences weakness and endures sufferings and hardships "because of Christ" (ὑπὲρ Χριστοῦ).[733] That is, Paul is able to willingly embrace a way of life ὑπὲρ Χριστοῦ because he *trusts* in the Lord's ongoing gracious care. The apostle's trust in the Lord's help recalls his reliance upon God to sustain him in his apostolic existence and, ultimately, to raise him from the dead – just as God has already raised Jesus (1:8-10 and 4:14).

The second dynamic is Paul's source of empowerment. In 2 Cor 12:9b the apostle speaks of ἡ δύναμις τοῦ Χριστοῦ, "the power of Christ." Here Paul evokes a reality that he has described in various ways in 4:7-13: ἡ δύναμις τοῦ θεοῦ (4:7); ἡ ζωὴ τοῦ 'Ιησοῦ (4:10b and 4:11b); and τὸ πνεῦμα τῆς πίστεως (4:13). As I have already suggested, these phrases point to the same thing, namely, the *divine power* bestowed upon the apostle that enables him to proclaim the gospel through both his Christ-like existence and his verbal proclamation. This power is the *christing* Spirit who has formed – and continues to form – Paul into the εἰκὼν τοῦ θεοῦ as revealed by Jesus. Indeed, the apostle's choice of the verb ἐπισκηνόω in 12:9b is suggestive, as he intimates that the power of the risen Christ "pitches a tent upon" him.[734]

---

[733]Reading ὑπέρ as signifying the reason for doing something. See BDAG, s.v. ὑπέρ, 2. Cf. Phil 1:29 and 2 Thess 1:5.

[734]Because 2 Cor 12:9b marks the apostle's only usage of this verb, caution must be exercised about its significance. Still, I propose tentatively that Paul might have here in mind a concept used by the evangelist John. As the divine Word became flesh and dwelt (literally, "pitched a tent" – σκηνόω, John 1:14) among people through the incarnation and life of Jesus, similarly the δύναμις τοῦ Χριστοῦ now descends upon Paul to empower him to incarnate the *ethos* of Jesus. Cf. MATERA, who makes a similar connection between John 1:14 and 2 Cor 12:9. See *II Corinthians*, 285.

Some commentators (e.g., PLUMMER, *II Corinthians*, 355; HUGHES, *Paul's Second Epistle to the Corinthians*, 452 and n. 141; HÉRING, *The Second Epistle of Saint Paul to the Corinthians*, 94; MARTIN, *2 Corinthians*, 421; and THRALL, *II Corinthians*, 2.828-29) hold that Paul has the OT concept of *Shekinah* – the presence of God, dwelling with God's people – in mind here. There may be something to this line of interpretation, though I contend that John 1:14 (which Martin does cite) comes closer to the apostle's thinking here.

This effect of the power of the risen Christ in and through Paul is the third summarizing dynamic. In 2 Cor 12:10 the apostle offers a short list of hardships endured "because of Christ": weaknesses, insults, troubles, persecutions, and calamities. This list recalls 4:8-9 (as well as 6:4-10). In the immediate context, it evokes the more detailed hardship catalog of 11:23b-29. There Paul makes dramatically clear that he endures many sufferings and hardships. In addition, the apostle alludes to his self-giving existence out of love for the sake of others. This is evident from Paul's references to his toils (11:27), his anxious concern for the well-being of the churches (11:28), and his empathic regard for the weaker members of those communities (11:29). As we have seen in examining 2:14-17 and 4:7-14, the apostle's sufferings and – even more – his self-emptying mode of existence are the ways by which he embodies the faithfulness of Jesus as God's δοῦλος.

Having set forth how Paul continues the story of Jesus' πίστις, we are now in a position to investigate how the apostle participates in the ministry of reconciliation.

V. Paul Participates in the Ongoing Ministry of Reconciliation

In Chapter Four, my analysis of God's act of reconciliation (2 Cor 5:18-21) focused on the role of Christ. Recall that Paul alludes to and draws upon the reconciling character and agency of Jesus in these verses (esp. 5:21a). But there is more to this story of reconciliation. Although the apostle makes clear that God has acted definitively in and through Christ, the work of reconciliation is ongoing. Observe how, after stating that it is God 'who has reconciled us through Christ,' Paul adds a parallel participial clause in 5:18: "*and* [it is God who] has given to us the ministry of reconciliation (τὴν διάκονίαν τῆς καταλλαγῆς)." Moreover, the apostle reiterates in 5:19 that God's action "in Christ "– whereby God no longer reckons the world's transgressions against it – is closely linked to the bestowal of "the message of reconciliation" (τὸν λόγον τῆς καταλλαγῆς).[735] That is, God's work of reconciliation continues through the ministry and message of reconciliation. Although God's act of

[735]For a helpful schematic view of the parallel features of 2 Cor 5:18-19, see R. BIERINGER, "Paul's Understanding of Diakonia in 2 Corinthians 5,18," in R. BIERINGER and J. LAMBRECHT, *Studies on 2 Corinthians*, BETL 112 (Leuven: Leuven University Press, 1994) 413-28, here 422.

reconciliation encompasses all those who are "in Christ" (cf. 5:17), God has entrusted the ministry and message of reconciliation more narrowly to Paul (and, presumably, to other apostles or leaders).[736]

In what follows, I look to the ways in which Paul participates in the ongoing work of reconciliation. First, I treat briefly his own self-description in 2 Cor 5:20-6:2. Second, I inquire into what the apostle means by the striking expression 'becoming the righteousness of God' in 5:21b. Third, I investigate the significance of Paul's claim in 11:7 that he 'lowers himself.' Fourth, I show how the apostle himself embodies the ministry of reconciliation. Lastly, I propose that he understands reconciliation in terms of σωτηρία ("salvation" – 6:2 and 7:9-10).

A. Paul, the "Ambassador" and "Co-worker" of Christ in the Ministry of Reconciliation (2 Cor 5:20-6:2)

Paul indicates in 2 Cor 5:20 that he continues the story of Jesus as the latter's envoy or ambassador. In 5:20a he states: ὑπὲρ Χριστοῦ οὖν πρεσβεύομεν ("Therefore, we[737] serve as ambassadors for Christ"). The verb

---

[736]Determining the referents of the first person plural pronouns is particularly difficult in 2 Cor 5:18-19. Given that Paul has just spoken broadly of all Christians in 5:17 (τις ἐν Χριστῷ), the referent of God's having reconciled *us* in 5:18a is most likely all Christians. This inclusive referent is confirmed by the fact that, in the apostle's explanation of 5:18a, he refers to God's reconciling *the world* in 5:19a. Although it is true that, broadly speaking, the ministry of reconciliation has been given to the entire church (5:18b), Paul and others exercise a special role in this ministry, as is evident from 5:19c, where he mentions the (proclaimed) *message* of reconciliation. It is certainly understandable that some commentators (e.g., BULTMANN, *The Second Letter to the Corinthians*, 161-62; and FURNISH, *II Corinthians*, 317) hold that the pronouns are inclusive throughout. Nevertheless, the content and sense of 5:18-19 – not to mention, the narrower use of "we" in 5:20a – demand, I believe, a change of referent in 5:19c. BIERINGER points out that Paul makes a similar shift in 1:3-4. See "Paul's Understanding of Diakonia in 2 Corinthians 5,18," 425.

[737] The subject of the first person plural πρεσβεύομεν is Paul and those who, like him, have been called to positions of leadership (minimally, Timothy and Silvanus, as well as Titus). This seems to be demanded both by the specialized sense implied by "ambassador," as well as by the fact that in 6:1-2 – which parallels 5:20 in many respects, and follows upon it almost immediately – the apostle distinguishes between "we" and

πρεσβεύω means "be an envoy/ambassador."[738] As Philip E. Hughes has pointed out, an ambassador or envoy (πρεσβευτής) "speaks not only on behalf of but also in the place of the sovereign from whom he has received his commission."[739] Here the apostle serves ὑπὲρ Χριστοῦ, in Christ's stead as his representative. As Jesus manifested God and God's ways, similarly Paul and his fellow workers now serve as conduits for God's word – "God, as it were, appealing through us" (5:20a). Moreover, the apostle immediately offers an example of his speaking on Christ's behalf and in his stead (note the second use of ὑπὲρ Χριστοῦ): "Be reconciled to God!" (5:20b). Thus, Paul participates in God's work of reconciliation by exhorting people, as Christ's ambassador, to be reconciled to God. And as the twofold use of the phrase ὑπὲρ Χριστοῦ in 5:20 intimates, the apostle sees his ambassadorial role in terms of continuing the story of Jesus.

Paul offers a similar self-description in 2 Cor 6:1 with the participle συνεργοῦντες – that is, he identifies himself as a "co-worker." But a co-worker of whom? Several exegetes maintain that the apostle claims here to work with God.[740] The immediately (prior) adjacent antecedent of

---

"you" (i.e., the Corinthians).

738See BDAG, s.v. πρεσβεύω. In addition, see *TLNT*, 3.174-76. Cf. Eph 6:20 (and Phlm 9, where, according to some MSS, Paul uses the substantive πρεσβευτής).

739HUGHES, *Paul's Second Epistle to the Corinthians*, 209-10; similarly, BULTMANN, *The Second Letter to the Corinthians*, 163.

740So, e.g, HUGHES, *Paul's Second Epistle to the Corinthians*, 216; HÉRING, *The Second Epistle of Saint Paul to the Corinthians*, 46; BARRETT, *The Second Epistle to the Corinthians*, 183; FURNISH, *II Corinthians*, 341; MARTIN, *2 Corinthians*, 165; THRALL, *II Corinthians*, 1.451; BELLEVILLE, *2 Corinthians*, 162; BARNETT, *The Second Epistle to the Corinthians*, 316; and KISTEMAKER, *The Second Epistle to the Corinthians*, 208. Thrall sums up well the rationale: "In relation to 5.20, where God is the subject of παρακαλέω, it is most natural to suppose that in 6.1 it is with God that Paul sees himself co-operating." PLUMMER (*II Corinthians*, 189) and BULTMANN (*The Second Letter to the Corinthians*, 166), while advocating that Paul claims to work with God, hold that co-operating *with Christ* is also a possibility. This is the position that I take.

Other interpretations have been offered. ALLO proposes that here Paul expresses that he works with the Corinthians. See *Seconde Épître aux Corinthiens*, 173;

συνεργοῦντες, however, is the object of the prepositional phrase ἐν αὐτῷ (5:21b). This pronoun refers to "the one who did not know Sin," namely Jesus (5:21a). Thus, I propose that Paul claims here to be *Jesus'* co-worker. This reading finds further support in the apostle's twofold use of ὑπὲρ Χριστοῦ in 5:20. In addition, notice that Paul later refers in 6:1 to "the grace of *God*" (τὴν χάριν τοῦ θεοῦ). If God were the established antecedent of σύν (in the participle συνεργοῦντες), we would expect the phrase τὴν χάριν *αὐτοῦ*.

What does being Jesus' co-worker entail? The role is similar to that of Christ's ambassador, in which the apostle co-operates with Jesus by "making an appeal" (παρακαλέω, 2 Cor 6:1; cf. 5:20). Here Paul appeals specifically to the Corinthians not to receive God's grace in vain (6:1). Moreover, just as the apostle as Jesus' envoy sets forth a dramatic exhortation ("Be reconciled to God"!; 5:20b), so does he as Christ's συνεργός set forth a stirring proclamation: "Behold, *now* is an acceptable time! Behold, *now* is a day of salvation!" (6:2b).

A closer look at 2 Cor 6:1-2, however, suggests that Paul's role as Jesus' co-worker involves more than such verbal exhortation. The apostle's proclamation in 6:2b is his own restatement of two lines from LXX Isa 49:8 – "At an acceptable time I have heard you, and on a day of salvation I have helped you" – lines he cites verbatim in 2 Cor 6:2a. I will look more closely at this citation's context later in this section. For the time being, it is sufficient to point out that LXX Isa 49:1-13 contains God's commission of a figure referred to as God's δοῦλος (LXX Isa 49:3 and 49:5). As we will see, in contemporizing this text, Paul places himself in this very role.[741] This is not surprising, given that

---

cf. BACHMANN, *Der zweite Brief des Paulus an die Korinther*, 274. Observe, however, that in 6:1 the apostle is *appealing* to the Corinthians, not expressing his co-operation with them. BRUCE (*1 and 2 Corinthians*, 211) holds that Paul refers here to "fellow workers," presumably other apostles and leaders. This interpretation presumes, however, that the plural participle refers solely to Paul himself, which is doubtful.

[741] Indeed, other commentators have rightly recognized the significance of the context and imagery of LXX Isa 49 in their interpretation of 2 Cor 6:2. See PLUMMER, *II Corinthians*, 190-91; YOUNG and FORD, *Meaning and Truth in 2 Corinthians*, 76-77; DANKER, *II Corinthians*, 85; and G.K. BEALE, "The Old Testament Background of Reconciliation in 2 Corinthians 5-7 and Its Bearing on the Literary Problem of 2 Corinthians 6.14-7.1," *NTS* 35 (1989) 550-81, here 561-64. *Pace* LAMBRECHT, who summarily dismisses the possibility that Paul draws upon the Isaianic context in 6:2. See

he portrays himself as the co-worker of Jesus, the δοῦλος of God *par excellence*. Furthermore, observe that the term co-*worker* implies something more than speaking in the stead of another; it also connotes *doing* something, that is, *laboring* with another. Indeed, the expressions 'becoming the righteousness of God' (5:21b) and 'lowering oneself' (see 11:7) offer important clues to the fact that the apostle's collaboration in the ministry of reconciliation also consists of embodying the character and mode of existence revealed by Jesus, the δοῦλος of God.

B. Paul's Becoming δικαιοσύνη θεοῦ in Christ (2 Cor 5:21b)

It is now time to take up the second half of 2 Cor 5:21, where Paul expresses the *purpose* of God's having made Christ – "the one who did not know Sin" – to be "sin." Second Corinthians 5:21b reads: ἵνα ἡμεῖς γενώμεθα δικαιοσύνη θεοῦ ἐν αὐτῷ ("in order that in [Christ] *we*[742] might become the righteousness of God"). This is an extraordinary claim. The apostle does not say here that he receives the status of (imputed) righteousness as a gift, nor does he state that he (verbally) proclaims God's righteousness. Rather, Paul refers to the possibility of *becoming* (γίνομαι) the righteousness of God. In order to understand what the apostle means here, it is necessary to ask what is signified by the phrase δικαιοσύνη θεοῦ, and to see how he uses it elsewhere.

What does δικαιοσύνη θεοῦ mean for Paul? The answer to this question lies in the resolution of two interconnected issues: (1) What kind of genitive is θεοῦ?; and (2) Does righteousness refer primarily to something

"The Favorable Time: A Study of 2 Corinthians 6,2a in Its Context," in R. BIERINGER and J. LAMBRECHT, *Studies on 2 Corinthians*, BETL 112 (Leuven: Leuven University Press, 1994) 515-29, here 524.

742The pronoun ἡμεῖς adds emphasis. I take the referent here to be, primarily, Paul and others like him who have been commissioned to be Christ's ambassadors (5:20) and co-workers (6:1), and thus who have a special role in the work of reconciliation. Similarly, WRIGHT, "On Becoming the Righteousness of God," 203. Nevertheless, as we will see in the following paragraphs, the logic of the apostle's understanding of δικαιοσύνη θεοῦ implies that *all* Christians are to become the righteousness of God in some manner.

belonging to God, or to a human status before God?[743] Traditionally, θεοῦ has been taken as a genitive of origin, with the phrase interpreted as denoting the righteousness that God bestows upon people. More specifically, this line of interpretation has concentrated on the *effect* of God's act of justification of sinners.[744] Thus, for example, C.K. Barrett interprets 2 Cor 5:21b as indicating that "we are acquitted in [God's] court, justified, reconciled."[745] Ernst Käsemann rightly objected to this reading as one inappropriately centered on the "gifted" aspect of God's righteousness, thereby focusing too narrowly on the anthropological question. Rather, he proposed reading θεοῦ as a subjective genitive, thereby understanding the expression δικαιοσύνη θεοῦ to refer in the first place to *God*, and more precisely, to God's salvation-creating power. By insisting, however, that God's power is for the whole world – and not just for

---

[743]For a helpful diagram that sets forth all the possible answers to these questions, see N.T. WRIGHT, *What Saint Paul Really Said: Was Paul of Tarsus the Real Founder of Christianity?* (Grand Rapids, Mich.: Eerdmans, 1997) 101. In addition, see R.K. MOORE, "2 Cor 5,21: The Interpretative Key to Paul's Use of *ΔΙΚΑΙΟΣΥΝΗ ΘΕΟΥ*?" in *The Corinthian Correpondence*, BETL 125, ed. R. BIERINGER (Leuven: Leuven University Press, 1996) 707-15, here 712-13.

[744]R. BULTMANN is the classic expositor of this position. See, e.g., "ΔΙΚΑΙΟΣΥΝΗ ΘΕΟΥ," *JBL* 83 (1964) 12-16.

[745]BARRETT, *The Second Epistle to the Corinthians*, 180. Cf. BRUCE, *1 and 2 Corinthians*, 211: "Paul has chosen this exceptional wording in order to emphasize the 'sweet exchange' whereby sinners are given a righteous status by God. . ."; and HUGHES, *Paul's Second Epistle to the Corinthians*, 214: "It is, in a word, the sinner's *justification* of which the Apostle is speaking. . ." (Hughes's italics). The implication of the traditional position is that God's righteousness is imputed to believers. Other commentators, however, hold that δικαιοσύνη in 2 Cor 5:21 refers to the *moral* righteousness of Christians. That is, their righteousness is something that they actually possess by God's grace, rather than something imputed to them by God. See, e.g., WINDISCH, *Der zweite Korintherbrief*, 199; and ALLO, *Seconde Épître aux Corinthiens*, 172: ". . . la 'justice de Dieu,' en ce passage, signifie bien une *justice reçue en nous*." While this latter interpretation is closer to the mark, it fails to take into account the entire dynamic implicit in Paul's understanding.

Israel – Käsemann downplayed any covenantal connotations.[746] N.T. Wright has offered a crucial refinement of Käsemann's position. Wright holds that the genitive is both subjective and possessive – that is, it refers both to God's activity *and* to an attribute belonging to God.[747] Moreover, against Käsemann, Wright insists that for the apostle δικαιοσύνη θεοῦ is a technical term for the covenant-faithfulness of Israel's God. Wright's reading of δικαιοσύνη θεοῦ will (in the main) be borne out in my argument.[748]

Beyond 2 Cor 5:21b, Paul refers to δικαιοσύνη θεοῦ in Rom 1:17, 3:5, 3:21, 3:22, 3:25, 3:26, and 10:3 (2x), as well as in Phil 3:9.[749] Notice that Rom 3:5 is sandwiched between references to God's faithfulness (3:3) and God's truthfulness (3:7), a fact that supports reading δικαιοσύνη θεοῦ as a possessive genitive: righteousness as an attribute belonging to God. In addition, observe that, with the exception of Rom 10:3, all the other instances of the phrase in question occur in the context of the apostle's discussion of *how* God's righteousness has been revealed through the faithfulness of Jesus (πίστις Χριστοῦ). I refer my reader to the discussion of Rom 1:17 and 3:21-26 in Chapter Three, where I focused on the role and meaning of Jesus' πίστις.[750] For the present, it is sufficient to recall that Paul claims that "the law and the prophets" (Rom 3:21; cf. 1:2) bear witness to the revelation of God's

---

[746]See E. KÄSEMANN, "'The Righteousness of God' in Paul," in *New Testament Questions of Today*, trans. W. J. MONTAGUE (Philadelphia: Fortress Press, 1969) 168-82.

[747]See WRIGHT, *What Saint Paul Really Said*, 103: "Since, for Paul, God is the creator, always active within his world, we should expect, in the nature of the case, to find his attributes and his actions belonging closely together." In addition, WRIGHT observes that "a 'subjective' genitive implies that *the noun governed carries a verbal sense. . . .*" See "On Becoming the Righteousness of God," 201 (italics added).

[748]For more on WRIGHT'S interpretation, see "On Becoming the Righteousness of God," 200-208, including 202, n. 5, and the bibliography provided there. I express my misgivings with Wright's overall project above (see Chapter Three, Section I.B).

[749]In Rom 3:25-26 the phrase δικαιοσύνη αὐτοῦ clearly refers to *God's* righteousness. Rom 10:3 shows that Paul intends no difference in meaning by the variation of syntax (i.e., τὴν τοῦ θεοῦ δικαιοσύνην = τῇ δικαιοσύνῃ τοῦ θεοῦ).

[750]I will take up Phil 3:9 immediately below in this section.

righteousness through Christ's faithfulness, a testimony that intimates that this revelation is intimately linked with God's covenantal purposes. Moreover, the apostle's use of the passive voice verbs ἀποκαλύπτεται (Rom 1:17) and πεφανέρωται (Rom 3:21) suggests that *God* was acting in and through Jesus, thereby substantiating the subjective genitive rendering of δικαιοσύνη θεοῦ. In addition, the perfect tense of πεφανέρωται indicates that God's activity has *ongoing effects* in the present.

This aspect of the *continuing* ramifications of God's righteousness, I suggest, illuminates Paul's statement in 2 Cor 5:21b. In his thesis statement in Rom 1:17, the apostle writes that God's righteousness has been revealed ἐκ πίστεως εἰς πίστιν. We have seen that ἐκ πίστεως is Paul's shorthand for "out of/through Christ's faithfulness." What about εἰς πίστιν? The preposition εἰς here marks the goal or result of an action.[751] That is, God's righteousness has been revealed through Jesus' πίστις with the goal of bringing about faithfulness (presumably, in others). The apostle offers further clarification in his restatement of the thesis in Rom 3:22. There Paul states that the revelation of God's righteousness through Christ is εἰς πάντας τοὺς πιστεύοντας, thereby suggesting that the goal of God's activity is *human* faithfulness (cf. "all those who are faithful"). Similarly, in Phil 3:9, in the course of contrasting his own righteousness with the δικαιοσύνη that is ἐκ θεοῦ, the apostle makes clear that the latter is through the "faithfulness of Christ."[752] Furthermore, God's righteousness is described as ἐπὶ τῇ πίστει, as

---

[751]See BDAG, s.v. εἰς, 4.e-f. Cf. Rom 6:16; 2 Cor 7:9; and Eph 2:21. This usage shades into denoting purpose as well.

[752]Cf. HOOKER, *NIB*, 11.528: ". . . we expect the righteousness that is opposed to what [Paul] terms his own righteousness to be that which belongs to Christ himself. . . . This righteousness would then be understood as being '*from* God' but *through* the faithfulness of Christ. . . . we should note that it is appropriate if Paul has Christ's own faith or faithfulness in mind here, in view of what was said in 2:6-11 about Christ's self-emptying and obedience (the result of faith!) and consequent vindication. . . . it seems likely that the genitive is subjective and that Paul is thinking here of the righteousness that is shared by those in Christ because of the faithfulness of Christ himself." While I share Hooker's decision to render πίστις Χριστοῦ as a subjective genitive in Phil 3:9, I am uneasy about her uncritical conflation of the terms "faith" and "faithfulness" (see Chapter Four, Section V).

the righteousness "which leads to/is for the purpose of faithfulness."[753] As Phil 3:10-11 indicates, this πίστις involves following the pattern of living and dying as revealed by Jesus.[754] Hence, Rom 1:17 and 3:21-22 – along with Phil 3:9 – strongly suggest that the ongoing effect of God's righteousness (revealed in the past through Christ's πίστις) now entails human faithfulness, a faithfulness understood as embodying Jesus' manner of existence.

Romans 10:3, in which Paul twice mentions "God's righteousness," does not at first glance seem to conform to the foregoing interpretation. In particular, there is no explicit reference here to πίστις Χριστοῦ. Notice, however, that the apostle does contrast seeking (ζητέω) one's own righteousness (referring to his Jewish "brethren," cf. Rom 9:3) with submitting to God's righteousness – the same contrast made in Phil 3:9. Moreover, it is crucial to take into account how Paul grounds his statement about the Jews' misdirected zeal with his comment in Rom 10:4: "*for* (γάρ) the τέλος of [the] law is Christ εἰς δικαιοσύνην παντὶ τῷ πιστεύοντι." In saying that Christ is the τέλος of Torah, the apostle suggests that Messiah Jesus is the goal toward which the law and the prophets bore witness and pointed (Rom 3:21). Christ is "the end" of the law insofar as he brought to fulfillment all God's promises (cf. 2 Cor 1:20a).[755] Furthermore, observe what Paul claims is the purpose and result[756] of Christ's coming: δικαιοσύνη. This "righteousness" is "for everyone who is faithful." In other words, the apostle intimates in Rom 10:3-4 that God's righteousness is closely linked with what was made manifest by

---

[753]See BDAG, s.v. ἐπί, 16, for reading ἐπί + dative as marking purpose. Cf. Gal 5:13 and 1 Thess 4:7. Although Paul's formulation in Phil 3:9 differs slightly (τὴν [δικαιοσύνην] ἐκ θεοῦ), WRIGHT is wrong to dismiss its relevance to the discussion of δικαιοσύνη θεοῦ. See *What Saint Paul Really Said*, 104. *Pace* Wright, I contend that the context and content of Phil 3:9 – not Wright's schematic view of the intricacies of the Hebrew law court – ought to determine the reading of δικαιοσύνη ἐκ θεοῦ.

[754]Observe in Phil 3:10-11 the presence of cognitive terminology in conjunction with the character and story of Jesus: "that I might *know* [Christ] and the power of his resurrection and the sharing of his sufferings, being conformed in his death, that I may attain the resurrection from the dead."

[755]See, e.g., G. E. HOWARD, "Christ the End of the Law: The Meaning of Romans 10:4ff," *JBL* 88 (1969) 331-37.

[756]Reading εἰς in the same manner as in Rom 1:17 and 3:22.

Christ, *and* that God's righteousness continues to be effective in all human beings who are faithful.[757] This is the same pattern we observed in Rom 1:17 and 3:21-26, as well as in Phil 3:9.

Returning to the interpretation of 2 Cor 5:21b: It is no coincidence that earlier in the epistle Paul linked God's fidelity (1:18a), Jesus' ναί in fulfillment of God's promises (1:19b-20a, thereby expressing God's covenantal faithfulness!), and the "Amen" to God of those empowered by the Spirit (1:20b-22). Recall that both Jesus' Yes and the ἀμήν of others refer to *human* faithfulness to God and God's ways. First and foremost Christ, and then those who have been 'christed' by the Spirit, embody the goodness and character of God through their πίστις. In the more immediate context of 5:21b, Paul once again reminds the Corinthians that God is the source of saving activity – τὰ πάντα ἐκ τοῦ θεοῦ (5:18a). The phrase "all things" (τὰ πάντα) refers here to what is contained in 5:14-17. "All things" includes "the love of Christ," which was revealed in his dying for all, and which now impels people to live for the benefit of others (5:14-15). Such existence lived in loving service of others – which embodies Jesus' πίστις and is a manifestation of the "new creation" (5:17; cf. the reference there to τις ἐν Χριστῷ) – is thus included in God's saving activity ("all things"). I propose, furthermore, that the apostle repeats this pattern in 5:18-21. God has acted to bring about reconciliation (5:18a and 5:19a). Moreover, God has done so through the agency and character of Jesus, "the one who did not know Sin," whom God "made 'sin'" (5:21a).[758] And, as was the case in the passages reviewed in the preceding paragraphs, the dynamic of God's activity is directed to a purpose or goal involving human beings: "*in order that* we might become δικαιοσύνη θεοῦ" (5:21b).

So what does Paul mean by this remarkable statement? I suggest that he alludes to being empowered to incarnate the mode of human existence manifested by Jesus. The apostle refers here to living in obedience to God and

---

[757]Cf. the RSV's translation of Rom 10:4: "For Christ is the end of the law, that every one who has faith may be justified." Observe how this takes great liberties with the Greek text, especially in rendering the prepositional phrase εἰς δικαιοσύνην as a passive verb.

[758]Cf. P. STUHLMACHER: ". . . daß Paulus unter Gottes Gerechtigkeit die Treue des Schöpfers zu seiner Kreatur versteht. 2. Kor. 5,21 zeigte, daß Christus die Verkörperung dieser Schöpfertreue ist." See *Gerechtigkeit Gottes bei Paulus*, 2nd ed., FRLANT 87 (Göttingen: Vandenhoeck & Ruprecht, 1966) 208.

in loving service of others. Thus, whereas in Rom 1:17 and 3:21-22 Paul writes about how God's righteousness has been revealed in the past through Jesus' πίστις, in 2 Cor 5:21b he mentions how God's righteousness *continues to be revealed* through those who embody Christ's faithfulness. In this manner, the apostle continues the story of Jesus' πίστις.[759]

Two further observations from 2 Cor 5:21b support this reading. First, I look to the significance of the verb γενώμεθα. Recall that γίνομαι can denote a change of nature or an entry into a new condition.[760] Paul's use of γίνομαι in 5:21b echoes his use in 1:19, where he states that Jesus did not become (ἐγένετο) Yes and No, but in him the Yes has come to be (γέγονεν). As previously indicated, the perfect tense indicates that Jesus did something in the past – namely, he chose to obey God's will, and continued throughout his life to say Yes to God – that resulted in his entering a new condition that continues to have effects in the present. In fact, the apostle refers to these continuing effects in 5:17. Indeed, we have just seen how the references there to a "new creation" and being "in Christ" allude to those who follow Jesus' mode of loving, self-giving existence. It is little wonder then that Paul exclaims, "Behold! New things *have come to be* (γέγονεν)!"

The second textual clue in 2 Cor 5:21b in support of my reading of this passage is the prepositional phrase ἐν αὐτῷ: "in *Christ*" (the obvious referent of the pronoun). Paul inserts this phrase prominently in the end position, thereby adding emphasis. The preposition ἐν here marks the cause or reason: It is *because of Christ* that the apostle and others can embody the former's πίστις.[761] That is, Jesus modeled forth obedience to God and living for the advantage of others; moreover, Paul is empowered through the gift of the Spirit,

---

[759]Indeed, SAMPLEY suggests that 2 Cor 5:21 recasts the story told in Phil 2:5-11 and 2 Cor 8:9. His insight into the logic of 5:21b is right on target: "From the clues one can see widely in the Pauline corpus, being reconciled to God implies some responsibilities to represent the righteousness of God to others." See *NIB*, 11.96.

[760]See n. 383. *Pace* MOORE, "2 Cor 5,21: The Interpretative Key to Paul's Use of *ΔΙΚΑΙΟΣΥΝΗ ΘΕΟΥ*?" 214: "Here γίνεσθαι seems to make better sense when understood as the equivalent of εἶναι." On the contrary, a careful reader should take the apostle's choice of γίνομαι – and *not* εἰμί – seriously here.

[761]See BDAG, s.v. ἐν, 9.a, and n. 596. This use can shade into understanding ἐν in an instrumental sense. Cf. LAMBRECHT, *Second Corinthians*, 101.

who *christs* people into the likeness of Jesus (1:21b). Thus, God's righteousness continues to be revealed through the apostle's "Christ-shaped ministry."[762] Given that 5:18-21 speaks of God's work of reconciliation – work which included the reconciling demeanor and agency of Jesus – I submit that the ongoing revelation of God's righteousness in Paul is characterized specifically by the apostle's reconciling demeanor and agency as well. As we will see, he uses a striking phrase to express (at least in part) this mode of reconciling behavior: ταπεινοῦν ἑαυτόν.

C. *Paul and ταπεινοῦν ἑαυτόν (2 Cor 11:7)*

In 2 Cor 11:7 Paul asks ironically: "Did I commit sin by lowering myself (ἐμαυτὸν ταπεινῶν) in order that you might be lifted up (ὑψωθῆτε), because I preached the gospel of God to you as a free gift?" The context of the apostle's rhetorical question is that he has come under attack for not taking financial support from the Corinthians for his work among them (11:7-11). Apparently, other missionaries/evangelists (the so-called "superlative apostles"; cf. 11:5 and 12:11) have come to the community and taken remuneration (see 11:12). Paul's insistence that he not take payment from the Corinthians – while simultaneously asking them to give generously to the collection for the church

---

[762]The phrase is WRIGHT'S. See "On Becoming the Righteousness of God," 206. Wright translates 5:21b: "so that in him we might become God's covenant-faithfulness." Whereas Wright stresses the notion of God's covenant-faithfulness, my accent falls on how that faithfulness is revealed through the πίστις of Jesus (first and foremost), as well as through those like Paul who incarnate the mode of Christ's faithfulness. Nevertheless, our interpretations are similar in many respects. Indeed, I agree wholeheartedly with his assessment that Paul "actually *becomes* the living embodiment of his sovereign. . .," i.e., of Jesus (ibid., Wright's italics).

The following remarks by M.D. HOOKER are apposite here: "It is clear, then, that Paul's notion of interchange does not mean simply that Christians 'become what he is' in the sense that they share in Christ's status before God; if they are made 'the righteousness of God in him,' that implies *moral* righteousness – and when we ask Paul what behaviour is appropriate for those who are 'in Christ,' then he appeals to the example of Christ himself." See HOOKER, "Interchange in Christ and Ethics," *JSNT* 25 (1985) 3-17, here 9-10.

in Jerusalem – has brought him under a cloud of suspicion.[763] My interest here is with the apostle's self-understanding of his *modus operandi*, namely that he "lowers himself." Although he makes sparse use of the verb ταπεινόω and the adjectival form ταπεινός, it is significant to note that four of the seven combined instances occur in 2 Corinthians.[764]

What is the significance of Paul's use of the phrase ταπεινόω + the reflexive pronoun (signifying "lower/humble oneself")? Strikingly, the apostle uses this construction in only one other place, Phil 2:8, where *Jesus* is the subject: "[Christ Jesus] lowered himself (ἐταπείνωσεν ἑαυτόν), becoming obedient unto death, death on a cross." Observe that Paul is in the midst of exhorting the Philippians to concern themselves with others' interests rather than their own, and to regard others as better than themselves (Phil 2:3-4). Indeed, the apostle proposes Jesus as the prototype (2:6-8) for living in service of others "by means of humility" (τῇ *ταπεινο*φροσύνῃ, 2:3)[765] and in obedience to God (cf. γενόμενος ὑπήκοος, 2:8). As Jesus lowered himself by becoming obedient even unto death, an act of love through which God has brought about reconciliation, so Paul lowers himself by preaching the good news of God (including the message of reconciliation!) as a free gift, that is, without imposing on or taking advantage of the Corinthians (cf. 2 Cor 11:21a).[766] Thus, the idiom ταπεινόω + reflexive pronoun in 2 Cor 11:7 strongly suggests that

---

[763]In discussing the cultural background of 2 Cor 11:7-11, scholars point to two main aspects. First is the Sophists' practice of charging for instruction, utilizing the premise that what is taught for free is worth nothing. See, e.g., PLUMMER, *II Corinthians*, 302; and HUGHES, *Paul's Second Epistle to the Corinthians*, 383. Second is the Greek bias that held in low esteem the practice of someone like Paul supporting himself by a trade (e.g., tentmaking). See, e.g., R.F. HOCK, *The Social Context of Paul's Ministry: Tentmaking and Apostleship* (Philadelphia: Fortress, 1980) esp. 50-65. My approach here is to focus on the clues that *the apostle himself* gives to us.

[764]The verb appears twice in both 2 Cor (11:7 and 12:21) and Phil (2:8 and 4:12). The adjective occurs in Rom 12:16, as well as in 2 Cor 7:6 and 10:1.

[765]THOMPSON rightly comments that the example of Jesus lies behind Paul's exhortation to the Philippians to embody ταπεινοφροσύνη. See *Clothed with Christ*, 216.

[766]So, too, ZMIJEWSKI, *Der Stil der paulinischen "Narrenrede"*, 124-25.

the apostle considers his activity as following in the reconciling manner of Jesus.

Second Corinthians 10:1b supports this claim. In this passage Paul concedes that he has been "lowly" (ταπεινός) among the Corinthians. The apostle's placement of this "admission" is notable. It occurs in the wake of his exhorting the Corinthians "by the gentleness and forbearance of Christ" (10:1a). That is, Paul aligns himself here with the *ethos* of Jesus, namely his πραΰτης and ἐπιείκεια.[767] And recall from the discussion in the previous chapter that these characteristics of Jesus pertain in particular to what promotes reconciliation – patience, slowness to anger, non-retaliation, and the willingness to forgive (even enemies and persecutors).[768]

---

[767]Notice that in Matt 11:29 Jesus' being "gentle" (πραΰς) is connected with his being "lowly/humble in heart" (ταπεινὸς τῇ καρδίᾳ). GÜTTGEMANNS observes the ὅς-introduction in 2 Cor 10:1b, the presence of Χριστός immediately before ὅς, and the particular characteristics of Christ highlighted in 10:1a. He then intriguingly suggests that 2 Cor 10:1b sounds like the beginning of a christological hymn (cf. Phil 2:6-11; Col 1:15-20; and 1 Tim 3:16). See *Der leidende Apostel und sein Herr*, 135-41. Although Güttgemanns is reductionistic in the way he understands Paul to make Christ manifest (namely, *only* through the apostle's weakness), his suggestion has merit in that the apostle does see himself as continuing the story of Jesus. MATERA notes the ambiguity of the Greek, observing that ὅς appears at first glance to refer to Christ. See *II Corinthians*, 217.

[768]Cf., moreover, 2 Cor 7:6, where Paul describes God as "the one who comforts the *lowly*" – ὁ παρακαλῶν τοὺς ταπεινούς – and then associates himself with the lowly whom God comforts. This recalls the story of Jesus' faithfulness alluded to in 4:13. Part of this story involves God's responding to and saving the righteous sufferer, who twice describes himself as "brought down low" (cf. ἐταπεινώθην, LXX Pss 114:6b and 115:1b). Hence, once again the apostle parallels his story with that of Jesus.

The fourth instance of ταπειν- terminology in 2 Cor can also support my interpretation. In 12:21 Paul expresses his fear that "my God might humble me before you" (ταπεινώσῃ με ὁ θεός μου πρὸς ὑμᾶς). The context here is that the apostle is afraid that he might find the community exhibiting, e.g., jealousy (ζῆλος), selfishness (ἐριθεία), and arrogance (φυσίωσις). Observe that these characteristics are the opposite of what Jesus manifested – love (2 Cor 5:14-15), living and dying for others (Gal 2:20b and Eph 5:2), and lowering himself (Phil 2:8). Although Paul's "being lowered" in 2 Cor 12:21 does not seem to be directly for the sake of lifting up the Corinthians (as in 11:7), I submit that it is a consequence of his submission to God's will, which entails the apostle's endurance of constant pressure and anxiety for the churches

That the apostle patterns himself after Jesus is also evident from the oath formula in 2 Cor 11:10a: ἐστιν ἀλήθεια Χριστοῦ ἐν ἐμοι ("[as the] truth of Christ is in me").[769] I submit that Paul indicates more by this expression than merely the notion of "truth-telling,"[770] although this is certainly included in the formulation. The apostle uses this phraseology to claim that his manner of lowering himself for the sake of the Corinthians is an embodiment of the manner of existence revealed by Jesus.[771] This is in line with 4:2, in which Paul self-*commends* "by means of the manifestation of the *truth*" (τῇ φανερώσει τῆς ἀληθείας). The latter expression involves his bearing the νέκρωσις τοῦ

---

he founded (cf. 11:28-29), and which includes the possibility of having to mourn for recalcitrant members (12:21). Cf. MATERA, *II Corinthians*, 300: "Paul's work, however, is not his own but belongs to God. . . . When Paul speaks of God humbling him before the Corinthians, therefore, he does so because he is doing God's work and not merely his own. Put another way, Paul is *not* saying that God will humble him to punish him. Rather, Paul is revealing his profound understanding of himself as God's coworker who endures everything for the sake of God" (Matera's italics).

[769]For reading 2 Cor 11:10a as an oath formula, see BULTMANN, *The Second Letter to the Corinthians*, 206. HUGHES (*Paul's Second Epistle*, 389) prefers to describe it as an asseveration. THRALL rightly points out that "[o]pinions differ as to whether we have here an actual oath formula, but in substance the assertion performs this function." See *II Corinthians*, 2.687.

[770]*Pace* FURNISH, *II Corinthians*, 493.

[771]MARTIN rightly reads Χριστοῦ as a subjective genitive – i.e., as "Christ's truth" (see *2 Corinthians*, 347). Keeping in mind WRIGHT'S observation that the governed noun in a subjective genitive carries a verbal sense (see n. 747), "Christ's truth" here would refer, at least in large part, to the *way* Jesus *manifested* or *embodied* truth. THRALL proposes that, by stating Christ's truth is '*in* me,' Paul refers to the indwelling of Christ within him (see *II Corinthians*, 2.687-88). I would qualify Thrall's statement in the following manner: By the 'christing' power of the Spirit, the apostle is empowered to manifest in his own life and words the mode of human existence revealed by Jesus, the true and authentic image of God. HUGHES captures this well: "As it is [Paul's] great mission in life to propagate the truth of Christ, so it is essential that his own language and conduct should be in conformity with the example of absolute truthfulness set by Christ." See *Paul's Second Epistle to the Corinthians*, 389. In fact, 2 Cor 11:10 gives flesh to Paul's claim in 6:8 that, although he and his co-workers are considered to be "deceivers, yet [we are] true (ἀληθεῖς)."

'Ιησοῦ and being handed over διὰ 'Ιησοῦν (4:10-11). And it is no coincidence that the apostle's motive in 11:7-11 – ἀγάπη (11:11) – reflects the "love of Christ" (5:14), the love through which God has brought about the work of reconciliation (5:18-19).

The very context of 2 Cor 11:7-11 suggests, furthermore, that ταπεινοῦν ἑαυτόν involves more specifically the work of reconciliation. Paul lowers himself by proclaiming the gospel to the Corinthians without receiving any support from them; he refuses to be a burden to them (11:7-9). It is crucial to point out that the apostle's defense of his working among the Corinthians without taking payment from them is not a new development. In fact, he had previously discussed this very topic with the community in 1 Cor 9:1-27 (esp. vv. 12 and 15-19). There, in a consideration of the propriety of eating meat sacrificed to idols (1 Cor 8 and 10), Paul held himself up as an example of one who sets aside his own rights for the sake of his brothers and sisters. The apostle's concern in 1 Cor 8-10 was to build up the community, an entity threatened by some who were "puffed up" by their own knowledge and sense of superiority (e.g., 1 Cor 8:9-12 and 10:24-33). By forgoing his rights to remuneration, Paul set an example of seeking not his own advantage, but that of others. This coheres with his exhortations in Phil 2:3-4 to act *not* out of selfishness or conceit, but rather to regard others as better and to serve their interests. Observe that this attitude and way of behavior are what are necessary not only for building up community but also for *facilitating reconciliation* among its members.[772] Indeed, it is striking how the apostle himself embodies the ministry of reconciliation throughout 2 Corinthians. It is to this topic that I now turn.

D. Paul Embodies the Ministry of Reconciliation

In 2 Cor 5:18-19 Paul describes God's act of reconciling people to God's self, thereby restoring the divine-human relationship that had been marred by human transgressions. While the apostle makes clear that God has acted definitively through Christ, nevertheless the work of reconciliation is an ongoing

---

[772]Paul's succinct summary of his mode of behavior in 1 Cor 9 is telling: He says that he has made himself a slave (δουλοῦν ἑαυτόν) to all (9:19). I submit that it is as δοῦλος that the apostle concludes his treatment in 1 Cor 8-10 by exhorting the Corinthians: "Be imitators of me, as I am of Christ," the δοῦλος of God *par excellence* (1 Cor 11:1).

phenomenon. Indeed, Paul himself participates in the dynamic of restoring relationships that have broken down.[773] In addition to proclaiming as Jesus' envoy the message "Be reconciled to God" (5:20), the apostle "co-labors" with Christ in the διακονία τῆς καταλλαγῆς by working to foster reconciliation among the Corinthians, between himself and the Corinthians, and between the gentile churches he founded and the church in Jerusalem.

In 2 Cor 2:5-10 Paul refers to an unnamed person (τις) who in some manner had caused pain to him.[774] Observe how the apostle, notwithstanding, immediately broadens the scope of the harm involved in the incident to include harm to the entire community. That is, he insists that *all* (πάντας ὑμᾶς, 2:5b) have been hurt by this incident. In fact, Paul twice uses the perfect tense λελύπηκεν (2:5a) to indicate that what happened continues to have deleterious effects. The apostle also alludes to a punishment (ἐπιτιμία) administered against the offending person by the majority of the community (2:6), an action that came about after he had written to them in anguish and tears (2:4). Now, in 2:7-8, Paul exhorts the community to forgive and comfort this person, and to confirm their love for him. In short, the apostle urges the Corinthians to restore the offending party to their community. Moreover, Paul himself takes the initiative and sets an example to the Corinthians by offering his own forgiveness – ᾧ τι χαρίζεσθε, κἀγω (2:10). Indeed, the apostle's pressing concern for reconciliation among members of the community is evident from his final

---

[773]Cf. GARLAND, *2 Corinthians*, 291-92: "The ministry of reconciliation therefore involves more than simply explaining to others what God has done in Christ. It requires that one become an active reconciler oneself. Like Christ, a minister of reconciliation plunges into the midst of human tumult to bring harmony out of chaos, reconciliation out of estrangement, and love in the place of hate."

[774]Both the identity of the offender and the nature of the offense to which 2 Cor 2:5-10 (and 7:8-12) alludes are debated. For a good presentation and critical assessment of the various hypotheses, see THRALL, *II Corinthians*, 1.61-69. Thrall's own theory – which is highly speculative in its own right – is that a member of the community had entrusted money to Paul for the collection, money that was then stolen by another member of the congregation. See THRALL, "The Offender and the Offence: A Problem of Detection in 2 Corinthians," in *Scripture: Meaning and Method: Essays Presented to Anthony Tyrrell Hanson for His Seventieth Birthday*, ed. B.P. THOMPSON (Hull: Hull University Press, 1987) 65-78.

exhortation to them (13:11): "Be restored (καταρτίζεσθε),[775] . . . think the same (τὸ αὐτὸ φρονεῖτε), live in peace (εἰρηνεύετε). . . ."

In 2 Cor 7:8-13a Paul again mentions the incident to which 2:5-10 alludes. The context reveals that there is still something amiss in the relationship between the apostle and the Corinthians, as he twice appeals to them to open their hearts to him (6:13 and 7:2), and he defends his conduct among them (7:2). After hearing from Titus that the community had responded favorably to Paul's previous letter, he recounts to them their eagerness to redress the situation (7:11). The apostle's strategy is apparently to encourage *continued* reconciliation between himself and the community by reminding them of a recent experience in which they expressed loyalty to him. All this points to the fact that at least part of Paul's motivation in writing 2 Corinthians is to effect a further restoration of the relationship between the Corinthian community, his "children" (6:13), and himself, their "father" (1 Cor 4:15).[776] According to the apostle, to be unreconciled to him is tantamount to being unreconciled to God. Paul stands firm on this premise: He serves God's cause as Christ's ambassador

---

[775]I read καταρτίζεσθε with the meaning expressed in Gal 6:1 (albeit there in the active form). I translate the verb in the passive voice, although a middle (reflexive) voice rendering might better capture Paul's sense (i.e., "Be restored to one another"). Indeed, this nuance of the verb is suggested by the imperatives that follow. Notice, moreover, that the apostle's admonition to "think the same" echoes his exhortation in Phil 2:5: τοῦτο φρονεῖτε ἐν ὑμῖν ὃ καὶ ἐν Χριστῷ 'Ιησοῦ. Cf. M. M. MITCHELL'S work on the rhetoric of 1 Cor. Observing the presence of the passive voice verb καταρτίζομαι in 1 Cor 1:10 and 2 Cor 13:11, as well as of the noun κατάρτισις in 2 Cor 13:9, she suggests: "One can argue that with the appearance of both verb and noun in 2 Cor 13:9-11, that the Corinthian correspondence has come full circle from its beginning in 1 Cor 1:10." See *Paul and the Rhetoric of Reconciliation*, 74, n. 48. Indeed, Paul's statement in 1 Cor 1:10 – "that you be reconciled *in the same mind* (ἐν τῷ αὐτῷ νοΐ)" – is very suggestive in light of the apostle's insistence that they have the νοῦς Χριστοῦ (1 Cor 2:16).

[776]Cf. SAMPLEY: "Paul's painful letter had the desired effect, and he is now in the position to practice and model the reconciliation and forgiveness (2:10) that *he so eagerly wants increased between himself and the Corinthians*." See *NIB*, 11.53 (italics added).

and co-worker (2 Cor 5:20-6:1).[777] The apostle's belief helps to account for the passionate tone in 2 Cor 10-13. In these chapters, Paul fears that, by rejecting him and his way of being an apostle, the Corinthians, in effect, follow another gospel (11:4). The very impulse to write 2 Corinthians attests to the apostle's participation in the ongoing ministry of reconciliation.

Paul further demonstrates his commitment to facilitate reconciliation by his unwavering diligence in organizing and promoting the collection for the church in Jerusalem (2 Cor 8-9; cf. 1 Cor 16:1-4 and Rom 15:25-28). I will examine passages from 2 Cor 8:1-9:15 in more detail in the following chapter. For the time being, it is sufficient to point out that the apostle tellingly refers to the collection as ἡ διακονία ἡ εἰς τοὺς ἁγίους – "the *ministry/service* for the holy ones" (8:4 and 9:1; cf. 9:12-13). Paul's frequent use of διακονία here recalls how he describes God's ongoing work of reconciliation, namely, as ἡ διακονία τῆς καταλλαγῆς ("the *ministry* of reconciliation," 5:18). This more than suggests that the apostle sees the collection within the context of the work of reconciliation. It is also important to take note of the content of 9:12-13 (where Paul twice refers to the collection as διακονία). The apostle states clearly in 9:12 that the collection will not only bring relief to the Christian community in Jerusalem, but will also result in their giving thanks to God. And in 9:13 he claims that the Corinthians themselves will glorify God through their generosity. The ultimate result is this: God will be blessed. And as Keith F. Nickle has observed, "The most urgently needed blessing which Paul foresaw was [the Corinthians'] reconciliation with the Jewish Christians and the

---

[777]Similarly, BEALE, "The Old Testament Background of Reconciliation in 2 Corinthians 5-7," 557: "If this alienation between Paul and his readers continues, it will also be an alienation from God since Paul represents God's authority and it is actually God who is 'entreating' through him." Cf. MCCANT, *2 Corinthians*, 54: "Reconciliation to Paul is the equivalent of reconciliation to God."

restoration of the unity of the Body of Christ."[778] Indeed, the notion of reconciliation is so important for the apostle that he speaks of it as "salvation."

E. Reconciliation as σωτηρία[779]

Immediately after entreating the Corinthians not to receive God's grace in vain, in 2 Cor 6:2a Paul cites verbatim two lines from LXX Isa 49:8: καιρῷ δεκτῷ ἐπήκουσά σου καὶ ἐν ἡμέρᾳ σωτηρίας ἐβοήθησά σοι ("at an acceptable time I have heard you, and on a day of salvation I have helped you"). Observe that in both the Isaian text and 2 Cor 6:2a, *God* is the speaker of these words.[780] In order to understand how this citation functions in the apostle's exhortation – as well as how he appropriates it in 6:2b – it is necessary to answer two preliminary questions: (1) To whom does "you" refer in the Isaian text?; and (2) What does σωτηρία ("salvation") mean here?

The two instances of the pronoun "you" (σου/σοι) in LXX Isa 49:8 refer to the figure identified in 49:3 and 49:5 as God's δοῦλος. God called this figure before he was born (49:1 and 49:5). In the face of the despair experienced by the δοῦλος in his service to God (49:4), God responded with words of encouragement (49:8, the lines cited by Paul). Moreover, God empowered the δοῦλος to help restore God's people (cf. Jacob and Israel), as well as to be a light to all the nations so that God's *salvation* might reach to the

---

[778]K.F. NICKLE, *The Collection: A Study in Paul's Strategy*, SBT 48 (Naperville, Ill.: Alec R. Allenson, 1966) 122. In commenting on Paul's use of the term κοινωνία in conjunction with the collection (see 2 Cor 8:4 and 9:13), Nickle states: "His application of [the concept κοινωνία] to the collection project testifies to the deep concern he felt about the tense and suspicious relationship existing between the two branches of the Church and to his ardent longing that the fissure be eliminated" (ibid., 124). Nickle concludes that the apostle had three strongly interconnected reasons for organizing and executing the collection: (1) to exercise Christian charity among fellow believers; (2) to promote and express reconciliation and unity among the churches; and (3) to symbolize and enact the eschatological pilgrimage of Gentile Christians to Jerusalem with the hope of moving the Jews to accept the gospel (ibid., 100-143).

[779]I am indebted to L.T. Johnson for suggesting the following line of inquiry.

[780]LXX Isa 49:8 begins οὕτως λέγει κύριος. 2 Cor 6:2 begins λέγει γάρ, where the unnamed subject is clearly God (cf. 'do not receive the grace *of God* in vain' at the end of 6:1).

ends of the earth (49:5-6). Of what does this σωτηρία consist? It entails (at least in part) a sense of "making steadfast" (στῆσαι) and of "bringing back" (ἐπιστρέψαι) God's people (49:6), whose journey is described in terms of a new exodus back to their homeland (49:9-12). In addition, LXX Isa 49:5 intimates that σωτηρία involves τοῦ συναγαγεῖν τὸν 'Ιακωβ καὶ 'Ισραηλ πρὸς αὐτόν – literally, "the gathering of Jacob and Israel to [Yahweh]." The verb συνάγω, whose primary meaning is "gather, bring together," merits close attention. The word can signify a renewing of relationship as well, thus shading into the connotation of "reconcile."[781] This suggests that the salvation to which LXX Isa 49:6 and 49:8 refer involves the restoration of relations between God and God's people. And as 49:5-6 intimates, God's δοῦλος has a special role to play in God's plan to bring this reconciliation into being.[782]

Returning to 2 Cor 6:2, the first issue to be determined is this: To whom does Paul intend that these lines from Isaiah be addressed (lines which, remember, are *God's* words)? To whom does σου/σοι refer? Several commentators argue that "you" refers to the Corinthians. Indeed, it is true that 6:1 ends with the pronoun ὑμᾶς, referring to the Corinthians, and that 6:2 functions as the basis (cf. γάρ) for what precedes it. The argument goes, therefore, that the apostle grounds his exhortation to the Corinthians (not to receive God's grace in vain) with a scriptural citation that operates as God's encouragement to them.[783] The main problem with this interpretation, however, is that it gives the singular pronouns a plural referent. In addition, it fails to take

---

[781]See BDAG, s.v. συνάγω, 2. Cf. *Barn.* 19:12: οὐ ποιήσεις σχίσμα, εἰρηνεύσεις δὲ μαχομένους συναγαγών ("You shall not cause division, but shall bring peace by bringing together/reconciling those who quarrel").

[782]For Paul's use and appropriation of Isa 40-66 throughout 2 Cor 5-7, see BEALE, "The Old Testament Background of Reconciliation in 2 Corinthians 5-7," 550-81. For an exhaustive study of how the apostle draws upon Isaiah, see F. WILK, *Die Bedeutung des Jesajabuches für Paulus*, FRLANT 179 (Göttingen: Vandenhoeck & Ruprecht, 1998).

[783]So, e.g., LAMBRECHT, "The Favorable Time," 527; THRALL, *II Corinthians*, 1.453; and BARNETT, *The Second Epistle to the Corinthians*, 318. HANSON points out that the Targum version of Isa 49:8 interprets the singular pronouns in this passage as a second person plural. According to Hanson, this supports the position that "you" in 2 Cor 6:2 refers to *all* Christians. See *The Paradox of the Cross in the Thought of St Paul*, 56. The problem with this line of argument, however, is that *Paul* retains the singular forms! If the apostle had meant to expand the referent, he could have easily done so.

into account Paul's use of the story of reconciliation in Isaiah. I submit instead that the apostle applies the lines from Isaiah to himself. That is, Paul sees himself in light of the Isaian δοῦλος who receives encouragement and help from God to carry on "the ministry of reconciliation."[784] In fact, in Gal 1:15-16 the apostle describes his call and mission in a manner that clearly evokes the call and mission of God's δοῦλος in LXX Isa 49:1-6.[785]

In 2 Cor 6:2a, then, Paul casts *himself* in the role of God's δοῦλος. Just as the Isaian δοῦλος plays a pivotal role in calling back God's people, so too the apostle – who is Christ's[786] envoy and co-worker, and through whom God makes

---

[784]So, PLUMMER, *II Corinthians*, 190-91. In addition, see BEALE, "The Old Testament Background of Reconciliation in 2 Corinthians 5-7," 562-64; DANKER, *II Corinthians*, 85; W.J. WEBB, *Returning Home: New Covenant and Second Exodus as the Context for 2 Corinthians 6.14-7.1*, JSNTSup 85 (Sheffield: Sheffield Academic Press, 1993) 128-45; and KISTEMAKER, *The Second Epistle to the Corinthians*, 210.

[785]In Gal 1:15 Paul says that God "set me apart from my mother's womb (ἐκ κοιλίας μητρός μου) and called (καλέσας) [me]"; cf. LXX Isa 49:1: "from my mother's womb [the LORD] called (ἐκ κοιλίας μητρός μου ἐκάλεσεν) my name." In Gal 1:16 the apostle states that he was commissioned to proclaim Christ "among the gentiles" (ἐν τοῖς ἔθνεσιν); cf. LXX Isa 49:6, where the δοῦλος is sent "for the purpose of light to [the] gentiles" (εἰς φῶς ἐθνῶν).

[786]Does Paul also have the story of Jesus in mind here? The description of God's δοῦλος and of his mission in LXX Isa 49:1-6 was taken by some early Christians as an apt depiction of the story of Jesus (cf. Luke 2:30-32 and Acts 26:23), and it seems plausible that the apostle may have understood it as such. Indeed, HANSON remarks: "Paul would certainly understand this passage as applying primarily to Christ, the original servant. He too was uniquely called. When he was put to death on the cross he seemed to have laboured in vain. But by raising him from the dead God has saved him, vindicated him, and is now making him the means of salvation to non-Jews as well as to Israel." See *The Paradox of the Cross in the Thought of St Paul*, 56.

It is striking how the lines cited in 2 Cor 6:2a do coalesce with the story of God's δοῦλος in LXX Pss 114-115, to which the apostle alludes in 2 Cor 4:13. The latter story begins with the psalmist (= Jesus) confessing that "the Lord has heard the sound of my supplication" and "inclined his ear to me" (LXX Ps 114:1-2a), and continues by recounting how God delivered and vindicated him. Observe that this story tells from the perspective of the δοῦλος what the Isaian text reports from God's point of view (esp. starting in LXX Isa 49:5). Thus, I submit that by citing the lines from LXX Isa 49:8 in 2 Cor 6:2a, it is possible that Paul not only recalls the story of the Isaian

an appeal (5:20-6:1) – has a crucial role in bringing people back to God. Indeed, Paul's message is precisely this: "Be reconciled to God!" (5:20). Then, after appropriating God's words of encouragement to himself in 6:2a, he addresses the Corinthians in 6:2b by contemporizing the words from LXX Isa 49:8: "Behold, *now* is an acceptable time! Behold, *now* is a day of salvation!" That which makes "*now*" (νῦν) "a day of salvation" for the Corinthians is the fact that God has reconciled the world to God's self through Christ, and has initiated the ministry of reconciliation (2 Cor 5:18-19). In effect, the apostle invites the community to see the present as a special time to "be reconciled."[787] Moreover, Paul's employment of LXX Isa 49:8 suggests that, for him, reconciliation is tantamount to salvation. In the Isaian passage, reconciliation with God is explicit. Recall as well that the ministry of reconciliation also involves reconciliation with Christ's envoy and co-worker (2 Cor 2:5-10 and 6:11-7:13a), as well as with all those who are ἐν Χριστῷ (8:1-9:15).[788] Hence, I submit that

---

δοῦλος but also alludes to the story of Jesus. This possibility is strengthened if, in 2 Cor 5:21a, the apostle does in fact draw upon Isaiah 53, another of the (so-called) servant songs. See, e.g., BRUCE, *1 and 2 Corinthians*, 210; MARTIN, *2 Corinthians*, 157; BELLEVILLE, *2 Corinthians*, 159; and DUNN, *The Theology of Paul the Apostle*, 217.

All of this underscores the complexity involved in Paul's use of stories and intertextuality. I suggest as a possible line of further inquiry the apostle's use of the story of Isa 40-55 to shed light on the story of Jesus as well as on the story of Paul (and others who are 'christed').

[787]Although several translations insert the definite article, the phrases "acceptable time" and "day of salvation" are anarthrous (both in Paul's citation in 2 Cor 6:2a and his application in 6:2b). This suggests an open-ended character to the times referred to in this passage. That is, in light of what God has done in and through Christ, there exists "from now on" (ἀπὸ τοῦ νῦν; cf. 5:16) the possibility of a new way of being – here, living in reconciliation with God and one another. Cf. BULTMANN, *The Second Letter to the Corinthians*, 167: "This 'now' is present in the apostolic preaching at the moment the preaching encounters its hearers – even where it encounters them a second time, as it does the Corinthian community right now."

[788]Cf. LAMBRECHT, "The Favorable Time," 528-29: "For Paul reconciliation is not only God's gift which reaches us from what Christ did in the past. Reconciliation with God and, as Paul also implicitly intends, reconciliation of the Christians with one another, of the Corinthians with Paul, that reconciliation is equally a concrete task for humans, now in the present."

what the apostle means by the term "salvation" in 6:2 is reconciliation broadly understood.

That salvation is important for Paul in 2 Corinthians is evident from the presence of the term σωτηρία in the opening prayer period (2 Cor 1:3-7), an epistolary section in which he regularly anticipates key themes.[789] There the apostle states that if he is afflicted, it is for the Corinthians' "comfort and *salvation*" (1:6). The dialectical tension between the experience of afflictions and σωτηρία is described in the preceding verse (1:5) as sharing in both Christ's sufferings and consolation – that is, as *continuing the story of Jesus*. That σωτηρία is intimately connected with reconciliation is strongly suggested by what Paul says in 7:9-10, where he recounts the effect of the so-called tearful letter that he had written to the Corinthians (cf. 2:4). The "tearful letter" had produced within the community grief/sorrow (λύπη) that was "according to God" (κατὰ θεόν) and that brought about "repentance leading to[790] salvation" (μετάνοια εἰς σωτηρίαν). As we saw in the previous subsection, this letter was the catalyst for the beginning of the restoration of the Corinthians' relationship with the apostle. That is, their repentance led to the possibility of (further) reconciliation. This, I suggest, is what Paul intends by describing their repentance as leading to σωτηρία.

To summarize this section: The apostle plays a prominent role in "the ministry of reconciliation." As Christ's envoy, Paul exhorts people to be reconciled to God (2 Cor 5:20). As Christ's co-worker (6:1), he not only preaches reconciliation but also 'becomes the righteousness of God' (5:21b). By this expression, the apostle claims that God's righteousness – revealed most prominently through Jesus' πίστις – *continues to be revealed* through those who embody Christ's faithfulness. That is, Paul (and others like him, who have been 'christed' by the Spirit) continues to make manifest God's fidelity and love. In particular, the apostle participates in the dynamic of ταπεινοῦν ἑαυτόν, that is, of lowering himself so that others might be lifted up. As Jesus epitomized this dynamic in obedience to God (Phil 2:8; cf. 2 Cor 5:21a), so too does Paul (11:7). An essential aspect of this mode of existence is to lead people to be reconciled to God and to one another. One of the apostle's reasons for writing 2 Corinthians was to encourage such reconciliation – among the

---

[789]See Chapter Four, Section I, and esp. n. 338.

[790]Reading εἰς as denoting goal or purpose. See BDAG, s.v. εἰς, 4.

Corinthians, between the community and Paul, and between the gentile churches and the church in Jerusalem. In fact, the apostle offers clues that he understands reconciliation with God and with one another as "salvation" itself (6:2 and 7:9-10).

VI. Paul Manifests Christ's ἁπλότης and ἀγάπη

Following the *berakah* (2 Cor 1:3-7) and the dramatic statement of his hope and trust in God (1:8-11), Paul begins the body of his letter in 1:12-14. In this passage, the apostle raises one of the main themes of 2 Corinthians, namely, that he has conducted himself toward the community ἐν ἁπλότητι καὶ εἰλικρινείᾳ τοῦ θεοῦ (1:12).[791] The two key terms here, ἁπλότης and εἰλικρίνεια, both denote "sincerity," and I suggest that they form a

---

[791]Cf. FURNISH, *II Corinthians*, 129: "These verses [1:12-14] open the body of the letter and introduce its first major topic – namely, the sincerity and constructive goodwill with which Paul has acted in relation to the Corinthian congregation." AMADOR ("Revisiting 2 Corinthians," 110) calls 1:12-14 the *propositio* of 2 Cor. Similarly, FITZGERALD (*Cracks in an Earthen Vessel*, 157-58) and MATERA (*II Corinthians*, 47) argue that these verses function as an *exordium*. Cf. GARLAND, *2 Corinthians*, 42 and 83-84. While I am in basic agreement with Amador's broad rhetorical sketch of 2 Cor (see n. 141), I have strong reservations about delineating 1:12-14 as the thesis statement of this letter. As I argued in Chapter Two, 2 Cor defies a rigorous rhetorical overlay. The main problem with identifying this passage as the *propositio* is that it does not mention the other (and, indeed, the most) essential thrust of this letter – the apostle's challenge to the Corinthians (unless this challenge is contained *in nuce* in the statement in 1:14 that 'I hope we can be proud of you on the day of the Lord'). Furnish's position that 1:12-14 introduces *a* major topic is a better approach.

Although there is good textual evidence for reading ἁγιότητι instead of ἁπλότητι in 1:12 (in particular, P^{46}), there are three strong reasons – as noted by Metzger – for reading ἁπλότητι: (1) the context seems to call for the notion of simplicity or sincerity, not holiness; (2) ἁπλότης is a key term used throughout 2 Cor (as we will see in Chapter Six); and (3) Paul does not elsewhere use the word ἁγιότης. See METZGER, *A Textual Commentary on the Greek New Testament*, 507. For the case for reading ἁγιότης, see M.E. THRALL, "2 Corinthians 1:12: ἁγιότητι or ἁπλότητι?," in *Studies in New Testament Language and Text: Essays in Honour of George D. Kilpatrick on the Occasion of His Sixty-Fifth Birthday*, ed. J.K. ELLIOTT, NovTSup 44 (Leiden: Brill, 1976) 366-72.

hendiadys.[792] That is, Paul asserts that he[793] has conducted himself toward the Corinthians "in godly[794] sincerity" or "uprightness." In what follows, I attempt to demonstrate how the apostle supports and gives flesh to this claim throughout the letter.

Paul refers again to his εἰλικρίνεια in 2 Cor 2:17. There he contrasts himself with "the many who peddle" (οἱ πολλοὶ καπηλεύοντες) God's word. The apostle claims that, unlike "the many," he acts ἐξ εἰλικρινείας, that is, out of sincerity.[795] What does this mean? Paul himself provides the answer in what

---

[792]See BDAG, s.v. ἁπλότης, 1; and s.v. εἰλικρίνεια, 1. For reading this phrase as a hendiadys, see BULTMANN, *The Second Letter to the Corinthians*, 33. While it is true that Bultmann prefers reading ἁγιότητι rather than ἁπλότητι, he acknowledges that the latter would also produce with εἰλικρινείᾳ the effect of a hendiadys. MATERA (*II Corinthians*, 48) aptly renders ἁπλότης here as "single-hearted devotion."

[793]From 2 Cor 1:3 through 1:13a, Paul uses first person plural pronouns. Since he speaks specifically about "our" conduct *toward the Corinthians* in 1:12, the apostle most likely refers in this verse to himself and Timothy (cf. 1:1) – and possibly Silvanus (1:19) and/or Titus (7:15 and 12:18). Observe that, in 1:13b, Paul switches to the first person singular.

[794]Taking the phrase τοῦ θεοῦ as adjectival. See LAMBRECHT, *Second Corinthians*, 26: "[Of God] may be a so-called Hebrew genitive, more or less the equivalent of an adjective." For understanding the phrase as modifying both ἁπλότης and εἰλικρίνεια, see MARTIN, *2 Corinthians*, 18: " [Of God] clearly belongs to the two preceding nouns in a hendiadys."

[795]Reading ἐκ as expressing the inner life or motivation out of which something proceeds. See BDAG, s.v. ἐκ, 3.g.γ. Cf. Rom 6:17 and 14:23; 1 Tim 1:5; and 2 Tim 2:22. For a good discussion of Paul's "who" and "what" referents in the expression οἱ πολλοὶ καπηλεύοντες, see THRALL, *II Corinthians*, 1.211-15. Her conclusion is: "What he is denying, then, is that he waters down the gospel and that he has any concern for personal gain, such as might accrue to his reputation and his finances from the more obvious success that a superficially more comfortable message might bring him. It is because he is able to make this denial that he is adequate for the task of proclaiming a gospel that has the effect of provoking rejection as well as acceptance. The πολλοί, by contrast, cannot make any such denial" (ibid., 215).

immediately follows – ὡς ἐκ θεοῦ κατέναντι θεοῦ.[796] As we saw in the analysis of 2:14-17 above, these phrases in their context summarize both his obedient service to God (as God's δοῦλος) as well as God's making manifest the fragrance of the knowledge of Christ through the apostle's self-giving love for the sake of others. In other words, Paul explains that he acts ἐξ εἰλικρινείας by embodying *Jesus'* character and mode of existence. Recall, too, from Chapter Four that Jesus' ἁπλότης (11:3) refers not just to his "sincerity" or "integrity," but more specifically to his singleness of mind and purpose. That is, Christ's ἁπλότης signifies his disposition to love and serve God, as well as his whole manner of living (for the sake of others) that expressed this disposition. I submit that the apostle's use of ἁπλότης and εἰλικρίνεια in reference to himself also suggests Paul's own disposition as well as his way of being an apostle.

While it is true that, after 2 Cor 1:12, Paul does not explicitly use the word ἁπλότης in connection with himself, other passages do portray the substance of his single-minded love and devotion toward the Corinthians (and the expression of his love and devotion to God contained therein). In 6:11-13 and 7:2-3 the apostle, addressing the Corinthians by name – Κορίνθιοι[797] – uses language that evokes deep affection and committed friendship. Paul tells them that his heart "has been and continues to be wide open" (cf. πεπλάτυνται, perfect tense) to them (6:11). There is no restriction in his affections for them (6:12).[798] Indeed, he even refers to them as his children (6:13; cf. 11:2 and 1 Cor 4:14-15). Keeping in mind that ἁπλότης can also connote integrity and innocence, it comes as no surprise that the apostle forswears having ever wronged or taken advantage of them (2 Cor 7:2). Finally, Paul employs a most dramatic expression of friendship and love: The

---

[796]So, too, BULTMANN, *The Second Letter to the Corinthians*, 70; and LAMBRECHT, *Second Corinthians*, 40: ". . . the [following] formulae present themselves, it would seem, as a further explanation of 'out of sincerity.'"

[797]As PLUMMER observes, Paul addresses his converts by name only here and in Gal 3:1 and Phil 4:15. Concerning 2 Cor 6:11 and the following verses, Plummer rightly states, "The whole passage is affectionately tender." See *II Corinthians*, 203.

[798]Literally, Paul says in 2 Cor 6:12a, "You are not cramped in us." As THRALL points out, however, the phrase "ἐν ἡμῖν must mean 'in my affections,' in view of the following ἐν τοῖς σπλάγχνοις ὑμῶν" in 6:12b. See *II Corinthians*, 1.470.

Corinthians are so much in his heart that he is willing to die with them and to live with them (εἰς τὸ συναποθανεῖν καὶ συζῆν, 7:3).[799] By these words, the apostle reveals his affection, care, and devotion to the community as their father and loyal friend.

Paul draws again on familial imagery in 2 Cor 12:14-15, where he poignantly portrays himself as father to the Corinthians. The apostle has just concluded a passionate section (10:1-12:13) in which he presents himself as a trustworthy laborer and "servant of Christ" who has been sent by God to the Corinthians with "the good news concerning Christ" (cf. 10:13-16 and 11:23a). In announcing his third visit to the community, Paul makes it clear that he will not be a burden to them (12:14). The apostle's use of καταναρκάω ("be a burden") here recalls 11:7-11 (esp. 11:9[800]), where he insists that he lowers himself in order that the Corinthians might be lifted up. Paul assures the community that he does not seek his own advantage ("I do not seek what is yours"), but that of the Corinthians. As a loving father would do for his children, so does the apostle look after their interests and well-being.[801] He reminds the community that it is the role of parents to "store up" for their

---

[799]Cf. SAMPLEY, *NIB*, 11.101: "This is the ultimate pledge of friendship in which Paul sketches out his and the Corinthians' scope of commitment"; and BELLEVILLE, *2 Corinthians*, 190: "Paul expresses himself in the classical formula of his day for abiding friendship and loyalty." In addition, see PLUMMER, *II Corinthians*, 214; WINDISCH, *Der zweite Korintherbrief*, 222-23; HÉRING, *The Second Epistle of Saint Paul to the Corinthians*, 53; BULTMANN, *The Second Letter to the Corinthians*, 178; BARRETT, *The Second Epistle to the Corinthians*, 204; FURNISH, *II Corinthians*, 367 (for several classical allusions); and THRALL, *II Corinthians*, 1.483-84. *Pace* TANNEHILL, *Dying and Rising with Christ*, 93-94; and BARNETT, *The Second Epistle to the Corinthians*, 362, both of whom see in the death/life motif in 2 Cor 7:3 a reference to the death and resurrection of Christ.

[800]See BDAG, s.v. καταναρκάω. Paul only uses this verb in 2 Cor (11:9 and 12:13-14).

[801]Cf. MATERA, *II Corinthians*, 294-95. Matera rightly observes one of the strategic implications of Paul's insistence upon his role as founder/father of the community. Because he is their father, the apostle refuses to enter into a client-benefactor relationship with the Corinthians. For a detailed study of how the issue of patronage impacted the tension between Paul and the wealthy in Corinth, see P. MARSHALL, *Enmity in Corinth: Social Conventions in Paul's Relations with the Corinthians*, WUNT 2/23 (Tübingen: Mohr Siebeck, 1987).

children, and not vice-versa. Paul's use of θησαυρίζω in 12:14 echoes 4:7-14, where he describes how the "treasure" (θησαυρός, 4:7) of the Spirit's enlightenment/empowerment is manifested in his embodying the character of Jesus and continuing Jesus' story. Indeed, it is by doing so that the apostle "stores up" for the Corinthians – that he serves them to their advantage.

Second Corinthians 12:15 confirms this interpretation, as Paul offers, in effect, a précis of living in the pattern of Jesus' love. Here the apostle states: "*I*[802] will most gladly spend and be utterly expended for [you]." His choice of the verbs δαπανάω ("spend") and ἐκδαπανάομαι ("be utterly expended") is striking.[803] At one level, these verbs, with their economic connotations, serve to remind the Corinthians of all that Paul has done for them, and to inspire them to respond to him (at least in part) by giving generously to the collection. At a deeper level, I suggest that the apostle uses these verbs as synonyms of παραδίδωι and παραδίδομαι. That is, by saying 'I will gladly *spend* for you Corinthians,' Paul alludes to his choice to give himself up for them (cf. the *active*, reflexive sense of παραδίδωι; 4:10a and 11:7[804]). And by stating 'I will gladly *be spent* for you,' the apostle refers to his being handed over by God for them (cf. the *passive* sense of παραδίδομαι; 4:11a).[805] This recalls the two

---

[802]Note the inclusion of ἐγώ, which, as PLUMMER remarks, "is very emphatic." He renders the beginning of 2 Cor 12:15 thus: "But *I*, I will most gladly . . . ." See *II Corinthians*, 362.

[803]KISTEMAKER rightly remarks that here is an instance where Paul's word play (with the verbs δαπανάω and ἐκδαπανάομαι) can be reproduced in English – "spend" and "*ex*pend." See *The Second Epistle to the Corinthians*, 428. I add the adverb "utterly" in order to convey more clearly that the second verb functions here to intensify the first. Cf. 2 Cor 4:8 – ἀπορούμενοι ἀλλ' οὐκ ἐξαπορούμενοι. Similarly, FURNISH, *II Corinthians*, 55; and SAMPLEY, *NIB*, 11.170.

[804]In 2 Cor 4:10a Paul mentions "bearing" (περιφέροντες, active voice) the νέκρωσις τοῦ 'Ιησοῦ; and in 11:7 he refers to "lowering" (ταπεινῶν, active voice) himself in order that the Corinthians might be lifted up.

[805]Some commentators hold that Paul's use of ἐκδαπανάομαι – instead of expressing the passive sense of δαπανάω – signifies a distinction in *content* in reference to the verbs. For example, it is argued that δαπανάω refers to the apostle's using his financial resources (or allowing the Corinthians to save theirs), while ἐκδαπανάομαι refers to his sacrificing himself for the community. So, WINDISCH, *Der zweite Korintherbrief*,

perspectives – of God and of Jesus – in the story of Jesus (as we saw in Chapter Four). Observe, moreover, that Paul says that he will spend and be spent *for the sake of* the Corinthians (cf. ὑπὲρ τῶν ψυχῶν ὑμῶν). Furthermore, the apostle grounds his "giving himself/being handed over" for their sake *in love*: "While loving (ἀγαπῶν) you all the more, am I to be loved the less?"[806] Paul thereby conjoins in 12:15 the notion of ἀγάπη with "giving oneself up/being handed over" (cf. the active reflexive and passive forms of παραδίδωμι) for the sake of (ὑπέρ) others. This is precisely the mode of loving, self-giving existence that Jesus incarnated (5:14-15; cf. Gal 2:20; and Eph 5:2 and 5:25). So now does the apostle embody it.[807]

400; BRUCE, *1 and 2 Corinthians*, 250; and BULTMANN, *The Second Letter to the Corinthians*, 234. SAMPLEY, however, rightly observes that "[t]he second verb intensifies the first and *extends to it the very giving of oneself in sacrifice for another* . . . ." See *NIB*, 11.170 (italics added). Thus, *both* verbs refer primarily to Paul's self-sacrifice. BARRETT remarks that the compound verb ἐκδαπανάομαι has a perfective force (see *The Second Epistle to the Corinthians*, 324). That is, it connotes that Paul's self-giving is portrayed here as continuing until it reaches completion. Cf. BDF, § 318 (5).

[806]There are two interrelated textual variants in the second half of 2 Cor 12:15. The most important decision involves choosing between ἀγαπῶ (indicative) and ἀγαπῶν (participle). For a helpful discussion, see THRALL, *II Corinthians*, 2.846-47; cf. METZGER, *A Textual Commentary on the Greek New Testament*, 517. The participle has solid attestation and yields the more difficult reading. Thrall tentatively suggests reading the participle, as well as taking the opening εἰ as interrogative. My translation reflects her position.

[807]BARNETT also sees 2 Cor 12:15 as an example of Paul's description of how he continues the story of Jesus, although he focuses too narrowly upon the apostle's replication of Christ's suffering. See *The Second Epistle to the Corinthians*, 586. HUGHES captures better how the apostle takes on Christ's character and continues the story: "The magnitude of [Paul's] love for [the Corinthians] is, indeed, a reflection of the love of Christ, who came not to be ministered unto, but to minister, and to expend His life a ransom for many (Mark 10:45). It is *Christ's* love which constrains the servant of the gospel." See *Paul's Second Epistle to the Corinthians*, 463 (Hughes's italics). In fact, Paul's use of economic language to describe his self-emptying mode of existence recalls a similar usage in 8:9 to depict the enactment of Jesus' "graciousness" (χάρις). Cf. 6:9-10, where the apostle characterizes himself and his co-workers "as poor, yet we enrich many" (ὡς πτωχοὶ πολλοὺς δὲ πλουτίζοντες).

This understanding of the "love of Christ" (cf. 2 Cor 5:14) illuminates those passages in 2 Corinthians in which Paul claims to manifest ἀγάπη. In 2:4 the apostle asserts that his purpose in writing (previously) to the community was to let them know of his abundant *love* for them. Given how Paul associates love with self-offering, his description of writing this letter "out of much affliction and anguish of heart" and "with many tears" becomes all the more poignant. In 6:6 the apostle lists *genuine love* (ἀγάπη ἀνυπόκριτος[808]) as one of the marks of a "minister of God" (6:4). Like the δοῦλοι of God, God's διάκονοι give themselves up in love for the sake of others. In 8:7 Paul names "the *love* from us [i.e., the apostle and his co-workers] among you"[809] as one of many things that the Corinthians have in abundance. Here he tries (as in 12:15) to motivate the community to be generous in giving to the collection by reminding them of his living for their benefit. Finally, in 11:11, the apostle insists that it is because he *loves* the Corinthians that he does not seek for himself their financial support. Love is thus the motivation and basis for Paul's participation in the dynamic of ταπεινοῦν ἑαυτόν, whereby he lowers himself in order that the community might be lifted up.

In sum, then, throughout this letter, the apostle elaborates on his claim in 2 Cor 1:12 to act with ἁπλότης toward the community. Paul consistently reiterates his deep affection and care for the Corinthians, whom he regards as his children (6:13 and 12:14). Indeed, the apostle's willingness to give himself/be given up for them (12:15) expresses most eloquently his continuation of the story of Christ's ἀγάπη.

---

[808]See THOMPSON, *Clothed with Christ*, 91-94, for the use of this expression in Rom 12:9.

[809]Reading ἐξ ἡμῶν ἐν ὑμῖν instead of ἐξ ὑμῶν ἐν ἡμῖν. The former has solid early attestation (including P^{46}). See METZGER, *A Textual Commentary on the Greek New Testament*, 512-13. In addition, whereas the other items (e.g., "faith" and "knowledge") in the list are anarthrous, Paul gives special signification to the love that he is talking about in 2 Cor 8:7. Observe, moreover, how in the very next verse, where the apostle *does* refer to the Corinthians' love, he makes this explicit – τῆς ὑμετέρας ἀγάπης (8:8). Cf. THRALL, *II Corinthians*, 1.530: "Since Paul is the founder of the community he is, humanly speaking, the originator of the spirit of Christian love by which the community is characterised. He has shown what love is through the manner of his own work in Corinth. The reading ἐξ ἡμῶν ἐν ὑμῖν is preferable."

VII. Summary

Throughout 2 Corinthians, Paul engages in the rhetorical strategy of establishing his *ethos*. But he does so in a peculiar way. The apostle distinguishes between a negative manner of *self*-commendation (indicated by the syntax ἑαυτὸν συνιστάνειν; 2 Cor 3:1, 5:12, and 10:18) and a positive manner of self-*commendation* (signaled by συνιστάνειν ἑαυτόν; 4:2 and 6:4). He eschews the former and embraces the latter. The reason Paul self-*commends* is that he incarnates faithfully the *ethos* revealed in Jesus' story. Hence, the apostle demonstrates his own *ethos* – wherein he confirms his integrity and trustworthiness – by embodying Jesus' *ethos*.

The gift of the Holy Spirit enables Paul to take on the character of Jesus and thus to continue Jesus' story. By the empowerment of the Spirit, the apostle has been "*christed*" and "sealed" – marked as God's δοῦλος and stamped with the very character of Jesus (2 Cor 1:21-22 and 4:6). Moreover, it is through the ongoing work of the Spirit that Paul is transformed more and more into the image of Christ (3:18), the εἰκὼν τοῦ θεοῦ (4:4). That is, through the gift of the νοῦς Χριστοῦ, the apostle embodies Jesus' attitude, values, and manner of existence. In particular, Paul incarnates the faithfulness of Christ, the δοῦλος of God, by his own self-giving existence out of love for the sake of others (4:7-14 and 2:14-17). The apostle also participates in the work of reconciliation as Jesus' ambassador and co-worker, thereby continuing to make manifest God's righteousness by lowering himself so that others might be lifted up (5:20-6:2; cf. 11:7-11). Indeed, it is precisely where Paul portrays himself in a sustained manner as continuing the story of Jesus – in 4:7-14 and 5:20-6:2 – that he self-*commends* (4:2 and 6:4). The apostle likewise embodies the ἁπλότης and ἀγάπη of Christ to the Corinthians (esp. 12:14-15).

Paul presents himself to the community as embodying Jesus' *ethos* and continuing his story right up to the very end of the letter, where the apostle claims to share both in Christ's "weakness" and in his living by "the power of God" (2 Cor 13:4). The immediate context of this claim is the Corinthians' demand that Paul 'prove' that Christ speaks in him (13:3). As we will see, the term for "proof," δοκιμή, is very significant for the apostle in 2 Corinthians. Although Paul spends no little time self-*commending* here, he is in fact more concerned with challenging the Corinthians to prove their own character. Indeed, the apostle's use of δοκιμ- terminology brings us to *the* key rhetorical strategy of this epistle: his admonition to the Corinthians to take on the character of Jesus and thereby to continue his story. This strategy is the subject of the following chapter.

Chapter Six
The Corinthians Are Exhorted to Embrace the Character of Jesus

I. Introduction

Second Corinthians abounds in Paul's self-*commendation*. The apostle *is* concerned with establishing – or perhaps better, with re-establishing – his *ethos* in the eyes of the Corinthians, at least some of whom have come to doubt his character. Paul authenticates himself and his ministry by aligning his *ethos* with that of Jesus. The fact that he self-*commends* throughout this epistle accounts, I suspect, for the tendency among those who utilize rhetorical analysis to read 2 Corinthians as (primarily) forensic rhetoric. Indeed, the apostle does appear to be defending himself up to the very end of the letter, as he responds to a challenge from the Corinthians to prove that Christ is speaking in him (2 Cor 13:3-4).

Paul's ultimate strategy in writing 2 Corinthians, however, is not self-commendation. Rather, the apostle rhetorically turns the tables on the Corinthians to throw their challenge right back at them.[810] He admonishes them in 2 Cor 13:5 to examine themselves and, even more strikingly, *to put themselves to the test* (cf. ἑαυτοὺς δοκιμάζετε). I submit that in this verse Paul reveals his principal purpose in writing this letter, namely, to challenge the Corinthians to take on for themselves the *ethos* of Jesus and thereby to continue his story. In doing so, the apostle engages in what is more appropriately classified as *deliberative* rhetoric. That is, Paul attempts to admonish and persuade the community to make particular decisions and to engage in certain activities. As will be shown in the following pages, the apostle's strategy is to convince the Corinthians that these decisions and activities flow from their appropriating for themselves the very *ethos* of Jesus.

That the character of the community is a crucial issue for Paul in 2 Corinthians is evident from the cluster of δοκιμ- terminology in the letter's

---

[810]Of those commentators who use rhetorical analysis to investigate 2 Cor (reviewed in Chapter Two), only MCCANT recognizes that Paul's primary strategy is to challenge the Corinthians. See *2 Corinthians*, esp. 164.

climax. Observe how the substantive δοκιμή (2 Cor 13:3), the verb δοκιμάζω (13:5), and the adjectives δόκιμος (13:7) and ἀδόκιμος (three times in 13:5-7) all appear in these verses. This concentration of δοκιμ- terminology echoes the apostle's utilization of δοκιμή and its cognates *throughout* 2 Corinthians, usage that merits special attention. In fact, the highest concentration of Paul's employment of these terms in his extant work occurs in this epistle: four of the seven instances of δοκιμή[811]; two of the six occurrences of δόκιμος[812]; three of the seven uses of ἀδόκιμος[813]; and, three of the seventeen instances of δοκιμάζω.[814] Now, δοκιμ- terminology connotes both the *process* of testing whereby one's competence – even more, one's character – is ascertained, as well as the *result* of enduring such a test.[815] Thus, δοκιμ- terminology is intimately connected with integrity and genuineness – in short, with *ethos*.

A glance at how the apostle uses δοκιμή elsewhere in his writings is helpful. Romans 5:3b-4 suggests that Paul understands this term in light of the development of character. In this passage, δοκιμή is the third of a four-member *sorites*: "affliction (θλῖψις) brings about endurance, endurance (ὑπομονή) [brings about] character, and character (δοκιμή) [brings about] hope (ἐλπίς)." What is noteworthy here is the connection between the endurance produced by affliction and the cultivation of character. It ought to be clear from the previous chapter that the apostle is very familiar with afflictions (see esp. 2 Cor 1:8, 4:8-10, and 7:4-5). Moreover, he suggests that endurance is a critical mark of his authenticity and *ethos*. For instance, when Paul self-*commends* as a "servant of God," the first thing he lists is his endurance – ἐν ὑπομονῇ πολλῇ (2 Cor 6:4, followed by a catalog of sufferings endured). Similarly, at the end of his "Fool's Speech" (12:12), the apostle concludes: "The signs of the apostle were

---

[811]Rom 5:4 (2x); 2 Cor 2:9; 8:2; 9:13; and 13:3; and Phil 2:22. W. GRUNDMANN, citing the work of E. Lohmeyer, remarks: "This word [δοκιμή] is very rare, there being no instances prior to Paul." See "δόκιμος, . . .," in *TDNT*, 6.255-60, here 255.

[812]Rom 14:18 and 16:10; 1 Cor 11:19; 2 Cor 10:18 and 13:7; and 2 Tim 2:15.

[813]Rom 1:28; 1 Cor 9:27; 2 Cor 13:5; 13:6; and 13:7; 2 Tim 3:8; and Titus 1:16.

[814]Rom 1:28; 2:18; 12:2; and 14:22; 1 Cor 3:13; 11:28; and 16:3; 2 Cor 8:8; 8:22; and 13:5; Gal 6:4; Eph 5:10; Phil 1:10; 1 Thess 2:4 (2x) and 5:21; and 1 Tim 3:10.

[815]See BDAG, s.v. δοκιμάζω, 1 and 2; s.v. δοκιμή, 1 and 2.

performed among you *in all endurance* (ἐν πάσῃ ὑπομονῇ)." In addition, Paul encourages the Corinthians to appreciate the importance of endurance for themselves. In 2 Cor 1:6 the apostle tells them that the consolation of Christ is theirs when they suffer "in endurance" (ἐν ὑπομονῇ) the same sufferings that he (that is, Paul) does. I submit that, since (according to the apostle) endurance produces δοκιμή, the references to ὑπομονή in 2 Corinthians are further evidence that *character* is a central issue in this epistle.

Philippians 2:22 sheds more light on Paul's understanding and use of δοκιμ- terminology. In that verse the apostle refers to Timothy's δοκιμή – that is, to his character and worth. The distinguishing mark of Timothy's δοκιμή is that "he has served as a slave (ἐδούλευσεν) for the gospel."[816] Thus, Paul closely associates δοκιμή with the notion of living for others, with being a δοῦλος (cf. 2 Cor 4:5). Moreover, notice that Timothy's δοκιμή is also characterized by his seeking first "the [interests] of Jesus Christ" rather than his own interests (Phil 2:21). This attitude allows Timothy to have a genuine concern for the welfare of others (2:20; cf. 2:3-4). Given how the description of Jesus functions in Phil 2:6-11, it is clear that the apostle now presents Timothy to the Philippians as an example of embodying self-giving existence after the manner of Christ. Thus, Paul appears to link δοκιμή here with taking on the pattern of Jesus, who "lowered himself, becoming obedient" (2:8).[817]

That the apostle connects δοκιμ- terminology with the character of Jesus is confirmed by Rom 14:18. There he states that "the one who serves Christ as a slave (ὁ δουλεύων) in this way is acceptable to God and approved (δόκιμος) among people." The phrase "in this way" refers to "walking in love" (κατὰ ἀγάπην περιπατέω, Rom 14:15), conduct that looks first to the neighbor's good and seeks to build up community (14:19 and 15:2) rather than insisting on one's own way and rights (in that case, concerning what is proper to eat and drink). Once again, Paul associates δοκιμ- language with serving as a slave. Moreover, the apostle holds up the example of Christ as one who "did

---

[816]Reading ἐδούλευσεν in Phil 2:22 as a complexive aorist, and εἰς as indicating the goal of an action (see BDAG, s.v. εἰς, 4.d; cf. Rom 1:1).

[817]Indeed, it is striking that Paul's reference in Rom 5:4 to 'endurance producing character' is set in a passage that draws out the implications of being made righteous ἐκ πίστεως (5:1). Recall from Chapter Three that the phrase ἐκ πίστεως is the apostle's shorthand expression for Jesus' faithfulness. Thus, Paul's mention of 'endurance producing character' in Rom 5:4 appears to be linked to the character and story of Jesus.

not please himself" (15:3), thus indicating that being δόκιμος entails taking on the *ethos* of Jesus.[818]

In fact, Paul has already used δοκιμ- terminology in a similar manner in an earlier letter to the Corinthians. Two instances are of particular relevance. Both occur in 1 Cor 11:17-34, his exhortation to the community to partake worthily of the "Lord's supper" (κυριακὸν δεῖπνον). In 11:19 the apostle observes that factions in the community are necessary in order that οἱ δόκιμοι, "those who are genuine" – that is, those who have passed the test – might become manifest (φανεροί) among them. Here Paul seems to suggest that the various problems surrounding the celebration of the δεῖπνον would serve as the occasion for distinguishing the δόκιμοι from the ἀδόκιμοι. Then, in 11:27-29, the apostle indicates more precisely what the issue is. He challenges each person in the community to self-examination (cf. δοκιμαζέτω ἄνθρωπος ἑαυτόν, 11:28). This test consists of whether or not the Corinthians are adequately discerning (διακρίνω) "the body" (11:29). That is, Paul warns them that they cannot partake worthily of the δεῖπνον if they fail to recognize and treat one another as members of the body of Christ. In effect, the apostle's challenge to the community involves their testing themselves to see whether or not they are acting as those who have the νοῦς Χριστοῦ (2:16).

Returning to 2 Corinthians, it comes as little surprise therefore that Paul connects δοκιμ- terminology with the character and story of Jesus. This is particularly evident in 2 Cor 13:3-5. To anticipate an argument that I will make in greater detail below:[819] After acknowledging that the Corinthians seek to ascertain his δοκιμή (13:3), the apostle refers to Jesus' having been crucified ἐξ ἀσθενείας (13:4a). As we saw in Chapter Four, the phrase ἐξ ἀσθενείας connotes a mode of human existence marked by gentleness and humility, as well as by the willingness to endure afflictions in giving oneself for the sake of others. In effect, by this phrase Paul alludes to Jesus' entire mode of self-emptying existence that culminated with his crucifixion. The apostle then

[818]THOMPSON argues that the reference to ὑπομονή in Rom 15:4 – which follows immediately upon Paul's holding up Christ as an *exemplum* (15:3) – alludes to *Jesus'* endurance. See *Clothed with Christ*, 225-28. It is certainly true that the apostle refers explicitly to Christ's endurance (ὑπομονὴ τοῦ Χριστοῦ) in 2 Thess 3:5. Following the logic of Rom 5:3-4, then, it would seem that Jesus' endurance played a role in the development of his δοκιμή. Cf. HOOKER, "ΠΙΣΤΙΣ ΧΡΙΣΤΟΥ," 339, n. 2.

[819]See Section IV.D.

immediately aligns himself with this mode of existence (cf. ἡμεῖς ἀσθενοῦμεν, 13:4b). Paul is able to do so because of his intimate relationship with Jesus (cf. ἐν αὐτῷ). Moreover – and this brings us to the main thrust of his strategy – the apostle turns the tables on the Corinthians and challenges them to test themselves (13:5a). Then he promptly asks them: "Do you not realize that *Jesus Christ is in you*?" (13:5b). Hence, Paul not only establishes his own δοκιμή vis-à-vis the story and character of Jesus; he also admonishes the Corinthians to see whether or not *they* are participating in the same story. As we will see, the apostle employs δοκιμή and its cognates in this letter primarily to exhort the community to embrace characteristics that he attributes to Jesus (2:9, 8:8, 9:13, and 13:5-7; cf. 8:2).[820]

In what follows, I demonstrate how Paul encourages the Corinthians to embody the *ethos* of Jesus and thereby to continue his story. Although the apostle does so chiefly through his use of δοκιμ- terminology, he also uses other techniques to inspire the community to participate in the story of Jesus. First, I briefly show how Paul interconnects the stories of Jesus, himself (i.e., the apostle), and the Corinthians throughout this letter. Second, I examine how he draws out for the community the implications of the transforming power of the Spirit. Then, after sketching the rhetorical situation of 2 Corinthians, I offer an extended treatment of how Paul, through his employment of δοκιμή and its cognates, challenges the Corinthians to take on the character of Jesus. This more extensive section consists of four headings – ὑπακοή, ἀγάπη, ἁπλότης, and πίστις. Lastly, I propose an interpretation of the apostle's climactic

---

[820]It is surprising how little space commentators devote to the presence of δοκιμ- terminology in 2 Cor. One exception is BETZ, who is particularly sensitive to the central importance of δοκιμή – both in terms of the notion of proving/being proven as well as the criteria involved therein – for Paul's argument in 2 Cor 10-13. See *Der Apostel Paulus und die sokratische Tradition*, 132-37. However, Betz focuses on the apostle's usage of δοκιμ- terminology in 13:3-7, and thus does not bring the other instances in 2 Cor to bear on his interpretation. This is another deficiency of analyzing the text by means of partitions. In addition, YOUNG and FORD offer a brief but informative discussion of δοκιμή. See *Meaning and Truth in 2 Corinthians*, 98-100. Young and Ford rightly note the difficulty inherent in translating into English the richness of this term. And while they overstate the case for 2 Cor as forensic rhetoric, they do acknowledge that "this untranslatable word *lies at the heart* of Paul's apology, *while also enabling him to turn the tables on his critics*; because in the end, they cannot put him on trial; the final judgement in the heavenly court hovers over them all" (ibid., 99; italics added).

appropriation of LXX Deut 19:15 (in 2 Cor 13:1) in light of the findings of this investigation.

II. The Interconnection of the Stories of Jesus, Paul, and the Corinthians

Throughout 2 Corinthians Paul weaves together the story of Jesus, his own story, and that of the Corinthians. From the letter's opening paragraphs to its climax, he encourages the community to participate in the story and character of Christ. In this section, I sketch how the apostle invites the Corinthians into the story of Jesus by looking briefly at 2 Cor 1:3-7, 4:13-14, 6:2, and 9:8-10. The consideration is meant as impressionistic reflection rather than systematic exegesis.

That the stories of Jesus, Paul, and the Corinthians are interwoven is evident in the *berakah* in 2 Cor 1:3-7. (Recall that the apostle sounds forth important themes in his opening prayer periods.) In these early verses Paul utilizes the notion of "interchange."[821] After blessing God (1:3), he describes God as the One who gives consolation so that those thus consoled might in turn become agents of consolation (1:4). Then, in 1:5, with his reference to τὰ παθήματα τοῦ Χριστοῦ, the apostle brings the story of Jesus to bear on this pattern of interchange. That is, Paul claims to share abundantly in the sufferings of Christ, as well as in the consolation that comes through him.[822] Next, the

---

[821]I take the term from M.D. HOOKER, the meaning of which she sees as captured in an expression of Irenaeus: "Christ became what we are, in order that we might become what he is." For Hooker, "interchange" is not a matter of substitution or exchange. Rather, "Christ is identified with us in order that – in him – we might share in what he is." See "Interchange and Atonement," *BJRL* 60 (1978) 462-81, here 462-63. Technically, Hooker reserves the term for passages such as 2 Cor 5:21 and 8:9. I extend the term to passages in which Paul describes himself as embodying the character of Jesus and/or exhorts others to do the same. That is, I use it as a more strategic term than a descriptive one.

[822]Commentators wrestle with the question of how the sufferings of Paul (and others) can be identified with the sufferings of Christ. For a helpful review of positions, see THRALL, *II Corinthians*, 1.107-10. Thrall's own position is the correct one: "Paul believed that through the indwelling of the Spirit of Christ the believer's character and existence became conformed to that of Christ" (ibid., 109). KLEINKNECHT sees the point of connection in light of the tradition of the righteous sufferer. See *Der leidende*

apostle refers to a dynamic that we observed throughout the previous chapter, namely that the afflictions that befall him work for the consolation and salvation of the Corinthians (1:6a). Finally, Paul alludes to how the Corinthians can actively participate in the story of Jesus by suggesting that they will experience consolation insofar as they themselves endure (cf. ἐν ὑπομονῇ) the same sufferings (1:6b). Hence, the apostle implicitly exhorts the community to be sharers or partners (κοινωνοί) with him in the sufferings (as well as the consolations) of Christ (1:7).[823]

Whereas in the *berakah* Paul invites the community to share in Christ's sufferings, in 2 Cor 4:13-14 he intimates that the Corinthians will also partake in the glorious conclusion of the story of Jesus. As we have seen, the apostle alludes in these verses to the story of Christ, God's faithful δοῦλος. In the course of aligning himself with Jesus' faithfulness, Paul refers to God's vindication of Christ by raising him from the dead (4:14a). The apostle goes on to state that God "will raise us[824] also with Jesus and will bring [us], with you, into his presence" (4:14b). Here Paul refers to his own trust and hope in God to vindicate his self-giving mode of apostolic existence, just as God vindicated Jesus' πίστις. The pertinent point for the present discussion is that the apostle includes the Corinthians in this scene of vindication – God "will bring close

---

Gerechtfertigte, 245-47. This position, too, has merit, although Kleinknecht does not appreciate the extent to which Paul alludes to the story and character of Jesus in 2 Cor.

[823]As FURNISH aptly notes, while Paul's expression of confidence in 2 Cor 1:7 – formally considered – is in the indicative mood, it has an implicit hortatory function. See *II Corinthians*, 121. Reading the text in this way alleviates a problem concerning 1:6 raised by THRALL: "There is no indication elsewhere that the Corinthians were actually undergoing persecution or any other kind of hardship. . . ." See *II Corinthians*, 1.111; cf. MARTIN, *2 Corinthians*, 10. Furnish also correctly notes that "the same sufferings" in 1:6 are those "shared by the whole body of Christ, as members of which believers are summoned to be conformed to Christ's life-giving death . . . ." See *II Corinthians*, 121. *Pace* TANNEHILL, who draws too great a distinction between the sufferings of Paul and those of the Corinthians. Tannehill seems to understand the latter in terms of "the sufferings involved in creation's slavery to corruption and in the body's unredeemed state" (cf. Rom 8:18-23). See *Dying and Rising with Christ*, 96; cf. ibid., 114. For a discussion of the textual variants in 2 Cor 1:6-7 which arose because of homoeoteleuton, see METZGER, *A Textual Commentary on the Greek New Testament*, 505-6.

[824]The first person plural pronouns refer to Paul and his co-workers. See n. 674.

[i.e., to God]" (παραστήσει)[825] Paul *along with the Corinthians* (cf. σὺν ὑμῖν). In doing so, the apostle exhibits great rhetorical finesse, as he subtly encourages the Corinthians to embody Jesus' self-emptying mode of existence, as well as the trust in God that underlies such a manner of living. By including the Corinthians in the (future) scene of God's vindication of those who are faithful, Paul astutely challenges them to consider the way of life that leads to that vindication.

The apostle's strategy to include the Corinthians in the story of Jesus is less subtle in 2 Cor 6:2. Recall from the previous chapter that, by appropriating the words of LXX Isa 49:8 (in 2 Cor 6:2a), Paul takes on the mantle of the Isaian δοῦλος. That is, the apostle understands himself as commissioned and encouraged by God to carry on the ministry of reconciliation. This ministry of reconciliation is a continuation of the story of God's reconciliation of the world through the reconciling agency and demeanor of Jesus, God's faithful δοῦλος (2 Cor 5:18-19 and 5:21), whose envoy and co-worker Paul is (5:20 and 6:1). Then, in 6:2b, the apostle emphatically draws the community into this story of reconciliation: "Behold, *now* is an acceptable time! Behold, *now* is a day of salvation!" He encourages the Corinthians with a great sense of urgency to see themselves as involved in the "new creation" (5:17) that God has brought about, in and through Christ.[826] Paul admonishes them not to receive God's grace in

---

[825]For this reading of παραστήσει, see BDAG, s.v. παρίστημι, 1.e. Cf. 1 Cor 8:8. In addition, see HUGHES, *Paul's Second Epistle to the Corinthians*, 149; BARRETT, *The Second Epistle to the Corinthians*, 143; FURNISH, *II Corinthians*, 286; THRALL, *II Corinthians*, 1.343-44; and BELLEVILLE, *2 Corinthians*, 125. These commentators agree that Paul makes a future eschatological reference with the (future tense) verb παραστήσει in 4:14. *Pace* BAUMERT, who understands this verb as synonymous with φανερωθῇ in 2 Cor 4:10b and 4:11b, and thus as expressing an existential, present-life reality. See *Taglich sterben und auferstehen*, 284-99; similarly, MURPHY-O'CONNOR, "Faith and Resurrection in 2 Cor 4:13-14," 549-50.

[826]Cf. HUGHES'S comment on 2 Cor 6:2: "The quotation in its present setting may be applied in a variety of ways: firstly, to the Corinthians who in receiving the message of reconciliation had proved the reality of God's grace in Christ Jesus and His readiness to attend to their prayers; secondly, to Paul who in carrying the gospel to Corinth had experienced the power and help of God as sinners responded to his preaching; and, thirdly, to Christ Himself concerning whom, as the Servant of Jehovah, the words of Isa 49:8 were originally spoken." See *Paul's Second Epistle to the Corinthians*, 219. Cf. MARTIN, *2 Corinthians*, 168; and DANKER, *II Corinthians*, 85. I disagree with

vain (6:1), but rather to be reconciled to God (5:20), as well as to himself and to one another (including Christians elsewhere). Indeed, such reconciliation is an integral aspect of God's gift of σωτηρία.

Paul resumes his invitation to the Corinthians to participate in the story of Jesus by encouraging them to give generously to the collection for the church in Jerusalem. The apostle reminds the community in 2 Cor 9:8 of God's abundant provision of blessings that enables them to be generous in turn to those who are in need. Then Paul cites LXX Ps 111:9, which (as I proposed in Chapter Four) he reads with a christological lens (2 Cor 9:9). The apostle seems to allude here to the story and character of Jesus, to his generous caring (χάρις, cf. 8:9) and trust in God. That is, Jesus – whose living and dying for others, out of love and obedience to God, manifested God's δικαιοσύνη (Rom 1:17 and 3:21-22) – appears to be the most appropriate referent of the generous, God-fearing man whose "righteousness endures forever" (2 Cor 9:9b). In 2 Cor 9:10 Paul goes on to exhort the Corinthians to trust in God's beneficence so that they might give generously to the collection. In doing so, God will increase "the harvest of your righteousness" (τὰ γενήματα τῆς δικαιοσύνης ὑμῶν). In other words, by giving generously of themselves for the benefit of others, the Corinthians will participate in the ongoing revelation of God's righteousness (cf. 5:21b).[827] In this way they will perpetuate the pattern of existence set forth by

---

Hughes in that I argue that 6:2a refers to Paul (and possibly to Jesus), *but not to the Corinthians* (see Chapter Five, Section V.E, including n. 786). It is only in 6:2b that the apostle includes the Corinthians. Nevertheless, Hughes is on target insofar as he sees in this passage the convergence of the stories of Jesus, Paul, and the Corinthians.

[827]I anticipate the objection that I too easily conflate δικαιοσύνη θεοῦ with the righteousness that Paul attributes to the Corinthians in 2 Cor 9:10. The key to understanding the apostle's logic here is to understand how God's righteousness – revealed preeminently through Jesus' πίστις – *continues* to be made manifest through those who, like Paul, embody Christ's faithfulness (see Chapter Five, Section V.B). Thus, in 9:9 the one whose δικαιοσύνη endures forever is an appropriate description of Jesus, whose entire mode of self-giving existence – culminating with his death on the cross – is the ultimate expression of God's righteousness. The reference to the possibility (cf. the future tenses in 9:10) of the Corinthians' participation in righteousness pertains to their acting on the apostle's exhortation to be generous in giving to the collection, thereby exhibiting Jesus' pattern of self-giving for the sake of others. In all cases – whether it is Jesus' δικαιοσύνη, Paul's, or that of the Corinthians – the source of δικαιοσύνη is God (whose very essence and activity are marked by δικαιοσύνη).

Jesus, who, "although he was rich, became poor for your sake in order that out of his poverty you might become rich" (8:9). They will also join in the apostle's participation in that same dynamic – "as poor, yet making many rich" (6:10).

In fact, Paul continues, right up to the very end of the epistle (2 Cor 13:1-10), to call the community to join him in living the story of Jesus. I will treat these verses in greater depth later in this chapter. For the time being, the preceding paragraphs are sufficient to indicate that the apostle's strategy *throughout the letter* is to persuade the Corinthians to be fellow partners (κοινωνοί, 1:7) with him in embodying the character of Jesus. As we will see in the following section, that which makes them partners is the κοινωνία of the Holy Spirit (cf. 13:13). Indeed, it is the Spirit who weaves together the stories of Jesus, Paul, and the Corinthians.

III. The Transforming Effect of the Spirit on the Corinthians

I analyzed 2 Cor 1:21-22 at great length in the previous chapter. These verses describe the way in which God empowers Paul, through the gift of the Holy Spirit, to continue the story of Jesus' ναί, his ἀμήν to God. What the apostle articulates in this passage, however, is not limited to himself (and his co-

---

Indeed, 9:10 makes this abundantly clear.

BETZ is therefore correct in seeing that "the harvest of your righteousness" (9:10) is meant to be seen in continuity with the reference to "his righteousness remains forever" (9:9). See *2 Corinthians 8 and 9*, 114. However, his judgment that the meaning of the term "righteousness" changes in these verses is wrong. Rather, as GEORGI rightly notes, δικαιοσύνη here is the righteousness of God into which people are integrated. See *Remembering the Poor*, 99. FURNISH captures this well: ". . . those who give generously to the needy should know that their charitable act is a part of that larger righteousness of God by which they themselves live. . ." (*II Corinthians*, 449). Thus, there is more involved in the δικαιοσύνη of the Corinthians than merely their moral righteousness (*pace*, e.g., ALLO, *Seconde Épître aux Corinthiens*, 235; and BARRETT, *The Second Epistle to the Corinthians*, 238) or their philanthropy in almsgiving (*pace*, e.g., WINDISCH, *Der zweite Korintherbrief*, 278-79; and BELLEVILLE, *2 Corinthians*, 240). The connection with *God's* righteousness is essential.

I will return to this passage in Section IV.C when I discuss Paul's exhortations to the Corinthians to embody ἁπλότης.

workers). The Corinthians, too, are included in Paul's description.[828] Hence, God also establishes/strengthens (βεβαιόω) the community to take on the character of Christ (cf. εἰς Χριστόν) and thereby to continue his story of faithfulness. They are thus empowered because God has anointed – or better, "christed" (χρίω) – and sealed (σφραγίζω) them. Recall that the latter term connotes both that the Corinthians have been marked as belonging to God, and that they have been inscribed with the character of Jesus. Moreover, the Spirit has been given to the members of the community as ἀρραβών, a metaphor that implies not only that God's empowerment has been bestowed on them in the past, but also that it will continue to be effective in them.

Paul refers to this ongoing work of the Holy Spirit in 2 Cor 3:18. There he expressly includes the Corinthians (cf. *ἡμεῖς* πάντες) as recipients of the transforming action of the Spirit.[829] As we have seen, this transformation involves the Spirit-empowered contemplation and appropriation of the story and character of Christ (recall the triad of Ἰησοῦς-πνεῦμα-εὐαγγέλιον in 11:4). Jesus, "the image of God" (4:4), revealed what it means to be human in his perfect fidelity to God and God's will. Now, "the same Spirit of faithfulness" (4:13) enlightens (cf. 4:6)[830] and empowers the Corinthians – bestowing upon them the νοῦς Χριστοῦ (1 Cor 2:16) – so that they too might embody more and more in their lives faithfulness to God and God's will. Or, to use the apostle's terminology in 2 Cor 3:18, the Spirit transforms them ἀπὸ δόξης εἰς δόξαν ("from glory unto glory"; cf. 1:20). They are therefore truly "a new creation" (5:17).

This transforming action of the Holy Spirit within the Corinthians illuminates Paul's rhetorical play on recommendation letters in 2 Cor 3:1-3. In this passage, the apostle first raises the issue of (negative) *self*-commendation

---

[828]See n. 605 above, esp. the observation made by BELLEVILLE in "Paul's Polemic and Theology of the Spirit in Second Corinthians," 284.

[829]See n. 649 for a discussion of the possible referents of "we all." I agree with FEE'S assessment that the phrase refers, in the first place, to Paul and the Corinthians. See *God's Empowering Presence*, 314.

[830]Although *God* is named as the subject of ἔλαμψεν in 2 Cor 4:6, the action described here is (at least in part) explanatory of what Paul describes in 3:18, where the Spirit is named as the agent of transformation. Moreover, observe that the apostle makes clear in 1:21-22 that God is the one who bestows the gift of the Spirit.

(3:1a), and then proceeds to ask whether he needs, as some do, letters of recommendation to the community or from them (3:1b). That Paul expects a negative answer is evident from the particle μή at the beginning of his question. Then, in 3:2, the apostle explains why he needs no (literal) letter of recommendation: *The Corinthians themselves* are his letter of recommendation – ἡ ἐπιστολὴ ἡμῶν ὑμεῖς ἐστε.[831] Commentators tend to understand this metaphor as indicating that the very existence of the church in Corinth gives validation to Paul and his ministry.[832] This interpretation, while valid, does not go far enough. The apostle's elaboration in the following verse makes this evident.

Paul continues his argument in 2 Cor 3:3: "by becoming known[833] that you are a[n] ἐπιστολὴ Χριστοῦ delivered by us, written not with ink but with [the] Spirit of [the] living God, not on tablets of stone but on tablets of fleshly hearts." In other words, the Corinthians are the apostle's letter of

---

[831]Observe the inclusion of ὑμεῖς for emphasis.

[832]Thus, HAYS, *Echoes of Scripture in the Letters of Paul*, 127: ". . . the very existence of the church in Corinth is manifest evidence of the efficacy of Paul's apostleship." So, too, e.g., PLUMMER, *II Corinthians*, 79; BULTMANN, *The Second Letter to the Corinthians*, 71; FURNISH, *II Corinthians*, 194; TALBERT, *Reading Corinthians*, 143; HAFEMANN, *Suffering and Ministry in the Spirit*, 188; THRALL, *II Corinthians*, 1.222; LAMBRECHT, *Second Corinthians*, 46; and M.J. GOODWIN, *Paul: Apostle of the Living God* (Harrisburg, Pa.: Trinity International, 2001) 172-73.

[833]Taking φανερούμενοι as expressing manner or means. For reading this participle as signifying "become known," see BDAG, s.v. φανερόω, 2.b.β. Cf. 2 Cor 5:11. It is striking how many translators and translations render φανερούμενοι *as a main verb* of a new clause. For instance, the RSV reads: "*and you show* that you are a letter of Christ . . . ." Similarly, see PLUMMER, *II Corinthians*, 76; FURNISH, *II Corinthians*, 173; MARTIN, *2 Corinthians*, 44; THRALL, *II Corinthians*, 1.190; BARNETT, *The Second Epistle to the Corinthians*, 159; and KISTEMAKER, *The Second Epistle to the Corinthians*, 99. Failure to uphold the participial force of φανερούμενοι, however, misses an important element in Paul's argument. HÉRING (*The Second Epistle of Saint Paul to the Corinthians*, 21), BARRETT (*The Second Epistle to the Corinthians*, 96), and LAMBRECHT (*Second Corinthians*, 37) do maintain the integrity of the participle, although they understand it as expressing *cause*. While this reading is defensible on grammatical grounds, I submit that it misses an important nuance in the apostle's argument in 2 Cor 3:1-3.

recommendation insofar as they qualify to be known as a "letter Χριστοῦ." The vast majority of interpreters take the genitive Χριστοῦ as subjective, understanding the phrase in question to mean that the church in Corinth is a "letter" *from* or *by* Christ.[834] Although this is a plausible reading, I propose that the genitive here signifies the *content* of the letter (with Χριστοῦ rendered as an objective genitive). By the phrase ἐπιστολὴ Χριστοῦ, Paul means (metaphorically) a letter *about* Christ. And how do the Corinthians show that they are an epistle about Christ? They do so by taking on the attitude, values, and behavior manifested by Jesus – in short, by embodying his *ethos*.[835] That this is the case is suggested by the means by which this letter is "written": πνεύματι θεοῦ ζῶντος ("*by* [the] Spirit of [the] living God"). This is the same πνεῦμα τῆς πίστεως, bestowed in human hearts (3:3; cf. 1:22b), who "christs" and transforms the Corinthians into the image of Christ, God's faithful δοῦλος. Thus, in 3:3 the apostle once again draws upon the transforming power of the Spirit, the power that enables recipients to incarnate Jesus' self-giving mode of existence for the sake of others.[836]

This reading is reinforced by two further clues in 2 Cor 3:3. First is the participle φανερούμενοι, a word closely linked with ἐπιστολὴ Χριστοῦ.

---

[834]So, e.g., PLUMMER, *II Corinthians*, 81 (subjective genitive); FURNISH, *II Corinthians*, 182 (authorial genitive); THRALL, *II Corinthians*, 1.224 (genitive of origin); and BELLEVILLE, *2 Corinthians*, 90 (genitive of source).

[835]SCHOLLA captures this well: "Given the context, it seems that Paul intends to emphasize *'Christ' as the content of this living text*. Consequently, by identifying the Corinthians as 'a letter of Christ,' Paul underscores *the christological substance of their life*: Christ Jesus is not only the foundation of their faith, but he is historically manifest to all humanity through their life and action (1 Cor 3:11). In this way, Jesus' witness to God and to the world continues through the community of believers, they are the perceptible expression of God's eschatological victory – a living 'letter of Christ.'" See "Into the Image of God," 40 (italics added). Scholla's last sentence is another way of expressing what I mean by the Corinthians' participating in and continuing the story of Jesus. MATERA points out that Chrysostom likewise understood ἐπιστολὴ Χριστοῦ as referring to the community's embodying Jesus. See *II Corinthians*, 77.

[836]Cf. GOODWIN, who remarks that Paul is concerned with "people-formation" in 2 Cor 3:3. See *Paul*, 183. Goodwin, however, does not push this insight in the direction that I propose. He sees the expression "Spirit of the living God" primarily as an allusion to the apostle's initial proclamation to the Corinthians and to their subsequent conversion.

Paul's use of the passive voice of φανερόω in 3:3 anticipates the usage in 4:10b and 4:11b. In these latter verses, he employs the verb to describe how the power of the risen Christ is made manifest through his (the apostle's) participation in Jesus' manner of living and dying (cf. 'bearing the νέκρωσις 'Ιησοῦ', 4:10a; and 'being handed over διὰ 'Ιησοῦν,' 4:11a). I submit that Paul uses φανερόω in 3:3 in the same way, in connection with the manifestation of Jesus' mode of existence.[837] The second clue is the participle διακονηθεῖσα, which I have translated "delivered" (by the apostle and his co-workers). I submit, however, that the verb διακονέω here does not merely signify the notion of 'delivering a letter.'[838] A deeper look at the text reveals that διακονηθεῖσα in 3:3 anticipates Paul's reference to himself as a "minister of [the] new covenant" (διάκονος καινῆς διαθήκης, 3:6; cf. διάκονος θεοῦ, 6:4), a covenant that involves "the ministry of the Spirit" (ἡ διακονία τοῦ πνεύματος, 3:8).[839] In fact, it is through the apostle's giving of himself for the sake of the Corinthians (cf. 4:5) that they are in a position to become a letter about Christ.[840] In addition, διακονηθεῖσα in 3:3 anticipates his reference to the collection as "the ministry unto the holy ones" (ἡ διακονία ἡ εἰς τοὺς ἁγίους, 8:4 and 9:1), the

---

[837]Cf. KISTEMAKER (*The Second Epistle to the Corinthians*, 102), who observes that φανερούμενοι in 3:3 may be rendered as middle (as does HÉRING, *The Second Epistle of Saint Paul to the Corinthians*, 21) or passive voice: "Both translations are equally acceptable, but I prefer the passive construction, which has God as the implied agent." Kistemaker's instinct here is right, but I would refine his comment: It is the "Spirit of the living God" who is the implied agent.

[838]Cf. W. BAIRD, who argues that Paul intends no more by this verb (in 2 Cor 3:3) than "deliver" or "carry." See "Letters of Recommendation: A Study of II Cor. 3:1-3," *JBL* 80 (1961) 166-72. In his concern to show how the apostle uses the motif of the letter of recommendation thoroughly and consistently, Baird reduces the meaning of διακονηθεῖσα too narrowly, thereby missing the connections with Paul's other use of διακον- terminology elsewhere in 2 Cor. For a more detailed critique of Baird's position, see HAFEMANN, *Suffering and Ministry in the Spirit*, 200-205.

[839]Similarly, HAYS, *Echoes of Scripture in the Letters of Paul*, 127; and FEE, *God's Empowering Presence*, 303.

[840]Cf. MARTIN: "Yet [the Corinthians] would not have become this [i.e., ἐπιστολὴ Χριστοῦ] had Paul not 'ministered' (διακονηθεῖσα ὑφ' ἡμῶν) to them." See *2 Corinthians*, 51.

collection that is an enactment of "the ministry of reconciliation" (ἡ διακονία τῆς καταλλαγῆς, 5:18).

Indeed, I propose that Paul's reminder to the Corinthians in 2 Cor 3:3 that they have been "ministered to" (the literal meaning of διακονηθεῖσα) by him serves an important rhetorical function. While 3:1-3 appears to begin with the apostle's defensiveness, he quickly shifts to put the onus on the community. They are his recommendation letter, but only insofar as they take on more and more the character of Jesus, as Paul himself has done by being διάκονος in service to them. The apostle thus subtly challenges the Corinthians to consider whether or not their lives reflect the empowerment of the Spirit – whether or not the ἐπιστολὴ Χριστοῦ is truly being written in them.[841] His strategy is formulated, I suggest, with an eye toward the collection. Just as the Corinthians have been ministered to by Paul, so now they are to minister to the needs of the church in Jerusalem. Indeed, the apostle's tactic in 3:3 foreshadows his rhetorical strategy in 13:5, where he turns the tables again on the Corinthians by commanding them to test their own δοκιμή.

That Paul is concerned with the community's appropriation of the Spirit's empowerment is also evident from the very last words of the letter: "The grace of our Lord Jesus Christ and the love of God and the fellowship of the Holy Spirit (ἡ κοινωνία τοῦ ἁγίου πνεύματος) be with you" (2 Cor 13:13). This extended grace-benediction is conspicuous when compared with the apostle's other closing blessings. Paul usually concludes his letters more simply: 'The grace of the/our Lord Jesus [Christ] be with you.'[842] The apostle's addition of "the love of God and the fellowship of the Holy Spirit," therefore, merits special attention. My concern here is primarily with the κοινωνία τοῦ ἁγίου πνεύματος.

In his analysis of 2 Cor 13:13, G.D. FEE aptly observes: "It is arguable that in ways that may not immediately meet the eye this is a singularly

---

[841]Thus, I submit that the typical position of commentators, captured succinctly by BELLEVILLE – "Paul's posture in 2 Cor 3:1-3 is a *defensive* one" – is overstated and not sufficiently nuanced. See "Paul's Polemic and Theology of the Spirit in Second Corinthians," 290 (italics added).

[842]Cf. Rom 16:20b, 1 Cor 16:23, Gal 6:18, Phil 4:23, 1 Thess 5:28, 2 Thess 3:18, and Phlm 25, all of which follow this basic form with only slight variations. Cf. also Eph 6:24 and 2 Tim 4:22. In the remaining letters, Paul prays simply, "Grace be with you [all]." See Col 4:18b, 1 Tim 6:21b, and Titus 3:15b.

significant conclusion to all the *theological* and *behavioral concerns* of this letter."[843] In terms of *theological concerns*, Paul's blessing is a summary and reminder of how *God's* love (ἡ ἀγάπη τοῦ θεοῦ) has been preeminently manifested, namely through "the grace of the Lord Jesus Christ." This latter expression – ἡ χάρις τοῦ κυρίου 'Ιησοῦ Χριστοῦ – recalls 2 Cor 8:9, where the apostle alludes to the story of Jesus' self-giving love in schematic form.[844] Moreover, Paul makes clear in 13:13 that God's love continues to be revealed through the gift of the fellowship of the Spirit, the gift that empowers its recipients to continue the story of Jesus (cf. 1:18-22).

The apostle's prayer that the κοινωνία τοῦ ἁγίου πνεύματος be bestowed on the Corinthians also touches on *behavioral concerns* – specifically the behavior of the community. Commentators are divided over what Paul intended by the genitive πνεύματος. Is it an objective genitive, thereby indicating one's fellowship with or participation in the Spirit?[845] Or is it a subjective genitive, thereby signifying the fellowship among people that the Spirit produces?[846] I suggest that, in this case, making an either/or decision about the genitive takes away from the richness of the apostle's prayer. That is, the genitive πνεύματος connotes *both* that the Spirit draws people into fellowship with itself (cf. the references to the Spirit's presence ἐν ταῖς καρδίαις; e.g., 2 Cor 1:22 and 3:3) *and* that the Spirit empowers people to live in closer fellowship with one another (cf. the apostle's exhortations in 13:11, all of which pertain to promoting greater harmony – κοινωνία – in the

---

[843]FEE, *God's Empowering Presence*, 362 (italics added). A couple of paragraphs later, he adds: "In many ways this benediction is the most profound theological moment in the Pauline corpus" (ibid., 363).

[844]Recall SAMPLEY'S comment that 2 Cor 8:9 is the "big story" about Jesus told "in its most cursory form." See both *NIB*, 11.123 and n. 521 above.

[845]So, WINDISCH, *Der zweite Korintherbrief*, 428; BARRETT, *The Second Epistle to the Corinthians*, 344; FURNISH, *II Corinthians*, 584; FEE, *God's Empowering Presence*, 363, n. 232; and THRALL, *II Corinthians*, 2.919.

[846]So, PLUMMER, *II Corinthians*, 383-84; HÉRING, *The Second Epistle of Saint Paul to the Corinthians*, 103; BRUCE, *1 and 2 Corinthians*, 255; MARTIN, *2 Corinthians*, 505; BELLEVILLE, "Paul's Polemic and Theology of the Spirit in Second Corinthians," 289; BARNETT, *The Second Epistle to the Corinthians*, 618, n. 14; and MCCANT, *2 Corinthians*, 171.

community[847]).[848] Indeed, it is only with the Spirit's indwelling and empowerment that the Corinthians can take on the character and manner of Jesus, especially by living for the advantage of others (cf. 5:14-15).[849] In doing so, they will join Paul in participating in the ministry of reconciliation (which

---

[847]As rightly pointed out by BELLEVILLE, "Paul's Polemic and Theology of the Spirit in Second Corinthians," 289. Her comment, however, that "it is the activity of the Spirit rather than our participation in the Spirit that is highlighted throughout" 2 Cor makes too much of the distinction. The Spirit's activity is possible only insofar as there is (human) participation in the Spirit.

[848]So, too, J.M. MCDERMOTT and B. SCHNEIDER. MCDERMOTT rightly observes: "One need not limit Paul's grammar too narrowly; perhaps both meanings are intended at least implicitly. . . ." See "The Biblical Doctrine of KOINΩNIA," *BZ* 19 (1975) 219-33, here 223-24. Cf. MURPHY-O'CONNOR, *The Theology of the Second Letter to the Corinthians*, 136; and MATERA, *II Corinthians*, 314. SCHNEIDER makes clear that 2 Cor 13:13 does not imply that Paul is praying that the fellowship of the Holy Spirit come to the Corinthians for the first time; rather, "[h]e is praying and wishing that they be strengthened and grow and receive more. . . ." See "HE KOINONIA TOU HAGIOU PNEUMATOS (II Cor. 13, 13)," in *Studies Honoring Ignatius Charles Brady Friar Minor*, TS 6, ed. R.S. ALMAGNO and C.L. HARKINS (St. Bonaventure, N.Y.: The Franciscan Institute, 1976) 421-47, here 422 and 440-41 (the quote is from p. 440). SAMPLEY also holds that the genitive πνεύματος is "powerfully ambiguous." See *NIB*, 11.179. It should be noted that the phrase κοινωνία πνεύματος also occurs in Phil 2:1. THRALL comments that "here [in Phil 2:1] the sense of the expression is ambiguous." See *II Corinthians*, 2.918. This observation adds to the plausibility that the same is true in 2 Cor 13:13.

[849]Concerning Paul's invocation of the Spirit in 2 Cor 13:13, R.P. MARTIN remarks: "[Paul] is seeking to establish the Holy Spirit as *the authentic sign of the new age, already begun but not yet realized in its fullness*, and he is building his case on *the readers' participation in the Spirit as the hallmark of their share in . . . the new world of God's righteousness. . . .*" See "The Spirit in 2 Corinthians in Light of the 'Fellowship of the Holy Spirit' in 2 Corinthians 13:14," in *Eschatology and the New Testament: Essays in Honor of George Raymond Beasley-Murray*, ed. W.H. GLOER (Peabody, Mass.: Hendrickson, 1988) 113-28, here 127 (Martin's italics). Martin's observation that the Spirit is the hallmark of the Corinthians' share in God's righteousness takes on greater weight, I submit, when δικαιοσύνη θεοῦ is understood as I proposed in the previous chapter – that is, God's righteousness continues to be revealed through the Corinthians' Spirit-empowered living after the pattern of Jesus' πίστις.

entails restoring broken relationships). Hence, the apostle's final prayer in 13:13 functions as a reminder to the community of the Spirit's presence *and* of the community-building behavior that the Spirit enables.

In fact, Paul has already employed a similar strategy in 2 Cor 6:16b-7:1.[850] In these verses he calls upon the Corinthians to recognize the presence of the Spirit among them, and to live in accord with the identity that the Spirit bestows on them. In 6:16b the apostle writes: ἡμεῖς ναὸς θεοῦ ἐσμεν ζῶντος ("*We*[851] are [the] temple of [the] living God"). That this is an allusion to the Spirit's dwelling within the Corinthians is evident from a question Paul had asked the community in a previous letter (1 Cor 3:16): "Do you not know that you [i.e., the Corinthians] are God's temple, and that *the Spirit of God dwells in you* (τὸ πνεῦμα τοῦ θεοῦ οἰκεῖ ἐν ὑμῖν)?" Thus, I submit that the apostle's statement in 2 Cor 6:16b would have readily evoked for the Corinthians the reality of the Spirit's indwelling among them.[852] Indeed, Paul

---

[850]Of course, these verses fall within 2 Cor 6:14-7:1, the notorious "fragment" whose authenticity is hotly debated. It is beyond the scope of my study to engage this debate. For reading this passage as Pauline (as I do), see, e.g., G.D. FEE, "II Corinthians vi.14-vii.1 and Food Offered to Idols," *NTS* 23 (1976-77) 140-61; M.E. THRALL, "The Problem of II Cor. vi.14-vii.1 in Some Recent Discussions," *NTS* 24 (1977-78) 132-48; J. MURPHY-O'CONNOR, "Philo and 2 Cor. 6:14-7:1," *RB* 95 (1988) 55-69; and J. LAMBRECHT, "The Fragment of 2 Corinthians 6:14-7:1: A Plea for Its Authenticity," in R. BIERINGER and J. LAMBRECHT, *Studies on 2 Corinthians*, BETL 112 (Leuven: Leuven University Press, 1994) 531-49. In addition, see WEBB, *Returning Home*, for a full-length study that offers a contextual and integrated reading of 6:14-7:1 in light of Second Exodus and new covenant traditions. I agree with the position taken by N.A. DAHL that 6:14-7:1 functions in its context as an admonition against siding with the intruding missionaries against Paul. See "A Fragment and Its Context: 2 Corinthians 6:14-7:1," in *Studies in Paul: Theology for the Early Christian Mission* (Minneapolis: Augsburg, 1977) 62-69. In addition, see SCOTT, *2 Corinthians*, 151-56; and HAFEMANN, *2 Corinthians*, 279-80 and 288.

[851]Reading ἡμεῖς rather than ὑμεῖς. See METZGER, *A Textual Commentary on the Greek New Testament*, 512.

[852]Cf. BELLEVILLE'S criticism of FEE'S *God's Empowering Presence*: "[Fee] devotes an entire chapter to the Spirit in 2 Corinthians; yet he goes to the other extreme and includes any passage that, in his judgment, implies the work of the Spirit. This amounts to thirty-two passages, while explicit mention of the Spirit occurs in only twelve." See

immediately goes on to explain to them that God (through the Spirit) dwells in them (6:16c). As God's temple, they have a special relationship with God: The Corinthians now belong to the people of God (6:16d); even more, they are "sons and daughters" of God (6:18).[853] In addition to recalling to the community their Spirit-given identity as God's children, the apostle also points out to them the appropriate behavior that this identity entails. The Corinthians are to separate and cleanse themselves from all that keeps them from living out their identity (6:17). Positively expressed, they are to "bring about," "accomplish" – literally, "make perfect" (ἐπιτελέω)[854] – *holiness* (ἁγιωσύνη – 7:1).

To 'make holiness perfect,'[855] I propose, is Paul's shorthand for appropriating and manifesting the manner of human existence revealed by Jesus, the εἰκὼν τοῦ θεοῦ. This is what the apostle implies when he reminds the Corinthians that they are to be a "letter about Christ." And it is through "the κοινωνία of the *Holy* Spirit" – whose action is described as "christing" – that the community is empowered more and more to embody the *ethos* of Jesus. It

---

BELLEVILLE, "Paul's Polemic and Theology of the Spirit in Second Corinthians," 282, n. 8. While Belleville's critique has some merit, Fee is entirely justified in treating 2 Cor 6:16-7:1 as a passage pertaining to the Spirit (see *God's Empowering Presence*, 336-39). In fact, GOODWIN rightly argues that Paul's mention of the "temple of the living God" in 6:16b evokes his reference to the "Spirit of the living God" in 3:3. See *Paul*, 218-20.

[853]Cf. Rom 8:14-17, where Paul makes clear that those who are led by the Spirit are children of God. FEE challenges the interpretation of 2 Cor 6:16-7:1 that sees these verses primarily as a threat or warning, for the apostle's reference to ἐπαγγελίαι in 7:1 shows that he understands the citations in 6:16b-6:18 chiefly as promises. See *God's Empowering Presence*, 337. Indeed, it is true that Paul has already referred to "God's promises" in 2 Cor 1:20a. While these promises have been fulfilled preeminently by Jesus' Yes, the apostle suggests in 1:20b-22 that they continue to be fulfilled through the ongoing ἀμήν of those who have been "christed" by the Spirit.

[854]It is worth noting that, in Gal 3:3, Paul uses the passive voice of the verb ἐπιτελέω with cultic connotations: "Are you so foolish? Having begun in [the] Spirit, are you now being perfected by means of [the] flesh?" The reference in this passage is to circumcision. See, e.g., J.L. MARTYN, *Galatians*, 292-94. This cultic nuance is suggestive for 2 Cor 6:14-7:1, especially given the apostle's employment there of the imagery of the temple of God. Cf. 2 Cor 1:20 and 2:14-16.

[855]The RSV aptly offers this translation.

is to the ways in which Paul grounds his *specific* exhortations to the Corinthians in the character of Jesus that I now turn. This analysis returns us to the apostle's use of δοκιμ- terminology.

IV. The Corinthians Are Challenged to Take on the Character of Jesus

Throughout 2 Corinthians, Paul exhorts and challenges the Corinthians to take on characteristics he associates with Jesus. The apostle especially calls forth from the Corinthians obedience, love, singleness/generosity, and faithfulness. Before analyzing how he does so, it is first necessary to step back and clarify the "rhetorical situation"[856] of 2 Corinthians.

Paul exercised great care and concern for the churches that he founded (see, e.g., 2 Cor 11:28-29). At least with respect to the Corinthians, the apostle responded to questions and/or concerns written to him (e.g., 1 Cor 7:1a), as well as to oral reports about the community's conduct (1 Cor 1:11 and 2 Cor 7:6-7). Paul's letters were not written in a vacuum. Rather, he responded as a pastor to the particular situations and circumstances of his communities. Three such circumstances are germane to understanding the apostle's exhortations to the community in 2 Corinthians. Although I have already alluded to these circumstances in the previous chapters, it is helpful to present them at this point in succinct fashion. It is extremely important to keep in mind that the data from which we reconstruct the rhetorical situation of this letter are *limited*, and that they come *from Paul himself*. Hence, the rhetorical situation outlined below is from the perspective of the apostle, constructed out of his own perceptions.[857]

---

[856]Cf. L.F. BITZER'S helpful definition: "Rhetorical situation may be defined as *a complex of persons, events, objects, and relations presenting an actual or potential exigence* which can be completely or partially removed if discourse, introduced into the situation, can so constrain human decision or action as to bring about the significant modification of the exigence." See BITZER, "The Rhetorical Situation," *Philosophy and Rhetoric* 1 (1968) 1-14, here 6 (italics added). For a concise discussion of "rhetorical situation," see G.A. KENNEDY, *New Testament Interpretation through Rhetorical Criticism*, 34-36.

[857]YOUNG and FORD'S methodological modesty deserves to be quoted at length in this connection: ". . . it is important to admit ignorance if ignorance is all we have. A great deal of exegesis falls into the trap of circularity: the text is used to reconstruct the situation and then the situation is used to interpret the text. In reaction against this, *we*

(1) During Paul's (recent) second visit to Corinth, an incident occurred in which a member of the community somehow "wronged" (ἀδικέω, 2 Cor 7:12; cf. λυπέω, 2:5 – "caused pain" to) him. Moreover, apparently no one came (immediately) to the apostle's defense. He claimed that this incident caused harm to the entire community (2:5). Only later, in response to his 'tearful letter' (2:4 and 7:8), did the Corinthians – at least the majority of them (cf. ὑπὸ τῶν πλειόνων) – mete out a punishment to the offending member (2:6). Titus reported the community's actions back to Paul, as well as their zeal and longing for him (7:7). In writing 2 Corinthians, the apostle deals with the community's response and how they are now to relate to the punished member (2:7-10). Furthermore, clues throughout the text suggest that unresolved tensions still remain between Paul and the Corinthians (see e.g., 6:11-13). In short, there appears to be a need for further reconciliation between the community and the apostle.

(2) Paul continues to collect funds for the church in Jerusalem. He refers to the collection as "the ministry unto the holy ones" (2 Cor 8:4 and 9:1), a work that the apostle had initiated among the Corinthians the year before (1 Cor 16:1-4 and 2 Cor 8:10-11). The community, however, has yet to complete its contribution, one that they had promised to make (2 Cor 9:5). The collection appeal is compounded by the fact that Paul remains adamant about not accepting financial support from the Corinthians for his ministry to them, something that other missionaries/evangelists apparently do (11:7-12). He insists on preaching the gospel free of charge to the community, even though it is within his right as an apostle to be remunerated (1 Cor 9:1-18). Paul's insistence on not burdening the Corinthians on the one hand, and his cajoling them to be generous in giving to the collection on the other, have brought him under a cloud of suspicion (2 Cor 12:16-18; cf. 7:2).

---

have endeavoured to look at what Paul was saying and not be too concerned to deduce a precise reconstruction of what lies behind it. We have also come to the conclusion that a number of factors affected the way Paul perceived the situation and led him to characterize it in certain stereotyped ways. This reduces the possibility of drawing conclusions about the reality behind the text from the descriptions we find in Paul's letters. And indeed, for the purpose of interpreting this text, *it may be more important to understand how Paul saw the situation* than to grasp what it really was. All too often scholars have been so preoccupied with reading between the lines for clues as to what was going on that they have failed to engage with what Paul has to say." See *Meaning and Truth in 2 Corinthians*, 44-45 (italics added).

(3) Other missionaries/evangelists have emerged or arrived in Corinth. Paul dubs them "the superlative apostles" (οἱ ὑπερλίαν ἀπόστολοι; 2 Cor 11:5 and 12:11). According to him, they engage in *self*-commendation (ἑαυτοὺς συνιστάνειν) in which they boast of great exploits and accomplishments (10:12-18; cf. 11:23).[858] The apostle implies that they inappropriately make their presence felt, lording it over the community (11:20). He regards them as "peddling" (καπηλεύω, 2:17) and even "distorting" (δολόω, 4:2) God's word. Indeed, Paul insinuates that their behavior and message are tantamount to preaching "another Jesus" and "a different gospel" (11:4). These missionaries/evangelists apparently hold the apostle's bodily appearance and speaking abilities in low esteem (10:10 and 11:6a). Although there is no explicit evidence in this regard, it is easy to imagine their antagonism toward Paul, and their desire to turn the Corinthians against him. This might be easily accomplished by fueling the fires of suspicion that already surround the apostle in connection with the collection/remuneration issue: his solicitation of money for others while refusing it himself.

Paul writes 2 Corinthians in the context of these circumstances. They form the horizon against which to understand his specific exhortations. Observe that the rhetorical situation just described entails the Corinthians' having some strong reservations and questions about the apostle and his ministry. They seem to think – perhaps having been encouraged by the aforementioned missionaries/ evangelists – that he needs to be "tested" (2 Cor 13:3a). As we saw in the previous chapter, Paul's response throughout this letter makes it clear that, in his manner of being an apostle, he regards himself as embodying the *ethos* of Jesus. Yet what is most striking about Paul's response is that he insists that it is *the Corinthians* who need to be tested. As I will demonstrate in the following pages, the apostle challenges the community to commit to and follow his example by making decisions that will lead to their progressive incarnation of the character of Jesus. The "meat" of Paul's response to the rhetorical situation is not self-defense, therefore, but rather admonition and exhortation. Indeed, I suggest that, insofar as he does engage in (positive) self-*commendation*, such commendation largely functions to show the Corinthians what it means to embody Christ's *ethos*. The apostle's main purpose is to urge the community

---

[858]For Paul's understanding of this *negative* aspect of self-commendation, see Chapter Five, Section I.

to join him in participating in the story of Jesus through their obedience, love, singleness/generosity, and faithfulness.

A. Obedience (ὑπακοή; ὑποταγή; ὑπήκοος)

Paul calls forth obedience from the Corinthians in all three aspects of the rhetorical situation sketched above. In the following paragraphs, I discuss how he tests their obedience in 2 Cor 2:9, 7:15, 9:13, and 10:5-6. In each case, I submit that the apostle's overarching strategy is to encourage the Corinthians to embody the "obedience of Christ" (ὑπακοὴ τοῦ Χριστοῦ).

After mentioning the punishment meted out by the community to the person who "had caused pain" (λελύπηκεν)[859] to him (2 Cor 2:5-6), and after exhorting them to receive this person back with forgiveness and love (2:7-8), Paul states: "For this reason καὶ[860] ἔγραψα, in order that I might know your character (δοκιμήν), whether you are obedient (ὑπήκοοι) in all things" (2:9). The important thing to observe here is the apostle's stated *purpose* (ἵνα) in writing: Paul seeks to know the quality of the Corinthians' *character*.[861] The

---

[859]That Paul twice uses the perfect tense of λυπέω in 2 Cor 2:5 indicates that, in his estimation, whatever happened continues to have malignant effects.

[860]THRALL offers a good discussion of the problems attending the placement and meaning of καί in 2 Cor 2:9. See *II Corinthians*, 1.178. If one takes καί to mean "also" (e.g., HUGHES, *Paul's Second Epistle to the Corinthians*, 69 – "For to this end also did I write. . ."), then it seems that Paul offers here an additional reason for writing the letter referred to in 2:3-4. But as Thrall points out, one would then expect the following syntax: ἔγραψα γὰρ καὶ εἰς τοῦτο. If one takes καί to signify "indeed" (e.g., FURNISH, *II Corinthians*, 153 – "It was indeed for this purpose that I wrote. . ."), then the apostle seems to formulate in another manner the reason he gave in 2:3-4. But as Thrall indicates, the backward reference is somewhat remote. Moreover, the second reason seems more than a reformulation of the first. It should be noted that both of these scenarios presume reading ἔγραψα as a regular aorist. As we will see, a way out of this dilemma is to read ἔγραψα as an epistolary aorist. Cf. n. 866 below.

[861]Both MATERA (*II Corinthians*, 60-62) and SCOTT (*2 Corinthians*, 49) interpret 2 Cor 2:9 as Paul testing the Corinthians' character. Indeed, Scott observes that, whereas the apostle has been handling accusations leveled against his own character by the community (in 1:15-2:4), he "now turns the tables by stating that he was examining the Corinthians' character" (ibid). I would modify Scott's assessment by stating that Paul's

apostle challenges the community to show or prove their δοκιμή – here in terms of their obedience. In order to understand what this obedience entails, it is first necessary to determine the force of the aorist ἔγραψα. Is it a regular aorist, simply signifying something that occurred in the past, or is it an epistolary aorist?

The vast majority of commentators render ἔγραψα in 2 Cor 2:9 as a regular aorist. That Paul refers here to an act of writing in the (recent) past is plausible for two reasons. First, the apostle has just alluded in 2:3-4 to having written – using the same verb, ἔγραψα – to the community "out of great affliction and anguish of heart" and "through many tears" (2:3-4). Second, in 7:8 he mentions this same letter and acknowledges that it caus*ed* pain (ἐλύπησεν, 7:8) to the Corinthians. Now, if ἔγραψα is a regular aorist, then the test of obedience must also pertain to a matter in the past: whether or not the community would have dealt out some punishment (ἐπιτιμία, 2:6) to "the one who had offended" (7:12) Paul.[862] The significance of the apostle's testing the Corinthians' obedience in 2:9, however, would not lie in the act of punishment *per se*. Rather, Paul (in this scenario) would have been concerned that the community take some action to demonstrate that they recognized that he – as "an apostle of Christ Jesus through the will of God" (1:1) – had authentically proclaimed to them, both through word and deed, "the gospel of God" (11:7). In other words, Paul's test of the community's obedience would have involved,

---

test of the community pertains to something in the present. The apostle will 'turn the tables' on the Corinthians again in 13:5.

[862]So, e.g., HUGHES, *Paul's Second Epistle to the Corinthians*, 70; BRUCE, *1 and 2 Corinthians*, 185; and WITHERINGTON, *Conflict & Community in Corinth*, 365. Cf. SAMPLEY, *NIB*, 11.53.

in essence, whether or not they recognized and responded to what *God*[863] was calling them to do through him as Christ's apostle.[864]

It is also grammatically possible, however, to render ἔγραψα in 2 Cor 2:9 as an epistolary aorist.[865] If this is the case, then Paul would be referring to his present act of writing (that is, to what we now call 2 Corinthians). His test of the community would therefore also entail something in the here and now: Will the community forgive and comfort the offending person (2:7), thus heeding the apostle's explicit exhortation to reaffirm their love for this person (2:8)? The proof of the Corinthians' δοκιμή would thus be their obedience as manifested by reconciling a fellow community member. I propose that this reading makes better sense of Paul's line of thought in 2:7-11.[866] Observe that

---

[863]Cf. FURNISH, *II Corinthians*, 162: "... for Paul obedience is to God (Rom 10:30-32) .... Finally, Paul knows, it is God alone who judges whether one has stood the test of Christian obedience (10:18; 1 Thess 2:4; cf. 1 Cor 3:13). Nevertheless, as an apostle he does not hesitate to serve as an instrument of that testing by which the authenticity and fiber of one's faith is brought to light." BARRETT also recognizes that the apostle does not seek obedience to himself *per se*. Barrett's reasoning for doing so, however, is insufficient. His purpose is to avoid Paul's contradicting what he said in 2 Cor 1:24 (about not 'lording over' the Corinthians' faith). See *The Second Epistle to the Corinthians*, 92. I submit that the key here is to see *how* the apostle calls the community to "Christ-obedience," an obedience that is directed to God.

[864]THRALL, who reads ἔγραψα as a regular aorist, sets forth the major problems with this line of interpretation. Whereas in 2 Cor 2:4 Paul explained that he wrote to the community in order to confirm his love for them, in 2:9 he states that he wrote in order to exert his authority as their apostle. In addition, the apostle's remark in 2:9 that he seeks their obedience in all things seems to belie what he said in 1:24 about not lording it over their faith. See *II Corinthians*, 1.179.

[865]Indeed, Paul uses the epistolary aorist in 2 Cor 8:17 (ἐξῆλθεν); 8:18 and 8:22 (συνεπέμψαμεν); and 9:3 (ἔπεμψα).

[866]Thus, I propose the following translation of 2 Cor 2:9: "For this reason indeed I am writing, ..." For reading καί as explicative, see BDAG, s.v. καί, 1.c. Cf. 1 Cor 3:5 and 15:38. Observe BARNETT'S interpretation of 2:9: "[Paul's] real purpose in writing the 'Severe Letter' was the same as in writing the present letter, namely, 'that I might know the proof of you, that you are obedient in everything.' He called for discipline of the man then; *he calls for forgiveness of him now* (vv. 6-8); but the principle is constant, that they 'prove' themselves to be 'obedient.'" See *The Second Epistle to the*

his challenge to the community – to offer forgiveness as a demonstration of their obedience – not only follows naturally on his recommendation and appeal to forgive in 2:7-8; it also helps to explain the apostle's statement in 2:10 that he himself is willing to forgive. By manifesting obedience in this manner, the Corinthians would thereby participate in what he later calls "the ministry of reconciliation" (5:18). In this way, their obedience would ultimately be directed to God, who appeals (through ministers like Paul; cf. 5:20) to people to be reconciled.[867] In either reading, the key point is that, for the apostle, the Corinthians' "being obedient" (cf. ὑπήκοοι εἶναι) is essential to prove their character, their δοκιμή.

One final observation concerning this text: I note Paul's striking use of ὑπήκοος. This adjective appears only twice in his writings, here in 2 Cor 2:9 and in Phil 2:8.[868] In the latter passage, the apostle attributes ὑπήκοος to Jesus,

---

Corinthians, 128 (italics added). Similarly KISTEMAKER, *The Second Epistle to the Corinthians*, 79; HAFEMANN, *2 Corinthians*, 89; and MATERA, *II Corinthians*, 62. I am in basic agreement with Barnett, Kistemaker, Hafemann, and Matera's understanding of the passage. But notice that the only way that one can interpret the challenge to the Corinthians to forgive *as a test of their character* is to read ἔγραψα as an epistolary aorist (which Barnett, Kistemaker, Hafemann, and Matera do *not* do). HAFEMANN rightly observes that by being obedient in the matter of extending forgiveness, the Corinthians "will be following Paul's example in extending mercy to the Corinthians themselves, just as he follows the example of Christ (1 Cor 11:1)." Hafemann goes on to call such obedience "Christ-like obedience" (*2 Corinthians*, 89), which is how I propose reading ὑπακοὴ τοῦ Χριστοῦ in 2 Cor 10:5.

[867]It is germane to note that Paul uses the same verb, παρακαλῶ, in 2 Cor 2:8 (indicating his appeal to the Corinthians to reaffirm their love for the punished offender) and in 5:20 (signifying that God appeals through the apostle and ministers like him for people to be reconciled). It might be objected that my interpretation requires reading ἔγραψα in 2:4 and 2:9 in different ways. In addition to claiming that my interpretation of 2:9 makes better sense of the flow of 2:7-10, I suggest that the person entrusted with delivering and reading this letter (Titus?) would have known how to render the two instances of ἔγραψα.

[868]Commentators rarely observe this fact. FURNISH is a notable exception. See *II Corinthians*, 157. Nevertheless, he dismisses the significance of obedience in 2 Cor (esp. in comparison to Rom). On the contrary, I argue that the notion of obedience *is* crucially important in 2 Cor, especially in terms of the community's assumption of the character

who "lowered himself, becoming *obedient* unto death." Christ's 'obedience unto death' was the ultimate expression of his lifelong ναί to God and to God's will. It was thus the climactic articulation of Jesus' self-giving manner of existence, a mode of being encapsulated by the idiom ἐταπείνωσεν ἑαυτόν ("he lowered himself"; cf. 2 Cor 11:7).[869] Is it possible to draw a connection between these two instances of ὑπήκοος? While caution must be exercised, the fact that Paul refers later to the "obedience of Christ" in 2 Cor 10:5 is suggestive. I submit that, by employing the adjective ὑπήκοος in 2:9, the apostle draws upon the story of Jesus. By doing so, he hints at something that will become more evident in the following paragraphs, namely, that the Corinthians ought to emulate Christ's obedience to God and God's will – here, by reaffirming their own love for a recalcitrant community member (reading, as I propose, ἔγραψα as an epistolary aorist).

Paul next mentions obedience in 2 Cor 7:15. The context is Titus's return to the apostle after visiting Corinth (7:6-7). Titus reported to Paul the community's loyalty to him, as well as their mourning (most likely for their passivity during the incident involving the offending member). The apostle then shares with the community the joy and consolation he felt in the wake of this news from Titus (7:8-16). Finally, in 7:15, Paul recounts his co-worker's great affections for them "as [Titus] remembers the obedience of you all (τὴν πάντων ὑμῶν ὑπακοήν), as with fear and trembling you received him." Notice that what gives the apostle and Titus joy and consolation is *the Corinthians' obedience* (ὑπακοή). In this instance, their obedience was manifested in their grieving and repenting (7:9-10), which led them to take action. This action included the punishment (ἐκδίκησις) of the offending member, and expressed their desire for reconciliation with Paul (7:11).[870] By

---

of Christ.

[869]Observe that the participial phrase γενόμενος υπήκοος is dependent on the main clause ἐταπείνωσεν ἑαυτόν. For Paul's appropriation of ἐταπείνωσεν ἑαυτόν in 2 Cor, see Chapter Five, Section V.C.

[870]So, e.g., FURNISH, *II Corinthians*, 398: "It is likely that Paul is referring primarily to Titus' discovery that the congregation had responded to the tearful letter by punishing the wrongdoer." Observe, as Furnish himself does, that this interpretation mirrors the interpretation of 2 Cor 2:9 given by commentators who render ἔγραψα as a regular aorist. It might be thought that the latter interpretation is thereby confirmed. But it is not

reminding them of their positive response toward him, the apostle hopes to foster greater reconciliation and trust between himself and the community.

While the Corinthians' obedience was rendered, at one level, to Paul and his envoy Titus, at a more fundamental level it was given to God. This is suggested by the apostle's use of the phrase "with fear and trembling" (μετὰ φόβου καὶ τρόμου).[871] Paul uses this same expression in Phil 2:12, where he exhorts the Philippians to continue their ways of obedience (thereby following the example of Jesus in 2:6-11!), all the more so now that he (Paul) is absent. That is, their obedience – like that of Jesus – is to be directed *to God*, who is at work in them in order to desire *and* to do what God wills (Phil 2:13). Indeed, the phrase "with fear and trembling" in 2 Cor 7:15 echoes the apostle's earlier admonition to the Corinthians to bring about or make perfect holiness "in [the] fear of God" (ἐν φόβῳ θεοῦ, 7:1).[872] By receiving Titus with fear and trembling, the community thus responded to the envoy and – by extension – to

necessary to draw this conclusion. Paul could very well be highlighting the Corinthians' obedience in the past (concerning their reaction to Titus's bringing to them the 'tearful letter,' a reaction that included their punishing the recalcitrant member; cf. 7:8-16), *as well as* calling forth their continued obedience (in connection with their reaffirming their love for this person). Indeed, the apostle is just about to call forth the community's obedience with regard to the collection. The most compelling reason for reading ἔγραψα as an epistolary aorist in 2:9 is the tenor and thrust of Paul's presentation in 2:7-10.

[871]As WINDISCH observes, "τρόμος κ. φόβος findet sich schon in LXX mehrfach zusammen [e.g., Exod 15:16; Isa 19:16; and 4 Macc 4:10]. . . . Es kennzeichnet die Haltung des Menschen gegenüber dem *numinosum*." See *Der zweite Korintherbrief*, 241.

[872]As rightly pointed out by DANKER, *II Corinthians*, 115.

Paul as *God's* διάκονοι (cf. 6:4).[873] Hence, in the apostle's way of thinking, the Corinthians ultimately responded in obedience to God.

Paul's reference to the community's obedience in 2 Cor 7:15 also serves a rhetorical purpose vis-à-vis the next part of the letter. By extolling them for their obedience in the past, the apostle encourages them to *continue* in their obedience – now with regard to the collection for the church in Jerusalem (8:1-9:15). In exhorting the Corinthians to participate in this collection, Paul is careful to insist that he is not speaking to them "according to [his] authority" (κατ' ἐπιταγήν, 8:8a). Nevertheless, the apostle makes clear that he *is* putting them to the test (δοκιμάζω, 8:8b). And an essential part of this test is that the community follow the example of "our Lord Jesus Christ" – who emptied himself so that others might have life (8:9) – as well as trust more and more in God's providence to enable their generosity (9:6-12). Furthermore, observe that Paul once again brings up the issue of testing at the conclusion of this exhortation for the collection: "By virtue of the test (διὰ τῆς δοκιμῆς) of this ministry [i.e., the collection], you [Corinthians] will glorify (δοξάζοντες) God on the basis of the *obedience* (ἐπὶ τῇ ὑποταγῇ) of your confession with respect to the gospel of Christ" (9:13).[874] Thus, the apostle makes the Corinthians'

---

[873]KISTEMAKER describes this well: "... the phrase *fear and trembling* describes the believer's attitude in God's sacred presence. The Christians in Corinth received Titus as God's ambassador who spoke the words God had given him. Their repentance, then, exhibited fear and trembling in the presence of the Almighty and a desire to do his will." See *The Second Epistle to the Corinthians*, 263 (Kistemaker's italics). Cf. DANKER: "That this obedience is not a matter of submission to Paul as an earthly figure, is clear from the words *fear and trembling*." See *II Corinthians*, 115 (Danker's italics).

[874]My translation involves the following exegetical decisions:

(1) I read διά as denoting instrumentality or circumstance (here, "by virtue of"). See BDAG, s.v. διά, A.3.e. Cf. Rom 12:3 and Gal 3:18.

(2) I take ἐπί as marking the basis for an action (here, "on the basis of"). See BDAG, s.v. ἐπί, 6. Cf. 2 Cor 9:15.

(3) I read εἰς as signifying reference (here, "with respect to"). See BDAG, s.v. εἰς, 5. Cf. Rom 8:28; and 2 Cor 9:8 and 13:3b.

(4) I understand the Corinthians – not the "holy ones" of the church in Jerusalem – to be the subject of δοξάζοντες. So, too, do BRUCE, *1 and 2 Corinthians*, 228; BARNETT, *The Second Epistle to the Corinthians*, 445, n. 49; LAMBRECHT, *Second Corinthians*, 148; SAMPLEY, *NIB*, 11.131; and MATERA, *II Corinthians*, 207. Although the majority of commentators argue, on the basis of the reference in 2 Cor 9:12,

participation in the collection a test[875] of their character. Moreover, he connects this participation with their obedience (ὑποταγή).[876]

That Paul sees the community's obedience here in terms of the character and story of Jesus is strongly suggested by three textual elements. First, the Corinthians' obedience entails a faithful confession of "the gospel of Christ" (τὸ εὐαγγέλιον τοῦ Χριστοῦ). Just as was the case with the apostle in 2 Cor 4:5-14, the Corinthians themselves can offer eloquent confession or proclamation of this gospel *by acting in loving service for the sake of others* διὰ 'Ιησοῦν[877] – in this case, by taking active part in the collection for those in need, thereby

---

that the subject is the (would be) recipients of the collection, they play fast and loose with Paul's grammar to do so. As THRALL concedes (see *II Corinthians*, 2.588), the most likely preceding nominative plural that can serve as an antecedent, grammatically speaking, is πλουτιζόμενοι (9:11), the subject of which is the Corinthians. For Paul's use of the participle δοξάζοντες in place of a finite verb and without any connection to one, see BDF, § 468 (2). I render the participle as a future in order to capture the conditional aspect of the apostle's statement: 'If you are generous, [then] you glorify God.'

[875]Some commentators (e.g., BARRETT, *The Second Epistle to the Corinthians*, 240; FURNISH, *II Corinthians*, 444; and THRALL, *II Corinthians*, 2.588) take δοκιμή in 2 Cor 9:13 as referring to verification, that is, to the *result* of having been tested (and thus not to the *process* of testing). This reading understands the Corinthians' offering as, in effect, a proof. The problem with this interpretation is that *the Corinthians have not yet completed their offering*. Thus, it is best to read the apostle's statement as saying that the collection is a *test* of their character. This is in line with Paul's stated strategy in 8:8. Cf. MCCANT, *2 Corinthians*, 97-98; and SAMPLEY, *NIB*, 11.131. Sampley also rightly sees the connection between the collection and the *ministry* of reconciliation through the apostle's use of διακονία in 9:12-13.

[876]It might be objected that Paul uses ὑποταγή – not ὑπακοή – in 2 Cor 9:13, and that the meaning of ὑποταγή often shades into the notion of "submissiveness" (cf. Gal 2:5; and 1 Tim 2:11 and 3:4). Nevertheless, as FURNISH observes (citing Rom 10:3), there is warrant for understanding ὑποταγή in the sense of obedience. See *II Corinthians*, 445. In fact, GEORGI intriguingly suggests that ὑποταγὴ τῆς ὁμολογίας in 2 Cor 9:13 will soon be rephrased by the apostle in his letter to the Romans as ὑπακοὴ πίστεως (Rom 1:5 and 16:26). See *Remembering the Poor*, 105.

[877]Recall the richness of the phrase "because of Jesus," which connotes both rendering loyal service to Jesus and following his example. See Chapter Four, Section V.

following in the self-emptying manner of Jesus.[878] Second, Paul states that the Corinthians will glorify (δοξάζω) God on the basis of such obedience. This recalls 1:20b, where τὸ ἀμὴν τῷ θεῷ – the apostle's shorthand for human faithfulness to God after the pattern of Jesus' Yes – is intimately connected with "glory" (πρὸς δόξαν). That is, Paul intimates in 9:13 that the Corinthians' obedience, their ναί to God in the matter of the collection, will redound for glory.[879] And third, the apostle refers explicitly to Christ's obedience a few verses later (10:5).

In fact, Paul continues to call forth obedience from the Corinthians in 2 Cor 10:1-6. Near the end of this passage, the apostle writes: "[as] we take captive every thought ἐις τὴν ὑπακοὴν τοῦ Χριστοῦ, being ready also to punish all disobedience, when your obedience is brought to completion" (10:5b-

---

[878]I therefore understand the phrase that immediately follows "obedience" (τῆς ὁμολογίας . . . Χριστοῦ) as *epexegetical.* That is, the Corinthians' obedience in 2 Cor 9:13 consists of their confession with respect to the gospel of Jesus Christ, a confession rendered first and foremost by *action.* Cf. FURNISH, *II Corinthians*, 445. Concerning this confession, BARRETT correctly comments that it is ". . . not a matter of words only but *genuine obedience to God* who is the author of the Gospel." See *The Second Epistle to the Corinthians*, 241 (italics added).

BETZ argues that the key terms in 9:13 are "in the first place, legal administrative, and have only been Christianized secondarily." See *2 Corinthians 8 and 9*, 122. In particular, Betz proposes that ὁμολογία refers to a contractual agreement, and that ὑποταγή refers to the Corinthian (i.e., gentile) Christians' submission to Jerusalem. Betz's understanding of ὁμολογία, however, flies in the face of Paul's usage elsewhere (1 Tim 6:12-13), including the verb ὁμολογέω (Rom 10:9-10; 1 Tim 6:12; and Titus 1:16). Moreover, observe the strange twists and turns Betz must make in order to support his position. For example, he explains that the words "to [for the purpose of] the gospel of Christ" are "like all diplomatic language, ambiguous" (ibid., 124). That is, according to Betz, the Christians in Jerusalem would understand the words to suggest that the Corinthians have submitted to them, whereas Paul and the Corinthians would take the words as referring to the gospel of Christ, a gospel that transcends both Jerusalem and Achaia. *Pace* Betz, the apostle's language here is far from being diplomatic and ambiguous. Rather, Paul is boldly coming to the climax of his insistence that the collection serves as an occasion to test the community's character. While it is true that ὁμολογία and ὑποταγή can have legal connotations – as Betz expertly demonstrates – the apostle does not draw upon that sphere of connotation here.

[879]This observation adds support to the position that the Corinthians are the subject of δοξάζοντες.

6). I argued at length in Chapter Four that the phrase ὑπακοὴ τοῦ Χριστοῦ refers to "Christ's obedience," and that the preposition εἰς denotes activity towards a purpose or goal. In this case, Paul seeks to effect in the community "Christ-obedience"– that is, obedience as embodied by Jesus.[880] Since, however, the apostle is no longer explicitly discussing the collection,[881] it is first necessary to determine whether there is an additional situation or circumstance in regard to which he calls forth the Corinthians' obedience. Three clues emerge from the immediate context. The first concerns the issue of Paul's authority over the community (10:8). The second relates to the apostle's awareness that others are speaking critically about him (10:10; cf. 10:1b). And the third is the striking military imagery that Paul employs to press his point (10:3-6). These clues direct us to the third circumstance of the rhetorical situation outlined above. That is, the apostle's call for the Corinthians to embody Christ-like obedience in 10:5 takes place in the context of the emergence or arrival of other missionaries/evangelists.

One of the things at issue in these verses is "the knowledge of God" (2 Cor 10:5), knowledge that Paul has linked earlier with the story of Jesus (cf. 4:6).[882] More specifically, the apostle is concerned here with that which is opposed to or stands *against*[883] the knowledge of God. It is striking that Paul will shortly express his fear that the Corinthians' *thoughts* (νοήματα) are being led astray from the single-minded devotion to God and God's will, a devotion that was expressed in an exemplary manner by Jesus (11:3). The apostle explains his fear by citing his dismay regarding the Corinthians' apparent willingness to hear about "another Jesus" and to receive 'a different spirit and

---

[880]Cf. WILLIAMS, "Again *Pistis Christou*," 435, n. 16. Williams suggests that Paul sets forth Christ's obedience as the standard by which the Corinthians are to measure their own.

[881]Paul's concern for the collection, however, does *not* disappear in 2 Cor 10-13. Indeed, as we will see in addressing 12:15 in the following subsection, the second and third circumstances of the rhetorical situation are deeply intertwined.

[882]So, rightly, PLUMMER, who remarks in this context that knowledge of God is "that true knowledge of Him which comes through acquaintance with One who was the image of God (iv. 4)." See *II Corinthians*, 277.

[883]See BDAG, s.v. κατά, A.2.b.α. Cf. 1 Cor 4:6.

gospel' (11:4). Notice that Paul immediately mentions "the superlative apostles" in the very next verse (11:5), and then adamantly defends his own γνῶσις (11:6). While the apostle's insinuations in 11:3-6 are tantalizing, it is necessary to exercise caution so as not to offer greater precision to the rhetorical situation than the data would support. Yet it seems safe to surmise that, in Paul's estimation, there are missionaries or evangelists among the Corinthians who are exerting a deleterious influence on the community. It seems plausible (again, from his perspective) that their teaching – including what they proclaim about Jesus – is flawed. Indeed, returning to 10:1-6, it is pertinent to observe that the apostle claims to destroy "arguments" (λογισμοί, 11:4)[884] and to take captive "every thought" (πᾶν νόημα, 11:5).

The teaching or γνῶσις, however, is not an end in itself. Paul's *chief* concern is the transformation of the values, attitudes, and behavior of the Corinthians that follows upon the Spirit-bestowed gift of the "mind of Christ" (cf. 2 Cor 3:18 and 1 Cor 2:16).[885] Whatever the preaching of "another Jesus" may or may not have involved, according to the apostle it seems to have led to values, attitudes, and behavior antithetical to those of Christ – skewed values, attitudes, and behavior exhibited by the interlopers (cf. 2 Cor 11:20) as well as by some in the community (12:20). Indeed, Paul's use of ὀχυρώματα ("strongholds," 10:4b), ὕψωμα ("arrogance," 10:5a), and ἐπαίρω ("lift up," 10:5a; cf. 11:20) is revealing. In the context of 2 Cor 10:1-6, these terms connote reliance on one's own strength, pridefulness, and putting on airs.[886] Moreover, observe that, a few verses later (10:12-16), the apostle chastises those who engage in (negative) *self*-commendation (i.e., in competition and boasting in their own accomplishments, even at the expense of the truth). In short, Paul challenges a mode of existence that is diametrically opposed to that revealed by

---

[884]Cf. THRALL, who argues that, by his use of λογισμοί in this context, "Paul must primarily have in view the forms of argument used by the rival missionaries and their Corinthian supporters." See *II Corinthians*, 2.612.

[885]PICKETT rightly perceives that "even though the discussion is oriented to 'reasoning' (10.4), 'thoughts' (10.5; 11.3) and rhetorical arguments (11.1-12.10), *what is really at issue is conduct*." See *The Cross in Corinth*, 162 (italics added).

[886]Cf. THRALL, *II Corinthians*, 2.612-13. She holds that λογισμοί, ὕψωμα, and πᾶν νόημα refer to the arrogant attitude of Paul's opponents and critics. Similarly, LAMBRECHT, *Second Corinthians*, 155.

Jesus. If the logic of the ancient moralists is right – namely, that proper moral behavior follows upon correct perception; and conversely, that improper behavior follows upon faulty perception[887] – then it would be natural for the apostle to assume that those who advocate strength, pride, and *self*-commendation do not rightly grasp the story and character of Jesus. Indeed, it seems safe to say that Paul does not regard the other missionaries/evangelists as possessing the νοῦς Χριστοῦ. It is significant, therefore, that the apostle begins 10:1-6 by referring to the character and story of Jesus, especially to his "gentleness and forbearance" (10:1a). To say the least, these characteristics differ greatly from those associated with the interlopers.[888]

So what exactly does the "Christ-obedience" that Paul calls forth from the Corinthians entail (2 Cor 10:5b)? And how will their obedience be brought to completion (πληρόομαι, 11:6)? In order to "complete" the community's obedience, Paul calls upon the Corinthians to heed what he himself teaches and embodies as an apostle (1:1) and servant of Christ (11:23), and as their slave (4:5). It is Paul – and not those whom he dubs "the superlative apostles" – who proclaims faithfully God's message by means of incarnating the character of Jesus (cf. 4:2 and 4:10-11). Hence, to heed the apostle and his proclamation

---

[887]HUGHES captures the pattern of this logic very well: "This we know to be diagnostically sound, in respect of human psychology and physiology as well as of the religious life, for a man's inner motives are the fount of his action; mind and will determine his conduct; and his attitudes are the effect of the presuppositions of his philosophy of things." See *Paul's Second Epistle to the Corinthians*, 351-52.

[888]SAVAGE devotes the first part of his study to the social setting of the first century Greco-Roman world, particularly in Corinth, arguing that Paul's Christ-centered viewpoint clashes head on with the worldly outlook of the Corinthians. Indeed, the apostle's rivals seem to have played into the Corinthians' natural proclivities. See *Power through Weakness*, 19-99. In addition, see PICKETT, *The Cross in Corinth*, 160-211.

(both preached and embodied) is tantamount to obeying God.[889] Such obedience to God is modeled forth and empowered by Christ.[890]

For Paul the issue of the community's obedience is so urgent that he attempts to "take captive" (αἰχμαλωτίζω) every thought to force a correct understanding of what Jesus revealed. *Prima facie*, this seems at odds with his appealing to the Corinthians through Christ's gentleness and forbearance. But the apostle's use of military imagery in 2 Cor 10:3-6[891] functions to portray the gravity and difficulty of the situation. The community's obedience to Paul and his message – obedience that is ultimately directed to God's revelation through Jesus – is for the apostle a matter of life and death. The opposition forces, moreover, are powerful.[892] Thus, in Paul's estimation, the stakes are so high that he wages a "war campaign" in order to help the Corinthians appropriate and live

---

[889]Cf. FURNISH, *II Corinthians*, 463: "That it is *his* gospel his hearers are urged to obey means that they are summoned to accept his authority as a preacher of the gospel, but their *obedience* as such is to be directed to Christ" (Furnish's italics). I agree with Furnish, except as to his final point. For Paul, obedience is to be rendered *to God*, not to Christ. Cf., e.g, Rom 6:15-23 (esp. v. 22) and 11:30-32 (both of which Furnish himself cites!), as well as n. 863 above.

[890]MURPHY-O'CONNOR, who does not read ὑπακοὴ τοῦ Χριστοῦ as "Christ's obedience," nevertheless aptly comments on 2 Cor 10:4-5 that the authentic knowledge of God involves the "lived acceptance of the fundamental value of love manifested in the surrender of self in the 'dying of Jesus' (4:10; cf. 5:15)." See *The Theology of the Second Letter to the Corinthians*, 102. Implicit within the surrender of self is obedience to God.

[891]E.g., στρατευόμεθα ("we wage war," 10:3b); τὰ ὅπλα τῆς στρατείας ἡμῶν ("the weapons of our warfare," 10:4a); καθαίρεσις ὀχυρωμάτων ("destruction of strongholds," 10:4b); and αἰχμαλωτίζοντες ("as we take captive," 10:5b). While BETZ argues that Paul's imagery here is derived from the philosophic-sophistic controversy (see *Der Apostel Paulus und die sokratische Tradition*, 68-69), MALHERBE casts the net wider to include both the self-understanding of the Cynics and the self-sufficiency and -confidence of the Stoics (see "Antisthenes and Odysseus, and Paul at War," 143-73).

[892]Cf. Paul's allusions to the machinations of ὁ σατανᾶς in 2 Cor 2:11 and 11:14; his reference to ὁ θεὸς τοῦ αἰῶνος τούτου ("the god of this age") who blinds people's minds (4:4); and his allusion to Βελιάρ in 6:15.

out the character and story of Jesus.[893] The apostle's use of cognitive terms (cf. 'destroying arguments and obstacles to knowledge of God' and 'taking thoughts captive') suggests that part of his campaign involves challenging and refuting aberrant teachings.

Paul's campaign also includes his readiness to punish (ἐκδικέω) all disobedience (2 Cor 10:6). On what grounds will he do so? The new creation brought about "in Christ" (5:17) entails following in the manner of Jesus' obedience to God – expressed in his living for others out of love. Such a manner of living is not merely one of several options for those who are now the "temple of God" (6:16b). Hence, as a last resort, punishment is necessary *within the community* if any members refuse to submit to the ὑπακοῂ τοῦ Χριστοῦ, that is, to Christ-like obedience. In his role as their father (6:13; 12:14), the apostle will wield the stick against the community if necessary (13:2; cf. 1 Cor 4:21).[894] Indeed, the Corinthians themselves have already acted to punish one

---

[893]Indeed, I suggest that there is a connection between Paul's use of the triumphal procession in 2 Cor 2:14-16 and his metaphor of taking captives in 10:5. Recall my analysis of 2:14-17 (Chapter Four, Section IV.C). There I argued that the apostle's graphic image of being led by God as a captured slave signified that he was, like Jesus, God's obedient δοῦλος. Now, in 10:5 Paul uses the same metaphor, but his place in the metaphor has shifted. That is, the apostle now portrays himself as part of God's triumphal army, bearing weapons which are powerful because of God (10:4; cf. 6:7). Here, it is the Corinthians who are to be led captive. In other words, like Paul in 2:14-16, they are to be δοῦλοι who are obedient to God and to God's will, as was Jesus.

[894]Commentators are divided on the question of who is the target of Paul's threat. On the one hand, some (e.g., BARRETT, *The Second Epistle to the Corinthians*, 253-54; FURNISH, *II Corinthians*, 464; MARTIN, *2 Corinthians*, 306-7; and THRALL, *II Corinthians*, 2.615) argue that the apostle threatens to punish the interloping missionaries. For instance, what sense does it make for Paul to punish "all disobedience" of the Corinthians when their obedience is brought to completion? Moreover, it is proposed that 2 Cor 10:12-18 alludes to the agreement described in Gal 2:7-10 concerning the division of the mission territory, an agreement that the intruders have broken. On the other hand, others (e.g., HUGHES, *Paul's Second Epistle to the Corinthians*, 354-55; HÉRING, *The Second Epistle of Saint Paul to the Corinthians*, 70-71; BULTMANN, *The Second Letter to the Corinthians*, 187; and BARNETT, *The Second Epistle to the Corinthians*, 467) contend that the apostle threatens to punish remaining community members who persist in aberrant behavior. Indeed, what authority would Paul have over (much less an authority to punish) other missionaries?

member of the community who had caused pain and done wrong to Paul (2 Cor 2:5-6 and 7:11-12). Notice, furthermore, that this act of punishment was the consequence of the Corinthians' zeal (σπουδή) for him. And reference to their zeal for the apostle indicates that they have previously recognized and accepted his presentation of what God has revealed in Christ.

In sum: Throughout 2 Corinthians, Paul tests the character of the community by challenging them to obedience. The apostle shows his approval of the Corinthians' obedience in responding favorably to his tearful letter (cf. 2 Cor 7:15). He now tests them to forgive and receive back in love a recalcitrant member of the community (2:9). Paul also puts the Corinthians to the test vis-à-vis the collection by exhorting them to proclaim the gospel through their generosity (9:13). And he admonishes the community to heed him, not the superlative apostles, because he is the one who faithfully manifests the truth of the gospel through his preaching and manner of living. The apostle links these exhortations to the very "obedience of Christ" (10:5), who modeled forth and now empowers (through the Spirit) a mode of existence lived for others in fidelity to God's will.

B. Love (ἀγάπη)

As he did with obedience, so Paul exhorts the Corinthians to embody love in connection with all three circumstances of the rhetorical situation. In particular, he adduces δοκιμ- language as well as the example and empowerment of Christ to call the community to incarnate love vis-à-vis the collection (2 Cor 8:1-24). The apostle also expressly summons the Corinthians to ἀγάπη in 2:8 and in 12:15. In each instance, the point is to persuade the community to embrace and appropriate the "love of Christ" (ἀγάπη τοῦ Χριστοῦ, 5:14).

Furthermore, he threatens punishment of community members in 13:2. I agree with HUGHES'S assessment of the apostle's statement in 10:6 (that he will respond against disobedience when the community's obedience has been brought to completion): "This indicates two things: firstly, that the punishment he administers will not be indiscriminate, for the true-hearted will have ample opportunity for displaying their loyalty by openly taking their stand with him; and, secondly, that he confidently anticipates that the response at Corinth will be one of obedience, although there may be a few defiant spirits who will attempt to continue their opposition to his authority and message." See *Paul's Second Epistle to the Corinthians*, 354.

Toward the beginning of his exhortation to the Corinthians concerning the collection, Paul makes clear his strategy (2 Cor 8:8): "I speak [to you] not by way of command,[895] but . . . I am testing (δοκιμάζων). . . ."[896] Thus, he regards the collection as a *test*. And that which the apostle tests pertains to the very character of the Corinthians – namely, τὸ τῆς ὑμετέρας ἀγάπης γνήσιον[897] ("the *genuineness* of your love"). Observe that Paul, in the course of listing the qualities in which the community abounds, has just reminded them of his own (and his co-workers') love for them (8:7).[898] As we saw in the previous chapter, he expresses his love for the Corinthians in the same self-giving manner embodied by Jesus. Thus, the apostle's reminder in 8:7 is a subtle tactic to evoke ἀγάπη within and from the community.

Paul does not rely exclusively on subtlety, however, in challenging the Corinthians to embody love. In 2 Cor 8:8 he proposes a specific standard for testing the quality of their ἀγάπη – namely, the earnestness or zeal (σπουδή)

---

[895]For a discussion of the various interpretations of what Paul means by his disavowal of issuing a command, see THRALL, *II Corinthians*, 2.530-31. To get lost in speculation over this part of the apostle's statement, however, is misguided. Emphasis ought to be placed on what Paul himself indicates *is* his purpose – namely, to test the community (see the following note).

[896]Reading the participle δοκιμάζων as expressing attendant circumstance. Cf. KISTEMAKER, *The Second Epistle to the Corinthians*, 280. *Pace* FURNISH (*II Corinthians*, 404), who interprets the participle as denoting "prove" or "approve," in the sense of *having* put to the test. HUGHES correctly explains, "The purpose of what Paul writes at this point is *to put the Corinthian Christians to the test. . . .*" See *Paul's Second Epistle to the Corinthians*, 298 (italics added). So, too, BELLEVILLE, who refers to the apostle's "game plan" in 2 Cor 8:8. See *2 Corinthians*, 215. Cf. BETZ, *2 Corinthians 8 and 9*, 59-60; and SAMPLEY, *NIB*, 11.123.

[897]For Paul's use of a neuter singular adjective as an abstract noun with a dependent genitive, see BDF, § 263 (2). Cf. 2 Cor 4:17 and 8:2.

[898]See n. 809 for reading τῇ ἐξ ἡμῶν ἐν ὑμῖν ἀγάπῃ instead of τῇ ἐξ ὑμῶν ἐν ἡμῖν ἀγάπῃ in 2 Cor 8:7.

of the churches of Macedonia (8:1).[899] It seems that the Macedonians had undergone some severe test of their own character (cf. ἐν πολλῇ δοκιμῇ, 8:2a), and according to the apostle, they passed with flying colors. Paul informs the Corinthians that the Macedonians' extreme poverty (πτωχεία) overflowed in a wealth (πλοῦτος) of generosity in giving to the collection (8:2). In fact, they freely gave beyond their means (8:3). Moreover, the apostle emphasizes that – even more fundamental than their gift of money – the Macedonians gave their very selves (ἑαυτοὺς ἔδωκεν, 8:5).[900] Notice that the phrase ἑαυτοὺς δίδωμι echoes Paul's use elsewhere of παραδίδωμι + the reflexive pronoun (cf. Gal 2:20; and Eph 5:2 and 5:25), an expression that denotes a manner of living for the sake of others *out of love*.[901] The apostle thus explicitly holds up to the

---

[899]BETZ aptly describes διὰ τῆς ἑτέρων σπουδῆς – a reference to the Macedonians' participation in the collection – as the "method for conducting the test." See *2 Corinthians 8 and 9*, 60. *Pace* ALLO, who proposes the possibility that τῆς ἑτέρων σπουδῆς refers to the *Corinthians'* zeal for the church in Jerusalem (thus reading ἑτέρων as an objective genitive). See *Seconde Épître aux Corinthiens*, 216. While this interpretation is grammatically possible, both the context and the obvious contrast (in 2 Cor 8:8) between ἑτέρων in the first phrase and ὑμετέρας in the second suggest otherwise. Cf. HUGHES, *Paul's Second Epistle to the Corinthians*, 298-99, n. 23; and THRALL, *II Corinthians*, 2.532.

[900]PLUMMER (*II Corinthians*, 236); HUGHES (*Paul's Second Epistle to the Corinthians*, 292, n. 13); and FURNISH (*II Corinthians*, 402) note the placement of ἑαυτούς for emphasis. Commentators are divided, however, over how to understand what Paul means by the adverb πρῶτον in 2 Cor 8:5. Some hold that the apostle thereby signifies that the Macedonians gave themselves *first to the Lord* (and then to Paul). So, e.g., FURNISH (*II Corinthians*, 402): ". . . the *prōton* (*first*) is to be construed only with *to the Lord*, distinguishing the self-giving to him as more important than the self-giving *to us*" (Furnish's italics). Others argue that πρῶτον refers to the Macedonians' giving themselves first (either temporally or in terms of importance) before they gave money. This second option renders the text best, for as THRALL points out (*II Corinthians*, 2.526), the emphatic placement of ἑαυτούς connotes that this pronoun is one of the terms in the contrast implicit in the adverb πρῶτον.

[901]MURPHY-O'CONNOR seems to see the same connection: ". . . [the Macedonians] had conformed themselves to the self-sacrificing Christ (5:15) by modelling their behaviour on that of Paul who manifested the 'life of Jesus' (4:10-11). As their models had done, they had to take risks to assist others less fortunate than they. The urge to participate in the collection, therefore, came from the depths of their being as Christians."

Corinthians the generous response of the Macedonian churches in the work of the collection. The former can now prove the authenticity of their love by emulating the latter.

It is the love of Christ that underlies Paul's exposition in these verses. Recall from the analysis of 2 Cor 5:14-15 that the ἀγάπη τοῦ Χριστοῦ was expressed by his living and dying for the sake of others. In the present passage, the apostle offers the community the example of the "the graciousness (χάρις) of our Lord Jesus Christ" (8:9) in the verse that immediately follows his challenge to them to prove the genuineness of their love.[902] Jesus' graciousness was manifested most eloquently in the fact that, "although he was rich he became poor for your sake, in order that by his poverty (τῇ ἐκείνου πτωχείᾳ) you might become rich (πλουτήσετε)." This is the same dynamic – the emptying of oneself in order to enrich others – that the churches of Macedonia exhibited. And it is this dynamic that Paul raises for the Corinthians as the measure of genuine love. *Ultimately*, therefore, he calls them to embody the same love and graciousness exhibited by Jesus.

Observe, moreover, that the apostle's strategy in 2 Cor 8:1-9 draws on the same logic of 1:18-22. In the latter passage, he began by alluding to God's being faithful, then pointed to Jesus' Yes, and concluded with the Amen of those 'christed' by the Spirit. In the present passage, Paul starts in 8:1 with a reference to the graciousness (χάρις) of God (who is called the "God of *love*" in 13:11!), and then proceeds to recall the story of Jesus' χάρις (8:9). Yet, the apostle's real purpose here is to invite the community to join in the story: "in

---

See *The Theology of the Second Letter to the Corinthians*, 80. Indeed, the Macedonians participated in the dynamic described in the opening *berakah* (2 Cor 1:3-7). Their endurance of affliction worked toward the consolation and salvation of others. Hence, they have joined with the apostle in participating in the story of Jesus.

Cf. WINDISCH, who suggests that Paul's meaning here is that the Macedonians' care for the ἅγιοι in Jerusalem expressed their care for the body of Christ (cf. Rom 12:4-5 and 1 Cor 12:12-27). See *Der zweite Korintherbrief*, 247: "Fürsorge für andere Gemeinden ist Fürsorge für andere Gelider des Leibes Christi."

[902]MARTIN plausibly suggests that mention of ἀγάπη in 2 Cor 8:8 "prompts Paul to appeal to the highest illustration of love-in-action" in 8:9. See *2 Corinthians*, 262. BELLEVILLE states that the apostle appeals here to "the supreme example of generosity." See *2 Corinthians*, 216.

order that (ἵνα) you also might abound *in this graciousness* (ἐν ταύτῃ τῇ *χάριτι*, 8:7)."[903]

That the Corinthians' embodiment of love is Paul's principal consideration in 2 Cor 8:1-24 is apparent from the way he concludes his commendation of Titus and the two "brothers" whom he sends to Corinth to expedite the collection (cf. 8:16-24). In 8:24 the apostle exhorts the community to offer τὴν ἔνδειξιν τῆς ἀγάπης ὑμῶν ("the proof of your *love*"). Notice once again that Paul is concerned that the Corinthians offer a demonstration of their character. This is evident from the prominent (first) position of the phrase just cited, as well as from the emphatic expression ἔνδειξιν ἐνδεικνύμενοι.[904] In effect, ἔνδειξις/ἐνδείκνυμι functions here as the equivalent of δοκιμή/δοκιμάζω – that is, as a test to ascertain one's character.[905] The context suggests that the community will demonstrate their love by receiving the

---

[903]See SAMPLEY, *NIB*, 11.119, for a brief treatment of the rich signification of Paul's use of χάρις in 2 Cor 8:1-9:15.

[904]BETZ calls this expression a "*figura etymologica*." See *2 Corinthians 8 and 9*, 85. For Paul's employment of a participle with imperatival force, see BDF, § 468 (2). Cf. Rom 12:9-17. Several commentators (e.g., FURNISH, *II Corinthians*, 425) note the Semitic use of the imperatival participle. V.D. VERBRUGGE objects to this way of reading the participle ἐνδεικνύμενοι. He proposes that the participle "may best be connected with a conventional epistolary conclusion, similar to ἔρρωσθε (such as ἀσπάσασθε; cf. 1 Cor 16:20; 2 Cor 13:12) that a redactor has omitted." Thus, Verbrugge argues that 2 Cor 8:24 was originally a letter conclusion. See *Paul's Style of Church Leadership Illustrated by His Instructions to the Corinthians on the Collection* (San Francisco: Mellen Research University Press,1992) 257. His proposal, however, rests too much on a reputed redactor's reputed activity to be accepted.

It should be noted that there is a textual variant in some MSS, where the imperative ἐνδείξασθε is found instead of the participle ἐνδεικνύμενοι. The latter yields the more difficult reading. Moreover, as METZGER notes, ". . . it is easy to understand that copyists, unacquainted with the Semitic idiom, would change the participle to the finite verb." See *A Textual Commentary on the Greek New Testament*, 513-14.

[905]BARNETT also recognizes the parallels between these sets of terminology. See *The Second Epistle to the Corinthians*, 427, n. 69. DANKER points out that ἐνδείκνυμι was used in official documents in connection with testifying to one's character. See *II Corinthians*, 134.

mission of Titus and the "brothers," and especially *by having ready their contribution for the collection.*[906] The key point here is that, for the apostle, the Corinthians' "enrichment" of others will constitute a manifestation of their ἀγάπη, love that is modeled (8:9) and empowered (cf. συνέχω, 5:14) by Jesus.

In addition to the issue of the collection, Paul calls the Corinthians to actualize ἀγάπη within their own community. In 2 Cor 2:8 he admonishes them "to ratify[907] [their] love" (κυρῶσαι ἀγάπην) for the person who had been punished for having caused pain to the apostle. Paul indicates in the previous verse *how* they can ratify their love, namely, by offering to forgive (χαρίζομαι – observe the connection with χάρις!) and to comfort (παρακαλέω) the offending member of the community (2:7). In other words, to embody ἀγάπη here entails participating in the ministry of reconciliation (5:18), the διακονία that the apostle describes in the context of his allusion to "the love of Christ" (5:14). Recall that a crucial aspect of incarnating the ἀγάπη τοῦ Χριστοῦ is to recognize the value of others in light of Jesus' dying out of love for them, thus treating them κατὰ ἀγάπην (cf. Rom 14:15) rather than κατὰ σάρκα (2

---

[906]FURNISH'S understanding of Paul's strategy here deserves to be quoted at length: "This is not an admonition to love Titus and the two brothers . . . although of course Paul desires that they should. Nor is it a general admonition concerning love, like the one in 1 Cor 16:14. . . . *It is a renewal of the appeal of 8:7-15 to make their promised contribution to the fund for Jerusalem.* Paul has already referred to this action as a sign of genuine love (8:8). Now he urges his readers to make sure that *this love is embodied in action*, specifically in their participation in the relief work for the needy Christians of Jerusalem. It is toward the concrete, public expression of their love that this appeal is aimed. . . ." See *II Corinthians*, 439 (italics added).

[907]See BDAG, s.v. κυρόω, 1. Cf. Gal 3:15. THRALL observes that the predominant sense of this verb pertains to official and legal decisions and actions. She plausibly proposes that, in 2 Cor 2:8, Paul is calling for "some formal congregational resolution." Given that the community had imposed some punishment on the recalcitrant member, it would now be necessary to have a formal expression of forgiveness and reinstatement. See THRALL, *II Corinthians*, 1.177-78. Similarly, WINDISCH, *Der zweite Korintherbrief*, 89; ALLO, *Seconde Épître aux Corinthiens*, 40; HUGHES, *Paul's Second Epistle to the Corinthians*, 67, n. 14; FURNISH, *II Corinthians*, 157; and BELLEVILLE, *2 Corinthians*, 75.

Cor 5:16).[908] Observe, moreover, that Paul places the word ἀγάπην in the prominent end position of 2:8,[909] immediately preceding his *reason* for writing in 2:9. If ἔγραψα is indeed an epistolary aorist (as I have argued above), then the apostle is challenging the Corinthians to prove their character by obeying his exhortation to reaffirm their love for a fellow community member.

Lastly, Paul poignantly appeals to the Corinthians to love in 2 Cor 12:15. As discussed in the previous chapter, the first half of this verse serves as a précis of the apostle's living in the pattern of Jesus' love: "*I* will most gladly spend and be utterly expended for your souls." Then Paul poignantly asks in 12:15b, "While loving you all the more, am I to be loved the less (ἧσσον ἀγαπῶμαι)?"[910] At one level, the apostle's use of economic terminology in 12:15a functions to remind the community of all that he has done for them in the hope that they will respond by participating in the collection. The immediate context suggests, moreover, that he is calling the Corinthians to respond to him as their spiritual "father" and to his way of presenting the gospel. In 12:14 Paul has just reminded them that parents seek what is good for their children. In the brackets of 12:13 and 12:16-18, he refers to his refusal to take remuneration from the community (as well as to their subsequent mistrust of him). And in 12:11 he mentions once again the superlative apostles (cf. 11:5). Hence, I propose that, most fundamentally, the apostle's rhetorical question[911] summons the Corinthians to respond to him with love, not for his sake but for theirs (cf.

---

[908]See Chapter Four, Section VI. FURNISH takes notes of the unusual juxtaposition of ἀγάπη and a term signifying a legal ratification (κυρόω), and goes so far as to call this juxtaposition an oxymoron. See *II Corinthians*, 157. However, when viewed in light of 2 Cor 5:14-6:2 – where Christ's love is linked to the pragmatics of the ministry of reconciliation – the apostle's formulation in 2 Cor 2:8 makes sense.

[909]Paul's syntax is κυρῶσαι εἰς αὐτὸν ἀγάπην, not κυρῶσαι ἀγάπην εἰς αὐτόν.

[910]For the justification of this translation, see n. 806.

[911]Both BULTMANN and MARTIN are sensitive to Paul's rhetorical finesse here. Bultmann rightly identifies the apostle's "characteristic" strategy of raising a rhetorical question in 2 Cor 12:15b. See *The Second Letter to the Corinthians*, 234. Martin points out that, by posing the question, Paul avoids an outright condemnation of the Corinthians, while leaving the way open for them to respond in a more appropriate manner. See *2 Corinthians*, 444.

13:7-10).[912] Paul wants the community to recognize that he – and not the superlative apostles – faithfully presents the gospel, a presentation that includes his own self-giving comportment after the manner of Christ. It is to this same mode of being, expressed here in terms of ἀγάπη, that the apostle calls the Corinthians with his heart-rending question in 12:15b.[913]

To conclude: Throughout 2 Corinthians Paul entreats the community to incarnate ἀγάπη. With reference to the collection, they are to follow the pattern of existence modeled forth by Jesus, who enriched others by giving himself in love (something that the churches of Macedonia have already done; 2 Cor 8:1-9 and 8:24). In addition, the apostle wants the Corinthians to show forth ἀγάπη by receiving back an ostracized member of their community (2:8). Finally, Paul desires that they manifest love by embracing him and his manner of proclaiming the good news to them (12:15). In all three instances (explicit in 2 Cor 8:1-24 and 2:8; implicit in 12:15), the apostle *tests* the character of the Corinthians to see whether or not they are incarnating the character of Jesus – specifically, Jesus' embodiment of love.

C. *Singleness/Generosity (ἁπλότης)*

In his exhortation for the collection, Paul summons the community to exhibit ἁπλότης (2 Cor 9:11 and 9:13). The concept of ἁπλότης is significant in 2 Corinthians: Five of the eight instances of this term in the apostle's writings occur here.[914] In order to appreciate his strategy in exhorting the Corinthians to ἁπλότης, it is first necessary to look briefly at how he employs the term elsewhere. Then, after reviewing how Paul uses the concept in connection with himself (1:12) and Jesus (11:3), I analyze his references to

---

[912]Similarly, HUGHES: "Less love on their part will not diminish the greatness of his love for them; *for it is not to himself that he wishes to bind them, but to Christ*" (italics added). See *Paul's Second Epistle to the Corinthians*, 463.

[913]MURPHY-O'CONNOR correctly observes that what Paul really strives for in 2 Cor 12:15 is to get the Corinthians "to appreciate the ideal which he has set before them." This ideal is "the standard of human behaviour set by Christ (5:15)." See *The Theology of the Second Letter to the Corinthians*, 127.

[914]Rom 12:8; 2 Cor 1:12; 8:2; 9:11; 9:13; and 11:3; Eph 6:5; and Col 3:22. In fact, Paul is the only NT writer to use ἁπλότης.

ἁπλότης in 8:1-9:15. In effect, the apostle develops in these two chapters what might be called "the *topos* on ἁπλότης."

As we saw in the analysis of 2 Cor 11:3 in Chapter Four, the meaning of ἁπλότης points to the concept of "singleness," in the sense of a singleness of heart and loyalty.[915] It can thus connote "sincerity" and "frankness."[916] With Paul it also shades into meaning "generosity, liberality."[917] Outside of 2 Corinthians, the apostle draws on both definitions (i.e., generosity and singleness). In Rom 12:8 – in the course of encouraging the community in Rome to use their particular gifts for building up the "one body" (12:4-8) – Paul exhorts "the one who gives" (ὁ μεταδιδούς) to do so "with *generosity*" (ἐν ἁπλότητι). In Eph 6:5 and Col 3:22 the apostle looks to the word's other aspect, commanding the slaves in the respective communities to obey their earthly masters "in *singleness of heart*" (ἐν ἁπλότητι [τῆς] καρδίας). Of course, singleness of heart and generosity are not entirely distinct notions. Indeed, generosity in giving can be regarded as a manifestation of the sincerity and singleness of purpose of the giver.[918]

Returning to 2 Corinthians, Paul claims to have acted toward the Corinthians ἐν ἁπλότητι καὶ εἰλικρινείᾳ τοῦ θεοῦ ("in godly sincerity and uprightness," 2 Cor 1:12). The placement of this averment at the very beginning of the letter body suggests its importance. Recall, moreover, from the previous chapter that the apostle insists *throughout* the epistle that he conducts himself toward the community with single-minded love and self-giving. In fact, vis-à-

---

[915]In addition, see MALHERBE, "Through the Eye of the Needle," esp. 123-25. For a full-length treatment of ἁπλότης, see J. AMSTUTZ, *ΑΠΛΟΤΗΣ: Eine begriffsgeschichtliche Studie zum jüdisch-christlichen Griechisch*, Theophaneia 19 (Bonn: Peter Hanstein Verlag GMBH, 1968) esp. 103-16. Cf. NICKLE, *The Collection*, 104-5; YOUNG and FORD, *Meaning and Truth in 2 Corinthians*, 103-4; and DANKER, *II Corinthians*, 118-19.

[916]See BDAG, s.v. ἁπλότης, 1.

[917]See BDAG, s.v. ἁπλότης, 2. In fact, it is typically the case that Pauline texts are cited as the evidence for this signification.

[918]Cf. THRALL: "To give unconditionally is to give generously, with sincere, single-minded concern for the recipients: it is to give with inward integrity." See *II Corinthians*, 2.524.

vis the Corinthians, Paul follows his own counsel to the actual δοῦλοι in Eph 6:5 and Col 3:22: He offers himself single-heartedly in his service to the community as their δοῦλος (2 Cor 4:5). In addition, the apostle leaves no question about his generosity toward the Corinthians: "I will most gladly spend and be utterly expended for [you]" (12:15). Paul lives this way because he has aligned himself with the *ethos* of Jesus, who, as God's faithful δοῦλος (4:13), manifested a mode of self-emptying existence lived in love for the sake of others.

Jesus is the apostle's explicit model of ἁπλότης lived *par excellence*. As we have observed, Paul's reference to Christ's ἁπλότης in 2 Cor 11:3 alludes to the latter's integrity, as well as to his single-minded devotion to God and to doing God's will. This commitment marked Jesus' life as one of generous self-giving (χάρις, 8:9). Christ's radical trust in God as the giver of life undergirded his manner of living and dying. It is to this single-hearted devotion to God and God's will – manifested by a life of self-offering, and founded upon trust in God to provide – that the apostle has oriented his own life. And it is to the embodiment of Christ's ἁπλότης that Paul exhorts the Corinthians. Specifically, the apostle encourages them to incarnate ἁπλότης in their own lives by giving generously to the collection.

In the process of exhorting the community to embody ἁπλότης, Paul raises up the example of the Macedonian churches. The Macedonians exhibited ἁπλότης by following the pattern of Jesus' enrichment of others through self-giving. The apostle informs the Corinthians in 2 Cor 8:2 that the extreme poverty of the Macedonians abounded εἰς τὸ πλοῦτος τῆς ἁπλότητος αὐτῶν. Both the association of "wealth" (πλοῦτος) with ἁπλότης, and Paul's insistence that the Macedonians gave freely "beyond their means" (παρὰ δύναμιν, 8:3), suggest that their ἁπλότης be understood as *generosity*.[919] But this does not exhaust the richness of the apostle's meaning in this passage. As noted above, Paul emphasizes in 8:5 that, even more fundamental than their monetary gift, the Macedonians gave their very selves in responding to his

---

[919]So, e.g., PLUMMER, *II Corinthians*, 232 and 234; HUGHES, *Paul's Second Epistle to the Corinthians*, 287-88; HÉRING, *The Second Epistle of Saint Paul to the Corinthians*, 58; BETZ, *2 Corinthians 8 and 9*, 37; FURNISH, *II Corinthians*, 399-400; MARTIN, *2 Corinthians*, 248 and 253; KISTEMAKER, *The Second Epistle to the Corinthians*, 269 and 273; LAMBRECHT, *Second Corinthians*, 135-36; and THRALL, *II Corinthians*, 2.520 and 524.

request for the Jerusalem church.[920] The expression "giving oneself" (δίδωμι + reflexive pronoun) captures well what is meant by the χάρις of Jesus (8:9). Indeed, it suggests that the Macedonians' entire existence eloquently expressed their *singleness* of purpose and devotion.[921] Moreover, observe that the apostle adds that their whole-hearted response was, in the end, a response to "[the] will of God" (θέλημα θεοῦ, 8:5).[922] Thus, like Jesus, the Macedonians' ἁπλότης ultimately manifested their devotion to God.

These observations position us to understand better Paul's references to ἁπλότης at the conclusion of his exhortation for the collection. The apostle's

---

[920]For this understanding of how the adverb πρῶτον functions in 2 Cor 8:5, see n. 900 above. Recall that Paul's emphasis upon the Macedonians' gift of *themselves* is suggested by the prominent placement of ἑαυτούς.

[921]Thus, BARRETT'S rendering of ἁπλότης in 2 Cor 8:2 as "simple-hearted goodness" captures Paul's sense better than "generosity." See *The Second Epistle to the Corinthians*, 216. NICKLE expresses well this richer signification of ἁπλότης: "Under the prevailing circumstances, Paul could hardly have been referring to the extent of the performance itself [i.e., the actual monetary gift]. Rather *he was describing the attitude which elicited this performance*, and in verse 5 proceeded to outline the manner in which this attitude came to govern their act." See *The Collection*, 105 (italics added). DANKER'S remarks concerning the Macedonians' self-donation are also apposite: "To the Greco-Roman understanding this statement [i.e., 8:5] would further imply that the Macedonians are making an appropriate response to divine beneficence by imitating it within the realm of their own possibilities." See *II Corinthians*, 122.

[922]PLUMMER (*II Corinthians*, 236) and THRALL (*II Corinthians*, 2.527) rightly recognize that Paul's reference to God's will is connected first and foremost to the Macedonians' response of self-donation. HUGHES'S comment is right on target in this connection: "In accordance with the teaching and example of the Lord Himself and in accordance with the logic of redemption [the Macedonians] renounced any claim to themselves. . . . They held themselves and their few goods in readiness to perform what was right 'by the will of God.' In a word, all is done in humble and cheerful submission to the sovereignty of the divine will." See *Paul's Second Epistle to the Corinthians*, 292-93. *Pace*, e.g., MARTIN (*2 Corinthians*, 255) and BARNETT (*The Second Epistle*, 399-400), who read διὰ θελήματος θεοῦ in light of 2 Cor 1:1, and thus place the emphasis on the Macedonians' recognition of Paul as a divine representative. While it is true that they do so (as evidenced by their participation in the collection), the apostle's reference to God's will in 2 Cor 8:5 points primarily to the Macedonians' ἁπλότης – that is, to *their* response to God and to the divine will.

attempts in 2 Cor 9:6-10 to convince the Corinthians of God's faithful and abundant beneficence culminate in his encouragement of the community to take part in the ongoing revelation of God's δικαιοσύνη through their 'giving to the poor' (9:9-10). Then in 9:11a Paul continues this line of thought: "as in every way you are being enriched[923] εἰς πᾶσαν ἁπλότητα." For the apostle, it is *God's* generous provision (note the passive voice of πλουτιζόμενοι) that makes possible the "enriching" of others.[924] Furthermore, observe that the preposition εἰς here denotes purpose:[925] God enriches *in order that* people so gifted might in turn enrich those who are in need. Indeed, Paul makes this clear in 9:12, where he states that the collection – described once again as διακονία! (cf. 8:4 and 9:1) – will supply for the needs (τὰ ὑστερήματα) of the members of the church in Jerusalem. Hence, it is certainly not inaccurate to translate εἰς πᾶσαν ἁπλότητα as "for the purpose of all *generosity*," with the accent on the call to be generous in giving to others.

As was the case with the Macedonians' ἁπλότης, however, generosity directed to others does not fully capture the nuance of Paul's expression in 2 Cor 9:11. The apostle's repeated emphasis on *God's* loving provision also functions to encourage the Corinthians to examine their relationship with God. Paul intimates that their generosity will result from, and allow them to grow in, their trust in God. Notice that the apostle has already suggested in 8:13-15 that economic "equality" (ἰσότης) – or, at least, the equitable sharing of resources

[923]Reading the participle πλουτιζόμενοι as expressing manner.

[924]BARNETT correctly observes that πλουτιζόμενοι is a divine passive. See *The Second Epistle to the Corinthians*, 442, n. 37; similarly, KISTEMAKER, *The Second Epistle to the Corinthians*, 317. *Pace* HÉRING (*The Second Epistle of Saint Paul to the Corinthians*, 67), who proposes the possibility of reading the participle in the middle voice, thereby indicating "enriching others." But this misses the function of 2 Cor 9:11a, which FURNISH properly describes as summarizing the key point in the preceding verses – namely, that "the Corinthians can afford to be generous contributors to the fund for Jerusalem *because God provides for them* to be." See *II Corinthians*, 450 (italics added).

[925]As suggested by BETZ, *2 Corinthians 8 and 9*, 116; DANKER, *II Corinthians*, 142; and MURPHY-O'CONNOR, *The Theology of the Second Letter to the Corinthians*, 94. See BDAG, s.v. εἰς, 4.e-f, and n. 751 above.

– is part of God's plan for human beings.[926] That is, those who presently have in abundance are to share with those in want *because this is God's will.* Therefore, Paul calls the Corinthians to single-hearted devotion to the will of God. So, in addition to the notion of generosity to others, I submit that the phrase εἰς πᾶσαν ἁπλότητα also connotes "for the purpose of whole-hearted singleness" – a *singleness* of trust in God and of commitment to carrying out

[926]Indeed, Paul's citation from LXX Exod 16:18 – "The one who [gathered] much did not have too much, and the one who [gathered] little did not have too little" – indicates that this principle of equality has divine warrant and validation. Cf. THRALL, *II Corinthians*, 2.542-43. KISTEMAKER rightly notes that with his reference to Scripture, Paul directs the Corinthians' attention to God. See *The Second Epistle to the Corinthians*, 289. I would add that the apostle's concern is to challenge the community to see what is God's *will.* GEORGI suggests that Paul draws upon traditions that personified ἰσότης as a divine force. He proposes that the expression ἐξ ἰσότητος (2 Cor 8:13) is practically equivalent to ἐκ θεοῦ. See *Remembering the Poor*, 84-91, esp. 88-89. Although Georgi overstates his case – especially the cosmic and charismatic-mystical qualities of ἰσότης – he is correct in seeing that God's will is behind what the apostle says in 2 Cor 8:13-15. That is, *pace* BARRETT (see *The Second Epistle to the Corinthians*, 227), ἰσότης here is more than "a fundamentally moral concept." It is divinely warranted.

God's will.[927] Indeed, it is only from the source of their ἁπλότης vis-à-vis God that the community's generosity to others will flow.

Finally, at the climax of his exhortation, the apostle links the Corinthians' ἁπλότης with a *test* of their character (2 Cor 9:13). As we have seen, he states that, by virtue of the test (διὰ τῆς δοκιμῆς) of the collection, the Corinthians will glorify God on the basis their obedience (9:13b). But observe how Paul's line of thought continues in 9:13c: καὶ [ἐπὶ] ἁπλότητι τῆς κοινωνίας εἰς αὐτοὺς καὶ εἰς πάντας. The apostle also challenges the community to prove their character "on the basis of" their ἁπλότης.[928] Given that the test is the collection itself, Paul surely intends the notion of generosity here. The juxtaposition of ἁπλότης and κοινωνία, however, intimates that something more is going on. Literally, 2 Cor 9:13b reads: "and [on the basis of the] ἁπλότητι of *fellowship/communion* unto [the holy ones of Jerusalem]

---

[927]DANKER is particularly sensitive to Paul's rhetorical strategy here: "The purpose for which God has materially blessed the Corinthians is made even more explicit in [9:11]. Such blessing is designed to make the recipient a source of blessing for others. But God's enrichment of the Corinthians extends beyond the material realm. They are also inwardly enriched so that they can practice the kind of generosity (*haplotês*) that was characteristic of the Macedonians (8:2). The conjunction of thought here with the opening sentences of chap. 8 is a powerful piece of evidence for the unity of chaps. 8 and 9. From a rhetorical perspective, it is a master stroke." See *II Corinthians*, 142-43. I suggest that the inward enrichment Danker mentions involves the increased trust in God that allows one to give one's very self (as did the Macedonians).

BETZ remarks that the phrase ἐν παντὶ πλουτιζόμενοι is "an anthropological statement" that declares human beings' absolute dependence upon God and God's abundant care. See *2 Corinthians 8 and 9*, 115. This all but suggests that God's loving provision ought to evoke increased trust, which is an essential underpinning of ἁπλότης. In addition, FURNISH is surely correct when he observes, concerning 2 Cor 9:12, that the Corinthians' gift to the church in Jerusalem is also service to God. See *II Corinthians*, 451. Indeed, their ἁπλότης contains both elements.

[928]Reading ἐπί as marking the basis for an action (see above, n. 874). In addition, see BDF, § 272 for a discussion of the repetition or omission of the article in prepositional attributives. I take the anarthrous ἁπλότητι as the second object of the preposition ἐπί. HÉRING is exceptional among the commentators for making explicit that the Corinthians' ἁπλότης – in addition to their obedience – is a crucial part of the test. See *The Second Epistle of Saint Paul to the Corinthians*, 68.

and unto all."[929] In other words, the Corinthians' reaching out to relieve "the wants of the holy ones" (9:12) will be a sign of fellowship and a proof of unity between the communities, thereby continuing the story of God's work of reconciliation.[930] Again the apostle exploits the rich resonance of the term ἁπλότης in 9:13b: The Corinthians will prove their character by their generosity; moreover, this generosity will manifest a singleness of purpose in trusting God and in doing God's will. By supplying the needs of others, the Corinthians will promote κοινωνία among the churches. And such κοινωνία is the fruit of the Holy Spirit – the bestower the νοῦς Χριστοῦ – who empowers its recipients to live in communion with one another (cf. 13:13).[931]

---

[929]Paul's language here is particularly dense. It is little wonder that PLUMMER remarked: "In the fulness of his feeling the Apostle gives a compressed fulness of expression, the general meaning of which is certain, but the exact construction of which cannot in all particulars be disentangled with certainty." See *II Corinthians*, 266.

[930]Several commentators render κοινωνία as the Corinthians' "contribution" (e.g., PLUMMER, *II Corinthians*, 257 and 266; HUGHES, *Paul's Second Epistle to the Corinthians*, 338; and LAMBRECHT, *Second Corinthians*, 148) or – what is the same thing – as their "sharing" (e.g., FURNISH, *II Corinthians*, 440 and 445; BELLEVILLE, *2 Corinthians*, 243; and BARNETT, *The Second Epistle to the Corinthians,* 446-47). In all cases, these interpreters translate ἁπλότης as "generosity" or "liberality." DANKER, however, rightly challenges this line of interpretation. That is, he recognizes that ἁπλότης in 2 Cor 9:13 connotes the community's "avowed commitment to Christ who is Lord of all the people of God." Danker also observes that the context demands that κοινωνία signify the fact that "[t]hey are linked with Christ's people throughout the world." Hence, by κοινωνία the apostle here intends something much richer than "contribution" or "sharing" (although this is certainly implicit); he intends "fellowship" or "partnership." See *II Corinthians*, 146. I agree with Danker's analysis, although I would make one minor adjustment: The Corinthians' ἁπλότης – like that of Christ himself– is directed ultimately *to God.*

[931]Although the actual term is not prevalent, κοινωνία is a key theme in 2 Cor. In 1:7 Paul states that the Corinthians and he (along with his co-workers) are κοινωνοί in sufferings and consolation. Moreover, the language of interchange and the line of argument in 1:4-7 suggest that the apostle regards their κοινωνία as including Christ (see 1:5). In 8:4 Paul recounts the Macedonians' pleading with him to participate in "the κοινωνία of the ministry of the holy ones." That is, he makes clear that the collection is about promoting fellowship among the churches. And as we saw earlier in this chapter, Paul concludes this letter by praying that the κοινωνία of the Holy Spirit be with the

Before concluding, I suggest that Paul's rhetorical strategy in 2 Cor 8:1-9:15 resembles the use of *topoi*[932] in Greco-Roman moral literature. The apostle appears to develop in these chapters what might aptly be called the *topos* "Περὶ Ἁπλότητος," a *topos* that is the antithesis of the more common *topos* "Περὶ Φθόνου" ("Concerning Envy").[933] Notice how he refers to ἁπλότης near both

---

Corinthians (13:13). Indeed, it is significant to note that, at the beginning of 1 Cor, the apostle refers to God as πιστός (1 Cor 1:9). As this text goes on to suggest, God's fidelity is manifested through God's calling the Corinthians into κοινωνία τοῦ υἱοῦ αὐτοῦ Ἰησοῦ Χριστοῦ τοῦ κυρίου ἡμῶν ("fellowship with [God's] Son, Jesus Christ our Lord"). And an essential element of this fellowship with Christ is, as I have been arguing, the reception and appropriation of the νοῦς Χριστοῦ.

Pace BETZ (*2 Corinthians 8 and 9*, 124), who argues that κοινωνία in 2 Cor 9:13 is best understood in light of administrative and legal language. On the contrary, as NICKLE observes, "Because Paul understood the fellowship of the Church to be *an organic unity with and in Christ*, κοινωνία and its related forms was an important term used in his writings to express the intimate relationship both of believers with Christ and of believers with each other. In every use which he made of the word-group, this *theological orientation* was retained." See *The Collection*, 105-6 and 122-25. The quotation is from pp. 122-23 (italics added). Indeed, BELLEVILLE aptly points out that the κοινωνία mentioned in 9:13 is that union which is forged by the Spirit, the union that is referred to in 13:13. See *2 Corinthians*, 244.

[932]For a helpful definition of *topoi*, see J.L. JAQUETTE, *Discerning What Counts: The Function of the* Adiaphora Topos *in Paul's Letters*, SBLDS 146 (Atlanta: Scholars Press, 1995) 12-13: "Often used with considerable ambiguity, this term usually refers to rhetorical forms or traditions that are handed down and adopted as stereotypes. *Topoi* are 'the common possession of at least a certain strata of society and are used by an author in a finite and concrete way in the treatment of the subject.' *Topoi* structure arguments in a given rhetorical situation by utilizing literary 'commonplaces,' or they refer to discussions of popular moral topics employing maxims, diatribe or clichés." The quotation in the second sentence is from R.N. SOULEN, *Handbook of Biblical Criticism*, 2nd ed. (Atlanta: John Knox, 1981) 199-200.

[933]The *topos* Περὶ Φθόνου is found in Stobaeus's catalog of *topoi*. See *Ioannis Stobaei Anthologium*, vol. 3, ed. C. WACHSMUTH and O. HENSE (Berlin: Wiedmannsche Verlagsbuchhandlung, 1958) 708-21. For a study that effectively brings the *topos* on envy to bear on the interpretation of a NT text, see L.T. JOHNSON, "James 3:13-4:10 and the *Topos* Περὶ Φθόνου," *NovT* 25 (1983) 327-47. In addition to being the opposite of envy, ἁπλότης is the antonym of *double*-mindedness (διψυχία). It is

the beginning (8:2) and end (9:11 and 9:13) of this unit, in effect creating an *inclusio*.[934] In addition, Paul's employment of *exempla* (8:2-5 and 8:9), authoritative appeals (8:15 and 9:9), and maxims (9:6; 9:7b) is reminiscent of some of the ways in which moralists and ethical writers presented their *topoi*. More importantly, throughout these two chapters he offers a consistent and thoroughgoing deliberative discourse in order to convince the Corinthians to trust in God to provide, and to generously share their resources with others because this is God's will for humanity. Thus, I submit that the issue of ἁπλότης, with all that it connotes, serves as the connective thread of the apostle's argument in 8:1-9:15.

In sum: The term ἁπλότης is significant for Paul in 2 Corinthians. The apostle presents himself to the community as one who has conducted himself ἐν ἁπλότητι (2 Cor 1:12). He also holds up the ἁπλότης of the Macedonians for the Corinthians to emulate (8:2). Paul exhorts the latter to generosity to the collection and – even more fundamentally – to exclusive trust in God and devotion to doing God's will (9:11). In fact, the apostle makes the issue of ἁπλότης another *test* (9:13) for the Corinthians as he challenges them to take on the character of Jesus, the very model of ἁπλότης (11:3).

D. Faithfulness (πίστις)

At the climax of the letter, Paul acknowledges that (at least some of) the Corinthians have challenged him to prove his own character (δοκιμή, 2 Cor 13:3a). Specifically, they seem to have asked him for proof that Christ speaks in him. The immediately preceding context is the apostle's threat that he will not spare those who have sinned and not repented (13:2; cf. 12:20-21). Therefore, it might appear that the key issue here is whether Paul will prove his apostolic authority by exercising his power to punish. But as the following verses reveal, this is not his main concern. After offering a brief response (13:3b-4, see below), the apostle quickly throws the community's challenge right back at them. He admonishes the Corinthians to examine *themselves* (ἑαυτοὺς πειράζετε) and to test *themselves* (ἑαυτοὺς δοκιμάζετε) in

---

interesting to note that the issue of double-minded people comes up in Jas 4:8 in the passage analyzed by Johnson.

[934]SAMPLEY suggests that it is the notion of *testing* (2 Cor 8:2 and 9:13; cf. 8:8) that creates an *inclusio*. See *NIB*, 11.131.

13:5a.[935] We have seen how δοκιμάζω pertains to the issue of character. So, too, does the verb πειράζω. Indeed, Paul deploys it here to denote "make trial of" in order to ascertain the community's character.[936] Hence, by means of a direct counter-challenge – reinforced by the duplication of his command[937] – the apostle makes absolutely clear that, in his mind, the real issue is not his own character, but that of the Corinthians.

Paul's challenge to the community in 2 Cor 13:5a takes on a particular tonality. They are to test themselves to determine whether or not they are ἐν τῇ πίστει. That is, the apostle's climactic entreaty to the Corinthians draws attention to the issue of their πίστις. Observe the presence of the definite article before πίστις. Paul's challenge to the community thus implies that he is holding up to them a particular type of πίστις as a standard. Indeed, I submit that *the apostle's strategy is to test the Corinthians to see whether they are embodying the faithfulness manifested by Jesus*. In order to substantiate this claim, I present a three-step argument. First, I demonstrate how 13:5a follows logically on Paul's mention of δοκιμή (13:3) and his appeal to the story and *ethos* of Jesus (13:4). Second, I explain what the apostle's follow-up rhetorical question in 13:5b presupposes concerning the "christing" power of the Spirit. Third, I show how the ensuing verses (13:6-10) draw out the implications of his challenge.

Paul's reference to δοκιμή in 2 Cor 13:3 brings to the fore the issue of character in the letter's climax. The apostle's initial reaction to the Corinthians' challenge is significant: He immediately turns to the *ethos* of Jesus. After

---

[935]Noting the prominent (first) placement of ἑαυτούς, P.C. BROWN aptly renders 2 Cor 13:5a: "Test *yourselves*. . . . Examine *yourselves*." See "What is the Meaning of 'Examine Yourselves' in 2 Corinthians 13:5?" *Bsac* 154 (1997) 175-88, here 177 (Brown's italics). Indeed, several commentators note the initial position of ἑαυτούς for emphasis. See, e.g., PLUMMER, *II Corinthians*, 375; WINDISCH, *Der zweite Korintherbrief*, 419-20; MARTIN, *2 Corinthians*, 477-78; and LAMBRECHT, *Second Corinthians*, 222.

[936]See BDAG, s.v. πειράζω, 2. Cf. Rev 2:2, where the church in Ephesus is commended: "You have put to the test (ἐπείρασας) those who call themselves 'apostles' but are not, and you found them to be false."

[937]As noted by THRALL, *II Corinthians*, 2.888. SAMPLEY refers to this as "a powerful doubling of verbs with considerable semantic overlap." See *NIB*, 11.176.

reminding the community of the ongoing power of Christ among them (13:3b), Paul refers in 13:4a to the story and character of Jesus. As I argued in Chapter Four, this reference functions as an encapsulation of all the references to Jesus' *ethos* throughout 2 Corinthians.[938] Thus, when the apostle recalls that Christ was crucified ἐξ ἀσθενείας, he alludes to two interconnected features of Jesus' life. First, his entire mode of existence was characterized by gentleness and humility. Second, it was distinguished by his willingness to endure suffering and affliction in giving himself in love and service for the sake of others. But Jesus' story does not end in death. Indeed, Paul also emphasizes that Christ lives *now* through the power of God, who raised him from the dead. Observe how this encapsulation evokes all of the main features of the story of Jesus alluded to in 4:13, the story of the faithful δοῦλος of God anointed with "the Spirit of faithfulness" (τὸ πνεῦμα τῆς πίστεως). And recall how the apostle's citation of LXX Ps 115:1 (ἐπίστευσα – "I have been faithful") functions to express Jesus' testimony to his own πίστις. Hence, the reference to the story of Christ in 13:4a is, I propose, an allusion to his character, an *ethos* marked by faithfulness.

Then in 2 Cor 13:4b Paul claims to participate in this story of Jesus by taking on the latter's character. This is his succinct response to the Corinthians' challenge to prove his δοκιμή. The apostle insists that he too (along with his co-workers) partakes in the mode of self-emptying existence conveyed by the phrase ἐξ ἀσθενείας: "*We* [too] are weak" (ἡμεῖς ἀσθενοῦμεν).[939] He does so because of his intimate relationship with Christ (cf. ἐν αὐτῷ). Moreover, by the same power of God to which the previous half verse refers, Paul will continue to live[940] and minister among the Corinthians. The δύναμις θεοῦ will

---

[938]For a detailed discussion of 2 Cor 13:3b-4, see Chapter Four, Section X. I draw upon the exegesis proposed there in this and the following paragraph.

[939]Similarly, PICKETT, *The Cross in Corinth*, 193: "Thus [Paul] affirms that he is weak in Christ. . . because in the weakness of the crucifixion *Christ epitomizes existence for others*" (italics added).

[940]Recall from my analysis in Chapter Four, Section X that a strict parallelism between 2 Cor 13:4a and 13:4b breaks down in connection with the verb ζάω. Whereas ζάω refers to Jesus' resurrection life in 13:4a (cf. 4:10b and 4:11b), it refers in 13:4b to how Paul will continue to live and minister among the Corinthians through the power of God.

continue to empower the apostle to embody Jesus' self-giving mode of existence for the benefit of the community. In fact, this is an essential aspect of how Christ continues to be powerful among the Corinthians in the present (13:3b). Notice how this recalls Paul's self-presentation in 4:7-14. In particular, 13:4b evokes the apostle's statement that, like Jesus, he has the πνεῦμα τῆς πίστεως. And "christed" by this same Spirit (cf. 1:21), Paul and his co-workers can exclaim: καὶ ἡμεῖς πιστεύομεν ("*We* too are faithful," 4:13). Thus, just as 13:4a functions as a précis of Jesus' *ethos*, so also I propose that 13:4b serves as a précis of the apostle's character. That is, he answers the challenge to his character by alluding to his own faithfulness, a πίστις that reflects the πίστις of Christ.

We are now able to appreciate more fully Paul's counter-offensive in 2 Cor 13:5a, where he puts the community on trial to prove its character. When the apostle admonishes the Corinthians to examine themselves to see whether they are ἐν τῇ πίστει, it becomes clear exactly what this test entails. The πίστις to which Paul refers in this verse – recall the articular substantive – is the faithfulness which Jesus exemplified, and which the apostle now manifests.[941] Observe, moreover, that the preposition ἐν functions here to mark a state or condition.[942] Hence, the "condition" in which Paul exhorts the

---

[941]*Pace* BARNETT (*The Second Epistle to the Corinthians*, 608), who argues that the phrase "in *the* faith" refers to "the propositional and theological content of that *message* about Jesus which is to be the object of 'faith'" (Barnett's italics). To be sure, Paul does care that the Corinthians get the "right message." But in 2 Cor 13:5 – and, indeed, throughout 2 Cor – the apostle is mostly concerned about their *living out* the implications of the gospel message. KISTEMAKER rightly challenges understanding πίστις as "objective faith that is rooted in doctrine." The alternative he proposes, however – namely, that the apostle refers here "to subjective trust in Jesus Christ" – is also insufficient. See *The Second Epistle to the Corinthians*, 450. Kistemaker stands on firmer ground when he states that Paul has in mind the living faith of one who walks faithfully in the footsteps of Christ. For a helpful discussion and critique of the various ways commentators have interpreted what the apostle means by ἐν τῇ πίστει, see THRALL, *II Corinthians*, 2.888-89. She correctly opts for understanding πίστις here in terms of living the Christian life, although (like most other commentators) she fails to see the connection with Christ's πίστις. MURPHY-O'CONNOR intimates that he does see this connection when he mentions here "the standard revealed in Christ." See *The Theology of the Second Letter to the Corinthians*, 134.

[942]See BDAG, s.v. ἐν, 2. Cf. 1 Tim 2:2 and 2:15.

Corinthians to be (cf. ἐστε) is that which is characterized by the faithfulness of Jesus. In other words, the apostle encourages the community to join him in participating in the story of Jesus by aligning themselves with the latter's πίστις, which reveals itself in a manner of living marked by love and self-donation.[943]

That Paul has Christ's πίστις in mind in 2 Cor 13:5a is supported by his follow-up rhetorical question[944] in 13:5b: "Do you not realize about yourselves that Jesus Christ [is] in you ('Ιησοῦς Χριστὸς ἐν ὑμῖν)?" Observe that the apostle begins the question with οὐκ, thereby signaling that he expects the answer to be Yes! Therefore, his question serves to recall for the Corinthians that, indeed, 'Ιησοῦς Χριστὸς ἐν ὑμῖν. Paul's strategy here is to have the community consider the implications of this fact, implications that are discernible from what he writes elsewhere.[945] For example, in the course of

---

[943]SAVAGE comes tantalizingly close to drawing this same conclusion. He correctly sees the connection between what Paul argues in 2 Cor 4:13 and his injunction in 13:5. See *Power through Weakness*, 180. MARTIN captures well the apostle's logic in 13:4-5: "What Paul is doing is expressing the hope that the Corinthians will examine themselves to deal with the issue of whether or not they are walking in the way of Christ by following his apostle (1 Cor 11:1)." See *2 Corinthians*, 478. Martin's citation of 1 Cor 11:1, where Paul exhorts the Corinthians to be imitators of him as he is of Christ – μιμηταί μου γίνεσθε καθὼς κἀγὼ Χριστοῦ – is particularly appropriate.

As noted above (n. 820), BETZ is especially sensitive to the apostle's use of δοκιμ- terminology in 13:3-7. See *Der Apostel Paulus und die sokratische Tradition*, 132-37. Betz argues that this language betokens the issue of authentication among Paul, the Corinthians, *and the opponents*. On the contrary, the triad with which the apostle is concerned is the community, himself, *and Jesus*. Betz's emphasis on authentication is accurate insofar as one understands that it is ultimately grounded in the issue of character – specifically, in Christ's *ethos*.

[944]The particle ἤ serves to introduce a rhetorical question. See BDAG, 1.d.α; cf. 2 Cor 11:7.

[945]Of course, the Corinthians will have to work out for themselves the implications from what Paul has written to them and from what he has preached to them in person. Whereas we have access to the former, we do not to the latter – except insofar as the apostle alludes to it and draws upon it. Given our access to Paul's other writings, however, it is valid to draw upon them insofar as they shed light on the reasoning process that he invites the churches (that he founded) to engage in. This reasoning process,

describing what life in the Spirit involves, the apostle draws out for the church in Rome the ramifications of Christ's presence among them (Rom 8:9-10). In Rom 8:10a Paul uses the same expression found in 2 Cor 13:5b: Χριστὸς ἐν ὑμῖν. For the apostle, this expression is tantamount to the "Spirit of God dwells in you" (πνεῦμα θεοῦ οἰκεῖ ἐν ὑμῖν, Rom 8:9a), the Spirit that he immediately identifies as the "Spirit of Christ" (πνεῦμα Χριστοῦ, Rom 8:9b).[946] Thus, I submit that Paul's rhetorical question in 2 Cor 13:5b challenges the Corinthians to consider the power of the working of the Spirit of Christ within them. In fact, as we saw earlier in this chapter (in Section III), the apostle has already employed this same tactic in 6:16b.

What does this Spirit do within and for the Corinthians? The Spirit's work of "christing" and sealing (2 Cor 1:21-22) entails "inscribing" its recipients with the character of Jesus. And, as Paul has already informed the community in a previous letter, essential to the Spirit's work is the bestowal of the νοῦς Χριστοῦ (1 Cor 2:16). The apostle's rhetorical question (2 Cor 13:5b) is very suggestive in this regard. In raising the question, Paul employs the verb ἐπιγινώσκω, a word that signifies a deeper, more complete kind of knowing than γινώσκω.[947] Notice, too, that the object of this knowledge is the Corinthians themselves (ἑαυτούς). Thus, the apostle seems to imply that if the members of the community really knew themselves, intimately and thoroughly, they would recognize that they possess the mind of Christ. Moreover, recall that the term ἀρραβών (2 Cor 1:22) connotes the Spirit's giving "further payments" as part of its ongoing work. It is significant in this regard that Paul alludes to this ongoing work of the Spirit in Gal 4:19 by using language similar to 2 Cor 13:5b: "My children, with whom I again suffer birth pains until *Christ is formed*

---

presumably, would be the same for the Corinthians.

[946]THRALL also makes note of the connection between Rom 8:9-10 and 2 Cor 13:5. See *II Corinthians*, 2.891, n. 159.

[947]So, HUGHES, *Paul's Second Epistle to the Corinthians*, 481, n. 177; BARNETT, *The Second Epistle to the Corinthians*, 608; BROWN, "What is the Meaning of 'Examine Yourselves' in 2 Corinthians 13:5?" 182; and SAMPLEY, *NIB*, 11.176. FURNISH observes that ἐπιγινώσκω refers to knowledge that *leads to action*. That is, the verb "suggests knowledge complete enough to warrant appropriate action." See *II Corinthians*, 572. Similarly, BELLEVILLE, *2 Corinthians*, 331. In addition, see BDAG, s.v. ἐπιγινώσκω, 1.a. Cf. 1 Cor 13:12; 2 Cor 6:9; and Col 1:6.

in you (μορφωθῇ Χριστὸς ἐν ὑμῖν)!" Again we encounter the expression Χριστὸς ἐν ὑμῖν, now used in conjunction with "being shaped" or "formed" (μορφόομαι). Thus, I submit that the apostle's rhetorical question in 2 Cor 13:5b – one he asks in his role as the Corinthians' father (cf. 6:13 and 12:14-15) – functions to remind them of the Spirit's work of forming them more and more into the image of Christ (3:18).[948]

Paul's rhetorical question is penetrating in its own right. He adds to its effect by attaching an ominous concessive clause: εἰ μήτι ἀδόκιμοί ἐστε ("unless you are *not* tried and true [that is, genuine])."[949] Again the apostle makes clear to the community that the issue is character – or the lack thereof. The inverse of his logic is that the person who *is* δόκιμος is one in whom the Spirit of Christ, the πνεῦμα τῆς πίστεως ("the Spirit of faithfulness"), is

---

[948]Cf. the following remarks by W.B. BARCLEY: "Transformation in Paul's thought world. . . means conformation to Christ's image. The formation (μορφωθῇ) of 'Christ in' the Galatians (Gal. 4:19) is synonymous with taking on his εἰκών." See *"Christ in You": A Study in Paul's Theology and Ethics* (Lanham, Md.: University Press of America, 1999) 87. Commenting on the apostle's meaning of the phrase "Christ in you" in 2 Cor 10-13, Barcley observes that the reality of Christ's presence "produces a transformation in believers' lives that shows itself in concrete ways" (ibid., 42). In fact, it empowers the Christian community "to display *the character of Christ* in their present life together" (ibid., 38; italics added).

FURNISH sees both a formal and material connection between Paul's rhetorical questions in 2 Cor 13:5 and 1 Cor 3:16 ("Do you not know that you are God's temple, and that the Spirit of God dwells in you?"). He offers a fitting description of what the apostle means by πίστις in 2 Cor 13:5: ". . . he is thinking of [πίστις] as primarily obedience (cf. 10:6) – and not in a moralistic sense. . . , but in the sense that one's whole life, placed under the rule of Christ's love (5:14), *is to be conducted according to the guidance of the Spirit. . . .*" See *II Corinthians*, 577 (italics added). BULTMANN makes the same point more succinctly: "[πίστις means] . . . the obedience of faith actualized in the περιπατεῖν κατὰ πνεῦμα. . . ." See *The Second Letter to the Corinthians*, 244-45.

[949]See BDF, § 376. ALLO aptly surmises that Paul's intention here is to shake the Corinthians out of their complacency. See *Seconde Épître aux Corinthiens*, 339.

present. Such a person is thereby empowered to express τὸ ἀμήν (1:20), that is, to live in the self-giving mode of existence characterized by πίστις.[950]

This interpretation is bolstered by an appreciation of how it sheds light on the immediately following verses (2 Cor 13:6-10). In 13:6 Paul expresses his hope that the Corinthians will know that he and his co-workers are not ἀδόκιμοι. Stated positively, the apostle implies that he hopes that the community will recognize and acknowledge that he is δόκιμος, of good character. For the final time in 2 Corinthians, we see him using cognitive language (γινώσκω). In effect, Paul conveys to the community that if they truly have the νοῦς Χριστοῦ, they will recognize that his *ethos* resembles that of Jesus.[951]

In 2 Cor 13:7 the apostle goes on to stress that his real concern does not revolve around the issue of how he is perceived by the Corinthians, whether as δόκιμος or ἀδόκιμος (for he is confident of where he stands). Rather, his preoccupation lies in what the community *does* (cf. ποιέω).[952] Paul prays to God that they might refrain from 'doing what is wrong,' and instead 'do what

---

[950]BROWN argues that Paul uses irony in 2 Cor 13:5, in the sense of sometimes meaning the opposite of what is said. See "What is the Meaning of 'Examine Yourselves' in 2 Corinthians 13:5?" 175-188. On the contrary, the apostle's language here is straightforward. Brown's study is colored by two presuppositions. First is a dogmatic one, as he presumes a "once-for-all justification in Jesus Christ." Second is an interpretive one, as he reads the letter as forensic rhetoric. Thus, Brown argues that Paul's intent is to defend his own authority by pointing out to the Corinthians their own faith and salvation, both of which serve to substantiate his apostleship. While it is true that the apostle calls the community his letter of recommendation (3:2), his real concern is that they embody the character of Christ and thus show themselves to be a letter about Christ (ἐπιστολὴ Χριστοῦ, 3:3).

[951]BULTMANN captures well Paul's logic in 2 Cor 13:6: ". . . [Paul] assumes that when [the Corinthians] measure themselves by the proper measure they will also apply the appropriate measure to him and recognize his δοκιμή. As verse 6 shows, self-criticism is the presupposition for the criticism of others or of him." See *The Second Letter to the Corinthians*, 245. I would add that the "appropriate measure" to which Bultmann refers is the νοῦς Χριστοῦ.

[952]This is further evidence for reading 2 Cor more as deliberative rhetoric than as forensic rhetoric.

is good.'[953] In a manner similar to Moses (see Deut 30:19-20), the apostle places the alternatives before the community in very simple terms: They can choose to embrace and appropriate the *ethos* of Jesus, whose character is distinguished by πίστις [= ποιέω τὸ καλόν (doing what is good or right)], or they can choose not to [= ποιέω τὸ κακόν (doing what is wrong)].[954]

In 2 Cor 13:8 Paul states that he (and his co-workers) cannot do[955] anything "against the truth" (κατὰ τῆς ἀληθείας); instead, what he does is "for the sake of the truth" (ὑπὲρ τῆς ἀληθείας). I propose that 'acting for the sake of the truth' is synonymous with 'doing what is good' (13:7),[956] and thus also signifies living in a manner that expresses Jesus' πίστις. Indeed, the apostle's reference to the truth here evokes what he has said earlier in the text. In 4:2 he engaged in (positive) self-*commendation* "by means of the manifestation of the truth" (τῇ φανερώσει τῆς ἀληθείας). Recall that this verse is situated in the context of Paul's description of the Spirit-empowered

---

[953]SAMPLEY proposes that 2 Cor 13:7 is another example of Paul's willing self-abnegation for the sake of the community: "Without the explicit terminology here, Paul thinks sacrificially and presents himself as being prepared to give himself up for their well-being, a notion found between Paul and other groups of persons as well (cf. Rom 9:3; 1 Cor 13:3; Phil 2:17), a profound Pauline affirmation of continuing friendship with the Corinthians. Paul depicts himself as weighing their prosperity ahead of his own; for them to meet the test is more important than for him to do so." See *NIB*, 11.177. For a similar interpretation, see MURPHY-O'CONNOR, *The Theology of the Second Letter to the Corinthians*, 134. Murphy-O'Connor rightly emphasizes that what the apostle seeks is that the quality of life in the Corinthian community reflects Christ's cruciform existence.

[954]Cf. WINDISCH'S comment: "Das positive τὸ καλὸν ποιεῖν (vgl. Gal 6:10) ist treffender als die Litotes μὴ ποιεῖν κακόν: das Rechte ist Gehorsam gegen Gottes Willen. . . ." See *Der zweite Korintherbrief*, 422. Similarly, FURNISH remarks that 'doing what is right' is tantamount to doing the will of God. See *II Corinthians*, 578. Of course, doing God's will is at the heart of Jesus' πίστις. See my comment on 2 Cor 13:8 below.

[955]The verb ποιέω must be supplied from 2 Cor 13:7. So, too, FURNISH, *II Corinthians*, 573.

[956]In fact, FURNISH points out that "the truth" and "the good" are used interchangeably in Rom 2:8 and 2:10. See *II Corinthians*, 579.

transformation into the image of Christ (3:18), a transformation that is demonstrated by embodying Jesus' self-giving mode of existence (4:10a and 4:11a). To incarnate Christ's manner of living *is* the φανέρωσις of the truth. Similarly, in 11:10 the apostle stated that the "truth of Christ" (ἀληθεία Χριστοῦ) is in him. The context of this verse is Paul's insistence upon lowering himself for the sake of the Corinthians by ministering to them without taking remuneration from them. In other words, by giving himself for the sake of the community, he continues the story of Jesus among them. Hence, continuing the story of Jesus is what the apostle means in 13:8 by 'acting for the sake of the truth.'[957]

Finally, in 2 Cor 13:9 Paul repeats what he has already acknowledged in 13:4b – namely, that he is weak (ἀσθενέω), a fact in which he even takes joy.[958] As we have seen, this is his shorthand for claiming that he participates in Jesus' mode of existence.[959] Then the apostle tells the Corinthians that he prays for their κατάρτισις. This term – which denotes "maturation," even "the process of perfecting"[960] – evokes 7:1. Recall that in the latter verse, Paul

---

[957]BELLEVILLE refers to the compelling ἀγάπη of Christ in connection with 2 Cor 13:8: "Just as Christ's sacrificial love compels Paul to preach the gospel (5:14), so too his commissioning as Christ's apostle hems him in to doing only what advances the gospel." See *2 Corinthians*, 333. As we saw throughout Chapter Five, Paul's most eloquent proclamation of the gospel is his embodiment of the self-giving love of Christ.

[958]FURNISH (*II Corinthians*, 579) argues that 2 Cor 13:9a does not support (cf. γάρ) 13:8, but rather 13:7. While it is true that 13:9a serves as a basis for 13:7, it also follows naturally upon the apostle's statement in 13:8 – another grounding statement! – when one realizes that, in 13:7-8, he is alluding to the πίστις-marked mode of existence exemplified by Christ.

[959]BARRETT rightly comments that Paul's rejoicing in his being weak refers to his weakness in Christ, and that it entails the apostle's "unremitting service and self-abasement." See *The Second Epistle to the Corinthians*, 340. FURNISH is correct to link the apostle's statement here to 13:3-4, as well as to 4:7 and 12:9-10. See *II Corinthians*, 579. Indeed, recall from Chapter Five, Section IV that I analyzed the latter two passages under the heading of the apostle's incarnating Jesus' πίστις.

[960]See BDAG, s.v. κατάρτισις. E.J. GOODSPEED intriguingly renders 2 Cor 13:9b as follows: "That is what I pray for – *the perfecting of your characters*." See *The Parallel New Testament: The American Translation and the King James Version: In Parallel*

exhorts the community to "make perfect" (ἐπιτελέω) holiness, an exhortation that refers to appropriating and manifesting the *ethos* of Christ. Hence, the apostle's prayer in 13:9 is in line with his strategy throughout this letter. In fact, as 13:10 reveals, Paul's greatest desire is to build up the community.[961] But as he threatened in 13:2, again the apostle warns that he will not spare those who choose to do what is wrong (cf. 13:7).[962]

Thus, having been challenged by the Corinthians to prove his character to them, Paul turns the challenge right back upon the community. He admonishes them to test themselves, to see whether *they* incarnate the character of Jesus. Specifically, the apostle desires that they embody Jesus' πίστις – his manner of living that was marked by lowering himself in love, as God's δοῦλος, for the sake of others. Paul reminds the Corinthians that the πνεῦμα τῆς πίστεως dwells within them, and thus urges them to live out of this "christing" empowerment. In effect, the apostle's admonition in 2 Cor 13:5 epitomizes and

---

Columns, with Introductions and Explanatory Notes (Chicago: University of Chicago Press, 1943) 429 (italics added). Goodspeed's translation thus seems to exhibit insight into the issue of *ethos* in this passage.

[961]Cf. BARRETT, *The Second Epistle to the Corinthians*, 341: "The Lord's intention, for which he has equipped his apostle with the paradoxical kind of authority in weakness that has been repeatedly noted in the epistle, is that there should be built up in Corinth a community of Christians, founded upon the Gospel and expressing their Christian existence in mutual love." Cf. SAMPLEY, *NIB*, 11.177: "Edification and love are Paul's choices for the Corinthians. . . ."

[962]It might be argued that my analysis of 2 Cor 13:3-10 does not take sufficient account of Paul's threat to punish some in the community. Undoubtedly, the apostle considers this a possibility (cf. 10:6, 13:2, and 13:10). Commentators tend to overstress this element, however, in their treatment of what Paul means by using δοκιμ- terminology in these verses. The apostle's *primary concern* here is what it has been throughout the entire letter – namely, to exhort the community to embody more and more the *ethos* of Jesus in the various circumstances in which they find themselves. The issue of Paul's authority to punish is subservient to this purpose. My reading therefore attempts to bring to the surface what underlies the apostle's treatment here. The function of Paul's δοκιμ-language in 2 Cor is to summon the Corinthians to join him in participating in the story of Jesus by taking on the latter's character. For an example of an interpretation that is overly determined by the specter of punishment, see HUGHES, *Paul's Second Epistle to the Corinthians*, 477-85.

summarizes all of his previous exhortations. This climactic exhortation, which follows upon an allusion to the story of Jesus (13:4), functions as an "exhortation of application,"[963] and thereby participates in the three-step logic employed throughout this epistle: Paul (1) alludes to the story and *ethos* of Jesus; (2) situates himself as one who participates in this story by embodying Christ's character; and (3) urges the Corinthians to do the same. In fact, I suggest that the apostle intimates this very strategy in 13:1, which – following a brief excursus – is the subject of the next section.

EXCURSUS: Paul's Use of πιστ- Cognates in 2 Cor 6:14-15

I submit that the understanding of πίστις offered above illuminates Paul's meaning in 2 Cor 6:14-15. Immediately following a passionate plea to the Corinthians to open their hearts to him (6:13), the apostle exhorts them: μὴ γίνεσθε ἑτεροζυγοῦντες ἀπίστοις (6:14a). This is usually translated, "Do not become mismated with *unbelievers*!" Paul then fires off five rhetorical questions, each of which dramatically juxtaposes what he considers to be two incompatible entities. The fourth of these questions is: τίς μερὶς πιστῷ μετὰ ἀπίστου? (6:15b). As with the interpretation of 6:14a, this question is usually translated, "What does a *believer* have in common with an *unbeliever*?" The problem with this line of interpretation, however, is that there is nothing in the immediately preceding or ensuing context – not to mention, in the entire epistle (unlike, e.g., 1 Cor 7:12-16 and 14:20-25) – regarding "believers" or "unbelievers." Rather, the apostle's concern remains, as it has throughout the letter, whether the community manifests obedience, love, generosity/singleness, and faithfulness to God's ways.

What, then, *does* the context suggest? In 2 Cor 6:4-10 Paul self-*commends* via a *peristasis* catalog in which he dramatizes the hardships involved in his self-emptying manner of being a "servant of God" (διάκονος θεοῦ). Moreover, in 6:11-13 it is evident that (at least) some of the Corinthians lack affection for him, at least from the apostle's perspective. Indeed, Paul plaintively calls for them to open their hearts to him, a plea that he repeats in 7:2. In this latter verse, it also becomes clear that the apostle's behavior among

---

[963]See FOWL, *Story of Christ in the Ethics of Paul*, 175 (as well as Chapter Three, Section I.D above). The term signifies one of the ways in which Paul attempts to connect the story of Jesus with the story of Christians.

the community has raised some doubts about him. And more immediately, in 6:17a, he cites Scripture in order to admonish the Corinthians to "come out from" (ἐξέρχομαι) and "separate from" (ἀφορίζομαι) some unnamed group.

Assembling these clues, I propose that the situation Paul addresses here reflects some combination of the three circumstances of the rhetorical situation mentioned above (at the beginning of Section IV). Seeds of doubt and opposition have emerged because of money (cf. both the collection and the apostle's refusal to accept remuneration from the Corinthians); or because of the punishment of the recalcitrant member (which was dealt out by the majority of the community, but not by all; cf. 2 Cor 2:6); or because of the comportment of the interloping missionaries/evangelists; or from some combination of these factors. From whom does the apostle want the Corinthians to "come out"? Either from some within the community, or from other missionaries/evangelists, or from a combination of these two groups. The apostle thus asks the Corinthians to separate themselves from such persons who are ostensibly believers, whether they are disaffected community members or other missionaries/evangelists. Hence, Paul refers here *not* to unbelievers, but to those whom he regards as *unfaithful* – unfaithful perhaps in what they proclaim, but more plausibly, unfaithful in their living out the mode of self-giving existence revealed by Jesus. Thus, I propose translating the apostle's admonition in 6:14a as follows: "Do not be mismated with *unfaithful ones*!"; and his question in 6:15b: "What has a *faithful person* in common with an *unfaithful one*"?

The four other paired incompatibilities in 2 Cor 6:14b-16a, I submit, confirm this interpretation. The first pair is δικαιοσύνη ("righteousness") and ἀνομία ("lawlessness"). Paul's reference to δικαιοσύνη echoes 5:21, where he states that God has acted in Christ "in order that we might become the righteousness of God." Recall the interpretation of this passage offered in Chapter Five – to become the righteousness of God means to follow in the way of Jesus by lowering oneself so that others might be lifted up. The second pair is φῶς ("light") and σκότος ("darkness"). The apostle uses these terms in 4:4 and 4:6. In 4:6 he speaks of God's gift of enlightenment in the πρόσωπον of Jesus Christ. As we have seen, this gift is linked to the bestowal of the νοῦς Χριστοῦ and the transformation of people into image of Christ (3:18). Conversely, according to Paul, it is the unfaithful ones (ἄπιστοι) whose thoughts have been blinded (4:4). The third pair is Christ and Beliar. That the apostle mentions Christ recalls the latter's ναί (1:19-20), which anticipates the reference to his obedience (10:5). This reference stands in contrast to Beliar, who in some textual traditions is associated with disobedience.[964] The final contrast is between the ναὸς θεοῦ ("temple of God") and εἴδωλα ("idols"). Paul immediately reminds the Corinthians that they *are* the temple of God (6:16b), which calls to mind the Spirit's gift of "christing" and sealing (1:21-22). Indeed, it is the Spirit who empowers them to bring holiness to perfection (7:1). The point here is that, in every instance, the apostle seems to contrast a Spirit-empowered mode of existence – lived in fidelity to God, as revealed by Jesus – with behavior that is characterized by disobedience and lawlessness (which is tantamount to practicing idolatry). This same pattern, I submit, abides in the fourth pair, the πίστος and the ἄπιστος. Hence, it is better to translate these terms, respectively, as "faithful person" and "unfaithful person" – and *not* as "believer" and "unbeliever."

V. 2 Cor 13:1b – Jesus and Paul as the "Witnesses" to the Corinthians

In 2 Cor 13:1a Paul announces to the community that he will be coming to them for the third time. He then follows this announcement with a citation from LXX Deut 19:15: ἐπὶ στόματος δύο μαρτύρων καὶ τριῶν σταθήσεται πᾶν ῥῆμα (2 Cor 13:1b). The apostle cites this text almost verbatim (although, as I argue below, with a significant omission).[965] The citation's context in Deuteronomy is a series of legal injunctions. Within this context, the quoted words denote that more than one witness is necessary in order to convict a person of any crime or wrongdoing. The RSV is typical in how it renders the citation: "Any charge must be sustained by the evidence of two or three witnesses." This translation rests, presumably, on the legal context

---

[964]See, e.g. *T. Dan* 5:11: καὶ τὴν αἰχμαλωσίαν λήψεται ἀπὸ τοῦ Βελίαρ, [τὰς ψυχὰς τῶν ἁγίων] καὶ ἐπιστρέψει καρδίας ἀπειθεῖς πρὸς Κύριον (cited from "Διαθήκη Δάν," *The Greek Versions of the Testaments of the Twelve Patriarchs*, 130-143).

[965]LXX Deut 19:15 is also cited in Matt 18:16 and 1 Tim 5:19; cf. Heb 10:28. It is possible that it is alluded to in John 8:17 and 1 John 5:8. For a study that investigates the role of Deut 19:15 in the understanding of Hellenistic and Palestinian Judaism around the beginning of the common era, as well as the use of this text by NT writers, see H. VAN VLIET, *No Single Testimony: A Study on the Adoption of the Law of Deut. 19:15 Par. into the New Testament* (Utrecht: Kreminck en Zoon, 1958).

of Deuteronomy, as well as on Paul's threat in the following verse to bring punishment to some in the community (2 Cor 13:2).

Two basic lines of interpretation have emerged concerning the apostle's use of LXX Deut 19:15 in 2 Cor 13:1b. The first holds that he employs the citation literally. That is, Paul refers here to some formal judicial procedure that he will employ in Corinth if the situation calls for it (cf. 13:2). This procedure would make use of the Mosaic directive concerning the necessity of having more than one witness.[966] Mathias Delcor suggests a more specific scenario. On the basis of 1 Cor 6:1-4, he argues that the apostle in fact had earlier encouraged the community to have in place a court system to mediate disputes between members.[967] He goes on to propose that Paul himself served in the office of "supreme judge" for the handling of serious disputes (cf. 1 Cor 5:3). Delcor states that 2 Cor 13:1 "clearly implies" that the apostle is coming to Corinth in this capacity as supreme judge.[968]

There are clear problems with this line of interpretation. Against the more general proposal that Paul will implement some type of legal proceeding when he arrives, it is questionable – given the apparent divisiveness within the community, as well as his desire to promote reconciliation – whether he would

---

[966]See, e.g., HUGHES, *Paul's Second Epistle to the Corinthians*, 475: "The Apostle is forewarning the Corinthians that he will not hesitate to execute condign justice should the state of affairs require it during his forthcoming visit, but that everything will be carried through in strict accord with the principles of justice laid down in the Mosaic code and approved by Christ Himself as applicable to disputes within the Church (Mt. 18:16): an adequate number of witnesses will be called and their evidence considered before a charge is accepted as proven and sentence passed." In addition, cf. ALLO, *Seconde Épître aux Corinthiens*, 335; BARNETT, *The Second Epistle to the Corinthians*, 598; and HAFEMANN, *2 Corinthians*, 489-90. SAMPLEY (*NIB*, 11.175) claims that Paul sets down here the ground rules for disputes that he has with them and vice versa.

[967]See M. DELCOR, "The Courts of the Church of Corinth and the Courts of Qumran," in *Paul and Qumran: Studies in New Testament Exegesis*, ed. J. MURPHY-O'CONNOR (Chicago: Priory, 1968) 69-84, here 69-70.

[968]Ibid., 76.

ask community members to testify *against* one another.[969] And against Delcor, his proposal rests on a tendentious reading of 1 Cor 6:4,[970] while completely ignoring the apostle's scathing condemnation of lawsuits between community members in 1 Cor 6:7. In addition – and most importantly for 2 Cor 13:1 – there is no specific mention of any formal judicial procedure following 2 Cor 13:2, nor for that matter anywhere else in this letter.[971]

The second line of interpretation, which goes back at least as far as Chrysostom, claims that Paul employs the citation metaphorically. Several commentators argue that the apostle's visits – two of which have already been made, the third of which is imminent – constitute the "witnesses."[972] In effect, the first two visits have functioned as a warning to the community. In his third visit Paul plans to bring the crisis to resolution. Advocates of this position point to the connection between the apostle's use of ordinal numbers ("second" and "third" visits; 2 Cor 13:1-2) and cardinal numbers ("two or three witnesses"; 13:1). Moreover, there seems to be a deliberate linkage in 13:1 between τρίτον and τριῶν. Because the former refers to a visit, it is likely that the latter does as well. Indeed, Paul is quite capable of interpreting texts metaphorically, as he

---

[969]Similarly, PLUMMER, *II Corinthians*, 372. Indeed, Hughes's proposal (see n. 966) reads 2 Cor 13:1 too much in light of Matt 18:16.

[970]DELCOR translates 1 Cor 6:4 as follows: "If then you have such cases, set up judges who are acceptable to the church." See "The Courts of the Church of Corinth and the Courts of Qumran," 70.

[971]As FURNISH rightly notes. See *II Corinthians*, 575.

[972]See, e.g., VAN VLIET, *No Single Testimony*, 96, n. 8; BRUCE, *1 and 2 Corinthians*, 252-53; BARRETT, *The Second Epistle to the Corinthians*, 333; BELLEVILLE, *2 Corinthians*, 327; LAMBRECHT, *Second Corinthians*, 221; and THRALL, *II Corinthians*, 2.876. BULTMANN (*The Second Letter to the Corinthians*, 241) and FURNISH (*II Corinthians*, 575) offer a variation of this line of interpretation. They question whether the apostle's first visit can appropriately be considered a witness against the community. Thus, they propose that the first witness is the second visit, the second witness is the present letter, and the third witness is the pending visit. But, as Thrall notes, if the second visit is the first witness, then would it not follow more naturally that the so-called painful letter be the second witness? Moreover, the metaphor becomes unwieldy when the image of witness pertains both to visits and a letter. See THRALL, *II Corinthians*, 2.875-76.

shows elsewhere.[973] The point of his use of the citation, then, is to give added (scriptural) warrant to his threat to punish sinners. This second line of interpretation is certainly preferable to the first, and admittedly has much to commend it (especially the way it links the apostle's use of numbers in 13:1-2).

I suggest a third alternative, however, one that lies between the literal and metaphorical interpretations, and one that takes better account of the larger context (2 Cor 13:3-10; especially 13:3-5). My proposal rests upon taking a fresh look at some of the key terms in the citation from LXX Deut 19:15. First is the word μάρτυς. While this term can have the technical sense of denoting a witness in a legal proceeding, it can also signify a "martyr" – one who offers witness at the cost of life[974] – as well as a "witness" who bears testimony to the life, sufferings, death, and resurrection of Jesus.[975] Second is the term στόμα. While this word can designate that which comes from the mouth – for instance, the "evidence" given by witnesses – its most fundamental meaning is the "mouth" itself, that out of which utterances come.[976] And third is the word ῥῆμα. While this term can take on the more specific sense of a legal "charge," it is also used more broadly to mean "matter" or "issue."[977] With these non-legal definitions in mind, I submit that *Paul utilizes LXX Deut 19:15 to allude to Jesus and himself as the two μάρτυρες*. That is, the apostle finds in this line from Scripture an apt epitome of his various allusions to the story of Jesus and of his (Paul's) claims to participate in this story himself. And as we will see, the apostle's goal in citing the text is to convince the Corinthians to take part in the same story.

Jesus is the first μάρτυς held up to the Corinthians. As ὁ Χριστός, the one anointed with the πνεῦμα τῆς πίστεως, Christ is God's faithful and obedient δοῦλος. His manner of living was marked by loving, self-emptying

---

[973]THRALL cites the example of 1 Cor 9:8-10. See *II Corinthians*, 2.875.

[974]See BDAG, s.v. μάρτυς, 3. Cf. Acts 22:20; and Rev 1:5; 2:13; 3:14; and 17:6.

[975]See BDAG, s.v. μάρτυς, 2.c. Cf. Acts 1:8; 1:22; 2:32; 3:15; 5:32; 10:39; 10:41; 13:31; 22:15; and 26:16.

[976]See BDAG, s.v. στόμα, 1. Cf. Rom 3:19 and 10:8; Eph 6:19; and Col 3:8.

[977]See BDAG, s.v. ῥῆμα, 2. Cf. Luke 1:65; and Acts 5:32 and 13:42.

service of others, even to the point of giving his life.[978] But observe that the Scripture citation also links the term μάρτυς with στόμα. Now, how has Jesus borne witness with his "mouth"? Recall the interpretation of 2 Cor 4:13, where Paul cites the words of LXX Ps 115:1a – ἐπίστευσα, διὸ ἐλάλησα. These words function as the words of Jesus himself, whose story as God's faithful δοῦλος is told in LXX Pss 114:1-115:10. In effect, Jesus here "speaks" about – or better, "bears witness to" – the story of his faithfulness to God, who has delivered him from death. Moreover, it is surely no coincidence that, near the beginning of this letter, the apostle refers to the ναί that has come to be ἐν αὐτῷ, that is, through the agency of Christ (2 Cor 1:19b-20a).[979] Jesus' "Yes" expressed his ongoing obedience to God. And Jesus' self-giving manner of existence, the result of his commitment to doing God's will, was his most eloquent witness and testimony. Hence, Christ is the μάρτυς *par excellence.*

Paul himself is the second μάρτυς. Although he is not a martyr in the literal sense of the term (at least, not at the time he wrote this epistle), the apostle continually bears in his body the νέκρωσις of Jesus, and is constantly being handed over εἰς θάνατον on account of Jesus (2 Cor 4:10-11). He even claims that θάνατος is at work in him (4:12). Paul is also μάρτυς in the sense that he has borne testimony to the Corinthians of the story of Christ's life, death, and resurrection (1:19 and 11:7), and in the sense that he wants to continue to proclaim the gospel in other lands (10:15-16). Thus, the apostle is μάρτυς with his mouth (στόμα) as well.[980] Indeed, recall how he aligns himself with the

---

[978]Cf. Rev 1:5 – which refers to Jesus Christ as ὁ μάρτυς ὁ πιστός, "the faithful witness/martyr" – and Rev 3:14 – which calls him ὁ ἀμήν, ὁ μάρτυς ὁ πιστὸς καὶ ἀληθινός, "the Amen, the faithful and true witness/martyr." Cf. 2 Cor 1:19-20.

[979]See Chapter Four, Section IV (esp. n. 387) for this understanding of the phrase ἐν αὐτῷ.

[980]Cf. Acts 22:15 and 26:16, where Paul is specifically commissioned to be μάρτυς in this sense. It might be objected that my interpretation would require the phrase ἐξ στόματος, whereas the phrase in LXX Deut 19:15 and 2 Cor 13:1 is ἐπὶ στόματος. In response, ἐπί is an extremely versatile preposition, governing all three cases – indeed, BDAG lists 18 different entries, many of which have even further refinements! Moreover, while the apostle is adapting the scriptural text for his own purposes, he remains true to the phraseology he cites, perhaps because it was a well-known text (as suggested by the citations in n. 965).

story and *ethos* of Christ in 4:13. There Paul tells the Corinthians that, like Jesus, he too is faithful and therefore he too speaks out (λαλέω).

Observe, moreover, how the apostle makes clear in 2 Cor 2:17 and 12:19 that he speaks ἐν Χριστῷ, that is, "in close association with Christ." As we saw in the analysis of 2:14-17, Paul speaks ἐν Χριστῷ as one who is God's captive δοῦλος and a fragrant offering. Recall that both metaphors connote the apostle's self-emptying mode of existence after the manner of Jesus. In addition, Paul's reference to speaking ἐν Χριστῷ in 12:19 comes in the context of his being "utterly expended" out of love for the sake of the Corinthians (12:14-18).[981] In both instances, it is because the apostle is faithful to embodying Jesus' πίστις and ἀγάπη that he is competent to speak out (λαλέω) by proclaiming the gospel. In fact, it is Paul's taking on more and more the *ethos* of Jesus through the "christing" power of the Spirit that enables him to make his remarkable claim in 13:3-4: He not only speaks in Christ, but *Christ also speaks in him* (13:3a). This is ultimately the reason why the apostle can hold himself up to the Corinthians as the second μάρτυς.

And what about the *third* μάρτυς? Notice that 2 Cor 13:1b reads: ἐπὶ στόματος δύο μαρτύρων *καὶ τριῶν* σταθήσεται πᾶν ῥῆμα – thereby indicating two *or three* μάρτυρες.[982] It is at this very point that Paul deviates from the text of LXX Deut 19:15, which reads: ἐπὶ στόματος δύο μαρτύρων καὶ ἐπὶ στόματος τριῶν μαρτύρων σταθήσεται πᾶν ῥῆμα. Does the apostle shorten the citation for stylistic reasons? Or does he omit the key terms μάρτυς and στόμα in connection with "three" for rhetorical purposes? Might Paul be leaving open the question of whether the Corinthians will join him in participating in the story of Jesus by embodying the latter's *ethos*, thereby subtly challenging the community to become the third μάρτυς? I submit that this is Paul's tactic here, especially given that his strategy throughout this letter has been to exhort the Corinthians to embody the *ethos* of Christ. Indeed, the issue of Jesus' character is the key underlying ῥῆμα – in the sense of "issue" or

---

[981]Paul's insistence that he speaks ἐν Χριστῷ – including all that this entails – is the real import of 2 Cor 12:19, not his remark about defending himself (*pace* LONG, *"Have We Been Defending Ourselves to You?"*). In fact, observe what the goal of the apostle's "speaking in Christ" is: namely, οἰκοδομή, the "upbuilding" of the Corinthians (cf. 13:10).

[982]For reading καὶ as meaning "or" instead of "and," see BDAG, s.v. καὶ, 1.a.β. Cf. Jas 4:13 (in some MSS): σήμερον καὶ αὔριον ("today *or* tomorrow").

"matter" – in 2 Corinthians. If my interpretation is correct, observe how the apostle's scriptural citation effectively sets up what follows in 2 Cor 13:3-10 (as set forth in Section IV.D).

To review: The literal interpretation of Paul's use of LXX Deut 19:15 in 2 Cor 13:1b is inadequate. While the metaphorical interpretation is an improvement, it focuses so narrowly on 2 Cor 13:2 (where the apostle threatens to punish sinners) that it fails to take into account the larger context. A more cogent reading results when 13:1b is viewed in light of Paul's overall rhetorical strategy in 13:3-10 (and indeed, throughout this letter). In this reading, the two μάρτυρες are identified as Jesus and the apostle himself. They are witnesses, although not in a strict juridicial sense. Rather, they are witnesses to a mode of existence lived out of love for the sake of others, in obedience to God. Jesus is the μάρτυς *par excellence* – whose faithful Yes to God has fulfilled all of God's promises – while Paul is the second μάρτυς insofar as he embodies the *ethos* of Jesus. Now, in announcing his third visit to the community, the apostle leaves open-ended the question of whether or not the Corinthians will join the story by taking on Christ's character, thereby becoming the third μάρτυς.

VI. Summary

The foregoing analysis has illustrated how Paul attempts to persuade the Corinthians to join him in participating in the story of Jesus. From the opening *berakah* to the final climactic passage (2 Cor 13:1-10) – and indeed, even to the closing benediction (13:13) – the apostle summons the community to take on the *ethos* of Christ. He wants them to live out of the "christing" power of the Holy Spirit, and thus he continually reminds them of this gift and its implications (1:21-22, 3:2-3, and 6:16b; cf. 13:5b).

One of the most striking features of Paul's rhetorical strategy in 2 Corinthians is his employment of δοκιμ- terminology throughout the letter. This language connotes both one's character and the testing which ascertains that character. The apostle uses it in conjunction with the complex rhetorical situation that lies behind the writing of this epistle. This situation includes the status of a punished and disaffected member of the community; the collection for the church in Jerusalem and the controversy over Paul's refusal to accept direct remuneration from the Corinthians; and the emergence or arrival of other missionaries/evangelists.

The apostle's tactic is to test and challenge the community to actualize certain characteristics and attributes. So, in 2 Cor 2:9, he states that his reason for writing is to know their character – specifically, whether they are *obedient*. In 8:8 Paul tests the genuineness of the Corinthians' *love*. In 9:13 he portrays the collection as a test of their *obedience* and *generosity/singleness*. And in 13:5, at the climax of the letter, the apostle challenges them to test their *faithfulness*. It is no accident that he associates each one of these attributes – ὑπακοή (10:5), ἀγάπη (5:14), ἁπλότης (11:3), and πίστις (4:13) – with Jesus. The characteristics Paul exhorts the community to embody are precisely those modeled forth by Christ. Hence, it is no surprise that, when the Corinthians (or, at least some in the community) issued a challenge to the apostle to prove his character, he responds by demonstrating that he in fact follows in the pattern of existence manifested by Jesus. It is to this same mode of existence that Paul summons the Corinthians. By taking on the *ethos* of Christ, the community will also participate in his story, thereby proving the authenticity of their own character. This is the apostle's principal purpose in writing 2 Corinthians.

Epilogue

At the beginning of this book, I compared the attempt to interpret 2 Corinthians to taking a journey over rough, uncharted terrain. For the last three chapters, I have led my readers on a long and, at times, arduous journey using a particular compass and guide – namely, the *ethos* of Jesus. This exploration of the text has revealed that the landscape is not only traversable; it is also breathtakingly beautiful. Or, to change the metaphor, my analysis points to the character of Jesus as the linchpin that holds together the various components of Paul's argument in this letter. It is now time to summarize the results of this study and to spell out some of the implications that result from it.

In Chapter One I reviewed the history of interpretation of 2 Corinthians. I argued that attempts to understand the text by means of partition theories and by means of the identity and ideology of the so-called opponents – both of which have produced a bewildering variety of hypotheses – have led primarily to detours and dead ends. I concluded by suggesting that a different approach was needed, one that focused on the tenor of the apostle's presentation and argument.

Chapter Two dealt with the emergence of rhetorical criticism as a means of interpreting 2 Corinthians. Rhetorical analysis has succeeded in demonstrating the interconnection and coherence of certain themes and terms in this letter, as well as the development and organic nature of Paul's overall argument. In short, this approach provides a viable means for reading 2 Corinthians as a literary unity. While in practice rhetorical analysis of this letter taken some wrong turns – especially the propensity of some of its adherents to impose rigid schemata on the text, and to read it primarily as forensic rhetoric – this approach has provided me with an important heuristic device, the notion of ἦθος. It is *ethos*, the issue of *character*, that allows us to enter into the heart of the apostle's presentation in 2 Corinthians.

Chapter Three reviewed two recent developments in Pauline theology. The first trend is the growing appreciation of the importance for Paul of the story of Jesus. To a greater extent than scholars have traditionally recognized, the apostle alludes to and draws upon traditions concerning Christ's life, death, and resurrection. Advocates of this position argue that Paul's pastoral strategy was to shape the lives of the people in the churches he founded so that they might conform more and more to the character of Jesus, the story's protagonist.

This approach leads to the issue of Christ's *ethos*: Does the apostle actually refer to it in his writings? The second trend in Pauline theology provides the answer to this question by recognizing that Christ's faithfulness and obedience play a prominent role in Paul's presentation of the gospel, especially in his magisterial letter to the church in Rome.

In Chapter Four I began the exposition of my thesis. I argued that the apostle refers and alludes to several aspects of Jesus' character – especially (though not exclusively) as these aspects pertain to his humanity. The most obvious reference is to Christ's gentleness and forbearance. Paul also alludes to Jesus' obedience, his continuous ναί to God's will. In addition, by appropriating the story of the righteous sufferer of LXX Ps 114-115, the apostle evokes the faithfulness of Jesus, God's δοῦλος, who showed his (and God's) love for all people by living and dying for their sake. In fact, Paul draws upon Christ's self-emptying mode of existence for others throughout the letter. Moreover, he summons the tradition that Jesus was innocent and did not know Sin. In short, the apostle evokes a portrait of Christ as the εἰκὼν τοῦ θεοῦ, the prototype of a new mode of human existence, one lived with single-hearted devotion to God on the basis of trust in God to bring the dead to life. It is the recognition of this fact that provides us with the compass to help navigate our way through 2 Corinthians.

Chapter Five showed how the *ethos* of Jesus functions in Paul's self-presentation. The issue of self-commendation, both positive and negative, is critical for the apostle, whose own character had been called into question by some in the community. I demonstrated that – as one who has been "christed" and marked as God's διάκονος through the power of the Spirit, and as one who is being transformed more and more into the image of Christ – Paul is able to self-*commend* because he faithfully embodies Jesus' character. That is, he lives in the same manner of self-donation out of love for the sake of others, thereby manifesting the faithfulness of Christ. Furthermore, the apostle participates in the work of reconciliation as Jesus' ambassador and co-worker, particularly by lowering himself so that others might be lifted up. Paul claims that it is through his being δοῦλος to the Corinthians.that the power of Christ continues to be at work among them. In fact, it is this type of loving service that the apostle holds up as proof of his character – this is how Christ speaks through him – and as an example for them to emulate.

Finally, Chapter Six demonstrated the role that Christ's character plays in Paul's exhortations to the Corinthians. Whereas the apostle has been challenged to prove his own character, I argued that the real issue is the community's character. This is evident from Paul's use of δοκιμ- terminology. Throughout the letter he exhorts the Corinthians to participate in the story of Jesus by taking on the latter's *ethos*. The apostle does so by reminding the community of the "christing" power of the Spirit. In effect, he calls them to appropriate the gift that has already been bestowed upon them, namely the νοῦς Χριστοῦ. Paul's chief strategy, however, is to challenge and test the Corinthians to embody ὑπακοή, ἀγάπη, ἁπλότης, and πίστις – characteristics that he attributes to Christ in this letter – within the particular circumstances in which they find themselves, especially with regard to the collection for the church in Jerusalem. In the end, the apostle's main reason for writing 2 Corinthians is to summon the community to incarnate the *ethos* of Jesus.

What are some implications of this study? I propose nine:

1) Second Corinthians can and ought to be read as a literary unity. I submit that this study makes a strong case for the compositional integrity of 2 Corinthians, as Margaret M. Mitchell's magisterial *Paul and the Rhetoric of Reconciliation* has demonstrated beyond doubt the literary unity of 1 Corinthians. Of course, the unifying thread is different, for in the second letter it is the character of Jesus – and not the apostle's thoroughgoing attempts to persuade the community to live in harmony – that serves as the linchpin. Thus, I suggest that it is time to close the discussion on the viability of partition theories.

2) Focusing on *Paul's* expressed concern – in this case, to self-*commend* by aligning himself with the *ethos* of Jesus, and (even more) to persuade the Corinthians to embody that same *ethos* – yields a better reading of 2 Corinthians than attempts to interpret the text vis-à-vis the identity and ideology of the so-called opponents. This has simple but profound methodological ramifications. It is *prima facie* more sound to begin the interpretive task by laying a foundation of what is central to the apostle's consideration and strategy, rather than to start building upon historical reconstructions based on insufficient data.

3) The application of rhetorical criticism to 2 Corinthians as a means of interpretation, while helpful, is also limited. Rhetorical analysis succeeds in illuminating Paul's argumentative strategies and his use of certain conventions (e.g., digression, amplification, resumption, anaphora, pleonasm, paronomasia, *synkrisis*, irony, and satire). My study has shown, moreover, the usefulness of employing the *ethos* argument as a heuristic device for the interpretation of this letter. When interpreters attempt to impose rigid rhetorical structures on the text, however, the use of rhetorical analysis distorts more than it elucidates.

4) Although it is true that the rhetoric in 2 Corinthians is not as rigorously deliberative as it is in 1 Corinthians, the tone of the former is much more persuasive than scholars have generally admitted. In other words, the emphasis on the apostle's use of forensic rhetoric in 2 Corinthians has been overstated. My analysis therefore offers an important corrective in this regard.

5) This study demonstrates that there is considerable continuity between 1 and 2 Corinthians. In particular, the issue of appropriating the νοῦς Χριστοῦ is central to both letters. Paul's concern that the Corinthians take on the mind of Christ is, I submit, the main reason for the many references to the character of Jesus in 2 Corinthians. Thus, although Walter Schmithals's attempt to interpret the Corinthian correspondence through the lens of Gnosticism is misguided, he *is* correct in asserting that there is greater similarity than dissimilarity between 1 and 2 Corinthians. The similarity, however, pivots around the apostle's christology and pneumatology.

6) Recent proposals stating the importance of the story of Jesus for Paul find support in this study. I have shown how he alludes to and draws upon the story of Jesus throughout 2 Corinthians. My analysis focuses more on the issue of character than on plot *per se*. Nevertheless, I hope to have made a contribution to this development in Pauline theology by demonstrating how the apostle summons the Corinthians to participate in the story of Jesus. By taking on Jesus' character, the apostle and (he hopes) the Corinthians "continue the story of Jesus."

7) By focusing on how Paul alludes to Jesus' character throughout 2 Corinthians, this study should contribute to the debate over the interpretation of πίστις Χριστοῦ. I have demonstrated that the apostle alludes to Christ's πίστις in 2 Cor 4:13. My analysis suggests, moreover, that the discussion of the issue of Jesus' character in Paul's writings will be advanced by expanding the focus beyond the issue of Jesus' faithfulness. Indeed, a more fruitful approach may be to look at all of the Pauline writings to see how (if at all) the apostle refers to and utilizes the character of Jesus – as Michael Thompson's *Clothed with Christ* does for Rom 12:1-15:13.

8) This study demonstrates that both the character of Jesus and the working of the Spirit to inculcate that character (in the apostle himself and in the Corinthians) are central concerns for Paul in 2 Corinthians. I suggest that it is worth investigating the extent to which the apostle draws upon the Spirit's empowerment to embody Christ's character in his other letters. Such an investigation might contribute to the discussion of a "coherent core" in Paul's writings.

9) Finally, in terms of methodology, my analysis shows the fruitfulness of bringing the entire Pauline corpus to bear on the interpretation of 2 Corinthians. While the index of New Testament sources reveals that I appeal most frequently to Romans, 1 Corinthians, Galatians, and Philippians, my work has been aided by appeals to the so-called deutero-Pauline and pastoral epistles as well. This suggests that the Pauline corpus speaks with a more unified voice than many commentators have appreciated or acknowledged.

Selected Bibliography

A. Texts and Tools

ALFORD, H. *The Greek New Testament.* Vol. 2. Grand Rapids, Mich.: Baker, 1980; reprint of rev. ed., 1871-75.

Apostolic Fathers. 2 vols. Trans. K. LAKE. LCL. Cambridge, Mass.: Harvard University Press, 1985-92.

AQUINAS, T. *Summa theologiae.* 5 vols. Ottawa: Commissio Piana, 1953.

ARISTOTLE. *The "Art" of Rhetoric.* Trans. J.H. FREESE. LCL. Cambridge, Mass.: Harvard University Press, 1991.

Aristotle, On Rhetoric*: A Theory of Civil Discourse.* Trans. with introductory notes by G.A. KENNEDY. New York: Oxford University Press, 1991.

BAUER, W. *A Greek-English Lexicon of the New Testament and Other Early Christian Literature.* 3rd ed. Rev. and ed. F.W. DANKER (based on previous English eds. translated, adapted, revised, and augmented by W.F. ARNDT, F.W. GINGRICH and DANKER). Chicago: The University of Chicago Press, 2000.

Biblia Hebraica. 4th ed. Ed. A. ALT, O. EISSFELDT, P. KAHLE, R. KITTEL, et al. Stuttgart: Deutsche Bibelgesellschaft, 1990.

Biblia Sacra Vulgata. 3rd ed. Ed. R. WEBER. Stuttgart: Deutsche Bibelgesellschaft, 1990.

BLASS, F. and A. DEBRUNNER. *A Greek Grammar of the New Testament and Other Early Christian Literature.* Trans. and rev. R.W. FUNK. Chicago: University of Chicago Press, 1961.

BROWN, F., S.R. DRIVER, C.A. BRIGGS and W. GESENIUS, eds. *The New Brown-Driver-Briggs-Gesenius Hebrew and English Lexicon.* Peabody, Mass.: Hendrickson, 1979.

The Catholic Study Bible: The New American Bible [NAB]. Ed. D. SENIOR et al. New York: Oxford University Press, 1990.

CHARLES, R.H., ed. *The Greek Versions of the Testaments of the Twelve Patriarchs*. London: Oxford University Press, 1908.

CHARLESWORTH, J.H., ed. *The Old Testament Pseudepigrapha: Volume 1: Apocalyptic Literature & Testaments*. ABRL. New York: Doubleday, 1983.

Cicero: De Inventione: De Optimo Genere Oratorum: Topica. Trans. H.M. HUBBELL. LCL. Cambridge, Mass.: Harvard University Press, 1949.

DEMOSTHENES. *Démosthène: Lettres et Fragments*. Ed. and trans. R. CLAVAUD. Paris: Société d'Edition "Les Belles Lettres," 1987.

-----. *On the Crown (De Corona)*. Trans. S. USHER. Greek Orators 5. Warminster, England: Aris & Phillips, 1993.

GOODSPEED, E.J. *The Parallel New Testament: The American Translation and the King James Version* [KJV]: *In Parallel Columns, with Introductions and Explanatory Notes*. Chicago: University of Chicago Press, 1943.

JOSEPHUS. *Flavii Iosephi Opera*, Vol. 1: *Antiquitatum Iudaicarum*, Libri I-V. Ed. B. NIESE. Berlin: Weidmannsche Verlagsbuchhandlung, 1955.

Josephus: The Jewish War, Books III-IV. Trans. H. ST. J. THACKERAY. LCL. Cambridge, Mass.: Harvard University Press, 1997.

JUSTIN (MARTYR). *Iustini Martyris: Apologiae pro Christianis*. Ed. M. MARCOVICH. PTS 38. New York: Walter de Gruyter, 1994.

METZGER, B.M. *A Textual Commentary on the Greek New Testament*. 2nd ed. Stuttgart: Deutsche Bibelgesellschaft, 1994.

MOULTON, H.K. and A.S. GEDEN, eds. *A Concordance to the Greek New Testament*. 5th ed (rev. by MOULTON). Edinburgh: T. & T. Clark, 1996.

New International Version of the Holy Bible [NIV]. Grand Rapids, Mich.: Zondervan, 1988.

The New Jerusalem Bible [JB]. Gen. ed. H. WANSBROUGH. Garden City, N.Y.: Doubleday, 1985.

The New Oxford Annotated Bible: New Revised Standard Version [NRSV]. Ed. B.M. METZGER and R.E. MURPHY. New York: Oxford University Press, 1991.

The New Oxford Annotated Bible: Revised Standard Version [RSV]. Ed. H.G. MAY and B.M. METZGER. New York: Oxford University Press, 1973.

Novum Testamentum Graece. Ed. E. NESTLE, K. ALAND, et al. 27th ed. Stuttgart: Deutsche Bibelgesellschaft, 1994.

Philo. Vol. 8. Trans. F.H. COLSON. LCL. Cambridge, Mass.: Harvard University Press, 1954.

Philo von Alexandria: Die Werke in deutscher Übersetzung. Vol. 7. Ed. L. COHN, I. HEINEMANN, M. ADLER and W. THEILER. Berlin: Walter de Gruyter, 1964.

QUINTILIAN. *The Institutio Oratoria of Quintilian*. Vol 2. Trans. H.E. BUTLER. LCL. Cambridge, Mass.: Harvard University Press, 1960.

Septuaginta. Ed. A. RAHLFS. Stuttgart: Deutsche Bibelgesellschaft, 1979.

SPICQ, C. *Theological Lexicon of the New Testament*. 3 vols. Trans. and ed. J.D. ERNEST. Peabody, Mass.: Hendrickson, 1994.

WACHSMUTH, C. and O HENSE, eds. *Ioannis Stobaei Anthologium*. Vol. 3. Berlin: Wiedmannsche Verlagsbuchhandlung, 1958.

B. Commentaries on 2 Corinthians

ALLO, E.B. *Seconde Épître aux Corinthiens*. 2nd ed. Paris: Études bibliques, 1956.

BACHMANN, P. *Der zweite Brief des Paulus an die Korinther*. 4th ed. KNT 8. Leipzig: A. Deichert, 1922.

BARNETT, P.W. *The Second Epistle to the Corinthians*. NICNT. Grand Rapids, Mich.: Eerdmans, 1997.

BARRETT, C.K. *The Second Epistle to the Corinthians*. BNTC 8. London: A & C Black, 1973.

BELLEVILLE, L.L. *2 Corinthians*. IVPNTCS. Downers Grove, Ill.: InterVarsity, 1996.

BETZ, H.D. *2 Corinthians 8 and 9: A Commentary on Two Administrative Letters of the Apostle Paul*. Hermeneia. Philadelphia: Fortress, 1985.

BRUCE, F.F. *1 and 2 Corinthians*. NCB. London: Oliphants, 1971.

BULTMANN, R. *The Second Letter to the Corinthians*. Ed. E. DINKLER. Trans. R.A. HARRISVILLE. Minneapolis: Augsburg, 1985.

DANKER, F.W. *II Corinthians*. ACNT. Minneapolis: Augsburg, 1989.

FURNISH, V.P. *II Corinthians*, AB 32A. New York: Doubleday, 1984.

GARLAND, D.E. *2 Corinthians*. NAC 29. Nashville: Broadman & Holman, 1999.

GOUDGE, H.L. *The Second Epistle to the Corinthians*. London: Methuen, 1927.

HAFEMANN, S.J. *2 Corinthians*. NIVAC. Grand Rapids, Mich.: Zondervan, 2000.

HÉRING, J. *The Second Epistle of Saint Paul to the Corinthians*. Trans. A.W. HEATHCOTE and P.J. ALLCOCK. London: Epworth, 1967.

HUGHES, P.E. *Paul's Second Epistle to the Corinthians: The English Text with Introduction, Exposition and Notes*. NICNT. Grand Rapids, Mich.: Eerdmans, 1962.

KENNEDY, J.H. *The Second and Third Epistles of St. Paul to the Corinthians*. London: Methuen, 1900.

KISTEMAKER, S.J. *New Testament Commentary: Exposition of the Second Epistle to the Corinthians*. Grand Rapids, Mich.: Baker, 1997.

LAMBRECHT, J. *Second Corinthians*. SP 8. Collegeville, Minn.: Liturgical, 1999.

MARTIN, R.P. *2 Corinthians*. WBC. Waco, Tex.: Word, 1986.

MATERA, F.J. *II Corinthians*. NTL. Louisville: Westminster John Knox, 2003.

MCCANT, J.W. *2 Corinthians*. Sheffield: Sheffield Academic Press, 1999.

PLUMMER, A. *A Critical and Exegetical Commentary on the Second Epistle of St. Paul to the Corinthians*. ICC. Edinburgh: T. & T. Clark, 1915.

SAMPLEY, J.P. "The Second Letter to the Corinthians: Introduction, Commentary, and Reflections," in *NIB*. 11.1-180.

SCOTT, J.M. *2 Corinthians*. NIBC 8. Peabody, Mass.: Hendrickson, 1998.

TALBERT, C.H. *Reading Corinthians: A Literary and Theological Commentary on 1 and 2 Corinthians*. New York: Crossroad, 1987.

THRALL, M.E. *A Critical and Exegetical Commentary on The Second Epistle to the Corinthians*. 2 vols. ICC. Edinburgh: T. & T. Clark, 1994-2000.

WAN, S. *Power in Weakness: Conflict and Rhetoric in Paul's Second Letter to the Corinthians*. NTC. Harrisburg, Pa.: Trinity International, 2000.

WINDISCH, H. *Der zweite Korintherbrief.* KEK. Repr. of 9th ed. [1924]. Ed. G. STRECKER. Göttingen: Vandenhoeck & Ruprecht, 1970.

WITHERINGTON, B. *Conflict & Community in Corinth: A Socio-Rhetorical Commentary on 1 and 2 Corinthians*. Grand Rapids, Mich.: Eerdmans, 1995.

YOUNG, F. and D.F. FORD. *Meaning and Truth in 2 Corinthians*. Grand Rapids, Mich.: Eerdmans, 1988.

C. Other Works Cited

AMADOR, J.D.H. "Revisiting 2 Corinthians: Rhetoric and the Case for Unity," *NTS* 46 (2000) 92-111.

-----. "The Unity of 2 Corinthians: A Test Case for a Re-discovered and Re-invented Rhetoric," *Neot* 33 (1999) 411-32.

AMSTUTZ, J. *ΑΠΛΟΤΗΣ: Eine begriffsgeschichtliche Studie zum jüdisch-christlichen Griechisch*. Theophaneia 19. Bonn: Peter Hanstein Verlag GMBH, 1968.

ANDERSON, R.D. *Ancient Rhetorical Theory and Paul*. CBET 18. Kampen: Kok Pharos, 1996.

ARNHART, L. *Aristotle on Political Reasoning: A Commentary on the "Rhetoric"*. DeKalb, Ill.: Northern Illinois University Press, 1981.

BAIRD, W. "Letters of Recommendation: A Study of II Cor. 3:1-3," *JBL* 80 (1961) 166-72.

BARCLEY, W.B. *"Christ in You": A Study in Paul's Theology and Ethics*. Lanham, Md.: University Press of America, 1999.

BARR, J. *The Semantics of Biblical Language*. Oxford: Oxford University Press, 1961.

BARRETT, C.K. "Christianity in Corinth," in *Essays on Paul*. Philadelphia: Westminster, 1982. 1-27.

-----. "Paul's Opponents in 2 Corinthians," in *Essays on Paul*, 60-86.

-----. "ΨΕΥΔΑΠΟΣΤΟΛΟΙ (2 Cor. 11.13)," in *Essays on Paul*. 87-107.

-----. "Titus," in *Essays on Paul*. 118-31.

BARTH, K. *Church Dogmatics: Volume IV: The Doctrine of Reconciliation: Part 1*. Ed. G.W. BROMILEY and T.F. TORRANCE. Trans. G.W. BROMILEY. Edinburgh: T. & T. Clark, 1961.

-----. *The Epistle to the Romans*. Tran. E.C. HOSKYNS from the 6th ed. New York: Oxford University Press, 1968.

BAUMERT, N. *Täglich sterben und auferstehen: Der Literalsinn von 2 Kor 4, 12-5, 10*. SANT 34. München: Kösel-Verlag, 1973.

BAUR, F.C. "Die Christuspartei in der korinthischen Gemeinde, der Gegensatz des petrinishen und paulinischen Christentum in der ältesten Kirche, der Apostel Petrus in Rom," *Tübinger Zeitschrift für Theologie* 4 (1831) 61-206.

-----. *Paul, The Apostle of Jesus Christ – His Life and Work, His Epistles and Doctrine: A Contribution to the Critical History of Primitive Christianity*. Vol. 1. 2nd ed.. Trans. E. ZELLER. London: Williams & Norgate, 1876.

BEALE, G.K. "The Old Testament Background of Reconciliation in 2 Corinthians 5-7 and Its Bearing on the Literary Problem of 2 Corinthians 6.14-7.1," *NTS* 35 (1989) 550-81.

BELLEVILLE, L.L. "Gospel and Kerygma in 2 Corinthians," in *Gospel in Paul: Studies on Corinthians, Galatians and Romans for Richard N.*

Longenecker. JSNTSup 108. Ed. L.A. JERVIS and P. RICHARDSON. Sheffield: Sheffield Academic Press, 1994. 134-64.

-----. "A Letter of Apologetic Self-Commendation: 2 Cor. 1:8-7:16," *NovT* 31 (1989) 142-63.

-----. "Paul's Polemic and Theology of the Spirit in Second Corinthians," *CBQ* 58 (1996) 281-304.

-----. *Reflections of Glory: Paul's Polemical Use of the Moses-Doxa Tradition in 2 Corinthians 3.1-18*. JSNTSup 52. Sheffield: JSOT Press, 1991.

BETZ, H.D. *Der Apostel Paulus und die sokratische Tradition: Eine exegetische Untersuchung zu seiner "Apologie" 2 Korinther 10-13*. BHT 45. Tübingen: Mohr Siebeck, 1972.

-----. "2 Cor 6:14-7:1: An Anti-Pauline Fragment?," *JBL* 92 (1973) 88-108.

BIERINGER, R. "Die Gegner des Paulus im 2. Korintherbrief," in R. BIERINGER and J. LAMBRECHT, *Studies on 2 Corinthians*. BETL 112. Leuven: Leuven University Press, 1994. 181-221.

-----. "Paul's Understanding of Diakonia in 2 Corinthians 5,18," in *Studies on 2 Corinthians*. 413-28.

-----. "2 Korinther 5,19a und die Versöhnung der Welt," in *Studies on 2 Corinthians*. 429-59.

-----. "Teilungshypothesen zum 2. Korintherbrief: Ein Forschungsüberblick," in *Studies on 2 Corinthians*. 67-105.

BITZER, L.F. "The Rhetorical Situation," *Philosophy and Rhetoric* 1 (1968) 1-14.

BJERKELUND, C.J. *PARAKALÔ: Form, Funktion und Sinn der parakalô-Sätze in den paulinishen Briefen*. Oslo: Universitetsforlaget, 1967.

BORNKAMM, G. "The History of the Origin of the So-Called Second Letter to the Corinthians," *NTS* 8 (1962) 258-64.

-----. *Paul*. Trans. D.M.G. STALKER. Minneapolis: Fortress, 1995.

-----. *Die Vorgeschichte des sogenannten zweiten Korintherbriefes*. 2nd ed. Heidelberg: Carl Winter, 1965.

BREYTENBACH, C. "Paul's Proclamation and God's 'Thriambos' (Notes on 2 Corinthians 2:14-16b)," *Neot* 24 (1990) 257-71.

BROWN, P.C. "What is the Meaning of 'Examine Yourselves' in 2 Corinthians 13:5?" *BSac* 154 (1997) 175-88.

BUCHANON, G.W. "Jesus and the Upper Class," *NovT* 7 (1964/65) 195-209.

BULTMANN, R. "ΔΙΚΑΙΟΣΥΝΗ ΘΕΟΥ," *JBL* 83 (1964) 12-16.

-----. *Exegetische Probleme des zweiten Korintherbriefes*. Darmstadt: Wissenschaftliche Buchgesellschaft, 1963.

-----. *The Theology of the New Testament*. 2 vols. Trans. K. GROBEL. New York: Charles Scribner's Sons, 1951-55.

BYRNE, B. *Romans*. SP 6. Collegeville, Minn.: Liturgical, 1996.

CALLOUD, J. *Structural Analysis of Narrative*. Semeia Sup 4. Trans. D. PATTE. Philadelphia: Fortress, 1976.

CAMPBELL, D.A. "False Presuppositions in the ΠΙΣΤΙΣ ΧΡΙΣΤΟΥ Debate: A Response to Brian Dodd," *JBL* 116 (1997) 713-19.

-----. "The Meaning of ΠΙΣΤΙΣ and ΝΟΜΟΣ in Paul: A Linguistic and Structural Perspective," *JBL* 111 (1992) 91-103.

-----. *The Rhetoric of Righteousness in Romans 3:21-26*. JSNTSup 65. Sheffield: JSOT Press, 1992.

-----. "Romans 1:17–A *Crux Interpretum* for the ΠΙΣΤΙΣ ΧΡΙΣΤΟΥ Debate," *JBL* 113 (1994) 265-85.

CARREZ, M. "Le 'Nous' en 2 Corinthiens," *NTS* 26 (1980) 474-86.

-----. "Que Représente la Vie de Jésus pour l'Apôtre Paul?," *Revue d'Histoire* 68 (1988) 155-61.

CHEVALLIER, M.-A. "L'argumentation de Paul dans II Corinthiens 10 à 13," *RHPR* 70 (1990) 3-15.

COLLANGE, J.-F. *Énigmes de la deuxième épître aux Corinthiens: Etude exégétique de 2 Cor. 2:14-7:4*. SNTSMS 18. Cambridge: Cambridge University Press, 1972.

COPE, E.M. *An Introduction to Aristotle's Rhetoric*. London: Macmillan, 1867; repr. Dubuque, Iowa: Wm. C. Brown Reprint, 1966.

CRADDOCK, F.B. "The Poverty of Christ: An Investigation of II Corinthians 8:9," *Int* 22 (1968) 158-70.

CRAFTON, J.A. *The Agency of the Apostle: A Dramatistic Analysis of Paul's Responses to Conflict in 2 Corinthians*. JSNTSup 51. Sheffield: Sheffield Academic Press, 1991.

CRANFIELD, C.E.B. *A Critical and Exegetical Commentary on the Epistle to the Romans*. 2 vols. ICC. Edinburgh: T. & T. Clark, 1975-79.

CRUZ, H. *Christological Motives and Motivated Actions in Pauline Paraenesis*. EUS 23/396. Frankfurt: Peter Lang, 1990.

DAHL, N.A. "A Fragment and Its Context: 2 Corinthians 6:14-7:1," in *Studies in Paul: Theology for the Early Christian Mission*. Minneapolis: Augsburg, 1977. 62-69.

-----. "Promise and Fulfillment," in *Studies in Paul*. 121-36.

DANKER, F.W. *Benefactor: Epigraphic Study of a Graeco-Roman Semantic Field.* St. Louis: Clayton, 1982.

-----. "Paul's Debt to the *De Corona* of Demosthenes: A Study of Rhetorical Techniques in Second Corinthians," in *Persuasive Artistry: Studies in New Testament Rhetoric in Honor of George A. Kennedy.* JSNTSup 50. Ed. D.F. WATSON. Sheffield: Sheffield Academic Press, 1991. 262-80.

DEISSMANN, G.A. *Bible Studies.* Trans. A. GRIEVE. Edinburgh: T. & T. Clark, 1901.

DE LA POTTERIE, I. "L'onction du chrétien par la foi," *Bib* 40 (1959) 12-69.

DELCOR, M. "The Courts of the Church of Corinth and the Courts of Qumran," in *Paul and Qumran: Studies in New Testament Exegesis.* Ed. J. MURPHY-O'CONNOR. Chicago: Priory, 1968. 69-84.

DERRETT, J.D.M. "Ναί (2 Cor 1:19-20)," *Filología Neotestamentaria* 4 (1991) 205-9.

DESILVA, D.A. "Measuring Penultimate against Ultimate Reality: An Investigation of the Integrity and Argumentation of 2 Corinthians," *JSNT* 52 (1993) 41-70.

-----. "Meeting the Exigency of a Complex Rhetorical Situation: Paul's Strategy in 2 Corinthians 1 through 7," *AUSS* 34 (1996) 5-22.

DICICCO, M.M. *Paul's Use of Ethos, Pathos, and Logos in 2 Corinthians 10-13.* MBPS 31. Lewiston, N.Y.: Mellen Biblical, 1995.

DINKLER, E. "Die Taufterminologie in 2 Kor. I 21 f.," in *Neotestamentica et Patristica: Eine Freundesgabe, Herrn Professor Dr. Oscar Cullmann zu seinem 60. Geburtstag überreicht.* NovTSup 6. Ed. W.C. VAN UNNIK. Leiden: E.J. Brill, 1962. 173-91.

DODD, C.H. *New Testament Studies.* Manchester: Manchester University Press, 1953.

DU TOIT, A.B. "Faith and Obedience in Paul," *Neot* 25 (1991) 65-74.

DUFF, P.B. "Apostolic Suffering and the Language of Processions in 2 Corinthians 4:7-10," *BTB* 21 (1991) 158-65.

-----. "Metaphor, Motif, and Meaning: The Rhetorical Strategy behind the Image 'Led in Triumph' in 2 Corinthians 2:14," *CBQ* 53 (1991) 79-92.

DUNN, J.D.G. *Baptism in the Holy Spirit: A Re-examination of the New Testament Teaching on the Gift of the Spirit in Relation to Pentecostalism Today.* SBT II.15. Naperville, Ill.: Alec R. Allenson, 1970.

-----. *Christology in the Making: A New Testament Inquiry into the Origins of the Doctrine of the Incarnation.* Philadelphia: Westminster, 1980.

-----. "Once More, ΠΙΣΤΙΣ ΧΡΙΣΤΟΥ," in *Pauline Theology. Volume IV: Looking Back, Pressing On.* Ed. E. E. JOHNSON and D.M. HAY. Atlanta: Scholars Press, 1997. 61-81.

-----. *Romans 1-8.* WBC. Dallas: Word, 1988.

-----. *The Theology of Paul the Apostle.* Grand Rapids, Mich.: Eerdmans, 1998.

DUPONT, J. *La réconciliation dans la théologie de Saint Paul.* ALBO II 32. Louvain: Publications universitaires de Louvain, 1953.

-----. *ΣΥΝ ΧΡΙΣΤΩΙ: L'union avec le Christ suivant Saint Paul.* Bruges: Éditions de L'abbaye de Saint-André, 1952.

EGAN, R.B. "Lexical Evidence on Two Pauline Passages," *NovT* 19 (1977) 34-62.

FEE, G.D. *1 and 2 Timothy, Titus.* NIBC. Rev. ed. Peabody, Mass.: Hendrickson, 1988.

-----. *God's Empowering Presence: The Holy Spirit in the Letters of Paul.* Peabody, Mass.: Hendrickson, 1994.

-----. "II Corinthians vi.14-vii.1 and Food Offered to Idols," *NTS* 23 (1976-77) 140-61.

FILBECK, D. "Problems in Translating First Person Plural Pronouns in 2 Corinthians," *BT* 45 (1994) 401-9.

FIORE, B. "NT Rhetoric and Rhetorical Criticism," in *ABD*. 5.715-19.

FITZGERALD, J.T. *Cracks in an Earthen Vessel: An Examination of the Catalogue of Hardships in the Corinthian Correspondence*. SBLDS 99. Atlanta: Scholars Press, 1988.

-----. "Paul, the Ancient Epistolary Theorists, and 2 Corinthians 10-13: The Purpose and Literary Genre of a Pauline Letter," in *Greeks, Romans, and Christians: Essays in Honor of Abraham J. Malherbe*. Ed. D.L. BALCH, E. FERGUSON and W.A. MEEKS. Minneapolis: Fortress, 1990. 190-200.

FITZMYER, J.A. *Romans: A New Translation with Introduction and Commentary*. AB 33. New York: Doubleday, 1993.

FORBES, C. "Comparison, Self-Praise and Irony: Paul's Boasting and the Conventions of Hellenistic Rhetoric," *NTS* 32 (1986) 1-30.

FOWL, S.E. "Some Uses of Story in Moral Discourse," *Modern Theology* 4 (1987-88) 293-308.

-----. *The Story of Christ in the Ethics of Paul: An Analysis of the Function of the Hymnic Material in the Pauline Corpus*. JSNTSup 36. Sheffield: Sheffield Academic Press, 1990.

FRASER, J.W. "Paul's Knowledge of Jesus: II Corinthians V. 16 Once More," *NTS* 17 (1971) 293-313.

FULTON, S.P. *A Rhetorical Analysis of Second Corinthians with a View to the Unity Question*. Ph.D. diss. The Southern Baptist Theological Seminary, 1999.

FURNISH, V.P. *Theology and Ethics in Paul*. Nashville: Abingdon, 1968.

GAVENTA, B.R. "Apostle and Church in 2 Corinthians: A Response to David M. Hay and Steven J. Kraftchick," in *Pauline Theology. Volume II: 1 & 2 Corinthians*. Ed. D.M. HAY. Minneapolis: Fortress, 1993. 182-199.

GEORGI, D. "Corinthians, Second Letter to the," in *IDBSup*. 183-86.

-----. *The Opponents of Paul in Second Corinthians: A Study of Religious Propaganda in Late Antiquity*. Edinburgh: T. & T. Clark, 1987.

-----. *Remembering the Poor: The History of Paul's Collection for Jerusalem*. Nashville: Abingdon, 1992.

GOOD, D.J. *The Meek King*. Harrisburg, Pa.: Trinity International, 1999.

GOODWIN, M.J. *Paul: Apostle of the Living God*. Harrisburg, Pa.: Trinity International, 2001.

GREIMAS, A.J. *Du Sens*. Paris: Seuil, 1970.

-----. *Sémantique structurale*. Paris: Librairie Larousse, 1966.

GRUNDMANN, W. "δόκιμος, . . .," in *TDNT*. 6.255-60.

GÜTTGEMANNS, E. *Der leidende Apostel und sein Herr: Studien zur paulinischen Christologie*. FRLANT 90. Göttingen: Vandenhoeck & Ruprecht, 1966.

HAFEMANN, S.J. *Paul, Moses, and the History of Israel: The Letter/Spirit Contrast and the Argument from Scripture in 2 Corinthians 3*. WUNT 81. Tübingen: J.C.B. Mohr/Paul Siebeck, 1995.

-----. *Suffering and Ministry in the Spirit: Paul's Defense of His Ministry in II Corinthians 2:14-3:3*. Grand Rapids, Mich.: Eerdmans, 1990.

HANSON, A.T. *The Paradox of the Cross in the Thought of St Paul*. JSNTSup 17. Sheffield: Sheffield Academic Press, 1987.

-----. *Paul's Understanding of Jesus: Invention or Interpretation?* Hull: University of Hull Press, 1963.

-----. *Studies in Paul's Technique and Theology*. London: SPCK, 1974.

HARVEY, A.E. *Renewal through Suffering: A Study of 2 Corinthians*. Edinburgh: T & T Clark, 1996.

HAUSRATH, A. *A History of the New Testament Times: The Time of the Apostles*. Vol. 4. Trans. L. HUXLEY. London: Williams & Norgate, 1895.

-----. *Der Vier-Capitel-Brief des Paulus an die Korinther*. Heidelberg: Bassermann, 1870.

HAYS, R.B. "Adam, Israel, Christ: The Question of Covenant in the Theology of Romans: A Response to Leander E. Keck and N. T. Wright," in *Pauline Theology. Volume III: Romans*. Ed. D.M. HAY and E.E. JOHNSON. Minneapolis: Fortress, 1995. 68-86.

-----. "Christ Prays the Psalms: Paul's Use of an Early Christian Exegetical Convention," in *The Future of Christology: Essays in Honor of Leander E. Keck*. Ed. A.J. MALHERBE and W.A. MEEKS. Minneapolis: Fortress, 1993. 122-36.

-----. "Christology and Ethics in Galatians: The Law of Christ," *CBQ* 49 (1987) 268-90.

-----. "Crucified with Christ: A Synthesis of the Theology of 1 and 2 Thessalonians, Philemon, Philippians, and Galatians," in *Pauline Theology. Volume I: Thessalonians, Philippians, Galatians, Philemon*. Ed. J.M. BASSLER. Minneapolis: Fortress, 1991. 227-46.

-----. *Echoes of Scripture in the Letters of Paul*. New Haven, Conn.: Yale University Press, 1989.

-----. *The Faith of Jesus Christ: The Narrative Substructure of Galatians 3:1-4:11*. 2nd ed. Grand Rapids, Mich.: Eerdmans, 2002.

-----. "ΠΙΣΤΙΣ and Pauline Christology," in *Pauline Theology. Volume IV: Looking Back, Pressing On*. Ed. E.E. JOHNSON and D.M. HAY. Atlanta: Scholars Press, 1997. 35-60.

-----. "Psalm 143 and the Logic of Romans 3," *JBL* 99 (1980) 107-15.

-----. "'The Righteous One' as Eschatological Deliverer: A Case Study in Paul's Apocalyptic Hermeneutics," in *Apocalyptic and the New Testament: Essays in Honor of J. Louis Martyn*. Ed. J. MARCUS and M.L. SOARDS. JSNTSup 24. Sheffield: JSOT Press, 1988. 191-215.

-----. "The Letter to the Galatians: Introduction, Commentary, and Reflections," in *NIB*. 11.181-348.

HEMER, C.J. "A Note on 2 Corinthians 1:9," *TynBul* 23 (1972) 103-7.

HENGEL, M. *The Son of God: The Origin of Christology and the History of Jewish-Hellenistic Religion*. Trans. J. BOWDEN. Philadelphia: Fortress, 1976.

HOCK, R.F. *The Social Context of Paul's Ministry: Tentmaking and Apostleship*. Philadelphia: Fortress, 1980.

HODGSON, R. "Paul the Apostle and First Century Tribulation Lists," *ZNW* 74 (1983) 59-89.

HOLLADAY, C.R. *Theios Aner in Hellenistic Judaism: A Critique of the Use of This Category in New Testament Christology*. SBLDS 40. Missoula, Mont.: Scholars Press, 1977.

HOLLAND, G. "Speaking Like a Fool: Irony in 2 Corinthians 10-13," in *Rhetoric and the New Testament: Essays from the 1992 Heidelberg*

Conference. JSNTSup 90. Ed. S.E. PORTER and T.H. OLBRICHT. Sheffield: JSOT Press, 1993. 250-64.

HOOKER, M.D. "From God's Faithfulness to Ours: Another Look at 2 Corinthians 1:17-24," in *Paul and the Corinthians: Studies on a Community in Conflict. Essays in Honour of Margaret Thrall*. NovTSup 109. Ed. T.J. BURKE and J.K. ELLIOTT. Leiden: Brill, 2003. 233-39.

-----. "Interchange and Atonement," *BJRL* 60 (1978) 462-81.

-----."Interchange and Suffering," in *Suffering and Martyrdom in the New Testament: Studies Presented to G.M. Styler by the Cambridge New Testament Seminar*. Ed. W. HORBURY and B. MCNEIL. Cambridge: Cambridge University Press, 1981. 70-83.

-----. "Interchange in Christ," *JTS* 22 (1971) 349-61.

-----. "Interchange in Christ and Ethics," *JSNT* 25 (1985) 3-17.

-----. "The Letter of the Philippians: Introduction, Commentary, and Reflections," in *NIB*. 11.467-549.

-----. "Philippians 2:6-11," in *Jesus and Paulus*. Ed. E.E. ELLIS and E. GRÄSSER. Göttingen: Vandenhoeck & Ruprecht, 1975. 151-64.

-----. "ΠΙΣΤΙΣ ΧΡΙΣΤΟΥ," *NTS* 35 (1989) 321-42.

HOWARD, G.E. "Christ the End of the Law: The Meaning of Romans 10:4ff," *JBL* 88 (1969) 331-37.

-----. "Phil 2:6-11 and the Human Christ," *CBQ* 40 (1978) 368-87.

HUGHES, F.W. "The Rhetoric of Reconciliation: 2. Corinthians 1:1-2:13 and 7:5-8:24," in *Persuasive Artistry: Studies in New Testament Rhetoric in Honor of George A. Kennedy*. JSNTSup 50. Ed. D.F. WATSON. Sheffield: Sheffield Academic Press, 1991. 246-61.

-----. "Rhetorical Criticism and the Corinthian Correspondence," in *The Rhetorical Analysis of Scripture: Essays from the 1995 London Conference*. JSNTSup 146. Ed. S.E. PORTER and T.H. OLBRICHT. Sheffield: Sheffield Academic Press, 1997. 336-50.

HURTADO, L.W. "Jesus as Lordly Example in Philippians 2:5-11," in *From Jesus to Paul: Studies in Honour of Francis Wright Beare*. Ed. P. RICHARDSON and J.C. HURD. Waterloo, Ontario: Wilfrid Laurier University Press, 1984. 113-26.

JAQUETTE, J.L. *Discerning What Counts: The Function of the* Adiaphora Topos *in Paul's Letters*. SBLDS 146. Atlanta: Scholars Press, 1995.

JERVELL, J. *Imago Dei: Gen 1,26 f. im Spätjudentum, in der Gnosis und in den paulinischen Briefen*. FRLANT 58. Göttingen: Vandenhoeck & Ruprecht, 1960.

JOHNSON, L.T. *The First and Second Letters to Timothy: A New Translation with Introduction and Commentary*. AB 35A. New York: Doubleday, 2001.

-----. "Isaiah the Evangelist," *Mils* 48 (2001) 88-105.

-----. "James 3:13-4:10 and the *Topos* Περὶ Φθόνου," *NovT* 25 (1983) 327-47.

-----. "The Mirror of Remembrance (James 1:22-25)," *CBQ* 50 (1988) 632-45.

-----. *Reading Romans: A Literary and Theological Commentary*. New York: Crossroad, 1997.

-----. "Romans 3:21-26 and the Faith of Jesus," *CBQ* 44 (1982) 77-90.

-----. "II Timothy and the Polemic Against False Teachers: A Reexamination," *JRelS* 6/7 (1978/79) 1-26.

-----. "Transformation of the Mind and Moral Discernment in Paul," in *Early Christianity and Classical Culture: Comparative Studies in Honor of*

Abraham J. Malherbe. Ed. J.T. FITZGERALD, T.H. OLBRICHT, and L.M. WHITE. Leiden: Brill, 2003. 215-36.

-----. *The Writings of the New Testament: An Interpretation*. Rev. ed. Minneapolis: Fortress, 1999.

JOUBERT, S.J. "Behind the Mask of Rhetoric: 2 Corinthians 8 and the Intra-textual Relation between Paul and the Corinthians," *Neot* 26 (1992) 101-12.

KÄSEMANN, E. "Blind Alleys in the 'Jesus of History' Controversy," in *New Testament Questions of Today*. Trans. W.J. MONTAGUE. Philadelphia: Fortress, 1969. 23-65.

-----. *Commentary on Romans*. Trans. and ed. G.W. BROMILEY. Grand Rapids, Mich.: Eerdmans, 1980.

-----. "Kritische Analyse von Phil. 2.5-11," *ZTK* 47 (1950) 313-360. Trans. by A. CARSE in *JTC* 5 (1968) 45-88.

-----. "Die Legitimät des Apostels: Eine Untersuchung zu II Korinther 10-13," *ZNW* 41 (1942) 33-71.

-----. "'The Righteousness of God' in Paul," in *New Testament Questions of Today*. 168-82.

KECK, L.E. "'Jesus' in Romans," *JBL* 108 (1989) 443-60.

KELLY, J.N.D. *A Commentary on the Pastoral Epistles*. HNTC. New York: Harper & Row, 1963.

KENNEDY, G.A.. *New Testament Interpretation through Rhetorical Criticism*. Chapel Hill, N.C.: The University of North Carolina Press, 1984.

KERR, A.J. "'ΑΡΡΑΒΩΝ," *JTS* 39 (1988) 92-97.

KIJNE, J.J. "We, Us and Our in I and II Corinthians," *NovT* 8 (1966) 171-79.

KLEINKNECHT, K.T. *Der leidende Gerechtfertigte: Die alttestamentlich-jüdische Tradition vom "leidenden Gerechten" und irhe Rezeption bei Paulus*. WUNT 2. Tübingen: Mohr Siebeck, 1984.

KOESTER, H. "The Purpose of the Polemic of a Pauline Fragment," *NTS* 8 (1961-62) 317-32.

KOPERSKY, V. "Knowledge of Christ and Knowledge of God in the Corinthian Correspondence," in *The Corinthian Correpondence*. BETL 125. Ed. R. BIERINGER. Leuven: Leuven University Press, 1996. 377-96.

-----. "The Meaning of *Pistis Christou* in Philippians 3:9," *LS* 18 (1993) 198-216.

KRAFTCHICK, S.J. "Death in Us, Life in You: The Apostolic Medium," in *Pauline Theology. Volume II: 1 & 2 Corinthians*. Ed. D.M. HAY. Minneapolis: Fortress, 1993. 156-81.

-----. *Ethos and Pathos Appeals in Galatians Five and Six: A Rhetorical Analysis*. Ph.D. diss. Emory University, 1985.

KRAMER, W. *Christ, Lord, Son of God*. SBT 50. Trans. B. HARDY. Naperville, Ill.: Alec R. Allenson, 1966.

KUHN, T.S. *The Structure of Scientific Revolutions*. 2nd rev. ed. Chicago: University of Chicago Press, 1970.

KÜMMEL, W.G. *Introduction to the New Testament*. Rev. ed.. Trans. H.C. KEE. Nashville: Abingdon, 1973.

KURZ, W.S. "Kenotic Imitation of Paul and of Christ," in *Discipleship in the New Testament*. Ed. F.F. SEGOVIA. Philadelphia: Fortress, 1985. 103-26.

LAKE, K. *The Earlier Epistles of St. Paul*. 2nd ed. London: Rivingtons, 1914.

LAMBRECHT, J. "The Favorable Time: A Study of 2 Corinthians 6,2a in Its Context," in R. BIERINGER and J. LAMBRECHT, *Studies on 2 Corinthians*. BETL 112. Leuven: Leuven University Press, 1994. 515-29.

-----. "The Fragment of 2 Corinthians 6:14-7:1: A Plea for Its Authenticity," in *Studies on 2 Corinthians*. 531-49.

-----. "The Nekrōsis of Jesus: Ministry and Suffering in 2 Cor 4,7-15," in *Studies on 2 Corinthians*. 309-33.

-----. "Paul's Appeal and the Obedience to Christ: The Line of Thought in 2 Corinthians 10,1-6," *Bib* 77 (1996) 398-416.

-----. "Philological and Exegetical Notes on 2 Corinthians 13,4," in *Studies on 2 Corinthians*. 589-98.

-----. "'Reconcile Yourselves. . .': A Reading of 2 Corinthians 5,11-21," in *Studies on 2 Corinthians*. 363-412.

-----. "Transformation in 2 Corinthians 3,18," in *Studies on 2 Corinthians*. 295-307.

LEIVESTAD, R. "'The Meekness and Gentleness of Christ' II Cor. X. 1," *NTS* 12 (1965-66) 156-64.

LINCOLN, A.T. *Paradise Now and Not Yet*. SNTSMS 43. Cambridge: Cambridge University Press, 1981.

LONG, F.J. *"Have We Been Defending Ourselves to You?" (2 Cor 12:19): Forensic Rhetoric and the Rhetorical Unity of 2 Corinthians*. Ph.D. diss. Marquette University, 1999.

LONGENECKER, B.W., ed. *Narrative Dynamics in Paul: A Critical Assessment*. Louisville: Westminster John Knox, 2002.

-----. "ΠΙΣΤΙΣ in Romans 3:25: Neglected Evidence for the 'Faithfulness of Christ'?," *NTS* 39 (1993) 478-80.

MACDONALD, M.Y. *Colossians and Ephesians*. SP 17. Collegeville, Minn.: Liturgical, 2000.

MALHERBE, A.J. "Antisthenes and Odysseus, and Paul at War," *HTR* 76 (1983) 143-73.

-----. "Through the Eye of the Needle: Simplicity or Singleness?" *ResQ* 5 (1961) 119-29.

MANSON, T.W. "The Corinthian Correspondence (1)," in *Studies in the Gospels and Epistles*. Ed. M. BLACK. Philadelphia: Westminster, 1962. 190-209.

-----. "Romans," in *PCB*. 40-53.

MARGUERAT, D. "2 Corinthiens 10-13: Paul et l'experience de Dieu," *ETR* 63 (1988) 497-519.

MARKS, H. "Pauline Typology and Revisionary Criticism," *JAAR* 52 (1984) 71-92.

MARSHALL, P. *Enmity in Corinth: Social Conventions in Paul's Relations with the Corinthians*. WUNT 2/23. Tübingen: Mohr Siebeck, 1987.

-----. "A Metaphor of Social Shame: ΘΡΙΑΜΒΕΥΕΙΝ in 2 Cor. 2:14," *NovT* 25 (1983) 302-17.

MARTIN, R.P. *A Hymn of Christ: Philippians 2:5-11 in Recent Interpretation & in the Setting of Early Christian Worship*. Downers Grove, IL: Intervarsity Press, 1997. [Originally published as *Carmen Christi: Philippians ii.5-11 in Recent Interpretation & in the Setting of Early Christian Worship*. London: Cambridge University Press, 1967].

-----. *Reconciliation: A Study of Paul's Theology*. Atlanta: John Knox, 1981.

-----. "The Spirit in 2 Corinthians in Light of the 'Fellowship of the Holy Spirit' in 2 Corinthians 13:14," in *Eschatology and the New Testament:*

Essays in Honor of George Raymond Beasley-Murray. Ed. W.H. GLOER. Peabody, Mass.: Hendrickson, 1988. 113-28.

MARTYN, J.L. "Epistemology at the Turn of the Ages," in *Theological Issues in the Letters of Paul*. Nashville: Abingdon, 1997. 89-110.

-----. *Galatians: A New Translation with Introduction and Commentary*. AB 33A. New York: Doubleday, 1997.

MATERA, F.J. *Galatians*. SP 9. Collegeville, Minn.: Liturgical, 1992.

-----. *New Testament Christology*. Louisville: Westminster John Knox, 1999.

MCDERMOTT, J.M. "The Biblical Doctrine of ΚΟΙΝΩΝΙΑ," *BZ* 19 (1975) 219-33.

MCDONALD, J.I.H. "Paul and the Preaching Ministry: A Reconsideration of 2 Corinthians 2:14-17 in Its Context," *JSNT* 17 (1983) 35-50.

MEEKS, W.A. "Image of the Androgyne: Some Uses of a Symbol in Earliest Christianity," *HR* 13 (1974) 165-208.

MINEAR, P.S. "Yes or No: The Demand for Honesty in the Early Church," *NovT* 13 (1971) 1-13.

MITCHELL, M.M. "A Patristic Perspective on Pauline περιαυτολογία," *NTS* 47 (2001) 354-71.

-----. *Paul and the Rhetoric of Reconciliation*. Tübingen: Mohr Siebeck, 1991.

MOO, D.J. *The Epistle to the Romans*. NICNT. Grand Rapids, Mich.: Eerdmans, 1996.

MOORE, R.K. "2 Cor 5,21: The Interpretative Key to Paul's Use of *ΔΙΚΑΙΟΣΥΝΗ ΘΕΟΥ*?" in *The Corinthian Correpondence*. BETL 125. Ed. R. BIERINGER. Leuven: Leuven University Press, 1996. 707-15.

MUNCK, J. *Paul and the Salvation of Mankind.* London: SCM, 1959.

MURPHY-O'CONNOR, J. "Another Jesus (2 Cor 11:4)," *RB* 97 (1990) 238-51.

-----. "Christological Anthropology in Phil. II, 6-11," *RB* 83 (1976) 25-50.

-----. "Faith and Resurrection in 2 Cor 4:13-14," *RB* 95 (1988) 543-50.

-----. "Philo and 2 Cor. 6:14-7:1," *RB* 95 (1988) 55-69.

-----. *Paul: A Critical Life.* New York: Oxford University Press, 1996.

-----. *The Theology of the Second Letter to the Corinthians.* NTT. Cambridge: Cambridge University Press, 1991.

NICKLE, K.F. *The Collection: A Study in Paul's Strategy.* SBT 48. Naperville, Ill.: Alec R. Allenson, 1966.

O'BRIEN, P.T. *Introductory Thanksgivings in the Letters of Paul.* NovTSup 49. Leiden: E.J. Brill, 1977.

O'COLLINS, G.G. "Power Made Perfect in Weakness: 2 Cor 12:9-10," *CBQ* 33 (1971) 528-37.

----- and D. KENDALL, "The Faith of Jesus," *TS* 53 (1992) 403-23.

OLBRICHT, T.H. and J.L. SUMNEY, eds. *Paul and Pathos.* SBLSymS 16. Atlanta: Society of Biblical Literature, 2001.

O'MAHONY, K.J. *Pauline Persuasion: A Sounding in 2 Corinthians 8-9.* JSNTSup 199. Sheffield: Sheffield Academic Press, 2000.

-----. "The Rhetoric of Benefaction," PIBA 22 (1999) 9-40.

OOSTENDORP, D. *Another Jesus: A Gospel of Jewish-Christian Superiority in II Corinthians.* Kampen: J.H. Kok, 1967.

PATE, C.M. *Adam Christology as the Exegetical & Theological Substructure of 2 Corinthians 4:7-5:21*. Lanham, Md.: University Press of America, 1991.

PATTE, D. *What is Structural Exegesis?* Philadelphia: Fortress, 1976.

PETERSON, B.K. *Eloquence and the Proclamation of the Gospel in Corinth.* SBLDS 163. Atlanta: Scholars Press, 1998.

PICKETT, R. *The Cross in Corinth: The Social Significance of the Death of Jesus*. JSNTSup 143. Sheffield: Sheffield Academic Press, 1997.

POLLARD, P. "The 'Faith of Christ' in Current Discussion," *Concordia Journal* 23 (1997) 213-28.

PRYOR, J.W. "Paul's Use of Iēsous–A Clue for the Translation of Romans 3:26?" *Colloq* 16 (1983) 31-45.

ROBBINS, V.K. *The Tapestry of Early Christian Discourse: Rhetoric, Society and Ideology*. New York: Routledge, 1996.

SAMPLEY, J.P. "Paul, His Opponents in 2 Corinthians 10-13, and the Rhetorical Handbooks," in *The Social World of Formative Christianity and Judaism: Essays in Tribute to Howard Clark Kee*. Ed. J. NEUSNER et al. Philadelphia: Fortress, 1988. 162-77.

SAVAGE, T.B. *Power through Weakness: Paul's Understanding of the Christian Ministry in 2 Corinthians*. Cambridge: Cambridge University Press, 1996.

SCHMITHALS, W. *Gnosticism in Corinth: An Investigation of the Letters to the Corinthians*. 3rd ed. Trans. J.E. STEELY. Nashville: Abingdon, 1971.

SCHNEIDER, B. "HE KOINONIA TOU HAGIOU PNEUMATOS (II Cor. 13, 13)," in *Studies Honoring Ignatius Charles Brady Friar Minor*. TS 6. Ed. R.S. ALMAGNO and C.L. HARKINS. St. Bonaventure, N.Y.: The Franciscan Institute, 1976. 421-47.

SCHOLLA, R.W. "Into the Image of God: Pauline Eschatology and the Transformation of Believers," *Greg* 78 (1997) 33-54.

SCHRAGE, W. "Leid, Kreuz und Eschaton: Die Peristasenkataloge als Merkmale paulinischer theologia crucis und Eschatologie," *EvT* 34 (1974) 141-75.

SCHUBERT, P. *Form and Function of the Pauline Thanksgivings*. BZNW 20. Berlin: A. Topelmann, 1939.

SCHÜTZ, J.H. *Paul and the Anatomy of Apostolic Authority*. SNTSMS 26. Cambridge: Cambridge University Press, 1975.

SCROGGS, R. *The Last Adam: A Study in Pauline Anthropology*. Philadelphia: Fortress, 1966.

SEIDENSTICKER, P. "St. Paul and Poverty," in *Gospel Poverty: Essays in Biblical Theology*. Trans. M.D. GUINAN. Chicago: Franciscan Herald, 1977. 81-120.

SEMLER, J.S. *Paraphrasis II: Epistolae ad Corinthios*. Halle, 1776.

SOARDS, M.L. *The Apostle Paul: An Introduction to His Writings and Teachings*. New York: Paulist, 1987.

SOULEN, R.N. *Handbook of Biblical Criticism*. 2nd ed. Atlanta: John Knox, 1981.

STEWART-SYKES, A. "Ancient Editors and Copyists and Modern Partition Theories: The Case of the Corinthian Correspondence," *JSNT* 61 (1996) 53-64.

STOCKHAUSEN, C.K. *Moses' Veil and the Glory of the New Covenant: The Exegetical Substructure of II Cor. 3,1-4,6*. AnBib 116. Rome: Editrice Pontificio Istituto Biblico, 1989.

STOWERS, S.K. "'Εκ πίστεως and διὰ τῆς πίστεως in Romans 3:30," *JBL* 108 (1989) 665-74.

-----. "*PERI MEN GAR* and the Integrity of 2 Cor. 8 and 9," *NovT* 32 (1990) 340-48.

STROBEL, A. *Untersuchungen zum eschatologischen Verzögerungsproblem auf Grund der spätjudisch-urchristlichen Geschichte von Habakuk 2,2ff.* NovTSup 2. Leiden: Brill, 1961.

STUHLMACHER, P. *Gerechtigkeit Gottes bei Paulus.* 2nd ed. FRLANT 87. Göttingen: Vandenhoeck & Ruprecht, 1966.

SUMNEY, J.L. *Identifying Paul's Opponents: The Question of Method in 2 Corinthians.* JSNTSup 40. Sheffield: Sheffield Academic Press, 1990.

-----. *"Servants of Satan," "False Brothers" and Other Opponents of Paul.* JSNTSup 188. Sheffield: Sheffield Academic Press, 1999.

SUNDERMANN, H.-G. *Der schwache Apostel und die Kraft der Rede: Eine rhetorische Analyse von 2 Kor 10-13.* Europäische Hochschulschriften, Reihe 23: Theologie 575. Frankfurt: Lang, 1996.

TALBERT, C.H. "The Problem of Pre-existence in Philippians 2:6-11," *JBL* 86 (1967) 141-53.

TANNEHILL, R.C. *Dying and Rising with Christ: A Study in Pauline Theology.* BZNW 32. Berlin: Alfred Töppelmann, 1967.

THOMPSON, M. *Clothed with Christ: The Example and Teaching of Jesus in Romans 12.1-15.13.* JSNTSup 59. Sheffield: Sheffield Academic Press, 1991.

THRALL, M.E. "The Offender and the Offence: A Problem of Detection in 2 Corinthians," in *Scripture: Meaning and Method: Essays Presented to Anthony Tyrrell Hanson for His Seventieth Birthday.* Ed. B.P. THOMPSON. Hull: Hull University Press, 1987. 65-78.

-----. "The Problem of II Cor. vi.14-vii.1 in Some Recent Discussions," *NTS* 24 (1977-78) 132-48.

-----. "2 Corinthians 1:12: ἁγιότητι or ἁπλότητι?," in *Studies in New Testament Language and Text: Essays in Honour of George D. Kilpatrick on the Occasion of His Sixty-Fifth Birthday*. Ed. J.K. ELLIOTT. NovTSup 44. Leiden: Brill, 1976. 366-72.

-----. "Super-Apostles, Servants of Christ, and Servants of Satan," *JSNT* 6 (1980) 42-57.

TIEDE, D.L. *The Charismatic Figure as Miracle Worker*. SBLDS 1. Missoula, Mont.: Scholars Press, 1972.

VANHOYE, A. "Πίστις Χριστοῦ: fede in Cristo o affidabilità di Cristo?" *Bib* 80 (1999) 1-21.

VAN UNNIK, W.C. "Reisepläne und Amen-Sagen, Zusammenhang und Gedankenfolge in 2. Korinther i 15-24," in *Sparsa Collecta: The Collected Essays of W.C. van Unnik*. Part 1. Leiden: E.J. Brill, 1973. 144-59.

-----. "'With Unveiled Face,' An Exegesis of 2 Corinthians iii 12-18," *NovT* 6 (1963) 153-69.

VAN VLIET, H. *No Single Testimony: A Study on the Adoption of the Law of Deut. 19:15 Par. into the New Testament*. Utrecht: Kreminck en Zoon, 1958.

VERBRUGGE, V.D. *Paul's Style of Church Leadership Illustrated by His Instructions to the Corinthians on the Collection*. San Francisco: Mellen Research University Press, 1992.

WALLER, E. "The Rhetorical Structure of II Cor. 6:14-7:1 – Is the So-called 'Non-Pauline Interpolation' a Clue to the Redactor of II Corinthians?," *Proceedings of the Eastern Great Lakes and Midwest Biblical Societies* 10 (1990) 151-65.

WEBB, W.J. *Returning Home: New Covenant and Second Exodus as the Context for 2 Corinthians 6.14-7.1*. JSNTSup 85. Sheffield: Sheffield Academic Press, 1993.

WEBSTER, J.B. "Christology, Imitability and Ethics," *SJT* 39 (1986) 309-26.

WEISS, J. *Earliest Christianity: A History of the Period A.D. 30-150, Volume I*. Trans. F.C. GRANT. New York: Harper & Row, 1959.

WELBORN, L.L. "Like Broken Pieces of a Ring: 2 Cor 1:1-2:13; 7:5-16 and Ancient Theories of Literary Unity," *NTS* 42 (1996) 559-83.

-----. "Paul's Appeal to the Emotions in 2 Corinthians 1:1-2:13; 7:5-16," *JSNT* 82 (2001) 31-60.

-----. *Paul's Letter of Reconciliation in 2 Corinthians*. Ph.D. diss. University of Chicago, 1987.

WILK, F. *Die Bedeutung des Jesajabuches für Paulus*. FRLANT 179. Göttingen: Vandenhoeck & Ruprecht, 1998.

WILLIAMS, S.K. "Again *Pistis Christou*," *CBQ* 49 (1987) 431-47.

-----. "The 'Righteousness of God' in Romans," *JBL* 99 (1980) 241-90.

WILLIAMSON, L. "Led in Triumph: Paul's Use of Thriambeuō," *Int* 22 (1968) 317-32.

WISSE, J. *Ethos and Pathos from Aristotle to Cicero*. Amsterdam: Adolf M. Hakkert, 1989.

WITHERINGTON, B. *Paul's Narrative Thought World: The Tapestry of Tragedy and Triumph*. Louisville: Westminster/John Knox, 1994.

WOLFF, C. "True Apostolic Knowledge of Christ: Exegetical Reflections on 2 Corinthians 5:14ff," in *Paul and Jesus: Collected Essays*. JSNTSup 37. Ed. A.J.M. WEDDERBURN. Sheffield: Sheffield Academic Press, 1989. 81-98.

WOODCOCK, E. "The Seal of the Holy Spirit," *BSac* 155 (1998) 139-63.

WRIGHT, N.T. *The Climax of the Covenant: Christ and the Law in Pauline Theology*. Edinburgh: T. & T. Clark, 1991.

-----. *The New Testament and the People of God.* Christian Origins and the Question of God, vol. 1. London: SPCK, 1992.

-----. "On Becoming the Righteousness of God: 2 Corinthians 5:21," in *Pauline Theology, Volume II: 1 & 2 Corinthians*. Ed. D.M. HAY. Minneapolis: Fortress, 1993. 200-208.

-----. "Romans and the Theology of Paul," in *Pauline Theology. Volume III: Romans*. Ed. D.M. HAY and E.E. JOHNSON. Minneapolis: Fortress, 1995. 30-67.

-----. *What Saint Paul Really Said: Was Paul of Tarsus the Real Founder of Christianity?* Grand Rapids, Mich.: Eerdmans, 1997.

WÜNSCH, H.-W. *Der paulinische Brief 2 Kor 1-9 als kommunikative Handlung: Eine rhetorisch-literaturwissenschaftliche Untersuchung*. Theologie 4. Münster: Lit, 1996.

YAMADA, K. "Epistolary Theoretical and Rhetorical Analyses of 2 Cor. 1-9," *AJBI* 24 (1998) 83-116.

YOUNG, F. "Note on 2 Corinthians 1:17b," *JTS* 37 (1986) 404-15.

ZMIJEWSKI, J. *Der Stil der paulinischen "Narrenrede": Analyse der Sprachgestaltung in 2 Kor. 11,1-12,10 als Beitrag zur Methodik von Stiluntersuchungen neutestamentlicher Texte*. BBB 52. Cologne and Bonn: Peter Hanstein, 1978.

ZORN, W.D. "The Messianic Use of Habakkuk 2:4a in Romans," *Stone-Campbell Journal* 1 (1998) 213-30.

Indices

INDEX OF ANCIENT LITERARY SOURCES

1. INDEX OF CLASSICAL TEXTS

2. INDEX OF OLD TESTAMENT TEXTS
(both MT and LXX)

PSALMS

PROVERBS

ISAIAH

3. INDEX OF APOCRYPHA

4. INDEX OF PSEUDEPIGRAPHA

5. INDEX OF HELLENISTIC JEWISH TEXTS

6. INDEX OF NEW TESTAMENT TEXTS

(bold typeface indicates extended treatment)

ROMANS

1 CORINTHIANS

2 CORINTHIANS

COLOSSIANS

7. INDEX OF EARLY CHRISTIAN TEXTS

INDEX OF MODERN AUTHORS

INDEX OF SELECTED TOPICS

Stampa: Maggio 2005

presso la tipografia
"Giovanni Olivieri" di E. Montefoschi
Roma • tip.olivieri@libero.it